Rockin' and around Croydon

Rock, Folk, Blues & Jazz
in & around the Croydon Area
1960 – 1980

Chris Groom

publishing

ACKNOWLEDGMENTS

For their assistance in the production of this book, there are a large number of people to thank, and for an equally large number of reasons; therefore, in roughly alphabetical order, enormous thanks go out to:

Keith Aldridge, Peter Alexander, Frazer Ashford, Brian Auger, Cliff Aungier, Alan Barnes, Richard Barnes, Derek Barr, Angela Young & David Shimmell from the Fairfield Halls, Dave Bachelor, Rick & Terry Biddle, Kit, Pip and Bernard Blakemore, Tim Blewett, Adrienne Bloch, Johnny Blunt, Colin Boone, Steve Boyce, Chris & Fran Browning, Kevin Bryan, Pip Burley, Captain Sensible, Ivan Chandler, Mike Chapman, Christie's Images, D. Clarke, Mel Collins, Daryl Corbett, John Cox, all the staff (past & present) of the Croydon Advertiser, Darius Photography, Robin Denselow, all at Digicol Link, Laura Dockett, Ann Dunn, Diana Eccleston, John Edmed, John Failes, Matthew Fisher, Simon Fitzgerald, Rachel Fones, Peter Frampton, Robin & Cathy Godden, Mick Hack, Dave Hallson, Martin Hammond, Oliver Harris and the local studies department at Croydon Library, Jim Henocq, Andy & Roger Jarvie, Wizz Jones, Eden Kane, Hilary Kay, Kim, Ian King, Neil Korner, Ray Laidlaw, Graham Lambourne, David Lashmar & all at Beanos, Sally MacDonald, Graham Maisey, Steve Mason, Jim McCarty, John Martin, Kevin & Sue McLure, Jacqui McShee, Ralph McTell, Bill Miller, Jamie Moses, Mark Mumford, David Newton, Martin Nigby, Dave Pegg, Barry Plummer, Simon Porter & Kirsty at Duroc Media, James Pringle, Roger Probert, David Redfern & Dede Millar at Redferns, Julia Revell, Mike Roberts, Francis Rossi, Steve Roth and Simon Lunt of the Croydon Guardian, Jacqueline Ryan, Peter Sarstedt, Deanna Sewell, Rose Simpson, Keith Skone, Brian Smith, Jim Smith, Pennie Smith, John Stevens, Ray Stevenson, Alan Stranks, Ian Stuart, Keith Temple, Ben Turner at MM, Peter Twitchett, David Tyler, John Tyler, Mike Vernon, Val Williams, Val Wilmer, Mark Woodley and finally, Bill Wyman.

LEGAL STUFF

First Published in Croydon (and the UK) in August 1998 by WOMBeAT publishing.

WOMBeAT publishing
PO Box 775, Purley, Surrey CR8 2ZY

Researched, written and designed by
Chris Groom

Front cover photography: *Mike Kay • Solar Studios*

Every attempt has been made to credit the photographs reproduced herein; all photographers are credited alongside their work, where known.

Printed by *Broglia Press*
Enterprise House, 52 Holton Road,
Holton Heath, Poole, Dorset BH16 6LQ

Distributed by *Renault 5*, with difficulty!

ISBN 0 953161900

A catalogue record for this title is available from the British Library.

Rock, Folk, Blues & Jazz in & around the Croydon Area 1960 – 1980

Contents

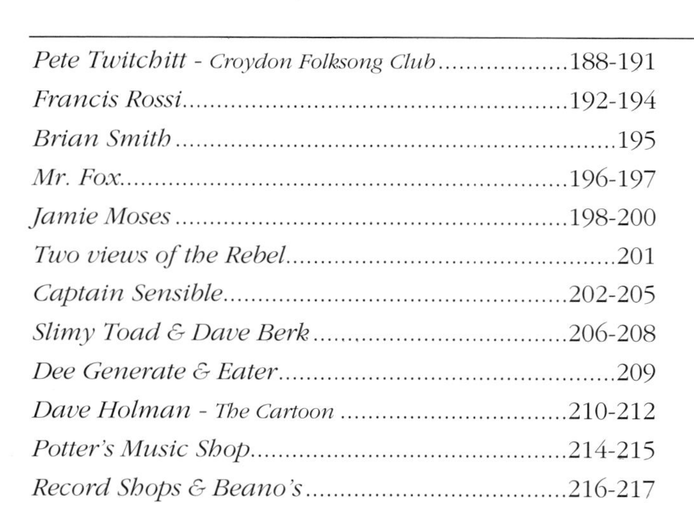

Not so much an introduction, more an explanation...

Why Croydon?

To be honest, there is a book of this kind to be based around any major town in Britain during the last thirty years, providing that town was home to a mid-size venue with several smaller satellite venues to support it. Croydon just happened to be my locality, but had I lived in Manchester, Newcastle or Glasgow I dare say I would still have put together something similar.

But this is not just a local history book, for I believe it has a much wider appeal as a document of who toured where, when and with whom! It also goes a long way to prove that if you are in the right place at the right time, there is always a good gig to be found - and to a lesser degree, it is an attempt to answer those cynics who say that 'nothing ever happens in Croydon'. Those of us who live around this area secretly know that this is simply not true and a glance through these pages should confirm the fact.

What sort of place was Croydon at the beginning of the Sixties? Strange as it may seem, the town wasn't the 'mini-Manhattan' or the 'Chicago of South East London', as someone recently described it, that it appears to be today. For a start there were no towering office blocks, the first of these was Norfolk House which didn't appear on the changing skyline until 1959. There was no Whitgift Centre, that space was still occupied by the Old Palace School and it was the school association with Archbishop Whitgift that gave the shopping precinct its name. The entrance to the school was on the main Brighton Road, which at that time ran straight through the centre of town, unhindered by 'pedestrianisation'.

There was no Fairfield Hall, simply a plot of empty ground - once the site of the original 'Field' where the local people held their annual 'Fair', an event that had originated in mediaeval times - and where, during the Second World War a captured Messerschmidt 109 fighter plane was positioned, with the local council charging admission to help raise funds for the war effort!

Croydon was chosen as a prime town for major redevelopment, positioned just 18 miles south of the capital on the main London to Brighton road and served by a direct rail link to East Croydon station. The town planners set their sights on building a new Croydon, an example of Britain's future at the dawn of the new decade, with the town centre providing employment, amenities and entertainment for the 'satellite' villages of Broad Green, Norbury, Thornton Heath, Addiscombe, New Addington, Selsdon, Sanderstead, Purley, Wallington and Waddon.

As always, to achieve such a vision there were sacrifices to be made; the Civic Hall and the Davis Theatre were demolished to make way for a state of the art entertainments complex which was situated on the waste ground next to Croydon College. The Old Palace school buildings and the 16th century Whitgift Hospital also bit the dust - the school was relocated to new positions in South Croydon and Shirley. In its place grew the first version of the concrete shopping centre that we know and love! On the opposite side of the Brighton Road were two huge department stores, Grants and Kennards. Situated where the Drummond Centre now stands, the most celebrated feature of Kennard's was the arcade, running right through the middle of the store - weird and wonderful at the best of times, but a magical place to be at Christmas.

"Croydon - it *sounds* like an illness.."

- Kenneth Williams

There are many suburban British towns which, for mainly comedy-related reasons are indelibly etched into the minds of the public, even if they have never visited the place in question. Balham, for example, will always be Peter Seller's "Gateway to the South"; Purley is either a "famous place, squire - nudge, nudge, say no more", thanks to Monty Python's Flying Circus, or the television home of 'Terry & June', June Whitfield and Terry Scott. Nearby Cheam is the setting for the fictitious Railway Cuttings where Tony Hancock complained his days away and as for Neasdon, well, if you want a place in which to set a situation comedy, then look no further. Its very name produces a knowing smirk on the face of many a non-resident.

Croydon seems to provoke a similar reaction from many people, although the reasons are not so easy to explain; there is no television comedy based there (although the town is often mentioned in passing), so perhaps it is because the public perception of Croydon is of a place where people go to shop, and to work, but not actually to live? Do people remember the radical town centre development at the start of the sixties and view Croydon as a town with it's heart ripped out and replaced by a concrete pacemaker?

But for all the massive changes to the structure of the town, one constant remained - the quality of the live music that Croydon had to offer. The 'sixties and 'seventies were obvious heydays for live music, in both quantity and innovative quality, and the drop in the number of concerts during the Eighties was due in no small part to changes in the music industry as a whole as much as the attitudes of the groups themselves.

Groups no longer toured endlessly before earning a record deal - home recording and the wider availability of recording facilities, enabled singles to be made and marketed (and indeed to reach high chart positions), without the artist ever playing before an audience. Consequently, when the demand for top-selling, chart artists finally forced them to perform, they were booked straight into the larger venues - the Hammersmith Odeons and Wembley Arenas, bypassing the clubs, pubs and small concert halls and understandably often producing dire performances at the end.

At the same time, after the Punk scene died out, (a musical form which at it's best had provided a much needed shot in the arm for unknown groups wanting to play live), and with the new wave of groups retreating to the comfort of their own homes to plan their attack on the singles charts, the small venues began to close down due to a general apathy towards watching or playing in a good live band.

The future, however, looks a good deal healthier.

The late 'eighties and early 'nineties have seen a definite swing back in favour of live music. There is a renewed interest in acoustic musical forms; youngsters are at last becoming disenchanted with the fickle state of the chart scene, delving instead into the traditions of Blues, Folk and Jazz with a healthy respect for what has gone before. You only needed to lend an ear to the Indie charts and listen to the number of heavily 'sixties influenced guitar bands; sales of 12-string Rickenbackers must have soared, that's for sure! For it's part, Croydon is witnessing something of a revival.

The Fairfield Hall went through a quiet patch, as not quite the influential top line venue it once was - it has matured and mellowed along with the groups and artists who cut their teeth on it's stage in their early days. It is now possible, however, to see plenty of established names appearing there and if you keep your ear to the ground and your eyes on the local paper, there are a multitude of younger 'stars' to be spotted among the support acts and in the smaller venues. Both the old *Cartoon* and the now defunct *Underground Club* certainly had their fair share.

The Fairfield complex has opened both the Arnhem Gallery and the Ashcroft Theatre to bands normally playing the pub & club circuit. The *Gun*, in Crown Hill has re-established itself as a fine live music venue, and the *Cartoon*, for a long time one of South Londons better, 'sweatier' rock gigs has only recently re-opened as the *Cool Room*, after a brief spell without a music licence. What Croydon needs now is a mid-size venue to bridge the gap between pub back room and Fairfield Hall, and it could cater for local and national live music on the same scale as it did during the late 'sixties and early 'seventies.

A word or two about the book itself. Either side of the central listings section are interviews with just a few of the people who made the Croydon music scene 'tick'; not all are musicians - there are views from the fields of record production, photography, journalism and concert promotion too - but they each have a fascinating story to tell, helping to piece together the bigger picture of the local scene. In every interview I have deliberately edited out my prompts and questions in an attempt to let the piece flow and hopefully to make it a more enjoyable read; in one or two cases the interviewee knew exactly what they wanted to say and once the tape was running, needed no extra help from me to pour out their story.

There were one or two local celebrities that it was impossible to track down, but who still warranted a mention and for these I have used first hand knowledge from other sources - a close schoolfriend of Gary Glitter and Jeff Beck's first manager, for example - and only the piece on David Bowie relies totally on previously published material.

The listings section, featuring month by month, year by year analysis, is by no means complete. That may seem a strange thing to say, having just completed six years research, but it would have been impossible to list every small local gig. Take, for example, a group like the Martin Jae Five. When they started, their performances were mainly small church hall dances and the occasional private function for friends and family, advertised by word of mouth and the odd hand-made poster nailed to a tree! Even as their local following grew and the venues got proportionally bigger there was little or no press advertising for the poor researcher to stumble onto twenty or thirty years later. And, as live performance was their 'raison d'etre', they really did work their proverbial butts off; five, six and sometimes seven nights a week. I viewed a few pages from the diary kept by the bass player and their workload - like that of every semi-pro. group - was truly astounding; driving their battered transit all over the country for one-night stands and still travel home and get up for work the following morning.

Multiply that by the scores of groups who worked out of the Croydon area and there is no way my gig lists could even come close. However, the major concerts are pretty well complete; say 99% for the Fairfield and 90% for the Greyhound, with the percentages dropping for venues like the Star and the Gun. With its 'flagship' status, the Fairfield Hall was well advertised, well served by two local newspapers - the Croydon Advertiser and Croydon Times - was often used by the national music press for reviewing purposes and still has its original bookings diary, which they kindly let me see. On the other hand, although the Greyhound advertised regularly in the music press, their concerts suffered a great deal from last-minute cancellations and replacements. I saw a collection of printed handbills where every other week's band was crossed out and the new group written in, sometimes being replaced a second time before the day of the gig! The Advertiser reviewed at the Greyhound in spasms, always giving the Fairfield preference on column space in each weeks edition.

As good a venue as the Greyhound undoubtedly was, it could be a nightmare to keep track of exactly who played there (and when) and some mistakes will inevitably have slipped through. As for the Star, the Orchid Ballroom and Wallington Public Hall, I have collected as much information as was recorded from various sources, but their lists are by no means complete - a shame, for both venues were of great importance to local music fans. Many other venues are mentioned here; if I found a gig that was of interest and I could find space, it was included.

I hope you enjoy this look back at Croydon music past, but remember - keep supporting live bands - Croydon's music future depends on it.

The Venues

The Fairfield Halls

Park Lane, Croydon, Surrey.

The Fairfield complex contains the largest concert hall in Croydon, with seating for between 1,500 and 2,000 people, as well as a theatre - The Ashcroft, named after Dame Peggy, the Arnhem Gallery, an exhibition/function hall named after Croydon's twin town, plus restaurant, cafeteria and licenced bars.

Opened on 2nd November 1962 by Queen Elizabeth the Queen Mother, the Halls, initially under the direction of general manager Thomas J. Pyper have since played host to a long and distinguished line of artists from every musical field; Duke Ellington, Ella Fitzgerald, Yehudeh Menuin, Julian Bream, the Rolling Stones, the Beatles, the Modern Jazz Quartet, the London Symphony Orchestra, and everyone else in between. The acoustics were designed before the days of heavily amplified rock music; in fact it is hard to imagine the likes of Deep Purple and Black Sabbath playing to its clinically seated, wood panelled interior - giving considerable problems to many a sound engineer. Having said that, the Fairfield has been a favourite place for musicians to record their live performances - both on vinyl and for radio broadcast.

The importance of the Fairfield Halls to Croydon's musical heritage is enormous; it was a major boost to the town's stature in the arts and entertainments world and became a regular addition to the gig lists of the top concert promoters. Some major shows, the Folk & Blues packages of the early 'sixties for example, were only booked into Croydon and the Fairfield became regarded as an alternative 'London' venue.

Although few of todays' top rock and pop artists stop here anymore (the 2,000 seat venues just aren't big enough for the likes of U2 and Madonna) the Fairfield can still attract big names, not only from the past - artists who cut their teeth on its stage the first time around - but also the present, recently hosting the likes of Suzanne Vega, Morrissey, Mike & the Mechanics, Mary Chapin-Carpenter and Croydon's own Eternal, who played their hometown gig just prior to a sell-out show at Wembley Arena.

Back in 1964 the Croydon Advertiser quoted a young girl's reply to her friend who enquired about the Fairfield: *"You must have heard of it. Everyone's heard of it, everyone's been there. Just where have you been recently. Australia?!"*

But the final word must go to Pete Townshend of the Who. In a 1974 interview for the late lamented ZigZag magazine he talked about their rock opera 'Tommy': *"The best performance of all was at Croydon, Fairfield Hall. It was the first time we played it including 'Sally Simpson' and a few other things we did specially. The sound in that place - oh, Croydon, I could bloody play there all night... it is just a good acoustic. It's as though the whole place was designed so that you could hear the conductor banging on his rostrum and not the orchestra. It's a freak, but it's great for rock".*

"The sound in that place - oh, Croydon - I could bloody play there all night.."

- Pete Townshend

Val Wilmer

A superb view of the familiar Fairfield stage in the main hall, with the Count Basie Orchestra in full swing while trumpeter Al Aarons takes his solo - 15th September 1963. Note the audience seated in the 'choir' section behind the band, more often hidden these days behind backdrops and amplification.

The Greyhound

Park Lane, Croydon, Surrey.

Situated at the foot of the towering St. George's House and right opposite the Fairfield Halls, the **Greyhound** was Croydon's second largest venue and for a long time during the Seventies was a close rival to its longer established and more affluent neighbour.

Basically a Courage pub with a large upstairs function room, the venue opened its doors to live music on November 23rd 1969, under the title 'Croydons Blues Club', with concerts promoted by **Mr. Fox**, a local record shop and mail order firm, who booked the more progressive rock and blues acts of the day. So successful were they, that 'Foxes' built up a chain of venues across the local area, including at various times the Starlight in Crawley, Wallington Public Hall and the Toby Jug at Tolworth. A lively stand-up venue, many bands returned two or three times a year, before moving up the concert hall hierarchy to the big place over the road.

Towards the end of the decade, the Greyhound became 'Surreys Premier New Wave Venue', mixing punk and heavy metal with the existing rock and blues bands. Sadly, live music petered out here during the early 'eighties.

The ABC Cinema

London Road, Croydon, Surrey.

Originally known as the **Savoy**, this Cinema was built in 1933 and was the second largest theatre in the Croydon borough, seating 2,276. It's successful run was temporarily halted in March 1953 when the auditorium and stage were gutted by one of the biggest fires ever seen in the area. The Savoy was partially restored and reopened until July 1958, when funds were sufficient for the full auditorium to be properly reconstructed.

In October of that year, the newly named **ABC** opened with a capacity of 2,118 seats and after the Davis Theatre was demolished in early 1960, the ABC cinema chain began to promote regular live concerts, among them Billy Fury, Cliff Richard, the Everly Brothers, Gene Pitney and a celebrated incident with P.J. Proby! The ABC was converted to a three screen cinema in 1972 and is today known as the Cannon.

The Star Hotel

London Road, West Croydon, Surrey.

This is the architypal 'pub back room', a tiny, smoky, dimly-lit venue, with no windows and a two foot high stage crammed into the corner. A popular jazz venue since the 'forties and home of the 'Croydon Jazz Club', the Star recognised the interest in 'beat groups' early on and began to host the 'Teen & Twenty' nights, giving early residency's to the Martin Jae Five amongst others. Around November 1963, the Star became one of the **Crawdaddy** clubs, under the management of Giorgio Gomelsky and consequently gave celebrated residency's to the Yardbirds, the T-Bones and the Authentics. It became the **Starlite Club** at the end of '65 and by 1966 the venue had turned its attention towards the blues, with regular appearances by Graham Bond, John Mayall's Bluesbreakers and Peter Green's Fleetwood Mac.

Jimi Hendrix played there in 1967, rumour has it that he had to be smuggled in through the rear windows because of the size of the crowd and Cream also played one of their early gigs there; it became the **Zodiac Club** in '68 but lost a lot of ground to the Greyhound at the end of the 'sixties. The Star continued to promote live bands throughout the 'seventies (although the level rose and fell as the management changed), it was a popular meeting place for punk rockers, Captain Sensible's local and at one point in the Eighties the venue tried to revive old glories by renaming the club the Crawdaddy.

Courtesy Croydon Library Services

The Star Hotel at Broad Green, circa 1969.

The Orchid Ballroom

Brighton Road, Purley, Surrey.

Originally known as Purley Ice Rink, the Orchid was for a while listed in the Guinness Book of Records as the largest ballroom in the UK, and has undergone many name and structural changes since its heyday in the mid-Sixties, when it was the spiritual home to TV's 'Come Dancing'!

In the early 'sixties, local big band leader Johnny Howard & his Orchestra were the residents, although the venue did offer teenagers a Beat Night on Mondays featuring the Fabulous Fleerakkers. The popularity of the new 'beat' groups prompted the Mecca chain to promote the new music as an alternative to its big-band dance nights and soon had gigs by the Who, Status Quo and Jimi Hendrix on their bill. One of their Monday night DJ's was Ian 'Sammy' Samwell and it was he who organised the Wednesday night concerts in direct competition with those at the Star. Samwell went on to become a regular promoter for Mecca, a record producer for Georgie Fame and the Small Faces, a songwriter - 'Move It' for Cliff Richard - and was an early member of Cliff's first backing group The Drifters.

Being primarily a dancehall, it was also a regular haunt of visiting American soul groups; Rufus Thomas, Otis Redding, Jimmy Ruffin, while Ben E King and various incarnations of the 'other' Drifters returning time and again, 'by popular demand'. In the early Seventies, the venue became **Tiffanys**, or 'Tiffs' to the platform-soled regulars who got down to the weekly disco nights or crowded in to see chart acts such as Wizzard, Slade, Mud and Suzi Quatro.

By the time it changed name again, to **Cinderella Rockerfella's** (sad, isn't it!), the venue had incorporated a squash and fitness centre and the live music nights had all but died out. Once it became **Jaz**, they had added a bowling alley and the only concession to live music were the occasional 'P.A.'s' (personal appearances), singers who turn up to sing or even mime over a backing track of their latest single. Currently known as the Metröpol... as Neil Young would say, it's better to burn out than it is to rust... but try telling that to the Savoy!

The Davis Theatre

73 High Street, Croydon, Surrey.

When it opened in December 1928, the **Davis Theatre** was said to have the second largest seating capacity in Britain, with 3,725 seats. Built by the Davis family, who had pioneered the opening of 'Picture Palaces' in London since before the First World War and designed by Robert Cromie, the auditorium was as vast as its decoration was lavish. Two years later, the Davis family arranged to build a 5,000 seater in Hammersmith, again designed by Cromie and in association with the Gaumont-British Picture Corporation. When it opened, the seating was down to 3,560 and it became known as the Hammersmith Odeon (now the Labatt's Apollo) - Cromie's auditorium design being similar to the Croydon Davis, but not so intricate in decoration!

After the war, live shows began to appear more frequently, including Jeanette MacDonald in July 1946 and the inaugural concert of the Royal Philharmonic Orchestra conducted by its founder, Sir Thomas Beecham. In October 1956, the Davis hosted the Bolshoi Ballet for its only performances outside of Covent Garden. The ticket queue is reputed to have stretched from the Theatre (opposite the South end of Surrey Street) right back up to East Croydon Station! Other names to have played at the Davis during the Fifties include Maurice Chevalier (February '53), Liberace (October '56), Bill Haley (7th October '56) and Buddy Holly (12th March '58).

Almost all of the jazz 'greats' played the Davis Theatre and the final live performance here was 'Jazz at the Philharmonic', on 10th May 1959 featuring Ella Fitzgerald & the Gene Krupa Quartet. Almost as a direct result of the planned Fairfield entertainment complex, the site was sold off for shops and an office block - sadly, the magnificent Davis Theatre was demolished in 1960.

The Gun Tavern

Church Street, Croydon, Surrey.

Although never one of the biggest venues, the Gun is certainly one of Croydon's longest running live music clubs. Situated on the corner of Church Street and Crown Hill, the pub became the home to the Croydon Jazz Club as early as 1952 and opened it's large side room as 'Croydon's Own Rock Club' on July 1st 1958, where for a mere two shillings, you could dance to Dickie Sayer & the Semitones! By 1965, the place was known as the **'Marquet Club'** (surely a play on the famous 'Marquee' in Wardour Street) and was in direct competition with the Star at Broad Green. In November '65, another name change, this time to the **'Club Nevada'** and guests included Gary Farr & the T-Bones and Van Morrison's Them. 1969 saw the Gun presenting a folk club that featured artists of the calibre of John Martyn and Roy Harper before it closed in March of that year. During the Seventies, it became once again predominately a jazz venue, with Don Weller's Major Surgery and a string of celebrated guests virtually monopolising the whole of 1975!

Fortunately the Gun is still very much alive as a music venue - jazz is still featured regularly on Sundays, although every type of musical taste is catered for during the week.

Courtesy Croydon Library Services

The Davis Theatre, circa 1959.

There are many other venues that deserve a fuller mention than space permits; for example, **Wallington Public Hall** was almost the equivalent of the Star, in terms of regular gigs and quality acts - Jerry Lee Lewis, Gene Vincent, Manfred Mann, the Stones, Cream, John Mayall, Status Quo, David Bowie - a great gig, and only the difficulty in sourcing dates and information prevented a fuller profile of the place.

The Olive Tree situated at Brighton Road, South Croydon was a coffee bar that hosted a regular music session in the basement. Although thought of as a folk club, anyone could turn up - the Quiet Five crammed in to play, Wizz Jones, Cliff Aungier, Ralph McTell, Jacqui McShee and Long John Baldry, while Jimmy Page, Rod Stewart and members of the Kinks and the Yardbirds were regularly spotted in the audience. And all over an espresso on a Sunday lunchtime...

Courtesy Croydon Library Services

The Gun Tavern, circa 1969.

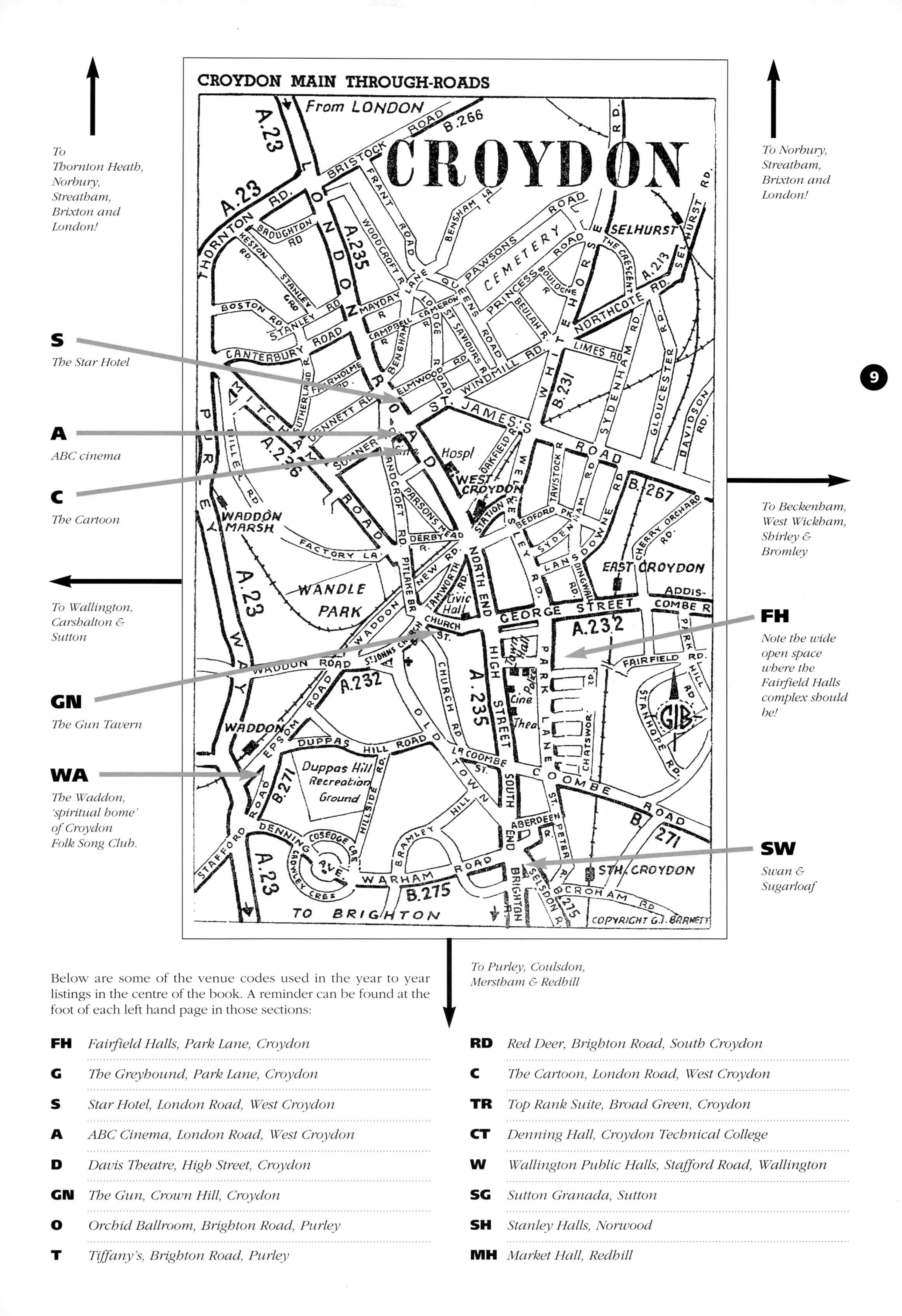

Below are some of the venue codes used in the year to year listings in the centre of the book. A reminder can be found at the foot of each left hand page in those sections:

- **FH** *Fairfield Halls, Park Lane, Croydon*
- **G** *The Greyhound, Park Lane, Croydon*
- **S** *Star Hotel, London Road, West Croydon*
- **A** *ABC Cinema, London Road, West Croydon*
- **D** *Davis Theatre, High Street, Croydon*
- **GN** *The Gun, Crown Hill, Croydon*
- **O** *Orchid Ballroom, Brighton Road, Purley*
- **T** *Tiffany's, Brighton Road, Purley*
- **RD** *Red Deer, Brighton Road, South Croydon*
- **C** *The Cartoon, London Road, West Croydon*
- **TR** *Top Rank Suite, Broad Green, Croydon*
- **CT** *Denning Hall, Croydon Technical College*
- **W** *Wallington Public Halls, Stafford Road, Wallington*
- **SG** *Sutton Granada, Sutton*
- **SH** *Stanley Halls, Norwood*
- **MH** *Market Hall, Redhill*

The Pre-Fairfield 'Fifties

Although this book was intended to begin at the start of the Swinging Sixties, it is impossible to ignore the major changes in popular music during the previous decade, in particular the arrival of American Rock'n'Roll during the late 'fifties. The entertainment industry during the 1950's was dominated by cinema and the theatre; live music consisted largely of variety shows and music hall packages, while dancehalls swung to the beat of the big band sound, with trad. jazz firmly established in the clubs and pubs of the area, in venues such as The Star, Broad Green, The Prince of Wales, Thornton Heath and The Palm Court in Purley.

Many big band vocalists had become stars in their own right - Bing Crosby, Alma Cogan, Frank Sinatra, Ella Fitzgerald. Sinatra never actually appeared in Croydon, although his son caused some confusion in 1964, but Frank senior came close on Sunday 14th June 1953 when he played at the Tooting Granada. Backed by Billy Ternent and his Broadcasting Orchestra, Sinatra ran smoothly through a set that included 'Tenderly', 'Night & Day', 'That Old Black Magic', 'September Song' and 'Birth of the Blues'.

Fifties Croydon had more than its fair share of theatres for the staging of live music - The Empire and The Grand among them - but the premier venue of the day was the **Davis Theatre**, situated in the High Street almost opposite the south end of Surrey Street. Sunday May 13th 1956 featured two shows by **Eartha Kitt** and the programme shows four other acts on the bill, including trumpet virtuoso Kenny Baker and American singing star Johnny Brandon. The 'Nabob of Sob' **Johnnie Ray**, so named for his emotional, tearstained performances, played here in early December 1956. Croydon Times reporter Leslie Hadfield noted that the massive steel safety curtain had to be lowered at the end of Ray's second show to prevent a mob of screeching, squealing teenage girls from rushing the stage. Outside, 4,000 yelling, screaming teenagers jammed the High Street until police could clear a passage for buses and cars; 300 girls, many with "I Love Johnny" emblazoned on their sweaters, jostled with police outside the stage door and blows were exchanged between a group of teddy boys and a few older men. But the Davis Theatre staff were already old hands at coping with such behaviour, as one member told the Times - "Following the visits of Liberace and Frankie Laine and other celebrities, we are quite used to this sort of excitement now..."

In America, Variety Magazine claimed that the new music was just a fad and would not last the year. But in February 1957 the Croydon Times announced the arrival in town of the new musical sensation - Rock and Roll! When **Bill Haley & his Comets** sailed into Southampton and caught the train up to London, our local paper had this to say;

Croydon Times – 8.2.57

'ROCK'N'ROLL KING IS COMING TO CROYDON - SO CALL THE POLICE!'

*ROCK'N'ROLL King **Bill Haley**, whose arrival at Waterloo Station on Tuesday night caused one of the biggest fan riots London has known, will appear at the Davis Theatre, Croydon on Monday and Tuesday, March 4 and 5. With his Comets band, he will give two shows on each evening - and squads of police will be on duty inside and outside the theatre each night, just in case the Haley fans should attempt to repeat the Waterloo Station scenes.*

Police will also be on duty at the theatre on Monday morning next, when the advance booking office opens. Prices will range from 5s. 6d. up to a guinea (21 shillings!)

Appearing with Haley and his Comets will be Vic Lewis and his Orchestra. Mr. Vernon Clarke, manager of the Davis Theatre, told a 'Times' reporter yesterday: "The Rank Organisation had booked up every date for Haley's tour of Britain, but when it was learned that we were interested and would like to present him in Croydon, Haley's agents decided to extend his tour."

Practically every top line American star who has visited Britain in the last five or six years has appeared at the Davis Theatre and the reputation of the theatre as a leading London entertainments centre is well known to American artists and their agents. In extending his tour, Haley is in good company, for last October the famous Bolshoi Ballet, who were originally booked only for Covent Garden, decided to stay in Britain several more days in order to appear at the 4,000 seater Davis Theatre. The story of the amazing mile-long queue which waited at the theatre for Bolshoi Ballet tickets hit the front pages of newspapers throughout the world.

Note: When the picture 'Rock Around The Clock', featuring Bill Haley and his band, was shown at the Davis Theatre some months ago, teenagers jived in the aisles and on the stage, and police had to break up hysterical crowds of youngsters in the street after the show.

In fact, Bill Haley's next feature film 'Don't Knock The Rock', was showing at the Eros Cinema in Croydon only two two weeks before his appearance at the Davis. Another local rock group, **Rory Blackwell & the Blackjacks**, had good reason to welcome the arrival of Bill Haley. Blackwell took his six-piece band down to Southampton in order to welcome Bill Haley to England and travelled back with him on the train to Waterloo, where both bands held an impromptu rock 'n' roll session on the platform. A jubilant Rory Blackwell told the Croydon Times: "Bill was very impressed with our performance and thought we compared well with many of the bands in the United States. I am pretty sure Haley will come along to our club and say 'Hello' after he appears in Croydon on March 5."

Since forming in September 1956, Rory and the Blackjacks played one night stands all over the country, appeared in the first ever British Rock 'n' Roll film called 'Rock, You Sinners' and opened a rock club at the Gun Tavern, Church Street, The Croydon Razzle-Dazzle Club, where they appeared every Tuesday.

Bill Haley's appearance at the Davis was reported in the Croydon Times: *'When the curtain went up on the second half, those seven figures in their famous tartan jackets were already in position, with 'King' Haley, kiss curl and all, rocking in their midst. They ripped immediately into some old favourites, 'Rockin' Through The Rye' and 'Razzle-Dazzle'. The audience, swaying and clapping to the beat, were well and truly 'sent' and if it had not been for the burly attendants who lined the walls there would certainly have been some rocking in the aisles.*

Haley, I felt, was always in complete control of the show. For 40 minutes the Comets dished out rock with flawless showmanship and polish. Their gimmick of playing their instruments while stretched flat on the floor was a huge success. Saving up his most popular numbers for last, Haley finished with an ear-splitting version of "See You Later Alligator' and 'Rock Around The Clock', which had the balconies quite literally shaking to the music. In an interview after the show, Bill Haley told me he had been rocked by his Croydon reception which was "tremendous".'

American rock 'n' roller Bill Haley takes a cup of tea backstage at the Davis Theatre with managing director Mr. Alfred Davis.

Note the familiar plaid jacket hanging on the dressing room door!

Courtesy Croydon Library

In the same week that Croydon's teenagers were rocking to Bill Haley, another local band was making its debut. The **Norrie Wescott Skiffle Group** first appeared at The Star on Friday 1st March; at the Star again the next night, at The Leslie Arms on Sunday and at the Gun's new rock'n'roll club on Tuesday 5th. The group featured local guitar tutor **Steve Benbow**. As the advertisement from the Croydon Times shows, 'Singing the Blues' star **Guy Mitchell** appeared at the Davis on 17th February 1957 just prior to Bill Haley, while only a month later on Sunday 7th April Count Basie & his Orchestra turned out.

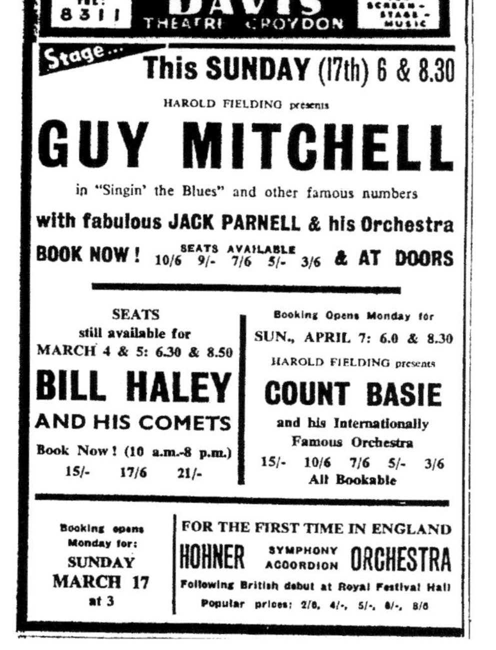

TEL: 8311 DAVIS THEATRE CROYDON FOR SCREEN - STAGE - MUSIC

Stage... This SUNDAY (17th) 6 & 8.30

HAROLD FIELDING presents

GUY MITCHELL

in "Singin' the Blues" and other famous numbers

with fabulous JACK PARNELL & his Orchestra

BOOK NOW! SEATS AVAILABLE 10/6 9/- 7/6 5/- 3/6 & AT DOORS

SEATS still available for MARCH 4 & 5: 6.30 & 8.50

BILL HALEY AND HIS COMETS

Book Now! (10 a.m.-8 p.m.) 15/- 17/6 21/-

Booking Opens Monday for SUN., APRIL 7: 6.0 & 8.30

HAROLD FIELDING presents

COUNT BASIE and his Internationally Famous Orchestra

15/- 10/6 7/6 5/- 3/6 All Bookable

Booking opens Monday for: SUNDAY MARCH 17 at 3

FOR THE FIRST TIME IN ENGLAND HOHNER SYMPHONY ACCORDION ORCHESTRA

Following British debut at Royal Festival Hall

Popular prices: 2/6, 4/-, 5/-, 6/-, 8/6

On 6th April the Civic Hall, Croydon held a Rock'n'Roll Special starring **Rory Blackwell & his Blackjacks**, **Bobby Breen's Rockers** and **Terry Dene**, billed as "Britains answer to Elvis Presley". The show was a bit of a flop, with only 90 people turning out in a hall with a capacity of 800; the organisers lost about £60.00 and Blackwell blamed the poor turnout on the fact that Count Basie was playing the Davis the following night!

Another of Britains earliest Rockers, **Wee Willie Harris** has good cause to remember the Davis Theatre. Bermondsey born Charlie Harris started singing around the clubs and coffee bars of Soho in 1956, playing a mixture of skiffle and a little early rock'n'roll either solo or in front of a group called Lo'Dons Ravin' Rockers. One of his first solo gigs was at the Croydon Civic Hall in April 1957 where he drew an audience of just 28 people! Harris began to hang around the celebrated 2i's Coffee Bar at 59 Old Compton Street, where he was eventually taken on the books of promoter Paul Lincoln, an Australian who co-owned the 2i's and was the manager of Terry Dene and the Most Brothers (featuring Mickie Most). Lincoln's first step was to persuade Harris to grow his hair and dye it an outrageously bright pink, followed by a change of name and wardrobe - vivid red drapecoat and pink socks to match the hair!

The launch of this colourful new image took place in Croydon at the Davis on 20th October 1957 in front of the invited national press, who splashed the story of how this new singer had insured his outrageous hairstyle for £12,000 all over the next day's papers. It may have been totally fabricated, but it turned Wee Willie Harris into a celebrity overnight.

Still an all-important attraction at the Davis Theatre, September 1957 saw appearances by jazz favourites **Earl Hines** and **Jack Teagarden**, whilst on the 27th October that year, **Count Basie** and his Orchestra, featuring vocalist Joe Williams, made a welcome return visit. Ticket prices once again ranged from 3/6d to 15 shillings.

The Grand Theatre, situated further south on the Brighton Road, tended to stage variety shows that ran for one whole week at a time. For example, singing star **Ronnie Carroll** topped the bill of the week commencing February 11th, changing to **Lita Rosa** on the 18th and "ooh now missus, 'ere's a funny thing..." one of Britains greatest comedians, **Max Miller** on February 25th. All of these acts played two shows a night with tickets ranging from 2/6 to 5/6d. Popular it may have been, but despite raising a petition of 40,000 signatures, the Grand closed down in April 1959 - Leon House now stands on the site.

Pre-Fairfield 'Fifties (contd.)

A further landmark concert for Croydon's rock'n'rollers took place on Wednesday 12th March 1958, when **Buddy Holly & the Crickets** took to the stage at the Davis Theatre. One of the true innovators of rock'n'roll music, Holly was in the middle of his first, and as it turned out, tragically his last UK tour. Following Bill Haley's somewhat 'eventful' British tour and the subsequent hysteria surrounding rock'n'roll groups, all national publicity was kept to a minimum and the twenty five dates went largely unrecorded in the press. Of course the fans had other ideas, giving Holly and two pals - bassman Joe B. Maudlin and drummer Jerry Allison - a heroes welcome. The Davis held two shows, with tickets ranging between 10/6d down to 3 shillings; for their money the fans got a bill that also featured Gary Miller, the Tanner Sisters and Des O'Connor as compere! One of the handful of local papers to cover the tour, the Croydon Advertiser was still restricted to a few brief lines, mainly reporting that a small section of the audience heckled the incongruous support acts: *"It's billing like this that gets the audience mad. The bad manners, justified as they may have been at times, were certainly not called for during Mr. Holly's boldly professional performance - a lusty, swinging, uplifting display of "rock", which I thoroughly enjoyed."*

Within a year, Buddy Holly was dead at the age of 22 - in trying to fulfil yet another concert date, his chartered plane crashed minutes after take off from Clear Lake, Iowa, also killing the pilot and two other stars from the tour, The Big Bopper and Ritchie Valens.

Columbia label before flying to Paris on Sunday.

Anka & Crickets name the dates

CANADIAN disc star Paul Anka will open his "quick"-return British tour in Scotland on March 1.

On this trip Anka will play one-nighters for agent Harold Fielding, backed by the 13-piece Vic Hammett Orchestra.

Other artists on the bill will include the Peter Groves Trio and the Kentones.

Tour towns

Anka will visit the Music Hall, Aberdeen (March 1); Caird Hall, Dundee (2nd); Usher Hall, Edinburgh (3rd); City Hall, Newcastle (4th); City Hall, Sheffield (5th); De Montfort Hall, Leicester (6th); Dome, Brighton (7th); Dominion, Harrow (9th); Colston Hall, Bristol (10th); Theatre Royal, Bournemouth (12th); Rialto Cinema, York (15th); City Hall, Hull (16th); Kings Hall, Belle Vue, Manchester (18th); Philharmonic Hall, Liverpool (19th); Savoy Cinema, Lincoln (20th); Victoria Hall, Hanley (21st); Davis Theatre, Croydon (23rd).

Dates not yet finalised are March 8, 13, 14, 17 and 22.

London debut

THIRTEEN more dates have now been fixed for Buddy Holly and the Crickets, who start their 25-day British tour of one-night stands at the Trocadero, Elephant and Castle, Saturday, March 1.

Added to the dates announced last week are:

Town Hall, Birmingham (March 10); Paramount, Worcester (11th); Davis Theatre, Croydon (12th); Granada, East Ham (13th); Granada, Woolwich (14th); De Montfort Hall, Leicester (16th); Gaumont, Doncaster (17th); St. George's Hall, Blackburn (18th); Regal, Hull (19th); Philharmonic, Liverpool (20th); Granada, Walthamstow (21st); Gaumont, Salisbury (22nd), and Colston Hall, Bristol (23rd).

ZZ FEDERATION

British Concert Tour of THE BRUBECK

AGENT PROTESTS

Melody Maker - issue dated February 15th 1958 Out every Friday, price 6d.

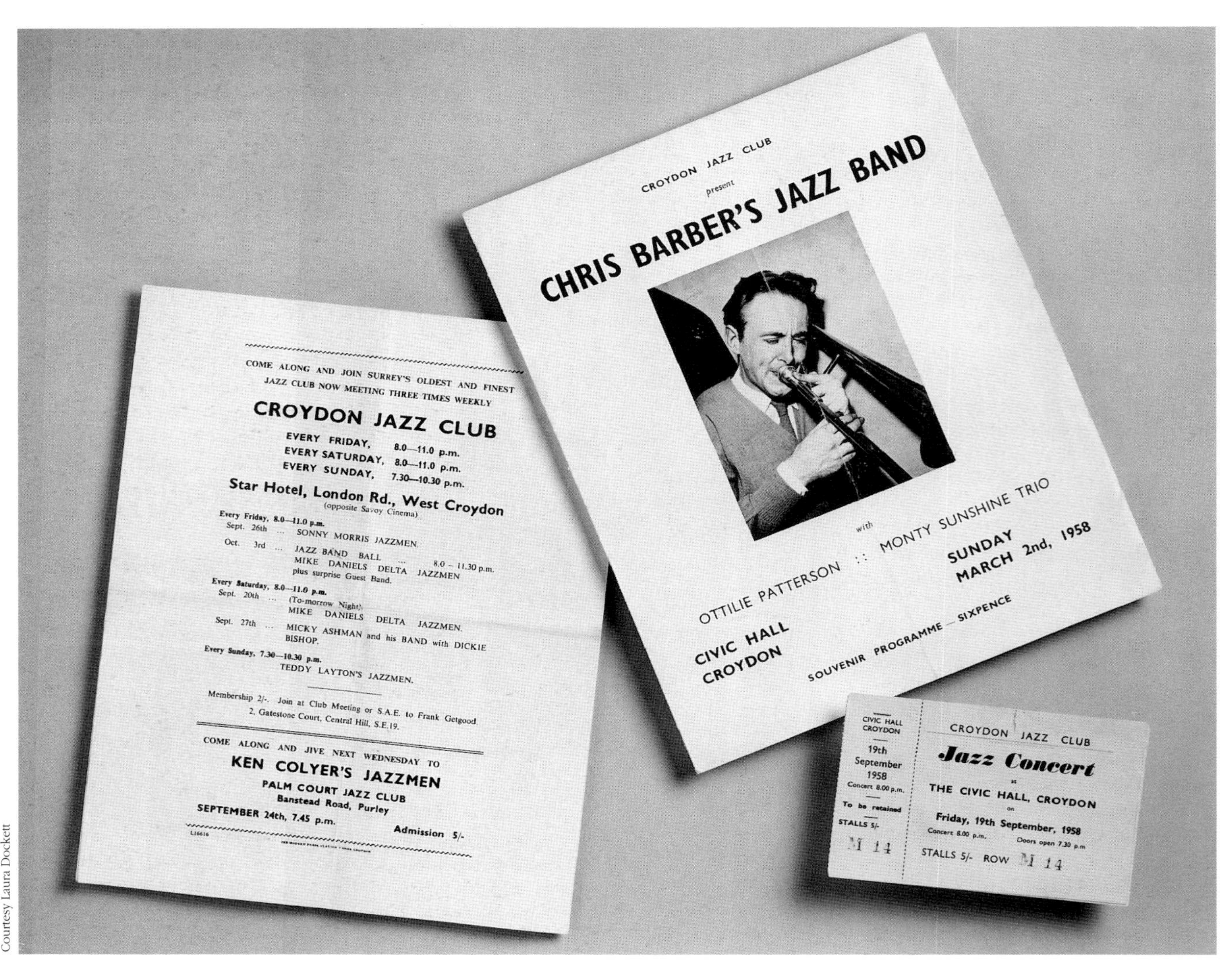

Courtesy Laura Dockett

A selection of items from the collection of jazz fan Laura Dockett. A keen dancer, Laura remembers jiving at Alf Spencer's Palm Court Jazz Club in Purley and at the Park Lane Ballroom, Croydon and was a member of one of the Peggy Spencer dance teams, operating out of the celebrated dance studio in Penge.

In the same month as the appearance by Buddy Holly, the Theatre hosted a concert by **Paul Anka** (Saturday 22nd March), backed by the 13 piece Vic Hammett Orchestra and supported by the Peter Groves Trio and The Kentones. The following night, opera fans were treated to a performance by **Mario Lanza**, one of the great tenors and occasional film star - 'The Student Prince' and 'The Great Caruso'.

The Croydon Advertiser ran a regular column called 'Swing Miscellany' to cover the local music scene of the day and it reported that the **Hot Rods**, from Thornton Heath won through two rounds of the National Skiffle Competition, organised by the Daily Sketch. A seven piece group, led by 17 year old Rodney Lyward, they beat off stiff opposition to go through to the regional finals held at Kingston on March 28th.

That same week, the **Cellarmen** won a local skiffle competition at the Civic Hall, Croydon. Their prize? - five guineas and a recording test! Swing Miscellany also reported that members of Croydon Jazz Club went to Twickenham to see the recording of Jack Good's pop programme 'Six Five Special', and that several of them could be seen jiving furiously to Don Lang & his Frantic Five.

The **Gun** opened 'Croydon's Own Rock Club' on July 1st 1958 and two shillings on the door gave you an evening with **Dickie Sayer & the Semi-tones**. Local lad Dickie Sayer later changed his name to **Dickie Pride** when he was taken under the wing of promoter Larry Parnes.

Elvis Presley may never have set foot in England, let alone visit Croydon, but his fans still managed to cause the local constabulary some considerable problems. Towards the end of September 1958, Presley's film 'King Creole' opened at cinemas all over the country and police were rushed to the Odeon in Croydon High Street where hundreds of fans were brawling and fighting in the queue outside the cinema. The trouble was calmed outside, but once the film had begun, pandemonium broke out. The Croydon Times reported that *"police entered the auditorium and ejected some of the leading troublemakers. Youngsters were jiving in the aisles, shouting, stamping their feet, whistling and jeering. Lighted cigarette ends were 'shot' across the packed rows of seats".*

One irate patron complained to the local press *"It was disgusting. If this goes on, Croydon will become a little Chicago".* Manager of the Odeon, Mr. K. Milborrow said that the cinema operated a blacklist system to 'vet' teenagers at the box office, but some of the troublemakers slipped through!

Croydon Jazz Club, although firmly based at the Star Hotel, also promoted larger concerts at the Civic Hall. Weekly admission was 3/- for members, plus an extra shilling for guests and a typical month saw appearances from the Sonny Morris Jazzmen, the Alex Welsh Dixielanders, Terry Lightfoots Jazzmen, Mr. Acker Bilk and Mike Daniels Delta Jazzmen (March 1958). Later that year, **Ken Colyer** played the Civic Hall (September 19th) and **Jimmy Rushing** was accompanied by Humphrey Lyttleton & his Band on October 10th, with tickets ranging from three to six shillings.

Val Wilmer

Sonny Payne, drummer with the Count Basie Orchestra. Davis Theatre, Croydon - 15th February 1959.

The great **Duke Ellington** and his Orchestra came to Croydon in October 1958 where 'jazzer' Val Wilmer managed to get past the stage doorman at the Davis to snap Clark Terry (see page 35) and in February 1959 Val returned to photograph the **Count Basie Orchestra**, including the shot of drummer Sonny Payne (below). For this visit, vocalist Jimmy Rushing had been replaced by blues singer Joe Williams and the orchestra were on top form - playing two sell-out shows following a recent 'top jazz band' award from the music press. Croydon Times reporter Jacqueline Kenney was suitably impressed: *"The way in which the band 'explodes' into each number has never been more prominent, and the overall effect was one of superbly controlled power... the greatest sound that ever issued from the USA."*

Jazz legend **Louis Armstrong** played two shows at the Davis on 8th March 1959, tickets priced 5/- to 15/-. His 'All-Stars' band featured pianist Billy Kyle, Trummy Young on trombone and clarinettist Peanuts Hucko. The show also featured Britain's Alex Welsh Band as support. Jacqueline Kenney had this to say - *"Louis is still the undisputed king of jazz, although many have their own opinion as to his being the greatest trumpeter."*

The final concert performance at the Davis Theatre was 'Jazz at the Philharmonic' on 10th May 1959. Top of the bill was **Ella Fitzgerald**, backed on the night by the Lou Levy Quartet. The show opened with the Oscar Peterson Trio, who were later joined onstage by saxophonist Sonny Stitt and the first half closed with the Gene Krupa Quartet. Ella appeared after the interval for a short, albeit sublime twenty minutes and the show concluded with trumpet star and showman Roy Eldridge.

Both houses were packed out in fitting tribute, partly to the star-studded jazz bill but also in farewell to a much loved theatre. The Davis continued to show films until its doors closed forever at the end of the month.

ALL-STAR MIDNIGHT MATINEE
to be held at
DAVIS THEATRE on MAY 1st
GIRLS—keep your date with DICKIE VALENTINE
not forgetting
MR. ACKER BILK'S PARAMOUNT JAZZ BAND
(by arrangement with the Croydon Jazz Club)

BERNARD BRESSLAW	SYLVIA LEE
ROY CASTLE	MORRIS & COWLEY
PETER CAVANAGH	DES O'CONNOR
DENNIS COLEMAN SINGERS	BOB & ALF PEARSON
FREDDIE EARLE	JACKIE RAE
THE HIGH FIVE GROUP	JOAN REGAN
AUDREY JEANS	CLIFF RICHARD
DESMOND LANE	DEREK ROY
	STAN STENNETT

These have promised to appear and a host of others
SEATS NOW BOOKABLE — BOX OFFICE OPEN
All proceeds to be shared between Croydon General, Waddon and Purley Hospitals and Variety Artists' Benevolent Fund
There are buses to take you home after the show

This ad. appeared in the Croydon Times dated 17th April 1959 - notice that sharing similar billing alongside Croydon's own High Five Group is a young Cliff Richard.

Ralph McTell

I met up with Ralph at the Half Moon, Putney in May 1993. Although he was born at Farnborough in Kent, Ralph moved to Croydon soon afterwards, living around the Waldrons/ Duppas Hill area for many years. Considered by many to be one of Britain's finest contemporary singer-songwriters, his work is full of references to his early life in and around Croydon - friends, neighbours, even his Sunday school teacher have all proved to be inspirations for his songs.

An undoubted classic, 'Streets Of London' gave Ralph a top five hit record in 1974 yet arguably it has been as much of a hindrance as a help to his career, as it tends to overshadow the wealth of other material he has written - 'From Clare To Here', 'Zimmerman Blues', 'Kew Gardens' and the locally-inspired 'Bentley & Craig'.

In 1959 I joined the army as a boy soldier; I was attending John Ruskin Grammar School, which was up near Shirley and to be honest I hated school - and I hated that school in particular. I had some good friends there, but not very many happy memories of the place and so I joined the army, which looking back was an even worse decision. In order to get out, part of the deal for my release was that I went back to school; well, the school option wasn't really open to me at that time, so I went to Croydon Technical College where I embarked on a course to try and obtain a couple of O-levels and I also attended the art department there.

By 1960 the 'Trad. boom' had occurred, which I quite enjoyed because I had always liked trad. jazz and there were quite a lot of musical activities happening in the art college - I remember the Temperance Seven coming to play there before they were really big, people like that. The college ran a jazz club and one evening after the club itself had finished, somebody put a record on by Jesse Fuller - actually I think it was Jesse Fuller, or it could possibly have been Rambling Jack Elliot, I'm not quite sure - but anyway, the song was 'San Francisco Bay Blues' which has become a bit of a blues standard - in fact Eric Clapton has just recorded it for his 'Unplugged' album. Now this may sound a bit corny, but hearing that old Jesse Fuller record quite literally changed my life; it was exactly the sort of sound that I'd been looking for, so I went straight out and brought myself a guitar. I had previously owned one guitar and never really taken it up seriously, but this time I went home everyday, got the guitar out and just worked and worked; I borrowed the EP that the song was on, I learned to play it or at least learned to play the chords and then I had to work on the technique. It really was so dramatic that I actually saved up some cash! - I had to get a job in order to pay back the money that I used to purchase my discharge from the army and at the same time as paying that back, I was working as a gardener on the weekends to save up enough for a decent guitar from Potter's Music Shop in South Croydon - £15 it cost me!

Eventually I brought a West German guitar called a Ross from Potters, which was the nearest thing to the 'jumbo' sound that I had heard - I didn't know at the time what these guitars were - it turned out they were known as Jumbo's or Dreadnaught's, and they had this fabulous deep sound.

Now around about that time I had discovered a pub called the Whitgift Arms at the bottom of Scarbrook Road, which was an old fashioned cider pub, run by a wonderful couple called Maurice and Reenie. It attracted the usual kind of 'cider heads', but gradually, and partly through my friend Les and I, it also attracted a fringe element, a sort of beatnik crowd and it wasn't too long before there was a bit of music going on in there. I still have a photograph of me aged about 17, playing my guitar outside that pub, I must have been showing off to my mates I suppose. That was the beginning of it, just a bunch of mutually encouraging friends - then someone else would bring another guitar down and one of the old boys would play the piano, in fact I wrote a song about it called "All Things Change". The early sixties was a very exciting musical period because you also had the Blues boom or at least the beginning of it, running in tandem with the trad. jazz thing. Before the Mods came along, there was a youth group called Modernists who wore shirts with detachable collars, little ties, very sharp suits and expensive shoes. They were mostly working class boys, and some of them were into the jazz thing but others were really driven by the blues and the Chicago blues in particular.

Of course, if you go back to the 1950's, you know that Buddy Holly played at the Davis Theatre and so, I believe, did Bill Haley and most of the big-name, mainstream jazz people - Ella Fitzgerald, Stan Kenton, Earl Hines; if only I had known, you know, what I know now! Croydon has always had a fairly healthy jazz scene; good old Bill Brunskill and his jazz band were still going up until quite recently, and for all I know they may still playing every week at the Lord Napier in Thornton Heath.

The Star up at West Croydon, opposite the old Savoy Cinema was a wonderful place; originally it was a jazz gig, but they also had the Yardbirds on a Friday night, certainly Clapton played there on a fairly regular basis and Jimi Hendrix once played there too. At weekends a group of us would either go up to the West End to dodge about, score a little bit of blow or whatever, or we could go over to Eel Pie Island in Twickenham to see a good rhythm and blues band. At that time it seemed to me that the music kind of went two ways; you either took the acoustic route or you got into the electric side of things. Quite a few of my friends, Jo-Ann and Dave Kelly and myself included, stayed firmly rooted in the 'blues', I always thought half way between Woody Guthrie and Blind Boy Fuller - acoustic sort of guitar things, with a bit of flatpicking and stuff - but at the time we had very few places to play.

We all used to go to a club at the Wheatsheaf pub by Thornton Heath Pond, which I think was held on a Monday night and run by three wonderful guys, Alan, John and Dave. They would play everything from R'n'B, to Sonny Boy Williamson-type blues, to sea shanties. This was the first time I ever heard it called 'folk' music; before that it had always just been music to us and I think it was probably the first place that I ever properly performed in public. Some friends of mine literally pushed me onto the stage one night and I played a few songs, to my surprise people didn't shout or boo, which was quite encouraging. Then an old mate of mine called Henry, who was a passionate music buff - he loved jazz but he also liked the blues and Woody Guthrie - he decided to open a club; I can't remember the exact sequence of this, but at some point we finished up playing at a place called 'Under The Olive Tree' in South Croydon. This was basically a basement coffee bar, local group Pat Dane & the Quiet Five used to play down there, in fact quite a few live bands came down.

The Olive Tree was situated on the main Brighton Road, well past the Swan & Sugar Loaf on the left hand side heading south, I doubt whether I could find it now. It was famous for a publicity stunt when it opened, because for some obscure reason they decided to bring a camel over from Chessington Zoo which absolutely refused to co-operate; it gobbed and snorted over everybody, but I should imagine they got a few good photographs out of it. Every Sunday afternoon they held a folk session, but it wasn't traditional folk as in 'hand over the ear' stuff, it was mainly local kids playing American folk music. I remember Wizz Jones played down there, Long John Baldry played there, Cliff Aungier... - it only held about 100 people, you know, and more often than not it was packed out. The place was only the basement area of a little terraced shop, so you can imagine the size of it, it must have been a fire hazard as well - oh yes, *and* there was no alcohol! I played there several times, in fact it was there that I got my first ever review in the Croydon Advertiser, it was just a one-liner, "a fella called Ralph opened the proceedings", that sort of thing, but I got to see my name in print, which was a bit of a buzz.

There was another acoustic club at the Gun Tavern just off Crown Hill, which was also run for a time by Henry, who booked Martin Carthy and that must have been the first time I ever saw Martin play. There was very much a jazz influence at the place, but out the back of the Gun was a little additional room which had live music on a Sunday afternoon. I don't think the club lasted for very long and I can't imagine the reason why, because when Roy Harper played there for the first time it was packed out. John Martyn played there too and these people were the overflow coming down from London clubs like The Troubadour, from Bunjies and from Les Cousins in Brigg Street, off Soho Square.

Henry opened yet another club around 1961, possibly 1962, at the Prince of Wales, once again an afternoon club which seemed to do quite well. Then he ran another at the Roebuck in Mitcham - you know, he was quite an entrepreneur this guy, considering he could only have been about 19 or 20, and yet it wasn't a profit making thing, so fortunately people's fees were quite moderate. I think it was about 2 bob or half a crown to get in to most places. It didn't seem to matter to us whether there was booze involved or not, it was just another place to play or to hangout and listen. That's about all of the folk and acoustic clubs that I can recall from the Croydon area and of those, the Star was probably the most influential.

We would also travel quite a bit to hear music - funnily enough, Henry and I would always come up here to the Half Moon, because on a Monday night they had Cliff Aungier, who is another Croydon boy, playing with people like Gerry Lockran and Royd Rivers. The 'Moon' would almost always book really good guest artists and we would come up from Croydon, watch the gig, have a curry on Putney Bridge and drive back; in fact for years, whenever I came up to the West End, the only way I knew how to get there by car was via Putney! But this place is so completely soaked in music you know, it's just unbelievable - simply hundreds of people have performed in the little back room here, Stephan Grapelli, Sonny Terry & Brownie McGhee played here, Tim Hardin, the Fairports, so many great people, it was a really good acoustic club.

Croydon was a very good environment to grow up in, because everybody seemed to be playing music and the scene was very diverse - someone might be into the Carter family and somebody else would be pure Woody Guthrie - then Bob Dylan arrived on the scene and it was around the same time that I started hitch-hiking and busking my way 'round Europe, 1962. Then I moved down to Poole in Dorset for a while, where there was another fairly healthy music scene, much the same sort of stuff - all acoustic. I don't know how we heard about them, but we contacted some art students who were living in a squat over a betting shop. It was actually a sort of storehouse for old fish boxes, it was a real tumble-down place, with about 8 or 9 people living

Dave Peabody

Ralph McTell braving the elements on Putney Common, 1983.

there by the end and there was some sort of music being played all night long. Somehow I managed to get a job for a little while in a tin foundry, a metal box factory somewhere down that way. But mainly it was just music, music, music...

I started to drift a little bit away from Croydon and to travel abroad a lot more - when I got married I had to get a proper job, some sort of career, so I enrolled in a teacher-training college over at Furzedown. I stuck with that for about a year, but it was during that year that I also got a contract for my first album and so... I left and embarked on a professional musical career, finally moving away from Croydon in about 1973, I think.

As a married man I found I was going less and less into Croydon, you know, things were changing rapidly, I think the old Whitgift School came down to be replaced by that big concrete shopping centre and a lot of the old meeting places were split up - I lost touch with a lot of people.

There are some lovely paintings, actually, in the Fairfield Halls that really bring back to my memory the way Croydon once looked. I was at college when they closed the old Eros cinema down, which had been a Music Hall as well, it had D-Wings and everything, and while they were demolishing it we used to muck about in there swinging on ropes and god knows what else, getting up to all kinds of mischief.

It must have been Chris Barber, I think, who first brought Big Bill Broonzy over to England in the 1950's, and Chris was involved in the Blues package tours which were put on at the Fairfield Halls. They featured Big Joe Williams, Sister Rosetta Tharpe, Memphis Slim and many other great musicians, Lonnie Johnson and Sonny Boy Williamson, too. Apparently, Big Joe Williams went missing after one of those shows and no-one could find him for several days - and then, so legend has it, he just turned up unannounced at the

Star and sat in with somebody's set.

The following year two of my major musical heroes came and played at the Fairfield Halls - the Reverend Gary Davis and Muddy Waters. Up until then, I had only ever seen a photograph of Muddy Waters, and to say I was a little disappointed by his appearance is an understatement; on his album sleeve was this picture of two black men dressed in rural clothes, chopping wood or something. So I still had this rather folksy image of it all, I didn't know about the slick Chicago scene and when Muddy came on with a Fender Strat and a tailored suit, a silver jacket or something, I wasn't quite prepared for the visual shock of seeing him - but of course the music was fantastic! Also on one of these tours was Lonnie Johnson, who had played with Louis Armstrong in the Hot Five. He was still 'playing great' in the Sixties when I heard him, so we really were blessed to have been able to see these guys perform.

"I once got into a car on the Purley Way and there was Rod Stewart sitting in the back - he was hitch-hiking down to Brighton as well..."

I believe that even the musicians themselves were shocked to discover just how popular their music was over here; in fact Granada TV recently discovered a film they made of that same package tour, recorded in Manchester and it's pretty much what they played at the Fairfield Halls - I saw it on TV for the first time about two or three years ago. It wasn't shown in the 'sixties, I think they just recorded the show and then shelved it - Granada have also got a wonderful bit of film of Sonny Terry and the Reverend Davis from that show; they took them out and filmed them on an old disused railway station, which is very atmospheric. Jesse Fuller came to Croydon as well, but sadly I didn't see him, I don't know what happened, but I never got to see Jesse play live. From that point of view the Fairfield did us all a great service - we just couldn't believe our luck to actually see these people for real.

I believe that after the old Savoy cinema at Broad Green changed its name to the ABC, they booked a lot of good package tours, as many of the cinema chains did, but they were more pop and rock acts - the Walker Brothers, Gene Pitney, the Everly's and PJ Proby, that sort of thing.

All this was happening at just the right time for me - by the time the acoustic 'boom' had really come of age and was even making inroads to the pop charts, I could already play quite well, so I had a bit of a head start on some of the others. I saw quite a few American musicians play at The Wheatsheaf by Thornton Heath pond; in fact the first time I saw a 12-string guitar played was by a guy called Fred Girlack. I just had to get myself a 12-string after that and then I heard the Stones use one on one of their early records, so I went out and bought a Harmony 12-string.

Everyone knows about Potter's Music shop, but there was another terrific instrument shop run by this old boy, just along from the Orchid Ballroom in Purley, which was chock full of Gibsons, Martins and Epiphones. I remember he had a beautiful old black Gibson with a rose motif on it, on sale for £45 and at the time I only had about 29 pounds; I fell in love with the damn thing, but I just didn't have enough money.

What was so exciting to me, or to anybody who was starting to play music in those days, was that you would learn from one another, note by note, chord by chord - there were no books, well, only Bert Weedons' 'Play-in-a-day' and so you had to do it all by ear. I do think that British folk and blues music evolved its own guitar styles, because it was done using our ears rather than studying from books. Martin Carthy, definitely produced his own style - and in a sense I also evolved my own, though it's nothing like as complex as Martin's. I learned from playing things like 'Freight Train' with a clawhammer-lick and listening to Blind Boy Fuller records, people like that. Eventually some sort of finger-style evolved and it was fascinating to work from old records, it forced you to learn in a different way.

The old Brighton Road use to run straight through Croydon on its way down to the coast and we would all go to these 'raves' in Brighton, either drive or take the 'milk train' down. I would get up at ridiculous hours to hitchhike a lift from someone on the Purley Way - I once got into a car and there was Rod Stewart sitting in the back, he was hitch-hiking down to Brighton as well! There were whole groups of us who used to gather on the seafront, sometimes there would be a jazz band and a few guitars, but I can tell you, if you've ever tried playing an acoustic guitar on the beach, it's almost impossible to hear!

I'm sure that the first time I ever saw **Wizz Jones** play was down on Brighton Beach and we subsequently got to know each other very well and became good friends. Eric Clapton maintains that he was listening to, and was influenced by Wizz at around the same sort of time, although Eric was getting more and more into people like Elmore James. I believe Wizz had his own skiffle group back in 1956, he came second in a competition at the Davis Theatre or something like that - a skiffle band called the Wranglers - after which Joe Brown invited him to join his band the Bruvvers, but Wizz declined - I'm sure Wizz can tell you more about that. Another Croydonian, comedian Roy Hudd was also involved in that competition, so possibly it was run by the Association of Boys' Clubs that Roy was involved with.

Around 1963/64, it seemed that I was on the move all the time - I would come back to Croydon for a bit of work and the Olive Tree was still there as a place to play, I had some good mates there. Then we all tended to move down to the Surrey Street area of Croydon, to pubs like the Dog and Bull and the Royal Oak. I seem to remember Don Cocker had a pub down there. I started to get a lot of gigs around the Bromley area, Orpington, Green Street Green and a little village called Downe, I used to play regularly at a club there.

I have to say that I prefer the memory of Croydon as it was, rather than the town it has become and I find the place gives me a very strange feeling when I go back now, I'm not all that easy there. It's just ghosts of things, I suppose. My life started again after I met my wife in Paris - we neither of us miss the old place much and all my family have moved out this way now; a bit nearer to London. Yeah, I've got nice, pleasant, hazy sort of memories of Croydon as it was and I prefer it that way, but I will say that it was a wonderful place to grow up in, and there was a hell of a lot of good music in the town. ”

Mike Vernon

A hugely influential figure in the British Blues boom - as a producer for Peter Green's Fleetwood Mac, Eric Clapton and John Mayall's Bluesbreakers (amongst many others), to the formation of his own Blue Horizon record label. When I met up with Mike, I made the fatal error of forgetting the tape machine! - this is an abbreviated version from my notes.

Although born in North Wembley on the 20th November 1944, Mike Vernon considers himself a Croydonian, and certainly a 'South Londoner'. He moved with his family to a house in Friends Road, Croydon when he was aged two and a half, where his father managed the electrical shop which adjoined the Davis Theatre.

Mike's education began at St. James Primary school, then on to Purley County Grammar for Boys, where he first met his long-time friend and fellow blues enthusiast, Neil Slavin, who was a year or two older. He later attended Croydon Art College, to study textiles. When he was aged eleven or twelve, the family moved to Kenley; his father bought the piece of land in Godstone Road and his grandfather designed and built the bungalow, where members of the Vernon family are still living today.

Mike and Neil formed their first band, **The Mojomen** - Mike sang and played harmonica, plus 'a bit of guitar', Neil played guitar, Vaughn Rees (brother of actress Angehard Rees) played drums and a fourth member named Williams or Williamson, also played harmonica. They were a blues come skiffle outfit, playing the songs they loved from the early Chess EP's that were starting to filter into this country at the time - Muddy Waters, Howlin' Wolf, Bo Diddley and the like. The band never really took off; they played regular gigs at the local Church Youth Club in Kenley and at a place in Upper Norwood, their greatest 'success' was playing the 'Barge' folk club in Richmond!

Mike and his friends regularly went to the Orchid Ballroom in Purley, dancing to the soul and R'n'B groups who played there; he particularly remembers the Flirtations, as he did indeed have a brief 'flirtation' with one of them! At this time, there was little press coverage of the blues and soul music they were listening to, so Mike and Neil started up their own magazine, co-editors of R'n'B Monthly. It could be bought by mail order from advertisements in the back of the specialist Jazz magazines of the time, but mostly it was sold at the gigs that they went to see; Mike could often be found selling his own magazine outside the Star at Broad Green, before going in to listen to the very bands he was writing about.

Mike got to know the Yardbirds very well during their residency at the Star, particularly Eric Clapton and even occasionally sang with them. Vocalist Keith Relf suffered from asthma and would often need to take a break or be unable to finish a gig; Clapton knew that Mike could sing and more importantly, knew the songs, and would coax Mike onstage to join them.

By this time, Mike knew that a career as a textiles designer was not what he really wanted to do; he wanted to work in the music industry and was prepared to start at the bottom to do so. After many applications (and refusals), he was given an interview by Decca Records in November 1963, where Mike's enthusiasm and 'gift of the gab', effectively talked himself into a job. He may have been the general dogsbody/tea boy, but he was in!

He admits to owing large debt of gratitude to Frank Lee, the head of department to which he was assigned. He gained experience in every aspect of the business, but surprisingly believes the typing course that Frank sent him on, to be one of his most valuable assets. Eventually, Mike was ready to try his hand at producing a record; yet it was an American bluesman that he suggested for his first project, not one of many homegrown blues bands that were touring the clubs. Nobody at Decca at that time, was aware of the British interest in blues music, but Frank Lee gave Mike the green light to produce 'Curtis Jones in London', featuring Alexis Korner, which sold around two thousand copies and surprised everyone at the company.

Mike followed up this relative success by producing albums for Otis Spann, Champion Jack Dupree (including Eric Clapton on guitar) and John Mayall's Bluesbreakers. Mayall had already recorded one album for Decca, but was unhappy and about to leave the company for another label; Mike persuaded him to stay and went on to produce 'Bluesbreakers', now regarded as one of *the* classic British blues albums.

One of Mikes' fondest memories of live music at the Star, is of an incident that occurred at a Bluesbreakers gig. Bass player John McVie was obviously drunk, (in fact he was hired and fired by John Mayall more than once for his heavy drinking), and was leaning on his two bass speaker cabinets for support. As you looked at the stage, the Bluesbreakers lined up with Eric Clapton on the left, then drummer Hughie Flint, then McVie and John Mayall to the right hand side. Immediately behind John McVie's speakers were a pair of double doors, like a french window, with a safety bar across them. With the band in the middle of a slow blues, McVie leaned back a bit too heavily; both speaker cabinets tipped over backwards, the top one pushing down on the safety bar, which opened the doors. With an almighty crash, out went the speakers and out went John McVie, disappearing with his feet in the air and still clutching his bass. Clapton, to the front of the stage and unaware of what had been going on behind him, only turned round when the bass stopped. Flint was trying hard not to laugh, but Mayall was lying across his keyboards, creased up with laughter. Fortunately, John McVie was unhurt, and to this day, it remains one of the funniest sights that Mike Vernon has ever witnessed.

Around this time, Mike had married and moved from Kenley to Hampstead Gardens to be nearer work, and in particular to the Decca recording studios at West Hampstead. The Blues records he produced were now making Decca a considerable amount of money, yet he was still only earning about £20 a week.

With his brother Richard, Mike decided to set up his own private label - **Blue Horizon**, initially with the intention of recording singles which could be sold through his magazine, R'n'B Monthly. Mike released around fourteen singles this way, including tracks by Eddie Boyd, Lowell Fulsom, Hound Dog Taylor and an early collaboration between Clapton and John Mayall which preceded the 'Bluesbreakers' album for Decca.

Mike then began work with the band that his label is most famous for - Peter Green's Fleetwood Mac. Mike had already worked with Green when he replaced Eric Clapton in the Bluesbreakers and when Peter Green decided to leave John Mayall, he turned to Mike Vernon to produce and record his new group. They started to record some tracks 'after hours' at the Decca studios and it was these tapes that were 'instrumental' in Blue Horizon obtaining a major distribution deal with CBS. ❞

Wizz Jones

A vastly underrated folk/blues guitarist, who is only now getting the attention he deserves and credited by the likes of Eric Clapton and Jimmy Page as an early influence on their playing.

I was actually born in Thornton Heath, but of course everyone thinks of it as Croydon; and I lived in Croydon right up until I left home at the age of 16. As far as the music scene went, the thing about Croydon was that it had the Variety places, you know, Music Halls, where you could go and see live music long before the rock'n'roll thing happened. My first experience of music was going to the Empire Theatre as a kid, and seeing someone like Sid Millward & His Nitwits!

Musically, it all seemed to happen at once during the late 'fifties; traditional New Orleans-style jazz, skiffle and then rock'n'roll were all emerging at much the same time. In Croydon there was a jazz club quite early on, but I first got hooked into skiffle - it was the in-thing at that particular moment, with Lonnie Donegan on the radio all the time - which led to everyone buying a cheap guitar and learning to strum a few chords. Once a few of your mates had done that, it was straight into forming a group and there were several skiffle groups in Croydon, two or three of them working around the local pubs. The group I put together was one of those, in direct competition with the other two and we were called the **Wranglers**. This was before the jeans! - we named ourselves after the cowboy/rodeo wranglers, although we used to laugh because in English, to wrangle is to argue over something and a lot of the time this was quite appropriate! We started to play around Croydon in 1957, I must have been about 18 years old at the time and we had a regular gig every Friday night at the Leslie Arms, in Addiscombe, you know, on the corner of Cherry Orchard Road.

We also had the Davis Theatre, which was an enormous theatre where they also put on live music; I remember that the embargo had just been raised on bringing acts over from America - there had been some problem with bringing artists in from the States and they had just worked out a system whereby they could come over on an exchange basis. I got to see people like Stan Kenton, Buddy Holly, Bill Haley, all the early rock'n'roll stars and at the same time there was all this jazz thing going on, you really didn't know which way to turn - one minute you were a New Orleans jazz freak and the next you were a rock'n'roller!

My little group the Wranglers played at the Orchid Ballroom in Purley quite a few times, they put us on with another group, a rock group, who I think were called the Solitares. The lead guitarist in my band, who was younger than me, in fact he was a friend of my younger brother, was a guy named Mike Borer although he later became better known as Micky King. He had taken up the guitar at the same time time as I did, but he was very good and quickly learned to play a lot of lead stuff; he would listen to all the Gene Vincent records and learn all those licks with no problem. We used to play together a lot, either in the band, or busking down on the beach in Brighton, but unfortunately, because he was so good, he got 'poached' by other groups. First he went off to play with another local rocker, Dickie Pride and eventually wound up in the band Cliff Bennett & the Rebel Rousers where he had some success, although I think Mike left them before their first hit.

After Mike left the band and the Wranglers split up, I was more often to be found hanging around Soho than Croydon, and going off on that beatnik/hippy tangent and discovering folk music. I had already discovered **Ewan MacColl** at his club in London; I was working at a warehouse in the City and I would catch the train every morning from East Croydon station, for about a year I commuted up to town. One morning I got on the train and Ewan MacColl was in the same carriage, I only knew him by sight, but I started talking to him and it turned out that he lived in Park Hill Rise, he was living there with his first wife, so I got to know him quite well, travelling out from Croydon on the train and because he was living locally. That in itself was a great introduction to the folk scene, being able to talk to Ewan MacColl on the way to work! We were chatting one day and I happened to mention that I was really getting into the Blues and Ewan said, 'Oh, there is a blues guitarist staying at my house at the moment, you should come back and meet him. His name is Big Bill Broonzy'. I couldn't believe it, I mean, christ, Big Bill Broonzy staying in Park Hill Rise and I never went! What a fool! Still, that's the story of my life.

The other Croydon connection that had an indirect influence on my career was the Bentley & Craig case. This was a major incident that has been well documented, but it resulted in the local police having to be seen to do something about all the juvenile crime and one of the things they did was to open a boys club, and a really good one at that, in Moreland Road, Addiscombe. All the coppers would arrive on their big, red Triumph motorbikes and the youngsters actually built up a rapport with the police, it really worked very, very well. Everything was there, every kind of sport you could think of, the whole place had a great layout, but on top of that it had a sort of arts and drama section run by an old lady called Gladys Cooper, I think, who must have been in her sixties or seventies and who had worked in the theatre. As a hobby, she was running the dramatic section of this boys club and two or three times a year they would put on a concert party, with sketches, dance and music. This was another inspiration for me, because watching those shows, a lot of those guys went on to become professional artists; probably the most famous one, who must have been 15 or 16 at the time, was Roy Hudd, a real comedian character, who really knocked me out. I was just starting to play with the Wranglers and as we were looking around for places to perform, and as they didn't have a group booked, Roy actually asked us to play at one of the boys club concerts. Somewhere I still have a photograph of us on stage at the Addiscombe Boys Club, which must have been one of our first ever gigs. Roy, of course, is now a real local hero, with great success not just as a comedian and a comic writer, but people forget that he is also a very fine actor. There was another guy who came out of that club crowd called Ernie O'Malley, who became a very good drummer and went on to play with Long John Baldry and toured the world with him.

'**Under the Olive Tree**' was a well known club in South Croydon, although that was much later, after I had left Croydon, been abroad, travelled around and had a wife and a baby by then. I can't quite remember how it happened, but we got to know the couple who ran the club and I wound up as the resident guitarist there every Sunday afternoon. That's where Ralph (McTell) and Phil used to come along to, before he formed that bluegrass group that he was in, the Hickory Nuts. He used to do floor spots there, in fact all kinds of people used to come along, I found out later that you had the likes of Jimmy Page and Eric Clapton sitting in the front row - no one knew them at the time, I only found that out later - all the Yardbirds used to come down, and there was a guy who used to hang around regularly called

Dave Brock. I always thought, well he's not much of a guitar player, he won't do much, but I saw him busking one day in the Portobello Road, and I said 'How's it going' and he said 'well, I've just formed a band, I don't know if we're going to get anywhere, we're called Hawkwind!'. Ralph's brother used to work at The Olive Tree, in the coffee bar - it was a strange gig because it was an held in the afternoon - which is probably why we would see people from various bands there, before they went off to their own gig in the evening.

I must have left Croydon in 1958/59; I was having a hard time at home and more or less got kicked out and as I say, spent my time hanging around the Soho scene, dossing around the all-night coffee bars. I didn't come back to Croydon until years later, probably when I did this residency at the Olive Tree - we would come down on a Sunday afternoon, leave the baby at my mum's house and go on to do the gig. People remember the Olive Tree, because it really was quite special, I mean the people who ran the place were quite far out people, I think they even had their own plane! Really quite offbeat people. There was a good folk club at the Gun for a while, too, that Ewan MacColl and Peggy Seeger went to quite often, in fact they may even have run it.

Dave Peabody

Wizz Jones 'giving it some'. 1980

As far as my busking with **Rod Stewart**, that is a myth that Rod keeps going, for some reason; and I don't mind, it's all good publicity! After I moved to Soho, he used to come in to the pub, Finches in Goodge Street, when I was playing and he'd play harmonica along with me - later, when I was running a club at the Porcupine in Leicester Square, he would come down there as well. I remember that Sandy was always arguing with him because he wanted to come in without paying, it was a real hassle trying to get him to pay! Rod was another one who came down to The Olive Tree, I would often bump into him there. I suppose he was a fan of mine, at the time, because he was into acoustic blues, like Clapton and Page, it inspired them and they just went on and did it themselves, you know. But as for Rod and myself, we didn't really busk together and we certainly didn't go to Spain together, that is a rumour that has expanded over the years. After Rod made a name for himself with The Faces, I ran into him again at the Half Moon in Putney. He had gone there with Long John Baldry and some friends to see Derrol Adams, who was an influence on all of us. Rod had been mentioning my name in a series of magazine interviews and I went over to him and said " Will you stop giving me all this publicity, I don't want to be famous!" We had a laugh over that.

The Wranglers went in for a talent contest, organised by Radio Luxembourg - we used to play at Brixton roller skating rink, because they used to have a band to play on a balcony overlooking the rink, while the kids were skating below. In the early days the 'band' always consisted of these old guys wearing wigs and playing violins, but when rock'n'roll happened they started to book younger bands; it was a terrible gig though, you couldn't hear a damn thing above the noise of the roller skates! However, it was another place to play and we played alternate weeks with another band called the Spacemen, which turned out to be Joe Brown's first group. Anyway, we entered this Luxembourg competition where the main prize was a recording contract, but even if you didn't win, every group got a 78rpm demo recording of their entry - everyone went up to this studio in London to record two songs and the demo's were sent to Radio Luxembourg to be judged. So we went up to this studio and recorded 'Mind Your Own Business' by Hank Williams and for the other side we did 'Traced Your Little Footprints Through The Snow' which was a hit at the time for Johnny Duncan. Now the reason we did that song was because Mike Borer was such a flashy electric guitarist that he could actually play the fancy run that appears in it and we all thought, we just can't fail to win! We listened to the other groups who were in the competition every week, and most of the skiffle groups were crap, no one could play guitar that well, certainly not as well as Mike. We really thought we *had* to win it. So each week they held a heat featuring three or four bands and the winner of that heat went on to the next weeks round; and of course the week we were on was the same week that the Spacemen entered, whose guitar player, we found out years later, was Joe Brown, who is a really good guitarist... and we lost! But we all got our own copy of the 78, which was some consolation.

The other unusual gig we played was at the Granada cinema, Thornton Heath; it was when they were showing one of Elvis Presley's early films, Jailhouse Rock probably, and the manager of the cinema booked us to play on stage every night of the week, just before the main feature. I don't know how we ever got that gig, we didn't have agents in those days; anyway, we would be playing away on stage and suddenly, without warning the curtain would go up and the film would start, with us hastily clearing all our gear off stage as fast as possible! That was a great thrill, playing maybe twice a night on that big old stage at the Granada.

The time I spent in Soho was great, it's pure nostalgia now, but it really was a wonderful time. You had such a wide mix of people coming in to Soho from outside; there were working class people like me, trying to escape my boring roots, trying to break free, and mixing in with public school boys, university students and rich kids - all mixing in together, it was great. It was like all good 'scenes'; sure it had plenty of casualties, but everything grew out of that period and so much has been written about the Soho scene - at the time everyone thought that we were all pioneers, the first people to do it, but obviously it had been going on for years, long before the sixties. When we all went to busk in France and thought how it was breaking new ground, but you've only got to read 'As I Walked Out, One Midsummer Morning' by Laurie Lee to find out that he was doing it in the bloody thirties, you know.

In some ways it was better in those days for the 'itinerant drop-out', because the mass media was nowhere near as big, it wasn't on television or in the magazines every day, you really were 'underground', so to speak. I don't think they realised how outrageous we were by comparison - I mean the fifties were so gloomy; everyone looked and dressed the same, you know, greatcoats and baggy, grey flannel trousers and trilby hats, but now when you walk down the street everyone looks different, it's great. I remember when Cecil Gee's first opened in West Croydon, and I first saw Teddy Boys walking down the road in their cutaway collars and their chukka boots, and I thought what on earth is that, it was so totally new and exciting. Incidentally, Eden Kane worked in that shop before he became famous; we only realised it when we first saw him on television, 'there's that bloke who used to work in Cecil Gee's'.

"I can remember buying my first ever blues record in Kennards - a 78 by John Lee Hooker called 'Hoogie Boogie'..."

The other great shop in Croydon was **Kennards**, with it's tannoy announcements and that wonderful arcade right up the middle. It was the first time I ever saw a jukebox, up on a balcony over the arcade; it was a big old brown thing that took pennies and threepenny bits and played 78's, I used to spend hours up there. In fact I can remember buying my first ever blues record in Kennards; it was a 78 by John Lee Hooker called 'Hoogie Boogie' and years later I heard Davey Graham playing a thing called 'Davey's Train Blues' and I said to him, 'that really sounds like 'Hoogie Boogie' and he said 'yeah, I bought that record in 1950-something' and I said 'so did I...'! It turned out that we had both bought this same blues 78 at roughly the same time.

I was a real pop music fan as a kid, I had these scrapbooks that I'd made with the lyrics to all the hit songs and little drawings of all the artists, it's a great shame that I didn't keep them. I was a mad music collector too; I had all the early Les Paul & Mary Ford records but I remember flogging them to a local junk shop one day when I didn't have any money. This guy Mike Borer, that I was talking about, he lived right across the road from me and we used to broadcast to each other by fixing a copper wire between our bedroom windows! It was potentially very dangerous, sometimes it would get knocked down by a lorry; we would put the output to the copper wire and the other to the gas pipe and using our old radios and record players we'd broadcast to each other, very often it would all go wrong and blow up! Real radio freaks we were.

I never went to Potters Music shop in Croydon, although Ralph is always talking about how good it was; it can't have been open when I was starting to play guitar. It's worth mentioning R.G. Jones of course, who had the recording studio in Morden and possibly one in South Croydon, but he was the 'bigwig' sound man for a lot of local gigs in the early days.

Also on the scene then was Steve Benbow, who must have been living in Croydon at the time, he was quite a well known performer working in the blues/jazz clubs, Alexis Korner's place, that sort of thing. He worked with Denny Wright and Lenny Hastings in some jazz things, but he also went out as a soloist and I followed him around quite a bit and learned a few of his songs. I didn't really know him to speak to at the time, but I remember one sunny afternoon in about 1958, Mike Borer and I were sitting in the town hall gardens, strumming away in the little sun house, when who should come walking past but Steve Benbow. He saw us playing and stopped to talk to us, which was an honour in itself, but then he got his guitar out - he had this great old Gibson Kalamazoo - and actually started playing with us, we were knocked out by that! It is strange how things like that stay with you for years, a great memory.

It is similar to the first time I saw the film 'Quadrophenia', because there is a scene in that film which is identical to something that happened to me years before. There used to be these 'milk-train raves', where groups of us would get the early train from Soho, leave London about three in the morning and get to Brighton about six. It was a cheap fare and everyone would just spill out into the cafes and then go jiving and busking on Brighton beach, you'd stay over Saturday night and sleep on the beach if the weather was alright. I remember this particular time, I was down there with Mike and we found somewhere to sleep, under a couple of old deckchairs underneath the promenade, and we were just settling down to sleep about two in the morning, when three or four teddy boys show up. They don't know that we're there, you know, and they're cursing and swearing and kicking all the deckchairs, making houses out of them, totally pissed; meanwhile Mike and I are sitting there shivering in our shoes wondering what to do. So I finally say to Mike, 'there's only one thing for it, get your guitar out and we'll both quietly start playing a twelve bar blues or something'; so we start playing and the teds all look up... 'what's that?'. And there is this scene in Quadrophenia where a couple of guys are under the prom. and scared when the mods turn up, and that is exactly how it was, only years earlier! Gradually the teds all heard it and came round the pile of deckchairs where we were, it was 'what are they going to do' you know? If this was a film, it would fade to black and then fade back an hour on, with the teds all raving and dancing, really enjoying themselves, banging on my guitar case and swinging Mike's cover round in the air. We had a great time all night and into the early morning, just jamming away with these guys; when I saw the film I really laughed at that scene, because the Mods and Rockers came along after the Beatnik/Teddy boy thing and the twain never really met for any of the various sets of people. We laugh about it now, but if you found yourself in amongst the wrong group there could be real trouble. ”

Local Boys Make Good...

The Searchers pictured early in 1966 after recruiting Selsdon drummer Johnny Blunt to replace the recently departed Chris Curtis. Left to right: Mike Pender, John Blunt, John McNally and Frank Allen.

Courtesy John Blunt

Courtesy Cliff Aungier

Wendy Aungier

A couple of Croydon boys out on the town. Ralph McTell and Cliff Aungier revisit an old haunt - The Roundhouse 'Blues & Barrelhouse Club' in Soho. Run by Cyril Davies and Alexis Korner, Cliff recalls spending a memorable evening there in the company of Sonny Terry & Brownie McGhee.

Right: Cliff revisits an old friend - a warm greeting from the late Brownie McGhee at Brownie's house in Knoxville, Tennessee.

Procol Harum circa 1968. Left to right: Robin Trower, BJ Wilson, South Croydon's Matthew Fisher, Gary Brooker and Dave Knights.

Private collection

Jacqui McShee

From the Olive Tree to the Royal Albert Hall - a one time regular face around the Croydon folk scene, Jacqui's glorious voice is synonymous with the music of Pentangle, the first group to successfully blend traditional folk and jazz influences.

To be honest, I have never actually lived in Croydon; I was born in Catford and when I was eight or nine we moved out to a place called Merstham, which is about eight miles south of Croydon. From age eleven onwards I went to school in Purley - to Purley County when it was a very strict girls school - I really couldn't wait to leave! I took my daughter up there a couple of years ago to try and show her my old school and there was nothing there, they'd flattened it. Which is sad in a way because it was a very nice old building - all the old science labs with their brass taps - and it's now a little estate of bungalow's. I didn't hang around much in Merstham as there was nothing to do and as soon as I left school I headed for the folk and blues clubs in London. I didn't start going into Croydon until about a year later, when I joined their branch of the YCND, the Youth Campaign for Nuclear Disarmament; a lot of the guys there played guitar and it was really through them that I started to regularly visit folk clubs and to meet people like Chris Ayliffe.

It must have been about 1963 when I first met Ralph McTell, again through YCND and my field of social activity was based around Croydon - mainly the pubs - because they were music pubs. The Gun often had something on a Sunday afternoon; I can remember going there to see Long John Baldry and Rod Stewart, because Cyril Davies had recently died and there were a couple of benefit concerts for him in Croydon, including this one at the Gun. Baldry and Stewart came down and sang with the other members of Davies's group, Baldry of course had been one of the Cyril Davies AllStars.

The other main club around that time would have been the Olive Tree and I expect Ralph has told you all about that. That was another Sunday lunchtime gig and that has always surprised me; because we were all about seventeen or eighteen then and every Saturday there was an all night party at somebody's house, so how we ever managed to actually get it together and *do* something on a Sunday afternoon I'll never know! It was probably because we'd all come out of the pubs at lunchtime, with nowhere else to go but the Olive Tree. Of course there was no alcohol served there, which was probably just as well as there were a treacherous set of back stairs leading down to the 'music room' - very narrow and very steep. Ralph fell down them when he had his leg in plaster, I can remember that and Baldry fell down them; I don't think I ever did thank goodness, but they were treacherous those stairs!

We had a bit of a jug band going back then; Ralph and I, 'Jug' Henry and an American guitar player called Gary Peterson; most of the places we played were found for us by Ralph's brother Bruce May.

The Olive Tree was run by a couple called Parker and in fact I'm still in contact with a guy called Eddie Parslow who used to work there. Eddie played guitar with Ralph and with my elder sister Pam who also used to sing there. Pam and I sang together for a while, before she became a nurse and went to work at Mayday Hospital. The Parkers later brought a place somewhere near East Grinstead and Eddie still did the odd bit of work for them, cottage renovation, that sort of thing and also for the Parker's children I think. There was also a local bluegrass group called The Hickory Nuts that featured Eddie Parslow's brother-in-law!

Jacqui and the boys pictured in a Pentangle tour programme from 1972. Left to right: Terry Cox, John Renbourn, Jacqui, Danny Thompson and Bert Jansch.

Courtesy Graham Maisey

I did go to the Star at West Croydon quite a bit, when it was more of a trad. jazz hangout; I suppose I was into jazz before I got into folk music, but that was only because Pam went there and being the younger sister I got carried along in her wake. We would go and see Ken Colyer and bands like that, right up until someone played me a John Coltrane record and then that was the end of it!

I started to sing with Chris Ayliffe and we went further afield for gigs; by that time I think the Olive Tree had stopped their live music on Sundays, although it was still open as a coffee bar. Chris was a twelve string guitarist who managed 'Watkins' music shop in Balham and he knew John Renbourn and Bert Jansch - it was Chris who pushed me in their direction, although I didn't realise what he was doing at the time. I left the Croydon music scene around 1965-66, probably '66 - I was still living in Merstham, but I just didn't spend so much time around Croydon.

'This is Pentangle' - the album sleeve from a German compilation, 1973. Left to right: Terry Cox, Bert Jansch, Jacqui, John Renbourn and Danny Thompson.

I helped to run a folk club at the **Red Lion** in Sutton, with some friends of mine, Alison, Dougie and Christine. We had people like Martin Carthy, the Malcolm Price Trio, John and Bert both came down to play individually. Guys like Steve Benbow and Redd Sullivan were around, but they seemed to me to have been on the scene for years - my sister had a record of Steve's that had a track called 'Looking Through The Knothole on Grandma's Wooden Leg'! I tended to gravitate towards people like Peggy Seeger; and Ewan MacColl of course, but as much as I admired Ewan it was Peggy I really went to hear. I can't say I really knew them, they were the high flyers back then, I looked up in awe to these people.

John Renbourn had been gigging with Doris Henderson and they had recorded an album together, but when John started work on his next solo record - 'Another Monday' on Transatlantic - he asked me to sing on a couple of tracks and the two of us went off and toured the folk clubs for about a year. One day we were travelling somewhere by train and John suddenly announced that we were going to rehearse with a band at The Horseshoe in Tottenham Court Road. That's how **Pentangle** started to come together. Every Sunday we would rehearse during the day and then play an evening gig in the pub - John and I would open the set, then Bert and John would play a set together. After an interval, Danny, Terry and I would come on and we'd all play the things we'd rehearsed that afternoon. For the first year we only played at the Horseshoe, plus a couple of college gigs.

After I left Merstham I moved down to Guildford and then more recently to Redhill; there was a period during the Seventies when I lost track of Ralph, but in the last few years we have started running into each other again. Ralph is funny about our past connections with the locality, I mean he *knows* that I've never lived in Croydon, but he always tells me, "You know, we've done well, considering we come from Croydon!" But it was a was a very lively scene, there was always someone playing or something happening.

Before the Fairfield Halls were built there was a terrific junk/antiques shop on that corner of Park Lane. It had these double glass doors as you went in, a wooden floor, an old fashioned bell that rang when the door opened and just inside the door was this enormous suit of armour. It was quite a dusty, creepy place but I loved it and used to get most of my Christmas presents in there! I was really sad when that place went and instead they built the Fairfield Halls and the underpass and it suddenly became 'the windy city'. You can freeze to death on that corner now.

I am sure that contributes something to the slightly 'cold' atmosphere that you can get at the Fairfield. Pentangle played there many times over the years but whenever I've sung at the Fairfield Hall I have to say that I've never been completely comfortable; partly because I was always so nervous about performing in public, but especially knowing that there were people out in the audience that I'd known for years. I could never really relax; mind you, I was never that relaxed onstage anywhere - but I am getting better, after all these years, I'm getting better!

We all used to go to the Capricorn Club in Greek Street that was run by Acker Bilk's brother, it was just a drinking club, but we would go there and play darts with all the music journalists. I beat one guy from the Melody Maker once and he never forgave me. We got to be quite good in the end, although Danny Thompson had always been a good player; the guys from Sounds and Melody Maker used to hold regular tournaments against the various bands - Steeleye Span were another good darts team!

Talking of journalists, I can remember **Robin Denselow** coming along to the Olive Tree quite a lot; he was a very gentle, sweet natured person and his younger sister would come down too, although I can't remember her name. Robin went on to become a successful music journalist, and then subsequently a political commentator on TV, but I once read a review of a Pentangle concert that he'd covered and I remember thinking 'you bastard, I thought we were mates'!!

On the other side of the coin, Karl Dallas reviewed one of our concerts for the Melody Maker, and he must have taken an acid tab or something, although I can't imagine Karl doing acid, but his review was out of this world, it was wonderful and yet it must have been one of the worst gigs we'd ever done. We were all miserable when we came off stage - you know sometimes it just doesn't work and it certainly hadn't that night! ❞

Paul Raven

aka Paul Gadd, Paul Russell, Paul Monday, Rubber Bucket and Gary Glitter...!

Gary was unfortunately 'unavailable for comment', so this piece is partly a brief retrospective of his early career, followed by an interview with one of his closest school friends, Rick Biddle.

Born Paul Gadd on 8th May 1944 *(are you sure?!)*, in Banbury Oxfordshire, he moved with his mother to the suburbs of Sutton in the summer of 1956. She had moved in with a man called Alan Russell and although they never married, Paul always referred to Alan as his stepfather and took his surname. Paul went to Sutton Boys School for a year, before moving to Davidson Road Secondary School in Croydon. He was given his first acoustic guitar in 1957 and rather than spend his early evenings hanging around Croydon, Paul travelled up to London to meet his stepfather from work, spending most of the waiting time in the Two-i's coffee bar, watching such acts as the embryonic Shadows and Vince Taylor & the Playboys. By the time he met his stepfather and they caught the last train home to Croydon, all Paul could think about was becoming a rock 'n' roll singer.

During 1958, he formed his first group with his best schoolfriend Trevor Dry on drums and another local boy called Mick Thompson on guitar. Their first public appearance was at the Sutton Granada, one of eight groups in a Saturday morning skiffle contest. Later they were joined by Pete Raynor, a good lead guitarist from Norwood and became **Paul Russell & the Rebels**, playing regularly at the Safari Club just off Trafalgar Square mainly due to the fact that Paul's father was a good friend of the proprietor. They moved to Addiscombe and Paul fell in love with a white Hofner Senator guitar that he had seen in a shop window in Thornton Heath. In order to buy it, Paul took a job selling the evening paper outside of East Croydon station. He would then cycle across to the Purley Way to catch the factory workers who were just finishing work and finish by having a coffee in the transport cafe on the roundabout (it had the best stocked jukebox in the neighbourhood!). On Saturdays he would sell the football edition of the paper in Surrey Street market.

A week after his fifteenth birthday, Paul left school and home, moving to a bedsit in Clapham in order to concentrate on his musical career. He changed his name to Paul Raven in January 1960 and released his first single *'Alone in the Night/Too Proud'* Decca F11202, although when he was later booked on a variety package tour, the band were still billed as Paul Russell & the Rebels, now with Brian Ramsey on drums. It was an odd bill, with Anthony Newley, Bernard Bresslaw and Mike Preston and was enough to convince the other band members *not* to turn professional! The Rebels split up as soon as the tour finished and Paul lost touch with them - Pete Raynor later joined the RAF and was killed in a rifle accident.

He also worked with a Peckham band called **The Twilights**; their bassist Brian Shields remembers Paul as a pretty good live performer *"but he did have trouble holding the last note of Roy Orbison's 'Crying' and I had to cover for him"!* In early 1965 he began working regularly with a local soul & blues group called the **Anzacs** and soon afterwards met up with Mike Leander who asked him to join the **Mike Leander ShowBand** and from April to October they set off on a massive tour supporting the Batchelors.

He then spent a long time touring the club circuit in Germany as **Paul Raven & the Bostons** and on returning to Britain in 1968, he teamed up again with Mike Leander and began working together in the studio on a song called *'Soul Thing'*, later to form the basis of the first chart hit for Gary Glitter *'Rock 'n' Roll Part 1'*. In the late summer of 1971, Mike came up with the name **Gary Glitter**, inspired by the Glam rock trend that was starting to flood the charts via Marc Bolan, Slade and the Sweet. The unmistakable double drum Glitterband sound of *'Rock 'n' Roll Parts 1 & 2'* was released in March 1972 and made number 8 in the charts - and the rest, as the cliche goes, is history.

R*ick Biddle takes up the story:* "I knew Paul at school, at Davidson Road School and I suppose he must have started there in 1958. He had moved into the area from Banbury, so he joined the school late and was in the year below me. He was one of those guys who had all the best clothes and a good hairstyle, he looked like a star even then, at fourteen or fifteen. He had a guitar, but it wasn't a beaten up old thing like the other kids had, his was a white Hofner. Paul and I used to go and watch all the Elvis films, I can remember going to see 'Loving You' with him and afterwards we did the usual thing, like all the kids did, of going back to his house and standing in front of the mirror copying all of Elvis's moves! But out of all of us, he was the guy who could imitate it straight away, you know?

At Davidson Road in those days there were some little huts that the school used as cloakrooms and most lunchtimes, there was a regular gang of us, five girls and three or four guys who would hang out there. Paul would bring his guitar to school and he had the 'front' to stand in this wash house and sing Elvis songs to us, with all these other kids standing at the windows peering in. It was obvious to us that he had star quality, because it took 'bottle' to do that, but really Paul was in a world of his own and you could see that, to him, he was onstage somewhere and not in some wash house in a Croydon school!

Then he formed a band with some other local lads, the lead guitarist was Pete Raynor, who was at school in Shirley and a guy called Trevor from our school who played drums; and they played their first ever gig at the Safari Club in Northumberland Avenue. When we left school, I lost contact with him for a while until he made his first record in about 1960. He was calling himself Paul Raven by this time and we knew he was trying to make it as a singer because we had seen a piece in the local paper about him. He had just made this record 'Too Proud', which was awful really, but he came round to our house one evening when I was up at the 2-i's club in London. Anyway, my brother Terry was there and let him in, and Paul was saying he wanted to ask me to be his road manager. Now, nobody knew what a 'road manager' was in those days and even if we had, chances are my mum would have put a stop to it! Paul had a copy of his record with him and said 'Would you like to hear this' and mum said 'Sorry love, we haven't got a record player'!

I remember a couple of embarrassing moments when he was Paul Raven; first when he had 'Too Proud' out, Paul appeared on a TV programme called Kent Walton's 'Cool For Cats'. He came out wearing a pullover and sang this song and it really was dreadful; the next week, Walton announced that Too Proud *was* actually available on record and it hadn't been just some schoolboy 'having a go' - which must have been quite embarrassing for Paul. The other time was on Juke Box Jury, when the jury voted 'Walk On Boy' a resounding 'miss' and Paul was the mystery guest who then had to come out and shake hands with them all.

The first time I ever really saw him perform onstage was at the Civic Hall, Croydon at that Gene Vincent show. By

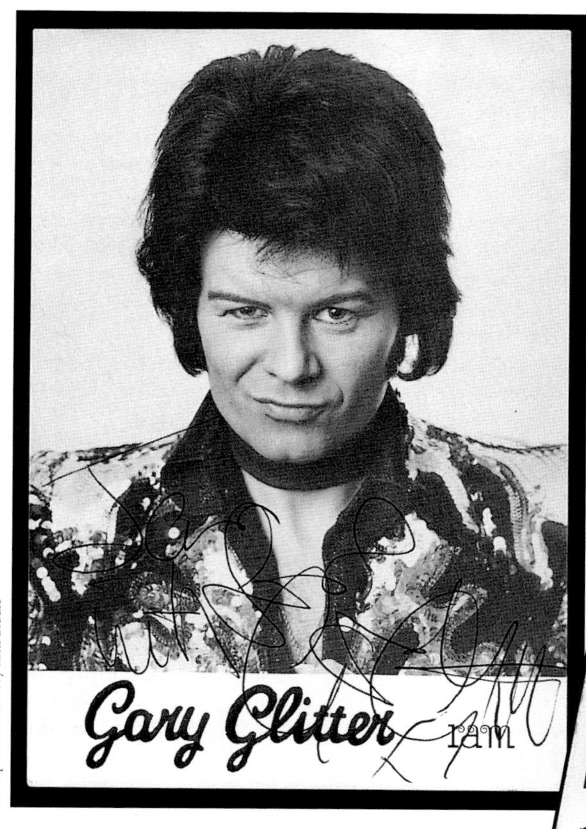

Both pictures courtesy Rick Biddle

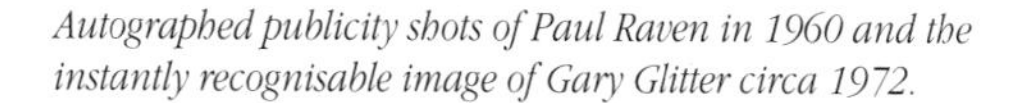
Autographed publicity shots of Paul Raven in 1960 and the instantly recognisable image of Gary Glitter circa 1972.

then he had recorded 'Walk On, Boy' which was a far better record and on that Vincent show he was magnificent. It was a pure Elvis act, with a few little added innovations, but he was really terrific. He prowled around the stage from side to side and would do things like knock the microphone stand over and then he wouldn't pick it up, which we've all seen many times since but back then it was rebellious and created a really tense atmosphere. During the guitar solo of one of his Elvis numbers he just collapsed on the stage and laid flat out on the floor, which I think Gene Vincent had done years before he came to Britain. I must say that although Paul put on a great show that night, Vincent himself was absolutely unbelievable, the best I've ever seen him.

Then I lost contact with him again, until sometime in the early sixties when I went up to the Albert Hall to see Bill Haley. Paul was there and he told me that he'd been over in Germany, playing at the Star Club in Hamburg and places like that. He talked about the Beatles and the other Liverpool groups, before we had really heard of them down in the South East. Then back in Britain, he was one of the warm-up acts on Ready, Steady Go! on TV, and by that time he had made a couple of good records and I really did think he was going to make it big. I used to see him quite a bit then, but he was always 'skint'; he'd ring me up to go and have a drink with him, and it was really an excuse for me to give him cigarettes and buy him a few beers! But that was fair enough, because he was kipping on friends floors all over London, would-be musicians and singers never made much money.

Paul rang me up one night to tell me that he was playing at Carshalton Hall, which was where the Charles Cryer Theatre is now and I arranged to meet him in the pub next door, the Fox & Hounds. His manager came in while we were sitting there and said "there's not a lot of people in tonight, why don't I tell the band to shoot off, and you can mime over the top of your records". And Paul said "Oh no, I can't do that, I don't care how many there are, I've got to be loyal to my public"!

Then he disappeared and I didn't see him again until 1972, when I was watching Top Of The Pops and there he was - with a shiny suit, platform boots and another new name, Gary Glitter! I couldn't believe it, he had a number one hit record with that 'Rock & Roll Part 1' and that was it - superstardom. I went down to the Winter Gardens at Margate to see him at the height of the 'Glitter' era; he put on a good show, but when I went backstage to see him he had definitely become a 'star' - he even called me Richard! 'Hello, Richard', he said; bloody ridiculous, he'd known me as Rick for years. I told him not to be such a prat, and he was alright with me after that, it must have brought him back down to earth for a while!

Finally Terry and I went to see him on a huge Rock'n'Roll bill at Wembley Stadium in 1974. Everybody was on that bill - Jerry Lee Lewis, Bill Haley, Little Richard, Bo Diddley, Gary Glitter, Wizzard. He didn't go down too well with the 'Teds', that day, but then neither did Little Richard, we booed him off stage so he wasn't in bad company! The crowd started to throw these beer cans at Paul and of course they were missing by miles, and he said to them "look, you're not hitting me, you're only hitting your friends at the front". Just as he said it, a can flew in a perfect arc across the stage and hit him full in the chest. To his credit, he simply turned to the direction from which it had come and said "You got me"! ❞

David Jones

*Arguably the most famous local pop personage, christened 'Bromley Dave' by the music press, as **David Bowie** he became one of the most influential figures of Seventies and Eighties music. Changing image and style with almost every album release, Bowie has already been well documented in a whole library of books; this then, is a brief look at David's early years prior to becoming 'Ziggy Stardust'.*

Born David Robert Jones to Peggy and John on January 8th 1947 at home in 40 Stansfield Road, Brixton. Towards the end of 1953 the family moved to 106 Canon Road, Bickley, South Bromley and from there to 4, Plaistow Grove, North Bromley near Sundridge Park British Rail station, in June 1955.

David began his education at Raglan Infants and Burnt Ash Junior school, from where he joined the 18th Bromley Wolf Cub pack. In September 1958, he joined Bromley Technical High School, Oakley Road, Keston where one of his teachers was Owen Frampton, head of the art department and father of Peter, also a pupil at the 'tech'.

It was here that he first met his longtime friend George Underwood and it was during a mock-fight with George that David injured an eye, leaving him with the distinctive feature of two different coloured eyes, one blue, one grey. David, George and Peter would occasionally sing and play guitar during their lunch breaks, mainly rock'n'roll and acoustic blues. By this time David was also listening to a lot of jazz and in early '62 he asked his father for an alto saxophone, subsequently pestering local musician Ronnie Ross for sax lessons; Ross, who lived in nearby Orpington, was an ex-member of the Woody Herman band.

Whereas Croydon's meeting place for musicians was Potter's Music shop, the Bromley equivalent was a record shop owned by Vic Furlong, near Bromley South station. In August 1962, drummer Dave Hadfield placed an ad. on their notice board looking for local musicians interested in forming a group; David replied, as did guitarists Alan Dodds and Neville Wills. After a one-off performance as the backing group for singer Jess Conrad, they became **The Konrads**, playing songs such as 'China Doll', 'The Young Ones' and 'Sweet Little Sixteen'. The line-up was completed by Rocky Shahan and two backing singers, Stella & Christine Patton. David was starting to write his own songs too, with Neville Wills helping out with the music and the Konrads would slip one into the set every now and then. By August 63, David had left Bromley Tech. and was working as a graphic artist for an agency in Bond Street, a post found for him by Owen Frampton. The Konrads were offered a studio audition by Decca, but were turned down (Decca had also recently turned down the Beatles) and David left the group soon afterwards. The rest of the band carried on and the highpoint of their subsequent career came with a gig supporting The Rolling Stones on a nationwide tour.

Private collection

David lining up for the school photo. Even then, there was a certain something that made him stand out from his classmates.

David's next group were the **King Bees** featuring school-friend George Underwood, Roger Bluck, lead guitar, Dave Howard, bass and Bobby Allen on drums. Their name was taken from the Muddy Waters song 'I'm A King Bee', which they probably learned from the Stones cover version. They were spotted by manager Leslie Conn who took David up to the Decca Studios in West Hampstead to record 'Liza Jane'. The unfortunately-named Conn, an ex-record plugger, then took the demo to Vocalion, a subsidiary of Decca records and had them press up 3,500 copies. Credited to Davie Jones & the King Bees, the single was released in June '64 and was even played on pop TV programme Juke Box Jury, whose panel voted it a 3 - 1 miss! The single sank without trace, and consequently original Vocalion copies now fetch up to a staggering £400.00!

David left the King Bees that summer and Conn provided him with a ready made group - **The Manish Boys**. Named after yet another song by Muddy Waters, they were an established band from the Maidstone area of Kent and David's first venture with them was a tour of Scotland on a package tour with Gerry & the Pacemakers and the Kinks. They also recorded a single 'I Pity The Fool' backed with David's own 'Take My Tip'. Produced by American Shel Talmy and featuring added guitar breaks from session man Jimmy Page, the single was eventually released on Parlophone but made no more impression than 'Liza Jane'.

In April 1965, a Margate based group called **The Lower Third** decided to turn professional and made the trip to London looking for their big break. They hung out at the Giaconda coffee bar, where they announced that they were auditioning for a fourth member. David auditioned and got the job as lead singer; very soon the band were being billed as Davey Jones & the Lower Third, causing a little friction among the other members, one of whom promptly went back to Margate. The band were regularly to be found amongst the audience at the Marquee, where they were particularly influenced by The Who. This influence was evident when they recorded their single 'You've Got A Habit Of Leaving', but record company problems, including the delay of the records release led to David parting company with manager Les Conn. In his place the band found Ralph Horton, one-time road manager for the Moody Blues, who secured the Lower Third a Saturday lunchtime residency at the Marquee, where they built up a strong following.

Horton then went to see music business entrepreneur Ken Pitt, to ask for some financial backing for his group. Pitt turned him down, stating that he would be far more interested in David as a solo artist, but helpfully pointed out that there were already other actors and singers in the business with the name David/Davy Jones. It was at this point in his career that David opted for the name **Bowie**, following his fascination with the story of Jim Bowie, the American with the distinctive hunting knife who died defending The Alamo mission in Texas, 1836.

Horton's second coup was to bring in producer Tony Hatch and secure a recording contract with Pye records, taking the band into Pye's Marble Arch studios to record 'The

London Boys', arguably David's best song to date and a live favourite with the Marquee crowd. Pye however, refused to release it, opting instead for 'Can't Help Thinking About Me' which flopped, despite some enthusiastic noises in the music press from Jonathan King.

By the end of January 1966, the gap between David and the Lower Third was widening. After playing a Saturday lunchtime gig at the Marquee, the band were told by Horton that they weren't getting paid, as the money was needed for 'expenses'. They were due to appear at the Bromel Club, Bromley that evening and the band refused to play; during the heated argument David was seen to be siding with the management and the band quit.

BROMEL CLUB
BROMLEY COURT HOTEL
Bromley Hill, Kent
Sunday, March 7th
MANFRED MANN
Monday, March 8th
BROTHERS GRIM
Admission 2/6
Wednesday, March 10th
DAVY JONES
and MANISH BOYS
Thursday, March 11th
DROVERS
Admission 3/-
All enquiries GER 3111 — LEE 7692

In February, it was David's turn to advertise for a new group and the obligatory ad. in the back pages of the Melody Maker was answered by Derek Fearnly, a bass player from Sutton. He was joined by a drummer from Harrow and two Yorkshiremen to become **The Buzz**, the first of David's groups formed specifically to be his backing band. David and the Buzz released a single on Pye, 'Do Anything You Say'/'Good Morning Girl', again to no avail and after a short tour of Scotland, the group were offered a Sunday afternoon residency at the Marquee, called The Bowie Showboat. When Horton approached Ken Pitt for a second attempt to boost the funds, Pitt finally agreed, having watched David perform at the Marquee.

David confided in Pitt that he was generally unhappy with Tony Hatch as producer and in particular with Pye's failure to release 'The London Boys' as a single. On Pitt's suggestion, David, the Buzz and a couple of extra session musicians went into R.G. Jones studios at Morden to re-record the song, along with a new Bowie composition, 'Rubber Band'. Pitt took these demo recordings back to Decca, who were suitably impressed to release the pair as a single and offer David the chance to record an album with producer Mike Vernon.

All along, Pitt had been pushing for David to remain a solo performer and in November he fired The Buzz, which David was visibly upset about, despite agreeing to the decision. Around the same time, Horton's poor judgement over a publishing deal convinced David to let him go as his personal manager - and Ken Pitt took over. Pitt's previous form as a manager included taking the Mann-Hugg Blues Brothers, renaming them Manfred Mann and suggesting that they record a song called 'Do Wah Diddy' - it became the band's first number one hit in mid 1964.

By early '67, David was in the studio recording tracks for his first solo album; in a show of loyalty he took Derek Fearnley with him as co-arranger and used other members of the Buzz on the sessions. The finished product, simply titled 'David Bowie' was released on the Decca subsidiary label Deram on June 1st having been preceded by a single 'The Laughing Gnome'. The media interest to both was good, as it was to the release of the single on Decca's American subsidiary, London records, which brought David into contact with U.S. producer Tony Visconti for the first time.

David had recently made the acquaintance of mime artist Lindsey Kemp and in June '68 was starting to look for more theatrical work - he auditioned for a part in the musical 'Hair' and for the film version of 'Virgin Soldiers', missing out on both. The film makers did take him on as an extra and he appeared as part of the crowd during a fight sequence; for his 'blink and you'll miss it' appearance, David received £40.

In January 1969, David unveiled a new song that was to finally launch his career as a solo artist - 'Space Oddity'. David moved to 24 Foxgrove Road, Beckenham, a large slightly run-down Victorian house where journalist Mary Finnigan had taken a ground floor flat. David, who was just coming out of one relationship, moved in to Mary's spare room. As both were perpetually broke, David decided to put on a small show to raise money. He went to the landlord of a local pub, The Three Tuns in Beckenham High Street and convinced him to let him use the pub back room on Sunday nights. What began initially as a folk session attracting up to fifty people, soon became known as the **Beckenham Arts Lab**, encompassing a range of activities from music to mime, from street theatre to light shows. It was not long before the audiences regularly topped two hundred. April 1969 - David went to see the debut concert by King Crimson at the Speakeasy in London and met Angela Barnett, an American staying with her parents in the UK. David was still living with Mary Finnigan, who was away for a short holiday, but on her return she found that Angie had also moved in to the flat. At first, Mary was understandably none too happy with this arrangement, but soon found that she and Angie had a lot in common- including David! For her part, Angie threw herself into the running of the Arts Lab.

Meanwhile, David was actively seeking a record deal with Mercury records, against the advice of Ken Pitt. This move hit problems at first, not least because Lou Reizner, who was head of Mercury's London office, was still annoyed at having lost Angie to David. And there was another side to this equation; David's emerging bi-sexuality led him to have an affair with Mercury employee Calvin Mark Lee, who had also been sleeping with Angie. In fact Angie's first sighting of David was in a photograph on the wall of Lee's flat and it had been Lee who first introduced them at the Speakeasy. As David said in a celebrated quote: "When I first met Angie, we were both screwing the same bloke!".

Behind Reizner's back, Calvin Mark Lee sent a demo tape of David to the Mercury offices in New York, where an English executive, Simon Hayes saw the potential and authorised a contract to release 'Space Oddity' as a single and to become the title track of a new album. Ken Pitt, as Davids manager, now found himself having to finalise a deal that he had opposed right from the start.

For the new album the choice of producer was Tony Visconti, although he surprisingly declined to work on the single, thinking it too commercial. The replacement was Gus Dudgeon, recently arrived from Decca and a man who had worked with David before; he had been the engineer on the Deram album. Some well known session men were brought in to record the single - Herbie Flowers played bass, Pentangle's Terry Cox on drums, guitarist Mick Wayne and keyboard wizard Rick Wakeman. Paul Buckmaster arranged the orchestral parts and the whole classic single was put down in just two takes. Prior to its release, the single was previewed to the crowd at the Stones Hyde Park concert and more importantly, was played by the BBC during the television coverage of Neil Armstrong's historic first moonwalk. Back in Beckenham High Street, David performed the song to the regulars of the Arts Lab, confident of a hit record.

This euphoria was soon nullified by the death of David's father on 5th August; only five days after the funeral, the Arts Lab held a Free Festival at Beckenham Recreation Ground where a somewhat subdued David was the headline act, backed by the group Junior's Eyes. Other performers included Bridget St. John, Tony Visconti and D.J. John Peel. In November 1969, 'Space Oddity' reached its highest position in the charts, number 5 in the music industry press or 6 according to the Melody Maker and New Musical Express.

David and Angie moved out of Mary Finnigan's flat into a large Edwardian house at 42 Southend Road, near Beckenham Place Park. With the grand name of Haddon Hall, the couple rented a ground floor flat for £8 per week. The success of 'Space Oddity' allowed David to 'up' his appearance fees to between £50 and £125, depending on the amount of travelling involved. He was booked to be the support act on a tour with Humble Pie, a group that included his old school friend Peter Frampton and then went on his own small tour of Scotland, again backed by Junior's Eyes.

That Autumn, David went into the studio to work on the Space Oddity album with Tony Visconti. Among the tracks was a song called 'Memory Of A Free Festival' written specifically about the event in Beckenham Rec.

In early 1970, David's first move of the new decade was to form his own group. Two of the members were already staying with him at Haddon Hall; producer Tony Visconti was also an accomplished bass player, and drummer John Cambridge from the group Junior's Eyes. Cambridge was from Hull, where he had been a member of The Rats, and when David announced that he was looking for a lead guitarist, John suggested his old friend Mick Ronson. In naming this new group, David told his manager Ken Pitt that he wanted "maximum publicity, one big hype". **The Hype** became the band's new name and they made their debut supporting Fat Mattress at the Roundhouse on 22nd February 1970. Photographer Ray Stevenson was heavily involved in the visual aspect of the group, discussing a 'superhero/comic book' style with David and Angie, who made the group's costumes. A good case could be argued that David & the Hype were the pioneering group of the whole 'Glam/Glitter rock' phase; also in the Roundhouse audience that night was Marc Bolan, already an acquaintance of Davids and who entered into the spirit of the evening by dressing up as a Roman Centurian - the Bowie entourage must have been quite a shock for the denim-clad rockers out to see Noel Redding's Fat Mattress.

After playing in a benefit concert for the mentally handicapped at the Royal Albert Hall on March 12th, David announced that he and Angie were to be married. David knew that now Angie was no longer a student, she could only legally stay in Britain on her U.S. visitors permit. Married status would make her a resident and allow her a work permit. However, he also knew that marrying an American would automatically give him the 'Green card' needed to live and work in the States. David and Angie married at Bromley Registry Office on 20th March 1970, with only John Cambridge, David's mother Peggy and a friend, Clare Shenstone to act as witnesses.

It wasn't long before Angie began to put pressure on David to dispense with Ken Pitt as his manager. Eventually David sent Pitt a letter to this effect, composed with the help of Tony Defries, a litigation clerk with ambitions to break into show business. The Defries family had moved from Rickmansworth, North London to Croydon during the 1950's, where Tony had attended Heath Clark school. He joined a London firm of solicitors and his first contact with the music industry came in 1964, when Mickie Most asked the company to act in a dispute between himself and the Animals. Defries worked on that case, and for Most in general for two years, also dealing with pop manager Allen Klein in New York.

By May 1970, David's association with Ken Pitt was over and Defries, along with his associate Laurence Myers, took over the management reins; Myers other pop clients at that time included the New Seekers and Gary Glitter. That same month, David received a prize for 'Space Oddity' at the Ivor Novello awards ceremony.

As well as the management reshuffle, there was a significant change to the personnel of The Hype, too. Whilst re-recording the song 'Memory Of A Free Festival', John Cambridge had trouble handling a tricky drum part. Angie stepped in once more, to convince David that a change of drummer was necessary and Mick Ronson brought in the man who had previously replaced John Cambridge in The Rats during their Hull days. Enter Mick 'Woody' Woodmansey, who arrived just in time to work on David's new album 'The Man Who Sold The World'.

Courtesy Alan Barnes

A ticket from Bowie's gig at Wallington Public Hall - February 1972.

The release of David's album 'The Man who sold the World', in late 1970, caused a minor storm of record company politics over the two sleeve designs. Bowie had commissioned Mike Weller, an artist who had designed posters for the Beckenham Arts Lab, to capture the mood contained in the lyrics. Weller designed a cover in cartoon style, depicting the main entrance to Cane Hill asylum in Coulsdon; he often visited a friend there and was aware that Bowie's older brother Terry was also in poor mental health, although he apparently did not realise that Terry was also a patient at Cane Hill. Standing in front of the building is an unshaven man wearing a stetson and carrying a rifle wrapped in a cloth. Part of his hat is 'exploding' and from his mouth comes a blank speech bubble. This artwork was given to the art department of Mercury records in Chicago and subsequently appeared on the November U.S. release of the album.

Meanwhile, Bowie had discussed the cover with the art director of Philips records who were to release the record in England, and decided on a photographic solution. When Bowie later presented the shots to Philips art department, they were 'surprised', to say the least. David is pictured lying on a couch wearing a floral satin dress, in a pose that art director Mike Stanford described as "totally unusual, and very provocative". Bowie believed that the 'dress' cover would also be used in the States and was horrified when the 'cartoon' cover appeared, despite his initial enthusiasm and approval of Weller's Cane Hill design.

David's songs were now being seen as a valuable commodity in themselves and he was offered a publishing contract with Chrysalis. Their representative Bob Grace took a demo recording of 'Oh You Pretty Things' to Mickie Most, who thought it ideal for one of his artists, ex-Herman's Hermits vocalist Peter Noone. Noone's single version went to number 12 in the charts.

On May 28th 1970, Angie gave birth to a son at Bromley Hospital, later christened Zowie Duncan Haywood Bowie. The event had a creative effect on David, who within days had written 'Kooks' for his son, the kooks in the lyrics of the song being Zowie's parents! With Angie's pregnancy and the arrival of his new boy, David had put performing on the back burner for a while; with the effect that once the recording sessions for the album were finished, Ronson and Woodmansey returned to Hull, where they reformed The Rats and put out their own single under the name Ronno. However it only took one quick 'phone call from David to get them both back down to Haddon Hall, bringing with them bassist Trevor Bolder to replace Tony Visconti. After a few weeks, Ronson, Bolder and Woodmansey moved into their own flat in nearby Penge.

In June 1971 the group played at the Glastonbury Fayre festival, finally coming on stage at dawn to play just as the sun was rising, along with most of the festival-goers! Only days later, recording began on a new album 'Hunky Dory' with keyboard player Rick Wakeman augmenting the Hype on the sessions. That September, David, Angie, Ronson and Defries flew to New York to deliver the completed acetate of the album and to sign a new contract with RCA records. While in the Big Apple, David met up for the first time with Lou Reed, Iggy Pop and Andy Warhol, about whom David had written a song on the Hunky Dory LP.

On returning to Britain, armed with the RCA contract, David headed straight for the studio to start work on yet another record, that would emerge as 'Ziggy Stardust & The Spiders From Mars'. It was to be more than just another album of songs, Ziggy became the first of many alter-ego characters that David would play onstage, as well as on record. Back at Haddon Hall, Angie was already preparing the costumes that would turn The Hype into The Spiders for the concert tour of February 1972.

Frazer Ashford

Bowie onstage at the Fairfield Hall, flanked by Mick Ronson and Trevor Bolder; Ziggy Stardust tour 1973.

The first gig of the tour was at the Toby Jug, Tolworth Towers on 10th February. It continued right across country, playing locally at Epsom and at Croydon, where a reported 1,000 fans were turned away from outside a packed Fairfield Hall. During a break in the tour, Angie asked hairdresser Suzi Fussey, from the Evelyn Paget salon in Beckenham to come over to Haddon Hall to cut her hair. On the spur of the moment, she asked Suzi to cut David's hair, coming up with what was to become the definitive Ziggy style - bright red, short and spikey top and sides, long at the back. The final show of the tour was at the Rainbow Theatre, Finsbury Park where David added the extra theatrical touches of light show and Lindsay Kemp's mime troop. The whole Ziggy Stardust concept was an overwhelming success - music journalist Robin Denselow reported in The Guardian that David was "a truly remarkable performer".

It was also the year that David first became involved with rock group Mott the Hoople, after going backstage to meet them at the Guildford Civic Hall. An excellent live act, they had consistent trouble in converting their vibrant concert performances into record sales. The band, who were on the verge of splitting up, were amazed when David offered them a new song - 'All The Young Dudes'. An obvious hit single, the band recorded it straight away, with David in the producer's chair and the record made number 5 in the charts.

David's next major British tour was to promote the album 'Aladdin Sane', beginning at Earls Court in May 1973 and playing 37 dates in just 45 days, every one a sell out. The tour carried on into Europe and then to the States, where David and Angie were spending more and more of their time. Inevitably it was only a matter of time before he finally severed his Beckenham connections and in October '73 David, Angie and Zowie left Haddon Hall and moved to a smart Victorian terrace in Oakley Street, Chelsea, where his neighbours included Mick and Bianca Jagger. ”

This piece drew heavily on the remarkable research of Peter & Leni Gillman, whose 'Alias David Bowie - A Biography' is essential reading for anyone remotely interested in Bowie's career.

Chris Browning

For any band, life on the road is far from being as easy and glamourous as it may sometimes appear; but at least the musicians get their two hour 'high' onstage - for their road crew it would seem to be non-stop hard graft. In 1963, ***Chris Browning*** *saw it as his chance to be a part of the music scene he enjoyed so much, working for a Beckenham-based pop group who were, unbeknown to Chris at the time, about to become even more popular.*

I was never a musician myself, far from it! At the time, I had left school and was training to be a plumber, but I loved music and just wanted to be involved in some way. I got to know a guy called Alan Williams, a keen photographer who had stated to work at 'The Rookery', Bromley Tech. - he had his own darkroom there and was instrumental in setting up the fine photographic section that the college has today. I was quite interested in photography and had helped him out on a few jobs and one day he told me there was an unusual assignment coming up. We ended up on Bromley Common taking some publicity shots for a local beat group called **The Preachers**.

After that first meeting I gradually got to know the band members fairly well; they were a popular local band and I used to go and see them play on a regular basis. I started to arrive at all these various gigs early enough to help them set up and then move their gear at the end of the show. The band and I had an unspoken 'understanding' that I would be there to help at each gig - it was strictly on an unpaid basis, my reward came in the form of a few drinks and the occasional meal with the band, plus the buzz I got from being connected with an up and coming pop group.

I seem to remember that the band started out as **The Alphabeats**, although I don't recall seeing them play under that name. The line-up at that first photo-shoot was Terry Clarke, Tony Chapman, Keith Temple and Steve Carroll; Terry was the lead singer and rhythm guitarist and like most 'frontmen' he attracted most of the early attention, although I think Tony and Keith were the main movers behind the Preachers.

Gradually, when the changes took place - I believe that Keith was still around then just before Andy Bown came in on bass - but obviously the first major change was the tragic death of Steve Carroll in a road accident, sometime in 1963. Tony was with Steve in the car and he was out for a long time with the injuries that he sustained, a broken collar bone, various ribs and so on. It was a very strange thing, because all four of them would usually go together in the same old van - in those days they couldn't afford to travel in style and certainly not in separate cars. But this particular night they were travelling to a gig in Worcestershire, or somewhere like that and they went two and two, which was very, very unusual. Tony and Steve went in the group's van, with Tony driving and all the bands equipment in the back. The force of the crash hurled the equipment forward and crushed him, that's how Steve was killed.

So they were forced into making various changes and I can remember that one of the guitarists they auditioned to take Steve's place was Jeff Beck! And they turned him down, not because he wasn't good enough, he obviously was, but more likely it appeared that he wouldn't fit in. To be honest, even Terry Clarke seemed to be a bit of a misfit; as I say he was very outspoken and always thought that he was the 'number one' - although he was well liked by all the fans at that time but then, as I say, he was their singer and frontman.

They tried various changes of format; I remember a keyboard player called Lewis Rich coming in for a while - great voice, absolutely tremendous 'bluesy' voice. The drummer that came in to take Tony's place was Mick Underwood, who came from a terrific group called The Outlaws - one of Joe Meek's groups - and Mick had played with some quality musicians, Ritchie Blackmore and the like. By this time the band had changed their name to **The Herd** and the line-up that ran for quite some time was Terry Clarke, Mick Underwood, Andy Bown and Gary Taylor and then they managed to secure the services of Peter Frampton, who at the time had been playing in a small local band called The Tru-Beats. No disrespect to the lads in the Tru-Beats, but Peter was completely wasted with them, he was a superb guitarist despite being a great deal younger than all the rest.

At that time, the Herd were the number one band in the area, and had been when they were still the Preachers, but more so as the Herd. They had regular stints at the Justin Hall in West Wickham and at the gig down by Beckenham Junction station and if you wanted to book a big local band, then the Herd were the ones you went for. David Meyer put on some good shows featuring the Herd and Chris Longman who ran the Justin, he also did them a lot of favours.

When it began to take off for the band and the distances they were travelling between gigs increased, then my involvement gradually decreased. In the early days if you got as far as Watford, then that was a long distance journey! What happened was that the band became involved with an agency in Manchester called Kennedy Street Artistes and consequently the work in the North of England came to the forefront. They went to a few places and died on their feet but at most other venues they went down a storm and were re-booked almost immediately - it wasn't long before their name really got around. Especially once they got to some sort of settled line-up. Eventually they kicked Terry out, and the last I heard he was in Australia. Andrew Steele who came in on drums after Mick, the last I heard of him was that he was in the Channel Islands running a couple of clubs or music venues.

Andy Bown, as we know, went on to a long association with Status Quo; funnily enough I remember going up to an awards show in North London somewhere, run by one of the Radio stations, where Quo were playing live. And the Herd boys were really putting them down for being so basic, because there's no two ways about it, musically the Herd were way ahead of a lot of the other bands who were around at the time. All four of them could read music, which was unusual at the time and both Andy and Peter did a lot of session work - a lot of their income came that way, initially. Not only were there changes to the band's line-up, but they had a few different managers too; I can remember Robert Stigwood being involved in the early days, Billy Gaff of course and Steve Rowlands the American actor, who was their manager when I was driving for them and then finally they wound up with Howard and Blaikley.

The association with songwriters Ken Howard and Alan Blaikley started with their regular appearances at the Marquee, because that's when the Herd really took off, you know, once they got that Monday night stint at the Marquee they just went from strength to strength. The night Ken and Alan signed them up, they told them that they would write them a hit record, and true to their word they did - 'From The Underworld' entered the charts in October '67 and reached number six.

There was a friendly rivalry between the Herd and the Move as to who could pull the biggest crowd at the Marquee; traditionally Monday night was the bad night to have any sort of residency, but the Herd soon turned that round and more

Courtesy Keith Temple

The Preachers pose on Bromley Common for their first official publicity photograph. Left to right: Terry Clarke, Keith Temple, Tony Chapman and Steve Carroll.

often than not, I'm sure they came off best in their 'battle' with the Move. The amazing thing about that place was that so many other artists would come along, in the crowd, to check out the opposition. I can remember seeing so many big names in the audiences; Long John Baldry, Jeff Beck, Rod Stewart...

On a similar line, the band used to have a regular gig up in Nottingham on the River Trent, where there were three or four of these big old boathouses which had been converted into dancehalls. It was nothing to have all four going at the same time, each with a big name band playing. One night the Herd were in one, and Baldry and his band were in the next one along; during his break, Long John Baldry came into see us and there was a big discussion about doing some sort of tour, that would be organised by the musicians themselves and would take the form of a glorified 'jam session', if you like... one of Baldry's scheme's that didn't come off.

The Marquee put together a package tour to showcase some of their best acts and sent them off around the country - the Spencer Davis Group, the Herd, the Move, the VIP's - and that show played at the Fairfield Hall in Croydon, in October 1966.

Wallington Public Halls was a successful place for the Herd to play, in fact they had been playing there since they were the Preachers and always went down well in Wallington. The Star in Croydon, of course and Silver Blades at Streatham was often good - and Chislehurst Caves was another strange venue - great sound but cold, as you can imagine, very, very cold!

A bit further afield, the Herd always had a good gig at the WitchDoctor Club in Hastings and then subsequently when they opened a sister club in Woolwich. I remember one gig we had booked down on the coast - it might well have been at the Witchdoctor - and I had to go over to collect Gary Taylor from his flat in Streatham to drive him down there, I think the rest of the band had gone on ahead. The date must have been July 1966, because when I got to Gary's flat he was just settling down to watch the World Cup Final on TV. Well, nothing was going to drag him away from the match, so we ended up watching England beat West Germany before jumping into the car as the final whistle went and racing down to the coast just in time for the gig!

Did you know that Andy Bown and Billy Gaff ran one of the clubs in Bromley, which they called Peyton Place - just to the left of Bromley South railway station there was a building that used to be a meat importers and the room above that was the club. I have a feeling that it was previously run by Chris Longham who we spoke about earlier, but it closed down; after that Billy and Andy acquired it and their opening night act was the Cream!

Although I've been singing their praises and saying how popular they were everywhere they played, strangely enough one of the venues the Herd never really took off at was Bromley Court Hotel, the Bromel Club. I don't know why - perhaps it was because they *were* a local band and people had grown used to seeing them in their local youth club or church hall. And bear in mind that Bromley Court Hotel was a big venue - people were used to seeing the likes of Cream, Hendrix, the Who, John Mayall's Bluesbreakers, you know...

The Bromel audience were certainly used to seeing top class entertainment and with no disrespect to the Herd, who were still more of an up and coming group really, they were probably considered to be more of a support band there; they certainly did one gig at the Bromel (November '65) as the Preachers with Lewis Rich, supporting a Croydon band called The Train and providing the backing for a duo called The Other Two.

Looking back, we had some great times travelling around, it was thanks to the band that I first got to go over to Europe - Holland, France and Germany mainly. There was a spell around the release of 'From The Underworld', where they went over to Bremen to appear on TV, which could well have been recorded for the Beat Club show. The band would go over for about four days, which was taken up with recording a couple of songs for TV, maybe a bit of press and radio, fit in one live gig while they were there and then come back. We would all drive up to Harwich and go over on the ferry - which at first was a new experience but gradually became a chore - catching late night or early morning ferries is no fun after a while. I went to Holland on a couple of occasions but I didn't manage to go on their St. Tropez trip, unfortunately!

I didn't travel everywhere with them - remember I was still working *with* them, rather than *for* them - I was never employed by the Herd, Barry Saitche was their actual road manager, he saw them right the way through. Barry and I were great mates though, I can remember the first van that we ever had - nearly every band went through a stage where they bought an ex-ambulance - we once did a gig at a Sussex College where we drove through the gates in our ambulance just as Dave Bowie and his band were arriving in theirs! But the first proper van that became known as a group van was the old Comma and the Herd eventually brought a green one, which soon became red and green as it was smothered in lipstick - the girl's would find it round the back of the gig and scrawl all over it. Then they briefly had a silver/blue Comma before they really hit the big time with a Ford Transit, which was quite something in those days - Barry and I spent one complete weekend making seats to go inside. Barry's father was in the decorating trade, I think, and he got us all the gear we needed and if I say so myself we really made a decent job of fitting that van out, we all travelled miles in that old Transit. At some stage they moved on to a van with windows, which was another step up - it sounds silly now, but in those days it was a big thing, some sort of status symbol with which you were rated by all the other groups. Remember, in the early days the band were only going out for £25 a night, and at one stage they were a five piece group, plus the money had to cover any other expenses.

"we eventually bought a green one, which soon became red and green as it was smothered in lipstick..."

Around about 1967-68, when the boys weren't quite at their peak, they were just breaking and they managed to secure a summer season at the Britannia Pier in Great Yarmouth. The Pier would have a big name band play every night during the summer, as part of a whole pop show and the Herd were there every Sunday; during the week you had the Searchers, the Merseys, Freddie & the Dreamers, the Merseybeats, Billy J. Kramer, all the Liverpool boys were still very big, plus each night you would get a support band or two. So that was a good booking for the Herd and we all had some hilarious times there.

Never ever let anybody tell you that being a member of a pop group was easy work - because I can tell you it wasn't. It was an awful lot of hard work, not just with the constant travelling but once the band reached a certain level of 'fame' if you like, they had to be seen to be on their best behaviour at all times, which is a strain in itself. Imagine you've just driven back down from Leeds or somewhere in the back of a van, grabbed two hours sleep and then you've got to be in the centre of London for a radio or press interview - and not just 'be there', but be bright-eyed and ready to really sell yourself and the band to the public - bloody hard work.

But the travelling... god it could be tough. You would leave the gig at one in the morning and get back home at seven or eight after you've dropped everybody off at their respective homes and then have to be back up at eleven o'clock because the band would be required at a publicity session perhaps, or worse, to be travelling again to your next long distance gig. Obviously if you had another gig in the same area you could stay overnight rather than travel back home, but getting accommodation could be a bit of a problem, because in those days some of the other bands were rather 'boisterous', shall we say! There's no two ways about it, certain groups did rather spoil it for the rest, but once you managed to get a good reputation there were one or two places where you would always be welcome - and the boys were one band who were always welcomed back and I think that spoke volumes for the group. Sure the band got up to a few silly antics like everybody else, but they were never disgraced in the way that some were - the Who are the obvious example I suppose, and the Move were another.

Most of the time, if it was humanly possible we'd travel back the same night - because don't forget that, apart from a couple of top name bands, the others really weren't earning huge amounts of money; the band weren't going out for thousands or even hundreds of pounds a night, eventually they were playing for about £125 or maybe £250 top whack - and that was big money, especially having worked up from £25 a night.

I always thought that the Herd gave good value for money, whenever they did a gig - their programme of forty five minutes to an hour was jam packed - they really put their heart and soul into it. Of course I may be slightly biased, but I can compare them to the other bands I saw at the time and their show was... 'punch' right from the word go and you could see from the reaction of the audience how good they were. It was professionalism on the band's part - and having come up the hard way, they were used to putting everything into a show, not only to win over the audience, but to impress the club manager and get another booking! To get yourselves re-booked - then you knew you'd had a good night!

I also remember another local band called Denny Mitchell & the Soundsations, who were quite successful and released at least one record... their highlight was in getting a spot on TV, on Thank Your Lucky Stars.

Once I packed it in and stopped travelling around with them I quickly lost contact with the band. I doubt whether any of them would even remember me now, I mean we're talking thirty years ago and people do change - possibly the one who would still remember me would be Peter, who I really did get on well with. He was basically very shy, you would never dream that he would go on to be hailed as the 'Face of '68' and then to handle all the superstardom, if you like, of his later career. I can remember going to his 21st birthday party and he just sat in the corner all night, away from everybody. The rest of us were getting stoned out of our minds and having a good time and he sat in the corner quietly talking to someone. But then, that was Peter. He was so into his music, as was Andy, and it's fair to say that they were the maturest, musically speaking, of the group.

Courtesy Chris Browning

A rare publicity shot of The Herd. Left to right: Andrew Steele, Gary Taylor, Andy Bown, Peter Frampton and Louis Cennamo.

Towards the end of their time together it was inevitable that the Herd were going to split up, you could see that. The members were all starting to do their own thing and I have to say, I always thought that Andy and Peter would stick together. If there was to be a break then it would be those two who carried on together, but no, Peter ended up with Stevie Marriott to form **Humble Pie**. Steve and Peter obviously knew of each other as musicians and they bumped into one another on numerous occasions - I remember one night outside the gig at Beckenham Junction, we'd either just finished playing there or we had gone down to see the Small Faces, but Peter and Steve sat on the wall outside talking for ages, while the rest of us were waiting to get away. Who knows, that may well have been the start of it. Humble Pie were a good band, no doubt about it, but Peter always looked a bit of a misfit with them, for some reason. Maybe he thought he had something to prove with more of a rock outfit, having done the 'pop star' bit with the Herd, I don't know. But Peter was a great guitarist, that's for sure, great guitarist. Even today, I still idolise 'God', you know, Clapton - but I honestly think that Peter was up there with the best of them.

Finally, going back to that 'Marquee' show with the Spencer Davis Group at the Fairfield Halls, I remember that all the equipment was set up during the afternoon and the guys came out for one almighty jam session. You had Steve Winwood on one organ and Andy Bown on another set of keyboards; Muff Winwood playing bass, Pete Frampton on guitar and various members of the other bands sitting in... and I still can't believe how lucky I was to have been there listening to all this, it was a real privilege to watch those guys play. There were only half a dozen or so people sitting around the stage watching and it sounds daft now, but at the time it felt like they were playing just for me, you know, if only someone had taped it. It was magic, pure magic. ”

Val Wilmer

Val's love of jazz and blues set her on course to become a leading journalist and photographer, her work in both fields has been widely published all around the world - Jazz Journal, Jazz News, Melody Maker, Downbeat, Let It Rock, Mojo, The Observer and The Guardian. In 1973, an exhibition of her music photography - 'Jazz Seen' , appeared at the V. & A. and she is the author of 'Jazz People', 'As Serious As Your Life' and 'The Face of Black Music'.

My mothers family lived in Croydon and Purley, and my fathers family originally lived in India, but he was really from another generation, my grandparents generation, as it was his second marriage. So although both of those areas are part of my family background, I was actually born in Yorkshire as my family had moved there during the War and only came back down to live in Streatham when I was about three years old. My father died when I was seven, so he played a relatively small part in my life, other than biologically! I have only ever lived in four places in my life; Herefordshire where I was born, Streatham with my mum, Balham for a while and here (Stoke Newington), for the last thirteen or fourteen years.

I was raised by a single mother, more or less; my grandparents Cissie and Ernest were around some of the time and I would often go to visit them, so I do have some Croydon and Purley background in my environmental upbringing.

My musical tastes came from listening to the radio; I wasn't really interested in music at all until I started to listen regularly to whatever was on the radio and I actually got into jazz through one of my mothers lodgers, it was around the same time that the New Musical Express was first published and he would but that on a regular basis and leave it around for me to read. The blues were a big part of the picture for anybody who was interested in jazz, it was part of the history of the music, you took it on board if you were someone with an interest in classical jazz, right from the beginning, rather than a 'BeBop' fan who was into the more modern styles.

There wasn't a great deal of blues played on the radio at that time, occasionally you would hear folk-blues by people such as Josh White and Charles Childer broadcast a few programmes about 'Journeys through America', but it would have been very, very limited.

I think my appreciation of jazz and blues has a lot to do with the period into which I was born; I was born just after the War and other people with similar tastes that I have met since all seemed to have come to the same conclusions about music that I did, no matter from which part of the country they came from. Whereas people born only a couple of years later seemed to get interested in rock'n'roll more easily than I did, those two years make all the difference. We should also acknowledge the pioneering work of researchers and writers such as Paul Rutherford and Max Jones in this country, who led us to a particular view of the blues and we certainly learned more about the music and the people from the music press, than the average person in the street. I learnt nothing about jazz and blues at school, I think only one other girl at my school had even heard of jazz and I must have been about fourteen when she suddenly gave me a 78 of Count Basie - it had been her fathers and she said 'Oh, you'd probably like this' and thrust it into my hands!

I was fortunate in that I got in touch with a lot of writers very early on - I have always been the sort of person to write to people for information and it's amazing what you can find out. By and large most of them were happy to write back; I am sure some were very intrigued that I was a schoolgirl interested in *their* music and there were probably a few jokes passed around, but early on it was more useful than a hinderence. Some were absolute pigs, but most were very kind to me and I still have many of their letters.

The first thing I wrote that was actually published was a biography of **Jesse Fuller**, in fact I was only thinking about this the other day - how did I come to write to him, why did I come to write to him? Well, Good Time Jazz was a record label, part of Contemporary Records, which used to have a mailout sheet printed up with news of their latest releases, all ornate lettering and beautifully designed. I don't remember how I came to have a copy, but in this particular issue was a picture of Jesse Fuller who had just released his first album and the label were very pleased with it. They may even have published a contact address, I don't know, but I wrote to him and to my astonishment, back came this letter by return of post, pages of it, very friendly, thanking me for my interest and we started corresponding. There was one period towards the end of my schooldays when I became quite ill and while I was confined to bed, I compiled a biography of Jesse and sent it off to *Jazz Journal*. They were always happy to receive contributions and they published it; in fact the magazine was subsidised by Decca and they payed people in records! When he eventually came to England I had been looking forward to meeting him, but when we eventually met up, he turned out to be quite a strange person, not very easy to get on with at all. He came to stay at my mothers house in Streatham for a short time. Later on I invited the great bass player **Charles Mingus** for dinner at mums house, and he agreed on the understanding that he brought the food. When Mingus arrived he made straight for the kitchen and started to hand round barbecue chicken straight out of the newspaper - I don't think my mother ever forgave him!

Jesse Fuller wasn't the first blues artist that I had met; the first two were **Sonny Terry and Brownie McGhee** at a concert of theirs at the Royal Festival Hall. When they came over with Chris Barber's band, my younger brother Clive and I went to see them and managed to meet them backstage, where we chatted and I took a few photographs. Over the years I would bump into them from time to time and say hello, but I never actually got to know them that well.

Jimmy Rushing was someone else that I wrote to; he had been a singer with Count Basie and when he came over to tour with Humphrey Lyttleton's band, I went with my mother to see him at the Civic Hall in Croydon. My mother was surprised to see that Lyttleton's band were using written arrangements; we were up in the cheap seats of the gallery and she craned forward and whispered loudly "Look, they've got *music*!" **Josh White** was another that I contacted and then **Champion Jack Dupree**, who stayed over here for quite a while at a hotel in London called Airways Mansions. This was an amazing place just off the Haymarket, whereas most places at that time were single rooms with a washbasin and occasionally a bath, the rooms there always seemed to have three parts to them, more like a hotel suite. Someone told me only recently that during the fifties one of the top rooms was equipped with a piano, which I find extraordinary, I have no idea how they could ever have got one up there. It was a regular stop for visiting musicians and they would often get together for jam sessions. It was certainly an education, I had never met people like that before, I had met plenty of jazz musicians, but the blues people were something else. **Memphis Slim** was another musician I was fortunate enough to meet at Airways Mansions when he was recording a couple of albums in

London and I took the cover shots for the sleeves.

There was a lot going on in Croydon for jazz people, for a start there was the Davis Theatre which hosted a great many jazz concerts, although the first time I actually went to the Davis it wasn't to see a concert - Guy Mitchell of 'Singing The Blues' fame was playing there and I went along to get his autograph! But many of the jazz greats played at the Davis, Ellington, Basie, Ray Charles, in fact I'm sure I saw Duke Ellington there twice, because one of the first jazz players that I got to know was Clark Terry, who played trumpet for him. I first met him at a concert at the Festival Hall and the following weekend they were down at Croydon; I can remember this vividly, having been given the job of finding him somewhere to get a coffee and a sandwich outside the Festival Hall, I took him to a place called RediSnax - all dark red tiles and probably part of a small chain, it sold dried up sandwiches and fry-ups, that sort of thing!

Val Wilmer

Trumpeter Clark Terry poses for a fan's 'snapshot' during a tour of the Duke Ellington Orchestra. Stage doorkeeper looks on, bemused! Davis Theatre, Croydon - October 1958.

A lot of the cinema chains were used for concerts in those days and were very attractive buildings, we lived quite near the Astoria at Streatham, which became the Odeon and the Tooting Granada was a lovely place too, similar to the old Rainbow in Finsbury Park. I went to see all the Folk and Blues tours at the Fairfield Hall, starting in 1963, they were nice, I think it was really quite something for those musicians to come over to this country and appear at big concert halls like the Fairfield. The backstage facilities were good, they had their own bar and a big dressing room.

I had always been keen on photography since the age of twelve or thirteen, using my mothers camera which was the old Box Brownie type and using that, I took some pictures of Sonny Terry & Brownie McGhee, which I later sold, so it couldn't have been too bad a camera. The first musician that I ever photographed was **Louis Armstrong** in 1956, he had been performing in London and my brother and I went out to the airport to see him leave and managed to take a couple of shots of him there. Louis was a big star at that time and hadn't been to England for a while, so they put on a run of concerts at Earls Court with this large revolving stage in the middle. All of the national newspapers carried daily coverage of the tour and the Daily Express ran a diary that Louis himself had kept of the visit and serialised it over about four weeks.

Another important factor in my musical education was growing up next to a record shop called **The Swing Shop**. The shop was in Mitcham Lane, Streatham and was run by a guy called David Carey who was, and probably still is a jazz drummer and vibes player, he drummed for Humphrey Lyttleton for a while. I must have been about twelve when I first walked in and naively asked if they had any jazz records! Bert Bradfield was working behind the counter at the time and he pointed me in the direction of a box of bargain priced 78's. I came away with a secondhand copy of 'Fidgety Feet' by Humphrey Lyttleton, for about two shillings. The Swing Shop was a meeting place for all sorts of people, musicians and writers; as years go by I keep running into people who used to go there regularly. Peter Guralnick, a very good American writer, who wrote the book 'Feel Like Going Home' amongst others, he used to visit the shop while he was studying at Cambridge. Jo-Ann Kelly, Simon Praeger and Steve Rye, Tony McPhee, lead guitarist with the Groundhogs, they all used to frequent the shop. We were roughly the same age and it wasn't so much that we all stood around talking about music, as the fact of all being on the same wavelength that was important. Another Streatham 'hangout' was a little place called *The Coffee Cabin*, where you could take your time over an Espresso to listen to their half-decent jukebox.

It is very sad that Jo-Ann (Kelly) is not around any more, she was a lovely person, very special. I can still picture her and me walking down the road, Streatham Hill or somewhere, with her younger brother Dave hobbling along behind us on a walking stick - he had broken his leg, I think.

I must point out that I was always primarily a jazzer, I mean I always liked the blues, but jazz was really my first love. After I left school I wrote a couple of things for Challenge, had several articles published by *Jazz News*, then *Jazz Week* and subsequently *Melody Maker*, *Downbeat* in the States, a piece on women in jazz for *Let It Rock*. There was also a magazine in America called *HitParader*, which was a monthly rock paper, I wrote loads of stuff for them around 1966, in fact I interviewed **Jimi Hendrix** for them. Later on I interviewed Hendrix again for Downbeat, and when they recently republished a series of articles from the past, my Hendrix piece was amongst the rock section. It's ironic really, because in the introduction to their recent retrospective, they say 'how interesting that Hendrix discusses the influence of blues artists like John Lee Hooker...' well, it was only because I specifically asked him about these people and had they given me more space I would have done a much more in-depth piece. Hendrix was a very affable and intelligent man, easy to talk to, and all that 'wild man' image was completely wrong, he was not like that at all, he was very gentle and helpful. I was still young and relatively new to the job and I was sent out to cover a particular angle in a short space of time. It is always easy with hindsight to say I wish I had asked this or that, but that's the way it goes.

I like to think that I'm known equally as a writer and photographer. I have done all kinds of photography, mainly documentary and worked at one point as feature photographer for The Times, but inevitably people think of you as one or the other, God forbid that you should do more than one thing!

With regard to those wonderful Blues package tours of the early sixties, Chris Barber was supremely important in bringing jazz and blues artists over to this country. Chris was in some sort of partnership with Harold Pendleton, he was the promoter who first put on the Richmond Jazz Festival and who used to run the Marquee Club. The Marquee was originally in Oxford Street, contrary to all the people who think it began in Wardour Street, but no, it started off in Oxford Street on the corner of Poland Street, in the basement of the Academy Cinema; it is now a Halifax Building Society branch or whatever. Harold and Chris, and possibly Kenny Ball as well, went into partnership with the Marquee and formed this organisation called The National Jazz Federation, which was supposed to be a body to 'further the aims of jazz', but was basically a glorified booking agency and management company. They also published a magazine called *Jazz World* and I first met Chris having written to him about something or other and he had said why don't you write about jazz for my paper.

At that time, Chris was riding high on the Trad. jazz boom and took his band over to the States quite a lot. He was very interested in authentic Black music and while he was over there he would arrange to bring back musicians to this country to play. Chris could afford to bring over the people he particularly liked; he was mainly responsible for bringing over Brownie McGhee and Sonny Terry, Muddy Waters, Sister Rosetta Tharpe, Louis Jordan, Edmund Hall who was the clarinet player with Louis Armstrong and Marie Knight, who sang with Sister Rosetta but actually came here to sing with the Humphrey Lyttleton band. Chris Barber was quite an incredible guy and deserves a lot of credit for opening up the touring possibilities for those people.

“...even I threw away some of my old negatives and now, I can't believe I did it. Documentary shots of black people in London during the early 'sixties.... historically those pictures were very important.”

The Musicians Union asked me to do some photographs for an exhibition called 'Keep Music Live', which was probably the first public exhibition I did, and some of the live shots I took were of one of the resident big bands playing at the Orchid Ballroom in Purley, most probably the Johnny Howard Orchestra.

A lot of places, the Musician Union and the Croydon Advertiser included, don't hold much in the way of archive photography, which does seem a terrible shame. Mind you, it is easy to say 'how terrible' now, but people didn't think that way in those days, I mean I threw away some of my old negatives and now, I just can't believe I did it. Documentary shots of Black people in London during the early sixties, they were only ordinary people but historically those pictures were very important. I did manage to keep some of them, thank goodness.

Thinking about those concerts at the Fairfield Halls, they were really quite important - the Fairfield was treated as another major London venue then and a lot of musicians would be in the audience to check out the artists on stage. I remember one Gospel show at the Fairfield where Dusty Springfield was in the front stalls, Eric Burdon and possibly Chris Farlowe were there to see people like Bishop Samuel Kelsey and Sister Rosetta Tharpe. Sitting with Dusty were Vicki Wickham, the producer of *Ready Steady Go!* and Madeleine Bell, a wonderful gospel singer who had come over from New Jersey to star in the play *Black Nativity*. It was really something else. Talking of musicians checking each other out, you could always spot Rod Stewart at blues gigs in those days, ever the skinny 'lad', people forget that he was a blues fanatic, him and Gary Farr.

Talking of Vicki Wickham and RSG!, one of the other presenters on that programme was Michael Aldred, who was a schoolfriend of my brother Clive. In October 1963, I was interviewing a musician in Lyons Corner House when Michael walked in with two young women. They came over and the older of the two, who turned out to be Vicki, told me "We've just been for an interview and we're all going to be in a new TV music programme". The younger woman was Cathy McGowan who, as it turned out also lived in Streatham. Vicki started as floor manager on the show, before working up to producer - Michael, Cathy and Keith Fordyce were the co-presenters. Soon after the show started, I began turning up at the Friday afternoon rehearsals to take stills of the performers, the Hollies, the Rolling Stones, Elkie Brooks, people like that. RSG! was responsible for giving many Black artists their first exposure on British television; John Lee Hooker, Buddy Guy, Charlie & Inez Foxx, Betty Everett, Fontella Bass - and for that reason, if nothing else, it became a very important show. And as a spin-off from that work, I also got to photograph the Beatles backstage at their Christmas shows. ”

For the complete story of Val's remarkable life in the jazz world, her autobiography 'Mama said there'd be days like this' comes highly recommended.

Val Wilmer

A superb portrait of a great musician. Louis Jordan, backstage at the Fairfield Hall - December 1962.

Val Wilmer

Star-studded card school backstage at the Fairfield Hall, during the Folk Blues Festival - 3rd May 1964. Left to right: Brownie McGhee, Muddy Waters, Belgian blues documenter Robert Adins, Cousin Joe Pleasants and bassist Ransome Knowling.

Cliff Aungier

A stalwart of the British folk and blues scene, Cliff has met and played with most of the blues 'greats'. London music fans owe him a particular debt of gratitude for being the co-founder, with his friend Gerry Lockran, of the music room at the Half Moon in Putney.

I was born in Stanley Road, West Croydon and went to the grammar school in West Thornton and then to Archbishop Lanfranc, technical modern. I left school with only a couple of abysmal 'O' levels and went into a years probationary training and student apprenticeship at the CEGB, the Central Electricity & Generation Board while at the same time, being interested in flying I was an air cadet with 97 Squadron in Croydon; in fact my old squadron leader is still around, bless his soul, ex-Mosquito pilot Bill Goodie.

Then after a year down in Brighton, or Southwick, Shoreham to be precise, I came back and did my five years at the CEGB in Industrial Instrument Technology, working in the gas turbine plant at Croydon power station. My brother Dave and I went back to Croydon only a few weeks ago (February '96), because I was interested to see how the old power station looked now. I spotted the two huge chimneys now with Swedish colours on and said to him "Let's go round the back to have a look at the plant, with those old Parsons steam turbines that I used to work on and the Rolls Royce Avon jet engines that drove them", and he said "They don't exist anymore, there's nothing there but the two chimneys and a damned Ikea superstore."

Anyway, at the same time I was doing an HNC course at Fairfield Technical college, which is where I first met **Ralph McTell** and **Gerry Lockran**, but by this time I was totally obsessed with playing the guitar and when I finished my student apprenticeship I was working so hard as a semi-professional musician, playing blues with Gerry Lockran and Royd Rivers, that I gave up any thoughts of a career in instrument technology!

Instead, I went for an audition at the BBC to host a new radio series, which I passed, and the programme went out as 'A Cellar Full of Folk'; at the tender age of 22, as they say, I turned my back on a proper job and I've been a musician ever since!

Going back to my first introduction to the blues, there was a television series that I really used to like by John Grierson of Scottish television called 'This Wonderful World'. It was a half hour show that featured all kinds of artistic clips and this particular night, all of a sudden there was this footage of **Big Bill Broonzy** playing guitar. My brother and I just sat transfixed in front of the TV; I liked all sorts of music at that time, I played trumpet in the Air Training Corp band, but the sound of Broonzy's guitar and those songs 'Guitar Shuffle' and 'Hey, Hey', songs that I still play today, they were something else, I just couldn't believe it. The next day at college, I got into conversation with Gerry Lockran and he told me that he played guitar in a skiffle group, he was interested in what I had seen of Big Bill on TV and we went rushing down to the local record shop to try and find some Broonzy on record. We went to a shop at West Croydon next to the ABC cinema and I couldn't remember the mans name, I was asking for Mr Blum Boogly?, Biggly Blombly? The man behind the counter said "My dear boy, look in the jazz section, you must mean Big Bill Broonzy" and I said yeah, that's it! So I brought a couple of records and got a guitar shortly afterwards and that *was* it. I pretty well stopped studying, which was probably a mistake, but the guitar took over my life, I learnt to play some Broonzy and off I went. After the CEGB days I turned professional and went to work with Gerry, Ralph many times and Royd. While we were both at college, Ralph and I used to practice the guitar in the toilets because the acoustics were so much better! Gerry was living in the Colliers Wood/Wimbledon area at the time and the two of us would climb onto his BSA Bantam motorbike, with a guitar between us and a pile of albums and drive all the way down to Brighton to see someone play in a club. In fact Gerry worked in a duo with harmonica player Royd Rivers before I did. I'll never forget the first time I played live, I was very shy about performing at first, it was in the folk club at The Wheatsheaf, Thornton Heath. I had become quite proficient at playing Broonzy stuff by this time and there weren't many others playing his material. I had met up with Bert Jansch who told me he'd seen the very same programme, but apart from Bert, Gerry and myself no one else was playing Broonzy. I regularly took my guitar along to the Wheatsheaf, I had brought a Levin guitar from Potter's Music Shop in Croydon, where else? It cost me £56, plus a case and my father just went potty that I could spend so much on a wooden guitar. Mind you, I now own a Martin and I didn't dare tell him how much that cost - I think I got Royd Rivers to cover my back on that one!

However, I used to take my Levin guitar with me every week to The Wheatsheaf and each time they invited floor singers out of the audience I would chicken out, go to the toilet, play darts, anything to avoid playing. This happened so many times, until one week when Martin Carthy was the guest. We had an interval and when I came back up to the room where the club was held, I found that a local group called the **Folkvendors** had pulled a fast one on me. The Folkvendors were Dave & Ted Smith, Alan Carter and Don Trendell and when I walked back into the clubroom I couldn't see my guitar anywhere. Dave Smith had put my guitar on stage ready for the next floorspot and as I turned to get out everyone barred my exit, so that I couldn't leave without playing. Dave announced me and I got up and played a couple of Broonzy instrumentals, not very well as I remember, but they seemed to go down well and it completely broke the ice for me. After that you couldn't stop me.

I heard Bert Jansch talking on a programme about Big Bill Broonzy and I totally agreed with him when he said that he envied **Wizz Jones** because Wizz had actually seen Big Bill play live. Remember, Big Bill had been dead two years before I even saw that TV programme - it's ironic really that I've met them all, and many of them are now gone; Brownie's gone and as far as I'm concerned he was the last of the legends. John Lee Hooker is still around, I know, and there are a lot of very talented blues players around, black and white, but for me Brownie McGee's death marked the end of an era. And I was so pleased to have met up with him again last year at his home in Knoxville, sadly for the last time, as it turned out. But as I say, Wizz saw Big Bill Broonzy play live and I envy him that, because Big Bill was the man who started me off, the reason I became a blues musician.

My brother David was in the same ATC band that I was, I played trumpet, he was a drummer and he had a guitar before I did - a Framus Black Rose, which was nothing at the time but quite sought after these days. He played it for a while, until he became more interested in racing motorbikes, so interested in fact, that he became Southern England Champion, grasstrack racing. He built his own frame and designed the whole sidecar outfit by candlelight in the back garden at Stanley Road! So I bought the guitar from him for about five shillings or so. Trouble was, I am left handed and my brother isn't, so I went through the process that many guitarists did in the sixties, of turning the thing upside down and re-stringing it. I had a copy of Bert Weedon's Play In A Day tutor... huh, 'play in a day'?, the lying so and so!... but of course the chord symbols are for right-handed people as well. So what I did was to turn the page round and shine a torch through the back, so that the chords came up left handed. I really should have patented that idea!

I played at a very important concert in Croydon, called **Folk At The Fairfield No. 1**, for which I still have the programme and it took place on Sunday 26th April 1964. The Folkvendors were on that bill, so was Steve Benbow, the late and great Alex Cambell, Dave Cousins & Tony Hooper appearing as the Strawberry Hill Boys, who of course went on to become The Strawbs. Martin Winsor & Linda Drew, John Pearse, Fitzroy Coleman, Colin Wilkie & Shirley Hart and finally the Malcolm Price Trio. A truly great line-up. The programme notes for Royd Rivers & Cliff Aungier say: *'Royd (12 string guitar and harmonica) and Cliff (guitar) have only been together for 4 months, but already they have a large following for their Sonny Terry, Brownie McGhee style of blues'*.

Courtesy Cliff Aungier

Cliff Aungier playing borrowed guitar (probably Ralph McTell's old Harmony), circa 1961-62.

The **Olive Tree** was another interesting Croydon venue, in fact when I discovered the Olive Tree it had the only jukebox I knew that had Broonzy on it, Muddy Waters, Alexis Korner & Davey Graham. I couldn't believe that I would walk all that way just for a cup of 'frothy coffee' and to listen to that jukebox. Actually it is only a few years ago that I was standing in the Half Moon, Putney chatting to Ralph McTell and he said 'there are a couple of people over there who want to say hello to you, who haven't seen you for over twenty years'. It turned out to be Annie and 'Fly' Parker, so-called because he was an ex-pilot, who used to own the Olive Tree.

Probably one of the earliest gigs I played was at the **Star Jazz Club** in Croydon, which I believe was the second oldest jazz club in Britain - it's changed somewhat now, of course, I popped my nose in a short while back... But the Star was a fabulous place in those days, it was Alan Elsdon, Humphrey Lyttleton and Chris Barber watched by all the Friday night, student duffle-coat brigade going out to get absolutely wrecked. What was it, one and sixpence for a pint of beer? and you could stand and listen to all that great music.

There was a pianist, Colin Branigan who always played during the interval, and these two guys who ran the club, Frank Getgood and 'Nobby' Clark. One evening, one of them saw that I played guitar and asked me if I would like to have a go at the interval spot the following week. I was still at college and playing regularly with Gerry Lockran, but not gigging very much. I looked at the tiny room, buzzing with the noise of all these people crammed in there and knew that I would have to amplify my guitar. So I went back to Ivan Morantz where I had bought my Martin guitar and paid 14 shillings for a pick-up - the gig fee was 15 shillings - and on the day of the gig I went down to the Star to do a sound check, all eager and nervous.

After the drummer had finished rehearsing, I went over to this little two or three valve amplifier, with a beer crate over the top, went to plug in and my jack plug was the wrong size! No time to change anything. Then later on when they announced me, I went to change the height and position of the microphone and found it was welded down low specifically for the horn players! I mean, I'd even received a telegram from Gerry to say good luck, that's how critical this gig was for me - I had to play the whole thing acoustically, I broke two strings and came off dripping with sweat. I went up to the bar where the whole of Alan Elsdon's band had been watching and the guv'nor came up, gave me the fifteen shillings and said "Very good, can you do it all again next week?"

Eventually, R&B came in and the trad. jazz all but stopped dead. I was there the night of the **Yardbirds** first gig at the Star. And I remember one very special night at the Star; the night before there had been a Blues package tour at the Fairfield Halls that I had attended and gone backstage to meet all these heroes of mine. Next night at the Star, there were only a handful of people, maybe twenty, twenty-five watching the Yardbirds, when the door opens and into the bar walked most of the blues guys from the Fairfield gig, all out for a night off. They had all their instruments with them and they were eating handfuls of chicken and chips straight out of the paper, that they'd just brought round the corner. Keith Relf was playing harmonica and **Sonny Boy Williamson** went over to him and said "No boy, like this". He dipped it in the beer, banged it on his knee and handed it back to Relf to carry on playing! They all did a number, two hours they were on and there wasn't a soul I could tell. I tried to get hold of my brother, I was calling people on the 'phone to get them along - a truly amazing night.

Oh, it was great, I'll never forget it - afterwards they were all looking around outside for somewhere else to eat before rejoining the tour bus and travelling up to Liverpool, where incidentally my wife Wendy saw the very same package tour. So these blues giants were all milling about outside the Star and **Lonnie Johnson**, who was a very fine jazzy-type guitar player, saw this old Ford pull up at the traffic lights. Lonnie jumped onto the running boards on the side, held on to the wing mirror and started rolling it from side to side; he pressed his face right up to the window and said to the startled couple inside "Hey, you guys, this is just like riding the blinds!" In fact, Lonnie stole the show from Sonny Boy the night at the Fairfield by playing an instrumental version of 'I Left My Heart In San Francisco', years before Tony Bennett covered it.

The first album I ever recorded, as part of a duo with **Royd Rivers**, was produced by **Jimmy Page**. He was working with John Marc, who had played in a duo with Alan Davies and was the Marc of the Marc/Almond Band. At the time I only knew Page as a session musician, but he went on to become huge as lead guitarist with the Yardbirds and subsequently with Led Zeppelin. In fact, Pagey not only produced my album ('Wanderin' - Decca), but he wrote the sleeve notes as well. I hadn't seen Jimmy for about eight or nine years, but I bumped into him at Fairport Conventions Cropredy festival a couple of years ago (1994). The first thing he said to me was, "I've still got my copy!"

In order to cut that album, I took an afternoon off sick from work and Royd and I went up to the studios at Decca and laid down between twenty and twenty two tracks in an afternoon. Straight through. And the engineer was one Glyn Johns, who has worked with everybody from Dylan to the Stones. I went down to the Diamond Record Shop near where I lived, every day for weeks to ask the owner if my album was out yet. On the day it finally came out, I was so excited I picked the record up off the counter and went rushing out of the shop only to hear him say "Excuse me, that'll be one pound, nineteen shillings please!" Do you know that I never saw a copy from the record company - things don't change, do they?

I used to go around with **Sandy Denny** quite a lot, places like Studio 51, the 100 Club, the Troubadour, Les Cousins, a folk club called The Student Prince, Bunjies of course, the smallest gig in the world! Sandy was a remarkable vocalist, and with respect, not a great guitar picker, but oh, that voice - and she wrote some fabulous songs. She married Trevor Lucas from Eclection, who I also worked with a lot, Doris Henderson's group - they were incredible times, there was so much going on. I played guitar for Sandy Denny on a couple of tracks on the album 'Alex Campbell and Friends".

"I'll tell you who else turned up one night - Paul McCartney. He paid his three shillings and sixpence like everyone else and stood at the back..."

I remember Alex at the Fairfield show, one incident in particular when he was talking away to the audience, ten to the dozen and his false teeth popped out! He'd had a few 'sherbets' by then Alex, bless him; his teeth came flying out and he caught them mid-flight and put them back in, without batting an eye. The audience absolutely fell about with laughing and someone in the crowd shouted "Howzat!"

The last time I saw Sandy, I had been working on an album at Olympic Studios in Barnes and Fairport were also in there doing some overdubs. I saw the studio door open, no red light on and I just walked straight through and there was Dave Swarbrick, standing alone in the middle of this huge studio room, with a woodbine on as usual, and I just thought he was rehearsing. I said "How are ya doing Dave", as I strolled past and there are the engineers in the box going crazy because they're rolling the tape.

It was tragic about Sandy and about Jo-Ann Kelly of course, another extremely fine singer - but you have to think of the good times and I have fond memories of them both.

Going back to the Croydon thing, we have **Peter** and **Clive Sarstedt**, both of whom I bumped into again recently at the Guildford festival which was organised by my friend Steve here, Steve Kennedy. In fact I released a single of one of Peter's songs, 'Time, Hope, Love, Life' on Polydor, but there were some contractual problems and the record company only released about ten or eleven thousand copies. I used to run into them all the time around the Sanderstead area and the various haunts around Croydon. Nice fellows.

Gerry Lockran and I started the club at the **Half Moon** in Putney sometime around 1963/64 and we ran it for about six years. It's changed hands many times since those days, but it was really very popular back then, not just because we were the residents! but the whole thing - the venue, the location was just right. Some occasions stand out, I mean we booked **Blind Gary Davis** at the Moon, **Arthur 'Big Boy' Crudup** courtesy of the National Jazz Federation and his fee was £25 plus a taxi home and a bottle of scotch! We would get so many floor singers wanting to play, that some nights there were up to twenty on the list and the room was filled with guitars, banjo's and fiddles stacked up by the door. **Tim Hardin** was, and still is a particular favourite of mine, I covered 'Lady Came From Baltimore' on one of my albums, but it was getting on towards the end when he played at the Moon, sad days for him. I was special guest to Hardin down at Dave Keys club in Portsmouth and again when he was booked to play four nights at the Half Moon, although he only lasted two; but he was still great once he was up on stage. Someday I would like to do a tribute album, he had such a great song catalogue - 'If I Was A Carpenter' was number one twice, 'Misty Roses' is a great song, 'Reason To Believe' which was a hit for Rod Stewart, 'Hang On To A Dream' is still, I think, one of *the* most beautiful songs ever written.

Gerry Lockran and myself used to go around sticking these little posters on walls, to advertise 'Folksville' which was the name of our club at the Half Moon. Many years later, I was playing football for the Blue Moon Allstars in some charity match, playing a World Service side at the BBC sports ground, in fact the referee was Ossie Ardiles. One of the opposition came up to me and said, "Cliff, Cliff Aungier you're playing a gig in Putney, tomorrow night, Monday", which I wasn't, I didn't have a gig booked to play Putney for some time. He said, well what about those posters down the road, under the bridge, then? So after the match I went along to check it out and there were three posters for the Folksville club that Gerry and I used to paste up. Those posters had remained at shoulder height, almost untouched - a bit dog-eared and faded perhaps - under the railway bridge at Merton for at least twenty years. The wall was covered in graffiti and other posters had come and gone, but there they were. I took some photos to prove it and showed them to Ralph McTell - he just said "I didn't think that araldite had been invented in those days!"

I recorded an album called 'Full Moon' with many good friends on it - Albert Lee, Ralph McTell, Clive Bunker from Jethro Tull - and the album was named because of the Half Moon connection, my wife Wendy and I both hit on the name at the same time. At that time I was playing a series of gigs as guest of the Paul Brady band and unknown to me, he had recently recorded a live album at the Half Moon that he had also called Full Moon. I met him at one of the sound checks soon after he found out and he held his head in his hands and said "I'm sorry, yours must have been first, it had to be first!" he was very apologetic. But what a talented musician Paul Brady is, and a great songwriter too.

After the Half Moon was up and running, I started a club called the **Dungeon Club**, which we held in a pub called The Copper just on the south side of Tower Bridge. We recorded a live album in conjunction with the BBC there and generally managed to attract some good guests to the club; Gordon Giltrap played - my old mate Gordon from Grove Park, Jackson C. Frank, Don Partridge begged us for a gig. When Don turned up I couldn't believe it, because in between us booking him and his appearance, his single 'Rosie' went to number two in the charts. I didn't think he would turn up for his eight guineas inclusive, but he did - and he was so happy about the record that he bought the whole club a beer! I'll tell you who else turned up one night - Paul McCartney. He paid his three shillings and sixpence like everyone else and stood at the back just checking the club out. We had a visitors book that everyone had to sign when they came in and about a week after McCartney came in someone stole the damn book! My wife Wendy was interested to hear about that because she spent her schooldays in Liverpool and knew the McCartney family quite well.

I left Croydon in about 1968 and set up a base in Willesden, North London renting a house with two other guys - an American semi-pro. tennis player and a Yorkshireman who was an educational administrator with ILEA - quite a strange trio. It was ideal for everything that was happening in Central London and it was almost at the end of the M1; we used to do some travelling up and down that motorway almost every other day, London to West Kirby and back in the same day, Southampton, Bristol, across to Southend, there were no such things as tour managers in those days! Knocking the bearings out of an old Cortina Mk.1.

I think the Gordon Giltrap story was the worst one. We were both booked to play Manchester College of Commerce and Gordon decided to travel up with me; we got part of the way and had a puncture - fixed that. We were two thirds of the way and got another flat, that was the end of the spares so we had to hitch to the nearest garage to get another tyre. Within about twenty miles of the venue, the fan belt pulley simply 'came out', so nothing worked, no lights, nothing! By this time, poor old Gordon, who wasn't a driver himself in those days was really panicking. Eventually we arrived, very late and the students had assumed that we weren't coming and half of the college were in bed. We knocked on some doors and got enough people together, some still in their pyjamas and Gordon and I did a half hour set each! To cap it all, something else went wrong on the way back and we arrived back to London in the middle of the next mornings rush hour.

The Lincoln Festival in 1970/71 was one of the best ever moments for me, Sonny and Brownie were there, Tom Paxton and James Taylor - it was a superb bill. I wasn't actually booked to play at Lincoln, but I had been playing a concert with John Williams the classical guitarist, at the York Theatre Royal and I got over to Lincoln very late and had to blag my way into the festival. I had two guitars with me and I managed to convince the guy on the gate that I was playing with Ralph McTell because I knew that if it came to the crunch, that Ralph would back me up. So I got in and headed straight for the hospitality area to see Ralph and when I repeated the story to the man outside hospitality, he smiled and said "Well, you're a bit late, Ralph opened the festival about four hours ago!"

Backstage there was Ralph with **Sonny Terry & Brownie McGhee** sitting around talking, when suddenly Sonny picks up a harmonica and starts blowing. Ralph joins in softly on a blues lick and whispers to me, go and get your guitar. I didn't need asking twice and I ran off to get the Martin out of its case, came back and started playing. Sonny, who was blind, listens to the sound of my guitar and said "That's a Martin", I mean to say the man, who wasn't a guitarist himself, could identify the make just by its tone. Brownie looks over at me and says "I knows you boy, I knows you, but I never knew you picked." Every now and then I would throw in some of his stuff and he would smile and say "Hey, where'd you get those licks from, boy"! but of course he knew all along. And Sonny shouted out "Hey you, Brownie McGhee, you leave that boy alone, cause when you long dead and gone he'll be playing with me in Knoxville Tennessee!" That was magic for me to hear that, and at the same time, while all this was going on there was a tapping on the door to the hospitality area and there were Alan Davies and Cat Stevens trying to get in, they were barred from getting in! That whole festival was just wonderful and although I've met Sonny and Brownie many times since then, it was only last year that I managed to go over to the States and visit Brownie at his house in Knoxville. I even managed to join in with a gospel choir down the road, while they were rehearsing for the Sunday, taped a bit of conversation with Brownie, had a bit of a jam - with him playing piano, took some photos and he seemed really happy and together. His daughter picked us up from a little bar across the way and drove us to the airport - we were chatting about the old times, Broonzy and so on, and he told me that his favourite place to play had always been the UK, even after all his travels. When I finally said goodbye I was numb with excitement, I couldn't believe what had just happened, you know? I didn't stop telling people about it for weeks.

The way it came about was partly through Stevie Rye. There was a local duo called **Praeger & Rye**, who modelled themselves on Sonny & Brownie in much the same way that Royd and I did and Stevie Rye sadly died a while back, in fact almost exactly a year after Jo-Ann Kelly died. I went to Jo-Ann's funeral and Steve being a fine harmonica player, had spent more time with Sonny & Brownie than most, particularly with Brownie. I got talking to Stevie about this and he gave me a 'phone number and a contact address for Brownie. I phoned Brownie up and suggested that we could maybe meet up if ever I came over to the States. He agreed to that quite happily and said "How is Steve Rye? His 'phone bill must be colossal boy, sometimes he's on it for three hours!" The next time I called Brownie was after Steve's death, he already knew by that time, but I promised to take him something of Stevie's over with me when I went to visit him. I took an Order of Service from Steve's funeral and Brownie was so pleased to have it, it obviously moved him, "Let me read it, boy" he said, as soon as I gave it to him.

After Steve's funeral we all went back to his house and I tentatively asked his brother John, an actor, if it was possible to have something of Steves to remember him by, maybe an old rusty harmonica or something. John told me to follow him, and he showed me this huge case full of harmonicas and said "By all means, take one". So I just picked one out, not really knowing what I was looking for, I don't play much harmonica myself and Simon Praeger said "Nice one Cliff, you've just picked out Steve's favourite harp".

Sadly now of course, we've recently heard about Brownies death (February 1996). I couldn't believe it when I heard, he looked so well when I saw him only a few months before. As I say, for me that really marked the end of an era for the blues. ”

File under 'spooky coincidence' - when Cliff was telling me about bumping into Jimmy Page at Cropredy, I mentioned that I had also been at that festival and spotted Jimmy (and Robert Plant) wandering about in the crowd. Cliff promptly produced a photograph taken during their meeting, showing the two of them standing shoulder to shoulder posing for the camera. Clearly visible in the gap between their heads is a punter standing about fifteen feet behind them, probably wondering who is having his photo taken with Jimmy Page.

Yes you guessed it, that punter is me! On seeing the photo I almost fell off my chair and, when I pointed it out to Cliff, he almost dropped his shot of whisky... well, almost.

The Kingpins

*Possibly '**the** Great Lost British Group of the mid-sixties" claims New Addington guitarist Ray Neale, who has kindly allowed me to use his article originally written for Record Collector magazine and published in issue 188, April 1995.*

The **Kingpins** were the mod-influenced vehicle for the talents of Ray Neale, who founded the group (not to be confused with similarly-named outfits who recorded for Oriole and Columbia) in 1964 as a 14-year old, living in New Addington, Croydon. Alongside Ray (rhythm guitar, vocals and songwriter) were his elder brother Keith (bass), Tony Martin (lead vocals), Glyn Stevens (lead guitar) and Jimmy Barnard (drums).

In mid-1965, the Kingpins won third prize in a local beat contest behind the Remainders (a forerunner of 70's stars Mud), with a distinctive sound due in no small part to Neale's home-made fuzz box. One of the competitions adjudicators was Ronald Jones, the proprietor of R.G. Jones recording studio and the Oak custom label in nearby Morden, who offered the band a prize of £10 and a free demonstration disc. Two tracks were duly recorded and pressed up on acetate. 'For Your Love' was a perfunctory rendition of the current Yardbirds hit, but 'Diamond Girl' written by Tony Martin was built around the kind of classic riff that had recently shaped the Kinks' 'All Of The Day and All Of The Night' and the Who's 'I Can't Explain'. With Martin's deliciously adenoidal whine well to the fore, the confident swagger of 'Diamond Girl' was firmly rooted in the mid-sixties garage band vein.

Courtesy Keith Aldridge

The Kingpins - circa 1964. Left to right (according to the signatures) are: Jimmy Barnard, Tony Martin, Keith Neale, Ray Neale and Glyn Stevens.

The band graduated to prestigious bookings like debutante coming-out parties. At one particularly select gathering, the band's set was interrupted by a well-spoken teenager requesting a Rolling Stones number. Despite being told that the song in question wasn't in the Kingpins' repertoire, the youngster blithely repeated his request. Eventually tempers became strained, and it was only after the show that Neale was informed that he frustrated Stones enthusiast was none other than a young Prince Charles!

In early 1966, a gig at swinging London's Cromwellian Club brought the Kingpins to the attention of Ember Records. With Geoff Coppins now replacing Tony Martin, the band were persuaded to cut sprightly covers of two American songs under the pseudonym of **Those Fadin' Colours** (although the label incorrectly credited them to *The* Fadin' Colours). Issued in April 1966, '(Just Like) Romeo & Juliet'/'Billy Christian' EMBER EMBS 229 boasted blistering guitar solos courtesy of the home-made fuzz box, although its punch was undermined by bursts of easy listening brass added by Des Champs. A photo session captured the band as Carnaby Street dandies, but when the picture sleeve appeared (in Greece of all places), their photo was replaced by that of another band!

By this time, the Kingpins were down to a trio of the Neale Brothers and Jimmy Barnard. They returned to R.G. Jones in April and June 1966 to record five tense and neurotic sub-three minute nuggets that succinctly defined their garage band sound. 'Maybe Sometime' erupted in a devastating frenzy of sound and language, with the line "that's what I call unkind..." seething with an almost unbearable sense of menace.

Although the young Kingpins - Ray was still only 16 - failed to convince the A&R men with their batch of aggressively recorded Oak acetates, they supported the Who, the Yardbirds, the Kinks, the Small Faces, the Troggs and even a callow youth called David Bowie.

By early 1967, drummer Barnard was replaced by Red Reece, a former member of Georgie Fame's Blue Flames. With the addition of guitarist John Wooloff and session pianist Colin Wood, the Kingpins made their final visit to R.G. Jones. The resulting four-track EP displayed refined instrumentation and morose introspection that anticipated the emergence of American blue-eyed soul songwriters like Joe South. By now, Reece was firmly locked into the downward spiral of heroin addiction that would shortly claim his life and he was replaced by Les Warren.

The activities of the group were temporarily suspended when Ray Neale replaced Stu James as lead singer/guitarist with the Mojos, who by this stage were led by drummer Aynsley Dunbar and future 'Professionals' actor Lewis Collins on bass. When Dunbar joined Jeff Beck in June 1967, Neale reconvened the Kingpins (who had continued to honour their commitments at the Hastings Pier Ballroom) with Les Warren and Ray's ever-faithful brother Keith. By the end of the year, they had adopted a new name - the **Orange Seaweed**.

Signing with the prestigious Harold Davison Agency (who also handled the Small Faces and Procol Harum), the Seaweed were placed with producer Jimmy Smith who, unimpressed with Neale's guttural vocals, told the startled singer: "You sound like an East End barrow boy. From now on I want you to sing like a poof"! A single featuring Neales newly emasculated vocals, 'Stay Awhile'/'Pictures In The Sky' PYE 7N 17515 was issued in April 1968, but proved to be their only release.

In the early '70's, after issuing a solo single entitled 'Morny', Ray formed a trio The Ray Neale Band for tours of, er... Turkey and Uganda. Switching to rockabilly, he joined Screaming Lord Sutch and the Savages in 1981 as lead guitarist, songwriter and occasional vocalist - Neale wrote 'Loonabilly Rock'n'Roll' inspired by the formation of Sutch's notorious Monster Raving Loony Party. Ray's own group, **Shotgun**, consisting entirely of former Savages, was formed in 1978 and regularly toured Europe as well as backing such legendary rockabilly names as Mac Curtis.

Ray Neale has been part of the 'soft white underbelly' of British rock for more than thirty years and has released a compilation - 'Kingpins For Sale' on Tenth Planet Records, which assembles the bands riotous demos in chronological order, providing not only a testament to his precocious talent, but a tantalising glimpse of what might have been.

Ivan Chandler

Ivan 'Chuck' Chandler has played keyboards for many major artists, including Dusty Springfield, Lulu, Cat Stevens and Kiki Dee. He led the jazz/latin group ICQ and still plays in the blues/rock band Running Blue. His 'day job' however, is with the music publishing and production side of the industry and consequently, Ivan was able to supply an invaluable and inexhaustible list of contacts.

I was born in North London, moved to Somerset for a while, and then settled in Brixton when my father got a job as an officer at the prison. I left school in 1962 when I was 16 and my first job was working in the pop music library at the BBC - and that's where this guitarist Stuart Cowell, who also worked there, said to me 'you've got to start joining local bands'. We used to rehearse at his house in Sanderstead; I'd only been doing classical piano up to that point, but working in the record library we could just pull out copies of things like 'Johnny B. Goode' - I still didn't really know what a 12 bar blues was. He had a Vox AC30 amplifier and you could pick up the sound of the television on it, from the aerial at Crystal Palace.

Later on, we joined a group in Croydon called the **Rumbles Blues Band**, whose singer, Kenny Leppard lived there. The piano at the rehearsal room we used was a tone flat, so to play in tune with the guitarist I had to play a tone up, and learn all our numbers in really difficult keys, 'In the Midnight Hour' for example - but looking back it was quite good training! We were Kenny Leppard, John Taylor on drums, Stuart Cowell on guitar and myself on keyboards. I bought a Bird organ with big black screw-in legs, because the Victor Brox Blues Train, they used one as well. Another Croydon band were the **A-Jaes** who John Taylor went on to play drums with. The magical place in Croydon of course, was the Star - I used to go there to see the Yardbirds, and when Eric Clapton was playing with them they were the most exciting band - and I can also remember seeing the Animals down there. Another band who played at the Star many times, but never really made it were the Authentics; their lead singer was a tall Irishman called Mick O'Neill, who occasionally sat in with the Yardbirds when Keith Relf couldn't make it.

At that time, I was playing in **Ralph Denyer's Rockhouse Band** - Ralph was from Tulse Hill - and we managed to get Georgie Fame's manager to persuade Rik and John Gunnell to take our band on. I was still going out to see bands and I remember seeing Julie Driscoll sitting in with a band at the Star - it might even have been with the Authentics, and must have been around '64 - and I went up to her afterwards and said to her, "look, I don't know much about the music industry but I think you've really got something" and she said 'well actually I've already got somebody who is interested in me, called Giorgio Gomelsky'. I don't know if that was the connection, but as you know, she went on to join Brian Auger's Trinity. I remember going to a Brian Auger gig at the Star, with guitarist Gary Boyle from the Echoes, Julie Driscoll and her sister - I quite fancied Julie's sister but I don't think she was interested in me! Like a lot of places then, you had to have the stamp on the back of the hand, which you could only see under ultra-violet light; that was the Star - always a great atmosphere. Locally, there was John Edmed, a highly rated steel guitarist who ran a music shop in Croydon and later ran Matthew Fisher's studio, the Old Barn in Croham Road.

There didn't seem to be the training or opportunity then at the Beeb, to learn studio management or producing, so I think I put an ad. in Melody Maker and got called up by **Dusty Springfield**'s secretary Pat Barnett, and I went along and auditioned in a rehearsal room with just a piano and Dusty, we played a couple of her songs - I remember one of the audition numbers was 'Shake', by Sam Cooke. I could read music and got the gig, and we did this tour as the **Echoes** in 1966, there were lots of people on that tour including Episode Six, the Alan Price Set and so on; I was with Dusty for about a year, just the one tour and then a pantomime at the Liverpool Empire - six weeks of madness!. She was the star but didn't have to dress up in costume or anything. Guitarist Gary Boyle left to join Brian Auger and we got this new guy in, Stuart Taylor, the drummer was called Peter Wolf, who went on to play with David Essex; Dougie Reese was the bass player, he was on the inside of it all - I think he was going out with Dusty's secretary and got himself sponsored by Vox, he had this awful Vox bass that sounded dreadful! Then we, as a backing group were offered out to other artists, so we worked with **Lulu** and with **Cat Stevens**. It was only his seventh gig and he was real nervous, I remember we did a little acoustic rehearsal round at the bass players house and I went back with Cat on the bus from North London; I was going back to Streatham and he got off at Shaftesbury Avenue because his dad owned a Greek restaurant there. His only hit at the time was 'I Love My Dog' but while we travelled on the bus he was telling me enthusiastically about this new song he'd written called 'Matthew and Son', which was going to be his next record. We also worked at the time with a dance group called the **Go-Jo's**, sort of an early Pans People, then we went on to work with Helen Shapiro, Paul and Barry Ryan, it gets worse after that! So, that was us, the Echoes. After that saga, I went to teacher training college for a year, but decided not to become a teacher and during the holidays, Dusty's secretary phoned me again and said **Kiki Dee** is looking for a musical director to handle all her arranging and live dates. I worked with Kiki for about six months, and she was very, very good. Actually, I lost my job with her when she signed for Tamla Motown - they said look, she's going to be away for three months at a time, they had me on a retainer to help her rehearse and do some TV shows and so on - but I was just about to get married and thought I'd better get a proper job! To be honest, although I enjoyed playing, it was never rewarding enough in itself, never quite broad enough. I was interested in so many different types of music, I thought it would be better to get into music publishing. When I lived in Streatham, I went to a piano teacher, Derek Abrahams, who lived in one of those roads opposite the Cats Whiskers (Streatham Bowl), he also taught Manfred Mann and Keith Emerson for a while. I guess many people were self taught, although others - Matthew Fisher for example, were well into their classical studies.

I later played in another backing group for **Johnny Johnson & the Bandwagon**; in fact there were often two backing groups, so we could double - you know, two gigs a night. It takes time breaking down your equipment, so there would be this second band at the next gig ready to go as soon as Johnny Johnson arrived. I suppose it was a bit of a trend back then. All the stuff we played was, you know, 'Mr Pitiful', My Girl'; everyone was playing everyone else's numbers back then. Streatham Odeon was another good venue, I saw Bo Diddley play there, on the same tour as the Stones, with Mickie Most supporting. That was a good gig that was; he's known as a producer now of course, but back then it was him and Dave, as the Most Brothers, playing stuff like 'Sea Cruise' with Mickie sliding all over the floor playing guitar! ❞

Neil Korner

After cutting his teeth in various local groups, Neil Korner played bass for artists as diverse as The Nashville Teens, Dana Gillespie, The New Vaudeville Band and Renaissance. He now lives in Selsdon, is in the process of putting yet another band together and is proud to say that his son is following in the family tradition by playing guitar and keyboards in a group at school.

I was raised in Mersham Road, Thornton Heath and then educated at Ingram Road School. Left school as a teenager to work in Croydon, and when I was seventeen I started playing guitar. I joined my first local group, **The Hi-Sounds**, and on discovering that I was the worst guitarist in the group, I became, or indeed was nominated as the bass player! Like many young bands of the time, we played mainly Shadows cover versions and entered the obligatory beat group competition - all the local bands went in for it - and I think it was held in the Justin Hall at West Wickham. After the Hi-Sounds, I decided to form my own group, called **Arnold's Engine** - and this was my first enthusiastic introduction to the blues and R'n'B; whether it be Sonny Boy Williamson or Muddy Waters, through to Chuck Berry and so on.

After Arnold's Engine, I put an advertisement in the Melody Maker for gigs; a chap 'phoned me up and his name was Matthew Fisher - Matthew was putting a band together, a rather large band it seemed at the time, called **Big Bully Coots & the Elastic Band** and I was recruited into their fold. This must have been around 1965 - Matt moved on to be the organist with Procol Harum, of course. For a short while, I was in another group with the first black guy I ever worked with, somebody Nelson, a really nice guy he was, played the organ, all Booker T. stuff, really getting into the soul thing. We rehearsed in his flat in Penge, which was actually next door to the one Bill Wyman owned.

I also worked a lot with Ivan Chandler in various soul outfits, more Booker T. material, including an interesting weekend with Johnny Johnson and the Bandwagon. On this particular occasion they found themselves without a bass player, and I was drafted in, with little or no rehearsal mind you, into a tight, uptight 'black soul act'. I remember going up to the gig in the van, trying to learn the material on the way! A weekend that I will never forget and I'm sure Ivan hasn't forgotten it either! Ivan was heavily into the 'Jimmy Smith, Georgie Fame' sort of scene - all based around that great Hammond organ sound, where the drummers were always jazz drummers and so that was the sort of gig I was playing at the time.

Going back to my Mersham Road days, it seemed that a lot of young musicians came from around that area and a few doors down from me was a guy called Peter Yerrell, another bass player, who started a matter of months before me and shot to fame bloody quickly. They fell pretty quickly too, but he got there very fast, and his group was called **The Snobs**. Well, one minute he was my neighbour in Mersham Road - it was 'hello Neil, hello Pete, how's it going' - and the next thing the bastard was in America on the Ed Sullivan show! We couldn't believe it. The Snobs used to dress up in all the 'flunky' gear; the wigs, the big collars, the 'regency style' of dress; 'Buckleshoe Stomp' was their record. Peter lives in Crawley now, and the last I heard he was still playing - local dinner dances, that sort of thing.

In 1966, the next band I joined turned out to be the **New Vaudeville Band**, and musically speaking, for me it was a big mistake. It was all a hype - the record label put out a single recorded by session musicians - 'Winchester Cathedral', with the attitude that 'if it sells we'll worry about it afterwards'. Of course, once it started to take off, they had to find a band to go out and promote it. I had placed another advertisement in the music press looking for gigs and I got a 'phone call from this guy Henry, who was a drummer and as it turned out, a friend of Geoff Stephens, who had written the song. Henry said to me, "Have you got a copy of the Melody Maker there? well if you look down the charts there's a single called 'Winchester Cathedral', and I said yeah, I see it, and he said "There is no group, I've been asked to put one together, do you fancy being the bass player!"

I went up to town to meet a couple of guys, we met in the basement of a music shop in Denmark Street and played a bit and they said do you want to join the band? When they explained to me what it was all about, well, I certainly wasn't used to this - turn on the radio and there is your 'hit record', that you hadn't played on - we put the band together bloody quick and within the week we were on Top of the Pops and other TV shows, there were photo sessions - it was shameful! To begin with Geoff Stephens tried to manage us, but when it became too big a job for him, **Peter Grant** took over, later to become the legendary figure behind Led Zeppelin's success. In fact it was Grant's idea to put us in those 1940's striped blazers and boaters.

We joined a package tour a couple of dates in, which was the Dusty Springfield tour playing the cinema chains, all the Odeon's and Granada's, where there were a large number of acts on the bill and each band only got to perform for about twelve or fifteen minutes. At that time, Dusty was backed by the Echoes and when I walked out to watch them take a soundcheck, there was Ivan Chandler sitting at the keyboards - I hadn't seen him for a little while, so that was nice, just bumping into him again like that.

I must admit, I tried to keep my involvement with the Vaudeville Band quiet, but several of my friends spotted me and blew the whistle - but at the end of the day, a gig's a gig - and besides, a short while later I was in the States. We were added to various bills in America as this novelty act from England, because the single was a huge hit over there too, and we played all these strange jewish hotels in the Catskill mountains of New York state. I got to know Peter Grant quite well too, as I had to share a room with him. Peter had a local connection too, you know; in his younger days he worked as a stage-hand at the old Croydon Empire theatre. He also fixed us up with a booking in Baltimore, Maryland on a gig with Curtis Mayfield, the Impressions and Patti Labelle & the Bluebells! I mean, we were the only white faces on the bill, but what a concert - the chance to see some of those soul guys up close, great bands, really tight!

I stayed with the New Vaudeville Band for just over six months, but for that sort of music you've really got to be an enthusiast and of course, I wasn't; I was a regular rock and roll bass player who had found himself in totally the wrong gig and so after about six months I just left. Once I was out, of course, I wondered "what was all that about?", having to wear straw boaters and 'forties suits! It was a lot of fun though, plus I managed to do a lot of radio, a bit of TV, a lot of recording and an awful lot of concerts - it was all great experience.

Next I joined a small soul band, I can't even remember their name, doing all Stax material and the next year we spent the whole of the summer touring in Germany, playing the U.S. Air bases and the clubs - and when we returned I joined the **Nashville Teens**.

Neil Korner onstage with the Nashville Teens during their Hungarian tour, summer of 1968. Surely this makes the 'Teens the first British band to play behind the Iron Curtain?

Below: the 'Teens line-up - Hungary, 1968. Left to right - John Hawken, Ray Phillips, Arthur Sharpe, Roger Groom and Neil Korner. Had the camera lens been wide enough, it would have picked up guitarist John Allen standing to the right of Neil.

Both photographs courtesy Neil Korner

When I came back from Germany, in the Autumn of '67, I read in the music press that their bass player Pete Shannon had left the band and I got straight on the 'phone to their manager, the infamous Don Arden at Galaxy Entertainments and said "You're going to be needing a bass player and I'm the man for the job". "Oh, are you" says Arden, "well, it just so happens there are a couple of the 'Teens in the office at the moment, you can talk to them". So Arden called one of them over and I told them who I was and what I'd been doing and who I'd played with. I told them I lived in Croydon and they said well, we're based in Weybridge, why don't you come down for an audition and we'll meet you at Weybridge station. We fixed up a date and I got on the train at Thornton Heath, changed at Clapham and sure enough there was a car with a couple of the Nashville Teens. We drove round to a little village hall that backed on to a pub. Inside the hall was all their gear set up, we ran through a couple of Jerry Lee Lewis songs, a couple of Chuck Berry's and they said fine, you obviously know how to play. We sat down for a chat and a drink and we got on very well, but they said we've got someone else to see, Don's sending him down a bit later on. When he turned up, he didn't really look the part - he was a mod who would have been better off in the Small Faces, and very young - but he did his thing and was glad to get away, I think. And that was it, I got the job and they didn't audition anybody else. The Nashville Teens were one of the finest bands I've ever had the good fortune to work with - John Hawken is one of the best rock 'n' roll piano players that this country has ever produced, certainly on a par with Ian Stewart who worked with the Stones. A great band, totally fucked up by Don Arden though, but I had a lot of fun playing with the Teens and they gained a great deal of respect playing on the circuit - and their circuit was playing the colleges and universities. I must have played every college and university in the country, every single one, round and round, up and down the M1; it was tough going sometimes, but then what was the alternative, a bloody day job! During my time with them, we recorded a version of 'All Along The Watchtower' with producer Vic Smith which was released in March 1968 and when the band left Decca records for Major Minor about a year later, we put out a version of Don Fardon's 'Indian Reservation'. Of course, Don had the hit with it!

Altogether I was with the Teens for about eighteen months to two years, from late '67 through '68 and well into '69 and left them not long after John Hawken moved on. Our guitarist John Allen left too, and Ray Phillips recruited some new guys to keep the band going. He recruited Roger Dean from John Mayall's band to replace me on bass and John Allen was replaced by Lennie Tuckey who later played guitar with Suzi Quatro and also ended up marrying her.

After he left the Teens, John Hawken 'phoned up Mickie Most, who he'd known from the early days of the Nashville Teens - Most had produced 'Tobacco Road' for them - to ask what was happening on the band front. Most shared an office in Oxford Street with Peter Grant, who had been my manager in the Vaudeville Band. John subsequently 'phoned me to say that Mickie Most was putting a country/rock band together around a special pedal steel guitarist called B.J. Cole, who had been spotted by Chris Dreja playing in a pokey little Irish band. And I later got a call from Peter Grant to say, 'If you're not doing anything, I've got this new band with your old mate John on piano, come up and play bass'. So we all went up to Studio 51 to rehearse, and it was a smashing little band, could have done really well, but it all fell to pieces, they decided they didn't want it. Of course, we all found out why, later on, because Peter had just taken on the New Yardbirds which emerged soon after as Led Zeppelin! Peter Grant had other people on his mind, namely Mr. Page and Mr. Beck!

Peter knew that I was more of a rock bassist and he told me personally about the signing of Jeff Beck; I have always wondered whether I might have been offered the gig, or at least had the chance to audition for the Jeff Beck group, if I hadn't just come out of the New Vaudeville Band. Because let's face it, it wouldn't have looked too good on the band's CV would it? - Beck's bass player ex-Vaudeville Band! But of all the guitarists around at that time, Jeff Beck was the one I would dearly have loved to play with, even just for a jam and Peter knew that. But it wasn't to be - the gig went to Ronnie Wood from the Birds, which is where he struck up the friendship with Rod Stewart, who came in as vocalist.

So, two of the other Yardbirds, Keith Relf and Jim McCarty decided to form another band and Peter said to them, well, I know a piano player who lives down in Surrey, called John Hawken, and that's basically how **Renaissance** came about. Keith also brought in his sister, Jane Relf on vocals. They had been together for about a year when Lou Cennamo, their first bass player left and the 'phone rang, it was John and there was my next gig.

I remember playing at the Croydon Greyhound with Renaissance, initially as support to Elton John, but Elton didn't turn up because of problems with their piano. We were okay because we always carried our own with us and went on to do the whole evening. The place was packed, in fact it was one of those evenings when you had the feeling it was too full for comfort, you know? I also got to travel Europe pretty widely with Renaissance, including the biggest crowd I ever played to, which was 25,000 at a festival in Germany. At the other end of the scale we were playing the support slot at places like Hemel Hempstead Pavilion, in fact at that particular gig the headline act was Deep Purple, and I always remember that it was keyboard player Jon Lord who outshone all the others, including Ritchie Blackmore.

I recorded one album with Renaissance and we also filmed an 'In Concert' special for Italian television. My favourite old Gibson was great for live work, but as this was being recorded I hired a Fender Telecaster bass from a local shop. The TV gig went well and the shop offered the bass to me for £120 - and I turned it down!

In 1977, the year Elvis died, I was playing with the **Frankie Reed Band**, again with John Hawken on piano, Tony Hall on sax and various other guys. One night Frankie introduced me to **Dana Gillespie**, film actress and singer and Dana invited me to play bass in her new band; although I didn't know it at the time, she also invited John and Tony to join as well, and fortunately Frankie Reed took it all in his stride! Dana's new band started to rehearse with guitarist John Knightsbridge and Ron Telemak on drums, Ron was later replaced by Tony Fernandez.

Dana was quite a celebrity at the time, well known for her relationship with David and Angie Bowie, in fact Angie used to come and visit the flat in Kensington where we rehearsed. And after a while it occurred to me that I knew Dana from somewhere else - in fact it was the Star in Croydon, and Dana used to visit the Star to see Hamish Grimes, who she quite fancied - Hamish was Giorgio Gomelsky's right hand man.

I stayed with Dana Gillespie's group for three years and I have to say now, it was one of the best bands that I have ever played in. It was strictly a London band, playing only London pub and club venues - places like the Golden Lion in the Fulham Road and a nightclub in Gerrard's Street. That particular club offered us four gigs a week, starting at midnight and playing through to about 1.15am and we ended up doing that for over a year, which gives you an idea of how well the band did.

One memorable night in Piccadilly, Dana arrived just in time for the soundcheck with a musician on her arm, who was a particular hero of mine, **Ritchie Haywood** - Ritchie was the drummer with Little Feat, without a shadow of a doubt one of the finest bands to come out of the States during the Seventies. She introduced Ritchie to all of us and told us that he would be sitting in with the band that night and I can remember feeling tremendously excited at the prospect of playing with such a drummer. Sure enough she announced him to the audience about three quarters of the way through our set, which would have been about one o'clock in the morning and the place erupted. When the guy played it was absolutely phenomenal, in the sense that his playing was so laid back, all the cliches about L.A./ West Coast drumming, but there was tremendous power which gave such an amazing contrast, that laid back feel plus the power - I've never heard a snare drum come down so hard in my life! And afterwards he came up to me and told me that he rated my playing and that he'd enjoyed the gig. It's a moment that I've always kept close to me, a real night to remember.

Unfortunately, not long afterwards Ritchie was involved in a serious motorcycle accident in Los Angeles, which left him badly injured for some time. About eighteen months later he came back to London and dropped in to see Dana when we were playing at the Golden Lion, Fulham Palace Road. The man clearly wasn't well, but he sat in with us once again and from the moment he sat behind the kit it was obvious that he'd lost none of that dynamic style of drumming, everything was still in place. It was wonderful to hear and needless to say, the musician-filled crowd at the Golden Lion gave him a tremendous welcome.

The only time Dana took the band out of London, we did a 'long weekend' in Dubai, out in the Persian Gulf, but apart from that we stayed in the capital and became a well respected band. The name of Dana's band was actually **Snakes Alive** and I like to think it was a musician's band, all the venues that we used to play were regularly frequented by other musicians, which was great, I enjoyed that gig a lot.

Like all good things, that band ran it's course and I moved on to a country rock band where I was actually playing nine gigs a week! Seven nights a week, plus Saturday and Sunday lunchtimes; good solid, regular work and not too difficult to work out why I did it. In 1986 I formed my own group called **Oak**, which was a very loud, heavy rock band playing power, ZZ Top style, that sort of material. I had John Knightsbridge on guitar, myself on bass, a drummer called Paul Elliott and a singer called Tony Mason from Orpington; we played the pub circuit, places like the Cartoon in Croydon and gigs in Leytonstone, all over London. ”

"Things may come and things may go... ...but the art school dance goes on forever"

So sang Pete Brown's Piblokto back in 1970, but the same line applies to those heady, after-school gigs at polytechnics, universities and colleges up and down the country - even Ewell Technical College. When Wallington's ***Terry Biddle*** *found himself fed up with the usual trad. jazz bands at his college, he decided to take over the social secretary's job and book the bands that he wanted to hear...*

I started at Ewell Tec. when I was just sixteen, which would have been around 1962 and it was a grave disappointment to me. I was going from school to a technical college, which was almost like being at university as far as I was concerned, people were grown up and wore their own clothes, not a uniform, that sort of thing. I expected, and hoped for, a real intellectual and political environment, which it really wasn't, and the dances in particular were a *real* let down, because they were all bloody Trad. jazz bands and not nearly enough people went to them.

So come the vacation for the next years term, I had just turned seventeen and I went and got myself the job of being entertainments 'chairman'. And I did that by going to the Wallington Public Hall and chatting to the bloke who ran it, who gave me the name of a few agents to contact. The Starlight Agency was one, I think, the sort of place you could go to book someone like say, Brian Poole & the Tremeloes who were a *proper* band as far as I was concerned. They gave me the job, not only because I was enthusiastic but because I had also written to Brian Epstein to try and book the Beatles! The first band we had on during my time was Alexander's Jazz Band, who the previous chairman had already booked and incredibly they packed the hall - and the hall we used at Ewell was in fact the refectory. That was the only drag, in that every Friday night you had to clear away all the tables and chairs and every Sunday morning you had to go in and set them all up again.

So it was a very good gig, but I decided that next time I would have a better one - the only trouble was I didn't know who to book. I turned to the back pages of the Melody Maker and everywhere you looked it was 'Georgie Fame this' and 'Georgie Fame that', so I booked him - and I got **Georgie Fame & the Blue Flames** for £45.00. They arrived and humped all their own gear in - I saw all these amplifiers and this great big Hammond organ, I'd never seen one before - and I was absolutely panic stricken, I thought how are we going to power this? Do they need a generator or something, it just hadn't occurred to me. And they said "no, no it's alright we've got a plugboard" - well, they plugged one 13 amp plug into a wall socket and they had about ten coming off it into this board! Georgie could only have been about three or four years older than I was, by the look of him and I said to them, 'there's no interval group, just stop when you want, then play on 'til about half ten, then an encore or two up to quarter to eleven'.

They warmed up for a bit and then started to play and it was an absolute bloody riot; people were up on each others shoulders, taking their shirts off and throwing them around... and at the end of the gig, Georgie looks around and said 'Crazy, man' and he picks up from under his seat the college principle's car parking sign, that somebody had pulled out of the ground and put on his Hammond organ! They got £45 quid for that and off they went then to the Flamingo club in London to do an 'all-nighter' - while I went home on the train, looking after all the money!

For the next gig I organised, which was the big college 'do' of the year at Cheam Baths Hall, I got the **Cyril Davies All-Stars** with Long John Baldry and the Velvettes and supported them with a local group called The Presidents. The funny thing about that gig was that I had just been up to Studio 51 with my brother Rick to see the Rolling Stones and I wanted to book them to appear with Cyril Davies - I missed getting them by a single day, we wanted them on the Friday night and they had just pencilled a gig in and could only do the Saturday. Of course I never got the chance to book them again! That gig at Cheam Baths actually broke their attendance record, there must have been over a thousand people crammed into the hall. The Davies group at that time was basically Screaming Lord Sutch's band - Carlo Little on drums, Nicky Hopkins on piano, Bernie Watson on guitar - and it was also strange because they all turned up in evening dress.

After that I was looking through Record Mirror and came across a group called the **Graham Bond Quartet**. At that time, although I hated the trad. scene, which I thought was boring and repetitive, I was a great fan of modern jazz, which was cool, sophisticated and 'intellectual' and one of my favourite records was Alexis Korner's Rhythm & Blues at the Marquee, which had Dick Heckstall-Smith on it. So when I read this article on the Graham Bond Quartet, it mentioned that Dick was playing with them and that Graham had previously played with Don Rendell - and I had an album with something by Don Rendell on it - so I decided that they were the group for me. I managed to book them for the princely sum of £40 and I designed a ticket for the gig with GBQ on it, because I didn't like the full name; people were so annoyed that I had booked an 'unknown' band for the college gig - who is this Graham Bond, they all said.

When Graham and the band eventually turned up, what an unlikely bunch of 'herberts' they were, they looked ancient and positively evil! When you're responsible for a gig you have to keep running back and forth - checking the ticket sales on the door, making sure the band are o.k., generally keeping an eye on things - and I kept missing bits of their first set, but I did hear people arguing about 'bloody modern jazz' and 'what do we want to hear this rubbish for'! So I made sure that I went out for the second half and I thought it was great; I was standing by them, they were playing on the floor again, no stage, right next to Jack Bruce who was on bass and it really did sound good. I had set out a couple of rows of chairs down at the front, a la Flamingo where I got the idea from, so that people could sit and listen or dance behind if they wanted to. The chairs were full of my mates who were nodding in that studious 'yeah, man, good' style; some were clapping and a few were actually clapping on the 'off beat', which was very hip in those days! Not clap on the beat which was rock'n'roll, of course. Other people were looking miserable and some were talking, until the band launched into 'Hoochie Coochie Man' and then everybody just went completely berserk. And for the final four or five songs - 'Night Time Is The Right Time', 'What I Say', 'Got My Mojo Working' and whatever else they did, everybody but everybody was on their feet, shouting and cheering. At the end, people were running towards the entrance, where I had set up a little display of posters, to pull one off to keep; and I found myself tearing one off and my best mate Rodney pulling on the other side! I won incidentally, and got it signed by the band and Graham said to me "Hey man, that was great, we've got to make a gig here all the time. You find us somewhere to play and we'll do the gig and all take the same money". Well, having since read his biography I can imagine that wouldn't have happened! Funnily enough I ended up giving the money to Dick Heckstall-Smith, because Graham said 'we're a corporate band...'

After that gig, Graham was the one everyone wanted to see, so I did a night using just local bands which was very popular and then booked Graham again. By this time we had built a stage and being able to see people and their reactions he was completely outrageous - standing up at the keyboard, playing alto sax and organ at the same time, Ginger crashing away on drums. Somebody in the audience had a whistle and during Ginger's drum solo, every time there was a break in the playing this guy would blow his whistle to fill the gap. Ginger looked up from behind his kit, with that look of his that said "If I find out who you are, I'm going to smash your x?*!x**?! head in"; but afterwards I asked Ginger what he thought of the gig and he said "Yeah, it was good that, mate it was alright, I liked that", people had brought in tambourines and harmonicas, it was a great atmosphere.

The next gig was my worst one of all, and unfortunately it was when I booked **John Mayall**. There was really heavy rain all afternoon and evening, the support band were pretty 'ropey' and John was unhappy about the whole thing. I remember saying to John "It'll be o.k. - all you have to do is play 'Mojo Working' and the audience will be right with you" and he said "but we don't do that one"! What was also odd was that the band all played sitting down and their guitarist Bernie Watson played the whole gig with his back to the audience. This was before Clapton joined them, one of the early line-ups of John Mayall's Bluesbreakers including bassist John McVie, one half of what would become the Fleetwood Mac rhythm section.

In the meantime I was travelling around to see Graham Bond and his band wherever I could, which was generally at the 100 Club in Oxford Street. I used to meet Graham beforehand in a pub round the back of Oxford Street and he would always say "It's o.k. man, I'll get you in for free" - and we never, ever got in for free! To give him his due, he used to have these huge rows with the management, saying how these kids had come all the way from deepest Surrey to see the band, but no, we never got in for nothing. So I kept in contact with them and Graham played the last night of my time as 'social secretary' at the Tec. where they must have pulled in about a thousand people - so many that we had to open the side doors and let everybody roam through. The other band who were booked to play the interval slot arrived very late and they were called the Fingernail Five, a band from the Flamingo. At first I refused to pay them and planned to put Graham on three times, but they insisted that there was just enough time to slot them in. When I said there's no time for you to set your drum kit up, their drummer told me "Don't worry I'll play Ginger's, I know him". I said "Yeah, I know him too, he won't like that" and when Ginger came back from the pub he saw what was happening and he just launched himself through the crowd towards this drummer. I was waiting for somebody to shout 'murder', when Ginger walked calmly back through the audience and said "Yeah I know him, it's alright".

I went to see Zoot Money's Band play at Wallington Public Hall and afterwards we got chatting about Graham Bond. Zoot said to us "Oh yeah, Graham's alright but you don't want to let him play anyone else's organ because he'll only go and break a key or something". He was just so ham-fisted, Graham, a huge guy and very full of himself, he loved being in the limelight, but he could be a very weird character. Except of course, at the time I didn't realise that anyone was doing drugs - although they probably all were, but I never saw any of that. It may have been evident a couple of years later, but not then.

And the number of times I helped carry that bloody organ off his lorry and onto the stage - anyway, the last time I booked Graham it was another really outrageous gig, he was absolutely tremendous. I had got myself a tambourine by then and this time the band were playing back on the floor - the 'stage' we used previously was made out of tables and a couple of them had been broken during the last gig - so Graham and the band played on the same level as the audience. He was really going for it - standing on his keyboard and roaring the crowd on - I was standing next to them and Jack Bruce pulled me in with the group, so that I could play tambourine into his vocal mike. He was singing the chorus of one particular song and I tried to join in, but I couldn't raise any sort of voice above the level of their music. Yet I could hear Jack's voice booming out and I just stood and looked at him in amazement - Jack took my tambourine, hit it two times and smashed the thing in half! Thanks, Jack.

Some little while later at the jazz festival in Richmond, I ran into Jack again and he introduced me to these people who either ran Klooks Kleek or the Ricky Tick club, one or the other. The funny thing was that here we were talking to a couple of the biggest concert promoters in London and Jack introduced me as running "one of the best gigs in the country"!

So they were the college gigs while I was actually there and running them but after I left, I subsequently went back to run the music side again for a little while. And I missed out a couple of things that I must tell you about: I organised a gig at Kingston with The Fourmost and they were quite good, but another band came in, a group of Jamaicans, a bluebeat band who arrived too late to play. So I booked them to come back and play at the college and I also had a guy called Duke Reid and his Sound System - a black guy who just played records. He was fabulous this bloke; he came in, found somewhere to plug his record player in and just started playing his own records in amongst the crowd who were starting to arrive - you hardly ever saw that sort of thing at that time. Then this bluebeat group turned up and they were led by a trombone player called **Rico** - who went on to play with The Selector in the early Eighties and then with Jools Holland - quite a few people.

Then a few years later, during my second stint at booking bands for the college, I managed to get **Cream** into the Wallington Public Hall - 4th February 1967. It was officially a Ewell Tec. gig, but we couldn't use the college refectory as it was being decorated! I went up to Robert Stigwood's office in London and met Ginger Baker there; he was still very friendly, it was "Hi, are we playing your gig...yeah?, good...

look forward to that, when is it?" all that sort of thing. The fee was £250 and they did two sets for that; there was a photograph that appeared in the Surrey Comet of the three of them with three girls and me peeping through the curtain behind!

The money side was quite incredible really, if you paid a band say, £50, then you might make £50. And I always wanted to pay the band their due amount - I mean it wasn't my money - so I was always happy to pay them the full whack, but I couldn't see how anyone actually made any money out of promoting these gigs. It must have been, and in fact I later found out the hard way, that some guys didn't pay them at all or they paid them very little money. Actually that Rico/bluebeat gig started off as a local promoter trying to rip me off and ruin the gig for me - we booked a band together and I wasn't too happy about the situation, so I put in Rico's band as a backup and it ended up saving the day for me really. I think I made about £5 profit on the John Mayall gig, whereas Graham Bond's best gig probably made us about £100. The guy who took over the college gigs from me had seen how popular his band were and wanted to book Graham again. By this time, his fee had grown to £80 a night and he asked me to phone up his agent and try to get a slightly better price! We were then charging 7/6 to get in and I think Cream were 8/6 or nine shillings, somewhere in that region.

Even after they formed Cream, Jack and Ginger were still alright; Jack was as quiet as ever, he just sat in the dressing room playing his guitar. Clapton, who I hadn't met before, arrived first at Wallington with this big fur coat on, accompanied by a henchman wearing an identical coat. Eric sat in there with one of those portable 45rpm record players and a box full of singles that he just played over and over again. Then Jack arrived and the two of them began tuning up and jamming a bit; Clapton said "Give me a G" or something and Jack rather sarcastically replied "Isn't your guitar perfectly tuned all the time?" They fiddled around a bit and then started to play 'Ticket To Ride" of all things; and after a minute Clapton said "On this bit here, I think I'll play this" - and he played some tricky section that had nothing in common with the song, and Jack looked at him as if to say, are you mad? Ginger and his wife arrived last, in his second Rover 2000 which was a big deal then, I think he'd smashed the first one up. During the interval Ginger, his wife and I went for a drink together, across to 'The Cavalier' pub in fact - most people think of him as a bit of a madman, but I always got on well with Ginger, he was probably the most down to earth of all three of them. Cream, and particularly Eric Clapton have been written about so often, yet reading about them now they seem like totally different characters; sure they all liked a drink and Jack and Dick Heckstall-Smith used to knock back the scotches in between the pints, but drugs? not a sign of them. ”

Matthew Fisher & Mike Roberts

When I met up with Matthew Fisher in South Croydon, I found that he had brought along an old friend, Mike Roberts, who had played in bands with Matthew since they were both teenagers - 'The Ban the Bomb Club, Denmore Road, 1960' was their debut according to Mike! Both were at one time members of Glen Athens & the Trojans and the Society Five, although Matthew is probably best known for his work with Procol Harum, including his part on a certain Number 1 hit single...

Matthew: 'To start right at the beginning, I was born in Addiscombe and the family moved to South Norwood when I was about fifteen or sixteen. Mike was born in Thornton Heath, I believe. As far as I can remember, there were three main bands that had connections with Selhurst School; we had **The Trojans**, **The Society Five**, which were combined in a sense, and **Paul & the Alpines**. Paul was a good bass player, but he had a terrible stutter...

Mike: Although **Glen Athens & the Trojans** appeared to be the usual five piece line-up - two guitars, bass, drums and a vocalist 'Glen', whose real name was Phil Saunders - we were slightly different in that I was one of two lead guitarists, who both had totally contrasting styles. There were several different line-ups, but the last one was together for at least a couple of years. By the time we finally called it a day in 1965, the band was Tim Guest and myself on guitars, Derek (Del) Needham on bass, the drummer was Dave Little and Phil Saunders the singer, who was 'Glen Athens'. By that stage though, we'd dropped the Glen bit and were just known as The Trojans'.

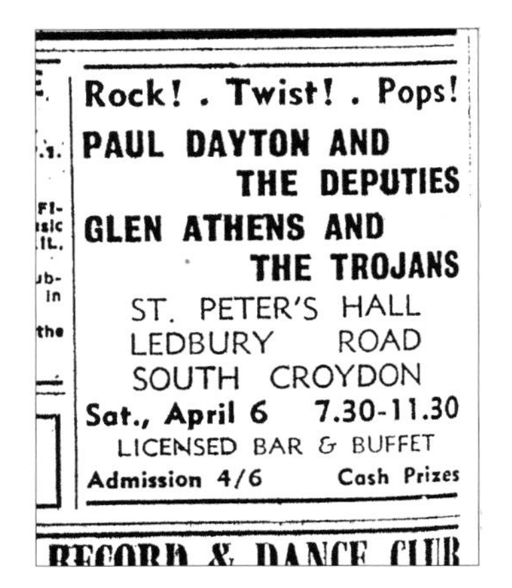

Matthew: 'Tim and Phil were in all the line-ups, right the way through and in fact, Tim is still playing in a little band somewhere. I originally played bass with them and dropped out of the Trojans when I decided to go professional and switched from playing bass to playing organ. I just couldn't get any work as a bass player and later went off to music school...

Mike: 'The Trojans released an EP on Spot Records which has got four tracks on it - three written by the group and one by some strange band who sound nothing like us! We made several other recordings, but that EP is the only thing that was released...'

Matthew: 'I didn't actually play on the EP, although I do remember coming back to a session to play piano on one of Mike's songs called 'Oh-Ah-Ah-Ooh'. And I did a session at RG Jones studio, again playing piano, which may have been after Mike left, it was for Decca with Mike Smith producing and I think we covered a Carole King song. Del Needham was there on bass and I remember being called back from music school to play on it. I also got the hard-sell from Rome Trudel, the Trojans manager, saying "come back, the band are really going places..."

Mike: 'Rome' Trudel was our manager for many, many years - he was a French Canadian and a very nice guy actually, but stuck in a bit of a rut - as the music scene changed, he stayed exactly the same. Later on a guy called Louis Chun became the Trojans manager'.

Matthew: 'The original line-up had John Gestico on bass, who was then replaced by Dave Coleman, then by me and finally Del Needham. There was another fairly stable line-up of the Trojans, which had Ray Cummings on drums, a rhythm player called Ken Howes and again this guy John Gestico on bass. Plus the ever-present Phil and Tim. This would have been while Mick and I were off playing in another band, **The Society Five**'.

Mike: 'Did you know that the Trojans came third in a National Beat contest? The Mecca Organisation ran this nationwide contest and one of the early line-ups, without either Matthew or I, came third - it was quite an achievement. They really thought they were going to take off, as the publicity blurb says on the back of our EP: *'From out of nowhere came the Trojans...!*

Like a lot of the bands at that time, the Trojans did a tour of Germany that included playing the Star Clubs in Karlsruhe and Giessen. We played over in France too, at a club called 'Le Kibitz' in Strasbourg. It was a very exciting thing to do when you're a teenager - most of us were about seventeen or eighteen, Del Needham was the eldest and he could only have been twenty. We shared the bill with a Scottish band called **The Fleet** who were very good, but a bit 'old-school', you know, a bit Cliff & the Shadows, whereas we were much more part of the British Beat scene that was coming through.

It was great fun but extremely hard work; we were playing six or seven nights a week, with the gigs on Friday and Saturday going on well into the early hours of next morning. In fact we were in Germany over Christmas, working Christmas Eve into Christmas Day and then spent the day itself huddled in a tiny, freezing cold hotel room. We filled a wastepaper bin with earth and stuck a single fir tree *branch* into it for our Christmas tree! We had just enough money to buy a few bread rolls, a little bit of cheese and a small jar of coffee - and we didn't have a kettle. The coffee was made with cold water in these little pyrex cups with separate plastic holders and then each cup was heated individually with a 'travelling' electric element. Happy Christmas, Trojans! The Croydon local paper ran a piece that painted a romantic picture of the band 'conquering' Germany, in particular a moment where we supposedly stopped on a snow covered mountain road to perform for the troops. What actually happened was that our tour bus, the famous van with the rocking horse on top, ran out of petrol halfway up this remote mountain road and it was the army who came along to get us started again! Still, it made for a good story in the paper.

Matthew: Of course, Croydon had its own 'Star' club, where everybody played and we would often go there to see a band. The Yardbirds did their stint at the Star during their 'Clapton' period, although personally I always preferred going to see the T-Bones, Gary Farr's group - I thought they were the better live band. I hated 'For Your Love', but then so did Clapton and he played on it! I only really got into the Yardbirds after Beck joined them and I much preferred Clapton's playing with John Mayall's Bluesbreakers.

Mike: The Trojans played the Star a few times earlier on and places like the Kings Head at Merton, which in those days was an out and out Irish pub. I remember one night, soon after 'Telstar' by the Tornados came out, and this big Irishman came up to the stage while we were playing and said "Play Telstar - or I'll thump the lot of yer...!" I think we had a go at it but it must have been a pretty rough old version.

Courtesy Mike Roberts

The Society Five. Left to right: Mike Roberts, Derek Spiller, John Wallace, Matthew Fisher and Mike Shun.

Matthew: It was at gigs like that where you needed to be playing a big old Fender Telecaster or a Jazz bass - or at least something heavy-bodied that you get a good swing on if things started to get rough!

Mike: I was playing a Burns in those days - in fact later on I reckon I could have owned the first left-handed Burns guitar *and* it was specially made for me by Mr. Burns himself. What happened was that I went up to a trade fair in London and I was on the Burns stand trying out a guitar. The boss saw me and must have been intrigued by the way I played, because I had learnt to play by simply turning the guitar upside down; so not only were the strings the wrong way up but I could use a tremelo arm upside down as well. Burns went away and made a left-handed version for me, which I used in the Society Five, although it meant I then had to re-learn to play with the strings the right way up, for a long time afterwards I could still play both ways.

Matthew: We haven't actually explained about the Trojans tour van. The band wanted a horse for the top of the van, as in *Trojan Horse* and they found one of those old Mobilo rocking horses, the ones with a hollow metal body attached to a metal frame with springs instead of rockers. It was mounted on top of the van at the front and I put a couple of bulbs behind the eyes of the horse and wired them up to light up independently. As the van approached an unwary pedestrian, one red eye would blink a couple of times and the poor guy would be left thinking he was going crazy, while we were all cracking up inside the van. Particularly effective in fog, this horse twelve foot up, looming out of the mist with flashing red eyes!

Mike: I seem to remember we also had a telephone receiver hooked up to the dashboard with a bit of old guitar lead and a bell that sounded like a ringing 'phone. The trick was to pull up at traffic lights next to a cyclist, sound the bell and pass the receiver out of the window to him, saying 'it's for you'. Funny thing is, some of them actually took it, if they managed to stay on their bikes in the first place! Matthew's attempts at wiring eventually blew the vans complete electric system, which filled the van with smoke while we all leapt out of the back doors laughing our heads off. Kids, eh?

We pulled a few stunts, but the only really naughty thing we ever did was the 'baseball practice' on that Shell garage. Between Wallington and Carshalton there used to be a garage and in those days the roadside signs had glass tops in the shape of the Shell logo, which were illuminated at night. Every so often, we would drive past late at night and take it in turns to lean out of the window and attempt to 'take out' the glass dome with a baseball bat - quite often we would miss - but the real test was to smash both lights, one at either end of the garage. I imagine that the garage stopped replacing them after a while. Bloody hooligans!

Matthew: Mike and I left the Trojans to form The Society Five, with drummer Andy Poulson. Actually we had quite a succession of drummers; Punjab was the first drummer, he was very good but he was Anglo-Indian and his parents were Jehovah's witnesses - they didn't like him playing in the band, so they bought him a motorbike on condition that he left the group, which he did. Then for a while we had this guy Roy Manleyson, who was okay as a drummer, but the point was that his dad had a car! Very important. His dad was great, his family were fine, but he was always complaining, always moaning, he just used to get us all down until we ended up screaming at him. John, our singer, once told him that before he joined we were the happiest band going, and now look at us... We just got completely sick of this guy and the last gig we played was in Caterham - at the time we were all dependent on our parents for transport, none of us could drive and we just decided that we had to get rid of Roy. So after a gig when we knew Roy's dad couldn't collect him, when the other mums and dads came to pick us up, we just left him at the hall, with his kit and no lift home. I think he took the hint.

One other particular gig stands out in the memory, when Mike nearly killed himself...

Mike: I had just brought a new amplifier from West Croydon Music Studios and when we got to the venue - which could have been the old ABC - the soundman offered to let us use the cinema's tannoy system as the P.A. I had already plugged my new amp in and the soundman gave me one of those big old tannoy microphones to hold while he went to plug that in. As the plug hit the socket, I was knocked about three feet off the ground and fell flat on my back; the fault was with my amplifier as it turned out and as I had been touching the strings on my guitar when the microphone was plugged in, I must have completed the circuit! The funny thing was, if you can call it funny, as I was

Matthew Fisher & Mike Roberts (contd.)

lying there 'twitching' and with six grooves burning into the palm of my hand, one of the band came over to me and told me to stop 'mucking about'...

Matthew: It was probably me, totally oblivious to you half-electrocuting yourself. Actually we realised what was going on pretty quickly and someone ran over to the socket and kicked out the plug!

Mike: 'Matthew went off to his professional gig and the Trojans did this tour in Germany and France; when we came back we did a few things, but quite frankly the band was dead on its feet. I ended up doing my first professional job at a holiday club in Devon and Matthew, who was looking for work at the time, ended up at a holiday camp in Minehead, Somerset, which was only about forty miles away.'

Matthew: 'Thinking back, before I went to music school I joined a Newcastle band called **The Gamblers**, who used to back **Billy Fury**. They did their own gigs as well, but if Fury had a tour or appeared on 'Saturday Club' we would be his backing group. That was strange, because that was the first time I ever turned on the radio and happened to hear myself coming out - it was months after we'd done this 'Saturday Club' or 'Easybeat' or some BBC recording, I turned the radio on and heard this organ playing and thought, Christ, that's me!' On one tour, Fury had two bands who used to back him on alternate numbers, The Gamblers used to do the more 'rocky' stuff and the John Barry Seven backed him on the ballads.

Courtesy Mike Roberts

Mike and Matthew gather round the mic. to practice those 'Beatle-esque' harmony vocals. The Society Five in rehearsal, circa 1965.

Going back to the earlier days, I played with several bands in a short space of time. Chronologically it was the Trojans, the Gamblers and Billy Fury, then I went off to music school - although it wasn't too long before I decided that I didn't like it and had to leave, which meant that I had to make some money to compensate the individual tutors for 'lost' tuition time! I needed a regular job and found one playing in a Butlins holiday camp with some band. It was a lot of fun, actually.

Then in a short space of time I did a few gigs with the **Downliners Sect, Peter Jay & the Jaywalkers** during the time when Terry Reid was their lead singer, and then I joined **Screaming Lord Sutch**, who had Ritchie Blackmore and Carlo Little in his band. There were a couple of groups that I only played with once or twice, when I first got my Hammond organ, I did a few gigs with **Tony Knight's Chessmen**. Finally I did something that I had always wanted to do, which was put an ad. in Melody Maker saying 'Hammond Organist seeks band...' and **Procol Harum** were one of the people who answered. At first, I actually wasn't too impressed; they had a lot of big ideas about this and that, which I had heard before, but I quite liked the songs and thought 'I'll give them three months or something'. At least they were a band that wrote their own material and that was something that I had been looking for, rather than a band that just played covers all the time. And of course, something did happen within that three months... *(Procol released 'A Whiter Shade of Pale', which became a massive hit worldwide)* ... and that was the beginning of the end for me really. In retrospect, I think perhaps the worst thing I ever did was join Procol Harum - things may have worked out an awful lot better for me if I hadn't. When I look back at it, everything was just going up, up, up, up... until then, when everything suddenly went 'woosh' - straight downwards! After that, nothing was really the same. I was only with Procol for a couple of years, '67 to '69, something like that...

Mike: 'But Matt, you're still with them...'

Matthew: 'That's a point, yes I'm still with them, I keep forgetting! Well I've got nowhere else to go now, at my age I don't think anyone else would want me. You see, right up until then I was quite confident of the fact that I could go up on stage with any band, and nobody knew who the hell I was, you know, I was just the organist. They would say, 'oh, he's good that organist, blah, blah, blah... who was that masked organ player!' that sort of thing, but once it got to the situation where I was up on stage and people actually knew who I was, knew my name, I didn't feel... I really didn't like it anymore. I had lost my anonymity, which I rather liked. So there we are.

I also remember playing a session at **Joe Meek**'s studio in 304 Holloway Road - I'd just left school, probably around 1964/65 and was hanging about with guitarist Roger Mingaye and a drummer Ian Broad, who had played with Freddie Starr's Midnighters. They told me that Joe was always looking for young musicians and keyboard players in particular, although I was still more of a bass guitarist at the time. I went up to meet Joe and was a little bit nervous - I'd heard all about his reputation - and after the session his comments were more about my dress sense than any musical ability - but I did get to play that strange old piano with the hammers full of drawing pins and gave me the chance to look around a real recording studio, probably for the first time.

I've always lived locally, barring a year in Wiltshire, although I was still working in Croydon and then spent six months in New York when I was producing for CBS. That was the end of 1971, beginning of '72; the culture was pretty interesting, reading in the next days paper about who had been murdered a couple of blocks away, but I didn't actually do much while I was there. It was a job that was offered to me at a time when I had nothing better to do, but to be honest it was a bit of a waste of time. I finished off an album that had been abandoned by another producer halfway through, by a little duo called Prairie Madness, which never really saw the light of day, although I'm told that there was a radio station in Milwalkee, of all places, that regularly played this album, it became a local cult album! When guitarist Robin Trower left Procol to go solo, I produced his first three albums, from which I still gratefully receive the occasional royalty cheque! ❞

Matthew still runs his recording studio in South Croydon, and as Mike said, still turns out for Procol when required! Mike is writing and recording songs, and in December 1997 won an award for 'Sarah Jane' - Great British Songwriting Competition sponsored by BMG/Miracle/Amnesty International.

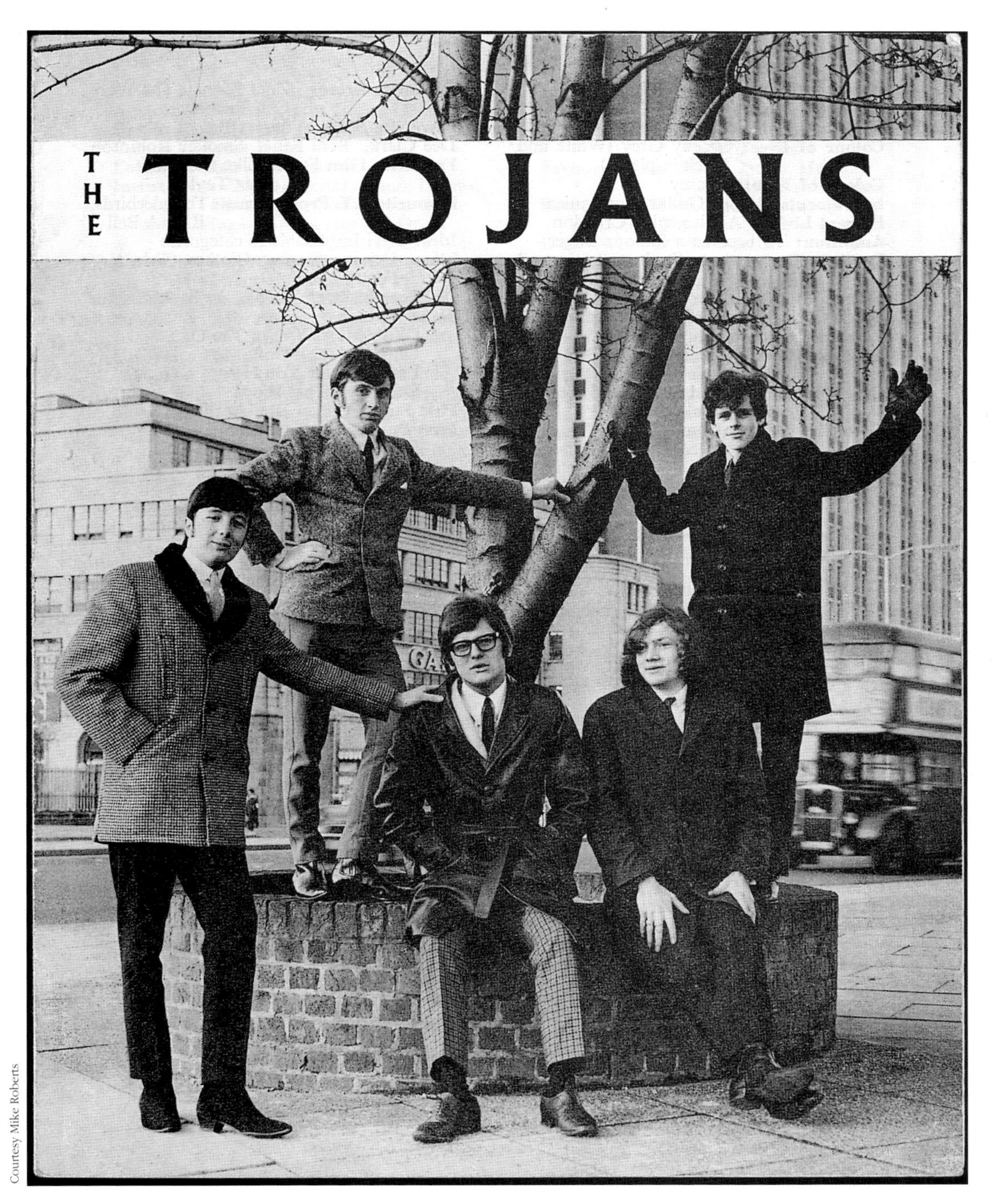

Courtesy Mike Roberts

The Trojans on the cover of the groups four page press release and photographed outside the newly built Fairfield Halls . Left to right: Tim Guest, Mike Roberts, Phil Saunders, Derek Needham and David Little.

Martin Nighy

Martin Nighy was the lead singer with one of Croydon's most popular and hardworking groups during the early Sixties, the Martin Jae Five.

I was born at Mayday Hospital, Croydon and grew up in Caterham, was educated in Caterham and then came back to Croydon as a teenager at fifteen to take up an apprenticeship at Dees of Croydon, the Ford dealer. So from the age of fifteen I was working in Croydon, but still living in Caterham.

I was always a singer, albeit a very self-conscious one and without very much confidence, but I loved music and singing and like all of the youngsters of the time, I can remember *specifically* when I first heard 'Heartbreak Hotel'. It was in the front room of somebody's house in Caterham, just one of a group of kids, aged maybe fifteen or sixteen; this girl had just got the record of Heartbreak Hotel by Elvis Presley and well, you've heard it a million times but, my skin crawled. I thought that's just the most incredible thing I've ever heard and it completely changed my view of music, because up until then I was into anything; anything choral, I used to sing in the church choir, I sang 'Sixteen Tons' and a few other things which were my contributions to the talent contests at the local youth club. I liked Bill Haley, traditional jazz and modern jazz, but when I first heard 'Heartbreak Hotel' I knew that was the type of music that I would like to be involved with. But I was still a closet singer, lots of practising in the bathroom at home where the echo was great or as a paperboy in the alleys, I used to cut through all the alleyways of Caterham on my rounds and of course you can get a great sound in an alleyway! I was very confused, because one minute I would be singing something by Mario Lanza - I loved that sort of voice - but having heard Elvis and the others, I was trying to imitate them. Obviously would have loved to have been a performer, but didn't have the confidence to be one. I went to work at Dees and there were two guys there, Mick Hack and John Stevens; Mick was a Brummie and he was an apprentice about my age, John also, and in their lunch hour they used to get a couple of guitars out - Mick was six string, John was bass and they would strum away and play around. I knew them and was very interested in what they were doing, but I didn't get involved initially. In fact, I was actually banned from singing and whistling, they said that I drove them mad with 'Singing the Blues'! That was during the Suez crisis and we had little or no work because there was no petrol for the cars, so we were given the job of painting the workshop... and the workshop at Dees was huge. We were up ladders, right up in the gables of the building and it was great for singing, but after being banned' at first I eventually got talking to Mick and John in the lunchbreak and started to sing along with them.

It was their idea to form a band and they found a drummer and a pianist and another guitarist - rhythm guitar was Bob Gamble, Earl Morgan became the main drummer, after we auditioned quite a few, but that really was the basis of the band and from there we started to go out and play a few gigs; we did the usual thing of travelling around in an old transit van. At first we were known as **The Hi-Five**; there was already a Croydon group called The Hi-Fi's - which was quite a trendy name at the time, you know, if something was High Fidelity it was 'state of the art' in recording equipment back then - and we liked the sound of that, so we changed it slightly to become the Hi-Five. As I say, we started to travel about a bit, doing a few jobs and it went quite well and at some point my ego took over and I became Martin Jae - my middle name is Joseph so I abbreviated the J from there and I had a parish priest in Caterham called Father Rae, which I always thought was a rather nice name, so I called myself Martin Jae - because I thought Nighy was totally off-putting. Something that my brother has since put me to shame about, because he is Bill Nighy the actor, and fairly well known now, and you see the name on television and outside the National Theatre and people actually know how to pronounce it, *(the Y is silent)* which is very unusual.

So, we quickly became **Martin Jae & the Hi-Five**, and then eventually after three or four years or so, it seemed better to be the **Martin Jae Five** which is how we stayed right up until the end.

That's how it all began, and from start to finish I suppose we were together from 1956/57, a hundred years ago!, till about 1965/66. I have a poster from a gig we did at the community centre in Addington in '65 and soon after that we split up and I joined up with local jazz pianist **Roy Budd**. I was honoured - I still can't believe that I was actually allowed to sing with Roy Budd. We had Roy's brother Ian on guitar and a guy called Dave on bass guitar and double bass, in fact I believe that Dave was the bass player on 'Tobacco Road'. Now, Ted Potter, who was the fulcrum of music in Croydon; you'll hear him mentioned time and time again, not just because he ran *the* music shop - you went there to get your guitar strings, your sheet music, instruments and amplification in those days - but also because Ted was just a wonderful guy. He was also a great jazz drummer, of course, an outstanding jazz drummer who knew all the jazz people - modern jazz, big band, you name it. It was Ted who was the prime mover in bringing Roy, Dave, Ian and myself together to form this strange sort of blues/jazz group. Roy was a wonderful pianist, and ultimately a great composer, as anyone will tell you, now sadly no longer with us. I can remember seeing Roy playing in the Friend's Meeting place in Croydon, this would be around 1959/60, when he would have been twelve or thirteen. He had curly hair like Little Lord Fauntleroy, this little cherub-like kid sitting up there playing piano like you've never heard before.

Roy could satisfy the jazz purists, but later on with us, he deigned to play more blues and rock, so we ended up with quite an interesting repertoire - we did some Stones stuff, some Matt Monro songs, because I quite liked his voice!, some rock, some blues and some of Roys' and it was great. We went round and played some gigs, not more than a couple of times a week; Ted's idea was that we should develop a unique style and perhaps do something with it - there was a big thing in the paper, with a picture of me signing a contract with Ted as my manager, you know, "Martin Jae goes professional". We tried a few things, but it sort of faded really, which just goes to show that I didn't have the determination that I should have had. I had a good day job, still with Dees and by 1966 I was Sales Manager; I was married, I was well paid and it was great fun selling cars, which I enjoyed tremendously. There were plans for the future, directorships, this and that - I was twenty five and stupid, in one respect, because I couldn't see myself or anyone, for that matter, as a pop singer making a living past thirty, which at 25 remember, was the benchmark. That's all I ever saw myself as, a pop singer, I was never a real rock'n' roller, although I would have liked to have been. I was never a rebel and I'm afraid that much to my disgust I was far too much in the 'Cliff' mould. I admire him, obviously, he has done very, very well but he doesn't *move* you like some of the real rockers would and in some ways he's manufactured himself into a 'pop singer'.

So what with being married and in a good job, I didn't really push it and it faded. I had a couple of recording tests, but the material wasn't very good and I guess I just wasn't anything different and of course, as we all know, you've got to have that something that is different, unique. By 1968/69 I had stopped performing in public, although if anyone asked me to sing I would, and I've since performed at the Ford conventions all over the world, but I was off the scene.

These days I'm still strumming at home; I never played guitar or any instrument in the band, but my engagement present from my wife was a Harmony six string guitar. By this time, Ted Potter had a guy named Dave Newton working for him, who also used to work with us at Dees as an apprentice car mechanic, but went to Potters' to learn how to repair instruments - guitars and basses initially, then latterly violins and bows - and I am told that he is now one of the leading bowmakers in the country. Anyway, they had a batch of Harmony guitars that had literally fallen off the back of a container and cracked; Dave repaired them and was selling them off for twenty five quid each, Mick Hack had one and I received one for my wedding present.

So I've satisfied both my singing and performing urges by learning a few chords and bashing out a few songs. It really is great therapy, if you're ever feeling a bit cheesed off, to go home and rattle out a couple of songs, even if you've sung them a million times, somehow you feel better. I'm no good on guitar, but I can hit a few chords and I still hear certain songs that move me so much I just have to learn them and try to sing them.

Last year (1994), the members of the Martin Jae Five met up again and played for a sort of reunion and it was one of the best things that has ever happened really, because Mick and I have carried on rehearsing ever since and I'm learning off him all the time. I've got a load more songs now and we're going to do a couple more gigs soon - it's feeble stuff, but it's good to be still doing it.

Not only did Ted Potter know everyone in the music business, but a great many people in the entertainment business too - Ted's mother was the sister of actor/comedian Will Hay - and Ted was a friend of the agent **Tito Burns**, who managed lots of people and in particular Dusty Springfield, he really looked after her career. Tito Burns wanted to create a mystery rock'n'roll band, build up a lot of hype and then try and do this big reveal - to create something out of nothing, with our band being the nothing!

There is a guy who lived on the borders of Wallington and Croydon called Bobby Richards, who was a composer/arranger; not by any means working in rock and only just on the edge of pop, really rather straight - a nice, nice guy and a very clever musician, but rather straight. He put together some compositions, really curious compositions which were indeed very different, but doubtful as to how popular they would be. So Tito had Bobby, with all his compositions and arrangements and he wanted a band, and in particular a band that wasn't too well known, but who were quite capable of managing these fairly complicated melodies and chord sequences. Ted Potter introduced us to Bobby and we went up to his house, sat around listening to these things - remember, I'm not playing, just observing because they don't need a singer. The result of that was that we recorded a demo and Tito Burns called us in and said OK, I would like you to do this, I'm going to call you **Group X**, you're not going to be known, everyone's going to say 'who are you?', we are really going to push this record and hopefully it will be extremely successful and then we'll take it from there.

And so the band went in to the studio and recorded 'There are Eight Million Cossack melodies and this is one of them'! I can remember sitting there after they'd got it down to everyone's satisfaction, given regard to the studio time and money available and Tito was saying, "Right, what are we going to call it?" Nobody knew what to call it, a few feeble titles came up but nothing useable and he said, I know, we'll use the opening line from Dragnet. Dragnet was an American TV police series that was popular here at the time, and there was a voice over the opening credits that said 'There are eight million stories in this city - this is just one of them'. I think Tito was getting a little bit tired by this time and he puffed on his big cigar and said it's going to be called 'There are eight million ...er, *Cossack* melodies.. and this is one of them' and he walked out. To be fair, the record *was* pushed quite a bit, we promoted it throughout the country and it got into the top fifty, I think, then fell out just as quickly! Then we recorded a second single as Group X, which again was pushed hard but didn't really make it and the mystery group thing just faded.

GROUP X

on

fontana

RECORDS

Courtesy John Stevens

Publicity shot for the mysterious Group X at the time of their hit single - 'There are Eight Million Cossack Melodies - and this is one of them', backed with 'Tenerife' which was released on Fontana 267 274TF. The follow up was 'Robi Calliope' b/w 'CrossBeat' on Fontana TF417.

In about April 1964, and back as the Martin Jae Five, we won the Mecca/Walls Ice Cream National Beat Contest; the band got £1,000 worth of Vox equipment and as I was just the singer and didn't play anything, I got to keep the cup! I was thinking only the other day that I wouldn't mind having one of those good old Vox AC30 valve amplifiers. One of the bands we beat were Dave Dee, Dozy, Beaky, Mick & Tich, although they weren't called that then.

This was a competition for bands throughout the country, with several knock-out heats held in the various Mecca Ballrooms, like the Orchid Ballroom in Purley. We went to four or five different venues and for whatever reason, were selected as being the best band on the night. This was doubtful; to be honest I heard some really good bands in that competition, much better than us! I was impressed with the Dave Dee outfit, but I'm convinced that the judges picked us because we were punctual, we were fairly clean and presentable and, I'm ashamed to say this, we were not too rebellious looking; a bit clean-cut, a bit *too* Brian Poole & the Tremeloes! Which to be fair, was a bit of a look at the time.

I really wish I could say that we were dirty, smelly and played bloody good music, but we weren't. However, we won the equipment and a recording 'test', which I presume we must have failed, because we went along and gave it our best, but we never got any work or anything from it.

Courtesy John Stevens

The Martin Jae Five - left to right: Martin Jae, Bob Gamble, Mick Hack, Brian Denny on drums, John Stevens and new sax player Bill Friars.

Martin Nighy (contd.)

As the Martin Jae Five we played regularly at the Teen & Twenty Club at the Star, Broad Green; we played the Park Lane Ballroom, which was just opposite where Croydon College is now and where the old Fire station used to be; we had gigs at the Purley Halls; the Co-op at Peckham Rye, we played there every saturday night for years, through all the fights!; The Castle, Tooting; the Market Hall at Redhill; the Wallington Public Halls when it was run by Fred Bannister, who went on to do big things as a promoter. The Stanley Halls at Norwood; the good old Orchid Ballroom, Purley, although we weren't properly on the Mecca circuit. We could have gone on and done a lot with Mecca but I really did not like the woman who ran that circuit and I had heard all sorts of horror stories about bands being sucked in and we didn't want that. Moving a bit further afield, we played the Lyceum Ballroom in the Strand, and we also played the Royal Albert Hall once, on a big bill with Dusty Springfield and the Hollies (a show called 'Top Beat', May 1964). I have to say that Dusty was one of my favourite singers, what a fabulous voice, but on tour you couldn't get near her, couldn't even step into the same lift as her!

Of the other local bands around at the time, I think we looked on the **Trojans** and the **Quiet Five** as 'threats'. I'm still in touch with Richard Barnes, who played bass with the Quiet Five. I also liked the **Del-Tones** as a band, they had a slightly rougher edge to their music that we lacked and I even got to sing with them a few times when their vocalist couldn't make it. They also had **Jeff Beck** as their guitarist at the time; Jeff was a motor mechanic then and I got to know him because he bought his parts and spares from Dees, where I worked. I remember one gig that I was due to do with the Del-Tones, Jeff was very late turning up and when he did arrive he had no guitar or amp with him. When the band asked him about it, he admitted that he had sold them to buy an engagement ring - and needless to say the gig didn't go ahead!

The next year, 1965, I got married and I think Mick also got married and then for various reasons the Martin Jae Five split up - I can't actually remember why, maybe I had in the back of my mind this gig with Ted and Roy Budd. I had a year or two singing with Roy which was just wonderful, I mean, real music. I always felt like just an accessory, in fact I was embarrassed to even attempt singing with him - I was no musician whereas he was simply outstanding - but I did it and I am very proud of what was done, with Roy and with the MJ5. ”

Mick Hack & John Stevens

Both Mick and John were members of the influential local band The Martin Jae Five. We have heard Martin's story, now over to the groups lead guitarist and bass player for their version...

John: 'Let's talk about Ted Potter, who owned the local music shop...

Mick: 'Potters really was *the* gathering place for the majority of local musicians; because we worked at Dees, the Ford dealership, John and I would stroll along there in our lunch hour. Jeff Beck used to go there, I mean he was also only just down the road, working at another garage...'

John: '...South Croydon Motors...'

Mick: 'Jeff used to walk up there in his lunchbreak during the week, Roy Budd we used to meet there on a Saturday - if we weren't working or gigging we always seemed to be at Potters. After a while, old Ted got wise to us and put all the musicians down in the cellar, where we could all sit and play and chat about the recent records or gigs we had been to or played in. Cliff Aungier was another one who came down regularly, in fact all of the various local musicians, be they rockers or folk and blues players would congregate there. Ted was really very good to us all, although he obviously got his piece of the action...'

John: 'Ted Potter was instrumental in getting us a sponsorship deal with Vox - certainly all our amplification was Vox made - and Ted himself drove over to Jennings at Dartford to collect all the gear. I played a Fender bass which I bought at Potter's in 1962 and it's still going strong.

Going back to Jeff Beck, at that time he was playing a regular gig at the Addington Community centre...'

Mick: '...back then, Jeff was more of a *rhythm* guitar player with, I believe Rodney Walsh & the HotRods, and the last time I saw the lead guitar player from that band, he was a milkman - how things change! When we were playing gigs at the Pyramid, which was next to the old Savoy cinema, in our interval we would walk across the road to the Star, where you'd get people like the Yardbirds, and I think Lonnie Donegan went in there quite a bit.'

John: 'Humphrey Lyttleton, Chris Barber - there was a big crossover thing going on, where you had the Trad. jazz guys and the blues and r'n'b groups all playing the same gigs. We played at Wimbledon Palais on a regular basis and that's where we used to run into the Yardbirds, and the Oscar Rabin Band. We would go over to Guildford on a Sunday, and get payed half a crown each - we played with Terry Dene there, we did a lot of support group work.'

Mick: 'To be honest, I don't remember being aware of all the big names that we played with, to me, I just played guitar in a band and it's only when you mention someone in hindsight that I think, yeah, I played on the same bill as them...'

John: 'We played support to Gene Vincent, Joe Brown, Jerry Lee Lewis, Mark Wynter, the Tornados, Lord Sutch, you know, a lot of very good people, but I have to say there were times when I thought that the main act weren't as good as we were.'

Mick: 'We were actually banned from playing at the Oddfellows Hall in Dorking, because one week there was a fight in the audience and in the local paper the following week, we found that we had "incited them to violence"!'

John: 'We travelled around a fair bit, not just locally but as far afield as Manchester, Stockport, Coventry and Devon. BelleVue was the big venue in Manchester, a huge place with a massive revolving stage. When we got there early to look around, we went into the restaurant by mistake and thought that it was the hall we were due to play in. We were later told that the week before we played there, the Beatles were the headline act and pulled in six and a half thousand people. And we actually got five thousand. Jimmy Saville was the DJ there, we met him a few times and the week after us they booked Hermans Hermits...'

Mick: 'We were booked to play on a prestigious bill at the Royal Albert Hall, with people like Dusty Springfield and the Hollies. I seem to remember that we borrowed the Hollies gear for the show, which was nice of them; although they had just returned from an overseas tour and were more interested in the new cameras and long lenses that they had all brought back. One thing that the Martin Jae Five never got to do was to play abroad, although like most other groups we had offers to go over to Germany.'

John: 'Pop music was starting to get more exposure on TV then and we played on a show called 'Thank Your Lucky Stars'. We travelled up to the Aston studios in Birmingham to record the show on a Sunday, along with people like Billy J. Kramer and Dee Dee Sharp - and Janice Nichols, their regular panelist and the "oi'll give it foive" girl, was twenty one that week and having a big party...'

Mick: 'But that side of it was really the cherry on the cake, because in between times we were slogging our way round places like the Addington Community centre and the Co-op Hall at Peckham. In fact, that gig at Peckham we played alternate weeks with the Dave Clark Five and it went on like that for months. This was all booked with Ed Waller, who was the man behind the gigs at the Park Lane Ballroom in Croydon and the Pyramid at Broad Green that we mentioned earlier. Ed also did the Tottenham Royal with the Dave Clark Five.'

John: 'All the others came later, but the Park Lane was his main one, and if you were given a booking there you knew you must be doing something right!'

Mick: 'I've likened it to Stringfellows these days, and it's fair to say that in the early days of the Sixties, the Park Lane Ballroom was where the 'in-crowd' used to hang out. Playing a gig there at Christmas could be horrendous, there were just huge numbers of people...'

John: 'Ed did us a lot of favours, but he was a true business man and in the end I think he did exploit the group a little bit, but one promoter who *was* really good to us was Fred Bannister.'

Mick: 'Fred Bannister was excellent, but the trouble with him was that we ended up working all over the place, these little one-off gigs that would turn up out of nowhere.'

John: 'If a group had any sort of a 'name', then Fred would try to promote them, in fact he tried to get the Beatles once - he did book the Stones into Wallington Public Hall - all the big names and a lot of American acts as well, Sam Cooke, Brenda Lee, Jerry Lee Lewis...'

Mick: 'From what I can remember, he started with the gig at Wallington, then he got the Market Hall at Redhill, the Co-op Hall in Dartford, the Stanley Halls in Norwood and later, during the 'seventies he started to get involved in much bigger things further north, with some of the big festivals like Reading and Knebworth.

There was another local promoter that we dealt with quite a bit, Ken Tapper, who lived at the top of the Purley Way. Ken had his own band, a dance band I think, but he started to book different groups for all kinds of gigs, and he certainly gave us quite a bit of work - although we did turn down a residency at Butlins which was offered to us.'

Mick Hack & John Stevens (contd.)

In those days I was quite naive about the business. Although I was born in Farnham, Surrey, the family moved up to Teesside when I was still a baby and by the time I came back down to Croydon at 17 to start my motor trade apprenticeship, well, I was just so naive, I really was. I had played guitar with a skiffle group before meeting up with John and Martin at Dees, and I was drafted into the group for their first 'big' gig at the Davis Theatre at the end of 1959; we were called Martin Jae & the High Five in those days and it was a huge variety bill with people like Cliff Richard, Bernard Bresslaw, Dickie Valentine, Roy Castle and Acker Bilk. I joined a band to play the guitar and all the other things that were going on, the politics and so on, just weren't things that I could relate to. When John and Martin were discussing the bands' next move, they never asked me, I would just have said, yeah, do whatever you like. Just tell me where we're playing and I'll be there. We never really had a manager as such, it was generally Martin who handled most of that side of things, although I suppose Ted Potter came as close to actually managing us as anyone ever did.'

John: 'Yes, all the promoters dealt with Martin, or if they couldn't get through to Martin they got in touch with me. I remember Robin Day 'phoning me once about a radio show.'

Mick: 'Although all three of us had started as apprentice fitters at Dees Motors, working on the benches, eventually Martin moved into Sales, John moved off into administration, but I stayed working with the tools. I seem to remember that whoever worked the switchboard would get a bit fed up with all the non motor-related calls that kept coming through to John and Martin!'

John: 'I'm sure that Martin will have told you all about the **Group X** recording thing, but he may not have mentioned our 'new' sax player. An integral part of the 'Cossack Melodies...' record was the sax sound, which was played by a session player but afterwards, Tito Burns told us to go out and get a sax player into the band so that we could promote the record live. We put an advertisement into the Melody Maker and duly took on Bill Friars, who was a New Zealander who had played in a band 'down under' and toured Australia backing Gene Pitney.

He wanted to try his luck with a group in Britain and the first thing he did when he got off the boat at Southampton was to pick up a copy of the Melody Maker and answer our ad. Almost the first time we all got to meet him was at the photo shoot for the Group X publicity, which is why, in the shot of us standing against a wall, Bill looks a bit 'adrift' from the rest of the band.'

Mick: 'After the Group X thing died down, the Martin Jae Five entered and won, a national talent contest. Our sax player was due to play one of his early gigs for us at one of the heats; however on the day he told us that he couldn't make the rehearsal as he had to drive down to Southampton to meet his father, who was coming over to visit. The rehearsal during the day went quite badly, but the actual heat that evening - complete with our sax player and his dad - went very well and we won through to the next round!

John: 'The finals were held at the Lyceum Ballroom in the Strand and we beat twelve other groups to win the contest; this was in May 1964. The prize was a £1,000 plus a recording contract with EMI and another Croydon group, Glen Athens & the Trojans finished third. I have a feeling that one of the other bands we beat on the way to the final was an early version of The Sweet, called 'Wright's Wigwam. It was quite a star studded event; the panel of judges included Jimmy Saville, Maureen Cleeve, the pop writer from the Evening Standard and Alan 'Fluff' Freeman was the MC. It was a fantastic evening, we really couldn't believe that we had won - and funnily enough if we hadn't won there was talk of the band splitting up. But we decided to carry on for a bit'

Courtesy John Stevens

A proof print from the photo session that supplied the "Cossack Melodies" sleeve - pictured left to right: Martin Jae, Bob Gamble, Bill Friars, Mick Hack, Brian Denny and John Stevens.

Mick: 'After the Martin Jae Five, John and I formed a band called **The Casual Four** which carried on playing from 1967 well into the mid-eighties, on and off! Because of my connection with Pye records, which I'll come to later, we all went down to Pye Studios and recorded an album for next to nothing...'

John: 'The Casual Four were regularly playing the clubs and everyone kept asking us if we had any records, so through Mick's contacts we went in and recorded the complete LP over one single weekend.'

Mick: 'Incidentally, around the time we made this record, Pye were planning to present Frank Sinatra with a gold disc for his sales of 'My Way'. So as a trial run for gold plating his disc, they used a copy of the Casual Four LP and subsequently gave us a framed and mounted gold disc of our record!

From the motor trade, where I had worked with John and Martin, I then got a job as a transport manager with the old Pye record company. When that folded I became a record company sales representative, in fact I often used to call on the very shop that I now own. The people who owned it were retiring and my brother and I bought the building, the **Art Nash** shop in Penge. The shop has quite a long history and is actually mentioned in Bill Wyman's autobiography, Bill used to have a flat nearby and he mentions it two or three times. Of course I love it, because for me it is both a job and a hobby, it's what I *do*, you know, and from that point of view I've been very lucky. I enjoy still keeping contact with the muso's, they come into the shop from all kinds of musical backgrounds, heavy metal, folk, classical and consequently I am always going to gigs.' 99

Courtesy Keith Aldridge

The poster for this 1963 pop show at the ABC cinema, shows a strong British line-up of artists, mainly from the Larry Parnes stable. According to the review in the Croydon Times, it was Joe Brown who stole the show, bringing a rare moment of hushed appreciation as he picked his way through a tricky piece of Spanish composition on the acoustic guitar. Backed by his ever-present Bruvvers, Joe completed his act with a superb rendition of 'Hava Nagila', at one point even pre-empting Jimi Hendrix by several years by playing his guitar behind his head!

Only just beaten into second place was Billy Fury, whose slick, stage act had the teenage fans in raptures. Richard Green wrote - "it was easy to see just how much Billy has been influenced by his idol, Elvis Presley, but nobody could accuse him of copying the American. Indeed, Billy's routine was as lively as a hatful of Mexican jumping beens and well ahead of today's other stars".

The Tornados not only backed Billy Fury but also played a well-received set of their own hits - "...proof indeed, that Britain's instrumentalists are every bit as good as their colleagues across the Atlantic". Praise too, for the other supporting groups, The Wildcats and The Ramblers, who helped back the solo singers Daryl Quist and local boy Dickie Pride.

John Edmed

From his early days as lead guitarist with Croydon's Partizans, John became a much sought-after session player and one of the top three pedal steel guitarists in the UK, before moving on to studio engineer and producer - working for a time in Germany with Frank Farian, the legendary figure behind Boney M.

I was born on 20th April, which is Hitler's birthday but not in the same year! and lived in Streatham until I was three, and in Thornton Heath from then until I got married and left home. I went to Whitgift School, but most of us who went there lived on the outskirts - when you think about the school situation, with Whitgift School being right in the middle of Croydon, it took out such a huge amount of the town centre that there wasn't much room left for housing and what there was, was much more expensive. The South Croydon, Coombe Road area was very, very upmarket and most of the more working-class family homes were on the northern edge of the town.

I left school at sixteen and a half and I only really played in one 'local' band, a group called **The Partizans**, who were actually formed by a couple of guys that worked in the city, where I worked at the time, translating for an insurance company which was, incidentally, the only day-job I've ever had! There was a drummer called Jim Smith, a bass player called Peter Hannaway and to start with, a singer called Ricky Freeman. They used to practice at a coffee bar in Soho called the Partisan, hence the name of the group, and I can't actually remember how I came to be inducted in to this band, but I joined them. In fact, the other original members all came from Southend, but quite quickly they were each replaced until the Partizans became much more of a local band! A guy called Gerry Lloyd played drums, he is now in Australia; John King played rhythm guitar, he's now an accountant; Graham Leech from Norbury on bass, a stockbroker; myself on lead guitar and a singer called Dave Draper who is still resident and I believe performing, somewhere in the Croydon area. We went through quite a few singers before Dave, but he was the only really permanent one.

Gus York

John Edmed at the mixing desk - Limewood Studios, Ashford, Kent 1980

Initially we played the same instrumental numbers that everyone else was playing; at the turn of the 'sixties there were really only the Shadows and the Ventures that you could copy. Apart from Elvis and Cliff Richard, there weren't that many serious solo singers in the rock idiom that had a career, and hence had a catalogue of songs that you could do! There were local groups like the Martin Jae Five, with old Martin Nighy, 'Mr. Smooth', doing his Cliff impersonation; you know, him and Mick Hack dressed up in their zoot suits doing a real presentation act, the 'glamour' stuff... but we were much more of a raw band I suppose, and as soon as the Mersey Sound broke, we very quickly got into that, as all the bands did. All of a sudden, come 1963/64 there was this huge demand for vocals! Prior to that, most bands didn't have much in the way of vocals, the singer got an easy life.

If you go down Melfort Road, just on the corner where the road becomes Norbury Crescent was The Endeavour, headquarters of the 67th Croydon Scout Group. In the early 'sixties a very enterprising guy called Robin Redson had the idea of staging what he called 'Jive Nights', with the idea of raising funds to build a new scout hut, the original being a battered Nissan hut - an old tin thing, backing onto the railway! We (the Partizans) were the first group that he actually conned into playing one of these Jive Nights and we were paid something ridiculous, like ten pounds, but of course it was an inordinate success and packed out the first night. He started out by having one every two weeks, but it became so big and with so many people that it had to move to St. Stephens Hall which was next to Winterbourne School. With a much larger hall, it soon became a weekly event and attracted The Partners, Glen Athens & the Trojans and all the other bands that were around at the time, all of us playing it in rotation - I think we eventually pushed the fee up to about twelve pounds and ten shillings!

It is important to remember that the music scene then was all very much new ground, nothing had been done before and there was so much live work around if you wanted it, so much demand and the thing to be seen doing was to be in a band. Towards the end of the Partizans career, we got some management, brought in a black singer, a Jamaican guy and went through a phase were we were doing our 'Mod' bit. He sang a lot of Otis Redding and some Fats Domino songs, and that was a good time for the band, we did quite well with that. The Partizans broke up after about four years, basically because I went after a 'pro' gig and the others didn't want that, they were all happy to carry on with their day jobs. In the end that gig didn't materialise, but there were a couple of spin-offs from it; sometime around 1968 the bass player, myself, a very, very good singer and piano player called Bob Johnson and an Indian guy called Terry Vance put together a band called **The Reform**, playing mainly Soul covers. I played in a band with Lenny Zakatek for about a year, a long time before he sang with Gonzalez and then there was the residency at the Surrey Hills Hotel. I did one season there with Peter Scott's band and when he left, I was offered the chance of putting together my own group in order to keep the gig at the Hotel, which I did for another three seasons.

At the same time, I was running the music shop at Broad Green which was owned by a guy of some notoriety, who also owned South East Entertainments at Lewisham. First of all we had the old Pyramid Record shop which was to the left of the ABC cinema as you face it, and then we moved to the other side of the cinema into the old cafe on the corner. We bought out the shop next to it, knocked them into one, turned the upstairs into an organ showroom and it did very well for him. Later on, myself and the guy who worked upstairs in the organ department, we opened our own music shop in Norbury and subsequently two more in the West End. In fact one of the shops is still there, still run by my partner; I got out in about 1980.

The Croydon scene was actually quite insular, in that it didn't go anywhere, all the bands revolved around half a dozen established venues - the Star was probably the best example. I once saw **Jimi Hendrix** play there; I seem to remember that the guy who ran the place booked Hendrix for next to nothing - fifty quid or something - about three weeks before 'Hey Joe' came out! Consequently by the time the gig came round, the record was at number one and you couldn't get near the place. In fact I thought he was much too loud for the Star, the noise was dreadful; I mean there is no doubt about the mans' ability with the guitar, but his sound was suited to a much bigger place. I saw him play later on at one of the London gigs and it was a lot better.

I used to go to the Star when it was known as the Crawdaddy Club, every week without fail and I am pretty sure that the Stones *didn't* play there; the T-Bones were *the* band, up from Brighton and led by Gary Farr, son of boxer Tommy Farr. Jethro Tull were good when they played at the Star, Ian Anderson in his tramps outfit and a plastic carrier bag with his flute and harmonica in it! Their old bass player Glenn Cornick came from Streatham. I watched the Yardbirds play there quite a few times, of course and as you know, Jeff Beck was another local boy. In fact not long after I had started playing and I was fascinated with Hank Marvin's sound, this kid who lived near us said 'You ought to come over and hear this band rehearsing at The Prince of Wales in Thornton Heath. So I went up there one night and it was this band of Beck's, **The Del-Tones**, and I was absolutely mesmerised by this guitarist who sounded just like Hank Marvin, same guitar, same sound, in fact the whole bloody band was a rip off of The Shadows! Even then Beck was special, completely special you know? He always had the knack of getting sounds out of the guitar that nobody else could do, he was a very good technician.

“...you took your life in your hands to try and stand up while playing, as the volume would have taken your head off!”

A venue you may not know about was the dance hall over the shops right next to the ABC cinema at Broad Green, quite a popular place it was, the MJ5 used to play there all the time. It was possibly called the Starlight, and it was a bit flash - the Partizans were never smart enough to get that gig!

I have to say that I never really ran into the Quiet Five, they were going before we started to play, although I believe that one of their guys, Nick Ryan, went on to become a producer - and has done very well for himself. There was no animosity between the bands in those days, we were able to keep out of each others way because we weren't all vying for the same slice of the action. Every band was different; The Martin Jae Five were all zoot suits and posey stage act, while others like the Del-Tones were the more Stones influenced, raw R&B, and later on there were the Soul groups - there was room for everyone. We would all meet up in the music shops like Potters and Croydon Music Studios, everyone was very friendly.

During the 'seventies, I became more or less a full time session musician, particularly the pedal steel work - Brian (B.J.) Cole and myself virtually had the pedal steel thing sewn up between us. For about four years, whatever recording session or TV show that he couldn't do, I took on and vice versa. Gordon Huntley was about the only other steel player around at the time and he was off working with Matthews Southern Comfort most of the time.

I also went out on tour with people like Elkie Brooks; I had just played on the single 'Pearls A Singer' which did very well in the charts and she needed a steel player for some of the material they were going to perform. This tour was in 1977, with Issac Guillory as the support act. I didn't play on every gig, but certainly I was at all of the bigger venues including the Fairfield Halls. Elkie has always been a bit of a 'fiery' personality, but remember she was under a lot of stress in her personal life at that time - I wouldn't have anything bad to say about her, no. I can understand the frustrations when you're trying to rehearse a band and it was a crucial time in her career, you know, it *had* to be good. She had some good players around her - Steve York on bass, Trevor Morais on drums and Pete Gage of course - but it was a difficult time because she was still married to Peter and Trevor had appeared on the scene as her sound engineer. I had known Elkie and Peter for a long time, before they were in Vinegar Joe together, in fact even before Dada, the band before that; Peter and I used to teach guitar at Ewell Technical College.

Unfortunately, the studio work for that type of specialist instrument started to die out with the synthesiser revolution, so I moved into the recording and production side of things.

I recorded some backing tracks for a local solo singer called Kelvin James, who put on his own ambitious show at the Fairfield Hall. In the audience that night was another vocalist called Marcia, who later said that she was interested in working with me and to cut a long story short, almost out of the blue I landed a job with Frank Farian, who was the German producer behind Boney M. That was wonderful schooling for me; he had so much money, that I was able to get hands-on experience with equipment that other studios simply couldn't afford. I was the engineer, co-producer and guitarist when needed, did a bit of everything really. I would mix things if required, play guitar on a track here and there or fly to Munich or London to record a string section for a Boney M record - I was on a retainer just to do his bidding really. I produced a couple of singles for Marcia from the band, when she was on her solo trip; Farian indulged her the solo records but he didn't really want her to tour, because even though she wasn't the *lead* singer with Boney M, she was still very much part of their act.

Another local musician was **Peter Oliver** from Sanderstead, who is probably best known as a member of the New Seekers. I first got to know him when he was forever coming into the music shop and later, when he appeared in the first stage production of 'Hair', it was Peter who got me that gig with the house band. The theatre had these huge banks of Fender amps along the edge of the stage and we were all sitting in the orchestra pit - you took your life in your hands to try and stand up while playing as the volume would have taken your head off! There was only one setting on those amps and that was 'flat-out', nobody ever turned their amp down halfway. That was a bit like a 'day job' really, good regular work and fairly easy if you could read music. Quite a few people got a break in those early productions - Marsha Hunt, Joan Armatrading, Sonja Kristina, Linda Kendrick and many more.

I did some recording with Peter when he signed for RCA and those sessions included Mike Roberts from the Trojans, Colin on bass from the hotel band and Cozy Powell on drums. In the early eighties I ran Matthew Fisher's studio in South Croydon for a while; I did some production work on some of the early records by the **Cure**, a band from Crawley who have gone on to be pretty big. More recently, I have worked on a CD with **Fast Freddie & the Fingertips**, who are also from the Crawley area, 'new-town soul' they call their brand of music!

I still see another local lad **Peter Sarstedt**, he has been here recently and we have been working on a follow-up to 'Where Do You Go To My Lovely?', which is a sort of sequel to that story. Peter is a very nice man; he still has a great voice and is a superb writer - he is probably the last of the true poets. In fact all the Sarstedts, Rick, Peter and Clive, were here just before Christmas. Actually now I come to think about it, an awful lot of people in the business did come from around Croydon. ”

Richard Barnes

From bass player and vocalist with The Quiet Five, via a successful spell as a solo singer, to an acting career in TV and stage productions such as Jesus Christ Superstar, Tommy and when this interview took place (October 1995), as 'the Narrator' in Blood Brothers.

I was born in a nursing home called either Shrublands or the Shrubberies, in Addiscombe or somewhere around the Croydon area; it was a sort of cottage hospital and I believe I arrived during the middle of a 'Doodlebug' raid! They shipped all the expectant mothers who were 'imminent' down to the basement and there I was born - so quite an ignominious beginning really!

Then it was home to Sanderstead, which has now become part of South Croydon and later I attended Whitgift School; there were two schools, Trinity School of John Whitgift and Whitgift School - I went to the latter, and it was there that I met up with most of the members of **The Quiet Five**. There were two incarnations of the Quiet Five really; the first featured a singer from Whitgift whose real name was Patrick Adamson, but who called himself Patrick Dane - and we were originally known as Pat Dane & the Quiet Five. Our keyboard player was Pip Burley, who is now a television producer; lead guitar was Nick Ryan, who I believe is now doing very well in record production and our original drummer was Paul Hoffman, who left fairly quickly to be replaced by Roger Brett. He was wonderfully mad, perhaps not quite as good a drummer as Hoffman, but he made up for it by being a real personality. In some of the larger venues that we played, the stage would have a hydraulic lift and on one classic occasion, we covered up all the mechanical parts of the lift with a load of drapes and at a given moment in the set, I think we gave him a drum solo, we pressed the button and *up* he went with his full kit on this platform, to about ten feet in the air, finished his solo and slowly came back down to rapturous applause!

Jacqueline Ryan

A youthful Richard caught backstage at the Fairfield Hall after one of the Quiet Five's many support appearances during 1963.

You could get away with stunts like that in those days, because there was precious little else to go with it; the stage lighting was non-existent then, if you were lucky you got a single coloured spot. The lighting people used to say, 'If it's a slow number we'll put a blue on, if its fast we'll put the red on and if it's real, out and out rock & roll we'll put the white on! And that was it. So anything else you could pull off in those days was just *so* exciting, because people had never seen anything like it. This would have been around 1961/62, just at the end of the real rock 'n' roll era and in the transition period just before the big Mersey Sound/British Beat thing that exploded.

Our manager at the time was based in Reigate, a man named John Smith, and he and his son promoted a lot of concerts locally including those at the Fairfield and later on, many of the big nationwide concert tours. For instance, we did a Gene Pitney tour with people like Peter & Gordon and the Dave Clark Five; he would give bands a start, by fixing up a mini-tour just when they were beginning to make an impact and later when they were better known, they would remember him, because he'd helped them out when they were starting. He quickly elevated himself from a very local promoter to a national one, albeit on a small scale by todays standards and he had a few good years there. He signed us, as I remember, when somebody dropped out of one of his concerts and he booked us to replace them, at Epsom Baths I think it was, you know, they would put a floor across the top of the baths for the audience. The Rolling Stones were top of the bill and we were one of the supports, along with another group called **The Vikings**. What happened was, their bass player wanted to go off somewhere else and some of the original Quiet Five didn't want to carry on, so it made sense for the two groups to amalgamate. This second line-up, still with Patrick Dane on vocals, lasted for about two years - Kris Ife on rhythm guitar, Roger McKew on lead guitar, John Howell on Vox organ, Ray Hailey on drums and I was still on bass. Then we became the Quiet Five proper; incidentally, I'll tell you how the name came about - you remember the Temperance Seven? Well, there were actually nine of them, so they were 'one over the eight' and they were drinkers, and they became the Temperance Seven! By the same token, there were six of us and when we played we were very, very noisy, very loud - hence the Quiet Five!

We played a lot of rock 'n' roll to start with and then gradually picked up on the newer beat music, basically just cover versions of whatever was popular. When we got our recording contract with Parlophone, one of the guys started to write our own material but they always seemed to end up on the B-side of the single and to be honest, the songs that were put out on record were never really representative of what we were like on stage, which was a bit unfortunate.
For example, one of our singles was a version of *Homeward Bound* by Simon & Garfunkel, we all thought 'they'll never make it with a name like that!' We had managed to get hold of a copy of their American album and that song had been top of the US charts for quite a while, so we thought, right, we'll release it in the UK and have a hit with it over here. Unfortunately, as soon as CBS were informed that we were covering it, they brought the Simon & Garfunkel single out in Britain and, quite rightly, it took off. Ours went about halfway up the charts and then, as their version shot past it, we began to slowly slide down. To his credit, we got a telegram from Paul Simon, saying thank you for being so instrumental in helping us to break in this country. He had always wanted to, he had toured extensively just on the folk circuit over here and he had a great love of England - I think that had we *not* decided to release that single, it would have taken a lot longer than it did for Simon & Garfunkel to break in this country.

Around this time we appeared in a local Songwriting competition, where the public entered pop songs and several local groups were booked to play them. (*Sounds Like Action - Fairfield Halls, November 1963*). In fact, I believe Richard Stilgoe was also there in one of the other groups, and years later he was performing at the same theatre in Sheffield as I was and he came up to me and said, 'Richard Barnes isn't it?' I said 'You're Richard Stilgoe, but how do you know me?' He said 'Well, we played on the same bill together' and then reminded me of this outrageous competition!

Courtesy Robin Godden

Patrick Dane & the Quiet Five - all six of them! Including Pip Burley seated at the keyboards, Richard Barnes with his bass, Pat Dane, Nick Ryan and Roger (Bugsy the Cool) Brett with snare drum.

Below: Richard as 'pin-up' material, around the time of his solo hit singles - 'Go North' and 'Take to The Mountains'.

At that time people were beginning to look at other ways of 'entertaining'; it was fine playing for a dance in a little local hall, but it was difficult for some of the bands to suddenly find themselves on a large stage with the audience *sitting down* watching them - they had to come up with something else.

One of our other claims to fame was being asked to play at the 18th birthday party for Prince Charles, on his actual birthday rather than his official birthday, in November 1966 in the private part of Windsor Castle. We turned up in our converted ambulance which carried all our gear, looking really scruffy and we arrived at a gateway into a secluded courtyard with a sentry on guard duty. Across the front of the vehicle was a sign that used to say 'Ambulance', but now read 'The Quiet Five' and this sentry had been warned that we were coming, so he opened the gate and then presented arms as we drove through! We went in as though it was just another gig, but it was totally bizarre; we were playing in the White Drawing Room, with all the family present, it was a completely private affair, just family and friends. But I mean, even the 'friends' were Lord and Lady this, that and the other. The Queen was twisting; I mean the twist was *the* dance that the Royal Family had latched onto, although I think it had died a death in the dancehalls by then, and the Queen was twisting away, but still with her little handbag attached to her arm! Princess Anne, who I suppose was about sixteen, kept disappearing behind this enormous folding oriental screen, with a succession of boys, presumably for a quick snog; Ian Ogilvy who had recently married into the family, was well-oiled enough to slip over on the pine needles under the Christmas tree and fall flat on his face. The Duke of Edinburgh was only ever seen right at the opposite end of the room by the bar, just lifting his arm every now and then, the whole thing was just amazing.

We got that gig because we had been playing quite a lot of 'Hunt Balls' for a couple of years and Lady Elizabeth Anson, who was responsible for booking people for these private functions, saw us at one of the Hunt Balls and recommended us to Prince Charles. The Quiet Five later played over in Greece for King Constantine, while he was still installed there, although the army were very much in evidence and it wasn't long afterwards, I believe, that the 'Junta' came and ousted him. Our other brush with Royalty was in Venice for a guy named Count Volpe; we played the whole evening, eventually finished about 5 o'clock in the morning and I went out onto this balcony to watch this beautiful sunrise. So I'm standing there looking down on this wonderful setting and I became aware of a young lady standing next to me. I didn't actually look at her straight away, just started to talk to her and probably attempting to chat her up - when I did look up I discovered that it was Gina Lollabrigida!

We also did the usual tour of some of the German clubs, not Hamburg, but we played Hannover and Frankfurt, Cologne, Essen, Dortmund - all the German cities had these music clubs because anywhere that was near US Army personnel, well those Americans wanted their nightlife. It was a lot of work, doing seven, three-quarter hour spots in one night and finishing at two, three and four in the morning. In one place, Frankfurt I think, we were kicked out of our hotel and had to sleep in our van. And the reason we were kicked out was because we had the audacity to complain to the hotel about the lack of hot water! I mean we were all getting ill from

Richard Barnes (contd.)

constantly washing in cold water and I eventually came back with pleurosy. Those were the days!

As far as local places went, we began by promoting our own gigs in a little village hall in Sanderstead, and we used to make quite a bit of money, actually, by cutting out the promoter. All we had to do was pay for the hall and the rest was ours, the crowd would turn up more or less by word of mouth. Most local pubs had a small back room or a hall attached where bands could play; there was a fairly major one in Brixton called the Valence, I think, down through places in Norbury and Thornton Heath, St. James' Youth Club in Kenley, and out to Westerham and Limpsfield. In all these places there were hundreds of kids, who by and large had to stay locally for their entertainment, they didn't have any transport, or leap onto a train or a bus to go into town like most do nowadays. It was quite a good little circuit and as a professional band we were on something like fifteen pounds a week each and that wasn't too bad in those days.

After the change of line-up, the band carried on into the Tamla Motown/Soul era and we tailored our set accordingly, instead of 'Rock Around The Clock' we would do 'Midnight Hour', that sort of thing, we moved with the times. There came a point where a couple of guys in the band got married and their wives would say, 'Oh, you're out on the road all the time, you're not making any money, what future have we got...' The rest of us would all say, Well, you knew he was in the band when you married him, which was a bit of a lame excuse really. The truth of the matter was that the band members were getting married and their wives wanted a reasonable standard of living, so people started to leave, we replaced them but the new line-up didn't have quite the same chemistry. So finally, towards the end of the summer 1968, we saw the writing on the wall and everyone went their own separate ways.

"In went the stake, out gushed the blood - and the director said "Right, that's great, we'll break for lunch"

By January 1969, I had managed to get myself a record deal with Phillips; I went to see a guy called **Gerry Bron** who at the time was managing Manfred Mann and an up and coming group called Uriah Heep! Gerry later formed his own record label - Bronze Records. He had promoted a few gigs for the Quiet Five and for the last few months of our existence he had all but become our manager, too. I went to him and said, 'Look, the group have disbanded, but I still want to carry on as a singer' and Gerry said 'Alright, I'll get you a record deal, my boy', it was as simple as that. He had taken over his fathers publishing business, which had started during the Big Band era, and Gerry was expanding it to cater for the rock side of the industry and I became one of his acts. I released four singles and one album in this country and an album on Capitol in the States; the American album was made up of half the tracks off the UK album and half were new tracks recorded especially for it.

To promote the records I spent a couple of years slogging round the Northern clubs and various other selected places, but the whole music business was very much group orientated at the time; if you were a solo artist with a number one, fine, but if you were down where I was, in the mid-twenties and thirties, there was enough interest from radio plays for people to come and see you, but it did mean you were restricted to playing places like Batley Variety Club and the Stockton and Wakefield Fiesta's. That was one of the reasons why I started to look for something different. We think of theatre as being bad enough, because we do eight shows a week, two on Thursdays, two on Saturdays, we're working Monday to Saturday inclusive, with just Sunday off. But singing on the club circuit it was seven *days* a week, and it's such a lonely way to live; you turn up and give the band their parts, you rehearse with them and then you're on, so you finish on a Saturday night in one place, the next morning about ten you're off in your transport to the next town on the list. Two o'clock in the afternoon you go and do your sound check, mostly with a new band, you go and find some digs, have a little bit of a rest and something to eat, then back into the club and do two shows. And so it went on.

When I started out, I think the first solo gig was Stockton Fiesta, I took my own band with me but the trouble with that was that you made no money. So after a while I just took my own drummer, who was a good friend of mine but after a year and a half, even *he* stopped wanting to do my gigs! Probably it was at this point that I began thinking 'there has to something else for me in this business'.

At the same time that my fourth single was out, I heard that they were auditioning for a new show called **Jesus Christ Superstar**; for a couple of years I had the desire to be on the stage in a more 'meaningful' way, because as a solo performer in those days, unless you wrote your own music, you didn't feel as if you had any integrity. If you broke big, like Tom Jones for example, as a solo singer with other peoples material, you were alright, but if you didn't, you thought that somehow you weren't succeeding because you didn't believe in the material... I had different people pushing me in various directions and I didn't agree with everything that was put forward. So to expand my horizons, I went for a job in Superstar and I put in an awful lot of work preparing for the big 'Jesus' number that they asked us to perform at the audition. And I got the part of Peter and understudy to Jesus, which was played by Paul Nicholas - that was the start of my stage career, the original production of Jesus Christ Superstar in 1972/73.

On the opening night there were nuns protesting outside, with placards saying 'This show is sacrilegeous' and what have you. Whenever something is new and even slightly controversial, you'll always get some people complaining, but after a while they get used to it - and in a way they just play right into the hands of the producer because that one protest raised the profile of the opening night by immense proportions. In fact some people came along and were quite disappointed to find that there *weren't* any nuns parading up and down outside, because it only happened the once, but of course the press covered it and *that* is what was on the front page of the papers the next day. They were great days, we played to capacity houses all the way, you couldn't get a ticket for love nor money - and neither could members of the cast. The only way we could get a ticket to bring a friend in was to queue early in the morning for returns and you were allowed two tickets per person. One particular time, I wanted to invite my flatmates and a couple of friends along and I needed six tickets in all. I only managed to get them by getting in the queue at ten the next morning and finding some others in the queue who only wanted one ticket and would get me a spare!

In 1976, I teamed up with songwriter **Tony Hazzard** and we went out on the road to perform as a duo. Tony had written the two songs of mine that were fairly successful in the charts, *'Take To The Mountains'* and *'Go North'*; Tony had also written *'Ha, Ha Said The Clown'* for Manfred Mann and *'Listen To Me'* for The Hollies, and he was a sort of house writer for Gerry Bron when I first met him. Part of the deal when I signed for Gerry was that I sang harmonies with Tony on the demos of his songs to send out to other people - this was the late Sixties and there were a lot of harmony acts around at the time. We loved singing together, there was an empathy there; we just had to watch each others lips and everything would be absolutely perfect. Unfortunately, he wasn't as prolific and successful enough in the long term, I think *'Ha, Ha Said The Clown'* was his only song to make number one. So through the long hot summer of '76, Tony and I rehearsed and we then went out on tour through the winter and into early '77. In fact Hazzard & Barnes toured as the support act to Camel, that popular progressive rock outfit! It was one of the few times that my work has brought me back to Croydon but I managed to get all the family along to the Fairfield for that one. I can remember saying to the audience 'I come from Croydon'... loud cheers... 'it's a great place to come from, as long as you don't go back'! And it brought the house down. Because I don't think anyone who lives in Croydon has a great love of the place; it's not that it's a bad place to live, but you get anywhere near that Whitgift Centre and you just think 'Oh God, isn't it ugly'.

When I grew up in Croydon it was almost like a small village, it was a small town with none of this high profile stuff around, it was simply somewhere halfway down the Brighton Road on the route to other places. It was nice and quiet and well-behaved, generally a nice place to live. Hard to imagine that the area where the Whitgift Centre is now, was once the grounds of Trinity School, where a lot of my friends used to go. That is fairly representative of what happened to certain towns during the Sixties; I mean, here is this wonderful school which we can't justify having around any more because there aren't enough people who can afford to pay to have their children educated in Croydon - so we'll pull it down and put up this concrete monstrosity of a shopping 'mall'.

So, in between the tour with Tony Hazzard and now, I did quite a bit of work in the theatre, and a little bit of television, but really, I have always been pigeon-holed as a musical person - and occasionally someone is good enough to give me a crack at a bit of straight acting. During 1977 and '78, I did three things for the BBC; there was a programme for children's television called 'Orion'. There was a group at the time whose singer was Jon Anderson out of Yes, they were called Flaming Youth and along with songwriters Howard & Blaikely they came up with this thing called 'Ark II', but it was renamed 'Orion' for TV and it was set in space. Then straight after that I did 'Count Dracula', which was a very high profile production, with Frank Finlay and Susan Penhaligon. Early one morning at the BBC studios, I had to stake Susan Penhaligon through the heart - it had to be done in one take, because there was a mock-up body and blood everywhere, so it had to be done first time. There was so much pressure, it almost became real - I whacked this stake into the dummy body with Susan's head poking out of the top, in went the stake, out gushed the blood - and the director said 'right, that's great, we'll break for lunch'! We all blanched at the idea and poor Susan said 'I'm afraid I have to go home! The set was like a mausoleum, cold and spooky with rats running all over the place and by the time we finished she had just about had enough.

After that, I did a musical play with Chris Farlowe and Sonja Kristina, where I was a sporty type student and Chris was a plumber, working in the university and we were rivals for Sonja's affections. It was called 'Curriculee, Curricula' written by a very well known screen writer, whose name escapes me at present. No matter how often I beat Chris at a number of sporting challenges, he eventually ended up with the girl. It was a really zany piece of work and I did a sequence in the shower, where I was taunting Chris Farlowe and I was completely naked - it was the first male full frontal scene filmed for TV. In fact it was then pre-empted by Dennis Potter's 'Pennies From Heaven', which came out before ours did, but they had recorded their nude scene after I had recorded mine. I was completely covered in soap, and while I was showering, I was singing a duet with Chris Farlowe in the form of a duel, during which time Chris came into the shower with a can of beer, shook it about a bit and pulled the ringpull, showering me with beer foam!

While filming Dracula I fell off a horse, and for two years after that I was in and out of traction to try and ease the problem with my back. Eventually Equity told me that I had to have an operation to repair a disc in my spine which had split open and it was 1981 before I was back to full fitness again. Then I did some more work on the stage; I was in a production of the musical 'Tommy', then a classic version of Joan of Arc called 'Jean' at Sadlers Wells that ran for about two weeks! and got absolutely panned by the critics. I went out on tour with 'Superstar', and worked in the West End production of **Chess**, which we then took out on tour.

There were a couple of lean years towards the end of the Eighties; I got married in 1987 and separated in '92 and I have the most wonderful seven year old daughter - I mean, no matter what my feelings are about how the marriage went, I can't regret it because she's there. I know every father thinks their daughter is special, and I'm no exception, she has the most wonderful character. She lives with her mother in Suffolk and I see her on Sundays, take her to school Monday morning and then drive back down here.

I made my debut in **Blood Brothers** on 28th November 1994 and I'll never forget it. I had two weeks rehearsal and I did most of my 'memorising' on the train, because I was still then living full time in Suffolk and the other people on the train stare at you as if you're mad! And two weeks rehearsal isn't enough really - I got through that first night by the skin of my teeth. I play the part of the Narrator, and link scenes; sometimes by explaining what has just happened but more often hinting at what might happen. It is a very useful trick, because in Blood Brothers there are areas in the play where, as time passes, the audience might forget that there is any *danger* involved - of the truth coming out. It keeps the audience on their toes and when I'm on stage, the other players act as if I'm not there. There's one particular scene where I walk around Stephanie Lawrence warning her of what might be and she is in this trance-like state, because I'm actually saying her thoughts; she turns, and every now and again we don't get the timing absolutely right and as she turns, I'm still there in front of her. And she'll look straight through me as if I'm not there - it's the most curious thing, even for me. It's an age old story, adapted by Willy Russell who has set the play in Liverpool and it works marvellously well - it's a good story, well told and by the end the audiences are completely won over.

I am still in touch with Martin Nighy from the Martin Jae Five. Martin and I have known each other for more years than either of us care to remember, since we were both in our respective local groups and we used to meet every week in Potter's Music Shop, which was the hub of everything musical in Croydon. It's important to keep these links, which is why I was so pleased when Pip Burley turned up out of the blue a while ago, he has kept tabs on the other members of the Quiet Five and is trying to organise some sort of reunion. It'll be fascinating to find out exactly what the other guys have been doing, because when you've been in a band for any length of time you do become close - you have to, if only to survive on the road - like brothers, in fact! ❞

Pip Burley

The original keyboard player with the Quiet Five, Pip moved on to work with the Big Bands of Joe Loss and Sidney Lipton, before eventually carving out a niche for himself in TV production - and picking up an Ivor Novello award along the way!

I can't tell you much about the music scene in Croydon prior to the late Fifties; in fact I am not sure that there *was* much of a scene in Croydon before that. It always seemed to me that Croydon really took off musically in the fifties with jazz and folk, and the very beginnings of rock and roll. It was that all-important transition period between the influence of Buddy Holly, Elvis Presley and all the solo artists that preceded them, and the groups; it happened *then* and I suppose because Croydon was this very, very large middle-class conurbation, I mean even then Croydon was 300,000 people strong, and amongst that large amount of population you were bound to get a reaction to whatever trend was passing through at the time.

So Croydon suddenly became the birthplace of a lot of groups, a lot of musicians in each of those three areas, jazz, folk and rock. It would be nice to think that the schools encouraged the young people to get involved in this whole new wave of popular music, but of course they didn't in those days, quite the reverse - they opposed it, in fact it was actively discouraged. I was at Whitgift School and there was no popular music represented within Whitgift at all; there was no swing band, no pop groups, nothing whatsoever. So what everyone did do, of course, was to meet out of school, in peoples garages for example and in the early days of the **Quiet Five**, we were very lucky in that a girlfriend of one of the bandmembers lived in a big house in Purley, off Foxley Lane in that large 'posh' residential part of town. She was a petite blonde pretty little thing, probably one of Pat Dane's or Richard Barnes, they were the only two who had girlfriends at that time, the rest of us had to catch up later! Her father had built a room for her in the garden, specifically I suspect, to keep her teenage friends away from the main house! and it was absolutely perfect to rehearse in and that's where we used to go.

I was born in South Croydon and I was lucky in that my father brought me a small piano when I was five years old (in fact I've still got it) and I took to it quite early on. I don't actually know why he bought it for me as my father wasn't particularly musical, my mother was quite musical but untrained, and by the time I was ten or eleven I could play pretty well, although I had not had lessons up to that point. The die was cast by then, and I started to take piano lessons although of course all the conventional musical training in the fifties was classical. I am glad I did it, but I was never going to be swayed away from popular music and it was during those five years that I really began to understand how music is put together. There has always been this great mystique amongst academic musicians, that they don't *really* want people to know how to compose and I'm not sure whether it is because they actually don't want you to know the 'secret', or more likely that many of them never fully understood it in the first place.

Music was traditionally all about becoming an instrumentalist and interpreting written work; largely what happened in the fifties was that we all started to think in terms of 'chords', and frankly it was due to people like Bert Weedon and his 'Play in a Day' guitar tutors - the guitar became hugely popular. At the risk of sounding mildly technical, we all started to think *vertically*, instead of *horizontally!* and that enabled thousands of people, who had never previously considered themselves as musicians, to suddenly start to play reasonably well. After all, when you see one chord symbol on a chart and you put your fingers in that certain position on the neck of a guitar, you produce six notes in perfect harmony - whereas up until then we had been searching around for each note individually. Mainly through the fifties, sixties and seventies, even very good guitar players who made it to the top of their profession, still couldn't read notation and if you gave them a melody line, a horizontal line of music, they couldn't play it. Chord symbols opened up music to a whole generation of people and it happened *then*, right at the start of the sixties.

The other interesting thing about it of course, is that it affords the individual musician the opportunity to express his or herself, and to contribute to the piece of music. Reading from chord symbols, they are only a structure, a skeleton, and the precise way the piece is played is left to the individual musician; rather than reading every note, every rest and every accent on a sheet of music. And that is great fun, because instrumentalists do like to put a bit of themselves into what they are doing and that was a direct transition from the roots of jazz music into popular music. As I say, this was all happening at the end of the fifties, beginning of the sixties and it enabled groups like the Beatles, who regardless of what one thinks of the soul of their music, to become wonderful composers, and to end up with a huge repertoire of very worthy popular songs.

I have to say that part of the appeal was that it was all a bit naughty and anti-establishment; it was almost an 'underground' scene, where the bands found the audiences and the audiences found the bands. **Potter's Music Shop** was enormously important to the Croydon musicians and Ted Potter himself was a huge influence. He was Croydon's Tin-Pan Alley if you like, the place where all the aspiring guitarists and pop musicians would meet up to play, swap ideas and of course to buy their gear. He was a very encouraging man, partly for commercial reasons and I think that he often found himself split between, on the one hand supplying the schools with all their classical requirements and on the other, providing the up and coming beat groups with guitars and amplification. When Ted died, and he died relatively young, his wife took over the business and effectively went the schools route, which was the end of Potter's little musical oasis for rock'n'rollers. In those days I also played guitar and my first guitar, a Hofner President was brought from Potter's. It was also a record shop, of course and the room above the shop was used for music lessons; if you couldn't get guitar or drum tuition at school, which you couldn't, Ted would get working musicians in to teach people. He was a drummer himself, I can't remember how good he was but he certainly taught the drums in the room over the shop. A very important nerve-centre to the Croydon music scene.

The **Olive Tree** in South Croydon was equally as interesting, although it had quite a short lifespan, but it was basically a single shop unit with a basement, which was used initially as a folk club, hence the name of the club was 'Under the Olive Tree'. If there was any early indication in Croydon of a 'beatnik, pot-smoking, beautiful people' style scene, then the Olive Tree was in at the beginning; they would all sit round on the floor, drink coffee and listen to 'Joan Baez look-alikes'. From time to time they would have bands in and the Quiet Five used to go down there, cram into a corner and play somewhat quieter than usual!

When I started, the keyboard player in a band played the piano, there were no organs around and certainly no synthesisers. There was a record around called *Telstar* by the Tornados which exposed the public to a completely new sound, and what that sound actually was, was an instrument that became known as the Clavioline. The Clavioline was a single note, two and a half octave attachment to the piano - it was a most extraordinary instrument - the idea being that you played the left hand on the piano and you played the right hand, with the few tones and textures that were available to you, on this little miniature keyboard.

The funny thing was, that in the context of a group with three guitars and a drumkit, the piano was almost inaudible; I used to go through night after night on stage wondering whether the audience ever heard a single note that I played! I had a vocal mike, so I knew that when I was singing I was at least making a contribution, but the rest of the time it rather felt as if I was banging out on the old box and no-one was hearing it. The other thing was that the piano is the most ungainly instrument to play in the context of a pop group; for one thing you are sitting down, you're either sideways on to the crowd or if the piano is in front of you they can only see the top of your head, all the problems that people like Russ Conway used to face at the time. The piano is a particularly unattractive visual thing on stage. So when this Clavioline came along, what we used to do was to set it up on its stand and forget the piano completely; for the first time, keyboard players stood up and faced the audience. Now you could only play one note at a time, it was a single note tone generator, which modulated each note to give you three or four sounds, probably the forerunner of the electronic organ. It didn't last very long, because people like Farfisa and Vox soon started to produce portable electronic organs, not that they were *that* portable in the early days, it could be a hell of a job setting those things up.

Courtesy Kit Blakemore

Patrick Dane, lead singer with the Quiet Five - posing for a publicity shot circa 1963.

When I later left the pop scene and went on to play for Sidney Lipton, Joe Loss and Ken MacIntosh, I mean you wouldn't believe it but in the mid-sixties there were keyboard players travelling around the country with trailers hooked up to the back of their cars, lugging Hammond organs around to live gigs. It was always an unwritten rule with freelance musicians, as opposed to groups, that a musician handled his own kit. So whilst in a pop group you would expect all the members to treat all the gear as a sort of joint property, when it came to playing freelance, nobody gave you a hand. Now that's o.k. if you're the trumpet player, but how these guys got in and out of gigs with their enormous Lowry and Hammond organs, complete with pedals and fixed stools, god only knows. I never had to do that, I had an old Bird organ early on, which was a heavy thing, but it was just about portable.

Pianos were hopeless really, it was all downside with pianos; to start with you had to rely on the instrument that was there, every village hall, pub and small concert venue *had* to supply a piano. So that was what you got and as you can imagine, they varied enormously - some were virtually unplayable, some were out of pitch, which meant the rest of the band had to tune up or down, it was generally bad news. People tend to think that it doesn't matter, but it does. Years later, I remember being booked to play at Quaglino's, a lovely venue in the West End, for the after-show party of the first night of a new musical starring Eartha Kitt. I was to play solo piano in the downstairs room at Quaglino's, while Eartha and the cast, all her friends came in after the show, all on this huge 'high', having completed a successful first night, you can imagine the atmosphere. I sat down at this little upright piano, in front of all these glittering people, played my first chord and the thing was hopelessly out of tune; and I realised that I was condemned to play solo piano for two or three hours, in front of all these highly attuned people, knowing that the whole thing was going to be a cock-up! I tried to get the piano changed or to find a piano tuner in about ten minutes, but eventually I sat down and played; people walked past looking over their shoulders, Eartha Kitt gave me a wide berth, and eventually a man called Hubert Gregg, who was a great entertainer and a pianist himself, came up to me and said "Dear boy, my heart bleeds for you". He understood, you see, he'd been there himself at some point in his career and it's a horrible feeling.

So it was a huge release when electronic keyboards started to appear, or at least when they developed into reasonable instruments, they weren't at first, in fact they could be horrible. But at last the keyboard player could be heard, you could adjust the volume level and be in with a chance of competing with the rest of the group.

The first line-up of the Quiet Five was composed of Pat Adamson who called himself Pat Dane, who sang and played rhythm guitar; Richard Barnes on bass; Nick Ryan who played lead guitar; myself on keyboards and Paul Hoffman played drums. I think we all came out of Whitgift School; Richard certainly did, I did, Pat and Paul, and possibly Nick did too. We did a lot of good gigs, a very busy working band, it was a band that came out of the local community and who really served the local community. Our audience were much the same age as we were, eighteen and nineteen, which is something you don't get a lot of today and then gradually the line-up altered.

I think I was the first to leave and I have to say, the reasons behind my going were much to do with what we've just been talking about - the problems with instrumentation and the feeling that I wasn't able to make a real contribution. Although over the years I've played every type of keyboard under the sun, the piano was always my first love and as we've said, it just wasn't compatible with the pop group of the time. All of us were pretty unlikely characters to do well at anything; Pat always had a very easy charm about him, very good looking, very charming young man, he went on to work for Mobil and did very well - he now runs his own advertising agency. He kept the music going right through until his late thirties/early forties, I believe; and he was always the driving force behind the band, it was Pat's idea. Richard Barnes of course, stayed in the business, singing and performing in the theatre - when I ran into him recently he was playing in *Blood Brothers* in the West End, he still looks good and he is singing beautifully, in fact he doesn't look or sound much different to when I previously saw him, which must have been thirty years ago!

Paul Hoffman, who was a good jazz drummer, and had very much the personality and character of a jazz musician - very intense, very introverted; we were good friends, Paul and I for many years, well he ended up on the Foreign

Pip Burley (contd.)

Exchange and probably made more money than the rest of us put together! Nick Ryan stayed in the business and initially, I believe became an A & R man; and knowing Nick, has probably by now done extremely well for himself. Nick would admit, and I'm sure he won't mind me saying, that he was the least competent musically, but out of all of the Quiet Five, he was the most in love with 'the scene'. I never really was, in fact probably the least keen on the beat scene at that time; timing in life is hugely important and had I been born say, five years later it would have made a huge difference on my musical career. But Nick loved it and he was a very good technician, he was especially interested in the equipment, again something I never was. The whole principle of the 'roadie', is that the musician is there to play the instrument and not to get involved with the cables and the valves. So Nick had this tremendous enthusiasm for the business and was probably destined to go into production, guiding other people. Having said all that, I've got a old demo of the Quiet Five downstairs which I was listening to the other day and I must say he plays very well. He used to take a bit of stick, but Nick was probably better than we gave him credit for at the time.

"...the town could have become very arid, in a cultural sense. The Fairfield Hall saved its bacon."

Before the Quiet Five there was a saxophone player called Brian McGuigan, who was very well known to the band, in fact he actually did a few gigs with us and he was an extraordinary guy. He was a couple of years younger than the rest of us and I never knew him go to school or to do any work at all. His father owned a dance hall in Victoria and had made a lot of money, he probably said to Brian, 'look lad, don't go looking for work, you don't need to', a terrible thing to say to a child, and Brian took him at his word! When he was about sixteen, Brian would go out and eat in expensive restaurants, which was an extraordinary thing - when I started work, doing magazine layouts, I was on £8 a week, which was a good starting wage then and I couldn't afford to eat out the way he did! He used to frequent two restaurants in South Croydon, which were both run by the same man, the *Chalet Suisse* and the *Eidelweiss*, which were opposite each other at the junction of Croham Road and Selsdon Road, and Brian was always in there. Sometimes the two of us would go and do a gig for about twelve quid, a wedding reception or a church hall, finish about eleven o'clock at night and then we would go and blow the money on a big meal at the Chalet Suisse - a really stupid thing to do, but the sort of thing you do for the hell of it when you're that age.

The Quiet Five started off playing every village or church hall in the area, the whole 'parish scene'; Pat would ring up Oxted village hall and book it himself, then we would stick up a few posters and gradually word of mouth gets around, you know. We played a lot of parties early on, too, eighteenth's and twenty-first's. Concert wise we played a lot of the big local halls, Lewisham Town Hall, the Fairfield obviously and we'd travel too. I remember one night we did a gig in Croydon that finished at one o'clock in the morning; we were then driven up to London in the promoters own rolls-royce, a fat little man who owned this club in Soho. We got there about half two, unloaded the gear and pushed through a seething mass of people to the tiny little stage, set the gear back up (which wasn't easy) and then worked through until about half past four in the morning. At the end, we found out that while he was quite happy to drive us up to his gig, the roller wasn't available to take us back! I don't remember how we got back, but we all eventually got home about seven a.m. and there was a lot of that sort of work involved in the early gigs.

Once the Fairfield Halls opened up, the big package tours started coming through and we were fortunate enough to be added to a lot of those. We were on the same bill as the Beatles, early in their career and I can remember thinking how small they all were!

We had offers from prospective managers, but early on, Pat handled that side of things, he had the entrepreneurial spirit required even then, a good salesman. Shaw Taylor was very interested in the band; people now think of him as the front man on 'Police 5', but Shaw started his career as a disc jockey and was very successful in the music business. We did a couple of demos for him up at a studio in Notting Hill, a lot of production value, no money spared, but in the end Shaw didn't think that we were quite up to it. The Quiet Five were a very good live group, but at the end of the day, you've got to be able to perform on record. One of the great ironys of the public perception of popular musicians, is that they can't play and they can't sing and of course it's not true, it's simply not true. An artist singing out of tune just won't make it in this business, whether he or she is singing opera or a pop song and it is the same today, all the current batch of pop singers, be it George Michael, Take That or Madonna, these are very good singers. They may disguise the tone and texture of their voice to maybe make you think they are not, but they have to be able to sing. Even with today's new technology, we can shift pitch and bend it and correct an awful lot that is wrong, but if the artist can't actually sing they won't get any further.

The Quiet Five did actually go on to record a number of singles, but I had left before then to move into the Big Band scene. And I did pretty well there, made a bit of money and started to concentrate more on writing, arrangement and production.

I first met a chap called Kit Blakemore when he had just written a show for the West Wickham Operatic Society and he wanted somebody to write the musical score. Our drummer Paul Hoffman was going around with a stunning girl at the time called Julie who had played 'principal boy' in a couple of their productions, and she was a great principal boy, I can tell you! We got on rather well, Kit and I, he was an extraordinary man, tremendously energetic and full of ideas.

Kit had this idea for a big talent contest, to showcase not only the local bands, but to encourage new songwriters from the area. It was called 'Sounds Like Action' at the Fairfield Hall and he booked one big act, Heinz Burt & the Saints and made the rest of the bill up out of local groups, including the Quiet Five. I had just left the band and possibly so had Paul by that point, and Kit asked me to compere the show. Heinz was quite big at the time, he was the ex-Tornados bass player with the short-cropped platinum blond hair and I always remember watching them rehearse for that show. After they had finished, he went and sat in the empty front row to watch the next band set up and as I went over to speak to him, I could see that he was in floods of tears. I never actually found out why, but it seemed to me that the small amount of fame that he enjoyed then, was just too much pressure for him to carry. Later on that evening, I introduced him onto the Fairfield stage and he went out and performed an extremely good show, a true professional. Also on the bill was a girl called Mary Elaine who sang a couple of numbers. I don't actually think 'Sounds Like Action' was a great success, Kit's original intention was to hold it several years running but I don't think it ever made a second event. But give the man his due, he did it and he got reasonably good houses at both shows.

The Fairfield Halls was obviously a hugely important centre for music in Croydon. I don't remember how I came to meet him, but I knew Tom Pyper just before he was appointed General Manager at the Fairfield, in fact he was appointed before the building was opened, while it was still being designed. He used to live in West Wickham and whatever people thought about Tom, I mean he made friends and enemies over it, but he drove that project through to its completion. In those days, 1962/63 it was a remarkable building and was a thrilling place to be; you went through those doors and you knew that this was something different and important and indeed it turned out to be so. There was a point when the old Grand and Davis Theatres were knocked down during the relentless commercial and industrialisation of Croydon, that the town could have become very arid, in a cultural sense. The Fairfield Halls saved its bacon. I don't know what battles went on with the council to get that place built, but it did get done and it was just as well for Croydon that it did.

Once again, this was a 'trigger', another factor in the emergence of Croydon as a major musical centre. It is also worth remembering that the whole Danceband scene tends to get neglected, almost as though pop music and rock'n'roll were completely enclosed, within themselves. The fact was that all musicians would very freely roam across these musical boundaries and it was *the public* who imposed the boundaries in the first place. Indeed most musicians do so as a matter of necessity - the same guitarist playing in the rock group on a Friday night is the same one playing 'Moon River' in the danceband on Sunday, you know, it's a paying gig!

Ken Tapper is a name that should crop up a few times; he was alleged to have been a drummer although I never actually saw him play, but for a number of years he totally monopolised the danceband scene in the Croydon area. I would imagine that every musician in Croydon during the late fifties and early sixties, at one time or other played in a band for Ken Tapper, and many of us played *a lot* for him. One of the things he did was to get the 'franchise', if that is the right term, for the Arnhem Gallery, which as you know is part of the Fairfield complex. The Gallery in those days was used an awful lot for dinner-dances and private functions and it wasn't unusual for Ken to have up to ten or twelve bands out playing on a typical Saturday night! He would put his evening suit on and go 'round to every venue, have a chat with the band leader, talk to the client, take the money off the client, pay the band and then move on to the next one - and he did that for years! Ken lived in a big house in Purley and made a lot of money but eventually, and no one quite knows why, he committed suicide. And a less likely candidate for that type of end you couldn't imagine, for there seemed to be a man who had everything together; but with Ken died an era in the musical life of Croydon.

Johnny Howard was another band leader with local connections, for many years he was resident at the Orchid Ballroom in Purley. He went on to be the house band for Ready, Steady Go! on TV and hit his peak during the sixties; for a long time, the Big Band leaders, like Johnny and Eric Delaney really didn't know which way the popularity of their type of music would go. Now of course, we can see that the Big Band was in decline, but Johnny Howard enjoyed many years of considerable success and is still going today, as is Ken MacIntosh.

In the end, I went off in a completely different direction; I had always been interested in the Arts - music, drama, literature and so on, not that I was particularly good at any of them. When you are a freelance musician, which is what I became, life consists solely of practising and then waiting for the telephone to ring. In the late sixties, which was the era of the session musician, I mean those guys had it made, the top guys were doing three or four well-paid sessions a day, which even in those days was £100 a session. But they were good, they could go in to a studio, sit down and sight read anything, any style, no problem. I really wanted to get in on that scene, but it was 'dead-mans shoes', you couldn't get a break until one of the top men moved out, there were only so many jobs to go round. I got started in session work and did a fair bit, but I could see it would be a long hard ride, there were a lot of much more established people in front of me. I went back to more live work with the dancebands, who favoured having a core of younger musicians, what would happen is that halfway through the set, the older guys would go off for a break and the rhythm section would be left to play a set of Rolling Stones numbers and rock'n'roll standards, which the other members couldn't play. We'd bring the house down and then the others would come back and it would be back to Glenn Miller and Swing! That was good fun and out of those bands I subsequently formed a group called **The Nightimers**, who were very successful on the London circuit. It was lead guitar, bass guitar, keyboards and drums and we were kept busy playing functions four and five nights a week.

I also had a vocal group called The Semi-Tones for a while and had begun to write jingles, but in the daytime, while waiting for the 'phone to ring, I enrolled at The London College of Printing taking a course in typography. This graphic design route in my career, led me to a day job as a layout artist working on various magazines for a publishing company. To cut a long story short, when the old boss left I took the business over and built it up, and then started a small advertising agency. This was during the seventies, when you could indulge your entrepreneurialism - start a business and make a success of it!

I got out of the agency business about nine years ago, (1986) and went straight back into show business, and into television. I set up an independent production company and the first series we launched was 'The Darling Buds of May' with David Jason and Catherine Zeta Jones, which turned out to be a huge success; I also wrote the music for the series, which won an Ivor Novello award. We then made a series called 'A Touch of Frost', which is currently running, once again with David Jason in the lead role and we're now into our fourth series.

The music session that I am going to after this interview, is over in nearby Sutton with a fellow called Jon Hiseman and his wife Barbara Thompson, they provided the soundtrack to 'A Touch of Frost'. Now, I got to know both Barbara and Jon through the local scene, as they are both South London musicians - Jon's band Colosseum was born out of this area and Barbara, who is now widely regarded as one of the finest saxophone players in the world, constantly played the jazz pub circuit in and around this area. So for the last three or four years working on the music for 'Frost' has brought Jon, Barbara and myself back together again. Apart from the work itself, getting together with the two of them is very much the old feeling, often playing and jamming for the sheer fun of it, just as we did when it all began, back in the early 'sixties. ”

Peter Sarstedt

All three of the Sarstedt brothers have enjoyed considerable success within their own individual musical careers, Peter proving to be the songwriter of the family, with his lyrical folk-based material. Ostensibly named Rick, Peter and Clive, the boys have recorded and played under a variety of names; here Peter helps to sort out the family ties between Wes Sands, Eden Kane, and Pete Lincoln!

Originally, the family came from India to England, and arrived in Broad Green, Croydon on 1st March 1954, my mother and four children, my sister Loraine and my brothers Rick (aged 13) and Clive (aged 10). I was about eleven or twelve and it didn't take long for us to get involved with music, we always seemed to be heading towards that. I started to listen to Lonnie Donegan and skiffle while I was at Heath Clark School, Winterbourne Road; it sounded good and seemed so easy - it was, 'yeah, we can do that'. In our first group, my brother Rick played guitar and sang, I was on tea-chest bass, plus three other guys from school and that was us, the **Fabulous Five**. We rehearsed at home specifically to enter a skiffle competition at Croydon Town Hall, which was our first official gig; after that however, we only played at private parties!

By about 1956 or '57 Elvis had appeared in America, Cliff Richard was the British equivalent and my brother Rick, who by this time was fed up with skiffle, decided to become a rock & roll singer and play in the archetypal two guitar, bass and drums line-up. So Rick joined up as lead singer with **The Del-Tones** and began playing regular gigs at the Park Lane Ballroom in Croydon and local dancehalls such as the Public Hall, Wallington and the Stanley Halls at Norwood, plus anywhere else they could get to play. They started to get paid pretty early on, because it was at that point they found that having the young **Jeff Beck** on lead guitar was a bit of a bonus!

While Rick was off singing with his rock & roll group, my younger brother Clive and I formed our own band, **Pete Lincoln & the Sundowners**, playing straight forward rock 'n' roll - Little Richard, Chuck Berry, that sort of thing. I took over the lead vocals as Pete Lincoln, Clive played guitar, a guy called Jet Burgess played bass and 'Spud' Riley played drums. We were a little dance-hall type band; we played our first gig at St. Andrews Youth Club in Thornton Heath and then spent most of our time supporting people like Johnny Kidd & The Pirates, The Tornados, Lord Sutch, The Zombies and Neil Christian & The Crusaders when they toured the local clubs. We also had a regular dancehall gig in East Grinstead, plus a weekend spot at the *Fouz Hibouz (Mad Owls)* Nightclub in Streatham and spent many a Sunday afternoon backing the strippers in The Tropicana club, George Street, Croydon. We would often come up against bands such as the Martin Jae Five and there were some very good local groups, but I wouldn't say that there was a 'Croydon Scene' as such; it's not as if it was a village like Aylesbury for example - Croydon was quite a big place, even then and there was room for the bands in each Croydon district to have their own 'patch' - the bands in Thornton Heath didn't have to compete with the bands from Purley!

Jacqueline Ryan

A rare shot of Pete Lincoln (left) and the Sundowners, caught backstage at Wallington Public Hall during 1963.

Our drummer, Spud, was a real jazz afficienado and he had several friends on the jazz scene at the Star - while we were trying to play rock & roll, he and his friends would be listening to Coltrane and the modern jazz people. It must have been difficult for Spud, because there is a totally different feel to rock drumming as opposed to jazz drumming. That was our problem I guess, our drummer was just too educated and our bass player wasn't educated enough! Bands like the Del-Tones were authentic copyists of a style, they could *be* the Shadows, whereas we were much more ragged and more interested in the expression of the music rather than playing 'regimented' rock all night.

At the start of the 'sixties, Clive joined a band and went off to Germany to play the music clubs in Hamburg; there was so much work there, you could just answer an ad. in the Melody Maker - "bands wanted for work in Germany" - and off you went. At the same time, having 'cut his teeth' in the Croydon area, Rick had moved away to London to make some records under the name **Eden Kane**; he was a pretty good singer and he'd worked a lot, so he was ready for it - he got himself a manager and off *he* went.

This left me in a kind of limbo, and it was then that I started to get interested in the *beatnik* scene, the guys who were more into folk music. I ran into several local guys who were into this scene - Ralph McTell, Wizz Jones - I first met Ralph on Mitcham Common actually, by the Pie stall, so he says. So while my two brothers were away doing their thing, I started travelling and trying to find my own way around and began writing my own songs around 1963. In fact I got a job working for a guy in the West End who had a huge batch of about thirty lyrics and he'd say write me some songs around these. They were tailored for specific artists to record, I would tape them and he'd send them out to various people - but it was good way of learning the craft and making a bit of money at the same time.

After a few trips abroad I thought, well maybe I should join up with Eden Kane and there was a vacancy in his band for a bass guitarist. So I went back to playing bass for my big brother again, touring the dancehalls until about 1965 when Rick decided to leave the country and live in Australia, where he had been offered some good deals. This really left me alone again; I didn't have a job, I didn't have a band - I said to myself, OK, now you've really got to write more songs and get yourself work in the folk clubs. By 1966 I was travelling around Europe, which is when I wrote 'Where Do You Go To My Lovely' and I was performing it as part of my set in the clubs, three years before it was released on record. I was living in Copenhagen at that time, that was my base from which to tour round the clubs, coming back to England every now and then and it was not until 1969 that I 'lucked' into a record deal. My first album came out in '69 and it probably didn't help my early career, the fact that I was non-resident in Britain and travelling back and forth to

Frazer Ashford.

The Sarstedt Brothers make a rare appearance on stage together, promoting the 'Worlds Apart Together' album at the Fairfield Halls, June 1973. Left to right: Rick (Eden Kane), Peter and Clive.

Copenhagen. But then part of the 'ethos' and the myth of it all, is to be out on the road, travelling around and abroad, that was part of the whole 'feel' of it; and things fell into place for me that way and I had the opportunity to do it.

The same thing happened to Clive, in a way; he answered his ad. in Melody Maker and eventually found himself in Sweden, where he got married and he ended up staying there for a few years. Clive has had a chequered career, record wise. He did a few things for producer Joe Meek under the names **Wes Sands** and Clive Sands, working with some of the very talented musicians who played on Meeks records. Clive was always one for coming up with new names - it was him who called me Pete Lincoln for our first group together.

The Brothers Kane single - that would have been about 1965, just before Rick was about to leave for Australia. It was a last chance to get the brothers together and it had a sort of a Bee-Gee's sound to it, the song was 'Walking In The Sand', it was a bit weird as I remember. The only man who remembers that record is DJ Mike Reid! I recorded one single as Pete Lincoln on the Major Minor label, 'My Monkey Is A Junkie'. We taped a few things with The Sundowners, but nothing was ever released under that name.

It wasn't until 1973 that all three of us got together again, we all managed to convene in England at the same time and recorded an album as the **Sarstedt Brothers**, which was written about our history, our story, called 'World's Apart Together' (REGAL ZONOPHONE SRZA 8516). It traces the journey from India, through the early rock & roll days, the dancehalls of Croydon and it was a good project, it lasted about six months and then everyone went back to their various walks of life. Unfortunately the album wasn't a commercial success, but then that wasn't really the point; it was more of a memento for ourselves, you know - and we didn't have the energy to promote ourselves as a 'band', and be recognised as a band - we were already better known to the public as three individuals. We did just one concert together, to see if we could do it, which took place at the Fairfield Halls in June 1973 - to be honest, I don't think we're finished with that idea yet, there are plans for the three of us to tour this year (1995) using all the material that we have been involved with all these years.

Let's see, Rick moved to America in '66 or '67, nearly thirty years ago, to Los Angeles where he married and settled down and there he has stayed. When he has a tour fixed up, he comes back to England to play; he still has pretty much the same agents and promotion guys as he did back in the early days and they put together these tours with many of his contemporaries - Marty Wilde, Joe Brown and if Billy Fury was still with us, he'd be there. Although his music is still there, because Marty sings his old songs now. So Rick, as Eden Kane, is still in much the same business as he was on those old Larry Parnes tours.

Clive's biggest chart success was with 'My Resistance Is Low' which made the top ten in 1976, and to confuse things even further he recorded that as *Robin* Sarstedt, which is in fact, his middle name. As so often happens, that record was not representative of his musical tastes, he made it as some sort of a challenge. A friend of Clives said that this song could be a surefire hit and nobody would believe him; eventually they took it to Decca records and they said 'OK let's give it a shot' and sure enough it was a success. But completely the wrong 'bag' for Clive, because he is a rock & roll lead guitarist at heart, not a twenties style 'crooner'! And that one-off hit led to more confusion for his career than anything. Nowadays, we work together a lot and as a duo we can cover a wide range of styles, including an acoustic 'unplugged' set for the folk festival circuit and a sort of pop/rock set for the concert tours. He also plays two or three regular pub gigs around Hampstead, which is where he now lives and he plays those under the name Clive Sarstedt, to keep things simple!

We did a lot of the 'audition' shows that were popular then, promoters would get all the young bands to come along in the hope that there would be a talent scout in the audience; of course he got a full house and a free show and we got the chance to do our numbers on a big stage in front of a large crowd. That's where we used to meet all the other bands - in sweaty backstage dressing rooms, it was like being back at school, really. But out of all that the best bands were formed, one or two guys were picked from here and a good rhythm section from there, and they are the ones who lasted, the ones who made it. It was very much a semi-pro scene, not many had the dedication to try and make a living out of it, because that seemed impossible. But it wasn't, was it!

'Where Do You Go To...' came as a big surprise when it took off. As I say, I had been playing it for three years beforehand and nobody was jumping around too much - I just slipped it in amongst a bunch of other songs during my set. Although I was playing the folk clubs, I was coming in as a singer/songwriter, I was never the sort of 'Alex Campbell type folkie'; coming from India, where the music was very American influenced, I didn't have this great 'folk tradition' in me, that the British have, whatever I wanted to write about came straight off the top of my head. It was also pure luck that it was recorded, it was a definite afterthought towards the end of the recording session. We had finished off some numbers with orchestral backing, which turned out to be useless, so we sent the others home and thought, let's try this song with just a double bass and an accordion. It was all done very hurriedly, even the cellos were only added right at the last minute, we quickly wrote them a part and down it went. United Artists, my record company didn't have any hopes for it as a single, but my manager at the time, Chris Pearce played it to some of his friends at the BBC, producers and disc jockeys, who all liked the song and it became an 'in-house' hit within the Beeb! Some of the DJ's got me in to do some late night live broadcasts and I played it then; eventually when it did come out on record, it seemed that a lot of people already knew it, certainly the media did. So I knew that a lot of people liked the song, but one day somebody came up to me and said 'that single of yours sold 30,000 copies yesterday, Pete' and we knew that something incredible was going to happen to it. It then occurred to me that I had about thirty gigs already booked into my diary at about forty quid a night, which was my normal folk club rate then, and I was about to have a number one hit! Which was exactly what happened; I was recording Top Of The Pops during the day as the number one act and then playing the same old folk clubs in the evening for £40 - so we weren't prepared for the success, we were way behind our schedules and had to learn what to do as we went along.

The fact that people enjoy your work is a wonderful feeling; the downside was that you then become a media man, everything you do is geared towards your 'press' - all your press commitments come first, which really annoyed me. My priority was for me to be sitting down and writing more songs, and playing - at the time I was a young ambitious songwriter trying to emulate the performers like Dylan and write songs that mattered. Whereas the pressure was to be more like a pop star and the conflict became overwhelming; in the end I had to say 'look I'm sorry, but I've got to ease off'. For about a year it was great, I had a lot of good offers which was thrilling and I felt that I had achieved some of my potential. I just wanted to then carry on with my ambitions, which was towards the songwriting, competing with and improving on my best work, not having to worry about my 'look', or my image.

It's so easy to fall in with it all and lose some integrity; soon after I had the number one, I was offered the chance to do a Campbell's Soup advertisement! And nobody could see why I didn't want to do it - they told me that I was an idiot, they said 'who do you think you are, are you too good for advertisements?' I was twenty eight, I'd already had about three different careers and the last thing I needed was to get involved in childish arguments about these things. It became a bit of a problem, but what could they do? - so I carried on doing things the way I wanted to.

It wasn't the money; because there just wasn't enough time to generate that kind of money - in fact we owed quite a bit, because it costs quite a lot to get a 'pop star' up and running. So it wasn't that I took the money and ran... I ran before the money arrived! I suppose I wasn't used to working on that kind of level, because it really had become a sort of advertising-oriented, marketing exercise - you can't be concerned with what you were before, you're different now.

"...it wasn't that I took the money and ran... I ran before the money arrived!"

So I went with my instincts and my natural instinct is to hang back a bit, to be patient.

Clive knows now that his time in Hamburg stood him in good stead for what was to come. It really was learning the trade the hard way; it's funny, you start playing in a band to avoid 'work', but you end up working like a trojan, with no food, no money and staying in the most disgusting accommodation imaginable. But musically, there was no better way to learn. And he is now a natural stage character, all those other semi-pro bands who just fell away never properly learned how to 'perform' on stage - and if you don't really enjoy it or want to be on that stage, then you are not going to do it for long.

His hit single 'My Resistance Is Low' got into the top ten here and went all round Europe, it covered quite a lot of ground for something that started out as a bet! But he couldn't follow it up, because once again the marketing people wanted to channel him in the wrong direction - Clive and his friends had achieved what they wanted to do by having the hit, and he didn't want to make a career out of singing that type of song - he wasn't a 'twenties 'crooner', he was a rocker at heart.

The trivial pursuit type question often crops up, you know, 'Which three brothers have individually had hit records in the top ten...' that sort of thing. Rick and I both got to number one and if Clive had done the same that would have been quite a feat. And we are all very individual; we come from different areas of the business - Eden the 60's pop singer, me with my songwriting and Clive the rock guitarist, apart from his one-off hit single.

It is very hard to reach a point where you can dictate the terms, the pressures to exploit success are so great - and everybody assumes that *you* want to be exploited as well. They don't imagine that you have any sensibilities at all, otherwise why would you be in this business?... "surely you want to be naked, don't you, you want to be a creature of the tabloids, take your shirt off, what are you afraid of..." And you say, but I'm not like that, and they say well, why are you here?

It has to be the right material too; Rick didn't always have the right material, he was too polite and was happy to go with the style of the times, he just didn't rebel especially in the early days. In a way, the fact that Rick and other singers like him didn't rebel, was instrumental in the arrival of groups like the Beatles. They heard what was being recorded and thought 'we've got to change this, this is not rock & roll, this is giving rock & roll a good name'! Around 1962/63, before they finally cracked it, John Lennon actually said to Rick and I: 'You guys are bad for us, you and your brother are dinosaurs, what do you think you're doing? All turned out in band suits...' Because at that time the Beatles were still wearing leather jackets and jeans, the scruffy rebel look, ironically this was before they were later told to wear band suits, that light grey collar-less gear they had. That is when rock groups start to fall apart, of course - having set out to topple the establishment, they then *become* the establishment! That really messed John's head up; Paul already had the establishment mentality, but it really made John angry - like me, he was another one who wanted to be like Dylan... but couldn't be, because the rest of the group were always dragging him down the wrong road. He had to go off with the group in pursuit of fame; and then discovered that once he had got it, he didn't want it!

George Wilkes

The Sarstedt Brothers - Rick, Peter and Clive - pictured backstage at their one-off Fairfield Hall show - June 1973.

Fortunately, I wasn't burnt out by it, I can still come up with a fresh idea - I think I stopped early enough to avoid becoming embittered by it; I could feel myself becoming more and more bitter towards life and I didn't like it. I much prefer to work on something that I can involve myself in; my song 'Beirut' for example. It was an unlikely single but it got a lot of airplay, but the radio people thought that it was a bit too much like the news - at the time it came out, the civil war in Lebannon hadn't ended and it was possible to hear a news bulletin about the war and then my song would start... *"In Beirut that night, gunshots cracked the heat..."*! So the national radio stations stayed well clear of it, they can't be seen to be too political; it got played on the commercial stations such as Capital but the BBC would say 'when we are playing your record, we are in effect sanctioning what you say' and they thought 'Beirut' sounded too political.

Nowadays, though, Radio 1 seems to be all about urban, political views, it has really changed, now it seems that you can't get a record played unless it *has* a message, some sort of political content.

Luckily, it is an International game, and this 'global village' thing means that the records are being played everywhere, all the time; people in the most obscure parts of the world have heard my music and that is a great feeling. You say to them 'how do you know that song?' and they say 'oh, we get your records, we get all the records'. In America, 'Where Do You Go To...' did well in New York and Los Angeles, but not in the great parts of Middle America, which is where all the massive sales are. It sounded too European for them and they were not geared up to listen to it. In France they also ignored it because it sounded too French!, it was too much the 'coals to Newcastle' syndrome, with the accordion and talking about their own city, they didn't like it. The rest of Europe took to it, especially in Italy, they loved its air of romance.

Interestingly enough, the guy who played the accordion on it was 'discovered' playing in Leicester Square by Ray, my producer, who was a big movie fan and he had seen this blind accordionist sitting there playing day after day. On the day we decided to record it, Ray remembered this guy and went down to Leicester Square, found him and brought him back to the studio. I said to him 'well, this is going to be tough, because you obviously can't read music', so I played him the intro, the run down and he just followed it perfectly. He played a French button accordion, that is what was so good about it, because all the session players were playing the piano accordion which is basically a German instrument. This man had the most authentic tone and he just made it up on the spot; the other good thing about the recording was that we had Dave Holland on bass, one of the best acoustic bass players in the business. He was a jazz man - I mean, he was playing with the Miles Davis band around the time of the session and he did my recording just to earn a few extra quid. He stood next to me in the studio and said 'I'll just watch you play, Pete' and he got it, boom, first take! If you listen to the record it is a very fine, very rhythmic bass part and yet it wasn't written down, nobody else could have played it. So there are all these little improvised signatures going on, which I know helped to capture the moment and make the record what it is. Even the two cellos at the end were a spontaneous addition; a cello part was quickly written down, we got the two cellists back in to the studio, because the majority of the orchestra had gone by then, and they just played it. In fact there is a mistake, but by then it was too late to re-record it, so we left it in - to this day I still notice it when the record gets played, although I'm sure nobody else would know!

I've been working with a local producer recently called John Edmed; John is a great player, but his production method these days is so geared towards the computer that I become almost superfluous! I supply the songs, add my vocal at the end and he takes care of the rest - completely at odds with the old 'live' studio recording. I am really pleased with 'The Green Alphabet', though, I think that's our best work. It is a sixteen minute piece, an A to Z of environmental issues and hopefully it will be on the next record that I release. I think it works extremely well; John said 'leave it to me' and he produced this backing track that really kicks, it's like front-line dance music and I just 'scatted' my vocal over the top. It changed the song, but got the words across, in a sort of free-form vocal and the whole project turned out really well because the energy was just right. Yet sometimes we'll sit and agonise over the various parts of a recording, whereas I just want to play the whole thing through, do it in one take - it's horses for courses I suppose. But the Green Alphabet is a very interesting piece, it is the best recording that I have ever done using computers and John was the best man for the job. He is a good engineer too; I remember one time at Matthew Fisher's studio, John and the guys were experimenting with long tape delays and running the tape out of the machinery and right around the room to get the effect they wanted!

I think the trend amongst the great producers these days is to leave artists alone as much as possible; when Daniel Lanois produces Dylan or Ry Cooder, there *is* no production, that is the beauty of it. Let's hear what the artist has to say without imposing any artificial production values on him. It is so easy to fade up some echo or drown the vocal with extra chorus, but why do that? The post-modernist producer is a guy who doesn't interfere, he is there in the studio for guidance and empathy, and to make sure it gets on the tape - and I think that's good.

Bob Dylan in particular, is very much aware that he is 'talking to us' through his songs and he wants to avoid as many extra distractions as possible. I am still very much an admirer of Dylan's work - not that I can avidly discuss every track that he has ever made, but I still try and listen to what the man has to say. You can't simply copy him, though, that is one of the first things you learn not to try and do! Ralph McTell is another musician that I admire; he is so 'religious' in the way he goes about his craft, and this dedication to the task has evolved into such a great guitar sound. And then there is this historical context to his music, where he is constantly referring back to the great blues players that he loves so much. When you do a gig with him, you really get to see just how much care he takes over his work, which is why he has remained so popular. I also think that there is a similarity between our best known songs, songs which were basically written about a lack of work and which both became top ten hits. 'Streets of London' is such a tremendous anthem; I did a folk festival in Sweden with Ralph and with all the acts up on stage for the finale, he starts into 'Streets' and suddenly the whole audience is singing it, the whole bloody town is singing it! Everyone is singing 'Streets of London', word perfectly, in the middle of Sweden - it was amazing.

Workwise, the songs have never really dried up. I have quit the business a couple of times, but even when I left London to live in Copenhagen, I ended up forming a band there, with a couple of English guys and a Danish bass player and drummer. We rehearsed in the basement of the house that I lived in and went out to gigs in Norway and Sweden, it was a great little band and I was happy playing exactly what I wanted to. Once again, the record company didn't like it; you're a solo artist, Pete' they would say to me, 'you're not a band'. There was this stand-off between us all the time. In fact we did record one album with that band, but the record company wouldn't release it because it 'wasn't me'! Of course, at that time it was the probably the only record that really was me! I had a wonderful time in Copenhagen in the early Seventies, such a great musical place, with people of all nationalities mixing together to listen an play. After that I lived in America for a couple of years and then moved to Wiltshire for twelve years.

I personally think that my best years are still to come; I'm still an ideas man and even though the execution of those ideas doesn't always strike the right chord, so long as they still keep coming, then I'm in good shape! ”

Soul nights at the Orchid

One of the leading Mecca Ballrooms, the Orchid at Purley became a regular stop on the touring circuit for a large number of dance groups, in particular visiting American soul acts. Artists of the calibre of Otis Redding, Ben E King, Patti Labelle, the Ronettes, Soloman Burke and the Drifters all filled the huge, and thankfully well-sprung, dance floor with the soul boys and girls of South East London.

In the early 'sixties, the Orchid mainly catered for dance fans with the big-band sound of the Johnny Howard Orchestra, but were astute enough to recognise the teenage interest in rock'n'roll; engaging the Fabulous FleeRakkers on a regular basis. Having fine-tuned their talents on the youth of Purley & Croydon, the Fleerakkers became one of the first British groups to be snapped up by producer Joe Meek.

Frazer Ashford

Above and below - Jimmy Ruffin giving his all for the Orchid Ballroom crowd, February 1970.

Left: 'Walking the Dog' soul man Rufus Thomas, caught in the Orchid spotlight.

Frazer Ashford

On the evenings when there was no live music, the Orchid also ran teenage 'disc nights' - one of the DJ's being Ian 'Sammy' Samwell, perhaps best known as the writer of 'Move It' for Cliff Richard, and later as a producer for Georgie Fame and the Small Faces. It was largely due to Samwell that the Orchid started to book rock and soul acts, as a reaction to the success of the Star at Broad Green.

Arguably the Ballroom's best period was from 1964 to 1972, including a purple patch in late 1966 when you could have seen the Who, the Hollies, the Small Faces and Otis Redding on consecutive weeks!

During 1973, the Orchid changed its name to Tiffanys, and with it the overall style of music. The bands that were to become the basis of 'Glam-rock' were topping the charts and 'Tiffs' started to book the likes of the Rubettes, Slade, Mud and Wizzard... but that's another story.

Frazer Ashford

Mel Collins

One of the most successful (and certainly one of the busiest) British saxophonists working in the rock world, Mel has played with virtually everybody! But prior to playing with the likes of Alexis Korner and King Crimson, his roots lie in Croydon band The Dagoes and a short-lived group called Circus, which also featured Philip Goodhand-Tait on vocals.

As a musician, I can proudly say that I was actually born on the road, while on tour in the Isle of Man. My father is a musician and my mother was a singer and they were out on tour with the Roy Fox Band who were playing a summer season over on the Isle of Man. Soon afterwards we moved back to Banstead, Surrey - to Walnut Tree Close in fact. I went to Banstead primary school and then on to secondary school in Epsom; then I worked for a photographer in Sutton, where I was given the job of taking the passport photographs, the babies and weddings, all that sort of thing.

Back then I would go and see live music all the time - Eel Pie Island, the Marquee, the Flamingo - mainly up in London, but locally the Public Hall at Wallington was *the* place, and I can definitely remember seeing Screaming Jay Hawkins play there. He had a very exciting stage act, which would probably seem a bit corny now, but back then it was terrific. I can also remember seeing the Rolling Stones play at Epsom Public Baths.

There were a couple of little bands prior to my joining a Croydon group called **The Dagoes**, but they were really just learning to play, nothing serious. The Dagoes were my first proper attempt at being 'a musician', you know, turning professional and everything. We played quite often at a big ballroom in East Grinstead called the Whitehall, and although we were obviously just a tiny little support band, we were able to open for the likes of P.J. Proby, Bo Diddley and even the Byrds on one occasion, which was all very exciting. We built up our own small following as well and it may seem old fashioned to say so, but we really did learn our trade by doing the rounds of little gigs and the odd support spot. Bumming up and down the M1, playing all-nighter's, two shows in an evening, moving across town from one club to another and then get home at six o'clock in the morning. It was very hard going, but we enjoyed it - not so much when the van would break down at four o'clock in the morning, sixty miles from home, when the clutch goes and you're stuck at the side of a motorway in the middle of the night - but mostly it was great fun!

We had some dates lined up in Germany, but I couldn't go until I was 18, so we waited until September for my birthday, when I could get a work permit and then we went straight out there! Actually that only lasted about a month, because as soon as we came back most of the others went straight back to work - except me, I was determined to stick it out. I really felt that I was now a professional and I was going to stay professional! I've no idea where any of them are now, although I think that our drummer Trevor Rodrigues is probably still living in Thornton Heath.

Our keyboard player, Errol Dyer and I got a job with this band called **Jet Set & the Soulmates** - Jet Set were the group and the Soulmates were the singers - and their drummer was Gerry Conway, who you will know from his later work with Cat Stevens, Kate & Anna McGarrigle, John Martyn and so on. The singers were Larry somebody, Brian - I can't remember their surnames, it was so long ago - and Lisa Strike who went on to do a lot of session work. That gig only lasted about six months.

Then I answered an ad. in Melody Maker for a job with **Philip Goodhand-Tait & the Stormsville Shakers**, who were based in Guildford and that lasted a bit longer, about eighteen months. Initially they were a rock'n'roll band, but by the time I joined they were much more of a soul group; we were signed to the Gunnell Agency and really did the rounds, playing the all-nighters with the likes of Georgie Fame and Zoot Money - all these people. We travelled up and down the country playing all these clubs and eventually as the music scene changed and became more psychedelic - even Zoot Money's group became Dantalian's Chariot and started wearing robes - we also changed away from being an out and out soul band. Our other sax player left and I stopped playing so much sax and started to play more flute, which was very popular in the late 'sixties, and we also changed our name to **Circus**. We were recording with Mike D'Abo, he was producing us at the time and very soon after the name change, Philip Goodhand-Tait decided to leave. I was actually writing songs by then and Philip and I contributed most of the original material, but Philip really had his mind set on a solo career and he left to concentrate on that.

So I consider the true Circus to be the band after Philip left - just the four of us who recorded the one album for Transatlantic. The Circus album actually broke even, it sold about six or seven thousand copies, which wasn't bad for a first album, most record companies used to write off of a band's debut record as a bit of a loss leader.

And in fact, Circus were indirectly responsible for my joining King Crimson. We had a three month residency at the Marquee in Wardour Street and the manager John Gee had this new idea for a series of gigs - there was a healthy jazz scene in London then - and as Circus were a sort of folk/rock/jazz combo, John wanted to mix the rock'n'roll up with the jazz side of things. He put this gig together called 'New Paths', which was basically us together with Keith Tippett's band on a Wednesday night and King Crimson, who played on Sundays with John Surman's band. The idea was to have a jazz audience in that would appreciate us and also if you like, a pop/rock audience that could come and listen to jazz. Which was quite a nice idea, really.

We would go and see King Crimson on a Sunday and they would come and see us on a Wednesday and that's how I first got to meet Robert Fripp. He obviously liked what I was doing in Circus - after Philip left I was pretty much the leader of the band, anyway - and Crimson had been having a troubled time on tour in America, Mike Giles and Ian MacDonald had left the band, girlfriend problems, or whatever, and when they came back from the States they were minus a drummer and a sax player. Fripp came down to see us one night and asked me if I would be interested in joining. So that was the beginning of my leaving Circus to join **King Crimson**.

Originally it was just on a session basis, during the recording of the 'Wake Of Poseidon' LP, but when I joined the band permanently it was with the specific purpose of getting the band out on the road. Greg Lake was still involved at the time that I joined, but he quit to form Emerson, Lake & Palmer while Crimson were still looking for their new drummer. So for a while, Crimson was just Robert, myself and Pete Sinfield, trying to get the band together. It took a year in fact, before we got the personnel together who recorded the album 'Lizard', which was the addition of Gordon Haskall on bass and Andy McCulloch on drums. Once the album was finished, this was going to be the band that went out on the road, but on the first day of rehearsals Gordon Haskall decided that he couldn't work with Robert anymore. Gordon and Robert had actually been at school together, but they'd had such a hard time in the studio -

Courtesy CBS Records/Keith Morris

The huge nine-piece Kokomo line-up in 1975, as pictured on the back of their debut album.

Fripp isn't always the easiest of people to work with - but the first day of rehearsing the tour and Gordon turns round and tells us he's leaving!

To begin with, I was broken hearted, because Crimson was going to be my big break and I actually went away and reformed Circus, with the idea of recording a second album. Then suddenly Fripp got enthusiastic again, he'd found a new drummer in Ian Wallace and we started to audition for a new singer and bass player. Along came Boz Burrell, who actually auditioned as a singer, he wasn't a bassist at all, but most people know the story by now that Fripp taught him to play bass, the whole set note for note, so that we could go on tour! At the end of two years, we finally had a band to go out on the road and off we went.

After my time with Crimson, that's when I really started getting into sessions. We were in America, having just completed our last US tour and we were splitting up the band, Ian, Boz and myself were leaving Robert. He did actually ask me to stay on and help out with the next Crimson; he was already planning the next line-up, with John Wetton on bass, but I'd really had enough, at the time I really didn't want to work with Robert anymore and it was either leave or be destroyed, I think. We had been doing this big package tour in America with Alexis Korner and Pete Thorup opening the show, Black Oak Arkansas were also on the bill, then Crimson, then Humble Pie - which was fantastic, great value for money. Everyone would get together before the shows and later in the hotel bars and jam - Alexis, Steve Marriott, Boz and myself, which was great fun - Alexis and Steve had known each other for some time. King Crimson finished their part of the tour in Birmingham, Alabama and Alexis, who knew that we were all leaving, thought it would be good to work with a drummer, and asked Ian Wallace to join him and Peter for the rest of the tour, which he did.

So Boz and I jumped into the back of a car with two young ladies and went over to the tour promoter's house in New Orleans - he was lending it to us for a holiday. We had no cares in the world, no responsibilities and we spent two fantastic weeks there; being fed strawberries and cream while lying in hammocks in the garden and boogeying in town in the evenings - there was some great music to be found in New Orleans, which was another reason why we were there. Meanwhile the tour carried on round the country and two weeks later was scheduled to play at the Warehouse in New Orleans. Boz and I went down to see them play, Alexis, Peter and Ian, and then went backstage to meet them afterwards. By now, Alexis was keen to expand this new 'band' of his and asked Boz to join on bass for the final six weeks of the tour - they were huge tours, these American packages. As they were leaving the dressing room, Alexis looked back at me, I must have looked a bit lost and forelorn, and said "well, we can't leave Mel..." so then I was in the band and we all finished the tour together.

The tour finished in San Francisco and Alexis decided that he wanted to make an album, the result of which was the 'Accidentally Born In New Orleans' LP, which was exactly how the band came about. Then we all went back to England and carried on touring as **Snape** and that lasted for another six months. Some of these bands may seem short lived, but I think the reason may be that in those days you could always get work. There were plenty of places to play and you could just put a band together and do a few dates, especially established names like Alexis - I mean, we did a two month tour of Germany, just doing the rounds of little clubs. Not making much money, in fact I know that Boz came back owing Alexis money, in the end!

We realised that we weren't getting anywhere, musically speaking. It was great fun, it was fantastic to have come out of King Crimson, playing high-energy rock, with its complicated time signatures to just playing the blues with Alexis. And learning to play the blues, if you like, because up to that point I hadn't really been involved with that musical form at all. The Dagoes had been a beat group; the Stormsville Shakers started out as a rock'n'roll band who

Mel Collins (contd.)

turned into a soul outfit; Circus were this psychedelic folk/jazz thing and then Crimson - so yes, meeting Alexis was my first real introduction to the blues.

Alexis was very good, bless his heart, at being a catalyst, both he and John Mayall would find good musicians and put them together, then move on to form another band. And having given those young musicians the benefit of his experience he was content to let them leave and find their own way. After Alexis came the sessions, yeah and that side of things really built up. Crimson helped, I mean after playing with them my name was out there, I even made the Melody Maker polls for 'Best Instrumentalist'! It was funny, because there was me and Dick Heckstall-Smith playing 'rock' sax, if you like, and Dick always came out above me. They never actually had a sax section or a woodwind section, and if you didn't play guitar, bass, drums or keyboards you were stuck in the miscellaneous instruments section, with people like Ian Anderson from Jethro Tull, Fairport's Dave Swarbrick and Lindisfarne's Ray Jackson. But one particular year, just after the Crimson thing, I was one place ahead of Dick, which was very satisfying.

Fripp was very fair when it came to doing the session work. It was really only he and Pete Sinfield who had the record deal with Island, while the rest of us were on a percentage - it was Robert's generosity that he included us in on the deal, but we didn't actually have a contract with Island at all. So after King Crimson split up, there was no problem in playing sessions for anybody. I had learnt the hard way when I was with Circus, for whom I signed a record deal with Transatlantic. When I wanted to leave Circus to join Fripp, it caused a big problem, because Transatlantic wanted me to pay £1,000 to buy myself out of the contract - in those days a thousand pounds was... well, I thought I would lose the gig with Crimson because I simply couldn't see any way of raising that sort of money. The two guys who started EG Music, negotiated with Transatlantic on my behalf and knocked them down to £500; they paid it upfront for me with the deal being that they would pay £250 and I would find the other half, which I eventually did, out of my wages.

> *"...it was fantastic to have come out of King Crimson, playing such high-energy rock, with its complicated time signatures, to just playing the blues with Alexis."*

Playing live is still, for me, the most enjoyable thing - there's nothing like it. And it makes you play better, that's for sure, getting that buzz from an audience. I mean, I'm lucky in that I get to do the big stadium gigs, say with Clannad and I can come back and play a little club when someone like Tony O'Malley calls me up, or when Kokomo get back together for a benefit. They're two completely different things, and yet they're both as exciting - the stadium gigs are obviously not so personal, but that adrenaline rush as you wait backstage just before you go on and the noise of the crowd when the lights go up, it's incredible. You are kind of detached up on the big stage, but it can be really something special. Then it's really scary to go back and play a club date with people right there in front of your face - in some ways it can be easier playing a stadium because of that detachment.

Even after we left Alexis and Snape, the three of us - Ian Wallace, Boz Burrell and myself - carried on working as a team; we were just jamming with a lot of people really, **Dick & the Firemen** was one amalgamation, with Stevie Marriott again, Zoot Money and a couple of the guys from the Grease Band. Because of the sort of band it was, there was a lot of drinking and partying going on, so when it was good it was fantastic, but when it was bad it could be truly awful. That line-up eventually evolved into Hinkley's Heroes and meanwhile Roger Chapman and Charlie Whitney from Family were looking for musicians to make an album; in those days you could do that, actually form a band specifically to make an album - and that's how the **Chapman/Whitney Streetwalkers** came about. It also meant that they had a ready made band to take on the road and promote the record. It was a shame really, because I quite liked that first Streetwalkers album but I think the record company went bust just as it got released - you couldn't get a copy in the shops even if you wanted to, so that took a dive. If I played on the next album 'Red Card' it was purely on a session basis.

In May 1973 Neil Hubbard and Alan Spenner formed **Kokomo**, with Dyan Birch, Frank Collins, Paddy McHugh and Tony O'Malley who had all been in a pop group called Arrival. I came in on sax and we got Terry Stannard to play drums, Jim Mullen on guitar and percussionist Jody Linscott. Kokomo have been described as a 'white soul group', along with people like the Average White Band and so on. We released a couple of albums for CBS, but made most of money from constant touring and after a few line-up changes the band were really running out of steam.

During this time, Neil, Alan and myself worked with **Alvin Lee** from Ten Years After. Along with Ian Wallace from Crimson and Tim Hinkley on keyboards we recorded a live album for Alvin called 'In Flight', after which we went out on a few dates to promote it. The touring band was just Alvin, Ian on drums and me, plus Steve Thompson on bass and Ronnie Leahy on keyboards.

Back to Kokomo; at the end of 1976, Joe Cocker played a few gigs with us as 'special guest' - he was an old mate of Neil and Alan's from their days with the Grease Band - and in fact one of those gigs with Joe was at the Croydon Greyhound. But by January '77 Kokomo finally decided to split up, although as you know we all still get back together again for the occasional benefit gig or just for the hell of it - they're a lot of fun.

These days I live and work mostly in Germany; I play in the house band on a German TV chat show - their equivalent of the Letterman Show in the States. It's great - regular work with whichever musical guest is booked for the show - and we only get a short time to rehearse a couple of their songs and then back them live on the night. Fortunately I know a good reliable sax player who will stand-in for me, but who doesn't want my job full time - which means I can still take up any offers of touring with various bands - Clannad for instance, seem to have adopted me recently! ”

On the opposite page is a very condensed version of the Mel Collins 'family tree' - much of the information has already been covered in Mel's interview. If you get the chance, go and see Kokomo perform - they are still a great live band.

THE DAGOES

Following months of rehearsal under the watchful eye of manager Louis Chun, this Croydon group landed a four week contract to play the Star Club in Hamburg, in September 1965 - for which each member received £30 a week, plus expenses! Pinto, Sampson and Rodrigues all lived in Norbury, Payne and Dyer came from Manor Road, Mitcham.

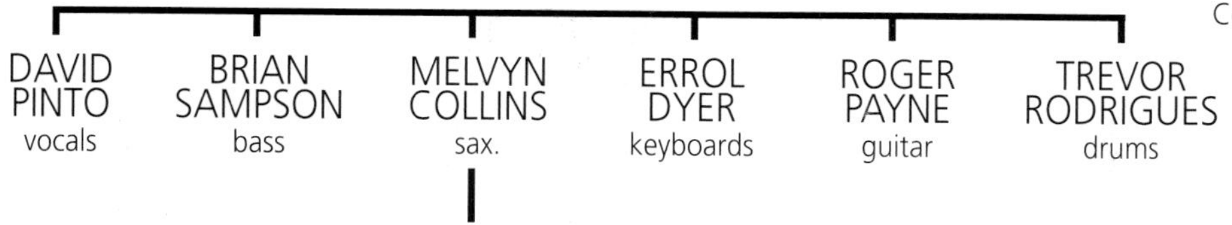

On leaving the Dagoes, Collins and Dyer spent about six months with a soul band - **Jet Set & the Soulmates** which also featured Gerry Conway on drums.

CIRCUS

Formed mid '67 and managed by ex-Manfred Mann vocalist Mike D'Abo, who gave them their name while the band were touring in Italy. Their first single 'Gone Are The Songs of Yesterday' flopped, followed by 'Do You Dream'/'House of Wood' issued March '68 and both written by Goodhand-Tait.

Left for solo career as singer/songwriter

Mel answered a traditional 'musician wanted' ad. in the music press. The group he joined were from Guildford - **Philip Goodhand-Tait & the Stormsville Shakers**. He was working in a Sutton photographic shop at the time and gave it up to play tenor sax and flute with the band. This is the band who later became **Circus**.

KING CRIMSON III

The brainchild of original founder Robert Fripp, this line-up (circa 1970) is the group around the time of their third album 'Lizard', although Collins and Haskell had worked as sessionmen on the previous record 'In the Wake of Poseidon'. But before this line-up had the chance to tour, Haskell and McCulloch quit.

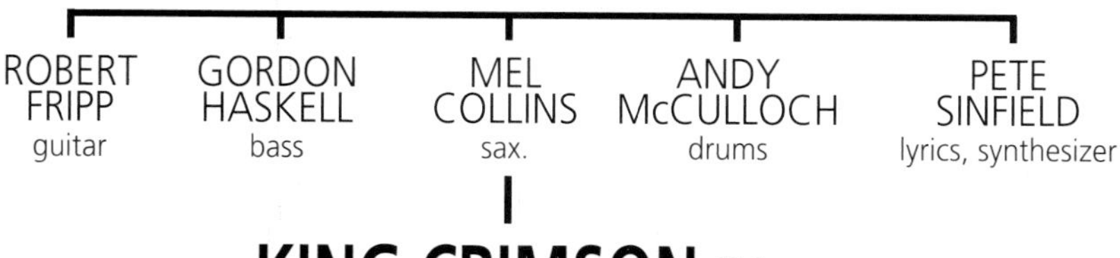

After Goodhand-Tait left, Circus veered off on a more folk/rock/jazz course. They recorded one eponymous album for Transatlantic and played a series of jazz meets rock 'crossover' gigs at the Marquee, which is where Mel first made contact with Robert Fripp.

KING CRIMSON IV

Ian Wallace replaced McCulloch on drums, but a new bassist and vocalist were harder to find. After much auditioning, Burrell was given he job of singer and decided he could play bass as well - Fripp taught him the entire set from scratch. In May 1971 they hit the road... with avengence!

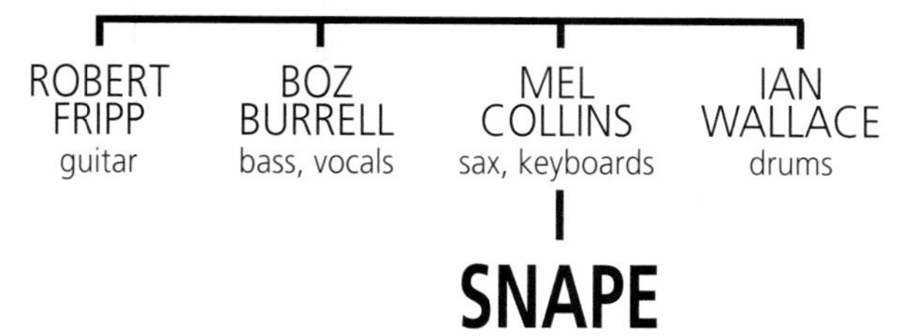

SNAPE

After the big Crimson split at the end of their American tour, Wallace, Collins and Burrell joined up with Alexis Korner and Peter Thorup to form Snape. This outfit recorded an album for Transatlantic - 'Accidentally Born In New Orleans' - in June 1973, which was pretty much the way the band actually got together.

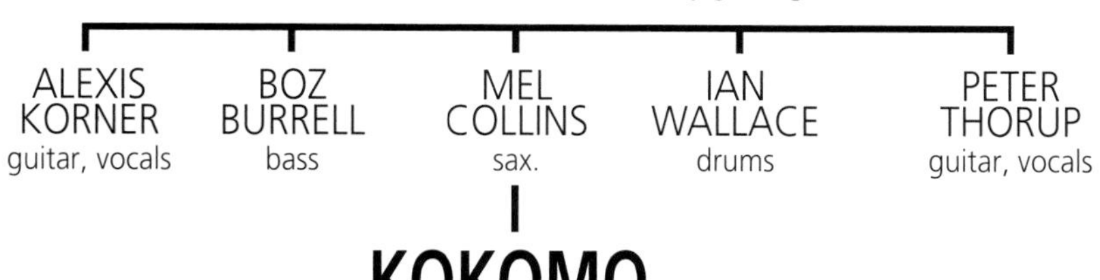

Soon after the split with King Crimson, and his brief spell in Snape, Mel played on the sessions for the first album by the **Chapman /Whitney Streetwalkers** in 1974. Roger Chapman and Charlie Whitney had just disbanded Family and along with Mel Collins, Tim Hinkley on piano and ex-King Crimson drummer Ian Wallace, the new band played a handful of UK gigs to promote the album. Wallace and Collins left after the tour, with Mel joining Kokomo.

KOKOMO

Formed in May 1973, a band of tremendous pedigree. Hubbard and Spenner from Joe Cocker's Grease Band; Mel Collins from King Crimson; McHugh, Birch, O'Malley and Frank Collins from Arrival. The huge ten-piece line-up shown here recorded their eponymous debut for CBS in 1975. Extremely tight and vocally very strong, Kokomo were always popular as a live outfit if a little short on record sales.

JIM MULLEN
guitar

ALAN SPENNER
bass, vocals

NEIL HUBBARD
gtr. vocals

MEL COLLINS
saxes.

TERRY STANNARD
drums

FRANK COLLINS
vocals

TONY O'MALLEY
piano, vocals

DYAN BIRCH
vocals

PADDY McHUGH
vocals

JODY LINSCOTT
congas

Roger Jarvie

Roger Jarvie was the founder member, bass player and subsequently the manager of the Del-Tones, a local group who opened up the doorway to rock stardom for a young guitarist called Jeff Beck.

I am going back nearly forty years here, with no newspaper cuttings or anything else to remind me of the exact timings or sequences, but here goes...

I first got involved with the 'pop' scene around 1956/57 whilst studying for A-levels at Whitgift Middle School/Trinity School in Croydon. We were all listening to 'Trad.' Jazz and to Lonnie Donegan, who was then playing banjo and guitar with the Chris Barber Band, setting the ball rolling for the launch of 'Skiffle' music. Some of us at school got together with a couple of guitars, a washboard and a tea chest and started messing about. We played in some of the local pubs and at the occasional wedding reception; we were pretty awful to begin with and called ourselves (appropriately) the **Discord Skifflers**. The line-up as I recall it, was Tony Jessop, Dave Boreham and myself from school, plus a couple of lads from outside - Bryan Bayliss and later on, a 'real' drummer called Alan Ruff, to replace the washboard.

Our biggest problem was that no-one could really sing; Brian was the best, and Tony was reasonable, but then I came across a lad from literally around the corner - Derek Burchell. When he joined us we really started to get it together. I became the group's manager and started to get us bookings at two local clubs that had opened in Croydon - including the Croydon Jazz Club, run by Frank Getgood at a pub in Broad Green, called I believe 'The Star'. Terry Lightfoot & his Jazzmen were the regular band and we played the interval, Terry and his band are still playing today. We began to move further afield and I was able to book the Skifflers into some of the top London jazz clubs - Ken Colyer's place, the Skiffle Cellar, Cy Lawries club etc.

We also did the interval at a pub in Kent where another new jazz band were getting started, which was Acker Bilk's group; at that time I was still playing on the tea chest and Acker's bassist kindly let me borrow his double bass. I remember Tony Jessop being a wizz-kid on electrics and he converted his rhythm guitar into an 'electric' by attaching a telephone mouthpiece to it and playing it through a converted radio set as an amplifier! Later on, as the pop scene became more sophisticated, he even made his own echo-chamber out of an old reel-to-reel tape recorder, using a looped tape with instant play-back.

Our transport in those days was either a lift from one another of our Trinity school friends in his fathers 'Bull-Nose' Morris - or public transport. By now I was playing my own double bass and managing the group; I used to literally carry the bass on my shoulder about a quarter of a mile from our house to the bus stop and then travel the three miles into Croydon on the platform of a number 12 bus! When we were playing in Soho, we would often have to go by train - in just the same way - carrying our instruments, including the bass and drum kit, then catch the last train back from Charing Cross to Croydon, or occasionally the early morning milk train.

At some stage - and my memory is very vague here - we packed up as the Discord Skiffle Group and I reformed a new group playing 'Pop'. Cliff Richard was on the scene then (in fact, it was when I heard Del, Derek Burchell, singing 'Living Doll' at a rehearsal in Ashburton Primary School hall, that I really thought we could go places. We also introduced a piano player, Ernie Able into the line-up and changed to have Mick Godfrey on drums. We were now into the real thing; I had a proper double bass and we also got ourselves a new lead guitarist, a little left-handed genius named Ian Duncan. We still played the Croydon gigs for Ed Waller and Frank Getgood, but we had also secured regular interval spots at the Wimbledon Palais, where the Oscar Rabin Band were based.

Then came a major turning point in the group's progress. Ian Duncan left us to play backing guitar for a solo singer called Peter Sarstedt - the younger brother of rising English pop star Eden Kane - so there we were with regular work and no lead guitar. At that time we had a young 'fan club' - about a dozen students and teenagers who followed us about on all the local gigs. One of them, a young art student about sixteen years old, asked for an audition as lead guitarist. My first reaction was 'no way', he was far too young to play with we 'established veterans', but as we had no other offers, we agreed to give him an audition. He came along to one of our rehearsals, in Bowaters canteen on the Purley Way one Thursday night, carrying a long cardboard box under his arm. I thought "Christ, he hasn't even got a guitar case, what kind of old junk has he got in that box". Then he opened it and took out a guitar that made all the rest of our equipment look ready for the scrapyard. The most beautiful red and gold Burns London guitar, and when he started playing we all froze in disbelief - he was magic - his name was **Jeff Beck**. So we snapped him up, but we also had to let his young friend John join on rhythm guitar as well (I've forgotten his surname).

As the group was based around Derek Burchell as the vocalist, and as his nickname was Del (not Del Boy!), I decided to call him Johnny Del and the group became **The Del-Tones**. So now we were really up and running, with regular spots at the Park Lane Ballroom in Croydon, Tonbridge Dance Club, Wimbledon Palais and Hammersmith Palais. I was kept busy as Group manager, arranging bookings, travel, rehearsals, an audition for BBC Radio Saturday Club, and the recording of a private disc, made before Jeff joined us. For this I received 10% of the group earnings - the standard Mr. Ten Percent!, but I made one big mistake, an oversight at the time in that I didn't get the group to sign contracts with me.

As we improved I remember having to go and see Jeff's parents, because he, John and the new bassist all decided to get new guitars and Jeff's mother had to guarantee his HP loan. She wanted to be reassured that Jeff would earn enough to pay off the monthly installments; little did she or I know that in less than five years, Jeff would be able to pay off the HP on the guitar, pay off the mortgage on the house and buy himself a Chevrolet StingRay, all out of about six months earnings!

The biggest night for the Del-Tones came when an agency contacted me looking for a group to back Gene Vincent on a one-night stand at Leyton Baths, East London. It was to be both the best and the worst night for the group - the best for the sheer excitement of backing one of the all-time greats and the worst because Jeff Beck was 'spotted'. Not long after the Gene Vincent show, Jeff dropped a bombshell on us, he was leaving the group. He had been offered the job of replacing Eric Clapton, lead guitarist with the Yardbirds, for a tour of the USA.

That was really the end of the Del-Tones; although Del carried on singing for a while with a band called the Crescents based in the West London area. Jeff may have played with them for a while too, at gigs such as the Boathouse, Kew Bridge and the Airport Bowl at Staines. But the rest, as they say - The Yardbirds, Rod Stewart, the Jeff Beck Group - is history! ”

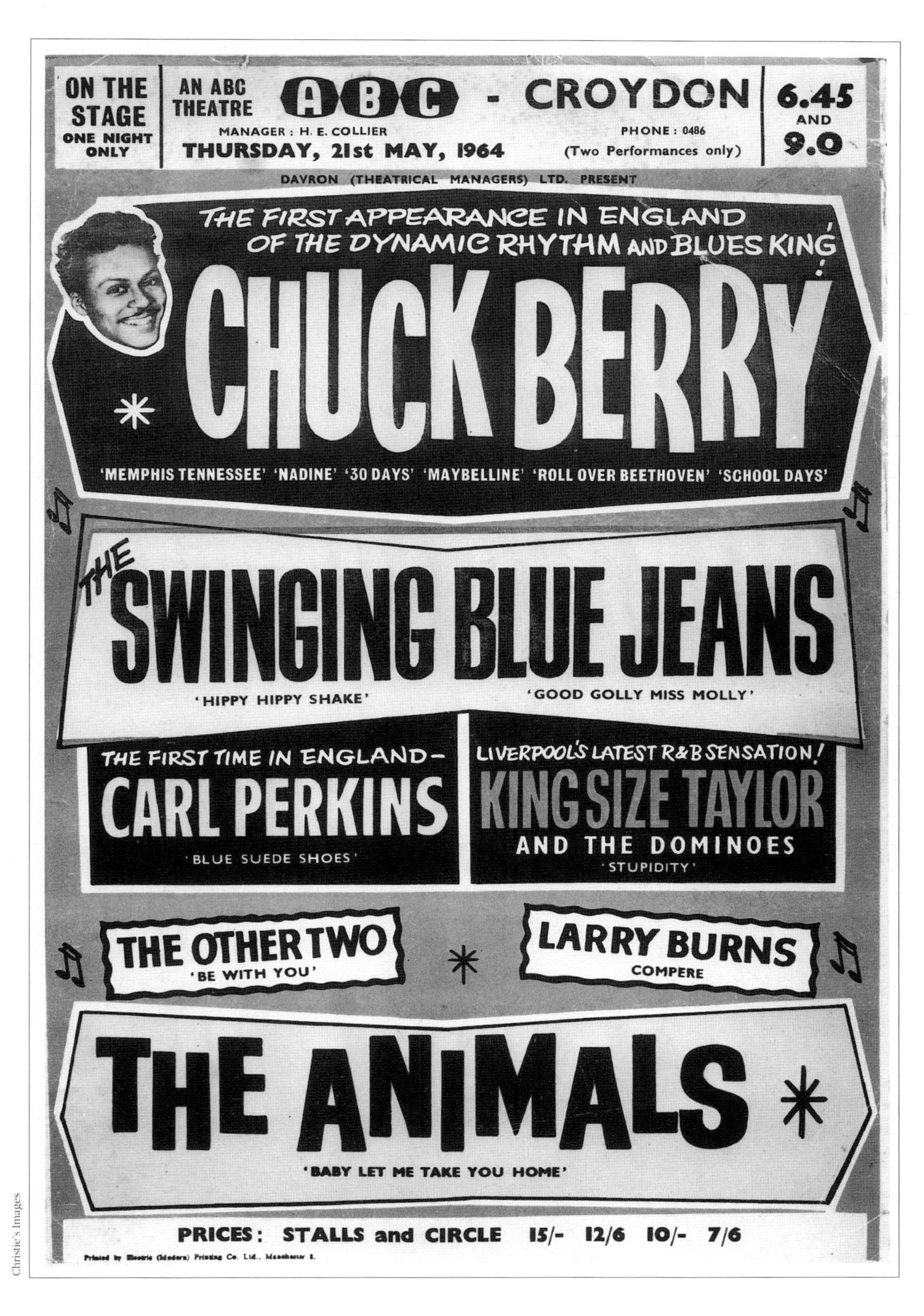

The poster for the Chuck Berry tour, May 1964. By the time the tour hit Croydon, the Swinging Blue Jeans had a 'previous engagement' and were unable to appear. Not mentioned on the poster is the fact that the backing group for female duo The Other Two were the Nashville Teens, who also performed their own set during the show.
Reviewing the concert for the Croydon Times, Roger Mercer went backstage after the show to talk to Chuck Berry, who said that he had received wonderful welcomes from British audiences wherever he had played. Berry went on: "To settle the controversy, the tunes I play, to me, are just music. Music shouldn't be labelled or put into any particular category".
He did add that if people had to argue about his music, then he was inclined to go along with the British view that it was rhythm and blues!

" ...the tunes I play, to me, are just music. Music shouldn't be labelled or put into any particular category. "

Chuck Berry

1960

JANUARY

15 MR. ACKER BILK **CH** (n/a)

FEBRUARY

MARCH

22 JOHN OGDON **CH** (1/6d)

APRIL

13 ADAM FAITH **SG** + JOHN BARRY SEVEN + LITTLE TONY (3/6d to 7/6)

29 KEN COLYER **CH** + MIKE DANIELS + TERRY LIGHTFOOT + MICKEY ASHMAN + ROGER SPEARING (10/-)

MAY

4 JOHNNY PRESTON + BILLY FURY **SG** + WEE WILLIE HARRIS + TONY CROMBIE + CHRIS WAYNE + THE ECHOES + DON ARDEN (3/6d to 7/6)

JUNE

3 CHRIS BARBER **CH** (n/a)

3 KEN COLYER **S** (n/a)

The new decade began with Croydon stuck in something of a live music limbo.

The good councillors of the borough had decided, in their "infinite Christian wisdom", that the town would become a modern, go-ahead, model 'sixties development and that nothing should stand in the way of their dream.

Plans were well underway to transform the town centre with the building of a new style, all-encompassing shopping centre (a forerunner of the American 'mall') and work had already begun on the million pound entertainment complex situated in Park Lane, although the proposed Fairfield Hall was not expected to be completed for two years. In doing so, the Davis Theatre had finally been closed down and by the end of May, was reduced to rubble - and it would not be too long before the Civic Hall met the same fate.

Whereas the major acts of the 'fifties had all flocked to play at the Davis, between November 1959 and November 1962 Croydon suddenly found itself left off the 'A-list' of suitable venues held by the top promotors. The pop package tours began to use the nations cinema chains as a method of covering all major UK towns, and it was the Granada-owned theatres that started the ball rolling; so local fans still had to travel out to either Sutton or Tooting for their regular pop 'fix'. However, once the ABC chain joined in, the one-time Savoy cinema at Broad Green, West Croydon became a useful and popular venue.

But if the big name acts had nowhere in Croydon to play, what else was on offer?

Local bandleader Johnny Howard and his Orchestra were the resident dance band at the Orchid Ballroom in Purley, featuring vocalist Tony Steven; while dancers in the Wallington area could waltz and foxtrot to the Alan Knight Band at the Public Hall every Saturday for an entrance fee of four shillings and sixpence.

Both venues were soon to become regular haunts for pop, beat and rock fans, but for the time being it was JAZZ that was Croydon's saving grace on the live music front line.

(n/a) = ticket price not available.

One of the hardest working bands in 'trad. jazz', **Mr Acker Bilk & his Paramount Jazzband** returned to the Civic Hall on Friday 15th January. This was only his second visit to Croydon, but whereas the first concert played to several empty seats, this time the show sold out over a week in advance with tickets selling faster than for the previous Chris Barber concert. All of which no doubt pleased Acker, in the "friendly-rivalry" stakes with Barber and Ball, and also cheered the promotors Croydon Jazz Club.

With the band attired in their trade-mark Edwardian suits, bowler hats and striped waistcoats they kicked off with a rousing version of 'Papa Dip', followed by a ragged 'In A Persian Marketplace'. However, that proved to be their lowest point and the band stormed through 'Who Rolled the Stone Away?', 'Good Morning Blues', 'Blaze Away', 'I'm Going Home' and 'East Coast Trot'. Mr. Bilk was on top form throughout, but there were also honourable mentions for drummer and vocalist Ronald McKay, Kenneth Sims on trumpet and Jonathan Mortimer, trombone.

Rock and folk fans continued to play second fiddle to the jazzers and as if to prove the point, the Croydon Advertiser (26th February) ran the following snippet of news:

Is Croydon becoming too dull... too stick-in-the-mud... too SQUARE?

*YES! scream many teenagers, who miss the star celebrity concerts in which the Davis Theatre specialised. But rock 'n' roll fans can take heart from the policy of the **Record Rendezvous** at Station Road, West Croydon.*

*This new store will be inviting popular recording stars to come and meet their Croydon fans. First on the list - at 3.00pm on Saturday next week - is **Lance Fortune**, a 19 year old veteran with recording, stage, film and television contracts in his pocket.*

The Sutton Granada cinema played host to the early package tours - with **Adam Faith** and the **John Barry Seven** playing on 13th April and **Johnny Preston**, **Billy Fury** and **Wee Willie Harris** appearing there on 4th May. Tickets for each show were priced at 3/6 to 7/6d.

River trips were an unusual outlet for musical entertainment and Croydon Jazz Club, in conjunction with Peckham Jazz, organised 'Rockin' Down The River' on Sunday 12th June. All aboard the Royal Daffodil moored in London, the day trip cruised across to Margate and back, to the sound of the full **Johnny Dankworth Band**, plus supporting groups and singers.

In May, the local paper ran a whole page synopsis about "...one of Croydon's often misunderstood arts..." It seems strange to think that jazz was looked on by some as an underground, possibly dangerous and subversive musical form - the introduction read:

"With jazz there is a tendency to not only refuse to listen to the music itself, but to condemn its devotees... What goes on in this misunderstood world?... Are jazz enthusiasts really as bad as some people imagine?

Croydon Advertiser – 6.5.60

Peter Thornton writes about the modern jazz stuff...

IT COULDN'T CARVE A NICHE

THE THING that has always amazed me about jazz in Croydon is that the modern stuff has never been a success. It seems almost inconceivable that, in a place of Croydon's size, modern jazz could not have carved out a niche for itself over the years. But it hasn't.

In the last two years or so, a few - a very few - modern jazz experiments have been tried in the town - all without success.

The Park Lane Jazz Club used to run a modern session on Saturday nights, but couldn't get enough support for it - even though the resident group had a variety of top-line modern jazz artists playing with them from time to time. Another experiment was the opening of a modern jazz club at the Star. This too, was doomed almost as soon as it began. It closed down, started up again after an interval of a few weeks and then as suddenly closed again.

On the face of it there seems no good reason why a town of 250,000 people should not support a modern jazz club. One can only assume that the younger generation in Croydon are so conservative that nothing but 'trad' will suit them. Another possible factor is that there are very few suitable halls available. The Church authorities, who own the majority of halls in Croydon, do not generally welcome jazz clubs.

Perhaps the chief reason for the failure of modern jazz in Croydon is the wealth of lush, modern clubs in the West End - all only about half an hour's journey away. the London clubs - with their accompanying incentive of "a night out in the West End" - cost only a few shillings more to visit than the local ones do. This I am sure, is the main reason why modern jazz is a flop in Croydon.

With traditional jazz however, the picture is different.

Croydon's rendezvous of traditional jazz - the Star - is enjoying, one might almost say suffering from - ever larger and more appreciative audiences. Here, at the headquarters of Croydon Jazz Club, the policy has been to have 'name' bands. Over the past few months we have seen Acker Bilk, Mike Daniels, Ken Colyer and other top-line bands of the trad. world.

The only note of change has been the introduction now and again of featured blues and folk singers - Sonny Terry & Brownie McGhee are the best example of this; mainstream in the form of the talented Humphrey Lyttleton band; and the unusual, in the form of the Diz Disley Quintet (which plays in the style of the Django Reinhardt Quintette du Hot Club de France, of the 'thirties).

All these guest groups have gone down well - including the mainstream of Lyttleton. But strange to say, the extremely good mainstream music of the Dave Shepherd group flopped when it did a regular Sunday night stand at the Star towards the end of last year.

Down the road at the Park Lane Jazz Club, traditional jazz took over when modern went out. But after a relatively short period even traditional went by the board. Now the Park Lane Ballroom is packed four nights a week for dancing to live 'cha-cha' and Rock'n'Roll.

The Palm Court Jazz Club in Purley is still going strong and features regular appearances of 'name' groups. Since May last year, when the Davis Theatre closed its doors, there have been no celebrity jazz concerts in Croydon. Fans who want to see the American 'greats' have to go in to London.

It seems to me that there is still ample opportunity for expansion in the jazz world in Croydon. Had there been a greater number of suitable halls available to potential club promotors in the past, I feel sure that we would now have more jazz clubs in Croydon. There should at any rate be room for another 'trad.' club - a town of a quarter of a million people could easily support more than one.

It is also true that over the past year or so, jazz in Croydon has been varied and entertaining, and the public has had its money's worth - but only from the point of view of the music. Much more could still be done to improve the actual conditions under which jazz is heard in Croydon.

Meanwhile, local folk singer **Steve Benbow** released a collection of traditional English folksongs on the newly formed 'Collector' label. Steve's album (JEB2) was the second release on the label and he was described by the Croydon Advertiser as 'a professional rustic downsman from Coulsdon'!

JULY

6 THE FLEERAKKERS **O** (n/a)

16 THE HI-FI's **PL** (n/a)

AUGUST

SEPTEMBER

14 MR. ACKER BILK **PC** (n/a)

OCTOBER

21 TERRY LIGHTFOOT JAZZBAND **S** (n/a)

28 MIKE DANIELS DELTA JAZZMEN **S** (n/a)

28 MIDNIGHT MATINEE **A** TOMMY TRINDER + DIANA NOBLE + THE RED PEPPERS + BILL PERTWEE + MIKE DANIELS DELTA JAZZMEN + JIMMY WHEELER + MORRIS & COWLEY (7/6 to 17/6)

NOVEMBER

11 EGGY LEY & HIS JAZZMEN **S** (n/a)

18 ALEX WELSH & HIS DIXIELANDERS **S** (n/a)

DECEMBER

9 HUMPHREY LYTTELTON **S** (n/a)

16 CLYDE VALLEY STOMPERS **S** with FIONA DUNCAN (n/a)

23 KEN COLYER **S** (n/a)

In his book 'Stone Alone', Bill Wyman recalls going along to the Wallington Public Hall with a friend named Stewart Wealleans to see a rock 'n' roll band called **Neil Christian & the Crusaders** and a few weeks later to see a well-known act called **Nero & the Gladiators**. Both of these acts (on record, at least), featured Jimmy Page as lead guitarist and it was live bands like these and the classic pop records of the day that inspired the young Bill Perks (he didn't change his name to Wyman until January '63) to form his own group.

Having moved into a flat in Birbeck Road, Beckenham, Bill and his brother in law Cliff Starkey plus a workmate Steve Carroll, began practising on a regular basis - copying Chuck Berry and Buddy Holly records. Bill at this time was playing a Burns six string. After a booking at the Starlight Ballroom in Penge, the group played various weddings and youth clubs, but Bill and Steve were also rehearsing with Stewart Wealleans and yet another guitarist, Brian Cade. This alliance eventually became known as **The Cliftons**; Brian Cade - lead guitar, Dave Harvey - vocals, Steve Carroll - guitar, Bill Perks, guitar and Tony Chapman - drums, they began serious rehearsals at the Lord Palmerston pub in Penge.

Bill only switched to bass guitar in August 1961 after seeing the Barron Knights at a dance in Aylesbury!, being impressed with the depth it gave to their sound. He bought a secondhand bass for £8 and took out all the frets in order to renovate it; Bill liked the sound it gave however and his instrument became arguably the first fretless bass in the country. The group regularly played a church youth club at St. Michael's Hall, Lower Sydenham with another good local group The Wranglers, later adding a sax player and moving to slightly larger venues including the London School of Economics and Chislehurst Caves.

Dancers at the Orchid Ballroom in Purley were promised an exciting 'new sound' from the **Swift-Burns Quartet**. The group played dance music and modern jazz, but led by the unusual combination of flute and electronic organ. All four came from the Croydon area, the group consisting of Johnny Trehorn, tenor sax & flute; Jack Raby, piano & organ; Ernie Spencer, bass and drummer Geoff Smith and their Purley residency followed a spell at the Jacaranda Club in London's West End.

(n/a) = ticket price not available.

The rise to fame of Croydon singer **Dickie Pride** was a leap of "lorry driver's mate to top recording artist in just eighteen months" according to the local press. Born Richard Knellar, the 19 year old from Heathfield Vale, Selsdon won himself a place at the Royal College of Church Music, but while he was singing psalms at college, he was performing with his rock group in the pubs and clubs around Croydon.

At that time he was using the stage name of Dickie Sayer and playing with his group The Semitones, whose guitarist Micky King from Thornton Heath, went on to play with Cliff Bennett & the Rebel Rousers. Dickie's big break came with a house-shaking performance at the Gaumont State Cinema in Kilburn.

Signed to Columbia records by Norrie Paramor, he was quickly taken under the wing of manager Larry Parnes, who gave him the name change to Pride - Parnes artists all had such names, Tommy *Steele*, Marty *Wilde*, Billy *Fury*, Georgie *Fame*, Lance *Fortune*, Duffy *Power* and so on. Pride had a top thirty hit with 'Primrose Lane' in 1959 and appeared on the ITV shows 'Wham' and 'Oh, Boy'.

His energetic stage performances earned him the nickname 'The Sheik of Shake', also the title of his first EP and he released subsequent singles 'Frantic', 'Betty, Betty' and a cover of Little Richard's 'Slippin' & Slidin'. Highly rated by 'Oh Boy' producer Jack Good, Dickie Pride never quite matched the success of his contemporaries and died far too young in 1969, aged 27, an early rock casualty of drug-related causes.

MR. ACKER BILK *

WEDNESDAY, 14th SEPTEMBER

PALM COURT JAZZ CLUB, Banstead Road

7.30 p.m. PURLEY 11.30 p.m.

Posters around Croydon advertised a new season of Saturday night dances at the Park Lane Ballroom, beginning in July with 'Pop music's Brightest band' - **The Hi-Fi's**. With over 50 appearances at Park Lane, the group had built up a solid reputation as Croydon's best rock 'n' roll band, but the 'bright' tag probably came from their penchant for wearing tangerine and purple jackets on stage.

The group comprised guitarist Len 'Sandstorm' Ford, Al Stainer on bass, pianist Brian Bennett, Mel Wright on drums and 19 year old vocalist Vern Rogers. The Croydon Advertiser noted that the dancers applaud the group for the quality of their dance music, but added - *"It cannot be denied, though, that many of the Park Lane teenagers would dance to anything as long as it had pace and a heavy handed drum beat!"*.

Apart from performing in the area many, many times, jazz musician **Humphrey Lyttelton** has another local connection, in that when he joined the Army on June 6th 1941, he was immediately posted to the Guards Depot at Caterham for training. In his autobiography 'I Play as I Please', he describes it thus: *"The Caterham initiation into the Brigade of Guards is famous. Nowadays it is spoken of, by those who know, in the same breath as the Foreign Legion. We make 'em or break 'em should have been the motto over the main gates...'*! After his initial training, Lyttelton was sent to Sandhurst and from there was drafted to Salerno, Italy to see active service with the Grenadier Guards. He contracted malaria and was sent back to Algiers to convaless and in December 1943 was flown back to England.

Shortly afterwards, he was back in Caterham at the Guards Depot, this time as an officer and with some time to play again: *"Throughout the war, many idols of the followers of popular music could be seen trudging along at the head of a column of Guardsmen. At one of the dances at Caterham, I sat in on trumpet with the band. Being struck by the clarinet playing of the bandsman sitting next to me, I asked him what his name was. When he said: 'Nat Temple, sir', I very nearly stood to attention and saluted!"*.

On August 30th a local beat group flew out to Germany for a month long engagement in Frankfurt. **Jay Chance & his Chancellors** were spotted playing at a gig in Soho and booked on the spot by a German theatrical agent. Remarkably, the group had only been playing together for four months, but had already clocked up many appearances at clubs, coffee bars and American air bases.

Formed by 17 year old Jay Chance - real name John Wolvett of Winterborne Road, Thornton Heath, the other members are Micky Gee (Michael Geary) of Stafford Road, Croydon, Micky Flyn (Michael Leonard) and Bryan Loam (Brian Collins), both from Bexley in Kent. They began their international debut at the Storyville House of Jazz in Frankfurt, but with an option to extend their visit at other venues who had shown an interest.

After a five-year trip to Europe, **Eggy Ley** and his jazzmen returned to the Star in November. One of the original British trad. players, Ley remembered performing in *"a sort of converted civic restaurant"* in New Addington over ten years before. The Advertiser described him as playing *"soprano saxophone in an elegant, fluid style, neither as bold or precise as Bechet nor as sensuous as Dodds, but quite satisfying all the same"*.

Croydon Advertiser – 16.12.60

'JAZZ AT THE STAR SPLITS THE PRO-HUMPHS AND ANTI-HUMPHS'

HUMPHREY LYTTELTON is almost certainly the best-known jazz musician in Great Britain. His music, while making him a favourite with young people has, through the wonders of the "telly", endeared him to their parents also. Mums approve of him in the same way that the BBC approves of him. (How far Auntie BBC accepts him is shown by the fact that he was even allowed to open a bazaar for the "Archers".)

A phenomenon of Lyttelton's success is that in forsaking the revivalist style, he has gathered new supporters - people who don't care what jazz sound he is creating, as long as the music is good. Many nasty things have been said about his jazz experiments. One cruel gentleman has even suggested that if he continues his present trend he will soon discover be-bop!

That this anti-Humph trend exists was evidenced at the Star, Broad Green on Friday, for many so-called 'authentic New Orleans purists' stayed at home. Their places were filled by people with no prejudices who simply came to hear Humph. H.L. seems to have found a pleasant mainstream instrumental balance. Though he no longer has a trombonist, his trumpet and the alto and baritone saxophones together produce a lusty and blended sound. When needed, in the essentially New Orleans tunes, Tony Coe doubles on the clarinet. In Friday's programme, I noted a fluent Joe Temperley baritone saxophone solo in "All of Me" and some crisp, effervescent ensemble playing in "Joshuz fit de Battle of Jericho".

Lyttelton went out his way to prove his versatility - allowing Coe to do most of the donkey work in a clarinet duet, and later taking over the drums in Coe's solo rendering of "After You've Gone". His trumpet playing, pungent and neatly phrased, tends to become rather shaky when it climbs into the higher register. I enjoyed the interval number, a version of "Sunny Side of the Street" in which he quoted from "The Peanut Vendor".

J.T.S.

In December the Star also played host to the **Clyde Valley Stompers** who, as their name suggests, had travelled down from north of the border to compete with the likes of Barber and Bilk. Sadly their intensive touring showed up in their playing which was *"jaded and mechanical"*, although Fiona Duncan sang well all evening, and was heralded as *"the best female vocalist to visit the Star this year"*.

JANUARY

6 DICK CHARLESWORTH **S** (n/a)

8 RICKY VALANCE & THE CRESTA'S **CH** + MARK ANTHONY (4/6 to 6/6)

27 MR. ACKER BILK **CH** (n/a)

FEBRUARY

7 JOHN OGDON **CH** (1/6)

10 GEORGE MELLY & MICK MULLIGAN **S** (n/a) *CANCELLED*

MARCH

3 GENE VINCENT **SG** + JOHNNY KIDD & THE PIRATES + SCREAMING LORD SUTCH +TERRY DENE + JOHNNY DUNCAN & THE BLUEGRASS BOYS + MIKE & BERNIE WINTERS (3/6 to 7/6)

3 ALEX WELSH **S** (n/a)

10 KEN COLYER **S** (n/a)

APRIL

MAY

20 VERN ROGERS & THE HI-FI's **ST** (n/a)

26 ALL-NIGHT JAZZ BAND BALL **CH** THE ARTISANS + MIKE DANIEL'S DELTA JAZZMEN (n/a)

27 ALL-NIGHT JAZZ BAND BALL **CH** NEW ORLEANS CHOIR & ORCHESTRA + KEN COLYER (n/a)

JUNE

9 MONTY SUNSHINE's JAZZBAND **CH** + BERYL BRYDEN (3/- to 5/-)

30 Mr. ACKER BILK **CH** (n/a)

(n/a) = ticket price not available

The first big Croydon gig of the year was the 'Sunday Beat Show' at the Civic Hall on 8th January, starring **Ricky Valance** - and the promoter David Smith was disappointed by the turn out of only a couple of hundred fans.

He was probably more upset by the performance of Ricky's backing group The Cresta's, who failed to complete his big hit 'Tell Laura I Love Her' even after three attempts, struggling to stay in the same key as the singer! Resplendent in a gold lame jacket, Ricky did manage to get through 'It's Now Or Never', 'Unchained Melody' and 'If You Were The Only Girl In The World'.

The Somerset-born singer **Mark Anthony** had lived in Croydon since he was 3 years old, his big break had been appearing on a show with Adam Faith. Also on the bill were Gary Luther and Lord Claud, plus the somewhat out of place Josie Stahl & Le Quatre du Jazz.

Coffee bars - very much part of a teenagers rock'n'roll lifestyle - where six of you take over the table in the corner and spend three hours over a couple of 'frothy coffee's' and plug the jukebox with all your spare cash. In February, the Espresso bar in London Road, Thornton Heath caused a bit of a stir when it was initially refused planning permission but opened on a technicality - only 'alterations' to the building had been refused - but as the bar was not altered and would still operate as a shop, there was no problem.

Some members of Croydon Council were less impressed; one told the Croydon Times - "We feel very amazed about the whole thing. I have nothing against an Espresso bar, but we know what happened at the (Thornton Heath) Pond before. It is the type of people who get in". Others held a special meeting to point out their 'considerable apprehension and alarm' to the Town Clerk. And all over a few cups of coffee and a bit of Chuck Berry, no doubt!

With rock 'n' roll concerts still at something of a premium in Croydon, it is worth noting that the Sutton Granada staged a 1961 AllStars show, featuring **Gene Vincent, Johnny Kidd & the Pirates, Johnny Duncan & the Blue Grass Boys, Terry Dene, Screamin' Lord Sutch** and guest stars **Mike & Bernie Winters!** The date was Friday 3rd March, two performances and tickets were 3/6d, 5/6d and 7/6d.

A jazz concert at the Civic Hall ended in a near riot, when fists and chairs flew between rival fans. **Acker Bilk** was the headline act and his 'Trad.' jazz audience clashed with those of **Blues Incorporated**, featuring Cyril Davis, who represented the 'new wave' of heavily amplified blues/jazz groups.

Blues singer **Memphis Slim** made an appearance with the Alex Welsh Band at Bromley Jazz Club, which took place at the White Hart, Bromley High Street on Tuesday 4th April. This was only three days after his performance with Josh White at the Royal Festival Hall.

Croydon Advertiser – 12.5.61

NEW TEENAGE SINGER BEGAN HIS CAREER AT A PARTY

To avid followers of the 'Top Twenty' hit parade and eager enthusiasts of juke box jingles, the name ***Eden Kane*** *will already be familiar. But the 'squares' may still be unaware of discland's newest citizen, the tall, dark and handsome six-footer from Norbury.*

Nineteen year old, green eyed Eden was born in India, where his father was an accountant to a prosperous tea merchant. When Eden's family returned to England, he became a pupil at Heath Clark Grammar School, Waddon, where he held the high diving championship and, as a member of the Air Training Corps, he won a gold medal and the Surrey high jump title. At sixteen he decided his vocation was architecture; but he could not settle down and tried other jobs including tailoring.

Then came the decisive day when he was handed a guitar at a party. Looking back, Eden says: "I found I could play intuitively and, at last, this sense of restlessness seemed to abate. I knew what I wanted to do". Singing came naturally and with some friends he formed the Fabulous Five which played in Croydon. When the group died, The Saints was formed, with Eden as lead singer and guitarist.

A talent contest put him on the road to fame and his new record "Well I Ask You", out today, is the result of nine months of singing lessons, drama coaching, voice production and piano playing. As far as his agents are concerned, he is "a certainty for the teenage girls' wig-flipping stakes"! What is more, he has "the ability to crash out a song with a beat that is likely to give him a longterm hit parade tenancy". Eden is having three screen tests for American films - and there is talk of a West End show.

Wallington-based group **Vern Rogers & the Hi-Fi's** made a return visit to Croydon to play a 'Rock 'n' Roll Ball' at the Stanley Halls, South Norwood on Saturday 20th May.

The group were the resident rock band at Croydon's Park Lane Ballroom up until its closure a few weeks beforehand and had since appeared at dance halls in London and the Midlands. They hoped that the concert at the Stanley Halls would be the first of another series of local dates. On 3rd June the group travelled to Bletchley in Buckinghamshire to back pop singer Ricky Valance, with a coach trip organised to take their Croydon fans to cheer them on. Hopefully they had more success than the Cresta's who backed Valance earlier in June!

On 23rd June they were back on home ground to play a benefit concert at St. Mary's Hall, Beddington in aid of Wallington & Carshalton CND.

If you happened to be an insomniac jazz fan, then Croydon's All-Night Jazz Band Ball was tailor-made for you. Organised by Croydon Jazz Club, around 500 people entered the Civic Hall at 11.00pm on Friday 26th May and emerged, blinking into the sunlight at 7.00am Saturday morning.

The Artisans kicked off the proceedings, as reported by the Croydon Times: *"Hot jazz blended with haloes of cigarette smoke and the aromas of fried onions, sweat and hot-dogs. Dress was informal; some young people wore top hats or bowlers as they cavorted to the music. A daring few even sported the latest lines in flour sacks".*

At midnight, the **Mike Daniels' Delta Jazzmen** took over and played probably the best set of the session, including excellent clarinet work from Johnny Barnes during 'Avalon'. They were followed by the New Orleans Choir & Orchestra with trombonist Eric Allandale and Will Hastie on clarinet.

Throughout the early hours of Saturday morning, everyone began to wilt visibly; *"the pace of the dancing slackened as more and more people shuffled off to dark corners. The East balcony - like a London news theatre on Cup Final morning - was soon full of sleeping people".* As dawn broke, the jazz became both uninspired and undistinguished and a few people started to leave, despite the plea from a sleepy Ken Colyer when he played 'Don't Go 'Way Nobody'.

As the clock struck seven and the last notes of 'High Society' drifted away, those hardy souls who managed to stay the distance crept out into the May morning air. "There's only one thing wrong with all-night jazz band balls" said the man with indigo quoits round his eyes. "They last all night!"

Croydon Times – 9.6.61

TEENAGE GROUP SIGN CLUB CONTRACT

A NEW teenage beat group, whose four members come from Croydon, have just been signed up by a Streatham club 'Les Foux Hiboux' (The Mad Owls). Called ***The Sundowners****, they are led by 18 year old* ***Peter Lincoln****, a former Heath Clark school pupil from Norbury Crescent, Norbury and were formed only two months ago.*

Peter, his brother Clive Sears and Tony Burgess of Lyndhurst Road, Thornton Heath gained experience with a small group before breaking away to form their own. On a tour of the coffee bars one night, they discovered drummer Michael Riley, who had been playing with a modern jazz group and invited him to join them.

Until their lucky break in Streatham, the boys found the going tough. West End auditions, including an interview at the famous 'Stork Club' merely led to a "we'll let you know some time". Now things are looking up; an audition with a well-known theatrical agent and a test with a major record company are promised in the near future.

The group rehearse four times a week and are not afraid of the hard road to success. There is always a demand for youngsters who have got 'what it takes' and their enthusiasm plus a new approach have already put them on the road to success. Peter and Clive are the brothers of singer ***Eden Kane*** *- and with his latest disc 'Well I Ask You' already in the hit parade, the boys have a lot to live up to.*

Jacqueline Ryan

Peter Lincoln poses backstage at Wallington Public Hall prior to a gig with his group The Sundowners.

Friday 30th June gave Croydon jazzers a choice - **Acker Bilk** and his boys in the Civic Hall once again or a college gig by the **Temperance Seven** at the Denning Hall.

JULY

15 THE SHADOWS **TG** + HELEN SHAPIRO + DANNY WILLIAMS (3/6 to 7/6)

AUGUST

SEPTEMBER

1 CHRIS BARBER **CH** (n/a)

8 GARRY MILLS & THE DECCADES **U** (5/-)

OCTOBER

6 TEMPERANCE SEVEN **CH** (n/a)

20 HELEN SHAPIRO **SG** + BROOK BROTHERS + DANNY WILLIAMS (3/6 to 7/6)

NOVEMBER

14 JULIAN BREAM **CH** (1/6)

17 RUSS CONWAY **SG** + BILL MAYNARD (3/6 to 7/6)

DECEMBER

1 GENE VINCENT **CH** + THE VISCOUNTS + GARRY MILLS & THE CHEROKEES + PAUL RAVEN + LANCE FORTUNE + SOUNDS INCORPORATED + VERN ROGER & THE HI-FI's (3/6 to 7/6)

12 JOHN OGDON **CH** (1/6)

12 EDEN KANE & THE BARONS **W** + PETE LINCOLN & THE SUNDOWNERS (4/-)

22 BOBBY ANGELO & THE TUXEDOES **SH** + VERN ROGER & THE HI-FI's (3/6)

If you fancied a little jazz on a Bank Holiday Monday, then not too far away was the Redhill Jazz Festival. Held on 7th August at the Memorial Sports Ground in Redhill, the advertised event promised music from 2.30 to 7.30pm, with *'space for jiving'* (very important) and refreshments, tickets five shillings in advance or six on the day. On show were four fine bands; Nat Gonella & his Georgians, Mick Mulligan and his band - featuring George Melly, Charlie Galbraith's All Star Jazz Band and the Preston Scott New Orleans Jazz Band.

On Tuesday 29th August, Croydon rockers **Sonny Stewart & the Dynamos** left town for a three month tour of Germany - first stop Hamburg, home of the celebrated Star Club. The group were booked in there for the first two months, after which they would play a series of night club gigs in Bonn, Stuttgart, Dusseldorf and Frankfurt.

Sonny (24) of King Henry's Drive, New Addington, formed the Dynamos in 1958 whilst living in Holmesdale Road, South Norwood, in the days when he was working as an apprentice engineer and rock'n'roll was just a hobby. After turning to music full time, the band appeared numerous times on television and radio, including 'Off The Record', 'Chelsea At Eight', 'Oh, Boy' 'Saturday Club' and the ITV teenage show 'Wham!'.

That "fabulous Decca recording star" **Garry Mills** made an appearance at the Utopia '61 Club on Friday 8th September. Backed by The Deccades, Garry ran through his hit records 'Look For A Star', 'Top Teen Baby', 'Running Bear', 'Bless You' and his most recent single 'I'll Step Down'. His biggest hit was 'Look For A Star', which reached number 5 in July 1960. The Utopia club was situated at 18 George Street, Croydon and admission for the concert was a mere five shillings.

Garry was back in Croydon in December, on the bill for the Gene Vincent concert at the Civic Hall - by this time though, his backing group were the Cherokees.

(n/a) = ticket price not available.

The Croydon Times ran a regular music column headed 'In the Groove with Dave Carter' which featured record and concert reviews, and interviews with up & coming local stars. Earlier in the year (26th May) he wrote about the 'Success Story' of Norbury's Eden Kane and in September it was the turn of another Croydon youngster...

Croydon Times – 22.9.61

PAUL FINDS IT TOUGH GETTING TO THE TOP

RECORD COMPANIES enjoy making predictions, blowing their own trumpets and banging the publicity drum for the personalities under contract to them. Their claims came true for Eden Kane, currently high in the charts with two hit discs, but the publicists were not so successful in their efforts for another Croydon youngster, ***Paul Raven****.*

After hearing Paul perform in a deserted Soho coffee bar, producer Bob Hartford-Davis confidently announced: "He's the boy I'm looking for - I could make him the singing idol of 1960!".

With the announcement that 100 guineas would go to charity if the claim were not fulfilled, came the singer's first record 'Alone In The Night', a bluesy-type ballad.

Unfortunately for Paul but fortunately for charity, the record hardly got off the ground. During the past 20 months Paul has persisted with his ambition to be a singing star. Besides gaining a lot of experience, he has switched to the Parlophone label for his latest attempt to break into the big time. Though there is an ample amount of beat to satisfy rocking enthusiasts, I cannot however, go overboard for his very ordinary main-side 'Walk On Boy'. As for the flip-over song, 'All Grown Up', one wonders if Paul is being given the right guidance. There is a distinct Presley influence, which in times past might have worked; but today the trend is for all-out originality among the successful British stars.

It takes much more than hard work, Paul, to put your feet firmly into the Top Ten position.

Paul's persistence did eventually pay off, ten years later! - see pages 24-25.

As well as Dave Carter's weekly column, the Times published a Top Ten chart compiled from local record shops - Potter's Music Shop, Record Rendevous of Station Road, West Croydon and Kennards Department Store, North End. Kennards chart was made up of the combined sales of record and sheet music; in September '61, 'Johnny Remember Me' by John Leyton was the Croydon best seller, with the Shadows 'Kon-Tiki' at number 5 and Eden Kane's 'Well I Ask You' in seventh position, on its way down having been a national number one earlier in the year.

Shown below is the inside spread of the programme for the Gene Vincent concert at the Civic Hall. There are a few notable local names involved; on the bill itself were Vern Rogers & the Hi-Fi's, a popular band also booked to play the Stanley Halls that Xmas and Paul Raven, later to achieve worldwide fame after various name changes.
The guest at the Wallington Public Hall is Norbury's own Eden Kane, whilst the support act Pete Lincoln is really Peter Sarstedt, Eden's younger brother. And it is no surprise to see that the Civic Hall concert was organised by Fred Bannister, a local promoter who ran the rock nights at both of the other venues.

Courtesy Mark Mumford

JANUARY

5 KENNY BALL **S** (n/a)

19 MR. ACKER BILK **CH** + ALEXIS KORNER's BLUES INCORPORATED (n/a)

FEBRUARY

8 ADAM FAITH **SG** + JOHN BARRY SEVEN + DESMOND LANE + BRAD NEWMAN + DAVE REID + JOHNNY LE ROY 2 shows (3/6 to 7/6)

10 BOBBY VEE **TG** + THE SPRINGFIELDS + TONY ORLANDO + CLARENCE 'FROGMAN' HENRY (4/6 to 8/6)

27 TEMPERANCE SEVEN **CH** (n/a)

MARCH

4 CLIFF RICHARD & THE SHADOWS **A** + THE DALLAS BOYS + THE TREBLETONES + PATTI BROOKS (6/6 to 10/6)

14 SWIFT-BURNS QUARTET **VH** (3/6)

23 BILLY FURY **SG** + JOHN LEYTON + MARTY WILDE + JOE BROWN + SHANE FENTON + JACKIE LYNTON + THE TORNADOS + RICKIE STEVENS + PETER JAY & THE JAYWALKERS + TONY MELODY 2 shows (3/6 to 7/6)

31 KEN COLYER **CH** (n/a)

APRIL

8 GENE VINCENT **TG** + BRENDA LEE + NERO & THE GLADIATORS + SOUNDS INCORPORATED + RORY BLACKWELL & THE BLACKJACKS + BOB BAIN 2 shows (4/6 to 7/6)

20 CHRIS BARBER **CH** + OTTILIE PATTERSON (n/a)

25 THE CRESTERS **S** (2/6)

MAY

2 GENE VINCENT **SG** + JESS CONRAD + EMILE FORD + THE ALLISONS (4/6 to 8/6)

21 SCREAMIN' LORD SUTCH **SH** (n/a)

25 DAVY KEIR JAZZBAND **CH** (n/a)

JUNE

When Acker Bilk brought his own particular brand of British Trad. jazz to Croydon Civic Hall in January, either he (or his management) bravely gave the support spot to Alexis Korner's **Blues Incorporated**. The headline to the concert review in the local press summed up the audience reaction - "Cheers for Bilk, boos for Blues".

Korner's ground-breaking new group were making their first public appearance and as such, their performance was raw and under-rehearsed; their drummer Colin Bowden later admitted that it would have been wiser to have made their debut in a more intimate setting. But it wasn't their ability that caused the jeers, boos and cat-calls; just the non-comprehension of a trad. jazz crowd brought up on so unappetising a diet as 'Brit.Trad.'

Through his 'In the Groove...' column in the Croydon Times, Dave Carter continued to chart the progress of Norbury's **Eden Kane**. In January, Decca released 'Forget Me Not', in an effort to gain Eden his third successive hit single, but Dave remained unconvinced. He wrote: *"A giant question mark hangs over Tin Pan Alley today: Can Norbury's Eden Kane score a recording hat trick with his latest Decca release? The disc finds our python-loving vocalist* in a romantic mood, exhibiting his talents against an impressive backing created by Johnny Keating and his musicians. Almost completely out of earshot are the 'growling' noises which marked Eden's two previous hit parade winners, 'Well I Ask You' and 'Get Lost'.*

The mature delivery of the lyric, say Decca, comes as a result of his recent sinus operation, but I can remember him singing ballads in this pleasant style when I visited him at his Norbury home long before his brief visit to a London hospital."

Eden had been busy making stage appearances throughout Britain and Europe, deliberately keeping up a high profile which had raised his salary to £1,000 per week, yet Dave Carter worried about the 21 week gap since his previous record was in the charts! *"Fans are fickle and long absences can be extremely dangerous. After all, stars are made, not born"*, he warned.

The new single had been recorded in the studios at St. John's Wood, back in October 1961 along with a batch of eleven other songs. But Dave's worries were unfounded - by the end of January 'Forget Me Not' was a top three hit.

(n/a) = ticket price not available.

* Eden Kane was reported to have owned a pet python named Samantha!

CH - Civic Hall • A - ABC • S - Star Hotel • O - Orchid Ballroom • SG - Sutton Granada • TG - Tooting Granada

Despite making his first appearance in Croydon at the Davis Theatre back in April 1959, **Cliff Richard** had to wait until March 1962 before headlining his own concert at the ABC Cinema, Broad Green.

By this time, Cliff was backed by The Shadows and was riding high on a string of hits, the latest of which was 'The Young Ones' having just been released in January.

As a schoolboy in the Forties, Cliff actually lived locally for a short while. Born in India, his family decided to move back to England in 1947 and the seven year old Harry Webb spent his first eighteen months in this country living at his grandmothers house in Carshalton. Once here, Harry was enrolled at Stanley Park Road Primary School where unbelievably, he became the target of playground racial abuse! His skin was still darkly tanned from the hot Indian sun and his accent had picked up some of the inflections from that part of the world. By the time this nastiness stopped, when his skin had paled and his voice adopted a South London accent, the family moved once again, to Waltham Cross in Middlesex.

Croydon Times – 18.5.62

'LOCAL BAND MAKE DEBUT'

A CROYDON TRAD. jazz band are to make their first professional appearance at the Civic Hall later this month - on the same bill as Acker Bilk.

Leader is ***Davy Keir*** *of Altyre Road, East Croydon, who has made many appearances as a professional musician - with such name jazzbands as Mick Mulligan, Joe Daniels, Sid Phillips, Freddy Randall, Dick Charlesworth and Ken Colyer.*

Davy Keir, a Scot who has lived in Croydon for seven years, plays trumpet, clarinet, alto-sax and trombone. He had his own band in Scotland, called the Nova Scotia Jazzband and the group included musician Alex Walsh. He has taken part in many recording sessions with well-known bands and appeared in concerts in Moscow.

His new group has been signed by the Lyn Dutton Agency, is managed by David Bilk and sponsored by Davids famous brother. The Davy Keir Jazzband play traditional music; says Davy: "We hope to avoid cheap gimmicks and build our success on good music, well presented and with lots of variety".

The group also includes another Croydon man - Colin Miller on drums. Colin, who was educated at John Ruskin grammar school, lives in Rymer Road, East Croydon. The other members are Cyril Keepper, clarinet; Jim Shepherd, trombone; Dennis Tonge, banjo; Graham Beazley, bass; and Brian Leake, piano.

ABC CROYDON ON THE STAGE Phone 0486

SUNDAY, 4th MARCH, at 5.15 p.m. and 7.45 p.m.

FABULOUS

CLIFF RICHARD

AND

THE SHADOWS.

THE DALLAS BOYS AND GREAT SUPPORTING COMPANY

ALL SEATS BOOKABLE — 6/6 · 8/6 · 10/6

ADVANCE BOOKING OFFICE OPENS TOMORROW, 3rd FEB., 10.30 a.m.

THEREAFTER WEEKDAYS 10.30 a.m. to 8 p.m.

If you were a pupil at Selhurst Grammar School circa '62, you may remember **Glenn Athens & the Trojans** playing at the end of term dance. Ex-pupil John Failes recalls that the group were formed by Phil Saunders, one of his contemporarys, and that they played *'Cliff & the Shadows-style music'* at local school dances, including Coloma Convent. Other schoolfriends may wish that they had safely kept their copies of the Groups EP - simply titled 'Glenn Athens & the Trojans' Spot 7E1018, it is currently valued at £300 - even allowing for some slight overpricing, it remains quite an investment!

John also remembers other Selhurst pupils who went on to be recording artists; Matthew Fisher, who *'even at a very young age was a brilliant pianist'*, went on to join **Procol Harum** and play keyboards on their No.1 single 'A Whiter Shade of Pale', and Viv Lythgoe, who formed a duo called **Cuppa T**. This pair recorded two singles on the Deram label, 'Miss Pinkerton/Brand New World' Deram DM144 and the locally-titled 'Streatham Hippodrome /One Man Band' Deram DM185.

The following gig review of Screaming Lord Sutch gives a good feel for the unusual stage act that he was perfecting as early as May '62. Under the guidance of local promoter Fred Bannister, Sutch appeared several times at the Stanley Halls and Wallington Public Hall over the next two years; although he never made a huge impact on the record buying public, his backing group **The Savages** proved to be an important launch pad for a large number of rock musicians. The group line-up circa May '62 was Carlo Little - drums; Ricky Brown - bass; Bernie Watson - guitar; Nicky Hopkins - piano, although May was also the month that Watson was replaced on guitar by Ritchie Blackmore.

By the end of the year, Hopkins, Watson, Brown and Little were all members of the Cyril Davies R&B All Stars, while Blackmore had joined the Outlaws. Sutch recruited Freddy 'Fingers' Lee on piano and a later line-up (called The Roman Empire) had Matthew Fisher on organ.

Croydon Times – 25.5.62

'ROCK 'N' ROLLER MAKES NORWOOD FANS SCREAM'

THE ROCK'N'ROLLER who claims he can scream louder than his fans, made the teenagers of South Norwood shriek with terror when he came to the Stanley Halls on Monday. Girls rushed for the exits and even some of the boys had horror-stricken looks on their faces, as ***Screaming Lord Sutch & his Savages*** *performed what has been described as 'the world's most ghoulish rock 'n' roll act'.*

Stanley Halls were jammed tight with crowds of youngsters all anxious to see the 'Screaming Lord'. After the Savages had rocked through a few frenzied numbers recorded by Jerry Lee Lewis and Chuck Berry, the curtains at the back of the stage were slowly drawn aside to reveal a black coffin with a small skull on the lid.

All was black, except for an eerie green spotlight focused on the coffin. Suddenly a blood-curdling scream came from inside the coffin and a white hand clawed its way out. Then,with another shriek the 'Screaming Lord' emerged dressed in a purple silk suit over which he wore a black cape lined with green. He had a black patch over one eye and his 18 inch hair hung down his back. With a fiendish expression on his face, he seized a large axe and hurled himself into a terrified audience, who scattered as best they could.

Earlier in a long interview with our reporter, his Lordship observed: "I've got it all worked out. Horror films are the biggest draw in the cinema these days, so I give my fans horror live - on stage".

The Screaming Lord - real name David Sutch - said that he was a plumber's mate and once worked in a tennis ball factory, until he found where his talents lay. His various guises include leopard skin and buffalo horns ("I've got four pairs of horns because people take them for souvenirs") and a King Kong outfit for when he charges out of a cage. Lord Sutch said: "I would like to become a national figure. My two ambitions in life are to make a horror film and to do a personal tour of Russia".

So far he has only had one record released, 'Til The Following Night' - a macabre number set in a graveyard. On the reverse is a pounding revival of Little Richard, 'Good Golly Miss Molly'. Sutch is pleased that sales of the disc have so far exceeded his expectations and told the 'Times' that another of his recordings 'Jack the Ripper' would be released in three weeks. Sutch is backed by Bannister Promotions and Mr. Frederick Bannister told us: "My only regret is that up to this moment I have been unable to get him on television".

JULY

5 DAVY KEIR JAZZBAND **S** (n/a)

AUGUST

13 THE FALCONS **A** (n/a)

20 BOB DAVENPORT & THE RAKES **WT** (n/a)

20 THE EAGLES **A** (n/a)

SEPTEMBER

29 DION & THE BELMONTS **TG** + DEL SHANNON + JOE BROWN & THE BRUVVERS + BUZZ CLIFFORD + THE ALLISONS + SUZY COPE + PEPPI & THE NEW YORK TWISTERS + WALLACE & DUVAL (4/6 to 8/6)

OCTOBER

11 SARAH VAUGHN **SG** + GEORGE SHEARING (6/- to 15/-)

23 THE EVERLY BROTHERS **A** + FRANK IFIELD + KETTY LESTER + THE VERNON GIRLS + THE TERRY YOUNG FIVE + DEAN ROGERS (6/6 to 10/6)

27 LITTLE RICHARD **TG** + JET HARRIS & THE JETBLACKS + SAM COOKE + SOUNDS INCORPORATED + THE BREAKAWAYS (5/- to 10/6)

NOVEMBER

9 MR ACKER BILK **FH** + DAVY KEIR JAZZBAND (5/- to 10/6)

10 HELEN SHAPIRO **SG** + EDEN KANE + THE KESTRELS (4/6 to 8/6)

16 BEE BUMBLE & THE STINGERS **FH** + BERT WEEDON + JOHNNY KIDD & THE PIRATES + TOMMY BRUCE + MICHAEL COX + THE ECHOES + VINCE EAGER (5/- to 20/-)

18 DICK CHARLESWORTH & HIS CITY GENTS **FH** + DIZ DISLEY + CYRIL PRESTON (3/6 to 7/6)

19 DAVE BRUBECK **FH** + RONNIE SCOTT QUARTET (6/6 to 15/-)

20 BILLY FURY **A** + MARTY WILDE + JOE BROWN & THE BRUVVERS + JIMMY JUSTICE + MARK WYNTER + MIKE SARNE + KARL DENVER TRIO + PETER JAY & THE JAYWALKERS (6/6 to 10/6)

24 BOBBY VEE **TG** + THE CRICKETS + RONNIE CARROLL + JOHNNY DE LITTLE (4/6 to 8/6)

24 THE BLUE COMBO's **K** (2/6)

DECEMBER

8 THE DELTONES **K** (2/6)

10 KENNY BALL **FH** + MIKE DANIELS DELTA JAZZMEN (3/6 to 8/6)

11 HELEN SHAPIRO **FH** + EDEN KANE + THE KESTRELS + THE VERNONS GIRLS + ARTHUR WORSLEY + RHET STOLLER & THE DYNAMICS + RED PRICE & HIS ORCHESTRA + BOBBY DENNIS (5/6 to 8/6)

17 CHRIS BARBER **FH** + LOUIS JORDAN + OTTILIE PATTERSON (3/6 to 8/6)

(n/a) = ticket price not available.

It was "A tremendous success"... that was the verdict on the Rock & Twist Festival held at Addington Community Centre on October 20th by the New Addington Red Cross. Six rock groups, mainly local bands, took part in the competition while the crowd of 160 competitors showed off the latest dance crazes - The Madison, The Twist and the Locomotion. During the intervals, music was supplied by the resident group **The Partners** with vocalist Ray Purkiss.

The competing groups were **The Astronauts**, **The Alpines**, **The Deputies**, **The Emeralds**, **The Firebugs** and **The Vampires** (who wore grotesque devil-like masks and black capes). Judged by volume of applause, Acton group The Firebugs won the first prize of £5 followed by The Emeralds (£3) and The Deputies (£2). There were also cash prizes for the best dancing couples.

Under the heading "New Name, But Same Swinging Pop Talent", the Croydon Times announced that **Martin Jae & the Hi-Five** were changing their name to the **MJ5**; their first gig using the new name was a charity show in October for the Spastics Society at the Lantern Hall in Sydenham Road. The group of Martin Jae, vocals; Johnny Stevens on bass; Bob Gamble, rhythm guitar; Mick Hack, lead guitar and Earle Morgan on drums were playing four or five nights a week, plus every weekend at regular gigs in Redhill and at Addington Community Centre. In addition they had just been offered a Friday night residency with the Teen & Twenty Club at the Star, Broad Green.

The band had played support to Johnny Kidd & the Pirates, Lance Fortune, Joe Brown & his Bruvvers and most recently Freddy Cannon at Wallington Public Hall. They also got the job of backing Susan Singer, Helen Shapiro's cousin, when she appeared at Redhill.

A little bit of 'rock-package rivalry' was going on between the ABC and Granada cinema chains. In September, the Tooting Granada kicked off with Dion, Del Shannon and Joe Brown. The ABC Croydon countered with the Everly Brothers and Frank Ifield on October 23 and four days later, Tooting hit back with Little Richard and former 'Shadow', Jet Harris. The ABC put on an all-British bill of Billy Fury, Marty Wilde and Joe Brown, while Tooting favoured America with Bobby Vee and the Crickets.

Around October '62, the Rolling Stones were having problems finding a regular drummer. They were forced to find people who could 'sit-in', for almost every individual booking; Mick Avory, who went on to join the Kinks, Carlo Little, who worked with Cyril Davies and Screaming Lord Sutch and Charlie Watts, who played part time with Blues Incorporated. Although Watts was the man they wanted, he was unable to join permanently at that time and the Stones settled for a young drummer called Tony Chapman.

Originally from Liverpool, Chapman had been playing with the Beckenham-based, semi-professional group the **Cliftons**, which also featured bassist Bill Perks (Wyman).

In December, the Stones original bass guitarist Dick Taylor left to start a course at the Royal College of Art (Taylor later joined the Pretty Things), and Tony Chapman was asked whether he knew any bass players who needed a regular gig. Chapman suggested Bill Wyman and an audition was arranged at the Wetherby Arms in Chelsea. Despite being seven years older and more used to playing stage shows backing Dickie Pride, Wyman had the advantage of possessing two enormous Vox amplifiers - this fact alone almost guaranteed instant membership into the group!

Not long afterwards, the Stones decided to try again to secure Charlie Watts as their drummer and once Charlie was in, Tony Chapman was out, fired in early January 1963 after a gig at the Ricky Tick Club in Windsor. Chapman's day job as a commercial traveller meant that he was often out of the area and as such, only semi-reliable. When he left, he asked his friend Bill to leave with him and start their own group, but Wyman declined.

Chapman had played with Croydon group the **Strangers**, later to become the **Preachers**, who were regular performers around the area and particularly popular at the Market Hall in Redhill. Tony Chapman said: *"When I left the Stones, I formed the original Preachers with Steve Carroll. Just before Steve was killed, we changed the name to the Herd, and then Andy Bown joined. Then we got another guitar player called Taylor. Then Billy Gaff got involved and eased me out.* (Gaff became the Herd's manager, and went on to greater success managing Rod Stewart.) *Later, I formed the second Preachers with Peter Frampton".*

Locally, the early Stones played the Red Lion in Sutton High Street several times; the first in November '62 without either Wyman or Watts and again in December, but by this time Bill had joined. For further information, see the 'family tree' on pages 98-99.

In August, Croydon's ABC Cinema screened the new film 'Play It Cool', starring Billy Fury and Anna Palk and to help promote it they staged a 'Twisting' contest on Friday 10th - the final night of its week-long run. Twisters were backed by East Croydon group the **Falcons**, who had played live before each screening of the dance-craze film on Tuesday, Wednesday and Thursday evenings and prizes included a copy of every record featured in 'Play It Cool'.

Croydon Times – 26.10.62

'Big success for the Everly Brother(s)'

*The story of the **Everly Brothers** over past weeks has not been a happy one. They have been the subject of a great deal of comment in the national press, ever since elder brother Don was rushed to hospital twice - and subsequently flown back to America - after reported food poisoning.*

Younger brother Phil decided to undertake a heavy tour of Britain without Don... and on Tuesday night he arrived at the ABC Croydon.

But all was not well, although his performance on stage was to be congratulated, he was not feeling up to standard, for over the past week or so he has been suffering from an attack of flu and a stomach cold. However his illness was not apparent whilst he was on stage - and considering the worries he has had during his current visit to Britain he did remarkably well.

It must also be remembered that Phil is not used to singing the straight version of a song - he is the brother who harmonises and taking this into account, he kept very well in tune throughout his performance. He opened his repertoire with 'Walk Right Back', which he followed with 'So Sad'. He duetted with a member of his backing group The Everly Trio, to sing 'Let's Twist Again' and closed his act with one of the Everly's biggest hits 'Bye Bye Love'.

With Everly on the bill was Ketty Lester, who got off to a bad start, but soon put this right, particularly with a Negro spiritual 'Fare Thee Well'. Her vocal abilities were also displayed during her version of Gershwin's 'Porgy, I Is Your Woman Now'.

Also popular was Frank Ifield, complete with background harmonica. His appearance brought the first screams of the evening, when he opened with 'Alone Too Long' and later sang his latest release 'Lovesick Blues'. He sang the flipside 'She Taught Me How To Yodel' as an encore.

But I still present my phantom bouquet to Phil Everly, who although under obvious strain, refuses to go back home before completing his British tour.

The major event of the year, and one that would have an enormous impact on Croydon's cultural status, was the opening of the **Fairfield Halls** in Park Lane. "Croydon Corporation's luxurious new entertainment & social centre" was officially opened by her Majesty Queen Elizabeth, the Queen Mother on Friday 2nd November before the inaugural concert by the BBC Symphony Orchestra. Conducted by Sir Malcolm Sargeant, with soloist Yehudi Menuhin, the show was sold out well over a month in advance. The concert was broadcast live by the BBC Home Service and presenter Robert Gunnell described the new centre as "one of Greater London's most dramatic developments in many years". The Fairfield's general manager Tom Pyper, was quoted as saying that the Fairfield...

"was not built for 1962,
but for 1992 and 2002".

The first popular music performance at the new complex was a jazz concert by **Mr Acker Bilk** on 9th November, but local rock'n'roll fans had to wait until the 16th for their turn. In a concert organised by Sanderstead comedian Derek Roy, the headliners were **Bee Bumble & the Stingers**, a group of University graduates from America, riding high on their hit single 'Nut Rocker'. Also playing were Bert Weedon, Johnny Kidd & the Pirates, Tommy Bruce and Vince Eager.

The Ashcroft Theatre began it's first run on 5th November with a new play called 'Royal Gambit' starring husband and wife team Michael Denison and Dulcie Gray; whilst the following night saw the first Dale Martin promotion of International Wrestling in the main hall, a regular event that was to become something of a tradition at the Fairfield.

They say that as one door closes another one opens, and much the same can be said about live music venues! With the Fairfield up and running, yet another old Croydon venue bit the dust towards the end of December, when the Civic Hall in Crown Hill was finally demolished.

Art colleges right across the country have long been recognised as a creative melting pot for aspiring writers and musicians, as well as for the occasional artist! In late '62, a certain **Ray Davies** left the art college at Hornsey to begin a course at Croydon College of Art, where he received a £200 grant from the local authorities but according to his mother, never spent a penny of it! Ray left Croydon towards the end of 1963, to pursue a more lucrative musical sideline with his brother Dave - by forming The Kinks.

By August 1964, Ray's 'You Really Got Me' entered the charts and headed straight for number one.

JANUARY

- 9 ROLLING STONES **RL** (n/a)
- 23 ROLLING STONES **RL** (n/a)
- 25 DUKE ELLINGTON **FH** (7/6 to 17/6)
- 27 JOHNNY & THE HURRICANES **TG** (4/6 to 8/6)

FEBRUARY

- 6 ROLLING STONES **RL** (n/a)
- 20 ROLLING STONES **RL** (n/a)
- 22 ACKER BILK **FH** + THE DAUPHIN STREET SIX (3/6 to 8/6)

MARCH

- 6 CLIFF RICHARD & THE SHADOWS **A** + THE VERNONS GIRLS + PATSY ANN NOBLE + THE TREBLETONES (7/6 to 12/6)
- 6 ROLLING STONES **RL** (n/a)
- 9 KEN COLYER **S** (n/a)
- 20 ROLLING STONES **RL** (n/a)
- 21 CHRIS MONTEZ & TOMMY ROE **A** + THE VISCOUNTS + THE BEATLES + DEBBIE LEE + TONY MARSH + THE TERRY YOUNG SIX (5/6 to 8/6)
- 23 BOB WALLIS STOREYVILLE JAZZMEN **S** (n/a)

APRIL

- 3 ROLLING STONES **RL** (n/a)
- 6 MONTY SUNSHINE **S** (n/a)
- 13 SHIRLEY BASSEY **FH** + MATT MONRO (6/6 to 14/-)
- 20 KEN COLYER **S** (n/a)
- 21 GERRY MULLIGAN QUARTET **FH** + JOHNNY DANKWORTH ORCHESTRA (6/6 to 15/-)
- 22 BILLY FURY **A** + THE TORNADOS + MIKE PRESTON + DICKIE PRIDE + THE ECHOES (5/6 to 8/6)
- 25 JOHN LEYTON + THE BEATLES **FH** + GERRY & THE PACEMAKERS + THE BIG THREE + BILLY J. KRAMER & THE DAKOTAS (3/6 to 8/6)

MAY

- 4 ARTISAN JAZZBAND **S** (n/a)
- 4 DEL SHANNON **TG** + JOHNNY TILLOTSON + THE SPRINGFIELDS + THE EAGLES + KENNY LYNCH (5/- to 9/6)
- 4 THE PARTNERS **K** (2/6)
- 9 JERRY LEE LEWIS **FH** + GENE VINCENT + HEINZ + THE OUTLAWS (6/6 to 10/6)
- 17 KENNY BALL **FH** + CYRIL DAVIES ALLSTARS (3/6 to 8/6)
- 18 UNIT SIX **K** (2/6)
- 21 JULIE GRANT **W** (3/6)
- 25 THE QUIET FIVE **K** (2/6)
- 28 JERRY LEE LEWIS **W** + THE OUTLAWS + TOMMY BRUCE & THE BRUISERS + THE ALPHABEATS (6/6)

JUNE

- 1 THE QUIET FIVE **SPH** + PAUL DAYTON & THE DEPUTIES (4/6)
- 7 ACKER BILK **FH** + THE DAUPHIN STREET SIX (3/6 to 8/6)
- 8 PETER DELL & THE DELTONES **SPH** + PAUL DAYTON & THE DEPUTIES (2/6)
- 8 THE DEPUTIES **K** (2/6)

(n/a) = ticket price not available.

This year saw the three Croydon appearances by the **Beatles** and in retrospect, it would be easy to imagine these concerts as being among the highlights of the year. In fact, the band were still in their infancy, having just released their first two singles and barely warranting a mention from the somewhat biased reviewers in the Croydon Advertiser!

On their first visit, March 21st at the ABC Cinema, the Fab Four were well down a bill that was headed by two American singers, the *'Exiting'* Chris Montez and the *'Fabulous'* Tommy Roe. By April 25th, they were back as part of 'The Mersey Beat Showcase', this time at the Fairfield, along with fellow scousers Gerry and the Pacemakers, The Big Three, Billy J. Kramer and the Dakotas and Vic Sutcliffe. John Leyton, who was joint top of the bill for this tour, could not appear at Croydon.

The Advertiser sent along reviewer W.I. (in those days their writers had the protection of just initials at the foot of their review) - you'll see why, as they opened the third paragraph with this little gem;

"Either you like beat, or you don't. I don't. But then, I don't really care who is in the Top Ten because I do not want to pour money week by week into the drain-like coffers of the pop record industry." He or she continued; *"Last weeks show was not entertainment, unless you are entertained by one helluva din, and the band clapping and foot stomping of hysterically screaming youngsters."*

Phew! Had they printed the journo's full name the *"rampant teenage mob"* would have buried him up to his neck in jelly babies.

It was fairly common practice for the cinema chains to give local groups a chance to perform prior to showing the main feature film. The Croydon ABC booked **Chas Dean & the Castaways** for a week, to be on stage 8pm sharp Monday to Friday. The group consisted of Mick Genno - lead guitar, Brian Curtis - rhythm guitar, Bob Larson - bass and Roger Harman on drums.

Thornton Heath was a hotbed of live music in early '63 - a jazz club was held every Wednesday at the Prince of Wales, Parchmore Road - the resident band being the **Brian Thompson Jazzmen** and thriving folk clubs at both the Fountain Head, Parchmore Road and the Wheatsheaf, Thornton Heath Pond.

Croydon Times – 17.5.63

'ROCK STAR LEWIS SENDS THEM WILD'

JERRY LEE LEWIS (Fairfield Halls)

Riots broke out at the end of the ***Jerry Lee Lewis*** *rock n' roll show at the Fairfield Halls last week. The packed house refused to leave the hall after the second show on Thursday had finished shortly after 11p.m. They surged forward trying to break through the long line of attendants in front of the stage. At one point more than 50 youngsters were on stage, and over 1,000 packed solid were pressing forward...*

Scuffles broke out while the crowd chanted wildly: "We want Jerry, we want Jerry". Despite the fact that the house lights went on, very few people left the hall and those who were not in the crush at the front of the stage remained in their places, frantically waving their arms and banging their seats. Eventually Jerry Lee Lewis appeared once again, bounded to the piano and gave as his final encore a frenzied rendering of "Good Golly Miss Molly". The number ended with Jerry Lee standing on top of the piano with the microphone.

Youths surged round the piano, and jumped down from the back of the stage. An attendant was struck, and three people were thrown headlong from the stage.

...eventually Don Arden, the show's promoter, walked over to a microphone and tried to address the crowd. "I would like Jerry to sing all night", he shouted, to which there was a loud cheering. "But this is just not possible. I'm sorry" (boos). He added: "I will try to negotiate for Jerry to visit the halls again". At this there was another burst of cheering. Don Arden then asked the audience to leave "as quietly and peacefully as possible".

...after the show, Mr. Tom Pyper, general manager, told The Times: "There is no question of banning future rock 'n' roll shows. What happened at the Jerry Lee Lewis show was simply youthful enthusiasm. Our attendants kept their position. Although there was some pushing around, we had the matter under control. No one was hurt and there was never any question of calling the police. We gave the hall a complete check-up the following morning and there was no damage done; our seats are designed to stand a lot of tough wear"!

...one person who witnessed the performance was Coun. A G Weller, J.P., and he was overheard to remark after the show: "It is certainly an education".

WALLINGTON ROCK SESSIONS
STAFFORD ROAD

WE PROUDLY PRESENT
A BIG BEAT FESTIVAL
Tuesday 28th May
STARRING
The World's Greatest Rock Artist
JERRY LEE LEWIS
PLUS
TOMMY BRUCE
AND THE
BRUISERS
THE OUTLAWS
Plus the ALPHA BEATS
ADMISSION ONLY 6/6

PLEASE NOTE - JERRY LEE LEWIS and the OUTLAWS will appear between 8.15—9.15 p.m.
So come early
Doors open 6.45 p.m. Non-Stop Show 7.00-11p.m.

JIVE OR LISTEN

Courtesy of Keith Temple

Not long after his 'wild' Fairfield show, Jerry Lee returned to play Wallington Public Hall. Preachers bassist Keith Temple was playing with the AlphaBeats on this bill.

The early part of '63 saw the first record release by 21 year-old local singer **Vern Rogers**, 'Be Everything' on Oriole Records. Vern, (real name Roger Newell) of Headley Avenue, Wallington was a former Purley Grammar school student who had been performing in local dance halls for five years with his group **The Hi-Fi's**.

After one nationwide tour, his manager decided he was ready to make a record and a demo disc was sent to EMI. At the same time the smaller, independent record label Oriole asked Vern to audition - and he signed a contract the next day. That was in the summer of '62, Oriole boss John Schroeder waiting for the right song to come along before Vern could record his first single. 'Be Everything' is an American song arranged by Frank Barber, a mid tempo number with Vern trying to sound at his heartbreaking best, plus plenty of echo on the chorus, at that time considered essential for a Top Ten record!

The B-side sounds remarkably like Eden Kane, his big Croydon rival, although Vern denied that he had consciously copied Eden's style, *"I was only given the song three days before I recorded it"*, he said.

When legendary producer Joe Meek took on the job of personal manager to **Heinz**, he found that a promotor had booked him on the Jerry Lee Lewis/Gene Vincent tour. This turned out to be ill-advised; Heinz was not yet prepared for this new role as solo star outside of playing bass for the Tornados, and to make matters worse, the audiences were predominantly male and leather jacketed, while Meek was grooming Heinz to be a lady-killing pop star.

Meek even persuaded the Outlaws to back him on the tour, a group which at the time contained Ritchie Blackmore on guitar and Chas Hodges on bass. Despite having a decent band behind him, at the concerts in Bristol, Birmingham and Croydon, the 'Teds' were after his blood - Meek himself attended the gig at the Fairfield Halls and watched as the first few rows of the front stalls stood up and turned their backs on Heinz for his entire act!

Despite his disappointment at the treatment of his protégé, Meek waited in the wings when Heinz left the stage and pushed him back out to take an encore.

JULY

6 KEN COLYER **S** (n/a)

23 SOUNDS INCORPORATED **W** + PETER DELL & THE DELTONES (n/a)

AUGUST

13 THE SEARCHERS **W** (n/a)

SEPTEMBER

3 CYRIL STAPLETON & HIS ORCHESTRA **O** (n/a)

7 THE BEATLES **FH** + MIKE BERRY & THE INNOCENTS + PAT DANE & THE QUIET FIVE (n/a)

18 COUNT BASIE **FH** + SARAH VAUGHAN (6/- to 20/-)

OCTOBER

4 BILLY FURY **A** + JOE BROWN & HIS BRUVVERS + MARTY WILDE + THE TORNADOS + DARYL QUIST + KARL DENVER TRIO + DICKY PRIDE + RAMBLERS (6/6 to 10/6)

11 FREDDIE & THE DREAMERS **FH** + TOMMY ROE + THE SEARCHERS (00)

18 MUDDY WATERS **FH** + LONNIE JOHNSON + SONNY BOY WILLIAMSON + BIG JOE WILLIAMS + WILLIE DIXON + MEMPHIS SLIM + OTIS SPANN (6/- to 21/-)

23 CYRIL DAVIES **S** (n/a)

30 GERRY & THE PACEMAKERS **A** + DEL SHANNON + JET HARRIS & TONY MEHAN + CILLA BLACK + DUFFY POWER + THE BACHELORS + THE BLUE DIAMONDS + BRYAN BURDON (6/6 to 10/6)

NOVEMBER

1 SHIRLEY COLLINS **AL** (n/a)

2 ERROL GARNER **FH** (6/- to 20/-)

2 THE YARDBIRDS **S** (n/a)

6 JOHN LEYTON **FH** + HEINZ & THE SAINTS + JOHNNY KIDD & THE PIRATES + DEE DEE SHARP + THE SUNDOWNERS 2 shows (3/6 to 8/6)

9 THE YARDBIRDS **S** (n/a)

14 'SOUNDS LIKE ACTION' **FH** + HEINZ & THE SAINTS + PAT DANE & THE QUIET FIVE (6/6 to 10/6)

15 BOBBY RYDELL + HELEN SHAPIRO **A** + THE SPOTNIKS + THE CHANTS + BERT WEEDON (6/6 to 10/6)

16 THE YARDBIRDS **S** (n/a)

21 DUANE EDDY **FH** + GENE VINCENT + THE SHIRELLES + CARTER LEWIS & THE SOUTHERNERS + THE FLINTSTONES + MICKIE MOST (5/- to 10/6)

23 THE YARDBIRDS **S** (n/a)

25 STAN KENTON **FH** 2 shows (6/- to 17/6)

30 THE YARDBIRDS **S** (n/a)

DECEMBER

6 CHRIS BARBER's JAZZBAND **FH** with SONNY BOY WILLIAMSON (3/6 to 7/6)

7 THE ROLLING STONES **FH** + GERRY & THE PACEMAKERS + THE OVERLANDERS + THE CHECKMATES + PETER McLAINE & THE CLAN + PAT DANE & THE QUIET FIVE (5/- to 10/6)

7 THE YARDBIRDS **S** (n/a)

14 THE YARDBIRDS **S** (n/a)

21 THE ANIMALS **S** (n/a)

22 THE YARDBIRDS **S** (n/a)

28 THE YARDBIRDS **S** (n/a)

(n/a) = ticket price not available.

The 7th September was an eventful day in the life of the **Beatles** and their fans. Their fourth single, *'She Loves You'* reached number one in the Melody Maker chart, a position it was to maintain for seven weeks. They made a television appearance that evening, on ATV's *'Big Night Out'*, and performed live on stage in the Fairfield Hall.

In fact, their appearance at the Fairfield Halls caused such 'hysteria', it was rumoured that pop concerts there would be banned. The Croydon Times ran an article headed:

TEENAGERS GO WILD, BUT 'POP' CONCERTS ARE TO CONTINUE

in which various incidents were reported to the police. The Beatles played to two packed houses and during the first, three girls required medical treatment, one suffered injury to the soles of her feet from 'continual stamping'! A line of stewards stretched across the front of the stage to prevent the girls from reaching their idols, and then had the impossible job of clearing the hall before the second house took their seats.

A reporter for the Croydon Times said - *"From my seat in the fourth row of the stalls I had extreme difficulty in hearing the performers and I was constantly deafened by a group of girls who let out ear-piercing shrieks. Two rows of seats (mine being one of them) were tipped over and I received a blow on the forehead when I was ejected from my seat. Girls were dancing in their seats, half sitting, half standing and those at the rear could see very little".*

Police were called to the rear of the Fairfield late on the Saturday night, when a crowd of 500 teenagers pushed open the tall iron gates at the entrance to the artist's car park and tried to storm the stage door. Stewards managed to stop them in time, but at 11.15pm, half an hour after the end of the second show, there were still hundreds of fans milling about outside.

In a letter to the local paper, a local resident wrote: *"The long periods of female screaming outside the Fairfield were an experience I failed to understand being allowed - they were a blatant public nuisance. I could not understand why the girls so wished to indulge in such hysteria. Can public disturbances on such as scale be justified and condoned, or must I accept them as a typical expression of musical appreciation emanating from our new Croydon centre of culture?".*

The general manager of the Fairfield, Mr Pyper, was away on holiday at the time, but a management spokesman was quoted as saying *"There is no question of banning future shows here. They are very popular and we like to give the people what they want".*

In the same issue of the paper, this is how the whole show was reported:

Croydon Advertiser – 13.9.63

'HOW TO TOP THE POPS'

FOR A BEAT GROUP to reach No. 1 position in the British pop record charts for the third time in the face of fierce competition from Cliff Richard, Billy Fury and Elvis Presley, it requires, among other things, outstanding material, an original approach and plenty of personality. ***The Beatles*** *have these things and more.*

During their two shows at the Fairfield Halls on Saturday, they demonstrated why they have shot to the top at such a rapid pace. They were self assured, smart in appearance and gave the customers what they wanted - although what this is precisely, poses rather a doubtful question.

It has been said somewhere that "The quality of Mersey is not strained." On Saturday it was very severely strained - the Noise Abatement Society would have had a hey-day!

Continuous high pitched screaming throughout the group's entire act from a capacity audience, composed mainly of teenage girls, prevented any attempt at a critical assessment of the Beatles' performance.

During their 15-minute appearance on stage, the numbers they played included, I believe, "Please Please Me", "From Me to You", a frenetic "Twist & Shout" and their current success, "She Loves You".

My sympathies went out to a bewildered compere, Ted King, who ought to be paid danger money, and to the harassed hall stewards, who looked as unbelieving as Mr. MacMillan probably would at a Trades Union Congress.

The first half of the programme opened with a likable group from Australia, ***Ian Crawford & the Boomerangs****, who sang everybody else's hits and one of their own, "Everlovin' Me".* ***Mike Berry & the Innocents*** *scored with a near-ballad, "Eighteen Yellow Roses" - "It's a bit square, but we hope you'll like it" - in an otherwise undistinguished appearance.*

Local interest was somewhat surprisingly provided by five Old Whitgiftians, ***the Quiet Five****, led by Patrick Dane, of Hillsmead Way, Sanderstead. A good-looking group, (or was that sun tan lotion?), they played a lively version of "Jezabel" to open, but did not produce a very convincing or original sound to match their polished stage technique. This is where the Beatles score every time.*

J.H.

In October the Beckenham & Penge Advertiser reported the success of West Wickham's first festival of pop music, titled **'Wickham Goes Pop!'**. The organiser was David Meyer who formed Wickham Enterprises for the specific purpose of staging shows for pop groups and fans in that area. Held at Wickham Hall, all seats were sold out four weeks in advance and Meyer planned a repeat show at the Assembly Hall in November, plus other dances at Shirley Parish Hall and the Justin Hall, West Wickham.

Seven local groups played for just under four hours at Wickham Goes Pop, including two Beckenham youngsters who were destined for much bigger things; **The Tru-Beats** boasted the fourteen year-old Peter Frampton on guitar, while **The Konrads** featured young David Jones on sax, later to change his name to Bowie.

The headline act were **The Rebounds**, the only professional group on the show, who backed Croydon vocalist Vern Rogers. Wickham group **The Psykons**, led by Robin Hill were given a terrific reception, as were **Del & the Panthers** with lead singer Derek Weatherley. Youngest group on the bill were **The Constrees**, made up of scouts from the 45th Beckenham Troop, but unfortunately The Burnettes, who were all members of Wickham Park Sports club had to stand down. Their singer Pip Blakemore did appear, however, having put together another band at very short notice.

The compere of the show was Brian Showell, who is still involved in the local music scene, as manager of Showell's record shop in West Wickham. He remembers being impressed by the Tru-Beats, and particularly by Frampton, who played cover versions of various instrumental hits by the Shadows.

It was something of an anniversary for the Konrads who were formed almost exactly one year before, when they made their debut at Shirley Parish Hall; and quite a successful first year for the group, too - Alan Dodds from Shirley, David Hadfield and Neville Wills from Orpington, Rocky Shahan and David Jones from Bromley - who had supported many top bands, including a joint billing with Johnny Kidd & the Pirates, and built up a 'fan club' of over two hundred!

Jacqueline Ryan

On Wednesday 23rd October, the newly redecorated Star Hotel launched a regular midweek Rhythm & Blues session with a performance by the **Cyril Davies Group**. The group consisted of two guitars, piano, drums and Cyril on harmonica, with Long John Baldry on 'earthy' vocals. The Croydon Advertiser reported that rhythm & blues had become popular in Britain thanks mainly to the work of Muddy Waters and only a few days beforehand, the American Negro Blues Festival had played its only British date at Croydon, following a successful tour of Europe.

The line-up for this concert should have blues enthusiasts drooling; the 74 year old **Lonnie Johnson**; **Memphis Slim**; **Willie Dixon**; **Michael Murphy**; the youngest member of the tour **Otis Spann**; harmonica wizard **Sonny Boy Williamson**; **Big Joe Williams** and **Muddy Waters**.

Liverpool born singing star **Michael Holliday** died in Croydon General Hospital on 29th October aged 38, having been found unconscious from a drug overdose at his home in Bishop's Walk, Addington, where he had lived for over six years. The inquest's verdict was suicide; in a letter to his wife, Holliday indicated that he was going to kill himself because of tax problems.

During the 'fifties he was a hugely successful ballad singer very much in the style of Bing Crosby, his top selling records including 'The Story Of My Life', but the emergence of beat groups pushed his style of music further into the background.

Yet another new folk club opened at the Alhambra public house on November 1st, featuring **Shirley Collins** and the **Folkvendors**. As with many old Croydon pubs, the Alhambra is sadly no longer standing, but was situated on the Wellesley Road, near the bus terminus.

In his autobiography 'Stone Alone', Rolling Stones bassist Bill Wyman remembers: *It was quite a typical day (7th December 1963) in the lives of a busy pop group in that period: after cutting the demo tracks, I went shopping for a leather jacket at Cecil Gee, we did a photo session and then drove by van to Croydon for two shows at the Fairfield Halls. On the bill with us were Gerry & the Pacemakers, who insisted on topping the bill; so we closed the first half. Gerry suffered the dangerous consequences of following us: lots of fans left the show at the interval, not bothering to wait to see his show. The Croydon Advertiser reported that hysterical girls howled successfully for an encore' from us. We celebrated a fine gig with a small party afterwards at my mum and dad's house in Penge.*

THE STONES CONNECTION

THE ROLLIN' STONES

R'n'B group, led in the early days by blues fanatic Brian Jones. Tony Chapman was the most regular of several drummers who sat in with the band for early gigs (when they still dropped the 'g' of Rolling), and it was he who convinced his old mate Bill to audition as bass player when Dick Taylor left to join the Pretty Things.

BRIAN JONES
lead gtr.

MICK JAGGER
vocals

KEITH RICHARDS
rhythm gtr.

Bill Perks changed his name to Wyman and Tony Chapman was edged out when the band finally got the drummer they wanted - the more experienced Charlie Watts from Blues Incorporated. With this line-up in place, the Stones went on to become quite successful - what more needs to be said about them!

Well, actually there is one question about the Stones that remains unanswered - whether or not they ever played at Croydon's Star Hotel? The jury, as they say, is still out on that one. I've met people who swear they saw them playing in that little back room, others who "would remember if they did" and some who think it most unlikely. For me, the big clue is the fact that Bill Wyman's diary doesn't list the gig - and who am I to argue with that.

TWIST 'N' JIVE
THE FABULOUS
KONRADS
plus THE TRUBEATS
SHIRLEY PARISH HALL
WICKHAM ROAD.
Saturday, 2nd Nov.
7.30-11.15
Admission 5/-

This ad. from November 1963 shows the Tru-Beats supporting the 'fabulous' Konrads. I can't vouch for exactly how fab they were, but they did include the young David Bowie on sax.

THE TRU-BEATS

Led by Nicholson, a popular band from around the West Wickham/Beckenham area. Played at 'Wickham Goes Pop' beat show (October '63), where the 14 year old Frampton played 'frighteningly good Shadows covers', according to compere Brian Showell!

For a short period, there was a Herd line-up that included Louis Cennamo on bass - with Gary Taylor and Frampton both fighting it out for the lead guitar role! Cennamo later joined Renaissance.

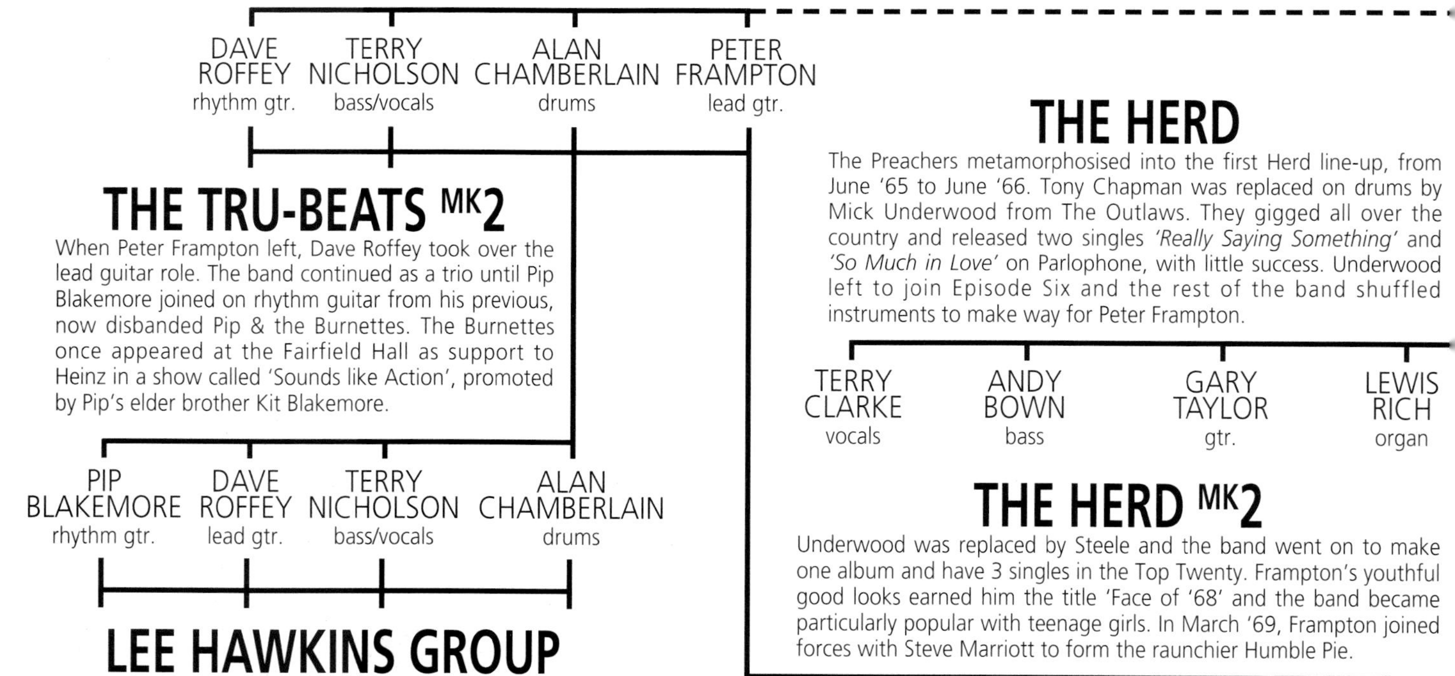

DAVE ROFFEY
rhythm gtr.

TERRY NICHOLSON
bass/vocals

ALAN CHAMBERLAIN
drums

PETER FRAMPTON
lead gtr.

THE TRU-BEATS MK2

When Peter Frampton left, Dave Roffey took over the lead guitar role. The band continued as a trio until Pip Blakemore joined on rhythm guitar from his previous, now disbanded Pip & the Burnettes. The Burnettes once appeared at the Fairfield Hall as support to Heinz in a show called 'Sounds like Action', promoted by Pip's elder brother Kit Blakemore.

PIP BLAKEMORE
rhythm gtr.

DAVE ROFFEY
lead gtr.

TERRY NICHOLSON
bass/vocals

ALAN CHAMBERLAIN
drums

LEE HAWKINS GROUP

Through Terry's connections with (then) obscure Detroit and New York record labels, the bands repertoire moved from 'Merseybeat' to Motown and soul. The band took up a residency at Tiles! in Oxford Street and played many of the London and South London Mod clubs. There was no Lee Hawkins - the group members wanted a name that sounded like the Spencer Davis Group!

THE HERD

The Preachers metamorphosised into the first Herd line-up, from June '65 to June '66. Tony Chapman was replaced on drums by Mick Underwood from The Outlaws. They gigged all over the country and released two singles *'Really Saying Something'* and *'So Much in Love'* on Parlophone, with little success. Underwood left to join Episode Six and the rest of the band shuffled instruments to make way for Peter Frampton.

TERRY CLARKE
vocals

ANDY BOWN
bass

GARY TAYLOR
gtr.

LEWIS RICH
organ

THE HERD MK2

Underwood was replaced by Steele and the band went on to make one album and have 3 singles in the Top Twenty. Frampton's youthful good looks earned him the title 'Face of '68' and the band became particularly popular with teenage girls. In March '69, Frampton joined forces with Steve Marriott to form the raunchier Humble Pie.

PETER FRAMPTON
lead gtr.

ANDREW STEELE
drums

ANDY BOWN
keyboards

GARY TAYLOR
bass gtr.

To Humble Pie, Frampton's Camel & then to huge solo stardom with 'that' double live album!

Made a solo album or two, rejoined Frampton in Frampton's Camel and has played keyboards for Status Quo on and off since 1974.

thanks as always to Pete Frame

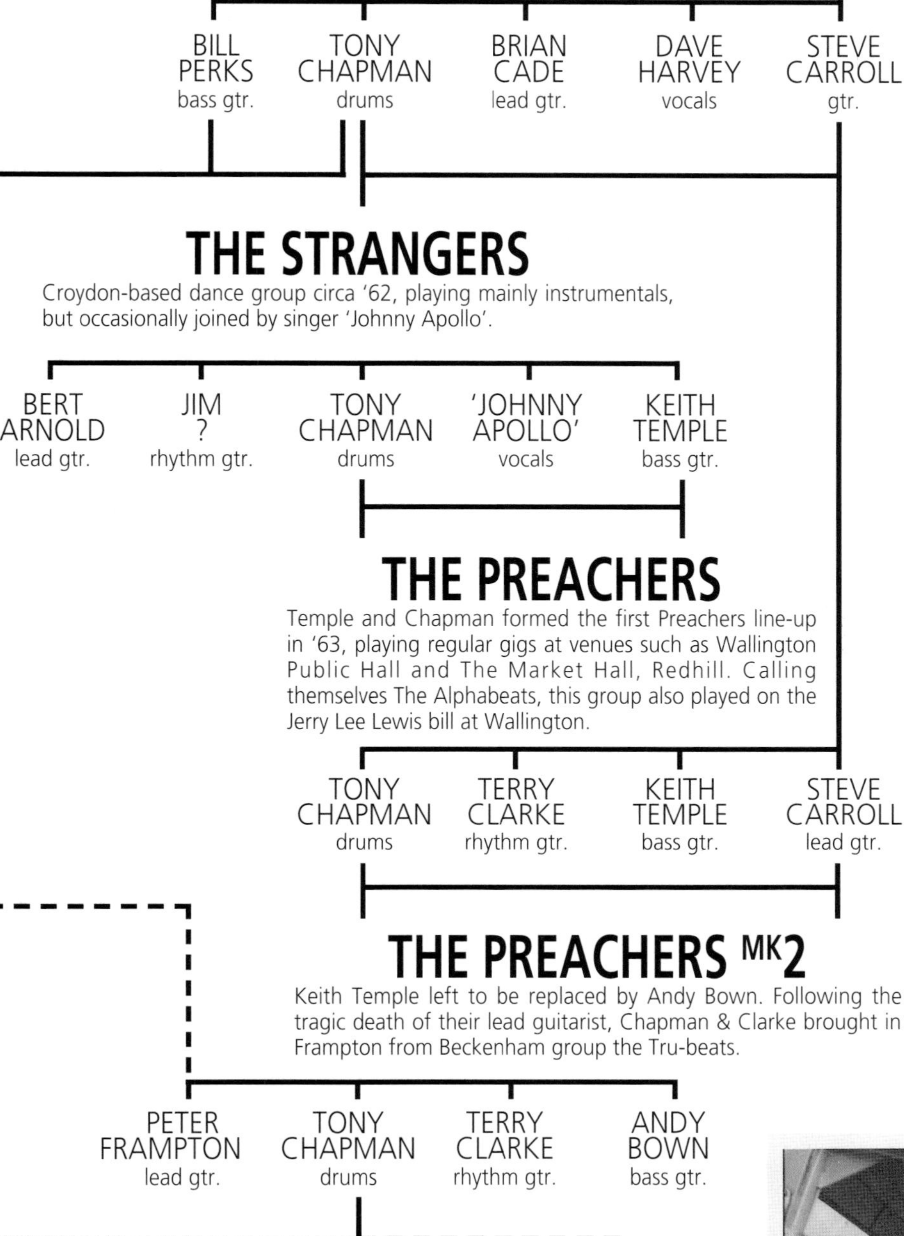

MICK UNDERWOOD drums ← replaced by — TONY CHAPMAN drums

PETE GOSLING keyboards

Underwood joined Episode Six with Ian Gillan and Roger Glover, yet didn't follow them into Deep Purple. However he later took over the drumstool in the second Gillan line-up.

When drummer Tony Chapman was 'eased out' of the Preachers in favour of Mick Underwood, Chapman joined forces with organist Pete Gosling. Later, when Frampton, Bown and co. changed their name to the Herd, Chapman retained the old Preachers name and his new line up recorded one single, *'Hole in my Soul/Too Old in the Head'* COLUMBIA DB 7680. This group were rumoured to have recorded an album which was never released - but according to Pete Gosling the master tapes still exist and it may yet see the light of day.

To Moons Train and production work.

Organist Pete Gosling was a member of the Denny Mitchell Soundsations, along with Mitchell himself, Mike Breslin, Peter Lynton and Howard Landon. This hard-working local group recorded a single for Decca - *'For Your Love / I've Been Crying'* F.11848 in 1964, (but not the Yardbirds tune - both sides are credited to 'Tubbs').

Bill Wyman and Pete Gosling crossed paths in 1965 when Bill's newly formed production company linked up with a group called The End. Wyman and Gosling co-wrote the 'Shades Of Orange' single for the group and together they formed the Merlin Music publishing company. Wyman later produced an album for Gosling's own group - Moon's Train, but that recording never saw the light of day. Gosling also worked with 'Stone Brian Jones on a soundtrack for the film 'A Degree Of Murder' - on which he played mellotron.

While travelling to a gig, the groups van was involved in a tragic accident in which Steve Carroll was killed. Tony Chapman was also badly injured and put out of action for several weeks. By a twist of fate, the other two members were travelling in a separate vehicle - whereas on any other night all four would have been in the van.

Jacqueline Ryan

The Preachers pose pre-gig, in the back of their tour van - shortly after Bown joined, in May 1964. Left to right: Tony Chapman, Andy Bown, Steve Carroll and Terry Clarke.

"... St. John's ambulance men worked overtime to cope with the increasing number of victims of the Mersey beat..."

FAIRFIELD HALLS
ASHCROFT THEATRE · FAIRFIELD HALL · ARNHEM GALLERY
in the FAIRFIELD HALL CROYDON

5.30 | THURDAY, 25th APRIL TWO CONCERTS | 8.00

JOHN SMITH presents
MERSEY BEAT SHOW CASE

Featuring
The Beatles
"Please please me"

GERRY & THE PACEMAKERS
"How do you do it"

THE BIG THREE

BILLY KRAMER & THE DAKOTAS

VIC SUTCLIFFE
Compere

GUEST STAR
John Leyton
"Cupboard Love" etc., etc.,

Courtesy Graham Maisey

The handbill from the Beatles concert at the Fairfield Hall, 25th April 1963 - complete with sellotape marks for authenticity! This was the second of their three appearances in Croydon and this time they had moved up a notch in the popularity stakes and were due to share top billing with John Leyton. Those of you lucky enough to attend either of the two shows will know that John Leyton did not appear and that after the stage was swept, the Fab Four were able to live on jelly babies for the rest of the tour!

According to Graham Maisey who supplied the handbill, the Beatles were good, but the Big Three were excellent!

'A fans-eye view...'

All the photographs on this page were taken by **Jacqueline Ryan**, a sixties 'beat' fan with a fascination for live music, photography and an eye for a good shot. Her regular hangout was the Public Hall at Wallington, where she photographed the visiting groups, had them developed and printed during the week and sold spare prints to her student friends at the following Tuesday night gig! Jackie's enterprising 'little sideline' ended abruptly when promoter Fred Bannister and his wife found out and asked her to stop. Still heavily into 'sixties music, Jacqueline is now secretary of the Troggs fanclub and more of her pictures can be seen in Alan Clayson's book 'Beat Merchants'

Jacqueline Ryan

Jacqueline Ryan

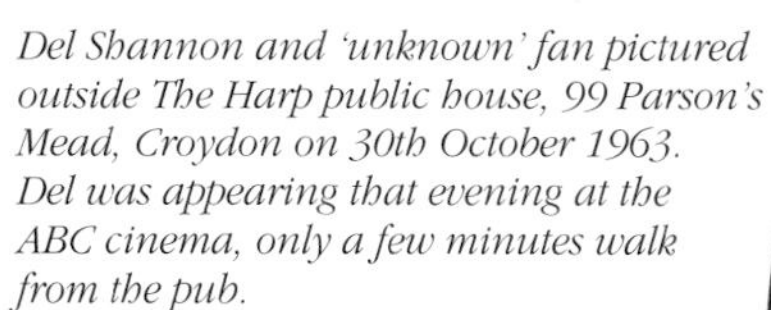

Del Shannon and 'unknown' fan pictured outside The Harp public house, 99 Parson's Mead, Croydon on 30th October 1963. Del was appearing that evening at the ABC cinema, only a few minutes walk from the pub.

The Pretty Things performing at Wallington Public Hall, 1963. Left is vocalist Phil May adding a bit of harmonica.

Centre picture shows Graham Nash of the Hollies, again at Wallington. It never ceases to amaze me that this Manchester beat group member ended up singing high harmonies in an American West Coast supergroup only a few years later.

Jacqueline Ryan

The Nashville Teens onstage at Wallington Public Hall, 1963. Left to right: Ray Phillips, Art Sharp, John Allen, Barry Jenkins and Pete Shannon. Pianist John Hawken is also in there somewhere!

Courtesy Jacqueline Ryan

Gene Vincent and Jacqueline herself, backstage at Wallington Public Hall, 1963.

'Sounds Like Action!'

This adventurous one-off show, staged at the Fairfield Hall on Thursday November 14th was the brainchild of **Kit Blakemore** from West Wickham. The show worked on various levels; the two performances comprised a rock concert starring Heinz & the Saints, plus support from local beat groups making it a showcase for local talent - and as if that wasn't enough, it incorporated the final stages of a nationwide 'Write a Top Pop Song' competition as well.

In August '63, Kit had formed a musical production company called 'Action', along with his 18 year old brother Pip and Brian Richardson. A member of the Songwriters Guild, Kit's background included work in the advertising world and with the local amateur dramatic society. Pip also worked in the family advertising business and was the singer with West Wickham group 'Pip & the Burnettes'. The new company began by writing jingles for television but quickly saw the popularity of the early pop shows organised by David Meyer, a local businessman. 'Sounds Like Action' was to be their first attempt at producing a live show.

Advertisements in the national music press invited entries for the songwriting competition; the ten best songs would be performed during the shows by the local groups and a panel of celebrities would be asked to choose two winners, one at each performance. Each winner would receive a trophy, £25 prize money and the chance to have their song recorded by the local group who performed it.

For the show itself, Kit knew that he needed a 'name' act to sell the show in addition to the local groups and for reasons of expediency, booked **Jess Conrad** to headline. Also on the bill were Croydon favourites **Patrick Dane & the Quiet Five**, **Peter Dell & the Deltones** (not to be confused with Johnny Del & the Del-Tones, who boasted the young Jeff Beck), **Pip & the Burnettes**, **the Psykons**, **Carol Elvin** and **Mary Elaine & the Starfires**.

With barely a month to go, Jess Conrad pulled out, having been whisked away to film in Budapest and Kit was left to find a new 'star turn'. Conrad's agency, the George Cooper Organisation, sent through a rosta of their other acts, plus their going rate. Top of the tree was Joe Brown (and his Bruvvers) for £350, closely followed by the Tornados at £225 and ex-Tornado Heinz Burt, backed by the Saints, for the same amount. Johnny Kidd and Marty Wilde both charged £150, Mike Preston and Duffy Power £75 each and then a host of singers around the £60 to 65 mark - Vince Eager, Danny Rivers, Dickie Pride and Michael Cox.

Kit opted for **Heinz & the Saints** and in a rare show of music business compassion, the agency agreed for him to do the show at Jess Conrad's rate of £135. The contract was signed on 2nd October for Heinz Burt Limited (hereinafter known as 'the Company') to provide the services of Heinz & the Saints (hereinafter known as 'the Artistes') to appear in two performances on the evening of 14th November 1963. An additional clause stated that Heinz would be onstage throughout the show, but that the artistes would not be required to play more than 30 minutes in each performance. The document was signed by Joe Meek in his capacity as a Director of Heinz Burt Limited!

Never one to do things by halves, Kit also commissioned Joe Meek to put together an electronic musical 'theme' especially for the evening; the busy Meek agreed to his request, probably because as Heinz's manager he had a vested interest in the show's success.

The night before the concert, Kit went up to the Beeb to record an interview for the Home Service 'South East' programme, talking about the 'Write a Top Pop song' contest. It was broadcast early on the evening of the show itself, which scarcely allowed enough time for it to be useful as a piece of promotion.

Two events conspired to work against Kit's show. On 7th September, the Beatles played the Fairfield and by all accounts their beat show ripped the place apart - emphasising the change in the British pop scene with the new beat groups taking over from solo singers - and with hindsight Kit is convinced there was no way his concert could compete after that. Action's Brian Richardson went along to the show to 'check out the opposition', and his notes underline the popularity of the groups; every lead vocalist was inaudible against the constant screaming of the fans and compare Ted King stood absolutely no chance of making himself heard.

Then on 7th November, barely a week before 'Sounds Like Action', Heinz appeared at the Fairfield on the John Leyton package tour and also played another low-key gig in the Croydon area. Heinz's agent denied that this double-booking would have harmed Kit's show - but surely many Heinz Burt fans stayed away, having seen him the previous week.

The Press reaction to the shows was mixed - the Croydon Advertiser gave a lukewarm review, while the Croydon Times hailed the idea a great success. However, this was hardly surprising, as they were sponsoring the song competition! It is fair to say that the battle of the local bands was won by Patrick Dane & the Quiet Five, who performed the winning song at both performances - 'You Sure Had Me Fooled' at the first house and 'Ten Thousand Tear Drops' at the second show. Strangely enough the writer of Ten Thousand Tear Drops turned out to be one Terry Dwyer, rhythm guitarist with the Starfires!

Once the dust had settled, it was time to balance the books. The Fairfield Hall bill just about broke even; 'Sounds Like Action' took £203 at the box office and sold £5. 15 shillings worth of programmes, while the expenditure came to £219. 19 shillings and 7 pence. This included £120 to hire the main hall, £3 for the hire of a mini piano, nearly £43 on press advertising and just over £10 box office commission. At the end of the day, Kit owed the hall £11. 7 shillings and 1 penny! That figure may not sound too bad today, but in 1963 it was a lot of money to find if you didn't have it.

The other expenditure was much more of a problem. All the artistes had to be paid - a total of £215. 13 shillings, Action's own advertising bill came to £148. 5 shillings and then of course, there was the hire of one black cat costume at £4 (don't ask!). Including the deficit to the hall, the total money outstanding was £377. 12 shillings and 2 pence - Kit began to see the problems that David Meyer had experienced with his Wickham Pop shows and decided that perhaps 'Sounds Like Action II' would have to wait!

I caught up with the irrepressible Kit Blakemore to find out exactly how the show came about...

The foundation of it all was the fact that I wanted to write songs - which was something I has started to do many years ago, in particular when I was out in Egypt - and sometime between 1960 and 1962 I decided that I would seriously get on with the job of becoming a songwriter.

I was working for my dad at the time, a Croydon-based company called Blakemore Advertising, and it appeared to me that I would become locked into the family business for ever; so this songwriting was an outlet, something I could do for 'me'. I started off by writing a few ballads, but there was one particular song which went down very well, even my father was enthusiastic about it, called 'I Want To Go Steady With You', the sort of song you could imagine Cliff Richard singing. After that, there was a great outpouring of songs from me, which far outstripped any firm ideas I had about how to market them. My real strength was as a lyricist - I used to write a very crude top line and then a local pianist would arrange the songs for me.

Around the same time, a friend from my time in the RAF was trying to get into scriptwriting and I got involved with him in terms of helping to build contacts into this very difficult world - in fact I was almost better at advising him than I was at advising myself! My songs began piling up, but I began to get a few leads; I wrote to Tommy Steele, enclosing a tape of one or two songs and he introduced me to Hugh Mendel at Decca. I went along to see Hugh Mendel and it was one of those classic interview stories - where you arrive there and suddenly find that you've forgotten the lead to the tape recorder, so you have stand in his office and sing all the work through without any backing. He did have a piano in his office but I was dreading that he'd ask me to play it!

I wrote a song for the Eurovision Song Contest and went down to the Brighton Dome to play it for that year's artist; he was the guy who sang 'Looking High, High High'. These were just two out of a succession of meetings and interviews and it gradually became apparent to me that, even though I was a member of the Songwriters Guild and did everything by the book, that I would never get anywhere if I didn't make some kind of impact. I needed to find some sort of back door because if you took it front on, there were too many other people all doing the same thing.

All this time I was still with Blakemore Advertising, which was useful because I could get all the photocopying I needed and it was relatively easy to get time off, and I exercised my writing ambitions by writing pantomimes for the local amateur dramatic society and squeezing in my own songs wherever I could. I can't remember exactly where the idea for 'Action' came from, but I've always been a great one for coining words and I decided that I needed some sort of identity. It was amazing that within two or three years there were all sorts of other companies called Action Productions and Action this, Action that... but it was a word that I registered early on as a business name, although it wasn't a limited company. It gave me the ability to go in anywhere, show a card and feel that I had some sort of base, that people would know where I was coming from, even though they'd never heard of 'Action'.

There is a lot of artificiality about show business, a lot of wishful thinking - which is illustrated only too well when you meet anyone in showbiz and say 'Hi', because they immediately respond as if they *know* you, as though they *care* about you, how great it's going to be to work with you... all that sort of thing. Standing on the outside, it appears to be very well organised but once you're on the inside you find out just how frail it really is, the whole business has no real substance. So that's how 'Action' the company came about, but where was it going to go? Somewhere along the line I got the idea that I would

Courtesy Kit Blakemore

The final flyer for 'Sounds Like Action' - the concert. Due to a last minute mix-up from Conrad's agency, copies of both handbill and poster were originally proofed with Jess Conrad & the Debonaires as the headline act.

organise a song contest - a national songwriting competition which would be called the 'Write A Top Pop Song Contest'. I was aided and abetted in this by a guy called Brian Richardson, who worked for Sultzer, a company in London that manufactured diesel engines, but he was very enthusiastic about the project and also had a contact in the business, because his cousin was the singer **Jess Conrad**. All these rather tenuous links gradually started to come together as we planned the contest.

I felt like some 'white knight' who was about to take on the world of showbusiness on behalf of all the unknown songwriters - at the time, the hit parade was dominated by a handful of songwriters who supplied all the performers with what I thought was fairly dreadful material, by and large. I thought it was high time that other people got a chance. Clearly I wasn't being totally altruistic, I could see that I could also get something out of this; I had written enough songs but I couldn't get them published, it was difficult to get any acknowledgement... apart from people like George Metstead who ran a group called The Chessmen, who did use some of my songs and gigged all round town.

Courtesy Croydon Library Services

The Quiet Five congratulate S.A. Matthias, composer of 'You Sure Had Me Fooled', the winning song at the first house of 'Sounds Like Action'. Looking on are Richard Barnes cradling his bass guitar and vocalist Pat Dane, second from the right.

Here in West Wickham there was a guy known locally as *'Mr. Pop'*, David Meyer, who ran these great big open air pop shows and concerts at Wickham Hall where all the up and coming local groups, pre-Beatles, would appear. So there was a succession of very exciting shows like 'Wickham Goes Pop' where all this new rock and roll music was played, although it has to be said that to run these shows, Mr. Pop mortgaged his house to the hilt and subsequently lost every bean he had in the process. But he did set some sort of benchmark as to what you could do if you wanted to promote a pop concert; we decided that our contest had to be advertised nationally, we would have to organise the vetting of the material, the selection of the finalists and the finalists would have their songs performed in the concert - *and*, let's have the concert at the Fairfield Hall.

We started by visiting the Fairfield and collecting all the 'bumpf' about the concerts that were being booked there at the time to find out exactly what you had to do. Their management said "we won't even entertain a show that isn't advertised properly, local press, 16-sheet poster sites, national music press and you've got to have a draw, a name act". Initially Brian said 'well, I'm sure Jess would do it' and sure enough Jess Conrad agreed to be our top of the bill. We then started to look for the other acts to support him, local groups like Pat Dane & the Quiet Five, The DelTones, Pip & the Burnettes and the Psykons. We got the Croydon Times to sponsor the show and they ran quite a big advertising feature on it. We designed various posters and leaflets for the concert and put a small amount of advertising in the national press, but the entries just flooded in - boy, did we ever make a job for ourselves. I can't remember the exact details of the judging process, but it was very, very exact - it had to be seen to be done fairly; we had a shift of pianists in order to rattle through the huge number of songs that came in. Some were rejected straight away, some were put to one side, some were almost impossible to play but we even tried to *make* it work for them, you know - and by the end of the day, we ended up with twenty songs, ten for each half of the show. We did give everyone a fair crack of the whip, taking twenty out of how ever many came in, it was a hell of a lot, the mail was unbelievable. We had also advertised in the NME and the Melody Maker, so we got a response from everywhere.

Then we had to find a panel of judges for the contest itself, and I can tell you who most of them were - there was John Schroeder from Oriole Records and Shaw Taylor, who before he became known for *Police 5* was heavily involved in the music business. There was a lady called Pamela Duncan, a well-known face from *Emergency Ward 10* and from TV advertisements, like 'Jim's Inn' - actually, I'd better explain that. There used to be advertising spots on TV called *'Admags'*, where you had a meeting place like a pub, all very chatty and friendly, a bit like the Rovers Return in Coronation Street. But in their conversations they would actually be selling various products - 'Oh, I see you're trying some of that new sauce... really, so Safeways sell it now, do they?' In fact, Admags were banned after a while, but 'Jim's Inn' was the best known, starring Jimmy Hanley and our panelist was a regular on that. We also had Mitch Murray who had written hit songs for Gerry & the Pacemakers. So these people all had to be contacted; I had contact with Shaw Taylor and Pamela because I had been on Admags myself, for a client of Blakemore Advertising; we had an account with a guy who had invented a baby's feeding bottle for dispensing semi-solid's!

When it came to the actual production, I drew on all my experiences with the West Wickham shows, and I shared the compere's role with Pip Burley, who was a keyboard player that I had been working with and who had only recently left the Quiet Five, one of the groups in the show. We worked it as a sort of double act - Pip was great, he was the one with all the patter. After the show we formed a bit of an alliance, Pip co-wrote a whole production of 'Tom Thumb' with me which included about 24 original songs - it took us all of 1964 to write the show and we put it on in '65, with Pip putting together a little band and performing the music.

So we were steaming up to November '63 and everything was coming together quite well; the song competition had been well advertised and drawn a huge number of entries, we'd whittled them down to 20 good numbers, we had our 'jury' of celebrities, the local groups were booked to perform the songs - and I can remember thinking to myself, 'there is nothing I can't do'. It was a wonderful time in my life, I would go and speak to anyone, try and organise absolutely anything and it didn't worry me one jot. We were enthusiastic of course, but at the same time we learned so much about the business side of things and the organisation, although ironically my own songwriting had to be put on hold while the show went on.

I went to see John Schroeder in London and he agreed to audition anyone who came out of the contest, he was always on the lookout for new talent. My meeting with him was the first time I ever heard the name Stevie Wonder - he showed me a photo and said "You see this guy? Watch him, because he's going to be big". John made his name with Helen Shapiro, he wrote 'Walking Back To Happiness' and produced it for her, before becoming A&R man with Oriole.

There's a lovely little off-shoot story to the show, because shortly before the night of the contest I decided that we needed an opening number and what I wanted was the sound of motorbikes revving up and the roar of the engines gradually giving way to the music of my opening song, which was called 'Sounds Like Action'. Someone said to me, there's only one bloke who could do that properly - **Joe Meek**. So I got straight on the 'phone to this Joe Meek, told him what I wanted and went up to Holloway Road to see him. When I got there I saw this line of old Victorian buildings, shop fronts with a couple of floors of flats above, the type you see all over North London, all very grim and forbidding. I remember trolling up this never-ending flight of stairs until I got to a long landing, dimly lit by one bulb and I turned towards a door right at the end that said 'studio'. Even before I got to the door I was challenged, this voice shouted out 'who's that?', the whole thing was a bit odd, a bit sinister. I had been looking forward to meeting Joe Meek, this man who had masterminded 'Telstar' for the Tornados, who was becoming a legend even then. So I announced myself to the disembodied voice and timidly knocked on the studio door - it opened about twelve inches and a hand came out with a tape in it. The voice said "There you are, gotta go now, we're busy" and shut the door! Presumably they had been in the middle of a recording session, and heard me clumping up the stairs; so I never actually met Joe, in fact I don't know if it was Joe that handed me the tape, but I took it and off I went! But that's how we opened the show, with a bit of a Joe Meek recording. The next thing I heard about Joe was that he'd shot himself at his studio in Holloway Road - all very bizarre.

"I tacitly admitted defeat at the hands of the Beatles.."

By this time, Jess Conrad had pulled out of the show due to prior commitments; it was quite late on, we even had some publicity material printed up with his face on, but we looked around and booked **Heinz & the Saints** as our top of the bill. I'm sure that part of the reason that Joe was interested enough to help us, was the fact that his protege was now our main act. On the night of the contest Heinz made a decent fist of it, but really his career was on the slide even then, the advent of the Beatles all but finished him off. Which was a shame because his stage act was so dynamic, he could be electrifying - having said that, apart from his bleach blond hair he didn't have much personality, but that wasn't what was asked for in those days. It was all in the sound and the man who provided that was the hero.

Heinz and the Saints played their own set, but the songs in the competition were performed by the local groups - Pat Dane & the Quiet Five, the Psykons, the Del-Tones, Pip & the Burnettes, the Starfires etc. Carol Elvin performed her own songs; I can't remember where I found her, she was living with her mother in South Croydon somewhere and although she was unknown to me, her act was very, very professional. To be honest, we were just enthusiastic amateurs scrabbling at the edge of the music scene and we hadn't made enough contacts to be totally at one with what was going on.

There were two shows, with ten different songs judged at each, so in fact there were two winners to the overall contest. At the early show we only had about 700 people in the audience and the second house was watched by around 1,200, maybe a bit more. So there was money from the box office, but at the end of the day I had to take out a second mortgage to pay off the hall. The Fairfield cost £650 to hire, including all the stewards, programme sellers, front-of-house staff, which seems like peanuts today but in 1963 it was a disaster - "where am I going to find 650 quid?".

Shortly after the show we asked all the songwriting members of 'Action' to provide new material to help push the group along, and some did and some didn't. Mary Elaine gave me one particular song which I then took to a man called Al Berlin, who sounds more like a gangster than a music publisher; he listened to it and quite liked it, but he said to me "I'm not so keen on the song, but I do like the quality of Mary's voice". So I left the tape with him to mull over and the next thing I know is that Mary is on my doorstep and accusing me of peddling one of her songs to Cilla Black! She wouldn't listen to reason, just had her say and then disappeared in a puff of smoke, quite convinced that I had sold her song to Cilla. Pip Burley and I wrote three numbers which we took to Oriole and played them to John Schroeder in his studio; I remember two of them, 'Three Wise Monkeys' and 'Dangerous Game' as being pretty good songs - Schroeder was certainly enthusiastic about them and really gave them the treatment. Pip had this singer in tow called Norma Bell who was really, really good and she did a terrific job of singing 'Three Wise Monkeys' - while 'Dangerous Game' had a sort of Brubeck/Take Five feel to it.We recorded these songs in a hall in South Croydon, which was built on to a private house in St. Peter's Road, in order to take them up to Schroeder and then we re-recorded them in the studios at Oriole. When the finished track was put together it was so exciting to hear it played back, it sounded magnificent and I thought, well we're made, you know.

I had already left Blakemore Advertising in January '64 and now things had become pretty fraught and fragile; there were drastic changes in my personal life, I was broke, I needed a job and I really couldn't wait on the *possibility* of coming up with a hit record. My father knew the editor of the NME, and arranged a meeting with him, the idea being that he would talk me out of going deeper into the pop business, which he succeeded in doing! After about six months of having nowhere to live and no money, with my bank manager constantly bailing me out, I bluffed my way into another agency job. There was a postal strike on at the time and I phoned them up out of the blue and said in a very aggrieved voice, 'well, have you made your mind up about giving me the job, or not?' They were a bit flustered and said we can't find your application anywhere, it must be the strike, come up as soon as you can for an interview. I went up to the Austin Knight agency in London and the long and the short of it was that I was offered a job as a copywriter.

So I was out of the professional music business and back into the world of advertising with a London agency, although I continued to develop my amateur career in various shows - producing local versions of The Wizard of Oz and writing pantomimes, that sort of thing - but the songwriting ambition just slipped away from me. I tacitly admitted defeat at the hands of the Beatles, because after they came on the scene there was no way anyone was going to buy ballads any more, and I had seen enough of the business by then to realise just how tenuous it all was.

David Redfern

Croydon Advertiser – 13.12.63

'Great Rhythm & Blues Artist'

THE JAZZ and blues concert at the Fairfield Hall on Friday, gave Croydon another chance of hearing the basic playing of an authentic negro rhythm and blues harmonica player and singer, Sonny Boy Williamson, who on this occasion shared the bill with the popular Chris Barber Jazzband.

It seemed inconceivable that a rhythm and blues player could be backed by a jazz complement, yet when the ear did become accustomed to the careful phrasings of horn and reed, between loud harmonica and voice, compatibility with the unexpected became another affirmation of this great artist's versatility.

The first half of the concert, devoted entirely to the Barber band, gave the impression of being no more than a curtain raiser. The second half began with 'Sweet Georgia Brown' and Sonny Boy Williamson made his entrance, applauded with true admiration to the microphone. Each number was introduced by a personal anecdote, beautiful in its simplicity, as were the tunes themselves - the music of his life.

Particularly appealing was his 'Bye, Bye Birdie', a kind of fragile daydream on harmonica... Chris and the band left the stage at this point and Sonny made his own rhythm, by foot tapping, clicking his fingers, swaying his body to and fro and giving the audience a hypnotising performance.

Two striking portraits of a true blues legend - Sonny Boy Williamson with the Chris Barber Jazz band, onstage at the Fairfield Halls.

David Redfern

"... sure the hoses were turned on them - the kids were a menace..."

Trouble at a concert by "grand-daddy" **Bill Haley**? Surely not. Yet that was the quote from a not-so-friendly Fairfield Halls attendant after a crowd of fans surged outside the stage door hoping for a glimpse of Haley or Manfred Mann.

The attendants used the fire hoses to spray the teenagers, in an attempt to quell what they saw as a potential problem and in return, were pelted with stones and bottles by the kids. One girl said: *"I didn't care about seeing the stars - I was only waiting there for a friend. They've got a cheek soaking me like that".* An official from the Halls declined to comment.

Croydon Advertiser – 2.10.64

'Still the King of Rock'

THE GRAND-DADDY of rock'n'roll, Bill Haley made a triumphant return to Croydon on Friday, appearing at the Fairfield Hall and playing to a 'packed and "sent" audience.

Just as the Beatles have topped the beat world, so Bill Haley has remained king of rock. His record sales total 40 million. Those for one record alone, 'Rock Around The Clock', are 15 million. I missed Bill Haley's last tour of Britain, being then of too tender an age to take much active interest in pop music. Friday was therefore the first time I had seen him - I very much hope it will not be the last.

Everything in the performance of Bill Haley & the Comets showed the self-assurance and slick professionalism only possessed by top-bracket entertainers. They were not aloof on the stage - they played to the audience, for the audience. Their numbers included 'Rock Around The Clock', 'See You Later Alligator' and 'Shake, Rattle & Roll'.

Opening the show, the Untamed Four proved themselves a very worthy group, playing only two numbers, the rhythm 'n'blues standard 'Hi-Heel Sneakers' and 'Boom Boom', a John Lee Hooker number. Second to appear were the Rockin' Berries, a group for which I predict a very bright future. They performed their new release 'He's In Town', a number in the Four Seasons style. Through the capable mimicry of their lead singer Clive Lea, they performed 'Transistor Radio', a song including "take-offs" of Billy Fury, Cliff Richard, Gene Vincent and Norman Wisdom. I thoroughly enjoyed their act and expect them to be appearing in the top ten.

Mixed reactions greeted two groups in the second half - the Nashville Teens and Manfred Mann. Neither played as well as they could, and the second, though trying very hard, did not hit the form of previous months. The mixed receptions arose from the fact that while both were very popular with the gentle sex, the Bill Haley fans, predominantly male, booed every number, and emphasised their protest by leaving before the end.

A packed second house showed that the promoters had done their work well. The lighting was first rate and the amplifying system had been improved. All in all this was the best pop show at the Fairfield for a long time.

H.J.L.

Courtesy 'Tracks' - rock'n'roll memorabilia

The handbill for the Bill Haley concert at the Fairfield Hall, 25th September 1964. Manfred Mann were late replacements for Brenda Lee, who was meant to be the original co-star on this tour. And whatever happened to Bobby Patrick's Big Six?

JANUARY

- 4 YARDBIRDS **S** (n/a)
- 7 BERN ELLIOTT & THE FENMEN **W** (4/-)
- 10 ACKER BILK **FH** (n/a)
- 11 YARDBIRDS **S** (n/a)
- 14 THE SEARCHERS **W** (5/-)
- 18 YARDBIRDS **S** (n/a)
- 21 THE UNDERTAKERS **W** (4/-)
- 25 YARDBIRDS **S** (n/a)
- 25 GEORGIE FAME & THE BLUE FLAMES **W** + JIMMY WILLIAMS COMBO (4/- to 5/-)
- 27 FRANK SINATRA JR. **FH** + THE TOMMY DORSEY ORCHESTRA + THE PIED PIPERS (4/-)
- 28 MANFRED MANN **W** (4/-)

FEBRUARY

- 1 BILLY WOODS COMBO **W** (4/- to 5/-)
- 8 CORVETTES & THE IMPALA'S **W** (4/- to 5/-)
- 15 YARDBIRDS **S** (n/a)
- 15 IMPALA'S **W** + GLEN ATHENS & THE TROJANS (4/- to 5/-)
- 18 CYRIL DAVIES BENEFIT SESSION **G** *featuring* LONG JOHN BALDRY + WIZZ JONES + ROYD RIVERS & CLIFF AUNGIER (n/a)
- 19 DUKE ELLINGTON **FH** (n/a)
- 21 TRIBUTE TO CYRIL DAVIES **FH** *featuring* SONNY BOY WILLIAMSON + THE YARDBIRDS + ALEXIS KORNER (n/a)
- 22 TONY RAE & THE EMBLEMS **W** + SHADES OF GREEN (4/- to 5/-)
- 23 DUSTY SPRINGFIELD **FH** + FREDDIE & THE DREAMERS + MIKE BERRY & THE CRUISERS + THE MERSEYBEATS (n/a)
- 29 IMPALA'S **W** + TONY RAE & THE EMBLEMS (4/- to 5/-)

MARCH

- 13 KENNY BALL **FH** (n/a)
- 28 YARDBIRDS **S** (n/a)

APRIL

- 4 COMMANCHES **W** (5/-)
- 5 STEVE MARRIOTT's MOMENTS **S** (n/a)
- 6 ELLA FITZGERALD **FH** + THE OSCAR PETERSON TRIO (n/a)
- 11 YARDBIRDS **S** (n/a)
- 12 THE ROLLING STONES **FH** + THE OVERLANDERS + THE WORRYIN' KIND + THE BARRACUDAS (00)
- 18 YARDBIRDS **S** (n/a)
- 21 YARDBIRDS **S** (n/a)
- 24 STEVE MARRIOTT's MOMENTS **S** (n/a)
- 26 FOLK AT THE FAIRFIELD No. 1 **FH** *featuring* ALEX CAMPBELL + STEVE BENBOW + CLIFF AUNGIER + THE STRAWBERRY HILL BOYS + COLIN WILKIE & SHIRLEY HART (00)
- 27 ROY ORBISON **FH** + FREDDIE & THE DREAMERS + CLIFF SANDFORD + TONY SHERIDAN + WAYNE FONTANA & THE MINDBENDERS (00)
- 28 ROLLING STONES **W** (n/a)
- 28 YARDBIRDS **S** (n/a)

MAY

- 1 SHIRLEY BASSEY **FH** (n/a)
- 2 AUTHENTICS **S** (n/a)
- 6 AUTHENTICS **S** (n/a)
- 9 AUTHENTICS **S** (n/a)
- 10 U.S. FOLK, BLUES & GOSPEL CARAVAN **FH** *featuring* MUDDY WATERS + BLIND GARY DAVIS + SONNY TERRY & BROWNIE McGEE (n/a)
- 16 YARDBIRDS **S** (n/a)
- 21 CHUCK BERRY **A** + THE ANIMALS + CARL PERKINS (7/6 to 15/-)
- 21 STEVE MARRIOTT's MOMENTS **S** (n/a)
- 27 YARDBIRDS **S** (n/a)
- 31 DAVE BRUBECK **FH** (n/a)

JUNE

- 1 BILLY J. KRAMER **FH** + THE MERSEYBEATS + TOMMY QUICKLY + JULIE GRANT (00)
- 3 AUTHENTICS **S** (n/a)
- 5 MR. ACKER BILK **FH** (n/a)
- 13 GREBBELS **S** (n/a)
- 15 DAVE CLARK FIVE **FH** + THE APPLEJACKS + MILLIE + PAT DANE & THE QUIET FIVE + THE FALLING LEAVES + THE WORRYIN' KIND (n/a)
- 20 AUTHENTICS **S** (n/a)
- 27 T-BONES **S** (n/a)

If '63 was the year of the Beatles, '64 was the year of the Stones. They twice rolled into Croydon to headline shows at the Fairfield Hall and are remembered here by regular concert-goer, **Jim Henocq**.

I remember going with a pal to see the ***Rolling Stones*** *and we desperately wanted tickets for the later of the two performances. The only tickets we could get were for the early evening show, so we decided to wangle our way into the second performance, which we did. The tickets issued were a raspberry red and a mauve colour, which fortunately for us looked very similar in a darkened room. We saw the first concert, which was excellent, I remember everyone getting hyped-up as the Stones would poke their heads around part of the stage set during the other acts and the girls screamed the place down!*

We hung around till the second performance was well under way, then coolly went upstairs, flashed our tickets in the gloomy light and said that we had just been to the toilet. The steward only gave our tickets a cursory glance and we were in! The second concert was even better than the first, with people screaming and dancing in the aisles. At the end, everyone rushed round to the stage doors at the rear, waiting for them to come out. After some time, my pal and I got fed up with waiting and went back to catch our bus, via the front entrance. To our astonishment, Mick Jagger & Keith Richards walked out through the main entrance, as bold as brass, with nobody taking a blind bit of notice; got into a Ford Consul (or a Zephyr), it had a bench seat and with Jagger driving, went off down Wellesley Road leaving the mayhem behind them!

Jim was also a regular visitor to the Star, going along with his elder sister to see bands at the Crawdaddy Club. Jim

Wallington Big Beat Sessions
STAFFORD ROAD

TUES JAN 7th — **BERN ELLIOT AND THE FENMEN** (MONEY)

TUES JAN 14th — **THE SEARCHERS** (Sweets For My Sweet, Sugar & Spice) ADM 5/-

TUES JAN 21st — FROM MERSEYSIDE **THE UNDERTAKERS**

TUES JAN 28th — BRITAIN'S TOP R & B GROUP **MANFRED MANN** (Cock-a-Hoop)

2 GROUPS AT ALL SESSIONS

7.30 - 10.30 ADM 4/- (Except Jan 14th)

As this monthly handout shows, the Public Hall at Wallington was attracting some good groups – the Manfred's had yet to have their first hit, while the Searchers could command an extra shilling on the strength of their two 'top five' singles!

FH - Fairfield Hall • A - ABC • S - Star Hotel • TR - Top Rank • O - Orchid Ballroom • W - Wallington Public Hall

says - This was the 'in' place to be, with entry being gained by first looking old enough to get into the pub and then having the back of your hand stamped with the fluorescent 'Crawdaddy' rubber stamp, to show that you had paid. This became something of a 'badge of honour' and I remember leaving the mark on my hand as long as possible, to prove to my school friends that I had been there. Eric Clapton was a great favourite and I certainly saw the Yardbirds play there many times.

After Eric left the Yardbirds, he came back to the Star with his new group, ***Cream****, for what must have been one of their first gigs. The darkened club room was absolutely jam packed, in a way that wouldn't be allowed these days because of fire regulations and the water was dripping off the walls. The sheer volume of Creams' music was stunning - I have never experienced anything quite like it, before or since.*

As Jim mentions, the **Yardbirds** regularly attracted large audiences to The Star Hotel at Broad Green. They were presented with a residency by their manager Giorgio Gomelsky, the man behind the famous Crawdaddy clubs, which now included The Star. Amongst the fans who turned up every Saturday to see them was Deanna Sewell, from Norbury. Deanna and her chums befriended the Yardbirds, in particular guitarist Eric Clapton with whom she shares not only the same birthday, but the same love of early blues. She remembers arriving one night to find another group about to perform, and without asking who they were, Dee went straight into *'Where are the Yardbirds?'. 'They're in Newcastle'* came the reply, *'we've swopped gigs for the night'.* The Yardbirds were playing the Club A Go Go; the Animals were in Croydon!

Deanna was also party to one of Gomelskys more bizarre schemes. In July, he suggested that the Yardbirds take a weeks working holiday in Lugano, Switzerland; to relax in a lakeside village by day, and play a couple of local clubs in the evening – and here's the punchline – the group would take a busload of local fans with them, for moral support! Rhythm guitarist Chris Dreja remembers it well:

"...imagine going over the Alps in a transit van, with Bill Relf (Keith's dad) driving! Giorgio really did organise those fans as well; the other van was full of these girls from places like Barnes - a sweet bunch. How their mothers were persuaded to let them go, I'll never know!... Bill got lost on the Alps and none of us slept - there was no tunnel then so it meant going up those incredible passes, around bends with an 8,000 foot drop on the other side, where we freaked Bill out by lurching to one side, screaming".

Deanna Sewell

Taken in the bar of the Star at Broad Green, this picture shows the young Yardbirds and friends in posing mood; left to right we have Sonny Boy Williamson, resplendent in leather coat, Chris Dreja, Jim McCarty, manager Giorgio Gomelsky, Eric Clapton and Paul Samwell-Smith. Kneeling is Hamish Grimes, Giorgio's right hand man, on the far right is a fan and the tall guy behind Giorgio and Eric is possibly a Yardbirds 'roadie'.

Special mention must be made here for the **Woodstock Hotel** in North Cheam, which provided a regular gig for many, many local bands. The hotel hosted live music on Wednesdays, Fridays and Sundays with an entrance fee of 3 or 4 shillings and during the first few months of 1964 you could have bopped and jived to the **A-Jaes**, the **Buccaneers**, the **Cheetahs**, the **Conchords**, the **Del-Tones**, the **Embers**, the **Hysterics**, the **Keymen**, the **Orbits**, the **Partisans**, the **Quadrabeats**, the **Ramrods**, the **Saracens**, the **Shifters** and the **Society Five**. Such was the demand for beat groups, that the Hotel also ran a Thursday night spot and split the residency between Denny Mitchell & the Soundsations and Tony Holland & the Pack-a-Beats.

The relatively new British rhythm & blues scene lost one of its finest exponents when **Cyril Davies** died in January at the age of 32. Davies was largely responsible for bringing the music to towns like Croydon, and Croydon in return staged two benefit concerts, with all proceeds going to Cyril's wife.

The bigger of the two was at the Fairfield with Sonny Boy Williamson, the Yardbirds and Alexis Korner, but the first was a far more personal affair, held at the Gun Tavern on a cold Sunday afternoon and headlined by Long John Baldry, the vocalist from Cyril's R&B AllStars.

This moving tribute was packed with Croydon's own folk and blues artists - Wizz Jones, Cliff Aungier & Royd Rivers, the Hicory Nuts and club 'regulars' Chris, Jacqui and Ralph, who were Chris Aycliffe, Jacqui McShee and Ralph McTell. This show was reviewed for the Croydon Times by local journalist Robin Denselow who called it *"four hours of the best folk music I have heard in Croydon, outside of the Fairfield Halls".*

With America still reeling from the 'British Invasion' headed by the Beatles, Croydon beat group **The Snobs** crossed the Atlantic at the end of April to try their luck in the States. The group dressed in powdered wigs and regency-style frock coats and were best known in this country for the single 'Buckleshoe Stomp'/'Stand & Deliver' - DECCA F11867. They made their first U.S. TV appearance on the 'Red Skelton Show' alongside guests Mickey Rooney and Jackie Coogan and were so well received that Skelton arranged for two further performances, for which they used the famous Hollywood Bowl as a rehearsal room.

The Snobs played two successful ballroom dates in Los Angeles, where on each occasion the State police had to be called in to calm the excited crowds, while the group's manager, Ivor Spencer, even had a request from an American manufacturer for a licence to market the Snobs' 18th Century powdered wigs! After flying back to Britain on 4th May, the group received offers to play a 20 date residency in Las Vegas and to visit Australia and Japan.

Referring back to the **Rolling Stones**, their appearance at Wallington Public Hall on 28th April must have been a real 'back to basics' gig for them; on the 26th they had played two shows at the NME Poll Winners concert, Empire Pool Wembley, while on the 27th they headlined two performances at the 'Pop Proms' in the Royal Albert Hall!

Then in November, Bill Wyman returned to the Public Hall in Wallington, primarily to watch American Bluesman **Jimmy Reed** who had been a huge influence on the early Stones and to meet up with his old friend Stewart Wealleans, who was working there as a DJ. During the evening Bill also joined Beckenham group **The Herd** on stage for a couple of numbers.

JULY

- 5 FOLK AT THE FAIRFIELD No. 2 **FH** *featuring* ALEX CAMPBELL + SHIRLEY COLLINS + FITZROY COLEMAN (00)
- 8 WOODY HERMAN **FH** (7/6 to 17/6)
- 20 RAY CHARLES **FH** (7/6 to 20/-)

AUGUST

- 3 STEVE MARRIOTT's MOMENTS **S** (n/a)
- 25 STEVE MARRIOTT's MOMENTS **O** (n/a)

SEPTEMBER

- 16 'GEORDIE SOUND' SHOW **FH** (5/- to 12/6)
- 17 GRACIE FIELDS SHOW **FH** (5/- to 15/-)
- 18 CLANCY BROTHERS **FH** (7/6 to 20/-)
- 25 MANFRED MANN **FH** + BILL HALEY & THE COMETS (5/- to 15/-)
- 27 NINA & FREDERICK **FH** (5/- to 12/6)

OCTOBER

- 16 TOM JONES **FH** (n/a)
- 19 THIRD AMERICAN BLUES FESTIVAL **FH** *featuring* LIGHTNIN' HOPKINS + HOWLIN' WOLF + SONNY BOY WILLIAMSON + WILLIE DIXON (15/- to 21/-)
- 23 P J PROBY **FH** + DAVID JOHN & THE MOOD + THE SUNLINERS + THE QUIET FIVE (5/- to 12/6)
- 23 KEN COLYER's JAZZMEN **S** (n/a)
- 24 WAYNE FONTANA & THE MINDBENDERS **W** (n/a)
- 25 THIRD AMERICAN BLUES FESTIVAL **FH** (15/- to 21/-) Second date added - *see above.*
- 28 ERROL GARNER **FH** (6/- to 20/-)

NOVEMBER

- 4 THE ANIMALS **FH** + NASHVILLE TEENS + CARL PERKINS + ELKIE BROOKS + TOMMY TUCKER + THE QUOTATIONS + RAY CAMERON (5/- to 12/6)
- 13 FOLK AT THE FAIRFIELD No. 3 **FH** *featuring*
- 18 THE SEARCHERS **A** + DIONNE WARWICK + THE ZOMBIES + THE ISLEY BROTHERS + ALAN ELSDON & THE VOODOOS + TONY SHEVERTON + SYD & EDDIE 2 shows (6/6 to 10/6)
- 24 JIMMY REED **W** + THE HERD (n/a)

DECEMBER

- 4 ROLLING STONES **FH** + CLIFF BENNETT & THE REBEL ROUSERS + THE WORRYIN' KIND + TWINKLE + THE QUIET FIVE + THE SACK O'WOES 2 shows (6/6 to 12/6)
- 21 YARDBIRDS **FH** (n/a)

(n/a) = ticket price not available

Croydon's kids were given an early start to their appreciation of pop music by Ron Earwicker, manager of the Classic cinema on the Brighton Road, South Croydon. As part of the cinema's matinee entertainment for children aged between 7 and 14, Ron added a 'beat bonanza' to the existing **Three C's Club** and the idea really took off.

Originally the kids just brought along their favourite records to play in the break between films, but with the assistance of Ted Potter from Potter's Music Shop, a few local groups were booked to play including the Martin Jae Five and Glen Athens & the Trojans. The groups were given a half hour spot before the matinee film and different groups were booked two or three times a month.

Ron held a popularity poll to find out the children's favourite local groups - top of their list were **Vern Rogers & the Orbits**. He told the Advertiser: *"As the children are leaving the cinema they always ask who is on next week. And if I have to tell them that no group is booked they show their disappointment in no uncertain manner".*

Croydon Advertiser – 24.7.64

'Shattering Impact'

No artist in the field of entertainment today holds so much mass appeal as Ray Charles, whose popularity is to be found alike among the very young and the very old.

Sections of the public who would normally not be associated with such popularity revere him; other big name entertainers flock to see him and be mesmerised, as were we all at Fairfield Hall on Monday evening.

Under the sweltering heat of the television arc lamps, artists and audience roasted alike, but out of it all came a performance that will not be forgotten by any who were lucky enough to be present.

I can only describe this man as enormous - in size, personality and impact. The cracked voice throws out lyrics such as "See that girl with the diamond ring - she knows how to shake that thing", utterly meaningless in themselves, yet when he says them his whole being comes across with them and gives meaning to what is really nothing. The fact that they are meaningless doesn't matter, it's their rhythmic presentation in tone which captures the imagination.

F.W.P.

The outrageous Screamin' Jay Hawkins onstage at Wallington Public Hall for the opening night of his UK tour.

Under the banner of 'The Geordie Sound', a large package tour stopped at the Fairfield Halls on September 16th. It turned out to be more of a general Northern bill, as it was headlined by the **Merseybeats** (Liverpool) and gave Croydon an early look at Sheffield's **Joe Cocker & his Big Blues**. Also playing were the **Naturals**, the **Kinetics**, **Paul Ryan and the Streaks**, and the **V.I.P's**, who later went on to become Spooky Tooth.

The Drill Hall, Marlpit Lane, Old Coulsdon held a 'Fantabeat Dance' on Saturday 17th October featuring music from the 'famous' **Pat Wayne & the Beachcombers**. Tickets 5/-.

As part of a massive 35 date tour, the **Searchers** headed an intriguing package that came to the ABC on Wednesday, 18th November. The tour heralded **Dionne Warwick**'s first visit to England; it was the first major tour for the **Zombies** and a rare chance for the Croydon audience to see the **Isley Brothers**. As if that wasn't enough, the comic duo **Syd & Eddie** later became better known as Little & Large!

Don Arden's Galaxy Entertainments signed up the American 'shock-rocker' **Screamin' Jay Hawkins** to play his first British concert tour, backed by The Blues Set, a British pick-up group. Among the afficianados to witness this tour was music journalist **Bill Millar**, who recalls;

A group of us flocked to all the London shows, including the opening night at Wallington Town Hall. Jay was never in better form. He ran on and off the stage, did the splits, played piano, waved his cloak like a rabid bullfighter, and screamed a slew of rock and roll classics; 'Alligator Wine', 'The Whammy', 'Strange', 'Feast of the Mau Mau'. Sadly, the more his fans cheered, the more the locals booed. They came to the Town Hall every Tuesday to get pickled and practice their chat-up lines to the strains of Freddie & the Dreamers or Dave Berry & the Cruisers. They certainly didn't want anybody to complicate things by putting on a show. Eventually fighting broke out and we had to escape via the dressing room and the car park, skulking away in the dark behind the former Golden Gloves middle-weight!

I don't think he was quite so wild again, but elsewhere the audiences were ecstatic. Record Mirror reported a "fantastic display" at Soho's Flamingo Club and some amp-trashing at the Bromley Court Hotel where Jay "made flames shoot from his fingertips before playing his sax".

During November and December, Purley library held a series of talks and lectures on the History of Jazz, initiated by journalist, critic and one-time member of Lord Rockinghams XI, tenor sax player **Benny Green**.

Croydon Advertiser – 11.12.64

'Rolling Them In The Aisles'

A YOUNG GIRL in front of me leapt to her feet, held her head in her hands, opened her mouth to scream and fell to the ground, apparently unconscious.

Her friend turned, and seeing her lying on the ground, screamed and was likewise stricken unconscious. THE ROLLING STONES were onstage at the Fairfield. A nurse and several attendants ran a sort of shuttle service, carrying limp, tearstained girls from the hall. After the show, the corridor outside was filled with anxious friends and relations, like a 19th century shipping office after a ship had been reported missing.

In short, the Stones had a fantastic reception on Friday. A few hours before seeing them, I reheard their first release 'Come On', which rocketed them to stardom not so long ago. Their style has matured since then and in many ways they are now worthy of the adulation lavished on them by swooning females and appreciative males. One last thing about the Stones; they are not just a group - they are a cult, a way of life, and whatever the moral aspects of this cult, they have well and truly established it and are its figureheads. They are also its 'whipping boys', because the adult generation blames them for everything from hairstyles to the weather.

As for the rest of Friday's bill there were two groups that impressed me. One had the unusual name of the Sack o' Woes, and the other the familiar name of the Quiet Five (familiar to Croydon beat-fans, anyway). The Quiet Five have failed to make a lasting impression on the national beat world so far, but on the strength of their versions of 'Fun, Fun, Fun', 'Blowing In The Wind', 'I'm Crying', 'I Feel Fine' and 'Hold Me', this is something that ought to be rectified in the near future. Their impersonations are first class, but they still need to develop a style of their own. With the right publicity and choice of song, they could still make their mark.

Also on the programme was a young girl called Twinkle, with a very sick song about a 'ton-up' boy whose love she spurns, so he kills himself by crashing his motorcycle. Twinkle claims that she likes to sing sad songs, but in my opinion, (i) this song was not sad, it was sick; and (ii) she does not sing, she shouts! Cliff Bennett & the Rebel Rousers were disappointing and the Worryin' Kind failed to come over at all.

In all then a mixed bag, but the dynamite which the Stones detonated in the audience made the show well worthwhile.

H.J.L.

JANUARY

- 6 T-BONES **S** (n/a)
- 10 AUTHENTICS **S** (n/a)
- 8 BILLY J. KRAMER & THE DAKOTAS **FH** + THE ROCKIN' BERRIES + JULIE GRANT + DUFFY POWER & THE FENTONES 2 shows (5/- to 15/-)
- 27 SONNY BOY WILLIAMSON **S** + T-BONES (n/a)
- 29 CHUCK BERRY **FH** + LONG JOHN BALDRY & THE HOOCHIE COOCHIE MEN + MOODY BLUES + GRAHAM BOND ORGANISATION + WINSTON G. + FIVE DIMENSIONS 2 shows (6/6 to 15/-)
- 29 CILLA BLACK & P.J. PROBY **A** + TOMMY ROE + THE FOURMOST + SOUNDS INCORPORATED + THE REMO FOUR + TOMMY QUICKLY + BOB BAIN 2 shows (6/6 to 10/6)

FEBRUARY

- 3 TOM JONES **FH** (n/a)
- 5 1st AMERICAN NEGRO GOSPEL FESTIVAL **FH** + BISHOP SAMUEL KELSEY (6/- to 21/-)
- 7 DAVEY GRAHAM **OT** + SHIRLEY COLLINS (n/a)
- 13 THE DISSATISFIED **S** (n/a)
- 17 DUKE ELLINGTON **FH** 2 shows (7/6 to 17/6)
- 17 INGOES **S** (n/a)
- 24 GEORGIE FAME & THE BLUEFLAMES **O** (5/-)
- 27 INGOES **S** (n/a)
- 28 WIZZ JONES **OT** + PETE STANLEY (n/a)

MARCH

- 3 THE T-BONES **S** (n/a)
- 5 RADIO CAROLINE SOUNDS OF '65 **FH** MOODY BLUES + YARDBIRDS + RONNIE JONES & THE NIGHTIMERS + MARK LEEMAN FIVE 2 shows (6/6 to 15/-)
- 6 BRIAN AUGER **S** + INGOES (n/a)
- 13 THE AUTHENTICS **S** (n/a)
- 17 THE T-BONES **S** (n/a)
- 19 BIG BEAT NITE OUT **FH** THE KINKS + THE ANIMALS + THE PRETTY THINGS + THE CARAVELLES + DODIE WEST + SEAN BUCKLEY & THE BREADCRUMBS 2 shows (6/6 to 15/-)
- 31 THE BACHELORS **A** + MIKE PRESTON + FREDDY DAVIS + THE MIKE LEANDER SHOWBAND (7/6 to 12/6)

APRIL

- 4 GERRY LOCKRAN **SW** (n/a)
- 15 ELLA FITZGERALD **FH** + ROY ELDRIDGE QUARTET + OSCAR PETERSON TRIO 2 shows (7/6 to 20/-)
- 30 BILLY FURY **A** + THE PRETTY THINGS + DAVE BERRY & THE CRUISERS + BRIAN POOLE & THE TREMELOES + JOHN BARRY SEVEN + THE ZEPHYRS 2 shows (6/6 to 9/6)

MAY

- 5 GEORGIE FAME & THE BLUEFLAMES **O** (5/-)
- 5 THE JAZZHOOTERS **H** + KENNY WHEELER (n/a)
- 12 THE JAZZHOOTERS **H** (4/6)

JUNE

- 8 THE WHO **W** (n/a)
- 14 RAMBLING JACK ELLIOTT **FH** + REV. GARY DAVIS + BUFFY ST. MARIE + JULIE FELIX + DERROLL ADAMS (5/- to 15/-)
- 27 STRAWBERRY HILL BOYS **SW** (n/a)

(n/a) = ticket price not available.

The stage act of one **P.J. Proby** was never to be the same again, after he split his velvet trousers during a performance at the ABC, Croydon. In a review by Francesca Hare of the Croydon Times, Proby *"dressed quite immaculately in dark blue velvet from head to foot (including a blue velvet bow to tie up his bonny black hair). Oh, how P.J. performed. Girls screamed, girls fainted, girls rushed the stage and were beaten off by a strong band of stewards. We had over 30 minutes of Proby - with all his little mannerisms, plus a view of the waistband of his underpants (when he lifted the tail of his velvet shirt) and his knees - for halfway through his tight trousers began to split."*

Alan Stranks from Caterham was in the audience that night and he remembers the crowd going wild, not just for Proby, but for Cilla Black too, backed for the tour by Sounds Incorporated. *"The nearest thing I've seen since was the hysterical reaction to 'Osmond-mania' in the Seventies"*, Alan told me.

The Croydon show on the Friday night was the start of a nationwide tour. The trousers split again at Luton, where the safety curtain was brought down and by the Monday, Proby had been banned by the ABC Theatre chain and from appearing on national television; with great irony, P.J.'s next single was called *'I Apologise'!* Incidentally, the Croydon ABC received no complaints after the show.

In February **Carol Elvin** made her second attempt at chart success with the release of 'Don't Leave Me'/'Cos I Love You' Parlophone R 5228. The 24 year old singer and dancer from Heathfield Vale, Selsdon had worked in show business since the age of 15 during which time she had been a dancer, choreographer, principal girl in panto, cabaret singer and rhythm & blues guitarist, often working abroad. In 1963 Carol released her debut single 'Cos I Know' on Columbia, which was a hit with the critics yet failed to excite the record buyers; but Carol knew the pitfalls: *"If you look at this business as a business, and not through rose-coloured glasses, I think you can do all right. But it's hard - hard work all the way"*.

St. Peter's Hall in Ledbury Road, South Croydon held an R'n'B Ball on Saturday 13th March. A mere four shillings was all you needed to dance to *'the sensational'* **Misnamed Five**, from 7.30 'til 11.00pm.

FH - Fairfield Hall • A - ABC • S - Star Hotel • O - Orchid Ballroom • SW - Swan & Sugarloaf • OT - Olive Tree

March '65 was a turning point in the career of local favourites, the **Yardbirds**. Eric Clapton had quit the band over a disagreement about their musical direction - he was fast becoming a blues purist, while they were opting for more of a 'pop' sound. The last single on which Clapton played was *'For Your Love'*, which he hated; ironically it was their biggest hit!

First choice replacement was Jimmy Page, a top session guitarist who also regularly turned up at Yardbird gigs and was therefore familiar with their material. But Page didn't want to swap his session work for touring and recommended **Jeff Beck**, whose own R&B band the **Tridents** had built a strong reputation at venues such as Eel Pie Island. Beck had grown up around the Carshalton area and played in a variety of groups, including **Johnny Del & the Del-Tones**.

After a brief 'breaking-in' period, Beck made his Yardbirds debut at the Fairfield Halls on March 5th, where the band were second on the bill to the Moody Blues in 'Sounds of '65', a concert organised by Radio Caroline. He warranted a mention in the Croydon Advertiser - *"The lead guitarist of the Yardbirds, a five man solid rhythm and blues group, demonstrated his versatility in 'For Your Love', their latest record"* - but the 'Pirate' show overall did not receive rave reviews. The reviewer went on - *"The Yardbirds in particular, must learn to choose suitable numbers to play to a sitting audience, rather than keep pounding away at something that would make excellent dance music, but is a little boring to listen to".* He should have tried telling that to the regulars at the Crawdaddy!

In April, heats were held for the Banstead Youth Week Beat Contest with the incentive of a recording test by EMI for the winners and an audition with Decca for the runners-up (it's true - poor old Decca, just because they turned down the Beatles...). While the competitors were hoping for their big break, another local group were just releasing their first single on Parlophone - 'Voodoo Blues' by the **Shades of Blue**.

Formed in 1962 by lead guitarist Roy Tones, the group featured Wallington-born singer David Blake, pianist Peter Ware from Worcester Park, Colin Fuller from Ewell on bass and drummer Tony Gooden from Kingston. They went on to record a version of 'Where Did All The Goodtimes Go' for Pye records and subsequently moved to Decca where they recorded under the mysterious name of Toby Twirl.

Croydon Advertiser – 14.5.65

'Beat Groups play for Charity'

Two sounds and a face are among my most vivid recollections of a Beat Concert organised by Addington Methodist Youth Club on Friday, when five Croydon groups played for charity.

Held in a small church hall that had probably never heard its like before, the concert, though a little disjointed, provided an interesting evening if only for the appearance of new faces on the amateur beat scene.

*In more than four years of dealing with groups, bands and rhythm sections, I had heard only one of Friday's before - **Glen Athens & the Trojans**. With a polish that can only come after years of practice and experience, Glen Athens and his group come as near to being a professional group as possible; they were the stars of the evenings programme.*

*My two sounds: a lead guitar is perhaps the instrument that is most prominent in any modern group, but seldom is it really outstanding or even exciting. At the drop of a song title 'Lavender Blue', I had visions of a syrupy ballad; instead, 18 year old Dennis Danzelman from Cheam, and lead guitarist with the **Pumpkin Eaters** proved it to be a delightful melody. He told me he had twice rewired his instrument to get the right sound and after six years of playing with various groups, he is satisfied.*

*Another guitarist, this time at the other end of the stage line-up, was 26 year old Dave Boreham, from Norbury who played bass with the second group on, the **Dynamic Blacksmiths** of Croydon. They had a style and enthusiasm surpassed only by the Trojans. Dave's swinging bass with its live, interesting variations could be heard loud, clear - and in balance. Their singer became a little too enthusiastic at times and tended to shout, which was not the wisest of things to do in such a small hall. The band have been promised an appearance on TV's 'Opportunity Knocks', but any future success will be without their talented bass player, because Dave is retiring due to family commitments. Their drummer Phil Reed, a 20 year old Thornton Heath lad, provided my interesting face. He sat at his kit with a commanding, even imperial air. Phil seemed to put his all into his playing, without being tired, he had complete control.*

The Pebbles**, a five piece group and **The Blue Surge** from Wallington completed the evenings line-up. All of the groups gave their services free and made the evening swing along for three hours. My one criticism is that a beat concert should have had a little more variety.* ***R.S.

California 1965 - rock guitarist **Frank Zappa** marries Gail Sloatman. Surely there can't be a connection there, you may ask - well yes, actually there is. At the end of the 'fifties, Gail's father was an American naval attache working in London and the Sloatman family home was in Croydon.

It was here that Gail courted her first boyfriend, a young Eton schoolboy named Ian Ogilvy who was later to become an actor, and follow Roger Moore to play the second Simon Templar, 'The Saint' on TV. He also tried his hand at becoming a rock 'n'roller by joining a group called The Wombats, with another future actor Nicky Henson. Ogilvy remembers travelling from Earls Court to Croydon at every available moment - *"It took hours getting there, but the journeys were at least half the pleasure"* - along with Gail's enormous blue eyes, her soft appealing American accent and Mrs Sloatman's home made angel food cake!

At the completion of her father's work in Britain, the family returned to the States; not too long afterwards Gail became Mrs Zappa and they remained married until Frank's death in December 1993.

Croydon Times – 28.5.65

'Golden Guitar Back'

The Golden guitar is back in Croydon! The guitar, which was stolen recently from Potter's Music Shop in the High Street, was collected last week from Croydon police station by the manager of the shop Mr. D. Wesson.

"It was taken to Birmingham," Mr Wesson said, "where it was sold to a dealer. The Birmingham police, who knew of the theft, returned it to Croydon. We had all given up hope that it would ever be returned to the shop, as we value it very much."

The guitar, a gold plated Epiphone Sheraton is worth £300.

The Georgian Club at 6 Dingwall Road, East Croydon advertised their weekly modern jazz session as the 'Wednesday Hooter Club', featuring resident group **The Jazzhooters**. The band featured Kenny Wheeler, Cedric West and Chris Pyne, plus a superb rhythm section of Danny Thompson on double bass and Terry Cox on drums. Thompson's first musical job had been as an 18 year old working with jazzman Nat Allen at the Streatham Locarno and both he and Cox had played with blues 'godfather' Alexis Korner before joining Pentangle - who were arguably the first group to successfully mix folk, blues and jazz influences.

JULY

- 13 MOTIVATION **GN** (3/-)
- 16 THE WHO **WADDON FOOTBALL GROUND** (n/a)
- 17 DEDICATED MEN JUGBAND **S** (3/6)
- 20 THE CROW **GN** + MOTIVATION + THE DEATHLY HUSH (3/6)
- 21 THE CROWD **S** (3/6)
- 21 THE ANIMALS **O** (6/-)

AUGUST

- 1 ARLO GUTHRIE **SW** (n/a)
- 5 THE BYRDS **FH** + IVY LEAGUE + THE QUIET FIVE + THE IMPACTS + CHRISTINE QUATIER 2 shows (5/- to 12/6)
- 18 THE T-BONES **S** (n/a)
- 21 DEDICATED MEN JUGBAND **S** (n/a)
- 24 THE SNOBS **GN** + MOTIVATION (3/6)
- 25 THE T-BONES **S** (n/a)
- 31 GARY FARR & THE T-BONES **GN** + THE NOYSE (4/- & 5/-)

SEPTEMBER

- 9 THE MARK FOUR **GN** (n/a)
- 15 SANDIE SHAW & THE PARAMOUNTS **O** (6/-)
- 20 COUNT BASIE ORCHESTRA **FH** (7/6 to 20/-)
- 20 DRAMATIC DRUIDS **GN** (n/a)
- 27 THE VAMPIRES **GN** (n/a)
- 29 JOAN BAEZ **FH** (7/6 to 20/-)

OCTOBER

- 5 TREES **GN** (n/a)
- 11 THE FOURTH AMERICAN FOLK/BLUES FESTIVAL **FH** 2 shows (6/- to 21/-)
- 12 HEART & SOULS **S** + THE BOBOLINKS (3/-)
- 13 THE BARRON KNIGHTS **O** (6/-)
- 15 FOLK '65 **FH** DONOVAN + JULIE FELIX + BOB DAVENPORT + IAN CAMPBELL GROUP + TONY McCARTHY 2 shows (3/6 to 15/-)
- 31 THE TODAS **S** (n/a)

NOVEMBER

- 3 THE YARDBIRDS **O** (6/-)
- 16 THE ANZACS **GN** (n/a)
- 13 THE KINGPINS **GN** + THOSE FADING COLOURS (n/a)
- 16 THOSE FADING COLOURS **GN** (n/a)
- 20 THE SQUARE FIVE **GN** (n/a)
- 23 SOUNDS ANON. **GN** (n/a)
- 26 JULIE FELIX **FH** + THE SETTLERS + DAVEY GRAHAM (5/- to 12/6)
- 31 SONS OF FRED **GN** (n/a)

DECEMBER

- 1 DIZZY GILLESPIE QUINTET **FH** + THE JIMMY SMITH TRIO (7/6 to 17/6)
- 6 CHRIS FARLOWE **S** (2/6)
- 7 THE NOYSE **GN** (n/a)
- 10 THE WALKER BROTHERS **A** + BRIAN POOLE & THE TREMELOES + JOHNNY B. GREAT & THE QUOTATIONS (7/6 to 12/6)
- 14 THE TREES **GN** (n/a)
- 18 THE VAMPIRES **GN** (n/a)
- 27 TONY KNIGHT & THE CHESSMEN **S** (2/6)

(n/a) = ticket price not available.

In August, a 1,500 strong crowd filled the Fairfield Hall to see the American group who had recently knocked the Rolling Stones from the top of the British charts - **The Byrds**. It was the fourth date of an eighteen day tour for the band, and the Croydon audience was almost as star-studded as the bill; watching from the stalls were Paul Jones, lead singer with Manfred Mann, Ian Stuart, road manager and occasional pianist with the 'Stones, plus vocalists Julie Grant and Twinkle.

Unfortunately, according to Ray Spencer of the 'Advertiser, their sound on the night suffered badly from distortion and the vocals were indistinct and echoed round the hall. They played their hit 'Mr Tambourine Man' and previewed the follow-up single 'All I Really Want To Do', but a British manager was overheard backstage to remark *"I have better groups on my books charging £10 a session"*.

By contrast, the **Ivy League** went down a storm, performing their hit 'Tossing & Turning' with harmony and clarity not heard from the other acts on the bill. Perhaps they supplied the sound engineer for the evening!

As usual, Croydon's **Quiet Five** played on the bill and were reported to have signed up for a tour of Rumania in January '67.

The Crawdaddy Club at the Star ran one of their inimitable advertisements in the Croydon Advertiser in early July; it read - "For the first time in this noble paper we 'advetize' the new sound of the Dedicated Men Jug Band; that's on Saturday and then at the Marquet, Gun Tavern, Church Street on Tuesday 13th, everyone is welcome to rave under the floodlit apple trees and in the hall to the up and coming Motivation. And supporting group. 3/-, 8.00pm. Proceeds to hire the future appearance of Y-BIRDS and them-BONES. P.S. The more the merrier!"

ORCHID BALLROOM, PURLEY
MECCA DANCING
WEDNESDAY, 21st JULY
Personal appearance on the stage
The Animals
DANCING 7.30-11 p.m.
Admission 6/-

Touring the folk clubs of Britain at this time, was **Arlo Guthrie**, son of legendary American songwriter Woody Guthrie. Steve Benbow managed to book him into the club at the Swan & Sugarloaf where he probably performed in front of about twenty people; only three years later he was to perform at the Woodstock Festival in front of about twenty thousand!

ming Play and evening of singing with Peggy Seeger and Enoch Kent.

STEVE BENBOW'S OWN CLUB, Swan and Sugarloaf, Brighton Road, Croydon. ARLO GUTHRIE, STEVE BENBOW, PAUL SOLLY.

TAM O' SHANTER, Central Hotel, Birkenhead. THE BOR-

Earlier in the year, **Paul Simon** was also out and about in this country; learning 'Scarborough Fair' from Martin Carthy and writing 'Homeward Bound' on Widnes Railway station. I don't believe that he actually made it to Croydon, but he did play at Wimbledon folk club on June 5th and also dropped into the club in Redhill. Tim Blewitt from Croydon told me - *"I was standing in the downstairs bar at Redhill Folk Club, talking to this American chap who turned out to be Paul Simon. He was telling me about the fact that his LP cover had to be re-done. The original design had a picture of the musician photographed against a brick wall and it was only after the photographs were printed up that they noticed the wall to be covered in graffiti. That was unacceptable in those days and it had to be scrapped. I had never even heard of Paul Simon before that meeting - yes, the club at Redhill was really good for a while."*

While we're on the subject of the folk scene, local musician **Cliff Aungier** had his first LP released in July 1965. Recorded with harmonica player **Royd Rivers**, *"Wanderin"* was an album of folk and blues material on the Decca label, available in Britain in mono only, although a stereo version was released in America. The album was engineered by Glynn Johns and produced by session guitarist Jimmy Page, later to become a Yardbird and go on to form Led Zeppelin.

Cliff, aged 24 from Stanley Road, Croydon and Royd, 29, from Balham had toured solidly throughout folk and jazz clubs all over Britain with a style heavily influenced by Sonny Terry & Brownie McGhee. It was hoped that the record release would open the door for visits to Europe, particularly the folk-conscious areas of Germany and Scandinavia, as well as the USA.

Wickham Enterprises arranged a short tour at the end of July for their stage show *'An Evening with the Preachers'*, following a successful performance earlier in May. The star of the show was vocalist Paul Christian, former leader of Shirley pop group Paul & the Alpines and now backed by Beckenham recording group **The Preachers**, as were all the artists in the show. Paul, from Springpark Avenue, Shirley made his solo singing debut at the first show in May and the July/August tour visited local venues such as the Civic Hall at Orpington and Beckenham Public Hall.

Every night from 30th August to 4th September, 'Croydon's Late Night Spot' the Tropicana Club featured **Martin Jae** - *'Croydon's Top of the Hit Parade Vocalist'* - appearing with Johnny Hazell & his Quartet. Situated at 18 George Street, the club invited it's clients to 'Dine • Dance • Cabaret - 7.30 pm to 1.00am (or just drink)'!

Sandie Shaw's backing group at her September Orchid ballroom concert consisted of Gary Brooker, Robin Trower, BJ Wilson and Diz Derrick. Known at that time as **The Paramounts**, the first three members went on to become the mainstay of **Procol Harum**. Who knows?, perhaps the dance floor that Brooker later skipped light fandango's and turned cartwheels across, was based on his time spent playing keyboards behind Sandie, at gigs such as this.

An advertisement in the Bromley & Kentish Times read "Radio London comes to West Wickham (by arrangement with Wickham Enterprises). Yes, it's Britain's Brightest DJ's - KENNY & CASH - plus guest group The Sons of Fred." This gig featuring Kenny Everett and Dave Cash was due to have taken place at the Justin Hall on Friday 17th September, admission six shillings!

The Justin Hall in Beckenham Road, West Wickham was also the venue for **Alexis Korner's Blues Incorporated** on Saturday 16th October. Admission to the gig and membership of the club was free if you presented the box ad. from Melody Maker! Not a bad deal to see a band that at various times included Ginger Baker, Graham Bond, Dick Heckstall-Smith, Long John Baldry, Paul Jones, Hughie Flint, Danny Thompson... no wonder Korner is considered one of the founders of British R & B.

Croydon Advertiser – 15.10.65

'Jazzman Predicts Big Trad Revival'

CROYDON Jazz Club, the second oldest jazz club in Europe, celebrated in no uncertain terms their 16th birthday at the Star public house in London Road, West Croydon on Friday.

Topping the bill at the celebration dance were the ***Ken Colyer Jazzmen****, one British group which owe much of their popularity to their many appearances at the club. With them were the Thames City Jazz Band, a new group to Croydon, but one which will be paying many more visits in the future. The exact number of fans who crammed into the Star on Friday night remains a mystery, but there was not a square inch of ballroom space not occupied by an avid jazz fan, nor a square inch of bar not occupied by thirsty enthusiasts working off some of the heat.*

Frank Getgood, who runs the club, is certain that this is the start of a big revival for traditional jazz. Many years ago he gave Acker Bilk his first club engagement in Britain. Then came the big trad boom throughout the country, when the pop record industry bowed to the demands of the fans and trad records regularly topped the best sales charts. Depression followed. Audiences at the Star, said Mr. Getgood, dropped to the 40 and 50 mark. Smaller bands found the going too tough and dropped out of the business altogether.

But the next thing is going to be trad, Mr. Getgood hopes. He is one of the few club proprietors who have stuck to traditional jazz throughout the bad days. Now is the time when, he believes, that loyalty is going to pay dividends. Gates are steadily going up and up, averaging around the 100 mark. The birthday celebrations gave him a record audience and he means to keep them.

C.R.

Beat group **The Zombies** came bowling into Croydon on Wednesday 1st December. The purpose of their visit was to shoot some unusual publicity photographs so the group, including Rod Argent, Colin Blunstone, Chris White, Hugh Grundy and Paul Atkinson, made straight for the Tenpin Bowling Centre in Tamworth Road and had their picture taken while they played a few games.

The full line-up for the **Walker Brothers** concert at the ABC on 10th December featured Brian Poole & the Tremeloes, Johnny B. Great & the Quotations, The Soul Mates with Jet Set, The Rivits, The Tremors and Peter Quinton.

Croydon - 'buried alive in the Blues'

Croydon connoisseurs of blues, folk and gospel probably couldn't believe their luck when the Fairfield Hall was chosen as one of the regular venues to hold a series of fine package shows, collectively known as the **American Folk & Blues Festivals**.

This allowed them the rare opportunity to hear black musicians of the calibre of Muddy Waters, Sonny Boy Williamson, John Lee Hooker, Lonnie Johnson and Albert King, often for the first time in Britain and on one or two occasions, the Fairfield was the *only* British venue on the tour. These remarkable concerts were initially the brainchild of jazz stalwart Chris Barber, who set about organising these artists to tour Europe in conjunction with the National Jazz Federation.

"...nowhere could we have hoped for such a reception as we got in Croydon."

1963 – **Sonny Boy Williamson**
Muddy Waters
Lonnie Johnson
Victoria Spivey
Matt 'Guitar' Murphy
Memphis Slim
Willie Dixon
Big Joe Williams

The first of these celebrated events took place on 18th and 20th October 1963 under the title 'American Negro Blues Festival', with Croydon being the only British venue at the end of a successful European tour. This blues showcase was a mouth watering line-up for enthusiasts who, up to that time, had been forced to make do with hard-to-come-by American-imported records, rare snatches of the music on radio and cover versions from the likes of the Rolling Stones, the Animals and the Yardbirds.

There were three shows, over two days, with an estimated 6,000 people through the doors including travelling fans from Belfast and Birmingham; plus the hundred or so lucky enough to be at the Star Hotel - see story opposite. An official for the NJF said: "This has been an unprecedented success; nowhere could we have hoped for such a reception as we got in Croydon".

1964 – **Muddy Waters**
Sonny Terry
& Brownie McGhee
Cousin Joe Pleasants
Sister Rosetta Tharpe
Rev. Gary Davis
Otis Spann

The next of these shows to roll into Croydon was the 'Blues & Gospel Caravan' on 10th May 1964. Another sell-out, it was the 'hot gospel' of Sister Rosetta Tharpe that stole the show according to the Croydon Times. Sonny & Brownie played Big Bill Broonzy's 'Key To The Highway' and Sonny later joined Gary Davis onstage for a couple of songs. Despite being top of the bill, Muddy Waters only had time for four numbers, backed by Otis Spann, Ransome Knowling on bass and drummer Willie Smith.

Fortunately, Val Wilmer was on hand to record some of these shows in photographic form, for posterity.

Val Wilmer

Members of the First (and arguably the finest) American Folk & Blues Festival take their bow at the Fairfield Hall. Left to right: Memphis Slim, Sonny Boy Williamson, Lonnie Johnson, Victoria Spivey and Muddy Waters.

Val Wilmer

'Muddy introduces his next song to an enthusiastic Croydon audience' - the legendary Muddy Waters onstage at the Fairfield in October 1963. Also pictured are Ransome Knowling on double bass and Willie Smith on drums.

One of the most amazing gigs to take place at the Star Hotel occurred just after the first American Negro Blues Festival in October 1963. It was witnessed by British blues guitarist Cliff Aungier, who had gone along to his local club to watch the Yardbirds perform, when in walked many of the original bluesmen from the festival.

Cliff's own account is mentioned in his interview on pages 38-41, but here is how the incident was reported in the Croydon Times:

Val Wilmer

Muddy relaxing backstage before the show with a game of cards. Artistes bar, Fairfield Hall, October 1963.

Croydon Times – 25.10.63

Now Broad Green has a Rhythm & Blues 'War'

Take one smoke-filled room, add a number of fervent youths and mix in a beat group. Repeat the process four days later and you have the instant recipe for Croydon's rhythm and blues 'war'.

The contenders for the honour of attracting most fans to their sessions are the giant National Jazz Federation, who meet at the Star, Broad Green on Saturdays and Peter Malcolm who runs his club at the same venue on Wednesdays.

First into the field were the NJF, who kicked off last weekend in splendid style with The Yardbirds - who have been called the second Rolling Stones - and a surprise visit from most of the cast of the American Negro Blues Festival which was taking place along the road at the Fairfield Halls. In charge was Giorgio Gomelsky who, like the fans, was overjoyed when Matt 'Guitar' Murphy, Sonny Boy Williamson and Muddy Waters agreed to give impromptu performances.

Of the Yardbirds, Sonny Boy told the 'Times' - "This is the first time I have heard a group of young fellas wailing to suit me. And I take some suiting".

When news got round that the Americans were on the scene, the club room quickly filled and one of the most swinging nights Croydon had seen for a long time soon got under way. Before long it was impossible to dance, sit or drink in ample comfort. As a burst of frenzied applause rent the air, Mr. Gomelsky told our reporter - "Hear that? That is how much the young people of Croydon enjoy rhythm and blues. We have come here to fill a gap in the musical life of a town of 253,000. We do not want to attract the 'geezers, herberts and charlies', we are here to suit the true afficianados. If we can do that we will be more than happy".

But one man who was not so happy was Peter Malcolm who had wanted Saturdays for his rhythm and blues club, and who has to be content with Wednesdays. Mr. Malcolm had the Cyril Davies AllStars with Long John along to entertain in their own special way - and again gave the Croydon fans a night to remember. Said Mr. Malcolm; "When I was trying to book Cyril, I spoke to an agent who let the National Jazz Federation know what I was planning at the Star. The next thing I knew, they had booked the pub for Saturdays. It is quite unfair".

But between them, the NJF and Peter Malcolm have, in fact added to the musical life of Croydon. Doubters need only pay a visit to the Star any Saturday or Wednesday from now on to find out how true that is.

1964 – **Sonny Boy Williamson**
Howlin' Wolf
Lightning Hopkins
Sleepy John Estes
John Henry Barbee
Sugar Pie Desanto
Willie Dixon

On Monday 19th and Sunday 25th October the Third American Negro Blues Festival played to packed houses once again. The tour backing band was just as 'star-studded' as the main cast, with Willie Dixon playing bass alongside drummer Hubert Sumlin, guitarist Clifton James and Sunnyland Slim on piano.

1965 – **Bishop Samuel Kelsey**
Five Blind Boys of Mississippi, Alabama
Sister Lena
Inez Andrews & the Andrewettes
Philip Jones

The 'First Negro Gospel Festival' played two shows at the Fairfield on 5th February, still presented by the NJF. Bishop Samuel Kelsey appeared with (deep breath)... The Congregation of the Temple Church of God In Christ, Washington DC!

1965 – **Rev. Gary Davis**
Buffy Sainte-Marie
Derroll Adams
Ramblin' Jack Elliott
Julie Felix

The show on Monday 14th June was definitely more 'folk' than 'blues', with the two ladies of the tour taking most of the credit, Buffy Sainte-Marie in particular performing with a passion and intensity that threatened to overshadow the rest. Her standpoint was from a different angle; the injustices served on the American Indians - she has Cree Indian descent - rather than those against the Black American that is the basis of all blues music.

Quote of the night goes to Rev. Gary Davis; blind since birth and one of the finest of the original blues guitarists, he told the audience: *"You may have to tell me how a guitar looks - but I can tell you how it feels"*.

1965 – **Big Moma Thornton**
Roosevelt Sykes
Buddy Guy
J.B. Lenoir
Dr. Ross
Eddie Boyd
Mississippi McDowell
Big Shakey Horton
Freddie Bilow
Lonesome Jimmy Lee

On 11th October, the Fairfield Halls was chosen once again as a venue for the 4th American Folk & Blues Festival. Presented by the National Jazz Federation, this concert featured one of the biggest collections of blues artists assembled on a British stage. There were two shows, at 6.45pm and 9.00pm and ticket prices ranged from 6/- to 21/-. With this being the opening night of the tour, several press photographers were in attendance to cover the event, including James Barron whose pictures appear here.

1966 – **Bishop Samuel Kelsey**
The Harmonising Four of Richmond, Virginia

16th January, this time under the name of the 'Spiritual & Gospel Show'.

1968 – **John Lee Hooker**
Jimmy Reed
T-Bone Walker
Big Joe Williams
Curtis Jones
Eddie Taylor Blues Band

The return of the American Folk/ Blues Festival, Wednesday 30th October but unfortunately reviewed for the Advertiser by a jazz purist. Consequently Hooker was "dull and uninteresting", Walker was "gimmicky" and so on. However, points *were* awarded to 66 year old Big Joe Williams and his battered acoustic guitar and for the clear lyrics of Curtis Jones. Harmonica stylist Shakey Horton joined T-Bone Walker onstage for a duet and the whole affair was compered by the garrulous Al Smith.

1969 – **Albert King**
John Lee Hooker
Otis Spann
Champion Jack Dupree
Sonny Terry & Brownie McGhee

November 9th - another strong bill, despite the absence of John Lee Hooker who cried off sick. Otis Spann was playing his first UK tour as a solo artist, having just left Muddy Waters Band. Albert King stole the show in a big way - six foot four, 280 pounds and trademark Gibson 'flying V' blazing away.

1970 – **Willie Dixon**
Sonny Terry & Brownie McGhee
Champion Jack Dupree
Sister Rosetta Tharpe
Shakey Horton & Lafayette Leake
Bukka White

Wednesday 25th November, another 'American Folk Blues & Gospel Show', headlined by bassist Willie Dixon & his Chicago Blues AllStars - a five piece band featuring Lee Jackson on electric guitar. Highlight of the show was a moving performance by Sonny and Brownie - *"their sounds complement each other beautifully... Sonny has the gritty voice and an ability to make his harmonica almost talk... Brownie's voice is soft in contrast, his guitar playing superb"*.

James Barron / Redferns

Caught in the spotlight and struttin' across the stage of the Fairfield Halls is the young Buddy Guy. Note the minimal amplification - but at least the bass player got his own amp!

James Barron / Redferns

Pictured backstage in the Fairfield dressing room is blues singer Big Moma Thornton, practising some harmonica and looking a little apprehensive. Close by, however, is a reassuring bottle of Johnnie Walker. Thornton is probably best remembered as the composer of the original "Hound Dog", a watered-down version of which became a bigger hit for an upstart country rocker, Elvis somebody-or-other!

James Barron / Redferns

Dr. Ross playing one-man band fashion, a la Jesse Fuller. Seated in front of a bass drum and hi-hat cymbal, he plays guitar left handed, but rather than re-string the instrument, he has simply turned his Gibson acoustic upside down!

Croydon Advertiser – 15.10.65

'Not much true blues left now'

THE 1965 EDITION of the American Folk Blues Festival began their tour of Britain at the Fairfield Hall on Monday with much the same format as has prevailed since their first arrival in Europe in 1962.

The content has, however, deteriorated. Much of Monday's concert was nothing but a glorified rock'n'roll show, with gimmicks and presentation to match.

There were of course, exceptions, namely J.B. Lenoir, Roosevelt Sykes and Mississippi Fred McDowell, all of whom had a great deal to offer, but in strikingly different styles.

Powerful contemporary blues came from Lenoir about Alabama. The riots, murder of Negros and segregation may seem a long way off when read of in newspapers or seen on television, but they are brought uncomfortably close to home by this singers simplicity and sincerity, stemming from environmental influences. When he sings "I ain't never going back to Alabama", it is a statement.

More traditional in approach was Fred McDowell with his stories of the blues and how you get them. "Highway 61" can be likened to the lifespan itself, with its disappointments, frustrations and never ending toil. Simple though the lyrics may be, many are of double meaning and more often than not relate to the master and slave situation of the plantation days before emancipation.

Roosevelt Sykes is one of the few remaining barrelhouse pianists on the scene today. Basically boogie style music, it evolved around the gin mills and waterfront bars of the American coast and was highly popular until the 'thirties. Today, Sykes is the master of this domain and his ovation at the end of this concert would have been the envy of any pop idol.

F.W.P.

JANUARY

- 3 ZOOT MONEY **S** (n/a)
- 15 KINGPINS **GN** (n/a)
- 16 SPIRITUAL & GOSPEL SHOW **FH** BISHOP SAMUEL KELSEY (n/a)
- 17 JOHN MAYALL **S** (n/a)
- 17 KINKS **SB** (5/6)
- 22 THE VAMPIRES **GN** (n/a)
- 24 ARTWOODS **S** (n/a)
- 25 TREES **GN** (n/a)
- 29 GARY FARR & THE T-BONES **GN** (n/a)

FEBRUARY

- 3 CHRIS FARLOWE **S** (n/a)
- 7 GRAHAM BOND **S** (n/a)
- 8 SONS OF FRED **GN** (n/a)
- 9 CHARLIE & INEZ FOX **O** + THE LEAGUE OF GENTLEMEN (5/-)
- 14 THE TRAIN **S** (n/a)
- 15 GENE PITNEY **A** + LEN BARRY + D,D,D,B,M & T + SUE & SUNNY + THE JUST 5 (7/6 to 12/6)
- 22 THEM **GN** (n/a)
- 23 THE SMALL FACES **O** (5/-)
- 25 IAN CAMPBELL FOLK GROUP **FH** + IAN & SYLVIA + GORDON LIGHTFOOT + THE SETTLERS + TREVOR LUCAS (6/6 to 17/-)

MARCH

- 3 WOODY HERMAN **FH** (7/6 to 17/6)
- 7 ZOOT MONEY **S** (n/a)

APRIL

- 6 SPENCER DAVIS GROUP **O** (6/6)
- 7 OSCAR PETERSON TRIO **FH** (7/6 to 17/6)
- 9 NINA & FREDERIK **FH** (6/6 to 15/-)
- 13 ALAN PRICE SET **O** (5/-)
- 15 THE WHO **FH** + SPENCER DAVIS GROUP + NEW MERSEYS + BAND OF ANGELS (5/- to 12/6)
- 20 THE VIBRATIONS **O** (5/-)
- 20 MIKE & PEGGY SEEGER **FH** (6/6 to 17/6)
- 25 THEOLONIUS MONK QUARTET **FH** (6/6 to 17/6)
- 27 DAVE DEE, DOZY, BEAKY, MICK & TICH **O** (5/-)

MAY

- 4 HEDGEHOPPERS ANONYMOUS **O** (5/-)
- 6 'FOLK MEETS THE BLUES' **FH** (5/- to 15/-)
- 7 BO-STREET RUNNERS **S** (n/a)
- 10 JOHN MAYALL **S** (n/a)
- 11 PATTI LABELLE & HER BELLES **O** (5/-)
- 12 ORNETTE COLEMAN TRIO **FH** (7/6 to 17/6)
- 14 THE IN-CROWD **S** (n/a)
- 16 BOARDWALKERS **S** (n/a)
- 18 THE DRIFTERS **O** (5/-)
- 21 T-BONES **S** (n/a)
- 23 GRAHAM BOND **S** (n/a)
- 25 BEN E KING **O** (6/-)
- 27 THE KINKS **FH** + D.D,D,B,M & T + WAYNE FONTANA + GOLDIE + SEAN BUCKLEY SET (6/6 to 15/-)

JUNE

- 1 THE SHE TRINITY **O** (5/-)
- 8 ZOOT MONEY'S BIG ROLL BAND **O** (5/-)
- 9 ERROL GARNER **FH** (6/- to 20/-)
- 10 THE INKSPOTS **O** (7/-)
- 15 ROY C. **O** (5/-)
- 22 THE FORTUNES **O** (5/-)
- 29 THE SMALL FACES **O** (6/-)

(n/a) = ticket price not available.

A mixture of luck and misfortune hit two young Croydon groups at the beginning of '66.

Misfortune hit **The Vandals** in January when they were themselves the victims of real-life vandalism. £100 worth of the bands' equipment was stolen from the garden shed of bass player Eric Jones, in Green Lane Gardens, Thornton Heath, including a £75 drum kit, an £18 guitar amplifier, speakers, cases, microphones and stands - leaving the group with just their guitars, a bass amplifier and a pair of bongos.

The Vandals had only been together for six months, playing their first gigs during the last weeks of December 1965; the band comprising of Paul Likeman, Edward Kemp, Steve Hinkesman and the unlucky Eric, all attended Ingram Road School in Thornton Heath.

The good luck fell to the **Fadin' Colours**, who signed their first recording contract with Ember Records, one of the largest independent labels in the country. The group was formed out of two earlier bands, The Kingpins and Those Fadin' Colours with the assistance of American manager Jim Economides who had been associated with Bobby Darin, the Lettermen and the Beach Boys.

The new line-up consisted of Keith and Ray Neale from Ripley Close, New Addington; Jimmy Barnard of Leigh Crescent, New Addington; Geoffrey Coppins from Norbury and Glyn Stephens from Birdhirst Avenue, South Croydon.

Short of something to do around 3 o'clock on Saturday 12th February? If you fancied meeting a 'top pop group', then Rumbelows of Croydon was the place for you. They boasted a personal appearance by *the fabulous* **Small Faces** at their shop at 27 St. George's Walk, where Stevie Marriott, Ronnie Lane, Ian MacLagan and Kenny Jones would be happy to sign autographs and chat about their latest hit record - ('Sha La La La Lee' was just edging its way into the charts)

In fact, the band were busy doing a sensible piece of promotion, no doubt with a hefty push from manager Don Arden, because their afternoon stint in Rumbelows record department probably ensured a sell out gig at the Orchid Ballroom on the 23rd February.

American recording stars **Gene Pitney** and **Len Barry** played two shows at the ABC on Tuesday 15th February. With them on the bill were Dave Dee, Dozy, Beaky, Mick & Tich, Sue & Sunny, the Just 5 and the Mike Cotton Sound, who were presumably the backing group for most of the artists. The compere was Billy Boyle.

A week later, 'Club Nevada' at the Gun put on a rare Croydon appearance by Van Morrison's **Them**; the advertisement in the local press billed the gig as 'Fab Irish R'n'B! and with the advantage of hindsight, I think I would have opted for a night down at the Gun.

Mr Guy Williams chose Croydon as the location for the British office of GAPS - General Artistic Production Services Limited, an agency boasting a rosta of thirty five groups, including eight local bands.

Williams started the agency in Germany during 1964 to assist the invasion of British Beat groups who flooded in to play the clubs of Hamburg, Frankfurt and Berlin. Now situated in Cherry Orchard Road, Mr Williams told the Croydon Advertiser - *"I came to Croydon because it is an expanding place and as yet, there are no other agencies here"*.

Two of the Croydon groups on his books included **The Commanches** and **The Nestlers** and both were successfully touring Germany at the time of the article; the Commanches playing the Big Apple Club in Hamburg before moving to clubs in Italy and Switzerland, while the Nestlers played the Crazy Horse Club in Hamburg, before moving to Frankfurt and then Switzerland.

By Popular Demand! shouted the classified ad. announcing the return of **The Barbarians** to St. Peter's Hall in Ledbury Road, South Croydon. The gig on Saturday 19th February also featured sets by the Traumen and the Defiant Ones and your admission fee of four shillings and sixpence gave access to a fully licenced buffet. *Come early!*

Of the many folk clubs that were once thriving in the Croydon area, only one was still in existence in the middle of March '66 - **The Grange** Folk Club in Norbury Road, Thornton Heath.

Since the closure of the club at the Star Hotel earlier in the month - presumably to concentrate on the R'n'B boom - Grange organiser Peter Eagle believed his club to be the only one locally that was devoted solely to folk music. The Grange had been formed in December 1965 and ran the successful policy of booking a top guest every other week; including artists such as Bob Davenport, Tony McCarthy and Bert Jansch.

For any self-respecting beat group in 1966, it seems that the thing to do was turn professional and get yourself over to Hamburg or Frankfurt - personally I blame the Beatles...

Germany invaded by Trojans!

So popular was this 'invasion' that the local fans screamed, shouted and stamped - one young German girl even proposed to bass guitarist Derek Needham! Croydon beat group **The Trojans** toured Germany in February as their first professional engagement.

Their agent Louis Chun told the Advertiser - *"I knew they were ready to turn professional; they've been going for five years now, in fact they are Croydon's oldest group. In Germany there is plenty of opportunity for a good, young group if they are versatile and have at least three years working experience behind them"*. He confided that generally the future for groups was looking grim - *"Local groups are no longer the draw because the youngsters get so used to them and the really good groups are charging so much less in order to get work. There was a time when a good, semi-pro band could earn £15 a night, now they often work for as little as £3"*.

In March, the Trojans were booked to play Silver Blades at Streatham Ice Rink where three agents and record company representatives would be there to hear them.

For the full story of the Trojans (formerly Glen Athens & the Trojans) see the interview with Mike Roberts and Matthew Fisher on pages 50 - 53.

Croydon Advertiser – 18.3.66

'APPEARING WITH THE SEARCHERS'

*One man's misfortune is another's opportunity. Or that's how it was with 18 year old **Johnny Blunt**, who last week became the temporary drummer for **The Searchers** when their regular drummer, Chris Curtis, fell ill.*

*"It's fantastic," said Johnny, who plays regularly with **The Trees**, from Croydon.*

After only two rehearsals with the group, he found himself hurled into the hectic life of a professional, facing a mob of screaming girls, signing autographs and talking to the fans.

It makes a change from humping sacks of coal around, which is what Johnny, who lives in Copse View, Selsdon, has been doing for the past two months. Now he's a retired coalman and is conserving his energy for the rest of the tour with The Searchers. When it's over he would like to turn professional full time. If he can't he'll stick with his own group and wait for another chance.

The **Olive Tree**, a popular coffee bar and club in Brighton Road, South Croydon had attracted more than its fair share of bad publicity over the previous months. So the owner of the club, Mrs Ann Parker, took the step of limiting the membership and vetting the applicants - and providing they were accepted, were over 19 and paid the membership fee of £1.00, each new member was issued with their own key to the basement club!

The newly decorated venue was called the Ala Moana Club, after a surfing beach in Hawaii and the decor reflected that theme. Music on Tuesday and Wednesday nights was provided by the clubs well-stocked jukebox and there were even plans to turn the place into a discotheque on certain evenings.

They may have been following the well-trodden path from East Croydon station to the Star Clubs of Hamburg, but having just turned professional, five-piece Croydon group **The Partizans** still couldn't believe their luck when they were booked for a 17 date tour of Germany. All in their early twenties, the group had been playing pop and rhythm & blues in Croydon and the surrounding area for about five years. Unfortunately instead of returning home with a success story, their good fortune turned to disaster soon after they left England.

It began when the group split up to make the journey to Hamburg. Three members - Graham Leech (bass), Robert Johnson (organ) and Gerry Lloyd (drums) - travelled by rail with their manager, while the other two, lead guitarist John Edmed and singer Clement Leo Taylor drove across in the group's van. The rail travellers arrived safely only to hear that 'Chubby' Taylor had not been allowed into the country. Although he held a British passport, it had been issued in Barbados so, unlike the rest of the band, he had to apply for a visa. After several days unsuccessfully trying to organise one, the dejected Chubby called the band and agreed to meet up with them in Ostend.

Then came the next bit of bad news; John Edmed, of Watlingham Road, Thornton Heath was involved in an accident while driving the van through Belgium and was in hospital in Ghent. Luckily he was not badly injured, but enough to be hospitalised for three days. The van was a write-off but none of the musical equipment was damaged.

Back in England, the group 'licked their wounds' and decided that things could have been much worse. In fact, they found that the tour of Hamburg clubs was still open to them and that an offer of six weeks work in the South of France had come in - proving that every cloud really does have a silver lining.

JULY

- 6 CHRIS FARLOWE **O** (5/-)
- 13 THE ORLONS **O** (5/-)
- 20 CLARENCE 'FROGMAN' HENRY **O** (5/-)
- 27 SOLOMON BURKE **O** (5/-)

AUGUST

- 3 THE TROGGS **O** (5/-)
- 10 GEORGIE FAME & THE BLUEFLAMES **O** (6/-)
- 13 CLAYTON SQUARES **OT** (n/a)
- 17 CLIFF BENNETT & THE REBEL ROUSERS **O** (6/-)
- 24 THE WHO **O** (6/-)
- 31 THE HOLLIES **O** (6/-)

SEPTEMBER

- 7 SMALL FACES **O** (6/-)
- 14 OTIS REDDING **O** (10/-)
- 21 MODERN JAZZ QUARTET **FH** (6/- to 20/-)
- 21 VIBRATIONS **O** (5/-)
- 26 CREAM **S** (n/a)
- 27 SEARCHERS **O** (6/6)

OCTOBER

- 21 THE MARQUEE SHOW **FH** + SPENCER DAVIS + THE MOVE + JIMMY JAMES & THE VAGABONDS + WYNDER K FROGG + THE HERD + THE VIP'S (5/- to 12/6)
- 25 THE ACTION **W** (4/-)

NOVEMBER

- 2 DAVE BRUBECK QUARTET **FH** (6/- to 20/-)
- 4 SCREAMING LORD SUTCH **NA** (n/a)
- 9 ZOOT MONEY's BIG ROLL BAND **NA** (n/a)
- 11 'BLUESENSATION' **FH** + ALEXIS KORNER + LONG JOHN BALDRY + CLIFF BARTON + GERRY LOCKRAN + DUFFY POWER (6/6 to 15/-)
- 23 JULIE FELIX **FH** (5/- to 20/-)
- 28 SHOTGUN EXPRESS **S** (n/a)
- 30 DIZZY GILLESPIE **FH** + CLARK TERRY + COLEMAN HAWKINS + BENNY CARTER + ZOOT SIMS (6/- to 20/-)

DECEMBER

- 7 TOM JONES **O** (7/6)
- 10 THE COFFEE SET **S** (n/a)
- 12 THE TRAIN **S** (n/a)
- 22 GARY FARR & THE T-BONES **NA** (n/a)

(n/a) = ticket price not available.

Back in March, the basement club at the Olive Tree may have changed its name to the Ala Moana and added a discotheque night, but the club was still actively promoting live music. On 13th August the **Clayton Squares** played two 45 minute sets, for which they received £30.

The contract for this gig was signed by Stephen Ford on behalf of the club and the additional clauses section shows that the band wanted 'cash on the night' and had to arrive by 7.30. The Bryan Morrison Agency took 10% of the fee as commission, which was then split with Galaxy Entertainments.

While on the subject of contracts, on 22nd December Galaxy Entertainments booked **Gary Farr & the T-Bones** into the New Addington Hotel. Once again they were to play two 45 minute spots, but the band were on 50% of the gate against a guarantee of £35 - that sounds like a better deal to me, especially as the New Addington Hotel could hold three times the crowd you could cram into the Olive Tree. Cash on the night, with all transportation to be provided by the artists and the contract was signed on behalf of the venue by one T. Poole.

ORCHID BALLROOM
PURLEY
MECCA DANCING
WEDNESDAY 3rd AUGUST
THE TROGGS
DANCING 7.30-11.00 ADMISSION 5/-

The 'cool, sophisticated sound' of the **Modern Jazz Quartet** filled the Fairfield on 21st September.

This superb American foursome, comprising pianist John Lewis, Percy Heath on bass, drummer Connie Kay and Milt Jackson on vibrophone, had been playing together for eleven years - little wonder that Kay and Heath provided such a tight rhythm section. John Hewitt reviewed the concert for the Croydon Times: *"Two of the numbers played were in fugue form and inspired some interesting interplay between the introvert style of Lewis and the group's fast playing vibraphonist, Milt Jackson. 'Dido's Lament', a new arrangement by Lewis of Henry Purcell's closing aria from 'Dido & Aeneas', was strangely beautiful in its hymn-like sonority. Jackson, in his solo, chose the notes exquisitely, with precision and reverence".*

Orchid Ballroom • Purley
Telephone: UPLands 1174
MECCA DANCING
Wednesday, 24th August
THE WHO
Dancing 7.30–11 p.m. Admission 6'-

Approximately one hundred female pop fans flocked into the record department of Allders Croydon store to catch a glimpse of **Brian Poole & the Tremeloes** on Friday 21st October.

The reporter from the Croydon Times was completely nonplussed: *As the girls swarmed around the beat group to get a signed photograph, I wondered at the staccato conversations going on around me. I felt like the traditional infidel, a non-believer among so many ardent followers, or so I thought. "Doesn't he look different in real life," said a girl of about 16, wearing white stockings and a maroon mini dress, "his hair is shorter than I expected". She pushed herself forward to the front of many frantic females clutching for an autographed picture - once the photograph was in her hand, she smiled and began to hurry out of the record store.*

Croydon Advertiser – 28.10.66

'SHOWERS OF SUGAR, etcetera'

THE MARQUEE SHOW

IT WAS A BIT of a shambles at the Fairfield Hall on Friday night, what with the sugar lumps, the rice, the lavatory rolls, the Smarties, the confetti and numerous unidentified objects.

These were all hurled onto the stage during the second house of a pop show headed by the ***Spencer Davis Group****.*

Wynder K. Frogg set the pace, which turned out to be an easy shuffle. And ***Wynder K. Frogg*** *turned out to be five of them - two sax players, a drummer, an organist (WKF) and a guitarist. Vocally they were humdrum and uninspiring, but instrumentally they were novel and exciting. And they played their unique sound in an entirely unaffected and nonchalant way, apparently unaware that there was an audience at all. You felt more like a fly on the wall than a 12s. 6d ticket holder. When this group have found a more original vocal approach they will knock some of the better known names for six.*

The only group who managed to vary the tension in their songs were the ***V.I.P's*** *- musically rather conventional, they were nevertheless hardworking and thoughtful and their volume ranged from pianissimo to fortissimo. 'Staggerlee' was an example of their studied dramatic approach.*

Standing in a straight line, ***Jimmy James & the Vagabonds*** *let rip. They had good songs, such as 'My Girl' and 'I'll Be There' and an overpowering gaiety that had the audience dancing in the aisles. A great act of pure burlesque came from the* ***Herd****, whose entertainment value was high even if their musical competence was debatable. Dressed as though for the circus, the only thing they didn't do was saw a lady in half. They threw a screaming one a red rose, though, and she ripped it to bits, petal by petal.*

Following in the path of the Who, the ***Move*** *have apparently decided to try a little wanton destruction for their gimmick. The idea was to kick everything onstage over (or if possible, to bits) while still playing. A few sparks flashed here and there to indicate blown fuses. But they weren't really kicking you see, just pretending to kick; you could tell that because of the little figure crawling on his hands and knees behind the amps, lighting the flashes. He also lit a violent explosion to end the act, but unfortunately it didn't go off until the next group were ready to play.*

At least, however we had the great ***Spencer Davis Group****; or rather, we had Stevie (Winwood), for it was only when he was 'in charge' that they rose above mediocrity into something really great. Their best number, a blues, featured him as pianist and vocalist. It was called 'Nobody loves you when you're down and out' and it was only a pity he adulterated it by turning it into a semi-beat number halfway through.*

Stevie is not really an accomplished musician, it seems to me - he thumped away at the keyboard with dexterity, but little else and sang in a voice strongly reminiscent of Ray Charles. But his unassuming personality has a great magnetism about it and he throws himself into a song, evoking such an atmosphere, that you are conscious only of the music and the words.

This ability to lose himself in a number, and to take the audience whole-heartedly with him, is what makes him a great performer. Greater perhaps, than the rest of the group deserve.

R. C. de S.

A great idea for a package tour; to take some of the groups who played regularly at the celebrated Marquee club in Wardour Street, London and send them off round the provinces. There were a couple of hidden stars in amongst the support acts; the organist of Wynder K. Frogg was Mick 'Blue' Weaver, who went on to play with Amen Corner, The Strawbs and (very) briefly with Mott the Hoople. The V.I.P.'s became Spooky Tooth, whose guitarist Luther Grosvenor also made a brief appearance in Mott the Hoople under the name Ariel Bender!

In November, the **Shotgun Express** made an appearance at the Star, featuring vocalists **Rod Stewart** and Beryl Marsden, Peter Bardens on keyboards, Mick Fleetwood on drums, Peter Green on guitar and Dave Ambrose on bass.

Rod's old mate Long John Baldry was also back in Croydon earlier that month, as part of the 'Bluesensation' package that played the Fairfield Hall; this is what one half of the local press had to say:

Croydon Times – 18.11.66

'Folk blues still have far to go'

ACCORDING TO the 'with-it' men in the pop world, Folk/blues is sure to be the next phase in records. But judging by the poor attendance for the 'Bluesensation' concert at the Fairfield Hall on Friday, it is going to be a long time coming.

And this despite the presence of ***Long John Baldry****, one of the most popular, if not professional, exponents of this type of music in England. But certainly the 200 or so who did go along enjoyed themselves, as Baldry and the other acts especially Duffy Power, put on a smooth performance.*

Gerry Lockran opened the programme and his rendering of 'New York's My Home' was particularly compelling. Former pop singer Duffy Power was next, and showed immense improvement from his rock'n'roll days - his voice was controlled and he showed a wide range. He received a particularly appreciative round of applause for carrying on despite a microphone failure during 'Help Me'. Power writes a lot of his material himself and should be in the forefront if and when this music really attains mass appeal.

However the arrival of Long John Baldry made the audience forget all that had gone before. The sheer physical size of the man compels one to listen (he is 6ft. 7ins.), and when one does, the powerful and subtle rendering of songs like 'Gee Baby, Ain't I Good To You' leaves one lost in admiration.

Alexis Korner, who also acted as compere, concentrated too much on the quantity of the sound rather than the quality when his turn came.

Nevertheless - a swinging evening.

Can't see The Searchers for the Trees...

Croydon R'n'B group **The Trees** were founded by drummer Johnny Blunt from Copse View, Selsdon and cut their teeth rehearsing in a hall up at Monks Hill, close to the homes of most of the group members.

The band played many of their local gigs at the Gun in Crown Hill, or the 'Club Nevada', as it was known back in 1966. In February of that year John was 'headhunted' by **The Searchers**, who were looking for a temporary replacement for Chris Curtis, who had just decided to quit the group. John's friend Valerie had an influential brother at the Harold Davison Agency and when their representative came down to watch the band play, John initially thought that it was with the intention of signing the Trees. Instead, he was given a few days rehearsal and within a couple of weeks John had traded the backstreet halls of Croydon for the theatres and cinemas of Britain as the Searchers joined a package tour with P.J. Proby.

Not only did John find himself playing to slightly larger audiences (!), but he was now sharing a stage with some of his own favourite artists - particularly one trip with Roy Orbison and the Small Faces. Before each concert the various group members would get together and jam - and Steve Marriott, who always wanted to try out every available instrument, often tried his hand at drumming on John's old Ludwig kit, getting John to show him a basic backbeat.

In February 1969, John made the papers when he was busted for possession of cannabis. As it was a first offence, John expected a small fine and a slap on the wrist, yet thanks to an over-zealous judge he was not only fined heavily but was remanded for 17 days. The twenty-one year old drummer remembers attending the prison chapel, only to find himself sitting in the row in front of the Kray brothers - wearing handcuffs and immaculate blue suits! The Searchers made a good living touring the college circuit but by the end of the 'sixties found themselves veering more towards the cabaret-style venues and it was at this point that John decided to jump ship. He stayed into early 1970, long enough to show Billy Adamson the ropes and then joined up with an old friend from New Addington, Ray Neale. Ray and his brother Keith had formed **The Orange Seaweed**, originally as a fourpiece, but when their drummer and rhythm guitarist left, Ray recruited John on drums and carried on as a trio. Almost his first gigs with the Seaweed were on a trip to Africa, with bookings in Istanbul and Uganda, where John remembers a curfew imposed on the band and an armed guard posted outside their makeshift accommodation, for their own safety!

Two ex-members of the Trees, Roger Probert and Rick Stannard put together a new group - **No Doe Fox** and John worked with them initially as manager. When drummer Malcolm Mills left around 1973-74, John was drafted in once more and this time found himself taking off to Zurich for a tour of the U.S. Airbases. Probert moved to America to work in A&R for Atlantic Records - while Rick Stannard is believed to be in Australia.

When No Doe Fox returned from Switzerland, John got to keep the group's van and one of his first jobs back in Croydon was helping local record entrepreneur Dave Lashmar to move house!

It was not long before John was playing with Ray Neale again, this time as part of a duo called **Ramrod** - rockabilly, blues and straightforward rock'n'roll. They parted company when the late Tony Vincent lured John away to join the highly-rated **CSA**, while Ray linked up with Bob Burgos to form Shotgun (see page 213).

In the early 'eighties John formed **Reflections**, featuring Garth Watt Roy from the Q-Tips (brother of Blockhead bassist Norman Watt Roy) and Tony from the Café Racers, a band that formed the basis of Dire Straits. Reflections proved to be very popular on the local circuit, especially at Crocks in Redhill.

These days John can be found performing solo, as a guitar and vocal act under the name of 'Johnny B. Good' - although he still teaches drumming to disadvantaged children - and incidentally his old Ludwig kit is now being competently played by his son.

Courtesy John Blunt

The first Trees line-up in rehearsal at Monks Hill, Selsdon. Left to right: Roger Probert, Dave Bushell, Johnny Blunt, Ian Coughlan and Jim Bale.

... The Orange Seaweed and No Doe Fox!

THE TREES

Popular Croydon-based R'n'B group circa '64/66, often to be found in the Gun Tavern playing alongside The Vampires and The T-Bones. "We were the local 'party' band" according to Roger Probert, "and just before John left we were starting to be a pretty tight band." Founder member Johnny Blunt was thrust into the limelight, when chosen by The Searchers as the replacement drummer for Chris Curtis.

Incidentally, the Croydon 'Trees' are not to be confused with the folk band of the same name, who released two highly sought after albums for CBS - *'The Garden of Jane Trelawny'* and *'On the Shore'* in the late Sixties.

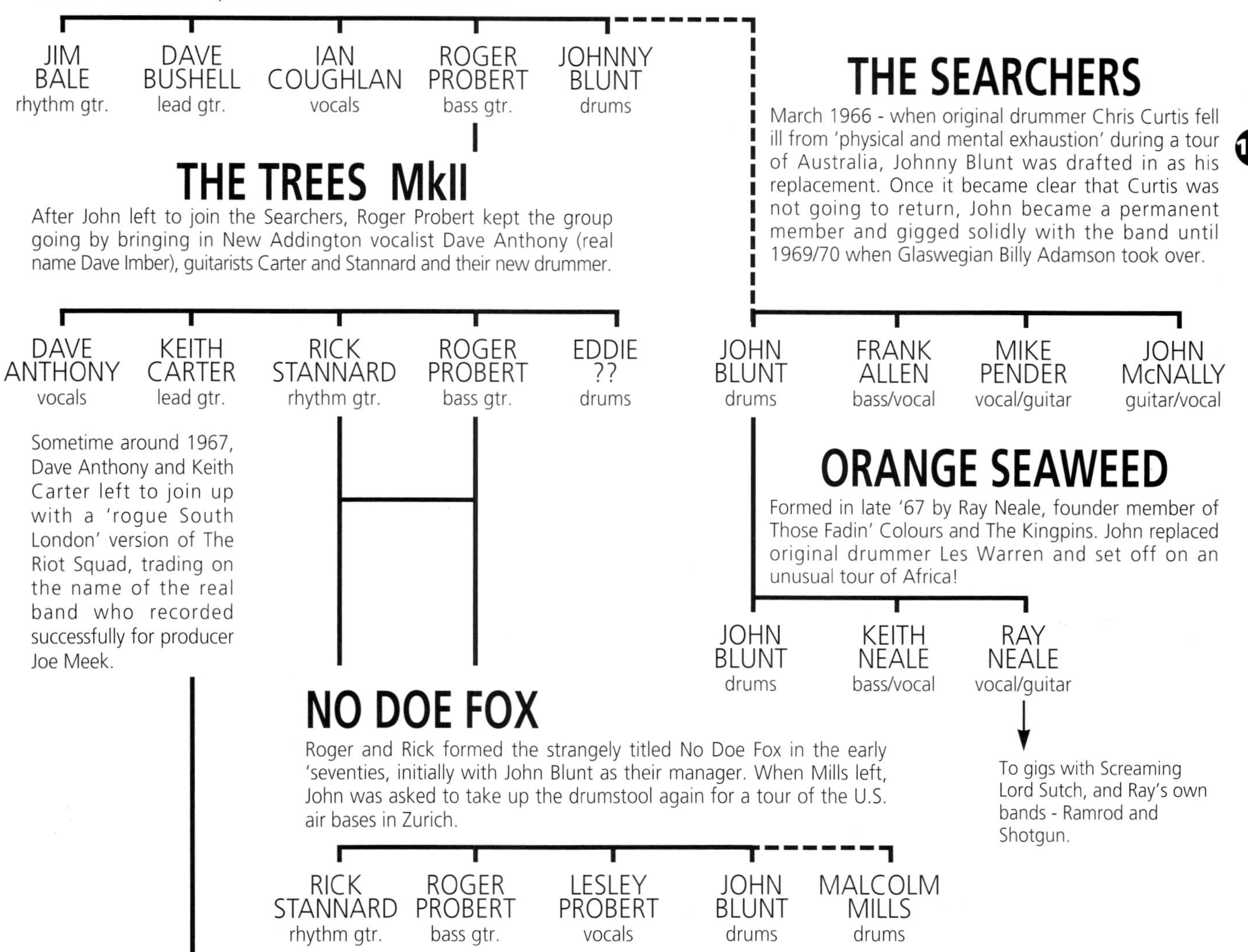

THE SEARCHERS

March 1966 - when original drummer Chris Curtis fell ill from 'physical and mental exhaustion' during a tour of Australia, Johnny Blunt was drafted in as his replacement. Once it became clear that Curtis was not going to return, John became a permanent member and gigged solidly with the band until 1969/70 when Glaswegian Billy Adamson took over.

THE TREES MkII

After John left to join the Searchers, Roger Probert kept the group going by bringing in New Addington vocalist Dave Anthony (real name Dave Imber), guitarists Carter and Stannard and their new drummer.

Sometime around 1967, Dave Anthony and Keith Carter left to join up with a 'rogue South London' version of The Riot Squad, trading on the name of the real band who recorded successfully for producer Joe Meek.

ORANGE SEAWEED

Formed in late '67 by Ray Neale, founder member of Those Fadin' Colours and The Kingpins. John replaced original drummer Les Warren and set off on an unusual tour of Africa!

To gigs with Screaming Lord Sutch, and Ray's own bands - Ramrod and Shotgun.

NO DOE FOX

Roger and Rick formed the strangely titled No Doe Fox in the early 'seventies, initially with John Blunt as their manager. When Mills left, John was asked to take up the drumstool again for a tour of the U.S. air bases in Zurich.

After The Trees, Roger Probert became musical director for visiting American artists such as Anne Peebles and Rufus Thomas. Due to these contacts, he later moved to the States to work in A & R with Atlantic Records. Probert currently lives in New York and is in the process of setting up his own live music venue.

THE SONS OF FRED

Keith Carter moved on to play with this band - signed to Parlophone and managed by Don Arden, the line-up also included guitarist Mick Hutchinson and recorded several singles including a version of Jimmy Reed's *'Baby What D'You Want Me To Do'*. According to Keith, the band could have fared much better had Arden not put all his effort into one of his other bands, The Small Faces!

For assistance on this Family Tree, thanks are due to Johnny Blunt, Roger Probert, Keith Aldridge (formerly Carter), Nick Cobban of the Croydon Advertiser and as always, the inspirational Pete Frame, without whom trees about The Trees would not exist!

Dave Anthony also sang with **The Moods**, a group who played the club circuit in Germany and six months in Copenhagen. Back in Croydon, he became lead singer with **The Trees MkII**, teaming up for the first time with guitarist Keith Carter.
On leaving the Trees, Dave Anthony and Keith Carter both joined forces with members of Liverpool group The Anzacs. These boys also went out under the name **The League of Gentlemen**, who were booked specifically to back visiting artists such as Don Covay and Lee Dorsey; they also appeared with Charlie & Inez Foxx at the Orchid Ballroom in February '66. By June, they were reincarnated as **Dave Anthony & the Anzacs** on another trip to Copenhagen and released Anthony's "Hey, Babe" as a single.
The band also gigged as The **Riot Squad** - but they were not connected with the original outfit produced by Joe Meek. Dave Anthony's line-up are rumoured to have recorded one single which, as he told the Croydon Advertiser, "died a natural death" - or reading between the lines, legal problems with the opposition!

JANUARY

- 11 THE SMALL FACES **O** (7/6)
- 11 FAT JOHN FIVE **S** (3/6)
- 18 THE WHO **O** (7/6)
- 20 MIGIL 5 **O** (6/3)
- 25 WOODY HERMAN **FH** 2 shows (6/- to 20/-)

FEBRUARY

- 6 JIMI HENDRIX **S** (n/a)
- 8 MAXINE BROWN **O** (6/-)
- 9 PINK FLOYD **AD** (n/a)
- 11 THE A-JAES **W** (6/-)
- 12 CLANCY BROTHERS & TOMMY MAKEM **FH** (7/6 to 21/-)
- 24 CLIVE PEERLESS JAZZBAND **S** (3/6)

MARCH

- 1 JIMI HENDRIX **O** (6/6d)
- 1 RONNIE SCOTT **T** + IAN BIRD SEXTET (6/6d)
- 10 FOSTER SHAW ALLSTARS **S** (3/6)
- 27 OTIS REDDING SHOW **FH** + ARTHUR CONLEY + SAM & DAVE + EDDIE FLOYD + THE MAR-KEYS + BOOKER T. & THE MG'S (6/- to 17/6)
- 31 BUDDY RICH **FH** (6/- to 20/-)

APRIL

- 2 THE NEW BREED **GN** (5/-)
- 9 CARL G. & THE ARROWS **GN** (5/-)
- 9 STEVE BENBOW **SW** (n/a)
- 14 PETE DYER'S JAZZBAND **S** (3/6)
- 15 THE LINCOLNS **GN** (6/6d)
- 26 FAB 208 NIGHT **TR** GENO WASHINGTON & THE RAM-JAM BAND + DAVE CASH (7/6)
- 27 JESSE FULLER **FH** + THE TINKERS (5/- to 12/6)

MAY

- 14 CLIFF AUNGIER **SW** (n/a)
- 22 COUNT BASIE ORCHESTRA **FH** (6/- to 20/-)

JUNE

- 2 KEN COLYER **S** (3/6)
- 23 DONOVAN **FH** (7/6d to 20/-) *CANCELLED*

(n/a) = ticket price not available.

Looking back, the tiny music room of the Star at Broad Green is the last place one would expect to have played host to guitar genius **Jimi Hendrix**. Yet in February '67, it was not so surprising; Hendrix was relatively new to England and the Star was a well-respected Blues/ R'n'B club.

One man who remembers the gig is Keith Aldridge, a local guitarist who as Keith Carter, played at various times in the Trees, and the Sons of Fred. Keith told me: "*The Star really was busy that night, the bars and backroom are very similar now to how they were then. The bands' drank in the saloon, because people were crowding in and out of the public bar to pass through to the backroom. It's a bit lighter in there now; then, there were just a couple of wall lights - the stage was not more than a foot off the ground, (it's been raised a foot and a half in recent years) and there was a piano over in the corner - it really hasn't changed at all. In the Star, you know they've got that alcove/French window with the stage slightly to the right? Well, they literally brought Hendrix in through that window, there was no way they could get him through the hall - just wouldn't have got him in, that's how packed it was. It was about ten shillings to get in - you thought 'Christ, ten-bob', because only three or four years earlier we'd gone there on a Wednesday and seen the Stones play, for half-a-crown.*

Before he'd even played, you noticed how impressive looking Hendrix was. I always thought of blues guitarists, in the flesh, as little men, especially after seeing Buddy Guy - but Hendrix was an ex-Yankee Paratrooper and he looked massive. If you look at films of him now, and see how easily his fingers run over the frets, you get an idea of how big he was.

They were basically playing stuff off the first album; a really nice 'bluesey' version of 'Rock Me Baby', I think he did a Buddy Guy song which might have been 'The First Time I Met The Blues', covers like 'Fire', but mainly slow blues like 'Redhouse' with lots of feedback and distortion - he was really enjoying himself. But then, to come from being relatively unknown in the States to being top of the bill, even at small clubs like the Star, must have been quite a kick. His record was in the charts, things were going well, he was being fed, working unbelievably hard - but then all bands did, I think people today must wonder 'How did they survive like that?'. It's always the early days of someone's career that are the most interesting. The later years, Monterey and Woodstock, are well documented already. I think all the other local dates (Bromley and Chislehurst Caves), are definites. Plus you can probably add the Aquarium in Brighton, around late January, early February 1967. I remember that because we, (Sons Of Fred) were in a chip shop after a gig. It was well after midnight and Hendrix's van pulled up outside on their way back from the coast into London. All you could see of him was this big fur coat. I don't remember anything being said about Hendrix losing his guitar - (rumour has it that one of Jimi's guitars was stolen after the Star gig) - *it's possible, but I would think doubtful - as I say, there were so many people there that night, you wouldn't have got in or out with anything like that. This was Hendrix's first tour of England; he had arrived around September '66 - drummer Mitch Mitchell had been sacked from Georgie Fame's band, I think for being drunk and disorderly and he (Hendrix) had advertised for a bass player. Noel Redding was looking to leave The Falling Leaves at the time - he went along thinking they wanted someone to play guitar. In fact, from what I remember being said at the time, Redding stood back at the audition in amazement when he heard Hendrix play - sort of 'Christ, if that's a guitarist, I think I'll play bass' (laughs).*

MONDAY cont.

STAR HOTEL
JIMI HENDRIX
LONDON ROAD
WEST CROYDON

Another regular at the Star, Deanna Sewell also remembers Jimi's appearance and recalls talking to Hendrix before the gig, in order to get his autograph. She managed to catch him early in the evening, before the place started to fill up and adds that he must have played the Bromley Court Hotel shortly afterwards, as Deanna and some of her friends were invited to go along by Jimi himself.

Noel Redding, bassist with the **Jimi Hendrix Experience** recalls that the band were paid £154. 14s. 4d for their appearance at the Orchid Ballroom, Purley on 1st March. Considering the fact that the Orchid held easily six or seven times the capacity of the Star, I wonder what the band were paid for their gig there, in February?

'Young Outlook', Croydon Advertiser March '67

"Stuck in the MUD -but it was lucky!"

WHEN A VAN loaded with equipment and the pop group ***The Mourners*** *made a wrong turn in a narrow Isle of Wight road, they were stuck for the night. For mud held the van in a vice-like grip and it was not until the morning that they were able to haul their vehicle free. And the mud has stuck! For the group, not satisfied with their name at that time, decided during the long wait overnight in their van that they would change it. To -* ***MUD****. Surely the shortest name in the pop world.*

Les and Pete Gray, from Hadley Road, Pollards Hill, Norbury, Robert Davis and Raymond Stiles from Mitcham are glad they did. For it has meant a change in fortune, as they have just had a record released which they hope will swing them to the top. Called 'Flower Power' and backed by 'You're my Mother', it might do just that. Les, aged 21 is lead vocalist; Peter, 19, the drummer, Robert, 19, lead guitarist and Raymond, 20, bass guitar. Their new record is released by CBS, no.203002. The boys are already getting a full diary. Recently they played at Springfield Stadium, St. Helier, Jersey and had a warm reception from fans when their plane landed. All this followed a £500 win earlier in the year in the Silver Blades Ice Rink Contest. Ronnie Beck noticed them, signed them up for CBS and that was the start of their future hopes.

The *"most exciting show to be seen at the Fairfield Hall in a long, long time"* - that was the Advertiser's verdict on the **Otis Redding** show on 27th March. A superb soul bill that also featured Sam & Dave, Arthur Conley, Eddie Floyd and The Mar-Keys, the 'house band' for the tour were Booker T & the MG's, onstage for the entire evening to back all the artists! According to journalist Nick Cobban, **Sam & Dave** stole the show with their polished, professional stage act, *"generating so much excitement, the roof might have caved in at any moment"*. Following their ten minute version of 'Hold On, I'm Coming', compere Emperor Rosko had some trouble in calming the audience down.

This was an important year for Croydon group the **Warren Davis Monday Band**, a seven piece outfit who earned their reputation playing soul music in the London clubs. The boys, Martin Grice, Pete Mole, Rob Walker, Bruce Usherwood, Andy Wilson, Paul Houlton and vocalist Warren Davis, aged between 19 and 23, released their first single *'Wait for Me'* COLUMBIA DB 8190 on May 12th and took the decision to turn professional a couple of weeks later. Davis was previously in a group called the Board Walkers and all the band members had been playing for five years. The 'Monday Band were given a residency at the Uppercut Club in Forest Gate and at the press reception to announce their new professional status, the Rolling Stones were expected to attend, as *Wait for Me* was written and produced by Bill Wyman.

Sport & General Press Agency

Mud load their old Commer van onto the train at Olympia before hitting the road. Left to right: Rob Davis, Pete Gray, Les Gray and Ray Stiles.

JULY

- 1 THE DUBLINERS **FH** (7/6d to 17/6)
- 21 THE ANIMALS **O** (6/-)

AUGUST

SEPTEMBER

- 4 THE HERD **SB** (6/-)
- 11 CHARLES AZNAVOUR **FH** (n/a)
- 13 GENO WASHINGTON & THE RAM-JAM BAND **O** (8/6)

OCTOBER

- 2 JACQUES LOUISSIER **FH** (n/a)
- 10 TRAFFIC **A** + THE FLOWERPOT MEN + THE MINDBENDERS + ART + TOMORROW *featuring* KEITH WEST (7/6d to 13/-)
- 12 JOSH WHITE **FH** (n/a)
- 16 MAX ROACH **FH** (n/a)
- 26 DAVE BRUBECK QUARTET **FH** (8/- to 21/-)
- 28 MUD **SB** (n/a)
- 30 FOUNDATIONS **O** (5/-)

NOVEMBER

- 6 'SOUL EXPLOSION' **FH** SAM & DAVE + LEE DORSEY + ARTHUR CONLEY (3/6d to 7/6d)
- 6 CREAM **SB** (n/a)
- 13 DAVE DEE, DOZY, BEAKY, MICK & TICH **O** (6/-)
- 15 MIRIAM MAKEBA **FH** (n/a)
- 24 DR. MARIGOLD'S PRESCRIPTION **SB** (n/a)
- 25 THE KONRADS **SB** (n/a)
- 27 GEORGIE FAME & THE BLUE FLAMES **O** (6/-)

DECEMBER

- 11 DESMOND DEKKER & THE ACES **O** (5/-)

The resident group at the Gun Tavern in Church Street were local soul outfit **The New Breed**, a six-piece Otis Redding-inspired band who had been playing together for only six months before being offered the residency in February. Four of the group members came from Croydon; Peter Anderson (17), John Couchman (18), Mark Mackenzie (17) and Joseph Black, while Roger Fox (19) and 'player manager' Chris Wilson (23) were both Londoners.

15 year-old vocalist Joseph Black was the last member to join and had started to write his own songs, but The New Breed were in no hurry to turn professional - as Chris explained *"We have had offers but turned them down, we've had chances to make a record but we have not taken them; we are going to wait until we are really good and then take our chance"*. As well as The Gun, the group also played regular gigs at the Sunday Spin club in New Addington.

In September, the Top Rank Club in Croydon held the area finals of a nationwide talent contest. This heat was won by a group from Twickenham called **1984**, who not only qualified for the finals to be held later in London, but were also offered a recording trial by CBS, one of the co-sponsors of the contest. The band featured Tim Staffell, Dave Dilloway, Richard Thompson (a drummer, not the Fairport guitarist), John Garnham and a certain **Brian May** on lead guitar.

When the band broke up early the following year, May and Staffell recruited a new drummer by the name of Roger Meddows Taylor, to become **Smile**, who gigged regularly around the college circuit, in particularly the Imperial College, London where May was studying for his BSc. During this time, vocalist Staffell introduced the group to a friend from art college who regularly travelled with them from gig to gig; and when Staffell finally decided to leave, his friend Freddie Bulsara took over as their lead singer. By early 1971, and several bass players later, the band were joined by John Deacon, Bulsara changed his name to Mercury and **Queen** were ready to embark on what was to become an incredibly successful career.

(n/a) = ticket price not available.

Working on tracks for his debut LP was 20 year old jazz pianist, **Roy Budd** from South Norwood. Recording with the Tony Hatch Orchestra, the album featured a few of Roy's own compositions including 'Summer Rain' the B-side of his new single 'Mr. Rose'.

Roy's parents started him off with piano lessons when he was six and by the time he was twelve he had appeared on BBC television's Black & White Minstrel Show and the Carol Levis Show. By the time Roy left Portland Road Secondary Modern school in Croydon, he was determined to make music his career. At sixteen he was playing four or five nights a week in a Thornton Heath jazz pub, subsequently moving to the Green Man at Blackheath where he met Ian Bird, who also ran Croydon's Tropicana jazz club.

Roy formed his own quartet and began playing a regular Sunday lunchtime session with local singer Martin Jae at the Dukes Head, South Croydon. It was during his six month stint at the celebrated Bulls Head in Barnes, that Roy made a great many contacts and began recording for radio shows such as 'Roundabout', 'Music Through Midnight' and 'Swingalong'.

Under the management of Radio Luxembourg DJ Doug Stanley, Roy also went on to compose the film score for the classic 'Get Carter', starring Michael Caine.

Two local singers both released their first solo records towards the end of 1967. **Tony Steven** was already well known as the vocalist with the Johnny Howard Big Band, singing five nights a week with them at Purley's Orchid Ballroom and appearing on thousands of radio broadcasts - for 'Easybeat', 'Swingalong' and the 'David Symonds Show'. Brought up in Eastbourne, Tony had been performing since the age of nine; he moved to Stafford Road in Wallington and turned professional in 1959 after successfully auditioning for the Johnny Howard band. Several record companies used Tony's voice on cover versions of the latest hits, but Columbia released his first single in December, entitled 'No Love Like Your Love' /'Try' DB8307.

Also making a bid for the charts was **Roger Earl Okin**, a 20 year old student from the University of Kent at Canterbury. Born in Carshalton and brought up in Streatham, he made his first public appearance on the children's TV show 'All Your Own'. An opportunist meeting at London Airport led indirectly to a contract with Dick James Music where two of Roger's songs were recorded by Cilla Black and Helen Shapiro. His own single was called 'Yellow Petals'/'I Can't Face The Animals' Parlophone R3644.

Croydon Advertiser – 13.10.67

"The night the Traffic slayed the girls"

IT WAS A STRAIGHT FIGHT. The hurtling girls versus the strong-armed men. And through it all, while the teenage cannon balls threw themselves bodily on to the stage and the men threw them back again, the pop groups kept right on playing. And the show, unfortunately, had to go on.

It was Tuesday night at the ABC Cinema, Croydon, where crowds of semi-hysterical girls beat on the stage door and a harassed official clung to the push bar on the other side, holding it closed with all his evaporating might. On stage it was less exiting.

The Mindbenders were noisy and out of date. The group called Art totally lacked personality and were so grossly over-amplified to counteract the screams that it was impossible to distinguish what they were playing. And the only accomplishment Keith West appeared to have was an ability to gyrate fanatically without splitting his skin-tight, green velvet trousers. Perhaps they had grown on him, like moss.

All this lack of professionalism was emphasised by the brilliant performance of the Flowerpot Men. Staggeringly dressed in the richest and most romantic of hippie styles, they sang in superb harmony and used the human voice as a proper instrument and not as a musical washboard.

Topping the bill were Traffic, Stevie Winwood's new group. Very little was audible, but that wasn't their fault. Every time Stevie opened his mouth, a thousand girlish screams drowned him.

All four boys in this group are remarkably versatile, between them playing guitars, harp, tenor sax, sitar, organ and flute, not to mention a variety of drums, bongo and otherwise. They touch blues, they touch jazz and they touch pop - an exciting mixture of sounds, absolutely unique and capped with Stevie's raw, wild voice. Traffic are beyond fashion, and too good for such a show.

R. C. de S.

Beckenham group **The Herd** were well on their way to national recognition, playing support to the likes of Cream and Jimi Hendrix at the Saville Theatre in London. Ready Steady Go! presenter Keith Altham wrote in the New Musical Express: *"My contender as the man 'most likely to get ripped to pieces by hysterical females' in 1967 is Peter Frampton, the seventeen year old vocalist/guitarist with the Herd. He regularly loses a shirt on personal appearances and quite recently was pursued around Streatham Ice Rink by a bevy of berserk 'birds' on skates".*

One of the major advances in concert amplification systems was pioneered by a local man, **Charlie Watkins** of Norwood. Using the advantages of transistors over the less stable valve amplifiers, he brought together two new concepts; first by separating the mixer from the power amplifier with the introduction of a small, five-input console called an Audiomaster. Secondly, because transistor amps could be coupled together without the instability problems experienced with valve circuitry, it was possible to build a large PA system from a number of smaller units, giving rise to the modular or 'slave' system. The line output from the Audiomaster was connected to the input of the first slave power amp; this had a parallel socket to allow the signal to be linked to a second slave, and from there to a third slave and so on.

At the '67 Windsor Jazz & Blues Festival, Charlie Watkins unveiled the world's first ever 1000 watt PA system. With its solid banks of speakers, this 'wall of sound' was a real revolution in sound reinforcement, both clear and powerful and soon every band in the country was using **WEM** equipment (Watkins Electric Music). Also, as several Audiomasters could be linked to provide more channels, it became common practice to mike everything up through the PA, rather than use the system exclusively for vocals.

As the year drew to a close, a year which hadn't exactly seen a glut of rock and pop gigs in Croydon, news filtered through of a new club about to open. The **Top Ten Club**, who operated successfully out of the East End of London, arranged with Mike Cafferty, landlord of the Swan & Sugarloaf in South Croydon to run a club night at the pub every Saturday evening. Groups rumoured to have been booked included The Who, Manfred Mann and the Foundations and the sessions were due to start on 2nd December... but did they?

JANUARY

8 SIMON DUPREE & THE BIG SOUND **O** (6/-)
15 THE PLATTERS **O** (5/-)
22 LOVE AFFAIR **O** (5/-)
26 THE DUBLINERS **FH** (7/6 to 17/-)
29 SAVOY BROWN **S** (5/-)
29 EDWIN STARR **O** (5/-)

FEBRUARY

2 KEN COLYER **S** (n/a)
5 CHICKEN SHACK **S** (5/-)
5 GEORGIE FAME **O** (6/-)
7 WOODY HERMAN **FH** (8/- to 16/6)
9 MONTY SUNSHINE **S** (n/a)
12 BLACK CAT BONES **S** (n/a)
19 THE COLOURED RAISINS **O** (4/-)
19 PETER GREEN's FLEETWOOD MAC **S** (n/a)
26 TEN YEARS AFTER **S** (5/-)
26 THE DRIFTERS **O** (5/-)
26 THE SMALL FACES **SB** (7/6)

MARCH

2 THE SEARCHERS **TK** + THE GLASS OPENING (7/6)
4 THE FOUNDATIONS **O** (6/-)
4 SAVOY BROWN **S** (n/a)
11 STATUS QUO **O** (5/-)
11 THE DOCKS **S** (n/a)
18 THE EQUALS **O** (5/-)
18 JETHRO TULL **S** (n/a)
25 PETER GREEN **S** (n/a)
28 ESTHER & ABI OFARIM **FH** (10/6 to 20/-)

APRIL

1 THE SMALL FACES **S** (6/6d)
1 CHICKEN SHACK **S** (n/a)
5 THE SCAFFOLD **FH** (7/6 to 20/-)
8 AYNSLEY DUNBAR **S** (n/a)
11 ARLO GUTHRIE **FH** (5/- to 15/-) *CANCELLED*
15 SAVOY BROWN **S** (n/a)
21 FOLK AT THE FAIRFIELD **FH** + DANNY DOYLE + ALEX CAMBELL + NOEL MURPHY + SWEENEYS MEN (6/6 to 15/-)
22 JETHRO TULL **S** (n/a)
22 SHOWSTOPPERS **O** (6/-)
26 THE DRIFTERS **O** (5/-)
29 BRUNO's BLUES **S** (n/a)
29 P.P. ARNOLD **O** (5/-)

MAY

5 CLANCY BROTHERS & TOMMY MAKEM **FH** (7/6 to 21/-)
6 JUDY COLLINS **FH** (5/- to 15/-) *CANCELLED*
6 DUANE EDDY **O** (6/-)
6 CHICKEN SHACK **S** (n/a)
13 ROBERT KNIGHT **O** (5/-)
20 ERIC BURDEN & THE ANIMALS **O** + ZOOT MONEY (7/6)
2? THE LOVE AFFAIR **TR** (n/a)
27 AYNSLEY DUNBAR RETALIATION **S** (n/a)
27 JAMES & BOBBY PURIFY **O** (5/-)

JUNE

3 EASYBEATS **O** (6/-)
10 RUBY & THE ROMANTICS **O** (5/-)
14 JULIE FELIX **FH** (7/6 to 21/-)
17 THE IMPRESSIONS **O** (5/-)
18 SHIRLEY COLLINS **Hi** (n/a)
24 THE CRICKETS **O** (5/-)

(n/a) = ticket price not available.

For the first half of the year, the Blues club operating out of the back room of the Star Hotel, London Road, West Croydon, went under the name of the **Zodiac Club** - with a sister venue being situated at the Eden Park Hotel, Beckenham. The club was run by Brian Mason and Steve Gledhill - Mason later moved his operation to the Greyhound. As shown in this Melody Maker advertisement, Croydon ran live music two nights a week, R'n'B on Mondays and Jazz on Fridays. **Jethro Tull**, who were very much a blues band at that time, returned to the club on 22nd April.

In February the Melody Maker Jazz LP of the month was 'An Evening With **Ornette Coleman**', released on Polydor 623 246/247. This live album was a recording of Coleman's Fairfield Hall concert back in 1965 and its '68 release tied in with a premiere of his new work 'Emotion Modulations' at the Royal Albert Hall on 29th February.

That same month the Croydon Advertiser finally picked up on a local group whose single had risen to number 12 in the charts. The song was called 'Pictures Of Matchstick Men' PYE 7N 17449 written by Mike Rossi - as the Advertiser put it: *"Mike, Roy, Alan, John and Ricki are the* ***Status Quo****, and they're rocketing to the top".*

Journalist Simon Tait went along to interview Rossi at his home in Park Avenue, Bromley. Mike said - *"Success is what we all aim at, of course, but there's only a few who can make it. We just hope we're among them. In the West End it's such a race to get anywhere. In London everyone seems to think it's their scene - that they're the biggest thing that ever happened. We want to steer clear of that and just play good stuff - we play anywhere outside of London and we seem to manage all right."*

I think it's fair to say that Mike (now called Francis again) and the Quo have more than managed all right ever since.

FH - Fairfield Hall • A - ABC • S - Star Hotel • TR - Top Rank • O - Orchid Ballroom • TK - Tangerine Klub, New Addington

Lead guitarist with the Kinks, **Dave Davies** was enlisted to open a new boutique called 'Fanny', in Station Road, West Croydon, living up to the group's hit as a 'Dedicated Follower of Fashion'. Despite opening on a Friday lunchtime in February, Dave still attracted a crowd of 100 teenagers who watched him burst through the white paper covering the doorway to the shop. Once inside, the kids were given badges, balloons and car stickers by manageress Renee Sale and her staff.

The Addington Hotel opened it's doors as the Tangerine Klub on Saturday 2nd March, with a first night line-up of **The Searchers** supported by **The Glass Opening**. Situated in the Parkway, New Addington, nearly 300 people turned out on opening night - paid their seven shillings and sixpence and got free membership into the bargain. However, interest in the 'klub' soon died down, the final straw being the non-appearance of the **Moody Blues** a few weeks later. Only minutes before the group were due on stage, the promoters took a call from the 'Moodys' road manager saying that the group would not be appearing because their mellotron had broken down! Nearly 500 disappointed fans were told that admission would be reduced and there would be 'dancing to discs' - but only 150 stayed on.

A local group called **Circus** released their second single on March 18th - *'Do you Dream'/'House of Wood'*; the band had only been together for nine months and their first record, *'Gone are the Songs of Yesterday'* was a flop. It was their manager, Manfred Mann vocalist Mike D'Abo who gave them their name, while the group - Philip Goodhand-Tait, Kirk Riddle, Ian Jelfs, Alan Bunn and Mel Collins - were touring in Italy. 19 year old Melvyn Collins, of Walnut Tree Close, Banstead gave up his job as a photographer to play tenor sax and flute with the band, after answering an ad. in the music press, although back in 1965 he was a member of Croydon group The Dagoes (see Mel's interview pages 76 - 79).

Two of the members of Circus went on to greater success in the music business. Philip Goodhand-Tait as an established singer/songwriter, while Mel Collins has played with almost everybody as a session musician; as well as touring with bands such as King Crimson, Streetwalkers and Kokomo.

The debut single from Croydon group the **Orange Seaweed** hit the record shops on Friday 26th April - entitled 'Stay Awhile' on the Pye label and produced by Jimmy Smith. The 'Seaweed had only been together for twelve months, but two of the boys had a much longer track record; Ray and Keith Neale were previously members of Those Fadin' Colours and the Kingpins. The Neale brothers from Ripley Close, New Addington were joined by drummer Les Warren from Hermitage Lane, Norbury and guitarist John Wolloff from Clapham.

Just a few miles down the road at the Sutton Granada, the **Gene Pitney** package tour were booked to appear on Friday 26th April. Gene, advertised as "America's International Singing Star" topped the bill and was supported by; Don Partridge, Status Quo, Simon Dupree & the Big Sound, Lucas & the Mike Cotton Sound, with Amen Corner opening the show. All this for prices ranging between 7/6d and 17/6d, with the whole concert due to run from 7 until 9pm working out at around twenty minutes per act! Value for money?

In May, hundreds of screaming teenage fans packed the Top Rank Suite at London Road, Broad Green, some breaking through the crash barriers and twenty being carried out, having fainted with the excitement.

Why? Cosmetic giants Yardley had organised a nationwide tour to publicise a new range of make-up for the 'teen and twenty' market, fronted by teen favourites **The Love Affair**. Their lead singer Steve Ellis was barely audible above the screams, let alone the music, occasionally reaching across the barriers in front of the stage to touch the fans. Keyboard player Lynton Guest was nearly pulled off stage when he tried the same thing. During the frenzy of the final song, girls rushed the stage and reportedly tried to take away one of the stewards as a souvenir!

For some time, the **'Hungry i'** coffee bar had been offering "non-stop pop music, played by a popular disc jockey" - Monday, Wednesday and Thursday from 8 'til 11pm. That was until two Croydon folk fans decided to step in and fill the Tuesday evening gap with a folk and blues night - although neither Jerry Leech or Anne Statter had any previous experience of running a club.

Situated at 79 London Road, West Croydon, the basement bar had room for about 60 to 70 people and the new organisers charged 1 shilling and sixpence membership and five shillings entrance fee. All profits were to come from the non-alcoholic bar and food which would then pay for future guest artists. They chose their first guest well, the 'sweet singer of Sussex' Shirley Collins, ably supported by Dick Hook, one of the resident singers from Redhill folk club...

Croydon Advertiser – 21.6.68

'Folk-club opens to encouraging audience'

*FOLK SINGER **Shirley Collins** played to a packed house of about 60 people when a folk and blues club opened on Tuesday (18 June) in the cellar of the **Hungry i** coffee bar in West Croydon. It was Shirley's first visit to Croydon and she sang the old English songs she learned from her grandmother and great-grandmother.*

Apart from Shirley, members of the audience sang and played music. The club, which plans to hold a residents evening at a later date, is being run by Jerry Leech, of St. James' Road, Croydon and his girlfriend Anne Statter of Canning Road, Addiscombe. Neither had any experience of running a club but their first-night response was encouraging.

Next week, (7.30), 'Spider' John Koerner will be featured at the club in London Road.

JULY

- 1 THE PLATTERS **O** (5/-)
- 1 ESTHER & ABI OFARIM **FH** (10/6 to 25/-)
- 5 PROCOL HARUM **D** (n/a)
- 8 THE FANTASTICS **O** (5/-)
- 15 REPARATA & THE DELRONS **O** (5/-)
- 22 PATTI LABELLE & HER BELLES **O** (6/-)
- 24 THE EQUALS **TR** (6/-)
- 29 CUPID'S INSPIRATION **O** (6/-)

AUGUST

- 5 BRUCE CHANNEL **O** (6/-)
- 12 THE RONNETTES **O** (5/-)
- 19 BEN E KING **O** (7/-)

SEPTEMBER

- 2 COLOURED RAISINS **O** (5/-)
- 9 BEN E KING **O** (7/-)
- 13 THE CORRIES **FH** + ROY HARPER + EDDIE & FINBAR FUREY (5/- to 15/-)
- 22 VICTOR BORGE **FH** (n/a)
- 23 EDWIN STARR **O** (6/-)
- 26 BUDDY RICH ORCHESTRA **FH** (8/- to 21/-)
- 29 'OLYMPOP' **FH** *See text* (10/- to 40/-)
- 30 THE DRIFTERS **O** (5/-)

OCTOBER

- 7 OSCAR PETERSON TRIO **FH** (8/- to 21/-)
- 7 THE FLIRTATIONS **O** (5/-)
- 10 JACQUES LOUISSIER **FH** (n/a)
- 14 THE PLATTERS **O** (5/-)
- 21 AMEN CORNER **SB** (n/a)
- 24 EARL HINES ALLSTARS **FH** (8/- to 21/-)
- 28 LOCOMOTIVE **O** (5/-)
- 30 AMERICAN FOLK/BLUES FESTIVAL **FH** JIMMY REED + JOHN LEE HOOKER + T-BONE WALKER + CURTIS JONES + BIG JOE WILLIAMS + SHAKEY HORTON + THE EDDIE TAYLOR BLUES BAND (9/- to 21/-)

NOVEMBER

- 3 THE DUBLINERS **FH** (7/6 to 17/6)
- 4 PP ARNOLD **O** (6/-)
- 11 CHARLIE & INEZ FOXX **O** (7/-)
- 14 TOM PAXTON **FH** (8/- to 21/-)
- 15 PENTANGLE **FH** (8/- to 21/-)
- 18 BRUCE CHANNEL **O** (6/-)
- 19 ROY HARPER **Hi** (n/a)
- 25 THE CHIFFONS **O** (5/-)

DECEMBER

- 2 THE OB-LA-DI, OB-LA-DA BAND **O** (5/-)
- 2 LOVE AFFAIR **SB** (8/-)
- 6 JULIE FELIX **FH** (7/6 to 21/-)
- 9 BANDWAGON **O** (7/6)
- 12 JIMMY SMITH TRIO **FH** (8/- to 21/-)
- 16 COLOURED RAISINS **O** (5/-)
- 30 THE FOUNDATIONS **O** (6/6)

(n/a) = ticket price not available.

High praise must go to the wide ranging booking policy of the **Mistrale Club** in Beckenham, situated at 2-4 High Street, adjoining Beckenham Junction Station. According to their press advertisements you could "dance and drink to some of the best music in pop, ska and blue beat, amid grecian pillars or round a vintage Rolls-Royce" - yes folks, the Mistrale had a vintage car smack dab in the middle of the dance floor! In May and June alone, their acts included Chicken Shack, the Pyramids, Bill Haley, Jethro Tull, the Coloured Raisins, Honeybus and Ike & Tina Turner!

MISTRALE CLUB
Adjoining Beckenham Junction Station
Friday, 18th October
THREE STAR BILL
TYRANNOSAURUS REX
The Pretty Things
Julian Kirsch
Members 7/6 Guests 10/-

Croydon Advertiser – 12.7.68

'Procol Harum play for Art Students'

PROCOL HARUM, the group which produced the No. 1 hit 'A Whiter Shade of Pale', visited Croydon on Saturday night to support Croydon Art College students' latest venture, their "Music Workshop". The five man group performed in an evening of entertainment at the Denning Hall, Park Lane, which also featured modern jazz, poetry reading and a musical comedy act.

One of the student organisers of the show, Malcolm St. Julian-Bown, told a reporter; "This evening is an extension of what we do every Wednesday at the Gun Tavern in Church Street. Procol Harum are playing because one of the group, Matthew Fisher, lives in South Croydon and knows several people at the college. They are all playing for free." Watched by an audience of about 300, Procol Harum played several songs including "A Whiter Shade of Pale".

*Light comic relief was provided by **Ron Geesin**, a Scottish composer from Kensington who sings into a battered paraffin can and declaims tortured Shakespeare. He was persuaded to perform by his wife Frances, who teaches at the college.*

FH - Fairfield Hall • A - ABC • S - Star Hotel • TR - Top Rank • O - Orchid Ballroom • SB - Silver Blades

On 29th September, an event took place at the Fairfield under the strange name **'Olympop!'**. Ticket prices ranged from ten shillings up to a massive forty shillings, but on the bill were Julie Driscoll, Brian Auger and the Trinity; the Alan Price Set; The Nice; Eclection; Spooky Tooth; Jethro Tull and David Ackles. The artists all performed for free, as the concert was in aid of the British Olympic Appeals Fund and the whole event was filmed *'in glorious colour'* by BBC2. Ackles appears to have been a late replacement for Alan Bown, who was mentioned in the advance advertisements but not in the review. This is what the Croydon Advertiser (4.10.68) had to say about Tull;

The evening began with ***Jethro Tull*** *who, on quieter reflection, seem to have been one of the best groups of the night. They're a four man blues group with a farmyard image - apt, since they have chosen the name of an agricultural equipment inventor for their title. Their excellent drummer, for instance, wears a squashed, manure-coloured felt hat and a dead-pan expression; while their lead singer is an incredibly dressed exhibitionist who looks like a tramp with his long wild hair and shapeless calf-length overcoat, a picture he encourages by constant scratching of his person during other peoples solos. He plays wild harmonica and Roland-Kirk influenced flute, moving his legs around like a demented pantomime horse, while his mouth is apparently pivoted on the microphone. The resultant music is loud, clear and disciplined blues.'*

The reviewer goes on to describe **Spooky Tooth**: *'...who look exactly like a parents' nightmare pop group, complete with fringes, frills, fur, lace, long wild hair and crotch-tight trousers'.*

The Purley Halls, Banstead Road, Purley was the unusual setting for a Folk 'n' Blues Concert, on Monday 28th October. Organised by Croydon's **Hungry i** folk club, the event featured **Al Stewart**, with Americans **Jackson C Frank** and **Marc Ellington**, local duo Simon Praeger & Steve Rye and Welsh guitarist John James completing the bill. Despite being the 'headline' act, Al Stewart only managed to perform three songs due to the concert running late. Mike Silver was the compere and tickets were 12 shillings and sixpence!

On Al: *"Of all the artists in the concert, he had the greatest hold on his audience. So great, in fact, that when a guitar string broke during his last number, he refused to break the spell of concentration as well. Another guitar was brought from offstage, he retuned it and resumed the song - instantly recapturing the suspended atmosphere".*

The American Folk/Blues Festival '68 rolled into the Fairfield on Wednesday 30th October. But what appeared to be another strong line-up of bluesmen certainly wasn't to the liking of the Advertiser's arts critic. I shall try to keep his vitriol to a minimum but this was how he opened the review: *"Nine musicians and an astrakan-hatted M.C., who kept calling us 'music-lovers' and described all the artists as 'great and fabulous', 12-barred their way into the Fairfield Hall, played getting on for three hours of non-stop 12-bar and then 12-barred their way out again. Maybe it was having to pay five shillings for the programme - twice the charge at jazz concerts - or maybe I'm green but these blues just made me see red. For having been weaned on the likes of Charlie Parker, Clifford Brown and Miles Davis etc, I was quite frankly disappointed. Was this, I wondered, the so-called 'roots of jazz'?"*

And therein lies the problem; the local paper, in their wisdom, sent along a jazz critic to review a folk and blues concert, and one with a more 'rootsy' line-up than some. No wonder the overdose of twelve bar blues wore him down. He found John Lee Hooker "dull and uninteresting"; T-Bone Walker was too "gimmicky" and Jimmy Reed was just too loud. So, did anybody take his fancy? Well he quite enjoyed the solo set by Texan Curtis Jones, on songs such as 'Lonely Soul', 'Sherry' and 'Lonesome Bedroom Blues' because - *"I liked the way you could hear the lyrics, limited though they may have been..."*

Highlight of the show however, was Big Joe Williams, introduced by compere Al Smith as 'the greatest country blues singer in the world'. *"I liked the solo efforts of this 66 year old, who tottered on with the aid of a complicated looking walking stick and played a battered guitar that looked as though it might have been born a few years earlier than its owner. Having thoroughly enjoyed every masterly chord of his repertoire - he played what must have been a dozen short and sweet numbers, producing a twangy, almost Hula sound on occasions - I was surprised to find that I was not alone in my appreciation. Three encores told their own story..."*

Croydon Advertiser – 8.11.68

'New job takes them straight to the top'

ONLY a few months after becoming fully professional, a local group have a booking to play at the London Palladium. It is the sort of opportunity most groups dream of, and it has come the way of a group called ***The Kinde****.*

Singer Barry Ryan, whose record 'Eloise' is expected to reach the top of the charts next week, has chosen them as his backing group. And the Kinde begin their new job on 1st December at the Palladium, where Barry starts a six-date British tour with the Beach Boys.

The Kinde consist of Tim Guest (20), lead guitarist from Thornton Heath who used to be with Glen Athens & the Trojans, another local group. John Heatherington (20) rhythm guitarist from Purley, bass guitarist Dave Chapman from North London and drummer Tim Galvin (20) from Norwood, the latest addition to the group. Both Tim Guest and John Heatherington went to Selhurst Grammar School and the group, who were formerly known as The Senators, began about three years ago.

Their chance to back Barry Ryan came through a friend, Keith Kirby who shares a flat with the singer and is now their personal assistant. Keith comes from Shirley and is an ex-pupil of Ashburton School.

The Fairfield Hall was packed for the visit of the **Jimmy Smith Trio** on Thursday 12th December. One of the leading exponents of the Hammond electric organ in jazz, or in any field of music for that matter, Smith was joined onstage by guitarist Nathan Page and percussionist Charles Crosby. An accomplished pianist as a youngster in Pennsylvania, after serving in the U.S. Navy he returned to his music and started to play bass, before switching to the organ and to the Hammond in particular around 1955-57.

The Croydon Advertiser critic was so impressed with the concert, he went backstage to talk to the 43 year old musician; here is what Jimmy Smith had to say: *"When I'm out there in front, I just don't know exactly what is going to be played next - no more than I can remember just what I've played when a show is over. All I know is that I'm going out there to play jazz - and you know jazz is something that just happens. Music must have feeling, and I try to make a spiritual contact with an audience. They know what they like, they know what they are listening for; I have to convey to them my feelings so that the ideas meet as if it were on a spiritual plane".*

Yeah, right on, Jimmy.

JANUARY

6 JIMMY JAMES & THE VAGABONDS **O** (5/-)
12 CLANCY BROTHERS & TOMMY MAKEM **FH** (7/6d to 21/-)
13 BILLIE STEWART **O** (6/-)
13 JOHN MARTYN **GN** + PAUL WHEELER (n/a)
20 JUNIOR WALKER & THE ALLSTARS **O** (7/6)
22 JOHN MAYALL **FH** (6/6 to 15/-)
24 ROY BUDD TRIO **FH** (6/- to 12/-)
27 MARMALADE **O** (6/6)
27 JACKSON C. FRANK **GN** (n/a)

FEBRUARY

3 COLOURED RAISINS **O** (5/-)
10 THE CATS **O** (5/-)
10 MIKE COOPER **GN** (n/a)
12 GENE PITNEY **FH** + JOE COCKER + MARMALADE + THE IVEYS 2 shows (8/- to 17/-)
13 'BLUES SCENE '69' **FH** (5/- to 15/-)
16 TYRANNOSAURUS REX **FH** VYTAS SERELIS + DAVID BOWIE + JOHN PEEL (8/- to 17/-)
17 THE BANDWAGON **O** (6/-)
24 ROY HARPER **GN** (7/6)
24 BEN E. KING **O** (7/6)

MARCH

2 INCREDIBLE STRING BAND **FH** (8/- to 17/-)
3 THE FANTASTICS **O** (6/-)
9 The STEVIE WONDER SHOW **FH** 2 performances (8/6d to 17/6d)
10 THE TYMES **O** (7/-)
13 MODERN JAZZ QUARTET **FH** (n/a)
17 G-CLEFS **O** (6/-)
24 MARV JOHNSON **O** (6/6)
31 BEN E. KING **O** (10/-)

APRIL

2 MARTHA REEVES & THE VANDELLAS **FH** + JOHNNY JOHNSON & THE BANDWAGON + MARV JOHNSON (8/6 to 17/6)
6 NINA & FREDERICK **FH** (n/a)
7 COLOURED RAISINS **O** (5/-)
14 DESMOND DEKKER & THE ACES **O** (7/6)
21 AMBOY DUKES **O** (5/-)
21 THE HERD **SB** (6/-)
24 COUNT BASIE ORCHESTRA **FH** (n/a)
25 PENTANGLE **FH** (n/a)
28 THE ORIGINAL DRIFTERS **O** (6/-)

MAY

5 BOB & EARL **O** (6/6)
5 AMEN CORNER **SB** (6/-)
12 OSCAR TONEY **O** (6/-)
18 WOODY HERMAN **FH** (n/a)
19 CHARLIE & INEZ FOXX **O** (7/6)
26 J.J. JACKSON **O** (6/-)
28 PETER SARSTEDT **FH** + THE HUMBLEBUMS (8/- to 17/-)
28 BOB & EARL **TR** (6/-)
30 PINK FLOYD **FH** (n/a)

JUNE

2 THE PLATTERS **O** (6/-)
9 THE BANDWAGON **O** (6/-)
16 GEORGIE FAME **O** (7/6)
22 THE NICE **FH** + ROY HARPER + THE IDLE RACE 2 shows (8/- to 21/-)
23 CHICKEN SHACK **O** (6/-)
23 THE EQUALS **TR** (6/-)
30 AMBOY DUKES **O** (5/-)

(n/a) = ticket price not available.

Blues Scene '69 was the apt title of a package tour featuring **John Lee Hooker**, Aynsley Dunbar's Retaliation, Champion Jack Dupree, Jo-Ann Kelly, and the Groundhogs, led by Tony McPhee.

Although on paper the line-up looks interesting enough, it wasn't quite so satisfying in reality. Hooker was on top form, as was Champion Jack Dupree - an excellent pianist with a ready wit, he was the most popular artist on the night.

According to the Advertiser, the 'white' blues artists didn't fare too well; Jo-Ann Kelly was disappointing, and so were Retaliation, led by former John Mayall drummer Aynsley Dunbar. The newly re-formed Groundhogs suffered from over amplification during their own set, but were vastly improved by the discipline of backing John Lee Hooker. Little wonder, when you learn that the original Groundhogs were formed for just that purpose, three years previously.

On Sunday 9th March, promoter Arthur Howes presented 'the Exciting Tamla Motown Star' **Stevie Wonder** for two shows at the Fairfield Hall. Compered by the Emperor Rosko, Stevie's package tour consisted of The Flirtations, The Coloured Raisins, The Big Movement and The Foundations, who had hit the charts with 'Build Me Up Buttercup'. Stevie's single at the time was 'For Once In My Life', which had been released in January and eventually made number three, one place less than 'Buttercup' which was released in December '68 and made the top two.

The Advertiser sent along reviewer S.D. who confessed to not understanding the attraction of Soul music - *"there seems to be little difference here from standard pop music, except that 'soul' utilises saxophone, trumpet and trombone to a greater extent. The basic idea is the same - turn your amplifiers up to deafening and start singing".*

Things became a little clearer as the audience warmed up - *"people in the choir stalls jumped to their feet and started dancing, the 'cool' young men sliding convulsively back and forth while the girls tried to punch their neighbours or shook like saplings in a gale... a tremendous roar greeted the appearance of Stevie Wonder, led across the hall on the arm of his director. Stevie may be blind, but he sings magnificently and plays the organ, harmonica and drums with skill and style".*

Croydon Advertiser – 21.2.69

'Music you can't put a label on'

DESPITE WHAT you might think, ***Tyrannosaurus Rex*** *are not a species of prehistoric animals; they are two musicians, and on Sunday they gave a concert in the Fairfield Hall. Marc Bolan writes and sings the songs that they play, thumping out the rhythm on an acoustic (but amplified) guitar. Steve Peregrine Took adds an assortment of sounds on bongos, African-talking drums, Chinese gong, pixiephones and maraccas.*

The music they play is difficult to describe. The current label for it seems to be 'underground pop', but it is musically much more interesting than the tasteless trivia commonly passing for pop. It is not folk, or blues or jazz - perhaps it is best not to give it a label at all.

Nothing that Marc Bolan sings is quiet. Indeed, for much of the time he doesn't sing at all; he attacks the microphone with a series of guttural cries, sometimes he barks at it, sometimes he moans into it, sometimes he hums. Although he would hate the comparison, Marc is perhaps the nearest thing there is in his style of music to a scat singer.

There are two obvious criticisms of Tyrannosaurus Rex. While their music is infectious and swinging (on Sunday one tune had some of the audience jiving in the aisles), it can also be monotonous - but in a literal sense. It is all the same tone and much of it has the same rhythm.

The second point is far more important. Marc Bolan's poetry is just as good as his music, yet he chooses to sing in a way which makes most of the words indistinguishable.

To really appreciate some of his songs - 'Pewter Suitor', 'Seal of Seasons', 'Wind Quartet' and 'The Sea Beasts' are particularly fine - one needs to hear them properly. The poetry is musical but it is also quite obscure and half its effect is lost if you can't hear what words Marc is singing.

Sunday's concert, introduced by disc jockey ***John Peel****, also featured* ***Vytas Serelis*** *who played a lengthy piece on sitar and* ***David Bowie****, who presented mime. Mime is such a rarely seen art these days, that it is almost impossible to compare performers. David was convincing in his act as an old man carried into the world of fantasy by smoking a fragment of 'pot'; also as a man who eventually becomes famous by donning a mask which eventually sticks to his face. John Peel added to the programme by reading poetry in his flat Liverpool accent.*

J.R.H.

The performance of folk singer **Roy Harper** at the Gun Tavern on Monday 24th February received a rave review from the local press. Described both as a rebel and *"an original and uninhibited performer"*, Roy played his folk-blues protest songs to an attentive and by and large, appreciative audience. *"The main problem seems to be that he hates too much. Every aspect of society sickens him and he ties up most of them in 'McGoohan's Blues', a twenty minute long protest which divides into two distinct musical halves. This sometimes takes on the flavour of a personal persecution complex, in which he is convinced that forces are out to destroy both him and the truth, these two things sometimes being the same".*

Unfortunately, the folk club at the Gun Tavern didn't last too long, despite having made such a promising start, and was forced to close shortly before local songwriter **Ralph McTell** was due to appear on March 10th.

Making only their second of what were to become many visits to the Fairfield Hall on 25th April, **The Pentangle** received a mixed review from the local press. The group's mixture of musical styles often left journalists grasping at thin air in an attempt to pigeon-hole them; the Advertiser began with - *"...this five-strong group have a capacity for music making which makes other talented groups seem sterile in comparison..."*, but went on to say - *"...whenever I hear the Pentangle, I wonder if they gain anything from having a drummer and a bass player... the group did not have us shouting for more"*. A remarkable thing to say about Terry Cox and Danny Thompson, one of the most subtle and flexible rhythm sections in folk, rock or jazz for that matter.

The traditional material went over best; songs such as 'Bruton Town', 'She Moved Through The Fair', 'Let No Man Steal Your Thyme' and 'Hunting Song' could hardly fail with the combination of Jacqui McShee's beautiful voice and the guitar work of John Renbourn and Bert Jansch.

FAIRFIELD, CROYDON Box Office 01-688 9291
SUNDAY 2nd MARCH 7.45 p.m.
INCREDIBLE STRING BAND
and FRIENDS
A NEMS ENTERPRISE
Tickets: 17/-, 15/-, 13/-, 10/-, 8/-

BALI HAI' CLUB
STREATHAM
ADJOINING SILVER BLADES
EVERY WEDNESDAY at 8 p.m.
JULIAN'S TREATMENT

The Fairfield audience was shall we say, 'less than full', for the May concert by Peter Sarstedt and support group **The Humblebums**. The Humblebums made light of it, thanks to the between-song banter of band members Billy Connelly and Gerry Rafferty. Full marks to anyone in the crowd that night who said 'that Billy Connelly ought to be a comedian'.

Private collection

Amen Corner get their skates on prior to an evening session at Silver Blades in Streatham.

JULY

- 2 JIMMY RUFFIN **TR** (6/-)
- 7 EDGAR BROUGHTON **S** (n/a)
- 14 ANDY FERNBACH **S** (n/a)
- 14 JIMMY JAMES & THE VAGABONDS **O** (5/-)
- 14 WILDMOUTH **GN** + NIMBUS (3/-)
- 21 JODY GRIND **S** (n/a)
- 21 HOUSE **GN** (2/6d)
- 28 THE EGG **S** (n/a)
- 28 SKIN **GN** (2/6d)
- 28 VIOLET BROWNE'S DECISION **O** (5/-)

AUGUST

- 4 STEAMHAMMER **S** (n/a)
- 4 MAX ROMEO **O** (6/-)
- 9 JO-ANN KELLY **S** (n/a)
- 11 VIOLET BROWNE'S DECISION **O** (5/-)
- 15 JODY GRIND **S** (n/a)
- 18 VIOLET BROWNE'S DECISION **O** (5/-)
- 25 GROUNDHOGS **S** (n/a)
- 25 VANITY FARE **O** (6/6d)

SEPTEMBER

- 1 COLOURED RAISINS **O** (6/-)
- 8 ALEXIS KORNER **S** (n/a)
- 8 FAT MATTRESS **O** (6/6d)
- 15 GLASS MENAGERIE **S** (n/a)
- 15 DESMOND DEKKER **O** (6/6d)
- 19 MIGHTY BABY **S** (n/a)
- 21 THE WHO **FH** 2 shows (8/- to 17/-)
- 22 GRAHAM BOND INITIATION **S** (n/a)
- 25 OSCAR PETERSON **FH** (8/- to 21/-)
- 26 ALEXIS KORNER **S** (n/a)
- 29 ATOMIC ROOSTER **S** (n/a)

OCTOBER

- 2 TOM PAXTON **FH** (8/- to 21/-)
- 6 BEN E KING **O** (10/-)
- 6 EDGAR BROUGHTON **S** (n/a)
- 10 FAIRPORT CONVENTION **FH** + NICK DRAKE + BRIDGET ST. JOHN (8/- to 17/-)
- 13 AYNSLEY DUNBAR **S** (n/a)
- 13 LEE DORSEY **O** (6/6d)
- 17 THE NICE **FH** + KING CRIMSON (12/- to 25/-)
- 20 THIRD EAR BAND **S** (n/a)
- 23 JACQUES LOUISSIER **FH** (n/a)
- 27 BLOSSOM TOES **S** + STRAY (n/a)
- 31 JOHN MAYALL **FH** (8/- to 17/-)

NOVEMBER

- 6 CLIFF RICHARD **FH** + THE SHADOWS (n/a)
- 7 INCREDIBLE STRING BAND **FH** (n/a)
- 9 ALBERT KING **FH** + JOHN LEE HOOKER + OTIS SPANN + CHAMPION JACK DUPREE (8/- to 21/-)
- 10 KEEF HARTLEY **S** (n/a)
- 16 FAMILY **FH** (8/- to 17/-)
- 17 JOHN DUMMER BLUES BAND **S** (n/a)
- 19 BUDDY RICH **FH** (8/- to 21/-)
- 23 JUICY LUCY **G** (n/a)
- 24 GRAHAM BOND INITIATION **S** (n/a)
- 24 ARTHUR CONLEY **O** (10/-)
- 30 KEITH RELF & RENAISSANCE **G** (n/a)

DECEMBER

- 1 STRAY **S** (n/a)
- 7 YES **G** (n/a)
- 7 DELANEY & BONNIE & FRIENDS **FH** (10/- to 20/-)
- 8 JUNIORS EYES **S** (n/a)
- 14 MOTT THE HOOPLE **G** (n/a)
- 15 WILD ANGELS **S** (n/a)
- 21 KEEF HARTLEY **G** (n/a)
- 22 EAST OF EDEN **S** (n/a)
- 27 TYRANNOSAURUS REX **FH** (8/- to 17/-)
- 28 DEEP PURPLE **G** (n/a)
- 29 STRAY **G** (n/a)

FH - **Fairfield Hall** • **A** - **ABC** • **S** - **Star Hotel** • **TR** - **Top Rank** • **O** - **Orchid Ballroom**

In August, arguably Britains finest blues singer made one of her regular visits to the Star Hotel, the venue where she took her first tentative steps as a performer. In those days, **Jo-Ann Kelly** and pianist Bob Hall would play the interval set between jazz bands for ten shillings a night; later, when club audiences requested an authentic blues sound, she was one of the few artists who could really deliver.

Born in Streatham, Jo-Ann (below) and her brother Dave would make regular visits to the 'Swing Shop', a celebrated local source of jazz and blues records. She began to sing with various blues bands and recorded with many of them - Tony McPhee's Groundhogs, Brett Marvin & the Thunderbolts and the John Dummer Blues Band as well as tracks with Dave Kelly, Bob Hall and harmonica player Steve Rye.

Michael Hasted

American singer-songwriter **Tom Rush** was due to play support to Fairport Convention at their Fairfield show on 10th October; but with only two weeks to go he pulled out and was replaced by two up & coming British artists - **Nick Drake** and **Bridget St. John**. This was to be one of Nick Drake's rare concert appearances - he wasn't always very comfortable in a live setting - and the Croydon Advertiser, like a teacher marking an end-of-term school report, had this to say:

"Drake, a Cambridge undergraduate, wore youthful cords, an open neck shirt and jacket, and a rather anxious expression. Both (he and Bridget) sing sad, personal songs in rather deep, hushed voices, interspersed with the slightly amateur incoherencies one associates with this sort of performer. But both are pleasing enough artists, with above average skills at the guitar and composition".

Croydon Advertiser – 26.9.69

'When Op is Pop'

AN OPERA at a pop concert? It seems hard to believe, yet ***The Who*** *managed to get away with it at the Fairfield Hall on Sunday. But then, The Who have grown up, and the opera was their 'Tommy' album - said to be their best-ever long player.*

The group's performance was far more professional than in the past. It was also less wild. Of course, Roger Daltrey hurled his microphone around; Keith Moon managed to splinter a few drumsticks and Pete Townshend thrashed his guitar about his body. John Entwhistle was very placid - he is usually the quietest of the four anyway. But when they wearily trekked away from the bright lights to their dressing rooms, all their instruments had survived. Apparently they have realised there is no need to smash up their equipment.

And if The Who have grown up, so have their fans. There wasn't a scream to be heard. It was obvious The Who were playing to the converted - fans who wanted to sit back, enjoy and appreciate Who sounds. "I hope you won't be bored", joked Townshend, as the group launched into their unrehearsed 'Tommy' presentation. And I'm sure there couldn't have been many in the packed hall - people were even standing at the sides - who were. A hard task to keep an audience happy on their own, non-stop for two and a quarter hours, but The Who managed it.

Most of the concert was devoted to the 'Tommy' album/opera - an involved story about a "deaf, dumb and blind boy". However, The Who did find time for some of their hits. Would they dare ignore numbers like 'Substitute' and 'My Generation'? They threw in some blues and songs like 'Fortune Teller' and 'Summertime Blues'. An ear-splitting version of 'Shaking All Over' was almost overpowering but nevertheless great. It does seem old-fashioned to admit that you couldn't hear the words. With most of The Who numbers it doesn't really matter, but I think I would have been able to appreciate 'Tommy' even more if I could have grasped more of the words. Sometimes the backing was too loud.

An idea new to me was the flashing of coloured slides on to back of the hall. Throughout 'Tommy' there were scenes to illustrate the opera; at other times The Who were projected - Roger Daltrey, for instance, bare-chested, hair resting on his shoulders, tassels flowing from his jacket. Quite a good idea this, even if the slides did occasionally manage to fall out of sequence.

An excellent evening, with far more professional entertainment than offered by the average pop concert. It was made even more enjoyable by the sophisticated behaviour of the enthusiastic audience, who gave The Who a standing ovation. Unfortunately, the group could only offer one encore - they were probably too exhausted to have gone on... and no wonder!

K.A.

This concert was one of the first live performances of "Tommy"; in fact local music 'buffs' Alan Stranks and Alan Barnes who were both in the audience that night, believe it may have been the debut of the rock opera on stage. This appears to be backed up by concert promoter Tony Smith in an interview with music journalist Michael Wale; *"The first really major thing I did in the rock scene was Tommy. I'd heard the album which completely blew me away and I went to Pete Rudge and Kit Lambert and suggested they did it all in one evening. We chose the Fairfield Hall in Croydon and used colour slides and lights for the first time. It was such a success, the first time the Who had done the concert straight through all on their own. It lasted two hours with no interval and everybody was really wary at first, because they didn't know what was going to happen. We subsequently did it again at the London Coliseum".* Also in the Fairfield Hall audience to see The Who on 21st September, was the relatively unknown session pianist, **Elton John**, who later went on to play a part in Ken Russell's film version of 'Tommy'.

The group **Blossom Toes** were booked to headline the Star on October 27th but when they failed to appear, support band **Stray** were presented with the chance to play both sets, apparently going down a storm. Thus began the long-standing 'love affair' between local audiences and Stray, who returned time and time (and time) again to churn out their own particular brand of blues/boogie.

In fact the working title of this book was going to be *'ello Croydon'*, a phrase I shall always associate as Strays' opening gambit whenever Del Bromham and the boys took to the stage! Del later told me that he was *"amazed that anyone else knew about the Blossom Toes /Stray/Star connection, I thought that I was the only person who remembered that!"*.

Croydon gained an excellent new venue when the Greyhound opened its doors to live bands on 23rd November, with **Juicy Lucy** having the honour of being the opening act. Lucy are best remembered for two things - a top twenty single 'Who Do You Love' in April 1970 and an arresting album sleeve that pictured a sultry young lady covered in fruit! The Greyhound prematurely billed itself as *Croydon's Blues Club*, a title that rightfully belonged to the Star, at the time.

American husband and wife team **Delaney & Bonnie Bramlett** brought along a few special friends on their British tour, namely Eric Clapton, Dave Mason and (at the second of two packed houses, at least), George Harrison. The backing group also featured Carl Radle, Bobby Whitlock and Jim Gordon who went on to become Derek's (Eric's) Dominoes, plus Rita Coolidge on vocals, percussionist Tex Johnson and a horn section of Bobby Keys and Jim Price.

Support on the night was from Ashton, Gardner & Dyke. The two Croydon shows were recorded and subsequently released as the 'On Tour' album (June 1970) ATLANTIC 2400013, and more recently on CD (May 1993) ATCO 7567-90397, although the recording is mis-dated 1970. The band recorded only two dates from their short seven-venue tour; the opening gig at the Royal Albert Hall and the last night at Croydon, but only released tracks from the latter - George Harrison did not appear at the RAH show and I imagine that the band were really getting into their stride by the time they got to the Fairfield Halls.

Tony Smith, with his father John, was also involved in promoting this tour and he told Michael Wale; *"The other funny tour I did that was not really a disaster, but a shame that more people didn't go, was Delaney and Bonnie. There was Eric Clapton, Dave Mason and George Harrison in that band and we made £50 on the whole tour from about eight or nine dates. We sold out the last date at the Fairfield Hall, for two houses, otherwise we would have lost £2,000. It was a shame really, because they were really nice concerts."*

LIVE! AT THE FAIRFIELD
FAIRFIELD HALL, CROYDON
Manager: Thomas J. Pyper, M.I.M.Ent.
SATURDAY, 27th DECEMBER, at 7.45 p.m.
JOHN & TONY SMITH PRESENT
TYRANNOSAURUS REX
IN CONCERT
WITH BOPPING FRIENDS
SEATS: 17/-, 15/-, 13/-, 10/-, 8/-. Bookable in advance from: BOX OFFICE, FAIRFIELD HALL, CROYDON. TEL: CRO 9291. Open 10 a.m. to 8 p.m.

JANUARY

- 1 SOFT MACHINE **FH** (n/a)
- 8 STRAY **S** + JO-ANN KELLY (n/a)
- 12 STEAMHAMMER **S** (n/a)
- 18 PINK FLOYD **FH** (10/- to 20/-)
- 18 MOTT THE HOOPLE **G** (n/a)
- 19 STRAY **S** (n/a)
- 23 SAM & DAVE **FH** + CLARENCE CARTER + JOE TEX & ARTHUR CONLEY (n/a)
- 23 BLUE MINK **G** + BOOKER T. & THE MG's (n/a)
- 25 CANNED HEAT **FH** + RENAISSANCE (n/a)
- 25 YES **G** (n/a)
- 26 IDLE RACE **G** + BREADLINE (n/a)

FEBRUARY

- 1 KEEF HARTLEY **G** (n/a)
- 2 RARE BIRD **S** (n/a)
- 8 BLODWYN PIG **G** + TRADER HORNE (n/a)
- 9 JO-ANN KELLY & FRIENDS **S** BOB HALL + SIMON PRAEGER & STEVE RYE (n/a)
- 11 AL STEWART **FH** + THIRD EAR BAND (8/- to 17/-)
- 15 PENTANGLE **FH** (10/- to 18/-)
- 15 TASTE **G** (n/a)
- 16 GRAHAM BOND INITIATION **S** (n/a)
- 18 KEITH POTGER & THE NEW SEEKERS **FH** (n/a)
- 22 DEEP PURPLE **G** (n/a)
- 23 CHAMPION JACK DUPREE **S** (n/a)

MARCH

- 1 LIVERPOOL SCENE **G** (n/a)
- 2 ALEXIS KORNER **S** (n/a)
- 8 MANFRED MANN **FH** + EGG (n/a)
- 8 LOVE **G** (n/a)
- 9 BOOKER T. & THE M.G.'s **O** + BLUE MINK + THE FANTASTICS (n/a)
- 15 DADDYLONGLEGS **G** (n/a)
- 16 TRADER HORNE **S** (n/a)
- 22 THE NICE **FH** (n/a)
- 22 FREE **G** (n/a)
- 23 CARAVAN **S** (n/a)
- 29 MATTHEWS SOUTHERN COMFORT **G** (n/a)
- 30 DAVID BOWIES HYPE **S** + UGLY ROOM (n/a)

APRIL

- 3 BLACK SABBATH **S** + WHITE LIGHTNING (n/a)
- 5 KEEF HARTLEY's BIG BAND **FH** (n/a)
- 5 EDGAR BROUGHTON **G** (n/a)
- 9 WILD ANGELS **S** (n/a)
- 10 STRAY **S** (n/a)
- 12 FLOCK **FH** + RARE BIRD (n/a)
- 12 HUMBLE PIE **G** (n/a)
- 17 THE EGG **S** + KEITH TIPPETT (n/a)
- 19 TAJ MAHAL **FH** + JOHNNY WINTER (n/a)
- 19 CHICKEN SHACK **G** (n/a)
- 26 SOFT MACHINE **FH** (n/a)
- 26 MOTT THE HOOPLE **G** (n/a)

MAY

- 3 SKIN ALLEY **S** (n/a)
- 3 TASTE **G** (n/a)
- 8 STRAY **S** (n/a)
- 10 COLOSSEUM **FH** (n/a)
- 10 EDGAR BROUGHTON **G** (n/a)
- 17 FREE **G** (n/a)
- 20 BARRABAS **GN** + GUN HILL (n/a)
- 22 COCHISE **S** + HIGH TIDE (n/a)
- 24 STEPPENWOLF **FH** (n/a)
- 24 JUICY LUCY **G** (n/a)
- 26 VAN DER GRAF GENERATOR **G** (n/a)
- 31 TRAFFIC **FH** + IF (10/- to 20/-)

JUNE

- 3 ROY HARPER **FH** + THE STRAWBS (n/a)
- 3 JO-ANN KELLY **GN** (n/a)
- 5 CLIMAX CHICAGO BLUES BAND **S** (n/a)
- 7 TYRANNOSAURUS REX **G** (n/a)
- 12 STRAY **S** (n/a)
- 14 DEEP PURPLE **FH** (8/- to 17/-)
- 14 BLACK SABBATH **G** (n/a)
- 15 MARV JOHNSON **O** (n/a)
- 19 TWINK, DEVIANTS & PINK FAIRIES **S** (n/a)
- 21 GROUNDHOGS **G** (n/a)
- 26 ALEXIS KORNER **S** (n/a)

1970

January 18th gave Croydon fans of progressive rock another early look at **The Pink Floyd** - in Floyd terminology this gig was 'post-Syd' but 'pre-Dark Side', or as Barry Shinfield put it...

Croydon Advertiser – 23.1.70

'Serious pop and the standing ovation'

THE CONCEPT of pop groups appearing "in concert" is established, and with it has grown a tendency towards over-enthusiastic audience response: standing ovations are the rule nowadays rather than the exception.

Like over-indulged superlatives, these outbursts of wild acclaim no longer mean very much. They are not, by any means, indicative of the success of a concert... which is all, perhaps an unfair preamble to a review of the concert by Pink Floyd at Fairfield on Sunday.

There was a standing ovation; there was an encore. It's almost too predictable now. Make no mistake, Pink Floyd are good. More than that they are originals and have been so since earlier days (after 'See Emily Play' and 'Arnold Lane') when they practically invented psychedelia.

They have experimented in electronic channels with admirable, often harrowing inventiveness - at least one member of the group, co-founder Richard Wright says his chief musical influence was Stockhausen. They are individually adept as musicians and command a range of instruments; Wright again, played organ, piano, trombone and vibraphone on Sunday and he can also play harpsichord, harmonium and 'cello.

They are the masters of creating atmospheric or mood music, which is built up by strident beat and chord sequences, with jungle noises and witch-cacklings. The volume is often frightening. There is - without over dramatising - a hidden terror, a hint of evil. What you hear is a kind of conglomeration of contemporary fears, frustration and madness. Anything can be legitimately used in creating the atmosphere: recourse to heavy timpani, violent assault on cymbal, flogging a gargantuan gong and the insistent thumping of fingers on microphones.

Pink Floyd are obsessed with the mystery of outer space - 'Set the Controls for the Heart of the Sun' and Inter-Stellar Overdrive' are two titles - and they portray it with imagination.

FH - Fairfield Hall • G - Greyhound • S - Star Hotel • TR - Top Rank • O - Orchid Ballroom • GN - Gun Tavern

The mums in the Fairfield audience who were seen *"writhing in their seats, clutching their ears in pain"*, had apparently seen the name **Manfred Mann** on the poster but failed to notice the **'Chapter III'** postscript. This was indeed a new chapter in the groups history, with Manfred and Mike Hugg left from the original group, aided by drummer Craig Collinge, Steve York on bass and saxophonist Bernard Living. For live work they added a four-piece brass section, giving them a sound that veered from soul to their favoured jazz rock. The only links to their pop past were the newly-arranged 'Mighty Quinn' and a piece called 'Travelling Lady' which started out as the B-side to 'Ragamuffin Man'.

David Bowies shortlived band **The Hype** played at the Star on March 30th, featuring guitarist Mick Ronson, producer Tony Visconti on bass and John Cambridge. This was to be the last gig before Cambridge was replaced on drums by Mick 'Woody' Woodmansey - Bowies 'Spiders from Mars' line-up was almost complete.

THE happy STAR HOTEL ✶ W. CROYDON
296 London Road, Broad Green
Monday, March 30th
LIGHTS
SOUNDS
DAVID BOWIES HYPE
+ UGLY ROOM
We are changing our night to Fridays and are pleased to begin with
BLACK SABBATH on FRIDAY, APRIL 3rd

The Fairfield concert by **Keef Hartley's Big Band** was really a concert by two bands - the first half was played by the basic 6-piece ensemble of Miller Anderson on guitar and vocals, Gary Thain on bass, saxophonist Lyle Jenkins, trumpeter Dave Caswell, Henry Lowther - trumpet and violin and Hartley himself on drums.

The ex-John Mayall drummer made several allusions to the fact that he was abruptly forced to leave his previous employer - *"We're all Mayall cast-offs"* he told the audience *"If you haven't had the sack from John Mayall, you can't join the Musician's Union!"*

For the second half, the big band enlarged to 14, with four sax players including Barbara Thompson, four trumpets and two trombones plus the violin, guitar, bass and drums. Henry Lowther's background covered the classics at the Royal Academy of Music, jazz with the likes of Johnny Dankworth and Ronnie Scott and rock with Mayall again, Manfred Mann and Colosseum. At this gig he was forced to play only violin as the recent removal of his wisdom teeth prevented his playing the trumpet!

Also in town: hard-working band **Writing On The Wall** plus **Easy Leaf** at the Star Hotel on Monday 9th March and **Genesis** at Carshalton College, Nightingale Lane, Carshalton on Saturday 20th June.

On average, you were paying ten shillings to twelve shillings and sixpence to see a live band in a small venue like the Gun or the Star. But what were the bands themselves being paid? As a rough guide, this is what the colleges and universities were being charged for weekend bookings towards the end of 1970:

Cheapest were the 'up & coming' bands like Skin Alley at £75 followed by Cochise and Hawkwind for £85, and the Pink Fairies for £100. Ralph McTell was on £150. The £200 - £250 range included the Strawbs, East of Eden, Mott the Hoople, the Groundhogs and Manfred Mann. £250 to £300 got you Elton John, Cat Stevens, Chicken Shack and Yes. Now we're into the big league! - Blodwyn Pig and T.Rex could command a £400 fee, Edgar Broughton wanted £500, while Pentangle and Soft Machine were on £600. 'Free' cost £750, and nearly top of the range were Family and Deep Purple who could ask for anything between £750 and £1,000. Way out in front though, were the Pink Floyd who charged a whopping £1,500 and all the lighting equipment the college hall could handle!

At 1.30am on the morning of Sunday 12th April, the American group **Flock** were still performing onstage in Paris. By six o'clock that afternoon they were in Croydon to play the first of two shows that kicked off the British leg of their European tour. Led by virtuoso violinist Jerry Goodman and guitarist Fred Glickstein, the group's advance publicity handout promised that "they create their own atmosphere of full-freak" - armed with this information, Barry Shinfield went along to discover exactly what 'full-freak' was...

It was soon apparent that it is Goodman who will make their name. He does all manner of things on the violin; Dave Swarbrick and Henry Lowther, the British pop violinists had better look out. Tucked affectionately under his chin, the instrument is almost an extension of his anatomy. The bow goes in and out of that curtain of hair at lightning speed; he kneels on the floor, he dispenses with the bow and plucks at the strings with his fingers, he uses a wah-wah pedal.

Flock play with confidence and authority - and they are completely relaxed. During the stamping of feet for an encore, Glickstein said "But we didn't even think you knew us". We do now.

During the research for this tome, I was fortunate to be allowed access to the actual booking sheets for the Fairfield Hall. As the promoters would often book a run of dates and then allocate artists from their rosta to fill them, it was possible to see who was initially pencilled in - sometimes two or three choices before the final act was 'inked-in' over the top. On the 19th April, for example, underneath **Taj Mahal & Johnny Winter**, is clearly pencilled **'Grateful Dead?'**. Now I don't know about you, but the very idea of the seeing 'the Dead' in Croydon is sufficiently mind-blowing! One for the 'if only' list, I think.

And later in the year, on October 25th, the bookings sheet has a concert scheduled for **'The New Nice'**, before finally inking-in Emerson, Lake & Palmer at a later date!

As it stands, the visit by **Johnny Winter** was a rare opportunity to see one of America's great blues guitarists, and with him his brother Edgar, a multi-talented musician who played organ, sax and even 'helped out' on drums. The Texan-born brothers presented an unusual sight on stage - for both are natural albino's, their long straight pure-white hair contrasting with the total black cotton and denim of their stage clothes.

For an added bonus, Johnny Winter walked over to the side of the stage and pulled keyboard wizard Keith Emerson from the wings for an impromptu jam session, a prolonged and highly successful instrumental that closed the first half and left the fans howling for more.

Unfortunately, Taj Mahal's more traditional blues set suffered by comparison and a large section of the audience had dispersed long before the end.

Soul and reggae fans were still well catered for by the Orchid Ballroom. On 12th January they put on a show cheekily titled 'Reggae, Steady Go' where a twenty shilling ticket gave you **Desmond Dekker & the Aces**, the Upsetters, the Pioneers, Symarip (of 'Skinhead Moonstomp' fame) and the Fireballs.

February followed up with the **Fantastics** on the 2nd, **Edwin Starr** on the 9th, **Jimmy Ruffin** on the 16th and **Oscar Toney Jnr**. on the 23rd, all tickets between six or seven shillings. Monday 9th March saw the Fantastics back again, but this time bottom of a superb bill that featured **Blue Mink**, DJ Johnnie Walker and topped by **Booker T. & the M.G.'s**.

Bob & Marcia promoted their hit 'Young, Gifted and Black' at the Orchid on 6th April and the seemingly ever-present **Ben E. King** returned on the 4th May, tickets ten shillings!

JULY

1 JUDAS JUMP **G** (n/a)
3 ALAN BOWN **S** (n/a)
5 FREE **G** + THORS ANVIL (n/a)
10 HAWKWIND **S** + WAYFARERS HALL (n/a)
12 SAVOY BROWN **G** (n/a)
17 GENESIS **S** (n/a)
19 MUNGO JERRY **G** (n/a)
23 INCREDIBLE STRING BAND **FH** (8/- to 20/-)
24 ARGENT **S** (n/a)
31 STRAY **S** (n/a)

AUGUST

2 YES **G** + SUPERTRAMP (n/a)
2 NICKY THOMAS **TR** (8/-)
7 QUIVER **S** (n/a)
9 ATOMIC ROOSTER **G** (n/a)
14 DUSTER BENNETT **S** (n/a)
16 EAST OF EDEN **G** (n/a)
21 AUDIENCE **S** + TRAPEZE (n/a)
23 HARDIN & YORK **TR** + KEEF HARTLEY (n/a)
23 FAIRPORT CONVENTION **G** (n/a)
28 URIAH HEEP **S** (n/a)
30 BLACK WIDOW **G** (n/a)

SEPTEMBER

4 LOVE AFFAIR **S** (n/a)
6 TASTE **FH** + STONE THE CROWS (n/a)
6 GROUNDHOGS **G** (n/a)
6 COLOSSEUM **TR** + DADDY LONGLEGS (n/a)
13 FREE **FH** + MOTT THE HOOPLE (n/a)
13 BLACK SABBATH **G** (n/a)
17 SUPERTRAMP **G** (n/a)
18 STRAY **S** (n/a)
20 DEREK & THE DOMINOES **FH** (n/a)
20 STEAMHAMMER **G** (n/a)
27 YES **G** (n/a)

OCTOBER

2 STATUS QUO **S** (n/a)
4 THE DUBLINERS **FH** (n/a)
4 EDGAR BROUGHTON **G** (n/a)
8 THE WHO **O** + THE JAMES GANG (20/-)
11 INCREDIBLE STRING BAND **FH** (n/a)
11 SAVOY BROWN **G** (n/a)
18 MOTT THE HOOPLE **G** (n/a)
23 SUPERTRAMP **S** (n/a)
25 EMERSON, LAKE & PALMER **FH** (10/- to 20/-)
25 BLODWYN PIG **G** (n/a)
28 BUDDY RICH **FH** (n/a)

NOVEMBER

1 PENTANGLE **FH** (8/- to 20/-)
6 THE ALAN BOWN **FH** (2/6d)
6 BURNIN' RED IVANHOE **S** (n/a)
8 GINGER BAKER'S AIRFORCE **FH** (8/- to 17/-)
12 RALPH McTELL **FH** (8/- to 15/-)
13 TREES **FH** (2/6d)
13 QUIVER **S** (n/a)
15 FAIRPORT CONVENTION **FH** + ROGER RUSKIN SPEAR (8/- to 20/-)
20 JOHN MAYALL **FH** 2 shows (8/- to 20/-)
22 DEEP PURPLE **FH** (10/- to 20/-)
27 AMAZING BLONDEL **FH** (2/6d)
29 LIFETIME **FH** (8/- to 17/-)
29 THE FACES **G** (n/a)

DECEMBER

6 CHICKEN SHACK **G** (n/a)
6 QUINTESSENCE **FH** + MIGHTY BABY (8/- to 17/-)
7 WOODY HERMAN **FH** (10/- to 21/-)
13 GROUNDHOGS **G** (n/a)
18 CAT STEVENS **FH** + AMAZING BLONDEL (8 to 15/-)
20 FLEETWOOD MAC **FH** 2 shows, 5.30 & 8.30 (10/- to 20/-)
20 EAST OF EDEN **G** + STATUS QUO (n/a)
24 STRAY **S** + BRAMSTOKER (n/a)
27 MOTT THE HOOPLE **G** (n/a)

1970

Following on from the Grateful Dead story, and to add to the list of Croydon concerts that 'nearly happened', the American psychedelic group **Iron Butterfly** were all set to play at the ABC cinema on Friday 10th July, until 'circumstances beyond our control' forced the management of the theatre to cancel. So, it was off home, burn some incense, put the album on the turntable and all together now - *'Ina gada da vida, baby...'!*

They were due to play two shows, with tickets priced between eight and twenty shillings and also on the bill would have been Warm Dust, featuring a young Paul Carrack, Cressida and Fairfield Parlour.

On 13th September, **Mott the Hoople** tried to record their Fairfield concert for release as a live album, but the plans went astray as the audience went 'wild' and stormed the stage. Mott's drummer, Buffin, later said - *'The Croydon recording was really for* ***FREE****, who were bill-topping (and rather suffered after our set - they'd slayed us in Sunderland though!)'*. However, Mott's 'Keep A Knocking' rock'n'roll medley from this gig did make it on to vinyl, as the final track on 'Wildlife' - Island ILPS 9144, released February 1971.

Four days later, a CND Benefit concert (that's the Campaign for Nuclear Disarmament) took place under the tour name 'Peace Pie!' It featured **Roy Harper**, the folk band **Trees**, Liverpool poet **Adrian Henri** and the **Radha Krishna Temple**.

A ticket stub from the Orchid Ballroom, where the Who were ably supported by The James Gang, an American trio that included guitarist Joe Walsh.

With a surfeit of good gigs to choose from, other concerts to add to the listings include **Family** + **Emily Muff** 26th July, (8/- to 20/-) at the Fairfield and **Johnny Johnson & the Bandwagon** at the Top Rank, 30th August (8/-).

Beddington Football Club presented a double bill consisting of local band **Katch 22** and **Mako** at Wallington Public Hall on Thursday 8th October, admission 7/6d.

Katch 22 were one of the more successful groups to come out of the Carshalton/Wallington area, a four piece band led by Martin Godbold, vocals and lead guitar, and his brother Robert on bass. Michael Eastman, rhythm guitar and Paul Bonner, drums and vocals completed the line-up.

One of their contemporaries from Elmwood School was Dave Francis, who told me, *'As friends of the band, we used to help them with their gear and then stay around to watch them rehearse; later on we would 'roadie' for early gigs at pubs such as the Greyhound next to Carshalton Ponds and the Fox & Hounds in Carshalton itself. Quite a few bands played at the Fox & Hounds, John Mayall being one of the most memorable'.* In 1968, a very young Katch 22 (judging by the sleeve) recorded their first album called 'It's Soft Rock & Allsorts' on Saga - EROS 8047 which contained several of their own compositions, Paul Bonner collaborating with an unknown friend, surname Wayne and with Michael Eastman, plus covers including Paul Simon's '59th Street Bridge Song' and 'Walk Away Renée'. Dave Francis also believes the band made a fleeting appearance in a late 'sixties film and were also featured in a TV toothpaste advertisement!

As the band got older and the music scene changed from pop to progressive in the early 'seventies, Katch 22 changed with it. They moved record label to Fontana and released singles with the more psychedelic titles of 'Pumpkin Mini' and 'The World's Getting Smaller'. They expanded their range of gigs to become regulars on the London circuit, under the management of John Smith Enterprises.

The Fairfield Halls hosted another of those superb blues concerts on Wednesday 18th November, featuring **Sonny Terry & Brownie McGhee**, more than ably supported by **Champion Jack Dupree** and **Willie Dixon & his Chicago Blues Allstars** featuring Lee Jackson on guitar. Opening the show were Bukka White, Shakey Horton and Lafayette Leake.

Sonny and Brownie's performance was reported to be *"a totally moving and absorbing performance. Their sounds compliment each other beautifully... Sonny has the gritty voice and an ability to make his harmonica talk and sing... Brownie's voice is soft in contrast, his guitar playing superb".*

Champion Jack Dupree - his name a hangover from his fighting days - was as much an entertainer as a bluesman, even playing the piano with his elbow!

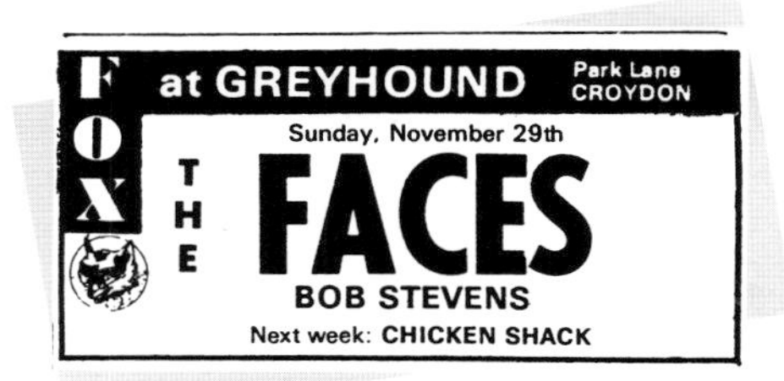

Croydon Advertiser – 9.10.70

'Martin comes home with the Mighty Baby'

NEXT WEEK, fans in Croydon will have the chance to see London-based group ***Mighty Baby*** *making a rare appearance at the Star Hotel, Broad Green. For lead guitarist Martin Stone the show will be much more than just another gig - it will be a homecoming.*

Twenty three year old Martin, whose parents live in Covington Way, Norbury, went to Whitgift School and first found his interest in music growing as he visited Croydon's folk clubs and pubs. "I started playing when I was about 11" he said, "but it wasn't until I listened to, and sometimes played with, Croydon's own musicians that I found out what playing really meant". At one time Martin was a reporter with the 'Advertiser'; that was in 1965 and it was at that stage that he found his commitment to music growing. "I was in a group called The Rockhouse Band, who backed a lot of American artists on visiting tours - John Lee Hooker, Rufus Thomas and others".

The most notable band Martin played with before joining Mighty Baby was ***Savoy Brown****, a well respected blues band who now spend most of their time playing on the other side of the Atlantic. Mighty Baby as a group started as The Action and this is how they were known when Martin joined them. They ended 1969 by playing support to the Rolling Stones at the Lyceum and Saville; it was also at the end of last year that the group's first album was released and received enthusiastic reviews from the serious music papers and trade press.*

The support act to both Derek and the Dominoes and John Mayall, were the under-rated **Brett Marvin and the Thunderbolts**, a jug-band style blues group destined to have their only chart success under the name **Terry Dactyl & the Dinosaurs** with 'Seaside Shuffle'. The band also included one John Lewis, who later changed his name to Jona Lewie, signed a solo deal with Stiff Records and had further hits in the Eighties with 'Stop the Cavalry' and 'You'll Always Find Me In The Kitchen At Parties'.

Jona's blues credentials go back to his first band at Kingston Poly. with Hawkwind's Dave Brock and playing keyboards on albums by Tony McPhee and Arthur 'Big Boy' Crudup.

Croydon Advertiser – 30.10.70

'Lunchtime Pop Music Concerts'

STUDENTS and young office workers in Croydon will be able to relieve the tedium of the day with lunchtime live pop music, next month. As an experiment, the Fairfield Halls are launching a series of four Friday concerts, beginning on November 6th.

The performances will be continuous, from 12.30 pm to 1.45pm and the price of admission, 2s. 6d, is attractively low.

A Fairfield spokesman commented: "We have been running the Tuesday lunchtime classical concerts ever since the building opened so we thought we would try this idea and see what the response is. We think we are one of the first - if not the first - place in the country to do this".

The first mid-day session will be by a group called ***The Alan Bown****, followed by* ***Trees*** *(Nov. 13),* ***Curved Air*** *(20) and* ***Amazing Blondel*** *(27).*

Tucked away in the folk listings of Time Out was this gem of a gig - under the title of 'The Blues Is What You Make It', the event consisted of a talk by guitarist **Dave Kelly** tracing the origins of the blues and illustrated with original recordings from his collection. This was followed by live performances by Dave and his sister **Jo-Ann Kelly**, **Simon Praeger & Steve Rye** and pianist **Bob Hall**. The date was Friday 13th November (lucky for those attending) at the Queens Hotel, Upper Norwood, presented by Crystal Palace & the Triangle Community Association, a mere 2/6 for members and 5 shillings for guests.

If John Mayall's first concert at Croydon's Fairfield Hall on Friday was something of a happening, the second house was even more of one. At the end, on stage were Mayall, Larry Taylor, Harvey Mandel, Sugarcane Harris and Keef Hartley with Rod Mayall, John's brother, on piano. Quite an occasion - and the audience fully realised it.

'Scene' column, Disc & Music Echo, 28.11.70

The 28th November issue of Time Out reviewed 'Anyway...' the new album released by **Family** on Warner Reprise. Side one of the LP was recorded live at the Fairfield Halls, while the 'studio' side two was recorded at Olympic in Barnes. According to reviewer Clive Loveless, the live version of 'Strange Band' is *"one of the most effective live rock recordings I've heard; it's off like a drag racer, blazing with so much vocal and instrumental power that you think the band's just got to fly apart at any moment..."*

JANUARY

3 STONE THE CROWS or YES? **G** (n/a)
7 JOHNNY JOHNSON & THE BANDWAGON **O** (n/a)
10 CURVED AIR **G** + ALAN BOWN (n/a)
15 UNIVERSE **S** (n/a)
17 EDGAR BROUGHTON **G** (n/a)
24 THE FACES **G** + DORIS HENDERSON'S ECLECTION (n/a)
31 RENAISSANCE **G** + POOR SUN (n/a)

FEBRUARY

4 T. REX **FH** (8/- to 15/-)
7 STRAY **G** (n/a)
7 FREE **FH** + AMAZING BLONDEL 2 shows (10/- to 20/-)
11 TOM PAXTON **FH** (8/- to 21/-)
14 STATUS QUO **G** (12/6)
14 KEEF HARTLEY **FH** + HARDIN & YORK (8/- to 17/-)
21 FAIRPORT CONVENTION **G** (12/6)
25 INCREDIBLE STRING BAND **FH** (50p to £1)
26 DEEP PURPLE **A** + ASHTON,GARDNER & DYKE (n/a)
28 LEON RUSSELL **G** (12/6)

MARCH

4 JUDITH DURHAM **FH** (40p to £1)
7 CURVED AIR **G** (12/6)
7 JOHN MAYALL **FH** + RANDALLS ISLAND (50p to £1.85)
14 COLOSSEUM **G** (12/6)
21 OSIBISA **G** + GRASS (12/6)
21 ELTON JOHN **FH** + HOOKFOOT (50p to £1.50)
26 QUINTESSENCE **FH** (40p to 60p)
26 DESMOND DEKKER **O** (80p)
28 MOTT THE HOOPLE **FH** + BRONCO (40p to 85p)
28 ARGENT **G** + DANTA (50p)

APRIL

4 EAST OF EDEN **G** + THIN LIZZY (50p)
11 GROUNDHOGS **G** (50p)
11 VAN DER GRAF GENERATOR + LINDISFARNE + GENESIS **FH** (50p)
16 STRAWBS **FH** + BREAK & KRANE (50p - 90p)
18 ATOMIC ROOSTER **G** + ROOT & JENNY JACKSON PEACE CORPORATION (50p)
25 SKID ROW **G** + ARMADA (50p)
25 INCREDIBLE STRING BAND **FH** (50p - £1)
30 NANA MOUSKOURI **FH** (n/a)

MAY

2 EDGAR BROUGHTON **G** + KARAKORUM (50p)
2 THE DUBLINERS **FH** (50p to 90p)
6 THE BYRDS **FH** + RITA COOLIDGE (50p to £1.25p)
9 STATUS QUO **G** (50p)
13 COUNT BASIE ORCHESTRA **FH** (50p to £1.30)
14 ROD McKUEN **FH** (50p to £1.25p)
16 CARAVAN **G** (50p)
23 FUNKADELIC **G** (50p)
23 T.REX **FH** (60p)
30 THE FACES **G** + TRAPEZE (50p)
30 KING CRIMSON **FH** + ROGER RUSKIN SPEAR (50p - £1)

JUNE

3 STEELEYE SPAN *in* 'CORUNNA!' **FH** (n/a)
6 QUINTESSENCE **G** (50p)
6 TRAFFIC **FH** + HEADS, HANDS & FEET (50p -£1)
10 CHAIRMEN OF THE BOARD **O** (80p)
13 EAST OF EDEN **G** (50p)
13 RORY GALLAGHER **FH** + JELLYBREAD (60p)
20 URIAH HEEP **G** + INDIAN SUMMER (50p)
27 GROUNDHOGS **G** + JERICHO JONES (50p)
27 HUMBLE PIE **FH** (n/a)

1971

Local musician Neil Korner was back on home ground at the end of January, when his new group **Renaissance** played at the Croydon Greyhound. Originally booked to play support to Elton John, Renaissance moved into top billing when Elton pulled out.

The membership of the group had changed completely since it was first formed by ex-Yardbirds Keith Relf and Jim McCarty, the new line-up had been together for seven months and consisted of vocalists Terry Crow and Annie Haslam, John Tout on piano, Mick Dumford on guitar, drummer Terry Slade and Neil on bass.

Neil Korner (no relation to Alexis), who was still living in Melfort Road, Thornton Heath at the time, had been a musician for ten years, working for the Apple record label and playing in various bands including the Nashville Teens. An interview with Neil appears on pages 44 - 46.

Journalist Barry Shinfield was decidedly unmoved by the lacklustre performance of **Free** at the Fairfield on Sunday 7th February.

"Why all the fuss" he asked in his Advertiser review, *"nothing one heard approached, for example, the Who at their perspiring best on stage. You couldn't lose yourself in the music of Free because it was so studied and laborious, and yet somehow so unspontaneous"*. Barry did note the queue outside the building, over 100 yards long, waiting for the start of the second house, and the fact that the fans made a big fuss over Paul Rogers and chums - *"inside, the first show was ending with a swaying flowerbed of frail young things dancing self-consciously like aspiring go-go girls at the foot of the stage, moving as exotically as they could to the music without working up too much of a lather"*.

Across the road at the Greyhound that same night, the gig by local favourites **Stray** literally went off with a bang. Towards the end of their set, with the band powering through the title track of their new LP 'Suicide', all the fuses blew, bringing both band and their enthusiastic crowd to a standstill.

Described as 'loud and brash, competent and cohesive', the group of vocalist Steve Gadd, Del Bromham on lead guitar, Gary Giles on bass and drummer Ritchie Cole, completely won over the crowd who cheered, danced and swarmed onto the stage at the end - once the fuses had been mended and the band were able to finish their set.

Croydon Advertiser – 26.2.71

'UPSETTING FOR THE FAIRPORTS'

*SOMETHING very upsetting happened to **Fairport Convention**, the pop group, early on Sunday morning at the house where they all live at Little Hadham, Herts.*

A lorry crashed into the room where violinist Dave Swarbrick was sleeping and the driver was killed. Despite the shock, the band decided not to cancel their engagement at the Greyhound in Croydon that evening. Inevitably though, their performance was affected. They found it hard to be enthusiastic and their usually lively music depends on this. Simon Nicol - lead guitarist and, since Richard Thompson left, the only remaining founder member - apologised twice for how badly they were playing.

For the most part, they lacked the heart to play their essentially happy electrified folk. At times glimpses of it - particularly from Swarbrick's vibrant electric violin - did shine through. Misfortune seems to beset them. Martin Lamble (their original drummer) was killed in a crash in 1969. Sandy Denny left, then Richard Thompson. Now, Sunday's fatal crash. But their fans can look forward to better things - the band have been working on a new album and it should be released in April.

May 28th saw yet another visit to the Fairfield from those masters of the yellow polo neck sweater, **The Spinners** (and they were back again in October); whilst on June 3rd, folk fans turned out to see 'CORUNNA', a play by Keith Dewhurst performed by **Steeleye Span, Pete Atkin** and members of the **Royal Court Theatre.**

There was a last minute programme change for the **Traffic** concert on 6th June. Ian Stuart told me - *'Heads, Hands & Feet were scheduled to support, but couldn't make it, so Traffic's Dave Mason substituted and then the group themselves played an extended set. It was a great gig - just listen to the 'Live at the Canteen' album for proof'.*

U20 FRONT STALLS | U20 FRONT STALLS
FAIRFIELD HALL, CROYDON
General Manager: T. J. PYPER, T.M.A., F.I.M.Ent.
EVENING 7-30 SUNDAY APRIL 11 | EVENING 7-30 SUNDAY APRIL 11
VAN DER GRAAF GENERATOR
AND SUPPORTING ARTISTS
50p | 50p
LATECOMERS will not be admitted until a convenient break in the programme. Tickets cannot be exchanged or money refunded.

Lindisfarne drummer **Ray Laidlaw** told me: *"My strongest memory of the old Greyhound is of a lovely afternoon in the summer of '71, when all of Lindisfarne were invited for tea at Peter Hammill's cottage in Purley".* (Hammill was the singer and writer with Van Der Graaf Generator, a group who shared the same record label, Charisma, and who were part of the famous '50 pence tour' with Lindisfarne and Genesis). *"It was just about the time that the news was spreading about the band and we were looking forward to a belting gig. When we arrived at the Greyhound, the queue was right around the building and the sold out signs were up. I think it was the hottest I have ever been in my life. It was after that show that I started to wear shorts on stage.*

About a year after that, we were backstage at a show in Chicago, when we met a girl who used to be a regular at the Greyhound. We were supporting David Bowie and she had been whisked away from Croydon to be Ziggy's hairdresser! I don't know who was the most surprised, the lady or ourselves".

Croydon Advertiser – 16.4.71

'FIFTY PENCE ROCK'

*'ROCK STARS on cut-price national tour' screamed the publicity sheet. It was referring to the current 15-day safari of **Van Der Graaf Generator**, **Genesis** and **Lindisfarne** through our highlands and lowlands to bring us their bargain rate pop music.*

The tour opened at Fairfield on Sunday where the price of a seat was a universal 50p. Cheap for a pop concert these days, but hard luck on Croydon because the price for the rest of the tour is only 40p and on the last night in Manchester, it descends to a mere 30p!.Nevertheless, although one would quibble slightly at the use of the word 'stars' to describe three groups nowhere near the top rung of British rock, they represented good value together. The pay-off for them will come, it is hoped, in increased record sales.

Van Der Graaf were top of the bill, but personally I found them the least engaging of the three. My objection to them springs from an admitted bias against heavy groups who try to knock you senseless with volume and have, if their fans look at it objectively, very little else. Or if they have individual instrumental talent, as Van Der Graaf obviously have, they are using it in the wrong way.

Genesis, appropriately began the evening. Their stage presentation was distinctive... with a singer who out-Jaggered Jagger and did so with panache. He could sing, as well and recounted some unnervingly macabre jokes... Lindisfarne were enjoyable too, and got at least as good a reception as Van Der Graaf. They are a talented folk-rock group with harmonica often taking solos and blending nicely with electric piano... their numbers were melodic, which is more than could be said for what was to come.

Barry Shinfield

Christie's Images

This tour marked a significant time in the career of Marc Bolan and T.Rex. Having enjoyed their first Number 1 single with 'Hot Love' in March, they went on to release the album 'Electric Warrior' in October, which also hit the top spot and stayed there for several weeks.

JULY

1 TAMI LYNN **O** (n/a)
3 BLACK AUGUST **GN** (40p)
4 STEAMHAMMER **G** (45p)
8 THE WILD ANGELS **O** (n/a)
13 VAN DER GRAF GENERATOR **G** (45p)
15 THE TREMELOES **O** (n/a)
16 JAMES TAYLOR **FH** + CAROLE KING + JO MAMA (n/a)
16 BILLY FURY **O** (n/a)
18 LINDISFARNE **G** + MIKE MARAN (45p)
22 FLEETWOOD MAC **O** (n/a)
25 HAWKWIND **G** (45p)

AUGUST

1 QUIVER **G** (40p)
8 MEDICINE HEAD **G** + BO IDLE (n/a)
15 ARGENT **G** (n/a)
22 TIR NA NOG **G** + MIKE MARAN (n/a)
27 SCREAMING LORD SUTCH **TR** (40p)
29 CHICKEN SHACK **G** (n/a)

SEPTEMBER

5 URIAH HEEP **G** + THIRD WORLD WAR (50p)
9 THE DRIFTERS **O** (60p)
12 EDGAR BROUGHTON **G** + GENTLE GIANT (50p)
19 KING CRIMSON **G** (50p)
26 WISHBONE ASH **G** + BURNT OAK (n/a)
26 JOHN MAYALL **FH** + EGGS OVER EASY (50p to £1)
30 QUINTESSENCE **FH** + MEDICINE HEAD (50p to £1)

OCTOBER

3 RORY GALLAGHER **G** (n/a)
7 NEW SEEKERS **FH** (50p to £1)
10 GREASE BAND **G** (50p)
17 ATOMIC ROOSTER **G** + SUNSHINE (60p)
21 JIMMY RUFFIN **O** (60p)
24 STEELEYE SPAN **G** + ANDY ROBERTS (50p)
24 T. REX **FH** 2 shows, (60p)
28 THE TAMS **O** (60p)
29 THE CORRIES **FH** (40p to 75p)
31 STATUS QUO **G** + NAZARETH (60p)

NOVEMBER

4 THE ELGINS **O** (60p)
5 BUFFY ST. MARIE **FH** + LOUDON WAINWRIGHT III (£1.25 to £1.50)
7 JACK BRUCE **G** + BARRABAS (n/a)
7 FAMILY **FH** + AMERICA (n/a)
10 BUDDY RICH **FH** (50p to £1.30p)
11 TOM PAXTON **FH** (50p to £1)
12 PENTANGLE **FH** (50p to 80p)
14 EDGAR BROUGHTON **G** (50p)
21 THE SUPREMES **FH** + LABI SIFFRE + BOB MILLER & THE MILLERMEN (n/a)
21 URIAH HEEP **G** (50p)
22 RALPH McTELL **FH** + THE DRANSFIELDS (50p to 80p)
25 AMAZING BLONDEL **FH** + JOHN MARTYN (40p to 75p)
28 FAIRPORT CONVENTION **FH** (50p to £1)
28 LINDISFARNE **G** + NAZARETH (n/a)
29 CLIFF RICHARD **FH** + MARVIN, WELCH & FARRAR + OLIVIA NEWTON-JOHN (65p to £1.50)

DECEMBER

5 AMERICA **G** (50p)
5 ELTON JOHN **FH** + ENGLAND DAN & JOHN FORD COLEY (65p to £1)
6 AL GREEN **TR** (50p)
12 OSIBISA **G** (n/a)
19 HAWKWIND **G** (n/a)
26 STATUS QUO (Xmas Party!) **G** (n/a)
30 BADFINGER **O** (n/a)

FH - Fairfield Hall • G - Greyhound • A - ABC • S - Star Hotel • TR - Top Rank • O - Orchid Ballroom

1971

You could be forgiven for thinking that a **Fleetwood Mac** concert would guarantee a large crowd; indeed when Alan Stranks from Caterham heard of their July gig at the Orchid, he simply *had* to be there. The new line-up were playing a handful of British dates prior to recording the *'Future Games'* album, so Alan and half a dozen friends 'piled into the van' and drove down to Purley to claim their place near the front. To their surprise, no more than thirty to forty people turned out to see Mick Fleetwood and Co., whereas only a year before, Fleetwood Mac had played two sell-out shows at the Fairfield. The reason? This '71 line up was 'mid-period Mac'; post Peter Green and pre-Buckingham/Nicks, which meant that along with Mick Fleetwood and John McVie, it contained Danny Kirwin, Christine McVie and newcomer Bruce Welch.

Here's a tenuous link - Fleetwood Mac were the best known band on Mike Vernon's Blue Horizon label and their 'labelmates' **Jellybread** played at the Addington Hotel on 17th July, while on 15th October a 'heavy blues' group called **Piranha** played a gig at the 'Y' Club in Dingwall Road. The band proved to be so popular, as was their admission price of 30p, that they were asked to return a couple of weeks later.

New Addington brothers Ray and Keith Neale were still plugging away at the music business with their band **Orange Seaweed**. Now down to a trio, the brothers were joined by new drummer John Blunt a 23 year old from Copse View, Selsdon who was once with local band The Trees and who briefly joined the Searchers in 1968.

Vocalist Ray, who also plays lead guitar and harmonica, landed them a contract for a three month tour of Africa, playing rock'n'roll in hotels and discotheques in Kenya, Uganda and Rhodesia. Each member of the group was guaranteed £45 a week and Ray told the 'Advertiser: *"we will be the first ever rock'n'roll band to play in Uganda and I think we should go down a bomb."*

Ray and the band spent two months in Istanbul during 1970, subsequently played at Liverpool's celebrated Cavern Club, Wimbledon Stadium and numerous RAF bases up and down the country. The group released their first record 'Stay Awhile' back in 1968 and planned two further singles - 'Josie On My Mind' and a version of the old Bill Haley song 'Skinnie Minnie'.

September saw the release of the debut single from **Leonard Rusk**, a Thornton Heath based group who take their name from lead singer Leonard Rusk! The group had been playing together for seven years, but under the name **Funky Fever** - including gigs at the Orchid Ballroom in Purley and a two year residency at the Star. On returning home from a tour of Spain and Portugal they decided to change their name in an effort to break into the charts - and recorded the single 'Nobody Needs You More', written for them by Philip Goodhand-Tait and John Cokell. Goodhand-Tait, who wrote the hit 'Everlasting Love' for the Love Affair in 1968, was once a member of the local group Circus before turning to a successful solo career.

The B-side of the record was 'I've Got My Pride' written by lead guitarist John Winder of Longdale Road, Thornton Heath and the other group members were John Donaldson, organ and piano, bassist Brendan McNeelance and William Slattery on drums. During the recording of the single, Leonard's wife Anna gave birth to a son, Leon - and the couple managed to spend a little bit of time together before the band went back out on the road.

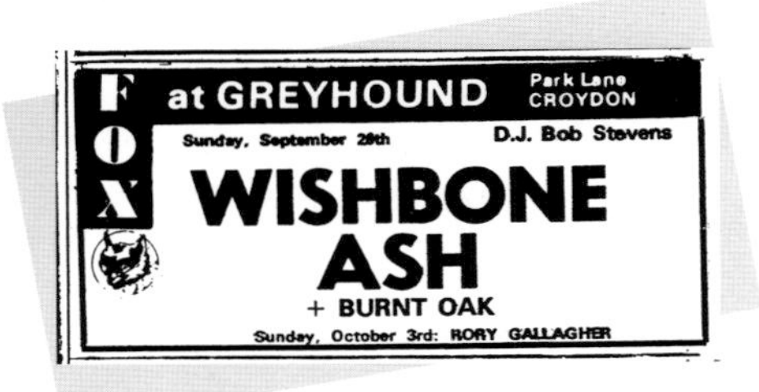

Disc & Music Echo – 13.11.71

'MATCH OF THE DAY'

*MATCH OF the Day at the Fairfield Hall on Sunday saw P.A. Gremlins lose 3 - 10 to a superb **Family** side. The hard-pressed Leicester team eventually triumphed over the dirty tactics employed by their opposition in the first half, when the Gremlins 'buzzed' Family's penalty area. Effective use by Family of their duo - Poli Palmer, who sprayed musical passes in all directions and Charlie Whitney (guitar) gained control of midfield from the kick off with "In My Own Time".*

A lesser group might have been discouraged by a series of fouls, but centre forward Roger Chapman took all they threw at him - and threw it back. This display should see them through to the finals in America next year, despite the formality of a second leg at the Rainbow on November 26th... Chapman proved to be the man of the Match, playing the entire game with a pain-killing injection of Scotch and coke.!

Martin Marriott

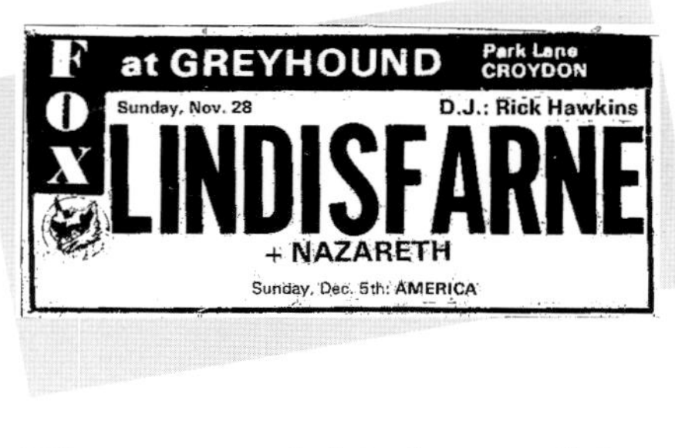

If anyone needed further proof that the music business is incestuous, then Cliff Richard's November package tour should be confirmation enough. To begin with, one of the support acts were **Marvin, Welch & Farrar**, a group comprising three ex-Shadows, Hank and Bruce from the original line-up and the recently added bass player John Farrar. Around this time, Cliff had been hosting his own TV show, on which the regular guest was the lovely **Olivia Newton-John**, and who was naturally recruited to appear on the tour. Cliff and Olivia were 'romantically linked' by the media, but in fact Livvy was seeing John Farrar, who had just finished producing her solo album, with musical assistance from... yes, Hank Marvin and Bruce Welch!

For once, music critic and unashamed Fairport fan Barry Shinfield missed one of their regular visits to the Fairfield, leaving Jane Hurst to rave about **Fairport Convention**. The November concert was notable for a near complete rendition of their latest album 'Babbacombe Lee', a concept album, if you like, about John Lee, 'the man they couldn't hang'.

Lee was sentenced to death for murder at the turn of the century and took the long walk to the gallows three times. Three times the trap door failed to open and under the law of the time, Lee walked free.

Fairport's Dave Swarbrick found a copy of Lee's autobiography in an antique shop and use it as the basis for the song cycle that makes up the Babbacombe Lee LP.

The concert closed with a rock 'n'roll medley for which the band of Pegg, Nicol, Mattacks and Swarbrick were joined onstage by former bass player and founder member Ashley Hutchings.

Shinfield did manage to review the **Amazing Blondel**, a bawdy yet innocent folk group quite unlike anyone else around at the time - 'the Monty Python of Elizabethan minstrelsy' as Barry called them. Supporting them was - *"an acutely nervous John Martyn, who sadly gave a disjointed, introverted performance. He seemed obsessed with his guitar playing to the neglect of his singing; as his voice can be uncommonly good, this seemed a waste".*

Disc & Music Echo – 11.12.71

*AFTER **ELTON JOHN**'s concert at the Fairfield Halls, Croydon last Sunday, there can be few left with the impression that Mr John's career IS over the hill. Despite the knockers, Elton proved he is still very much a number one musician. Featuring material from his new album 'Madman Across the Water', Elton whipped up the audience from the word go and kept them at fever pitch for the next two hours.*

Elton's audiences, and this one was no exception, seem unaware of the repetition of much of his material, or perhaps it's just that they don't care. Certainly he pulled out all the stops to ensure the reception he received, throwing in everything from favourites like 'Take Me to the Pilot', 'Your Song', 'All the Nasties', (a dig at the knockers), to an almost country sounding 'Honky Tonk Women'.

*But it wasn't until almost the end of the concert that Elton really raised the roof, when he was joined on stage by **Marc Bolan**. Earlier that evening Elton had promised: "We've got some surprises for you", but even the most ardent boppers in their wildest dreams wouldn't have expected to see the stage shared by both Messrs. John AND Bolan. Quite what they sang was largely unheeded by the standing audience (in fact it was a tuneless version of 'Get It On' - repeated over and over again), in favour of storming the stage.*

What Elton lacks in "idol appeal", Marc makes up for and what Marc lacks in musical ability Elton ably compensates. If those two were to team up on record...

Bill Kellow

And I wonder if Marc visited his parents while he was in the area? Local pub expert John Judd notes that Mr & Mrs Feld (Marc's mum and dad) once ran the Devonshire Arms, a popular Croydon public house which was demolished at the end of 1977 to make way for an additional wing of Mayday hospital.

On 5th December, Ian Dury's **Kilburn & the High Roads** played their debut gig at Croydon Art College and the same month were paid to put on an end of term show at Canterbury School of Art (where Ian was a teacher). At the time, their act mainly consisted of 'fifties rock'n'roll - 'Twenty Flight Rock', 'Lucille', 'I'm Walking' - and the line-up included Davey Payne on sax, the only member of the Kilburns to stay with Dury and join up with him again in the Blockheads. For a while the Kilburns were arguably the most popular band on the London pub circuit and were even given the support slot on a UK tour with the Who.

1972

JANUARY

2 KEEF HARTLEY **G** + CAROL GRIMES (50p)
9 STRAY **G** + SUTHERLAND BROTHERS (50p)
13 LOU CHRISTIE **O** (50p)
16 HEADS, HANDS & FEET **G** + MONTAGE (50p)
17 SLADE **TR** (70p)
23 BARCLAY JAMES HARVEST **G** + SKIN ALLEY (50p)
27 CURTIS MAYFIELD **TR** + CARL DOUGLAS & GONZALES (75p)
28 STEVIE WONDER **FH** (75p to £2)
30 STRAWBS **FH** (50p to 80p)
30 RORY GALLAGHER **G** + MR MOSES SCHOOLBAND (n/a)

FEBRUARY

3 EDDIE FLOYD **O** (60p)
5 PLAINSONG **CT** + CAROL GRIMES & UNCLE DOG (60p)
6 WISHBONE ASH **G** + TRAPEZE (n/a)
10 STAN KENTON **FH** (50p to £1.30)
13 MC5 **G** + BARRABAS (n/a)
20 MOTT THE HOOPLE **FH** + BRONCO (50p to 85p)
20 GENESIS **G** + BELL & ARC (n/a)
22 DEEP PURPLE **O** + BEGGAR'S DEATH (80p)
24 THE DRIFTERS **O** (n/a)
24 EDDIE FLOYD **TR** (60p)
24 DAVID BOWIE **W** (50p)
27 HAWKWIND **G** + KAHCAS JUTE (60p)

MARCH

2 BEN E. KING **O** (n/a)
2 PIONEERS **TR** (60p)
5 OSIBISA **G** + BEGGAR'S DEATH (n/a)
9 MARV JOHNSON **TR** (60p)
12 STRAY **G** + MR MOSES SCHOOLBAND (50p)
12 DEEP PURPLE **FH** (50p to £1.25)
17 JACQUES LOUISSIER **FH** (n/a)
19 HEADS, HANDS & FEET **FH** + PATTO + CLAIRE HAMMILL (40p to 75p)
19 BARCLAY JAMES HARVEST **G** + FOCUS (60p)
26 EDGAR BROUGHTON **G** + KILLING FLOOR (n/a)
26 SANDY DENNY **FH** + DAVID ELLIOTT (50p to 80p)

APRIL

2 ARGENT **G** + WICKED NUN (n/a)
4 GENTLE GIANT **G** (n/a)
6 STATUS QUO **W** (n/a)
9 STEELEYE SPAN **FH** + AMAZING BLONDEL (40p to 75p)
9 ATOMIC ROOSTER **G** + TRAPEZE (n/a)
16 THE DUBLINERS **FH** (50p to 90p)
16 ELECTRIC LIGHT ORCHESTRA **G** + ALEX HARVEY (n/a)
23 FAIRPORT CONVENTION **G** + CAPABILITY BROWN (n/a)
27 BLOODSTONE **TR** (40p)
30 STATUS QUO **G** + DRAGON MILK (n/a)

MAY

7 DR. JOHN **G** (n/a)
10 ROD McKUEN **FH** (n/a)
11 MARVIN, WELCH & FARRAR **FH** (£1.05)
14 ELECTRIC LIGHT ORCHESTRA **FH** + COLIN BLUNSTONE + F.F.& Z. (50 to 90p)
14 STRAY **G** + GRINGO (n/a)
17 MR. ACKER BILK **FH** (40p to 75p)
21 RALPH McTELL **FH** (n/a)
21 EAST OF EDEN **G** + BYSANTIUM (n/a)
25 SLADE **O** + STATUS QUO (65p)
28 URIAH HEEP **G** + MIKE MARAN (n/a)

JUNE

2 THE SPINNERS **FH** (n/a)
4 DON McLEAN **FH** + TIR NA NOG (n/a)
4 MOTT THE HOOPLE **G** + SHAMELADY (n/a)
11 ROY ORBISON **FH** + FRIDAY BROWN (50p to £1.30)
11 LINDISFARNE **G** + SPREADEAGLE (n/a)
18 RORY GALLAGHER **G** + SMITH, PERKINS & SMITH (n/a)
18 RITCHIE HAVENS **FH** + LINDA LEWIS (n/a)
25 DAVID BOWIE **G** + ROXY MUSIC (n/a)

Ian Hunter's 'Diary of a Rock and Roll Star' gives probably the best insight into the day to day workings of a rock band. Written during a tour of the States in November 1972, the Mott the Hoople lead singer lays bare the financial side of the business and strips away much of the 'glamour'. When later interviewed about the book by Michael Wale of Radio One, Hunter said - *"There are literally thousands upon thousands of groups that you think are big; groups that you think must have houses and flash cars, but who haven't, because so much money comes out of what you earn. I continually find it astonishing, what we're left with after maybe selling out a place. I mean, we've still got a piece of paper where we sold out the Fairfield Halls, Croydon and wound up owing 248 quid. We couldn't sell any more tickets, they'd all gone and we still... that was cos. we wanted the P.A. and the lights, you know, and we paid for a support group and this, that and the other. I mean, to be confronted with that the day after you've done the gig - I don't know, it's quite amazing".*

Not content with running their successful music nights at the Greyhound, Fox promotions booked **Deep Purple** into the Orchid Ballroom on February 22nd. 80 pence entrance fee (casual dress please), also gave you support group **Beggars Death**, regular Greyhound DJ Rick Hawkins and a guarantee of the gig going ahead, because as the ad. said - *generator available in case of power cut'.*

The following month, Deep Purple were back at the Fairfield, where their concert was reportedly filmed for use in a 15-second Thames TV commercial to promote their new album 'Machine Head', released later that month (March 30th).

FH - Fairfield Hall • G - Greyhound • S - Star Hotel • TR - Top Rank • O - Orchid Ballroom • W - Wallington Public Hall

Mott-mania was the description of Croydon's reaction to the latest visit of **Mott the Hoople**, when they pulled in an 1,800 strong crowd to the Fairfield Halls in February. Described as the most successful live group in the country at that time, in terms of getting the whole audience on their feet and rocking, the Fairfield was turned into a football terrace as they smiled, sang, danced and threw paper aeroplanes and toilet rolls across the auditorium.

Ian Hunter led the way, dressed all in black, a cape around his shoulders and wearing his trademark dark 'shades'. Playing a custom-built guitar with it's body in the shape of a Maltese Cross, Hunter growled his way through 'Walking With A Mountain' and 'Rock & Roll Queen' into which were woven snatches of the Stones' 'Jumpin' Jack Flash' and 'Satisfaction'. The finale was a brilliant pastiche of original rock'n' roll, with versions of 'High School Confidential' and 'Whole Lotta Shakin' Going On'.

Bronco were the support band, but as the Advertiser put it: *"The effect they spent an hour striving for was achieved by Mott in just three chords".*

One of the many bands who made their debut in Croydon were the **Electric Light Orchestra**, but their appearance turned out to be somewhat less than inspiring. In his book, *The ELO Story*, drummer Bev Bevan describes the occasion first hand: *"We were finally forced into making a live appearance at the Fox & Greyhound (sic) in Park Lane, Croydon on Sunday April 16th 1972. It was just a big pub where they played progressive music each week. I don't think the audience could believe it's ears. No-one could hear the cellos or violin, just the thumping beat of the drums and guitars. Then the French Horn would suddenly start and drown everything else with it's shrillness.*

Roy (Wood) insisted on playing cello, oboe, guitar and bassoon, and on each song there was a delay as he switched to a different instrument. The delays between the songs were longer than the songs themselves. And as he was wearing his long white wig and glasses, he could hardly see a thing. Roy was stumbling from one instrument to another with the audience of about 400 watching in total silence, their mouths open in amazement. David (son of manager Don Arden) was in the audience and spent most of the time hiding his face, hoping that no-one would recognise him or link him to what was going on. Afterwards he came backstage wearing a sickly smile and kept nodding his head, "Nice, fellas," he kept repeating, "Nice".

I felt shattered. It was worse than even I anticipated... like all disasters you always think it can only get better. Not necessarily with ELO; and word travelled fast!"

The Greyhound added a Tuesday night to their schedule on April 4th, in order to screen the feature film of the Jimi Hendrix Berkeley Concert, which had just gone on general release, and supported it with live music from **Gentle Giant.**

The house was surprisingly only half-full at the Fairfield Halls on 26th March, to see ex-Fairport vocalist **Sandy Denny**. Backed by Richard Thompson on guitar, Timmy Donald on drums and bassist Pat Donaldson from Sandy's short lived group Fotheringay, she veered from her own songs - 'Who Knows Where The Time Goes', to the traditional 'Lowlands of Holland' which she performed unaccompanied. Bert Jansch's 'Go Your Way, My Love' and the Everly Brothers 'Love Made A Fool Of You' were included, plus the direct Fairport link to 'Matty Groves'.

In May the Croydon Advertiser announced that: *The **Rolling Stones** are likely to be appearing in the Croydon area later this summer. Negotiations are now in progress to book them at a local venue, but the deal has not yet been finalised. The Stones are said to be 'very interested' in the engagement, which would draw fans from all over London and the South."* Tumbling Dice was high in the single charts and their LP 'Exile On Main Street' was due for release on 26th May. The gig never materialised, but it is interesting to speculate at where it was to have been held. The Fairfield is the obvious choice, but were they also thinking about playing the Crystal Palace Garden Party?

Supporting Don McLean on June 4th were folk duo **Tir Na Nog**, last minute replacements for a relatively unknown American singer-songwriter called **Billy Joel**. I wonder what ever became of him!

As this Melody Maker advertisement shows, **Roxy Music** made their first appearance in Croydon as support to David Bowie; in the same month that their debut album 'Roxy Music' was released and only a few weeks after the bands first official live performance - bottom of the bill at the Lincoln Festival. The bands prospects started to improve after the show at the Croydon Greyhound however, as Roxy were invited to support Bowie at Londons Rainbow Theatre and to open the show for Alice Cooper at the Empire Pool, Wembley, both in July.

Croydon Advertiser – 30.6.72

'The Fall & Rise of David Bowie'

THREE YEARS ago I interviewed David Bowie at the time of his hit record 'Space Oddity'. He had already been industriously working in the pop world for some years then (six, to be precise). So it was small wonder that he was not over excited about having a hit.

He took it all very calmly, "I can take it all in my stride - I'm not a particularly excitable person" I can remember him telling me. He also said "The money I'm making now will make a nice nest egg and, if the bubble bursts, I'll be able to live quite comfortably for a couple of years on the proceeds".

The bubble did burst - David Bowie died the death and left the proverbial limelight. True, there were odd bits of publicity, like him being photographed wearing a dress and pushing a pram with his son Zowie inside it.

But now Bowie has re-emerged with a clap of thunder. No publicity is bad publicity and the music press has leapt with glee at his ambivalent sexual stage image. He is camper than Marc Bolan. His stage act is new and exciting. And he believes in himself, firmly, rationally and objectively predicting that this year will make him a superstar (as they're called these days). His music supports this theory; I have seen him twice recently, the most recent being at the Greyhound, Croydon on Sunday. And Bowie - his stage persona and his music - and his band are so good, that I go along with his prediction.

He is dominant and magnetic from the first chord, most of the material is from 'Hunky Dory' and 'The Rise & Fall of Ziggy Stardust and the Spiders from Mars', his two current LP's. The best are 'Changes' (which was released as a single, but somehow did not catch on), 'Five Years' - the alarming prophesy of the 'end-of-the-world-is-nigh' ilk and 'Starman', his current single. Unaccompanied, except for his own guitar, he does Jacques Brel's 'Port of Amsterdam' and he also does a couple of Lou Reed numbers, encoring with a momentous version of 'Waiting For My Man'.

His band The Spiders from Mars, fronted by their excellent lead guitarist Mick Ronson, tore into 'I Feel Free' while Bowie slipped off to change into a sumptuous silver ensemble. When he was back, it was fun to him and the others have a go at the Who's 'Can't Explain'. As the act neared the end, posters dropped in their hundreds from the ceiling - all part of the ultra-commercialised David Bowie.

P.S. - I'm told that while 600 fans were inside the Greyhound, another 600 had to be turned away. The Bowie bug is biting.

Barry Shinfield

JULY

- 2 GENESIS **G** + SNAKE EYE (n/a)
- 9 AL STEWART **G** + TRAPEZE (n/a)
- 16 SOFT MACHINE **G** + SUNRISE (n/a)
- 22 JULIE FELIX **FH** + CURTISS MULDOON (45p to 90p)
- 30 LOU REED **G** + SUNRISE (n/a)

AUGUST

- 6 STATUS QUO **G** + J.S.D. BAND (n/a)
- 12 WILD ANGELS **CPH** (60p)
- 13 BARCLAY JAMES HARVEST **FH** (n/a)
- 13 EDGAR BROUGHTON **G** + SHAMELADY (n/a)
- 20 CAPABILITY BROWN **G** + JOHN PEEL (n/a)
- 27 TERRY DACTYL & THE DINOSAURS **G** + DAVE BUNDY (n/a)

SEPTEMBER

- 3 ELTON JOHN **FH** + LINDA LEWIS (n/a)
- 3 HAWKWIND **G** (n/a)
- 10 FREE **FH** (n/a)
- 10 VINEGAR JOE **G** (n/a)
- 15 JO-ANN KELLY's SPARE RIB **S** (n/a)
- 17 GENESIS **G** + TOM YATES (n/a)
- 22 DORIS HENDERSON's ECLECTION **S** (n/a)
- 24 PINK FAIRIES **G** + SNAKE EYE (n/a)
- 25 EVERLY BROTHERS **FH** + DAVE LOGGINS (70p - £1.50)
- 29 STEVE TILSTON **S** (n/a)

OCTOBER

- 1 CURVED AIR **FH** + NICK PICKETT (55p - £1)
- 1 CARAVAN **G** + MIKE MARAN (n/a)
- 6 MIKE MARAN **S** (n/a)
- 8 FANNY **G** (n/a)
- 12 TOM PAXTON **FH** (n/a)
- 13 JACQUES LOUISSIER **FH** (n/a)
- 15 DICK HECKSTALL-SMITH BAND **G** (n/a)
- 17 BLUE **RD** (n/a)
- 19 STEELEYE SPAN **FH** + AMAZING BLONDEL (n/a)
- 22 FOUR TOPS **FH** + THELMA HOUSTON (n/a)
- 22 ARGENT **G** + SENSATIONAL ALEX HARVEY BAND (n/a)
- 29 STRAY **G** + COTTONWOOD (n/a)

NOVEMBER

- 1 BUDDY RICH **FH** (n/a)
- 4 PATTO **G** + UFO (n/a)
- 5 PENTANGLE **FH** + WIZZ JONES + CLIVE PALMER'S C.O.B. (50p to £1)
- 5 STRAY **G** + UFO (n/a)
- 12 GENESIS **FH** + CAPABILITY BROWN (60p to £1)
- 12 FOCUS **G** (n/a)
- 17 CLIFF RICHARD **FH** + OLIVIA NEWTON JOHN + THE GREATER UNION (00p)
- 19 ROXY MUSIC **G** + KEITH CHRISTMAS (n/a)
- 24 RALPH McTELL **FH** + NATURAL ACOUSTIC BAND (n/a)
- 26 INCREDIBLE STRING BAND **FH** (n/a)
- 26 VINEGAR JOE **G** + RISING SUN (n/a)

DECEMBER

- 1 THE SPINNERS **FH** (n/a)
- 3 SOFT MACHINE **FH** (50p to £1)
- 3 PINK FAIRIES **G** + CONSORTIUM (n/a)
- 7 JSD BAND **FH** + JOAN ARMATRADING + HARVEY ANDREWS (n/a)
- 16 AMON DUUL II **G** + SNAKE EYE (£1)
- 17 RORY GALLAGHER **G** + JADE WARRIOR (n/a)
- 17 WISHBONE ASH **FH** + AVERAGE WHITE BAND (n/a)
- 24 CAPABILITY BROWN **G** + BUDGIE (n/a)
- 26 STRAY **G** (n/a)
- 31 STATUS QUO **G** + BYZANTIUM (n/a)

(n/a) = ticket price not available.

1972

Not renowned for it's rock gigs, the Surrey suburb of Coulsdon hosted a Charity walk for Bangla Desh on 23rd July. Intent on doing their bit for George Harrison's favourite cause, the artists appearing included Principle Edwards Magic Theatre, Colin Scott, Magic Carpet, Al Matthews and a band called Flight which featured Jack Lancaster from Blodwyn Pig.

For the Fairfield concert by **Free** on September 10th, the support band was supposed to be Smith, Perkins & Smith. Punter Ian Stuart recalls; *'Due to an accident, the support didn't turn up, so Free played an extended set, only stopping when they were forced to admit that they didn't know any more songs. A wonderful concert!'*

On Friday 15th September, a new folk club opened at the Star Hotel, London Road to an audience of about 100. The resident singer was Tom Yates and the first guests to perform at the 'Yellow Bird Club' were **Jo-Ann Kelly's Spare Rib**, primarily a blues band. After only two other folk nights, Doris Henderson's Eclection and Steve Tilston, the club folded due to 'falling attendances', before Mike Maran could appear on the 6th of October. However, as one club closes another one opens, and the first of four experimental folk evenings began on Tuesday 6th November at Scarletts discotheque in the Royal Oak Centre, South Croydon! Folk/rock band Tamarisk were the resident artists and the first guests were Dave & Toni Arthur.

The vastly underrated **Patto** played at the Greyhound on Sunday 4th November. This versatile four piece were described as *"clean textured, slightly jazz-influenced in their use of syncopated rhythms, with the various tones of saxophone, oboe, flute and organ each dominating the melody line in turn"*. The group played straight rock and roll with equal style and their vocals were clear and tight on versions of 'Baby, I Don't Care' and 'Stairway Of Love'. Dylan's 'Dear Landlord' and Randy Newman's 'The Dream I Had Last Night' would seem to be odd choices, but the closing number of 'Shakin' All Over' was a masterpiece of tongue in cheek humour and virtuoso playing.

Supporting Patto were **UFO**, who suffered the usual problems of badly mixed P.A. that it seems every support group is forced to contend with.

Croydon Advertiser – 6.10.72

'Cautious Caravan'

CARAVAN are a band whose talent as musicians and whose blues-jazz style I much admire and yet, somehow their performance at the Croydon Greyhound on Sunday was incomplete.

While their playing was attractive, they seemed to be holding themselves back from fully exploring their own potential. Replacing the advertised group Jo Jo Gunne, they were at their most effective in the numbers that possessed almost symphonic quality; the different movements combining to produce full and interesting compositions.

The first number began in cool, jazzy mood, then built up, increasing in pitch and tempo until it became almost frantic, before the whole thing suddenly dropped and became cool and gentle again. So it continued on a constantly changing journey. Their second number 'Waterloo Lily' composed by organist Derek Austin, had something of this quality, although heavier and more emphatic. This started much 'hotter' in feeling before switching to feature Geoff Richardson in a viola solo which, as the song suggests, evoked the sensuous, coolly seductive stroll of the tarty lady of the title.

Caravan's music appeals to the mind - sometimes it floats out of the top of the head; while at other times the more striking, discordant passages pierce the brain.

Sandy Harrod

What should have been a strong folk bill at the Fairfield on 5th November was turned on it's head by local man **Wizz Jones**, according to the Croydon Advertiser review. The headline act, **Pentangle** were *"a major disappointment... the most dissatisfying aspect was Jacqui McShee, whose vocals, although perfectly in tune, had little force and were hard to follow"*.

Wizz, on the other hand, engaged the audience with personality and 'direction', a quality apparently lacking from both Pentangle and the second act on the bill, ex-Incredible String Band member **Clive Palmer's C.O.B.** The one-time resident performer at Croydon's Olive Tree club, Wizz sang 'National Seven', 'Can't Keep From Crying Sometimes' and 'Touch Has A Memory' co-written by Pete Atkin and Australian presenter Clive James.

Croydon Advertiser – 1.12.72

'Gritty Rock Band'

VINEGAR JOE *are a gritty young rock 'n' roll band whose full potential has probably yet to be realised.*

The first time I saw them, several months ago, was in an almost deserted hall at Epsom, where they played their hearts out to a handful of locals. They are better known now and 300 or so received them well at the Croydon Greyhound on Sunday.

They are keen, almost desperate for audience participation and their girl singer, Elkie Brooks repeatedly exhorts the audience to dance. She's an extrovert in the Maggie Bell mould; her persona is blowsy, sexual, her slit satin skirt reveals a garter clinging to her thigh. She high kicks her slender legs. Her midriff is bare and pulsates to the music. You could imagine her tempting rough bristly cowboys in a Western saloon. Her long, raven hair seems to sway her from side to side.

Vinegar Joe also have another singer with a fine voice, Robert Palmer, three guitarists, an organist and drummer. They are at their best with fast rock 'n' roll numbers, which came more to the fore towards the end of their act. What went before was often undistinguished and the band were wasting their time by tearing into material that was basically unsuited to their penchant for rock'n'roll.

An example is their latest single 'Rock & Roll Gypsies', which is slow, unexciting and not rock 'n' roll at all. Vinegar Joe have tremendous energy, but they need the right outlet for it.

Barry Shinfield

Ian Stuart was back at the Fairfield Halls on December 3rd: *'This was a Charity Show in support of the Spastics Society; the full line-up was Soft Machine, Medicine Head, Ron Geesin, Ivor Cutler and DJ John Peel - I was selling programmes and got to meet Peel, a very pleasant evening'.*

While Barry Shinfield was getting all hot and bothered by Vinegar Joe at the Greyhound, the latest line-up of the **Incredible String Band** were over the road at the Fairfield Halls. Robin Williamson was still at the helm, with Malcolm Le Maistre alongside; the lovely Liquorice had departed, but an ex-jazz musician Gerry Dott had joined to widen the groups instrumental base. 'The Circle Is Unbroken', 'The Old Buccaneer' 'Wild Cat Blues' (Dott's influence) and Le Maistre's 'My Father Is A Lighthouse Keeper' were all typically well received by a packed house. The Advertiser was impressed - *'...the band have certainly travelled forward, and if their instrumental talents now seem more impressive than their ability in the field of songwriting, both their material and presentation are still those of creative innovators, rather than mere followers of convention'.*

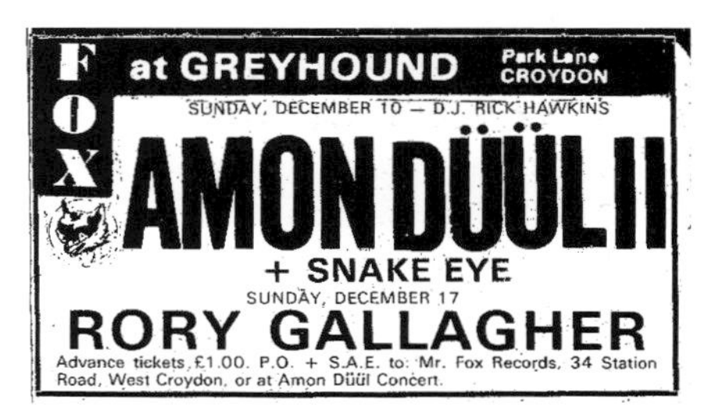

Despite the date on this ad., the Amon Düül II gig was recorded on 16th December using the Pye Mobile studio, engineered by Vic Maile and released as the album 'Live in London' UNITED ARTISTS USP102.

Frazer Ashford

The Incredible String Band caught in full flight, Fairfield Halls, 26th November 1972.

"...a mixture of camp 'fifties clothes and flashy Kensington Market stuff..."

Frazer Ashford

A rare view of the original Roxy Music line-up, onstage at the Croydon Greyhound 19th November 1972. Left to right: Brian Eno, Phil Manzanera, Andy MacKay, bassist Graham Simpson and Bryan Ferry. The hidden drummer is Paul Thompson.

Below: A mixture of nerves and concentrated effort, Bryan Ferry works up a sweat for the Croydon faithful.

Frazer Ashford

Croydon Advertiser – 24.11.72

'ROCKSY MUSAK'

AN UNFORTUNATE effect of the current popularity of 'visual' pop performers like Slade and Alice Cooper is that the music itself can get neglected while the main concentration is on looking good.

Not since the black rock'n'rollers of the mid-fifties, brought back by Sha Na Na has there been such visual excitement, such emphasis on putting on a show. And ***Roxy Music*** *at the Greyhound, Croydon on Sunday were very exciting to look at in their heavy make-up and stage movements.*

Dressed in a mixture of camp 'fifties clothes and flashy Kensington market stuff, they posed around the stage in an interesting and amusing way. Slight, blond Eno was wearing a shaggy silver tinsel jacket, voluminous embroidered trousers and blue eye shadow, as he elegantly flicked the switches of the electronic synthesiser.

Andy MacKay shook his bleached blond quiff, pursed his lips round a saxophone and pranced back and forth in short, tight yellow plastic trousers. Bryan Ferry stood at his organ keyboard like a cross between Gene Vincent and Richard III - wearing black eye make-up, black shiny trousers and a sparkly black jacket with padded shoulders.

But however thrilling they looked, their distinctive music began to pall for me after the first few numbers - it all sounded so alike. The rocking bit, with Ferry's tough singing, Mackay's blaring sax and Phil Manzanera's solid guitar work, followed by the space music bit of Eno's screeching, whining electronics.

I thought it was slightly self-indulgent and towards the end I had simply stopped listening. It just went on like 'musak' while I stood and watched them. But judging from the reception they got, I was the only person there who did not really like the music. For a band whose first performance was only six months ago, they were rewarded with a surprising amount of warmth.

M.C.

Frazer Ashford

The New Seekers look out over a sea of admiring Croydon fans - Fairfield Hall, 6th May 1973. Left to right: Paul Layton, Marty Kristian, Eve Graham, Lynn Paul and Sanderstead's Peter Oliver.

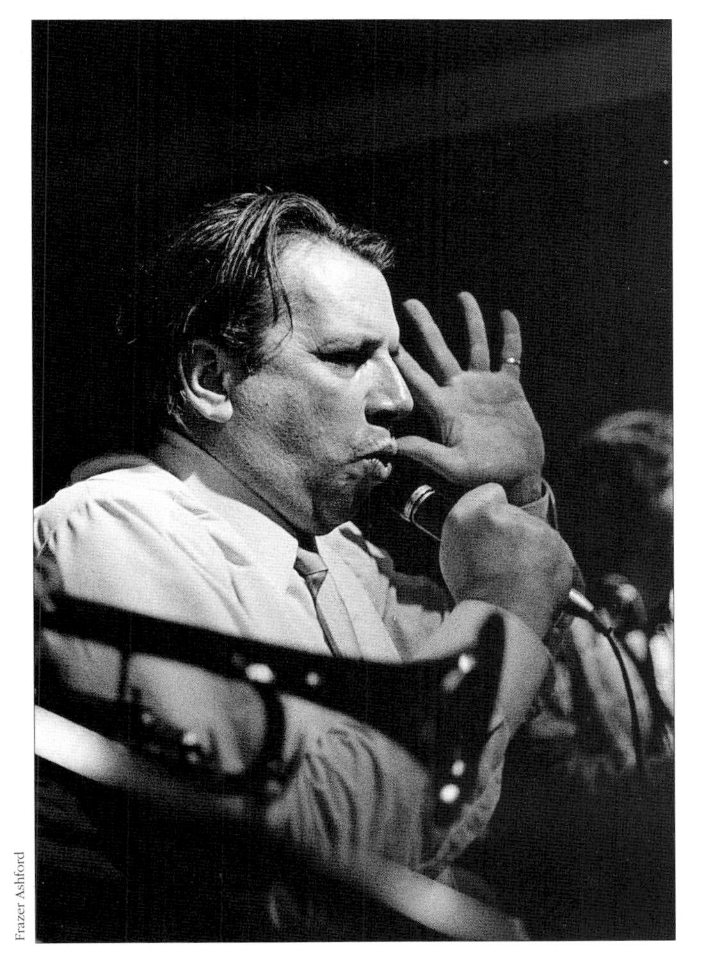

Frazer Ashford

George Melly – no doubt wishing he could 'shimmy like his sister Kate' – crammed onto the stage at renowned jazz pub and Youngs hostelry, the Lord Napier, Thornton Heath - 27th February 1973.

Frazer Ashford

The late Rory Gallagher with trademark battered Fender Stratocaster - Fairfield Hall, 11th December 1973.

JANUARY

- 7 GENESIS **G** (n/a)
- 21 FOCUS **G** (n/a)
- 28 DARRYL WAY'S WOLF **G** (n/a)
- 28 URIAH HEEP **FH** + SILVERHEAD (50p to £1.25)

FEBRUARY

- 4 WIZZARD **G** (n/a)
- 4 FAMILY **FH** + LINDA LEWIS (65p to £1.10)
- 11 GROUNDHOGS **G** + ANGEL (n/a)
- 16 SLIM WHITMAN **FH** + JAMEY RYAN (75p to £1.75)
- 18 STACKRIDGE **G** (80p)
- 22 AL STEWART **FH** (60p)
- 23 STAN KENTON **FH** (50p to £1.30)
- 25 STEALERS WHEEL **G** + MIKE ABSALOM (80p)
- 26 LABI SIFFRE **FH** + MAGNA CARTA (50p to £1)
- 27 GEORGE MELLY **LN** (n/a)

MARCH

- 4 BARCLAY JAMES HARVEST **G** + CAMEL (80p)
- 8 NEW WORLD **FH** (50p to £1)
- 11 THE SUPREMES **FH** + ARTHUR CONLEY (65p to £1.50)
- 11 KINGDOM COME with ARTHUR BROWN **G** (n/a)
- 18 STRAY **G** + CAT IRON (n/a)
- 22 JAKE THAKERAY **FH** (60p)
- 25 THE DUBLINERS **FH** (50p to £1)
- 30 JACQUES LOUISSIER TRIO **FH** (75p to £1.75)

APRIL

- 8 TEN YEARS AFTER **FH** + BECKETT (50p to £1.25)
- 8 THIN LIZZY **G** (n/a)
- 12 JULIAN BREAM & JOHN WILLIAMS **FH** (50p to £1.50)
- 15 SPIRIT **G** (n/a)
- 22 BIRTHA **G** + HEAVY HEART (n/a)
- 29 SPENCER DAVIS **G** (n/a)

MAY

- 6 THE NEW SEEKERS **FH** + OFARIM & WINTER (55p to £1.60)
- 6 LOUDON WAINWRIGHT III **G** (n/a)
- 17 FOCUS **FH** + HARVEY ANDREWS & GRAHAM COOPER (55p to £1.60)
- 20 CILLA BLACK **FH** (75p to £2.20)
- 20 AMON DÜÜL II **G** + FANG (90p)
- 27 FLEETWOOD MAC **FH** + NICK PICKETT (50p to £1)
- 27 FANNY **G** + MOONDOG (90p)
- 31 GROUNDHOGS **FH** + GENTLE GIANT + STRAY + MISTER CRISP (n/a)

JUNE

- 3 BARCLAY JAMES HARVEST **FH** + TERRY REID & BRIDGET ST.JOHN (65p to £1.50)
- 3 NAZARETH **G** (n/a)
- 8 RALPH McTELL **FH** + HUNTER MUSKETT (50p to £1.50)
- 12 STUKA **GN** (20p)
- 14 GILBERT O'SULLIVAN **FH** + MUD + TONY ADAMS (75p to £2.50)
- 17 WISHBONE ASH **FH** + CLIMAX CHICAGO (n/a)
- 17 STACKRIDGE **G** + SHAMELADY (n/a)
- 20 THE BEE GEES **FH** (n/a)
- 20 THE SARSTEDT BROTHERS **FH** (60p)
- 24 DAVID BOWIE **FH** (n/a)
- 24 JSD BAND **G** + BUDLIPPSPRINGER (n/a)

(n/a) = ticket price not available.

JANUARY - Britain enters the EEC; February sees a strike by the Gas workers and the first ever strike by Civil servants; in April, Chancellor Barber will introduce VAT; in October the Israelis will invade Arab territory, forcing the Arabs to cut their oil output by 25%, reduce export to Britain by 50% and withdraw oil export to the US completely. The miners and electricity workers ban overtime in support of a wage claim - by December there will be petrol queues, coal shortages and panic buying, the Government will declare a State of Emergency – but meanwhile, back in Croydon...

Croydon Advertiser – 12.1.73

'Yes, it's GENESIS back yet again'

STORMING BACK to Croydon for the third time since September, Genesis played a typically professional set at the Greyhound on Sunday, to the delight of the sardine-packed audience. Dwarfed by great banks of speakers and lights, Genesis took the stage and received a tumultuous welcome - the audience were won over before a single note was played.

What was played was extremely good, the arrangements although sometimes contrived were carefully worked out. Peter Gabriel, looking trendily camp, managed to alternate his vocals between the soft timbre of Jon Anderson (Yes) to the raspy attack of Roger Chapman (Family). The only unfortunate aspect of his performance was his battle to sing louder than the instruments - a common problem with most bands now.

What is most striking about Genesis is that they are concerned with what and how they play, their music has a point to it and is not just a sound. The arrangements are very forceful, favouring the use of mellotron while the guitar and drumming complement each other to set up a thumping , rippling beat. My only criticism is their similarity to Yes and, at times, to King Crimson. Their material sometimes possesses an incredible likeness to songs off the 'Yes Album' and Yes's 'Fragile'. Nevertheless, numbers like 'Return of the Giant Hogweed', 'Music Box' and 'Supper's Ready', continue to excite audiences and, as one of the numbered "sardines" was heard to say, "I must buy their LP". Genesis will not be poor.

Nick Beacroft

Croydon Advertiser – 9.2.73

'Deafening Rock'

IT JUST defies human comprehension. How can young people possibly ENJOY an unnecessarily loud rock concert like that at the Greyhound on Sunday? It seems the the greatest excitement to be had these days is the excitement of going deaf before your time.

Even when there was no-one actually performing, all efforts at conversation were blasted out of existence by records that were at such volume, half of Croydon must have been able to hear them.

The star turn were Roy Wood's ***Wizzard*** *and they maintained the assault on our eardrums. They were loud, very loud and repetitive to the point of tedium. Whatever subtlety their music may have contained, it was lost in the quest for volume. I caught just one song title ('Buffalo Station', I think), and noted that the piano player Bill Hunt, seemed to be obsessed with leaping about like Batman, banging two tambourines together.*

All that can be said in Wizzard's favour is that they have made a stab at originality, by including in their eight man line-up saxes and an electric cello. The mindlessness of the music was reflected in the audience,who seemed obsessed with,in the terms of popular idiom, "out-grooving" each other.

Possibly I and a friend were in a minority of two, judging by the general reaction. Perhaps at twenty two I have grown too old and cynical to appreciate the modern rock generation.

K. McD.

....a 'classic review' in my opinion and well worth repeating here in full! The reviewer appears to hold absolutely no interest in the artist, or in the 'rock idiom', for that matter. And as for that last line... or perhaps at 40, I have grown a little too sarcastic?

On the same day that Wizzard were deafening the Advertiser's latest reviewer, the lucky Nick Beacroft was over the road at the Fairfield to see **Family**. Emphasising the staying power of this ever popular band - *"at the forefront of the British music scene since 1966"* - the line-up had changed considerably since their early days, this gig featuring two new members: Jim Cregan on guitar, who joined them from the group Stud in 1972 and Tony Ashton from Ashton, Gardner & Dyke replacing Poli Palmer on keyboards.

The support was provided by **Linda Lewis** (Mrs Jim Cregan), an impish figure on stacked heel shoes, promoting material from her new album 'Lark'.

Frazer Ashford

Jim Patterson, lead singer with Budlippspringer caught in rehearsal at the Dog & Bull, Croydon.

Probably the only Croydon band ever to take their name from a town in Germany were **Budlippspringer**, a gritty, rock/blues band who played most Thursday nights in the back room of the Dog & Bull pub in Surrey Street.

A likable bunch of semi-pro musicians, they began playing at the pub in March '73, where they were spotted by the management of the Greyhound and booked to support the JSD Band in June.

Lead guitarist Bernie Brooks and drummer Alan Steltnor first played in a rock'n'roll band at Wimbledon Palais in the mid-sixties, called The Maniacs. Budlipp are named after Bernie's birthplace. A Scot, Jim Patterson was their lead vocalist and the bass player was Vic Young, who had only recently moved to the area from Australia.

DUE TO THE SELL OUT

BARCLAY JAMES HARVEST

concert at the Royal Festival Hall on Friday May 18th, an additional date featuring the orchestra will take place at the

FAIRFIELD HALL, CROYDON

SUN JUNE 3rd at 7·45pm

and special guest artiste Terry Reid for his 1st solo performance.

Barclay James Harvest information service. Tel 01-629 4448

A thirty five piece orchestra did indeed accompany the four man **Barclay James Harvest** in concert on Sunday 3rd June, but as the Advertiser's Nick Beacroft explained *"failed to mix the orchestra with electronic music effectively"*. He compared their efforts with similar experiments by Emerson, Lake & Palmer, Deep Purple and particularly The Nice, whose concert with the London Symphonia at the Fairfield Hall yielded the successful 'Five Bridges' album for Charisma Records.

Croydon Advertiser – 1.6.73

'SHADOW OF THE ORIGINAL MAC'

AT ONE TIME, ***Fleetwood Mac*** *were a highly respected band endowed with great resources of musical talent mainly emanating from guitarists Peter Green and Jeremy Spencer.*

They made a number of hit singles and their albums also entered the charts. But, as so often happens, differences emerged and Fleetwood Mac split, leaving only a skeleton of the original group. The name was retained, but those musicians now performing under the title Fleetwood Mac are poor substitutes for the original members.

In their concert at Fairfield on Sunday, there was none of the original guitar work that was so delicate as well as forceful. They began with the old hits, including the splendid 'Oh Well', and at that point the concert sounded hopeful. But then they turned to new numbers that had no relation to Fleetwood Mac as we knew them. They played long guitar solos that became a sort of self adulation and completely lost the audiences attention.

Christine Perfect of Chicken Shack fame was entirely wasted; you could not hear her playing the organ and her singing was equally inaudible - an astonishing waste of talent. Only one song had any impact and that was an oldie, 'Same Old Blues'.

Nick Beacroft

Pioneers of the 'twin lead guitar' sound, **Wishbone Ash** turned up at the Fairfield in June, with a mobile recording studio in tow to cut a live album. This led to an hours' delay while the engineers set up the sound equipment and also accounted for the non-appearance of the support act - *and* the resulting double-album 'Live Dates' only featured two tracks from the Croydon gig, 'The King Will Come' and 'Phoenix'.

Advertiser journalist Barry Shinfield explained the story behind their twin-lead style - when bassist Martin Turner and drummer Steve Upton advertised for a lead guitarist, they couldn't decide between Andy Powell or Ted Turner - so they forgot about getting in a rhythm player and asked them both to join!

The celebrated Ziggy Stardust tour that pushed David Bowie into the 'superstar' bracket hit Croydon on 24th June. The two shows sold out weeks beforehand almost on the same day that tickets went on sale. Several of my classmates took the day off school to queue for their £1.50 worth of 'gold dust'. In all, 4,000 fans crammed into the Fairfield to see the two magical shows, with another 1,000 distraught kids left outside on the pavement.

JULY

1 MAN **G** + BEGGARS OPERA (n/a)
8 ARTHUR BROWN'S KINGDOM COME **G** (n/a)
15 LINDISFARNE **G** (n/a)
15 PROCOL HARUM **FH** + ROD CRISP (50p to £1.25)

AUGUST

12 ELVIS PRESLEY CONVENTION **G** (£1)
28 ACKER BILK & HIS PARAMOUNT JAZZ BAND **FH** (50p to £1.50)

SEPTEMBER

2 HAWKWIND **FH** (n/a)
9 FAMILY **FH** + PHILIP GOODHAND-TAIT (75p to £1.25)
13 WIZZARD **T** + RAYMOND FROGGAT (£1)
16 ARGENT **FH** + GLENCOE (50p to £1.25)
16 STRAY **G** + CHARLIE (n/a)
18 RAMSEY LEWIS TRIO **FH** (75p to £1.50)
20 MAGNA CARTA **FH** + PETE ATKIN (60p)
23 JACK THE LAD **G** (n/a)
30 STATUS QUO **FH** (n/a)
30 TEMPEST **G** (n/a)

OCTOBER

7 THE KINKS **FH** + BLOODSTONE (75p to £1.50)
12 DON MCLEAN **FH** (75p to £1.50)
14 JSD BAND **G** (n/a)
16 LABI SIFFRE **FH** (50p to £1.25)
22 INCREDIBLE STRING BAND **FH** (60p to £1.10)
00 GEORGIE FAME & THE HARRY SOUTH BIG BAND **FH** (75p to £1.50)
28 MAN **G** + DEKE LEONARD'S ICEBERG (£1)
30 TOM PAXTON **FH** (50p to £1.75)

NOVEMBER

2 FOUR TOPS **FH** + DETROIT SPINNERS (£1 to £2.50)
4 AMON DÜÜL II **G** (£1)
9 STEELEYE SPAN **FH** (75p to £1.50)
13 BLACKFOOT SUE **T** (50p)
18 STACKRIDGE **G** + FILMS (£1)
22 CLIFF RICHARD **FH** 2 shows (75p to £2)
27 AL STEWART **FH** + CANTON TRIG (n/a)
30 RITCHIE HAVENS **FH** (75p to £1.75)

DECEMBER

2 MANFRED MANN'S EARTHBAND **FH** + BACK DOOR (75p to £1.25)
2 ALEX HARVEY **G** + BECKETT (n/a)
5 GEORDIE **T** (50p)
6 O'JAYS **FH** + BILLY PAUL + THE INTRUDERS (n/a)
7 DONOVAN **FH** + JAKI WHITREN (75p to £1.75)
9 John Hiseman's TEMPEST **G** (n/a)
11 RORY GALLAGHER **FH** + STRIDER (75p to £1.50)
16 FAIRPORT CONVENTION **FH** + AMAZING BLONDEL (50p to £1.25)
23 MAN **G** + MASON (£1.10)
30 STRAY **G** (n/a)

(n/a) = ticket price not available.

The Mael Brothers, Ron and Russell of the American band **Sparks** decided to set up a base in England in 1973 and brought a house in Southend Lane, Beckenham. The groups most successful single, 'This Town 'Aint Big Enough For Both Of Us' hit number two in the charts in May 1974 - I know Beckenham's not that big, guys but even so ...!

Space-rock group **Hawkwind** lit up the Fairfield Hall on Sunday 2nd September with a superb light show by 'Liquid Len', using his £2,000 worth of lighting equipment and backscreen projections to illuminate the hall. The five-piece band, including guitarist Dave Brock and Nik Turner on sax featured their recently finished work 'Space Ritual' and delighted their legions of fans with its' performance, punctuated by the poetry readings of Bob Calvert and the 'astral dancing' of the near-naked Stacia, who was almost pulled into the front row during the encore of 'Silver Machine'.

The Croydon Advertiser announced that the ever popular **Family** were splitting up and would play the Fairfield on 9th September as part of their farewell tour; while ex-Colosseum drummer Jon Hiseman would bring his new group **Tempest** to the Greyhound on 30th September, featuring guitarist Ollie Halsall (ex-Patto) and Mick Clarke.

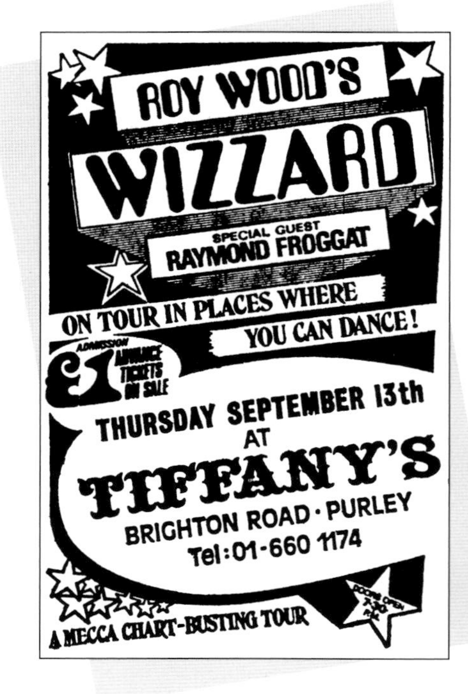

The **Lindisfarne** line-up for the Greyhound gig on the 15th July was the new Mark II version, containing original members Alan Hull and Ray Jackson, plus Kenny Craddock (keyboards), Tommy Duffy (bass) and Paul Nichols (drums). Hot on their heels on 23rd September, the other three original members - Simon Cowe, Ray Laidlaw and Rod Clements - turned up in their offshoot band **Jack the Lad**, augmented by vocalist Billy Mitchell and reviewed here by Nick Beacroft:

Croydon Advertiser – 28.9.73

'Too subtle for the rowdies?'

AMID CRUDE cries for 'rock'n'roll' and a shambling line of sweaty youths dancing the conga, a new band Jack the Lad, who had more subtle musical intentions, played an outstanding set at the Greyhound on Sunday.

The foursome includes former members of Lindisfarne; Rod Clements who plays bass and violin, Ray Laidlaw on drums, Si Cowe on lead guitar, mandolin and vocals and Billy Mitchell who plays guitar and mandolin.

Very sadly, their performance was almost spoilt by heckling and a general disinterest. But musically their songs were varied and never tedious, consisting of lyrics on almost every aspect of everyday living, from driving down a motorway to imaginary emigration to Utopia.

The Lindisfarne influence is certainly there, although they have avoided the Newcastle slant synonymous with the original band. Si Cowe and Billy Mitchell played mandolins at amazing speed during the two or three jigs the band play and thankfully, the jigs amused the rowdies by giving them something to dance their conga to. They really should have listened more closely; Jack the Lad have a great deal of potential and are going to be much more expensive to see soon.

Julia Revell from Caterham recalls the **Argent** concert in mid September as much for an unexpected interruption as for the music itself. It was during a period of terrorist activity when 'bomb scares' sadly seemed to be an everyday occurrence and crowded concert halls needed to be particularly watchful. As well as bag searches on the way in, the entire audience were 'evacuated' to the foyer during the interval while the Fairfield was thoroughly checked.

Julia was especially impressed with the support band **Glencoe**, a folk-influenced rock group featuring future Blockhead bassist Norman Watt-Roy, Graham Maitland, Stewart Francis and John Turnbull, a guitarist and vocalist who had played in Newcastle bands The Chosen Few and Skip Bifferty.

Croydon Advertiser – 5.10.73

'Wild Set'

*The tradition of very heavy but ever-so-simple rock music was maintained at the Fairfield on Sunday, when **Status Quo** played a wild set that had everyone - but everyone - rocking in the aisles.*

The music itself was dull and boring, insensitive, lacking in subtlety and thoroughly unrewarding. Yet put such music in the hands of Quo and they magically transform its deficiencies into assets. As the lights went down for the beginning of the gig the audience became excited - clapping and shouting. When the foursome strode on to the stage, the youths went mad, rushing to the front only to be turned away by the worried ushers.

Yet once the gig was underway there was no stopping the determined hairies. Everyone leaped out of their seats and rocked. Each number was violently blasted out of the shaking amplifiers that stood precariously on the edge of the stage, which was surrounded by long haired youths. The lyrics were rasped out by Francis Rossi, who looked out onto the chaotic concert hall as if this sort of thing happened everyday.

Rossi tried to cool the excitement down after a couple of numbers, saying "You gotta slow down, 'cause you gotta have a lot of energy with us". But the kids would not have it, they just carried on rockin' and reelin'.

The band had a good slick stage act, with Rossi and Rick Parfitt on guitars and Alan Lancaster on bass synchronising expertly with each other's movements. At one point they surrounded the drummer John Coughlan, and played in a circle around him. Their string of rock numbers included some new material from their latest album 'Hello', plus favourites like 'Don't Waste My Time', 'Caroline' and 'Mean, Mean Girl'.

The highspot of the evening was 'Roll Over, Lay Down', followed by a jig that had the audience bouncing around the hall. The Fairfield had been turned into a hot and stuffy dance hall full of rocking teenagers.

Nick Beacroft

Frazer Ashford

The Fairport 'Nine' line-up onstage at the Fairfield Hall, 16th December 1973. Left to right: Trevor Lucas, Dave Mattacks partially hidden behind his drumkit, Jerry Donahue, Dave Pegg and Dave Swarbrick.

Many fans will argue that the line-up who recorded the 'Fairport Nine' album was the Convention at their best. Certainly, journalist Barry Shinfield made no apologies for his more than enthusiastic review of the groups December concert. *"With breathtakingly brilliant Fairport Convention, it's the music that counts - Play It Again"* screamed Barry's headline and there was more to come. *"What folk has over rock is, in a nutshell, more range - and never is that more apparent than when presented with the expertise, precision and panache of a band like Fairport Convention. On Sunday the latest line-up, whose album Fairport Nine is a joy, did it all. And for old times sake, they brought on a chic-looking Sandy Denny to join them in their encores".*

The set included 'Polly On The Shore', 'Hexamshire Lass', 'Bring 'Em Down', and 'Tokyo' all from the new LP. Swarbrick's 'Cell Song', 'Dirty Linen' and the tour de force 'Sloth' with it's dramatic fiddle and guitar combinations *"faultless, imaginative, beautiful"*, yes, yes, yes, Barry tell me about it - god, I wish I'd been there!

1974

JANUARY

- 6 COCKNEY REBEL **G** (n/a)
- 13 PINK FAIRIES **G** (n/a)
- 15 PIONEERS **T** (50p)
- 20 OSIBISA **FH** (75p to £1.25)
- 24 WOODY HERMAN **FH** (60p to £1.50)
- 24 MUD **T** (50p)
- 27 JSD BAND **G** + JOHN ST. FIELD
- 29 ICE CREAM **SC** (n/a)
- 31 JAKE THAKERAY **FH** (60p)

FEBRUARY

- 3 CAN **G** + HOME (£1)
- 5 GEORGE MELLY **FH** + PETER SKELLERN (75p to £1.25)
- 10 NEKTAR **G** (£1)
- 15 NEIL SEDAKA **FH** (75p to £1.75)
- 17 LINDISFARNE **G** (£1)
- 22 THE SPINNERS **FH** (n/a)
- 24 BILLY FURY + MARTY WILDE **FH** + HEINZ & THE NEW TORNADOES + TOMMY BRUCE + CARL SIMMONS (50p to £1.25)
- 24 ENO **G** + THE WINKIES (90p)
- 28 RALPH McTELL **FH** + PRELUDE (50p to £1.50)

MARCH

- 5 GOLDEN EARRING **G** + ALQUIN (£1)
- 5 TOM JONES **FH** 2 shows (£1 to £3)
- 10 ELECTRIC LIGHT ORCHESTRA **FH** + BADGER (75p to £1.25)
- 10 QUEEN **G** (n/a)
- 13 JACQUES LOUISSIER **FH** (n/a)
- 14 GEORGE HAMILTON IV **FH** (n/a)
- 24 KIKI DEE **FH** + TONY BIRD (50p to £1)
- 24 COCKNEY REBEL **G** (£1)
- 28 ALVIN STARDUST **T** (75p)
- 31 HAROLD MELVIN & THE BLUENOTES **FH** + HOT CHOCOLATE (75p to £2.25)
- 31 HARVEY MANDEL **G** + PURE FOOD (n/a)

APRIL

- 1 THE DUBLINERS **FH** (75p to £2.25)
- 7 CARAVAN **FH** + TIR NA NOG (75p to £1.50)
- 14 REFUGEE **G** + ISSAC GUILLORY (£1)
- 21 ALVIN STARDUST **FH** + FABLE (50p to £1.25)
- 21 GROUNDHOGS **G** + CHARLIE (£1)
- 23 CHICORY TIP **T** (75p)
- 24 CLEO LAINE **FH** + JOHNNY DANKWORTH QUARTET (50p to £1.25)
- 25 AMAZING BLONDEL **FH** + DAVID ELLIOTT (60p)
- 28 THE STYLISTICS **FH** + JIMMY JAMES & THE VAGABONDS + JIMMY RUFFIN (£1 to £2.50)
- 28 STRAY **G** + MOTHER SUN (£1)

MAY

- 2 BUDLIPPSPRINGER **D** (n/a)
- 5 TRAFFIC **FH** + SOUR GRAPES (£1 to £2)
- 5 GREENSLADE **G** + AJ WEBBER (£1)
- 9 BUDLIPPSPRINGER **D** (n/a)
- 12 THE HOLLIES **FH** + JAMES GRIFFIN (n/a)
- 12 GONG **G** (£1)
- 18 PFM **G** (£1)
- 26 BLACK SABBATH **FH** + BLACK OAK ARKANSAS (£1 to £2)
- 26 MAN **G** (£1.10)
- 31 KENNY BALL & HIS JAZZMEN **FH** (50p to £1)

JUNE

- 2 LOVE **G** + CASABLANCA (£1.10)
- 7 JOHN RENBOURN & JACQUI McSHEE **FH** (£1 to £1.75)
- 9 BLOOD, SWEAT & TEARS **FH** (£1 to £2.50)
- 9 BARCLAY JAMES HARVEST **G** + RARE BIRD (£1)
- 16 STOMU YAMASH'TA's EAST WIND **FH** (n/a)
- 21 PRELUDE **FH** + PETER SKELLERN (n/a)
- 23 REFUGEE **FH** + GRYPHON (n/a)
- 26 GROUNDHOGS **FH** + STRAY (n/a)
- 30 FAIRPORT CONVENTION **G** (£1)

(n/a) = ticket price not available.

At St. Mary's Hospital, Addiscombe, on January 16th, Linda Moss gave birth to a daughter Kate, destined to become Croydon's most celebrated gift to the fashion world only nineteen years later.

When **Neil Sedaka** arrived at the Fairfield on February 15th, his touring band included the cream of the West Coast session musicians; bassist Lee Sklar, guitarist Danny Kortchmar and Russ Kunkel on drums.

The Rock'n'Roll revival show on the 24th also featured Heinz & the New Tornadoes, Tommy Bruce, Carl Simmons and a young Alvin Stardust (or an old Shane Fenton, depending on your point of view!) - more of him later.

On Sunday 10th March, the **Electric Light Orchestra** returned to the Fairfield Hall to a far better reception than they received on their debut at the Greyhound. This time led by Jeff Lynne after the departure of Roy Wood to form Wizzard, the revamped line-up were perhaps less innovative but had found a more accessible combination of rock, pop and classical music.

As the Advertiser pointed out, their sound was now *"...basic, solid rock and hits home because of it, but there are some interesting harmonic twists which lift it well above the ordinary"*. ELO had only just released 'Ma-Ma-Ma-Belle' as a single, but the style and direction was now set for the band to go forward and produce a string of chart hits - 'Evil Woman', 'Mr Blue Sky', 'Telephone Line' and the like. It may have been better for all concerned if Roy had persevered with them!

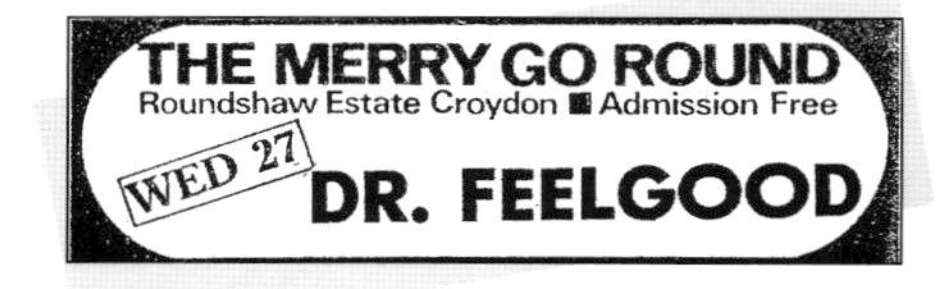

This is one gig that took me a little bit by surprise; (a) I didn't realise that the Merry Go Round pub ever staged live music, and (b) they didn't book just any old local band but in March we have Canvey Island's finest, **Dr. Feelgood** playing for free! Their mixture of high energy R'n'B standards was ideal for a pub crowd and the band were still a year away from releasing their first album. And for those of you who might have driven past without knowing it was there, the Roundshaw Estate is just off Foresters Drive, halfway between Purley and Wallington.

Croydon Advertiser – 15.3.74

'Queen lionised'

TASTEFULLY made-up ***Queen****, a band currently riding on a tidal wave of success, blasted out their own brand of rock music to the delight of a packed Greyhound audience on Sunday.*

The four man group who have recently received their fair share of television and radio exposure, shook the Greyhound with an interesting combination of heavy, rhythmic music and slow ballads. They brought along their own lighting and sound mixing equipment, which proved a tremendous advantage despite the hall's acoustics.

Although their opening number sounded weak and disjointed, they soon found their rhythm with 'Great King Rat'. Lead singer Freddie Mercury, looking like a smaller version of Alice Cooper with his eyes lined in black, moved feline-like across the stage rasping out the lyrics. Guitarist Brian May played some excellent rock backing and John Deacon provided a solid bass sound.

They slowed their eye-catching act down with 'Son and Daughter', an excellent number that fully demonstrated Mercury's versatile vocal range and revived memories of Led Zeppelin's beautiful 'Stairway to Heaven'. But the fans wanted fast rock and Queen gave them their last single 'Keep Yourself Alive' and the new chart release 'Seven Seas Of Rye'.

It was a shame they reverted to rock'n'roll at the end of the evening, when their own unique style had been so well received. The group have been voted as best band of 1973/74 by two pop newspapers and have recently backed Mott the Hoople on tour.

Judging by their following at the Greyhound, they should soon be regaled with success.

Nick Beacroft

Frazer Ashford

Kiki Dee - Fairfield Hall, 24th March 1974.

Purley Tiffany's continued to attract the 'pop' end of the market; having kicked off the year with the Pioneers, Mud and Alvin Stardust, Tiff's booked the Drifters (again!) on April 9th, Christie on April 30th, Barry Blue on May 1st, Paper Lace on May 7th and Hot Chocolate on May 22nd.

Alvin Stardust in particular just couldn't keep away from Croydon, playing here in three consecutive months and each time moving up a rung on the ladder. In February he was well down the bill of a Rock'n'Roll package tour, but his second single 'Jealous Mind' had just entered the charts. At the end of March he was at Tiffany's touring a number one record and by April 21st Alvin was headlining his own tour at the Fairfield, where he thrilled the audience of teenage girls, but the Advertiser's Barry Shinfield had seen it all before; *"A leather-gloved hand, rings worn over, caresses the microphone. The other arm is thrown out and one knee raised like a flamenco dancer who's suddenly cricked his back. 'Wait for me, Alvin... love me, Alvin' cries a little female voice from behind, and there was other competition for his attention on Sunday.*

Paper missiles containing addresses and 'phone numbers showered onto the stage. Diminutive, even in high-heeled boots, Alvin is currently making 12 year old girls go gooey... or all 'Coo-Ca-Choo'-ey... with his black leather pout and tight pants. A star of the late 'fifties when he was Shane Fenton, now he's re-emerged as a hybrid of Elvis Presley and Gary Glitter.

But he doesn't arouse the same hysteria. On Sunday night the shouting, screaming and storming of the stage were only half-hearted, almost academic. The kids in the audience should have seen Presley in his early days, or Gene Vincent, or Eddie Cochran. But they didn't, and are given Alvin instead".

One year on, and those Croydon favourites **Budlippspringer** were still rocking the Dog & Bull in Surrey Street every Thursday night. There was a new look to the band, however; vocalist Jimmy Patterson and lead guitarist Bernie Brooks remained, to be joined by Dave Betts on keyboards, drummer Pete Cooper and bass player George Walker, who had previously played with soul man Al Green.

Croydon Advertiser – 3.5.74

'Jimmy saves a soul night'

A HALF FULL Fairfield Hall presided like a wake over the coffin of a soul music tour that turned up in Croydon on Sunday. The gathering was small for two shows from yesterday's stars, ***Jimmy James & the Vagabonds*** *and* ***Jimmy Ruffin****, plus present chart successes* ***The Stylistics****.*

The concert was an epitaph to soul, which during its heyday in the 'sixties commanded the charts, discos and jukeboxes. Dance halls drew their life blood from the funky sounds of soul and the music made heroes out of artists like the late Otis Redding, Wilson Pickett, Marvin Gaye and Stevie Wonder. Now the stars have either retired from the scene or, like Wonder, have progressed to more mature music.

The concert was saved from complete disaster by the veteran Jimmy Ruffin. Faced with an audience cooled to frigidity by the weak Jimmy James & the Vagabonds, Ruffin picked a winning combination of old hits - 'What Becomes of the Broken Hearted', 'I Passed This Way Before', Farewell Is A Lonely Sound', 'Wonderful' and finished with 'Forever'. He had the audience clapping along and singing with him; the climax came when he sang 'Take Me Higher', using the same participation technique so well exploited by Sly Stone at Woodstock.

But the Stylistics sounded dated and uninspiring - most of their numbers, with the exception of Carole King's 'It's Too Late', were virtually indistinguishable. Dressed in gaudy blue tail suits, they sang their hits 'You Are Everything' and 'Betcha' By Golly Wow', but each number was too long - they lost the audience's attention and received little applause at the end.

Nick Beacroft

On May 12th, **Elton John** was due to perform at the Fairfield Hall, but his whole UK tour was cancelled due to 'exhaustion' following a gruelling tour of America. **The Hollies** stepped in to fill the empty date, with their support act **James Griffin** who prior to trying his hand as a solo performer, had been the guitarist and second vocalist with Bread.

The tour programme announced forthcoming solo records by Hollies Terry Sylvester and Allan Clarke and to help promote his own album, Clarke returned alone to play the Croydon Greyhound in September.

Probably the most successful band ever to wear tartan trousers, the **Bay City Rollers** appeared 'by public demand' at the Cats Whiskers Club, Streatham Hill on Monday 13th May. The cost of a ticket, a mere 75p!

1974

JULY

- 2 BUDLIPPSPRINGER **RD** (n/a)
- 4 JAZZ FESTIVAL **FH** (n/a)
- 7 COCKNEY REBEL **G** + BE BOP DELUXE (£1)
- 11 BUDLIPPSPRINGER **D** (n/a)
- 14 NEKTAR **G** (n/a)
- 21 BUDGIE **G** (n/a)
- 28 STRAY **G** (£1)
- 31 RONNETTES **SC** (n/a)
- 31 SYNDROME **GN** (n/a)

AUGUST

- 2 PROCOL HARUM **FH** + BE BOP DELUXE (n/a)
- 4 CAMEL **G** + COAST ROAD DRIVE (n/a)
- 7 RUBETTES **T** (95p)
- 11 JSD BAND **G** (n/a)
- 18 SUTHERLAND BROTHERS & QUIVER **G** (n/a)
- 22 BUDLIPPSPRINGER **D** (n/a)
- 25 STACKRIDGE **G** (n/a)
- 27 BUDLIPPSPRINGER **RD** (n/a)
- 28 LIMMIE & THE FAMILY COOKIN' **T** (50p)

SEPTEMBER

- 1 CARAVAN **FH** + SANDGATE (75p to £1.75)
- 1 EDGAR BROUGHTON **G** (n/a)
- 4 GLITTERBAND **T** (75p)
- 5 BUDLIPPSPRINGER **D** (n/a)
- 11 WIZZARD **T** (n/a)
- 15 STREETWALKERS **G** (£1.10)
- 15 LEE KOSMIN **D** (n/a)
- 25 GALLAGHER & LYLE **FH** + PAUL CARMEN (50p to £1)
- 25 COZY POWELL **T** (90p)
- 29 ALLAN CLARKE **G** (n/a)
- 29 GREENSLADE **FH** + AJ WEBBER (£1)
- 29 GONG **G** (£1.10)

OCTOBER

- 2 THE CRICKETS **T** (80p)
- 4 THE SPINNERS **FH** (75p to £1.50)
- 6 THE STRAWBS **FH** + BETTE WHITE (75p to £2)
- 6 CAN **G** (£1.10)
- 13 WISHBONE ASH **FH** + UPP (75p to £1.75)
- 13 MAN **G** + BADFINGER (£1.10)
- 15 THE TREMELOES **T** (60p)
- 16 PETER SKELLERN **FH** (£3.75 to £5)
- 17 TOR **SPH** (n/a)
- 20 BE BOP DELUXE **G** (£1.10)
- 24 AMAZING BLONDEL **FH** + GORDON GILTRAP (60p)
- 25 JOHN D. LOUDERMILK **FH** + GRAND OLE OPREY ROADSHOW (75p to £1.50)
- 26 MAX BOYCE **FH** (£3 to £6)
- 27 GEORGE MELLY **FH** (75p to £1.50)
- 27 THIN LIZZY + THE JAM **G** (n/a)
- 29 SHAKIN' STEVENS **FH** (£3.50 to £4.50)
- 30 LEO SAYER **T** + LIFE (£1)

NOVEMBER

- 3 HEAVY METAL KIDS **G** (£1.10)
- 10 HUMBLE PIE **FH** + McGUINESS FLINT (£1 to £1.75)
- 10 GROUNDHOGS **G** + PERCY (£1.10)
- 13 WISHBONE ASH **FH** (75p to £1.75)
- 17 OSIBISA **FH** + GARY FARR (75p to £1.50)
- 17 HATFIELD & THE NORTH **G** + KEVIN COYNE (£1.10)
- 18 STEELEYE SPAN **FH** + RICHARD DIGENCE (n/a)
- 21 TOM PAXTON **FH** (75p to £1.50)
- 24 SPARKS **FH** + PILOT (£2)
- 24 NEKTAR **G** (£1.10)
- 28 CLIFF RICHARD **FH** (n/a)

DECEMBER

- 1 STACKRIDGE **G** (£1.10)
- 5 PETE ATKIN **FH** + JULIET LAWSON (60p)
- 8 FAIRPORT CONVENTION **FH** + BRYN HAWORTH (75p to £1.50)
- 8 RONNIE LANE & SLIM CHANCE **G** (£1.10)
- 15 BUDGIE **G** (n/a)
- 15 LEE KOSMIN **D** (n/a)
- 17 SWINGING SIXTIES TOUR **FH** (50p to £1.25)
- 22 GREENSLADE **G** (n/a)
- 29 STRAY **G** (£1.10)

The concert by **Caravan** on 1st September was the first UK show to feature their new bass player Mike Wedgwood. It was recorded by the Pye mobile studio and broadcast live on radio. Initially, one track *'For Richard'* appeared on the retrospective double album 'Canterbury Tales' Decca DKL-R8/1/2 released in 1976, but the whole concert has since been released on Kingdom records in France, imaginatively titled 'The Best of Caravan Live'.

If keyboard-led instrumental and progressive rock/jazz was your 'bag' back in '74, then you were probably at the Fairfield Hall on Sunday 29th September to see **Greenslade**. Founder members Dave Greenslade and bassist Tony Reeves were both with Colosseum during the late 'sixties, so comparisons were inevitable. Their other keyboard player Dave Lawson joined from The Alan Bown, while drummer Andy McCulloch had played with both King Crimson and Fields.

The group played a tight set of material from their three albums, including the strangely titled 'Bedside Manners Are Extra', 'Sun Kissed You're Not'and 'Siamseesaw'.

Yet another line-up of the **Strawbs** appeared at the Fairfield on 6th October; still led by singer/songwriter Dave Cousins, the band featured ex-Stealers Wheel drummer Rod Coombes, Chas Cronk on bass, former Nashville Teens and Renaissance keyboard player John Hawken and guitarist Dave Lambert.

On 17th October a local band by the name of **Tor** played at St. Peters Hall, Ledbury Road, South Croydon. Sometimes gigging under the name **Rot**, the line up included one Rat Scabies on drums, Phil Mitchell - bass, Pete Starks - vocals, Glyn Evans - guitar and Slimy Toad - guitar. Toad later played in Johnny Moped with Captain Sensible on bass; Scabies would later meet up with the Captain to form leading punk group The Damned.

Rat told Rock Family Tree expert Pete Frame: *"Rot played nothing except well-over-the-top arty-farty stuff... a lot more complicated than Television are capable of doing. I hated every minute of it... they made me put towels over my drums because I was too loud! We had a residency at St. Laurence's Mental Home in Caterham, playing to the patients... but they were more interested in watching us set up our gear".*

FH - Fairfield Hall • G - Greyhound • S - Star Hotel • TR - Top Rank • O - Orchid Ballroom • D - Dog & Bull

The **Amazing Blondel** were a pale shadow of their former selves when they appeared at the Fairfield on Thursday 24th October. Their unique qualities seemed to have deserted them with the loss of John Gladwin, the trio paired down to a duo comprising Eddie Baird and Terry Winscott. To quote Barry Shinfield - *"They began as a hairy, bawdy, Rabelaisian trio, dispensing a winning blend of folk music and blue jokes, utilising all kinds of exotic instruments from the crumhorn and lute, to the pipe organ and cittern... creating a quite unique pastiche of Elizabethan music".*

"Their material is now a succession of dreary, hammy, Beatles-ish love songs... played on two electric guitars, with Terry Winscott contributing the occasional muted flute".

Croydon Advertiser – 15.11.74

'Earful of Pie'

*THERE MUST be experiences physically comparable - but cheaper, than being deafened by **Humble Pie**. Like having Buddy Rich play a 24-hour drum break on a bucket on your head. Or removing the wax from your ears with a pneumatic drill.*

The noise level of their pitched amplification battle at Fairfield on Sunday was measured at 105 decibels. That doesn't in itself mean a lot to me; but it was the first time that I have had to use a page from my notepad for earplugs. They made Rory Gallagher sound like Tiny Tim. Theirs is a now passé preoccupation with volume for volume's sake - a silly, mindless blast of pseudo-aggression. In an abstract way, (with ears safely muffled) you might have enjoyed the surly truculence of Steve Marriott, the groups diminutive leader, as he launched parabola's of spittle across the stage, or swigged from a brandy bottle. Or delicately, fastidiously announced the numbers: "I fink I'll dedicate this 'un to moi ol lady's ol man - it's called 'Six Day Creep'."

Another song 'Firty Days inny Ole' (Thirty Days In The Hole) encapsulated the physical essence of this concert. As the quartet returned like prima donnas after a lengthy false exit and ripped into their encore number 'Doctor', I really felt I needed one.

For pre-prandial delectation, McGuinness Flint served up a dated mixture of the heavy and the schmaltsy - indulgent, dull and over histrionic. But by comparison, however, they were a heavenly choir.

Barry Shinfield

This exceptionally loud Humble Pie line-up comprised guitarists Steve Marriott & Dave Clempson, Greg Ridley on bass and Jerry Shirley on drums.

When David Essex kicked off his nationwide tour at the start of November, he chose the pop group **Merlin** as his opening act. Merlin's lead guitarist was 19 year old Jamie Moses from Brian Avenue, Sanderstead and their keyboard player was Scully Wagon-Lits (aka Bob Webb) 20, from Mitchley Avenue, Purley. The group's single 'Wildcat' and an album, both on CBS records, were released to coincide with the opening gig of the 25 date tour, although Jamie and 'Scully' didn't get to play in Croydon - the closest concerts being held at the Sutton Granada and the Lewisham Odeon.

Towards the end of 1974, a band named **Flip City** played at the Gun, which at that time had something of a reputation as a bikers hangout. As Flip City had a repertoire that included material by Little Feet, Bob Dylan, the Grateful Dead, and Jesse Winchester, friends of the group were sceptical about exactly how well they would be received! However, vocalist and guitarist Declan Patrick McManus began chatting to the bikers and invited one of them up on stage to play harmonica, with the result that the rest of evening went off without a hint of trouble. Two years later McManus changed his name, first to D.P. Costello and then to **Elvis Costello** and went on to much greater success with his own unique brand of songwriting.

Playing support to **Thin Lizzy** at their Greyhound gig in October were an embryonic version of **The Jam**. The appearance was secured by John Weller, Paul's dad and group manager, who had 'a contact' at the venue. The band were a four piece at the time, with original guitarist Steve Brookes, Paul Weller, Rick Buckler and new bass player Bruce Foxton only coming on stage to play on the songs he knew!

Croydon Advertiser – 13.12.74

'What next, Fairport?'

*AFTER THE success of Pete Atkin on Thursday, the Fairfield really excelled itself with an appearance by **Fairport Convention** on Sunday. Simply all the superlatives have been exhausted by now in description of such inveterate campaigners.*

Bryn Howarth, the first act, said that Fairport were playing well, and he didn't exaggerate. The question is, where do Fairport go from here?. How does a band progress from such commendable playing as that on their extended version of 'Sloth'?

Sandy Denny, tired like the rest of band after 48 consecutive dates, but full of herself none the less, said in announcing the number that it was like undertaking a marathon journey. But it was a trip to be savoured; the moving little song has become a joyful vehicle for solos and these were stunning. 'Sloth' as heard on Sunday, is an essay in the musicianship of Fairport.

A lead solo from Jerry Donahue that was masterly in its understatement - whoever heard of a lead guitarist playing so softly that you could have heard a pin drop? Then a brief, imaginative contribution from Dave Pegg on bass, before the Swarb (Dave Swarbrick) who is simply a virtuoso and wove magical wands on violin, a breathtaking solo that made one lament the absence of a recording unit.

Earlier tunes included 'Dirty Linen', 'Cherokee Shuffle', 'Hexamshire Lass' and 'Fiddlesticks'; 'Six Days on the Road' and 'Matty Groves' were among other expected inclusions. And how the audience loved it; dancing in the aisles at the end of the night to encores they had positively insisted on.

But somehow it was 'Sloth' that summed up Fairport at the height of their powers. Familiarity can breed contempt, but not with a band of such consistent application and calibre. It was an emotional occasion for Fairport, being their final gig with drummer Dave Mattacks, who is leaving after five years' sterling service.

But they'll be back with a replacement next year. A Convention that needs preserving.

Barry Shinfield

Even during the early 'seventies, the dreaded revival/package tours were already doing the rounds. December's Swinging Sixties show featured varying line-ups of the Swinging Blue Jeans, the Love Affair, Cupids Inspiration, the Nashville Teens, the Mojos and a version of the Honeycombs *minus* female drummer Honey Langtree!

JANUARY

5 ACE **G** (n/a)
7 LEO SAYER **T** (£1.25)
12 THIN LIZZY **G** + JACKIE LYNTON's GRANDE (n/a)
16 THE RUBETTES **T** (£1.20)
19 MAHAVISHNU ORCHESTRA **FH** *feat.* JOHN McLAUGHLIN & JEAN-LUC PONTY (£1.25 to £2)
19 FRUUPP **G** (n/a)
26 SWEET SENSATION **FH** + MR. BIG (75p to £1.50)
26 EDGAR BROUGHTON **G** (n/a)
29 HOT CHOCOLATE **T** (80p)

FEBRUARY

2 JESS RODEN BAND **G** (n/a)
6 KENNY **T** (65p)
9 BUDGIE **G** + BURLESQUE (n/a)
12 MAC & KATIE KISSOON **T** (65p)
16 KIKI DEE **FH** + SAILOR (75p to £1.50)
16 LINDISFARNE **G** + NATIONAL FLAG (n/a)
18 AL STEWART **FH** + BRINSLEY SCHWARZ (75p to £1.25)
18 WAYNE GIBSON **T** (n/a)
23 BLACK OAK ARKANSAS **G** + SASSAFRAS (n/a)
26 ALVIN STARDUST **T** (80p)
27 LABI SIFFRE **FH** + MARIAN SEGAL & GLENN CARDIER (75p to £1.25)
00 NEIL SEDAKA **FH** + PHILIP & VANESSA (n/a)

MARCH

2 RUFUS **G** + SLOWBONE (n/a)
4 GILBERT O'SULLIVAN **FH** (£1.50 to £2.75)
6 JOHNNY JOHNSON & THE BANDWAGON **T** (65p)
9 THE SHADOWS **FH** (75p to £1.50)
13 RICHARD DIGENCE **FH** + ROBIN & BARRY DRANSFIELD (75p)
13 BLACKFOOT SUE **T** (65p)
16 MANFRED MANN's EARTHBAND **G** (n/a)
16 NOSMO KING & THE JAVELLS **T** (65p)
27 HELLO **T** (80p)
30 IAN HUNTER & MICK RONSON **FH** + JET (£1.25)
30 CURVED AIR **G** (n/a)

APRIL

1 RALPH McTELL **FH** + GAY & TERRY WOODS (£1 to £1.25)
3 OSCAR PETERSON **FH** (£1 to £2)
6 EDGAR BROUGHTON **G** (n/a)
13 DETROIT SPINNERS **FH** + BEN E. KING + SISTER SLEDGE + JIMMY CASTOR BUNCH (£1 to £2.50)
13 CAMEL **G** (n/a)
14 PAPER LACE **FH** + PETER OLIVER (75p to £1.50)
20 KOKOMO **G** (n/a)
25 TIM HARDIN **FH** + CITY WAITES (75p)
27 STRAY **G** (n/a)
29 RICHARD & LINDA THOMPSON **FH** + HEDGEHOG PIE (80p)

MAY

4 10 CC **FH** + FANCY (£1 to £1.75)
4 CAN **G** (n/a)
11 GREENSLADE **FH** + RAB NOAKES (75p to £1.25)
11 SNAFU **G** (n/a)
18 THE SENSATIONAL ALEX HARVEY BAND **FH** + SKYBAND (£1 to £2)
18 DR. FEELGOOD **G** (n/a)
25 JOHN MARTYN **FH** + HEDGEHOG PIE (75p to £1.50)
25 BE BOP DELUXE **G** (n/a)
26 DON McLEAN **FH** + LESLEY DUNCAN (£1 to £3)
28 THE SHADOWS **FH** (£1 to £1.75)
30 THE SPINNERS **FH** (£1 to £1.75)

JUNE

1 THIN LIZZY **G** (n/a)
5 CHRIS BARBER **FH** (75p to £1.25)
8 KEVIN COYNE **G** (n/a)
12 LOUDON WAINWRIGHT III **FH** (75p to £1.50)
15 BACK STREET CRAWLER **FH** + DOG SOLDIER (£1 to £1.50)
15 BUDGIE **G** (£00)
22 DONOVAN **FH** (£1 to £3)
22 BILLY COBHAM **G** (£1.20)
29 SUTHERLAND BROTHERS & QUIVER **G** (n/a)

FH - Fairfield Hall • G - Greyhound • S - Star Hotel • TR - Top Rank • T - Tiffanys

1975

Throughout the year, the jazz group **Major Surgery** held a Sunday night residency at the Gun Tavern. Led by the 'Falstaffian' figure (Time Out's description!) of tenor sax player Don Weller, the band included Harry Beckett, Jimmy Roche, Bruce Colcutt, Tony Marsh and Gordon Beck and would regularly feature guest spots from the likes of Barbara Thompson, Art Themen and Elton Dean.

Croydon-born Weller was intent on working his way round the local pub circuit; back in 1973 Major Surgery had been resident in the back room of the Dog & Bull - talking of which...

A new group named **Borzoi** were booked in to the Dog & Bull in Surrey Street, Croydon for a string of Sunday night dates towards the end of January. Named after a Russian breed of dog, their appearance at the Greyhound in Fulham Palace Road led to rumours that they were the latest rock group from behind the Iron Curtain, but in fact were more at home in Balham than Berlin. Borzoi's lead singer was Jimmy Patterson, one time vocalist with Budlippspringer, a popular band with the Croydon locals who also played many times in the back room of the Dog & Bull. The two groups shared the same manager, Ron Popham from South Norwood, who linked Jimmy with a trio called Lapwing to form the current Borzoi line-up, featuring Martin Godfrey on bass, Paul Gibbs from Surbiton on drums and guitarist Graham Dunne from Raynes Park.

A bit of obscure (and perfectly useless) local trivia for **Elton John** fans. When the original album 'Captain Fantastic & the Brown Dirt Cowboy' was released in 1975, the packaging was superb - gatefold sleeve, Alan Aldridge illustrated lyric book and poster, plus a 'scrap' book of reviews, photos and selected entries from Elton's diary. In this booklet are several shots of Elton and Bernie Taupin 'looning at Caterham' in April 1969; most of them could have been taken anywhere, but one was undoubtably shot in the centre of Wapses Lodge roundabout, at the junction of Burntwood Lane, Croydon Road and the Caterham bypass.

Elton's diary for Sunday 21st September 1969 also notes, "Going to see the Who at Croydon - took Catherine - they were excellent".

Croydon Advertiser – 2.5.75

'SUPERGROUP'

*A FOLK PHOENIX had to rise from the dying embers of Fairport Convention and Steeleye Span. It is **Richard & Linda Thompson**. Plus Dave Pegg. Plus Dave Mattacks. And it works exceedingly well. The evidence was there at Fairfield on Tuesday, when the band went down like the folk supergroup it is destined to be.*

Richard Thompson is one of the finest lead players in the land - "the best rock guitarist in the country", was one description I heard when they did a rock number near the end of the set. With the Fairport experience of Pegg on bass and Mattacks on drums, it is a band to hear; with a lovely touch of accordion from John Kirkpatrick.

The dream topping comes from the thrush's throat of Linda Thompson, whose voice has that marvellous Sandy Denny flight of pathos. Richard's voice has come on a treat too - and he now does justice to his solo vocals.

From their first album they did the lilting, bouncy 'I Want To See The Bright Lights Tonight' (which was released as a single and should have been a hit, but wasn't). From the latest album they chipped in with 'Mole In A Hole' and there was a stunning medley, 'Morris On' to enjoy too.

In the first half, Hedgehog Pie came out of hibernation to serve up some tasty Lindisfarne-flavoured Geordie folk and humour. Dylan's 'Forever Young' stays in the memory. Another band with a lot of charm and a very bright future.

Barry Shinfield

On Sunday 30th March, I finally got to see one of my rock heroes - **Ian Hunter**. I originally had tickets to see Mott the Hoople at Hammersmith Odeon, but the gig was cancelled when the original band split up. Ian Hunter & ex-Bowie guitarist **Mick Ronson** carried on and - fortunately for me - added the Fairfield to their tour.

As the band took the stage, a single spotlight picked out Hunter's head and shoulders and with a quick 'Allo', he launched straight into 'Once Bitten Twice Shy', followed by 'Lounge Lizard' both from the new solo album. The band included keyboards from Blue Weaver, who had been drafted into MTH for their final U.S. tour; Jeff Appleby on bass and Dennis Elliott on drums. Call me biased if you will, but their set really was magic!

The support band **Jet** featured ex-Nice guitarist David O'List, but were memorable only for the antics of their singer who would leap acrobatically on and off stage, carefully avoiding the latecomers who were still finding their seats in the front row!

An object lesson in rock theatre was much in evidence at the gig by the **Sensational Alex Harvey Band**. Harvey himself was a 40 year old Scot with a gruff voice and a stage outfit direct from a production of Long John Silver - striped t-shirt, frock coat and a scabbard containing not a sword but an umbrella! His inimitable lead guitarist Zal Cleminson wore the make-up of a clown, plus cod-piece and suspenders, all perfectly captured in Frazer's picture shown below.

The concert was reviewed for the Advertiser by Barry Shinfield, who was obviously not in the mood for Harvey's theatrics - *"Harvey's stage act toys with decadence and nihilism, not in the aesthetic intelligent manner of Jacques Brel or Lou Reed, but in an overtly theatrical, and ultimately absurd way. When Harvey throbs his groin in time to the music he looks more like a pantomime comedian or clown than a sex-idol or svengali - and this he probably knows."*

SAHB knocked out their version of 'Delilah', the old Tom Jones hit, after which Alex Harvey told the audience, "You kids are suckers for melodrama!"

The local press were less than happy about the treatment given to **Tim Hardin** by the Fairfield audience. Playing to a hall that was only two thirds full and with half of those not seeming to know the first thing about Hardin's background, he nevertheless conspired to produce a memorable performance - *"Tim Hardin has been singing these unbelievably melancholic, magical masterpieces for so long, that he now embellishes them, moving almost into jazz with his vocal delivery".*

After the break up of Free in 1973, their lead guitarist Paul Kossoff recorded a solo album entitled 'Back Street Crawler'. Two years later he put together a band using that name, with Terry Slesser, Mike Montgomery, Tony Braunagel and Terry Wilson. The Fairfield gig by **Back Street Crawler** was recorded for posterity and later issued as an LP entitled *'Croydon, June 15th 1975'* SDLP 1002 - well, that tells it like it is, I suppose! You won't find it in the record racks under 'B' though, but under 'K' - it was released under Paul Kossoff's name.

Frazer Ashford

Lead guitarist Zal Cleminson strikes a characteristic pose for the Sensational Alex Harvey Band' - Fairfield Hall, Sunday 18th May.

JULY

6 STACKRIDGE **G** + THE JAM (n/a)
13 GREENSLADE **G** (n/a)
20 MANFRED MANN's EARTHBAND **G** + CAMEL (n/a) *CANCELLED*

AUGUST

3 CAMEL **FH** + MICHAEL CHAPMAN (75p to £1.50)

SEPTEMBER

7 THE SUPREMES **FH** + SWEET SENSATION (£1 to £3)
11 CHRIS BARBER's JAZZBAND **FH** (75p to £1.25)
14 OSIBISA **FH** + MOON (£1 to £2)
14 LEMMY's MOTORHEAD **G** (n/a)
17 JIMMY JAMES & THE VAGABONDS **Sc** (75p)
19 ROY ORBISON **FH** + THE KARLINS (£1 to £2)
21 KRAFTWORK **FH** + AJ WEBBER (£1 to £2)
21 BABE RUTH **G** (n/a)
23 PETE ATKIN **FH** + ANDY DESMOND (75p)
25 THE DUBLINERS **FH** (75p to £1.75)
28 SNAFU **G** + BABY (n/a)

OCTOBER

5 THE PINK FAIRIES **G** + GASWORKS (n/a)
5 JOHN MAYALL **FH** + MOONRIDER (£1 to £2)
7 THE GLITTERBAND **T** (80p)
7 PETER SKELLERN **FH** + AMAZING BLONDEL (£1 to £1.50)
12 STRAY **G** (n/a)
15 THE CHIEFTAINS **FH** (£1 to £2.50)
17 THE PLATTERS **FH** (£1 to £2.50)
19 SAILOR **G** + PEGASUS (n/a)
23 TANGERINE DREAM **FH** (£1 to £2)
26 STACKRIDGE **G** (n/a)
26 THE HOLLIES **FH** + HOWARD WERTH & THE MOONBEAMS (£1 to £2)

NOVEMBER

2 FAIRPORT CONVENTION **FH** + DAVID LEWIS (£1 to £2)
2 STACKRIDGE **G** + MUFFTY (n/a)
4 RICHARD DIGENCE **FH** + CITY WAITES (75p)
7 CLIFF RICHARD **FH** 2 shows (£1 to £2)
7 ACE **G** (n/a)
9 SPARKS **FH** + PAUL JOSES BAND (£1.25 to £2)
9 NILS LOFGREN **G** (n/a)
13 TOM PAXTON **FH** + DAVE WILLIS & IAN HUNT (75p to £1.75)
14 FOUR TOPS **FH** + AL MATTHEWS (£1 to £3)
16 SUPERTRAMP **FH** + JOAN ARMATRADING (£1.25 to £2)
16 GONG **G** (n/a)
18 HOT CHOCOLATE **FH** + D'DANCER (75p to £1.50)
30 JOHN CALE **FH** + NASTY POP (75p to £1.50)

DECEMBER

3 KENNY BALL & HIS JAZZMEN **FH** (£1 to £1.75)
7 MAN **FH** (£1.25 to £2)
7 BUDGIE **G** (n/a)
14 THIN LIZZY **G** (n/a)
15 ALBION DANCE BAND **TS** (70p)
21 PINK FAIRIES **G** (n/a)
26 STRAY **G** + NASTY TRICKS (n/a)
28 KOKOMO **G** (n/a)

(n/a) = ticket price not available.

Following their support to Thin Lizzy at the Greyhound in November '74, **The Jam** returned again to support Stackridge on 6th July. The travelling Stackridge fans reacted by throwing turnips at the sharp suited boys from Woking, which apparently is a West Country 'custom'!

Croydon Advertiser – 8.8.75

'Camel give me the hump'

CAMEL are a band who have been flogging away for a while without an enormous following. Suddenly, by releasing a 'concept' album based on Paul Gallico's weepy novel, 'The Snow Goose', they fill the Fairfield on Sunday.

The album bobbed into the charts a few weeks back on release, then last week it was equal 28th in the MM compilation. After sitting through the music from beginning to end on Sunday, I'd say the fact that they have suddenly arrived can only be testament to the dearth of emerging group talent in this country.

Musically, 'Snow Goose' is ambitious but unfulfilled and totally removed from inspiration. Despite the recourse to back projection (what did William Blake have to do with it, for example?) the entirely instrumental treatment of the theme must have been a complete mystery to those unfamiliar with the book. Camel did point out that the programme (20p) would help those unfamiliar with the story, but I doubt it.

Despite their commensurate organisation as a band, and the accolade they deserve for the attempt, 'Snow Goose' is a big zero as a piece of composition. After a couple of tracks from an earlier Camel album 'Mirage', the audience sat through an uninterrupted rendition of 'Goose', though there were signs of restlessness. With no vocals and an over-reliance on Peter Bardens' repetitive keyboards, and in the absence of a strong melodic theme, this was not an experience I would care to repeat. More scope could have been given to Andy Latimer's voice, and praise must go to the drumming of Andy Ward. Otherwise, it is hard - but for the novelty value - to see what all the fuss is about for Camel.

More engaging were the guitar pyrotechnics of Michael Chapman in the first half. Chapman, a down to earth character from Hull, describes himself as an 'electronic dunce', but his masterly use of vibrato, reverb and phrasing continue to be a revelation.

Barry Shinfield

August 1975 and a young group whose set consisted of some rough 'sixties cover versions changed their name from Swankers to the Sex Pistols. Their manager **Malcolm McLaren**, ran a shop in the Kings Road specialising in rock'n'roll memorabilia and had just returned from a brief spell managing the New York Dolls in America, where he picked up many of the ideas that he would later use to mould into an image for the Pistols.

For a short time, McLaren had been a student at Croydon Art College, as was **Jamie Reed**, who carried through his design training and teamed up with McLaren and his band to produce some of the ground-breaking graphics by which punk is often remembered. I spoke to 'punk historian' Andrew Wilson, who told me - *"Jamie and Malcolm met at Croydon college - I don't know how Jamie, a Scot, came to be there but Malcolm was forever changing colleges. He would apply for the free first year grant, and then move on to a different college using a new name! The punks were all trying to get out of the suburbs and into the 'real' centre of London - I guess punk was very much a South London sort of thing."*

As part of their first British tour, those German electro-rockers **Kraftwerk** confounded a Fairfield audience in September. The four group members stood almost motionless amid a virtual laboratory of electronic equipment; Ralf and Florian programming melody and special effects, while Karl and Wolfgang handled the percussion. Against a backdrop of *teutonic* visuals that included a painting by Friedrich, an Expressionist horror film and an excerpt from the Faust legend, their music became *"layer upon layer of hypnotic sound... at times deliberately harsh and strident...at others, soaring phrases of majestic and intoxicating grandeur"*. Touring on the strength of their single 'Autobahn', the surprise hit - number 11 in May '75 - that cleverly conjured the sensation of high speed motorway travel, Kraftwerk (whose name means 'Powerplant') left most of the Croydon faithful intrigued and inspired by this new music - part of the generation that spawned *'techno'* in the 'nineties.

For a mere 75p, fans of rude reggae could dance to the **Judge Dread** Roadshow at Scamps nightclub in Crown Hill on 8th October. The 'Judge', real name Alex Hughes, first became part of the music industry when he began work as the doorman at Brixton's celebrated Ram Jam Club in 1963. He first hit the charts in August '72 when 'Big Six' made number eleven and five subsequent singles all broke into the top thirty - not that you'd have heard any of them played by the BBC!

October saw yet another visit from **John Mayall**, but not, by all accounts, with one of his classic line-ups. The band still featured Larry Taylor on bass and Don 'Sugarcane' Harris on electric violin; drummer Soko Richardson had the benefit of ten years backing Ike & Tina Turner, but lead guitarist Rick Vito had the impossible task of emulating such previous Mayall players as Peter Green, Eric Clapton, Mick Taylor and Harvey Mandel.

Croydon Advertiser – 21.11.75

'Tramp' on upper!

THANKS largely to their 'Crime Of The Century' album and the hit single 'Dreamer', ***Supertramp*** *have been widely regarded as "the band most likely to" for almost the whole of this year. Only a shortage of material and a somewhat lacklustre stage personality, it seems, has delayed their breakthrough.*

Now, evidently these matters have been seen to. The band have just released a new album 'Crisis? What Crisis?', to coincide with their current tour and they've also devised an exotic criss-cross light show to make each performance glitter and gleam like a fireworks display.

Sunday's hour and a half Fairfield set was Supertramp's fourth date of thirty. If, as seems likely, the audience acclaim of this show is matched elsewhere, the band will have emphatically confirmed their status as important pioneers of keyboard-based rock. They may not be shaped in the conventional rock-band mould - they have no charismatic frontman to steal the spotlight, nor do they have a polished 'chatman' to charm the fans. But, more important, all five are genuine musicians who can blend and balance sound to superb effect.

During the evening the glossy beams shifted from performer to performer, no individual was dominant. Richard Davis, Roger Hodgson and John Helliwell took turns on five different keyboards, the last two also doing good work on guitar and saxophone respectively. Dougie Thompson and Bob Benburg provided all-important support on bass and drums.

Supertramp's musical range is now so rich and varied it would be more difficult to categorise their style. The most popular characteristics are Hodgson's high pitched vocals and staccato piano technique, evident in 'Dreamer' and their very similar new single 'Lady'. But in addition, fine piano, wind balance and carefully worked out vocal harmonies proved consistent features of their other strong numbers - 'Sister Moonshine', 'Hide In Your Shell', 'Back To The Night' and 'Another Man's Woman'.

A.W.

Funk-rock band **Gonzalez** released their new LP 'Our Only Weapon Is Our Music' on EMI, featuring the lead vocals of 28 year old Lenny Zakatek from Guildford Road, Croydon. An Anglo-Indian born in Karachi, Lenny joined the group in August 1974, replacing Karl Douglas who had left to pursue a solo career that led to his million selling hit 'Kung Fu Fighting'. Prior to joining Gonzalez, Lenny had released a couple of solo singles of his own, produced by singer Lynsey De Paul but his career was put on hold for eight months while he recovered from a motor accident in which he went through a car windscreen.

Gonzalez were formed in 1971 by a group of session musicians with time on their hands - between studio work for the likes of Cat Stevens, Osibisa, Pete Wingfield, Bryan Ferry, Elton John, Linda Lewis and Ronnie Lane - and Lenny described their sound as 'Latin American funk'. The band also had a passion for football - being a twelve piece enabled them to field their own team and they beat an Island Records eleven by 5-2, with Lenny grabbing a hat-trick!

A former pupil of Ashburton School, **John Curd** found that there is a good living to be made from promoting rock concerts. He took his first financial gamble at the tender age of 16 when he booked a pop group into Shirley Parish Hall; about 400 fans turned up, and John was well and truly hooked.

Although most of his work involved London venues - the Lyceum in the Strand, the Hammersmith Odeon and the Roundhouse, for which he was the sole promoter - he turned his attention back to his home town and booked the September gigs for Osibisa and Kraftwerk into the Fairfield Hall, followed by Man in December. John's company, *Straight Music* operated out of an office in Chelsea and he only moved from his Shirley home to Battersea in 1974 to be 'nearer the office'!

Trinity School, Croydon was the slightly unusual venue chosen by the **Albion Dance Band** for their only London performance of the year.

The group were a veritable who's who of British folk music, led by the husband and wife team (at that time) of Ashley Hutchings and Shirley Collins. The Fairport connection was carried on by guitarist Simon Nicol and drummer Dave Mattacks, plus Eddie Upton (vocals), John Rodd (concertina), Will Duke (concertina & melodeon), John Sothcott ('early' instruments!) and Greg Gregory (percussion). Their act was split into three sections; early music, traditional Sussex and the 'dynamite' electric band. Billed as 'Croydon's Christmas Ceilidh' tickets cost 80p on the door, 70p in advance.

1976

JANUARY

- 4 HEAVY METAL KIDS **G** (n/a)
- 11 RENAISSANCE **G** (n/a)
- 18 PRETTY THINGS **G** (n/a)
- 24 ELKIE BROOKS **CT** (85p to £1.25)
- 25 RONNIE LANE **G** + RAB NOAKES (n/a)
- 31 KURSAAL FLYERS **G** (n/a)

FEBRUARY

- 2 WOODY HERMAN **FH** (£1 to £2)
- 3 LABI SIFFRE **FH** (75p to £1.50)
- 5 SLIM WHITMAN **FH** (£1.50 to £3.50)
- 7 MEDICINE HEAD **CT** (85p to £1.25)
- 8 STEVE MARRIOTTS ALLSTARS **FH** + RACING CARS (£1.25 to £2)
- 8 STRAY **G** (n/a)
- 15 SAILOR **FH** + ALFALPHA (£1.50 to £2)
- 15 COLOSSEUM II **G** (n/a)
- 17 RALPH McTELL **FH** + PRELUDE (£1.25 to £2)
- 22 MANFRED MANN'S EARTHBAND **G** (n/a)
- 22 ANDY FAIRWEATHER LOW **FH** + LIMEY (75p to £1.50)
- 25 THE FATBACK BAND **T** (£1.50p)
- 31 10CC **FH** (n/a)

MARCH

- 2 JULIE FELIX **FH** (75p to £1.50)
- 7 THIN LIZZY **G** (n/a)
- 10 ALAN PRICE **FH** (£1 to £2)
- 12 THE YETTIES **FH** (£1 to £1.50)
- 14 KOKOMO **G** (n/a)
- 17 THE TYMES **T** (60p)
- 21 STACKRIDGE **G** (n/a)
- 22 DAVE BRUBECK **FH** (£1.50 to £3.25)
- 28 GONG **G** (n/a)
- 28 CAMEL **FH** (£1 to £2)

APRIL

- 4 PINK FAIRIES **G** (n/a)
- 5 FRANKIE VALLI & THE FOUR SEASONS **FH** + R &J STONE (£1.50 to £3)
- 6 DRIFTERS **T** (£1.25)
- 8 STYLISTICS **FH** + BROOK BENTON (£1.50 to £3)
- 11 HEAVY METAL KIDS **G** + EVIL WEASEL (n/a)
- 11 OSIBISA **FH** + GONZALEZ (£1.25 to £2)
- 18 LEO SAYER **FH** + GLYDER (£1 to £2.50)
- 22 BERT JANSCH **FH** (£1 to £1.25)
- 25 BUDGIE **G** (n/a)
- 25 BACK STREET CRAWLER **FH** (£1.25 to £2)
- 28 CHRIS BARBER **FH** (£1 to £1.50)

MAY

- 1 THE STRANGLERS **PH** (n/a)
- 2 CARAVAN **FH** + STARS (£1 to £2)
- 2 EDGAR BROUGHTON **G** (n/a)
- 9 BABE RUTH **G** (n/a)
- 9 ELTON JOHN **FH** + MURRAY HEAD (£2 to £3)
- 11 GEORGE MELLY **FH** (£1.25 to £2)
- 16 CANNED HEAT **G** (n/a)
- 23 DARYL HALL & JOHN OATES **FH** (£1 to £2)
- 23 STRAY **G** + EVIL WEASEL (n/a)
- 30 PRETTY THINGS **G** (n/a)

JUNE

- 6 BACK STREET CRAWLER **G** + AC/DC (n/a)
- 6 DR. HOOK **FH** + UNICORN (£1.25 to £2.50)
- 13 KURSAAL FLYERS **FH** + CRAZY CAVAN & THE RHYTHM ROCKERS (£1 to £1.50)
- 13 FAIRPORT **G** (n/a)
- 17 KENNY BALL **FH** (£1 to £1.50)
- 20 ALBERTO Y LOST TRIOS PARANOIAS **G** + EVIL WEASEL (n/a)
- 20 CURVED AIR **FH** + STRIFE (£1.25 to £1.75)
- 27 ERIC BURDON **G** (n/a)
- 27 OHIO PLAYERS **FH** (£1.50 to £3.25)

FH - Fairfield Halls • G - Greyhound • S - Star Hotel • RD - Red Deer • T - Tiffanys • CT - Croydon Tech.

I was interested to see that the support group to Manfred Mann's Earthband (Greyhound 22nd February) was **Why Worry**. The Advertiser review called them - '*...the best (support) I have heard at the Greyhound yet...*' and they certainly were a fine band. When I was at Reigate Art College, Why Worry were considered to be one of the 'college bands', as their drummer, Colin Robson was a graphics student there. The word was that Colin had auditioned for the drummers job in the Earthband, and been shortlisted, before finally losing out to Chris Slade. I saw them play a couple of the College parties and also at a charity gig held inside St. Matthews Church, Redhill (churches make great venues) - where their set included a superb acappella version of the Beatles *'Nowhere Man'*.

And talking of support bands, listen to what the Advertiser had to say about another 'up-&-coming' group...

Croydon Advertiser – 11.6.76

'Bright hopes of rock'

YOU REALLY should have been there on Sunday evening. Croydon's Greyhound creaked, groaned and almost came apart at the seams as two of rock's brightest hopes powered their way through three hours of brain-tearing music.

***AC/DC** were supposed to be the support band; but they played some of the best rock music I have ever heard anywhere. This was rock as it was always supposed to be - driving, raw and full of nervous energy. If you can catch a listen to their 'High Voltage' album, it's totally devastating. I particularly warn you about 'Live Wire' which is likely to leave you incapacitated for about a week.*

*There was a very real danger that the stars of the night, **Back Street Crawler**, were going to be blown clean off the stage. But they are a tight little band, playing very much in the Free/Bad Company mould and finally emerged with credit. 'Voodoo Woman' opened the proceedings and almost immediately one's thoughts went to the late Paul Kossoff. He WAS Back Street Crawler and many wondered whether the group would survive without him. But Geoff Whitehorne is a very able guitarist and he did his stuff without ever trying to emulate Kossoff.*

Whisper it discreetly, but January saw two local musicians join **Paper Lace**, yes, the group who sang 'Billy Don't Be A Hero' and other such dubious, albeit successful, ditties. The guilty pair were Peter Oliver, whose previous form included the New Seekers and guitarist Jamie Moses from rock band Merlin. Jamie comes clean about this particular career move on pages 198 - 201.

Former Small Faces and Humble Pie frontman **Steve Marriott** brought his 'AllStars' to Croydon in February for what was only the group's third British concert. The band comprised bassist Greg Ridley from Humble Pie, ex-King Crimson drummer Ian Wallace and guitarist Mickey Waller.

One of the most unusual bookings of the year took place at the start of May, when **The Stranglers** found themselves playing the Purley Halls, Banstead Road, Purley and facing an audience of Young Conservatives. Jet Black, the groups' drummer takes up the story; *"We'd talked our way into a gig, a ball, which was a really posh do! Very un-Stranglers - all the ladies were in ballgowns and all the men looked like penguins! We emptied the hall of nearly all two hundred and fifty people within about three songs - only one guy stayed and he loved it!"*

In true punk fashion, before the band started to play they told the startled audience *"...you won't like us, so you might as well fuck off now!"*

A Surrey band, they were originally known as The Guildford Stranglers; the members all lived above an off-licence in the town and spent their early days gigging around local pubs including the Greyhound in Redhill.

The late, great **Alex Campbell** played to a sparse audience at the Swan & Sugarloaf folk club on Thursday 13 May. Richard Evans reviewed the gig for the Advertiser and reported that only fourteen people turned out to see him; seventeen if you count Alex himself, the guitarist who accompanied him, plus his agent! In his heyday, Campbell packed almost 2,000 into the Fairfield Hall - yet even by the time this folk club date ended, Alex had doubled the audience to twenty eight.

Croydon Advertiser – 14.5.76

'Thunder? It was Elton!'

THUNDERSTORMS expected in the South East missed Croydon, but broke out in the Fairfield Halls on Sunday night. The electric atmosphere, which had been building up all evening, exploded suddenly just after 8.40 when on to the royal-red carpeted stage appeared a diminutive figure with a cocky grin stretching up to his white-framed tinted glasses.

While the deafening, pulsating music competed with the sounds of the fans, ***Elton John*** *- in candy pink jacket emblazoned with large blue piano keys, navy blue tracksuit trousers, his feet splayed into spangling sneakers - started to chimp about the stage. And under two banana-shaped arcs of more than 70 multi-coloured lights, he answered the tumult of shouts and applause by waving an enormous gilt banana that hung from a chain round his neck.*

He dared Kenny Passarelli to do the splits; he delivered Eric Morecambe style face-slaps to guitarist Davey Johnstone and threw a piano stool across the stage. He stood on the sequinned Steinway and conducted the masses; and if he's fought for Watford F.C., he took a willing Croydon by the scruff of its neck. "It's good to be back in Croydon" he yelled and the audience cheered - he launched into 'Goodbye Yellow Brick Road', and they cheered again. They needed only two or three bars before they cheered 'Island Girl', 'Rocket Man', 'Benny & the Jets' and 'Hercules'... "That's my middle name" he said, "I changed it from Dorothy. It's more butch".

All were powerful, gutsy extended versions; original rough gems, without the polish plastered on in recording studios and sounding even more like the child of some marriage between Beatles' lyricism and Stones' rock... But it was too LOUD.

"Louder than Concorde (but not quite as pretty)", was the only useful bit of information imparted by the glossy 50p programme. So loud that it wasn't only the fans, but also the floor of the auditorium that was doing the rock'n'roll. It was a gruelling 120 minutes plus, and more than once Elton John, the larger than life-size version of Reg Dwight, took off his glasses, rested his head on an amplifier and wiped or covered his head in a towel. Halfway through he called for a tea break and again rested while ghostly strains of music wafted over the patient audience and an eerie green light bathed the stage.

Then they were off again; the satanic Ray Cooper - who'd been snarling at the audience from his percussion 'cell' above the piano - beat an enormous gong dramatically bathed in a red spotlight. When Elton finally went off stage, the thunder from the stomping and shouts brought him back - with costume and glasses changed - for two encores, 'Saturday Night' and 'Pinball Wizard'. "We're going home after this one, I can tell you" he said, leaving the stage utterly exhausted and nursing a sore thumb from an over-enthusiastic hand shake.

Murray Head, with his rough David Gates/Cat Stevens voice, had the unenviable task of providing the warm-up, which was successful in bringing everyone to the boil.

Susie Cornfield

American boogie band **Canned Heat** played a storming set at the Greyhound on Sunday 16th May, the last date on a five week European tour. The band included larger-than-life singer Bob 'the Bear' Hite, his brother Ritchie and guest guitarist Stan Webb from British blues band Chicken Shack, who was said to be in inspired form on the night.

On Wednesday 26th May, **Pete Brown** made one of his rare appearances at the Star Hotel, with his new band led by Ian Lynn. Pete Brown is probably best known as the lyricist who collaborated with Jack Bruce on many of the songs for Cream, but his work goes back to the early 'sixties when he toured clubs like the Star in the company of Graham Bond and also appeared at the celebrated Fairfield Hall concerts by Ornette Coleman in 1965.

On 11th June, the Croydon Advertiser reported the tragic death of deputy arts editor **Barry Shinfield** who had drowned in Sandwich Bay, Kent on the previous Sunday. Aged 29, Barry began his journalistic career with the Kentish Gazette in Canterbury and on the Folkstone Herald before joining the Advertiser in June 1969 as a news reporter. He moved to the arts department, where his record and concert reviews showed him to be a '*well-informed, provocative and often brilliant writer on pop music and the arts*'.

JULY

4 SASSAFRAS **G** (n/a)

AUGUST

SEPTEMBER

3 FIVE HAND REEL **G** (n/a)
5 FATBACK BAND **FH** + HEATWAVE (£1.25 to £2.50)
12 KOKOMO **G** (n/a)
12 MANFRED MANN'S EARTHBAND **FH** + RACING CARS (£1.25 to £2)
17 DON WILLIAMS **FH** (£1.50 to £3.50)
19 FRANKIE MILLER's FULL HOUSE **G** (n/a)
22 HOT CHOCOLATE **FH** (£1.25 to £2.50)
26 STRAY **G** + R.D.B. (n/a)
30 STAN KENTON **FH** (£1 to £2.25)

OCTOBER

3 SASSAFRAS **G** (n/a)
7 THE SPINNERS **FH** (£1 to £1.75)
8 ALAN PRICE **FH** + LAMPLIGHT (£1 to £2)
10 SUTHERLAND BROS. & QUIVER **FH** + MOON (£1.25 to £2)
10 CURVED AIR **G** + A BAND CALLED LIPS (n/a)
12 THE CHIEFTAINS **FH** (£1.50 to £2.50)
17 EDDIE & THE HOT RODS **G** (n/a)
24 BARCLAY JAMES HARVEST **FH** + EASY STREET (£1.50 to £2.50)
25 FOUR TOPS **FH** + EDWIN STARR (£1.25 to £3.25)
25 SLIK **T** (75p to £1.00)
28 CLIFF RICHARD **FH** (£1 to £2.50)
29 CLIFF RICHARD **FH** (£1 to £2.50)
31 WISHBONE ASH **FH** + SUPERCHARGE (£1.50 to £2.50)
31 GROUNDHOGS **G** (n/a)

NOVEMBER

7 FAIRPORT **FH** + ARBRE (£1.25 to £2)
7 CLIMAX BLUES BAND **G** + SQUEEZE (n/a)
14 TANGERINE DREAM **FH** (£1.25 to £2.50)
14 DEAF SCHOOL **G** + THE BABYS (n/a)
18 EVIL WEASEL **RD** (n/a)
20 DOCTORS OF MADNESS **DH** (n/a)
21 RANDY EDELMAN **FH** (£1 to £2.50) *CANCELLED*
21 FLAMIN' GROOVIES **G** + THE DAMNED (n/a)
22 JIMMY JAMES & THE VAGABONDS **T** (£1)
27 EARL OKIN **W** + DOWNES & BEER + SPINNING WHEEL (£1.50)
28 KURSAAL FLYERS **FH** + BURLESQUE (£1 to £1.50)
28 EDDIE & THE HOT RODS **G** + ASWAD + THE DAMNED (n/a)
29 THE DUBLINERS **FH** (£1.25 to £2)

DECEMBER

4 KOKOMO **G** + JOE COCKER + GHOST (n/a)
5 MAN **FH** + ALKATRAZ (£1.50 to £2.50)
7 THE WURZELS **FH** + THE NEW VAUDEVILLE BAND (£1 to £1.50)
9 BABE RUTH **RD** (75p)
16 JOAN ARMATRADING **FH** + PRELUDE (£1 to £2)
19 BUDGIE **G** (n/a)

(n/a) = ticket price not available.

In his book on **Supertramp**, author Martin Melhuish followed the group on their '75 tour (not '76) and noted this incident from the bands Fairfield Hall concert on November 16th:

"Because of its proximity to London, the Croydon gig was a fairly important one for the band. The press would be there in full force and they found out that A & M's Jerry Moss would be in attendance, along with the promoter for most of the British dates, Peter Bowyer.

On the first tour of England that Supertramp had done with Bowyer, the promoter had worn a white suit to each one of the concerts. As a bit of a joke on Bowyer, this time around, the band stipulated in their rider, (a document attached to the usual contract indicating the bands technical and backstage requirements), that the promoter had to wear a white suit. Of course, this stipulation was only meant for the eyes of Peter Bowyer, but somebody had forgotten to take out this clause when the contract was sent to other promoters. Figuring that it was just another eccentricity from a rock band, a number of the other promoters actually called up to ask if they too had to wear a white suit to the concert.

Supertramp had their quirks, but choosing a promoters evening wear was certainly not one of them, beyond the inside joke with Peter Bowyer."

The CBS single 'I Love To Love' finally catapulted 20 year old singer **Tina Charles** to the top of the charts. Born in Whitechapel and raised in Essex, Tina had been living in a Streatham flat with her partner Trevor Horn and had joined a club band called Nicki North & Northern Lights which had a residency in a Purley club. Also in that band was Martin Jay (no relation to the Croydon 'sixties vocalist) who decided to form his own group 5,000 Volts; and when they recorded their single 'I'm On Fire', Tina supplied the lead vocal. Under contract to CBS, Tina couldn't admit to being their singer and apart from the £200 session fee, had to sit and watch while 'I'm On Fire' rocketed into the charts all over Europe.

After the success of 'I Love To Love' and further subsequent hit records, Tina left Trevor Horn and moved to live in Caterham Valley with her new husband, and son Max. She quit the music business in 1979 to spend more time with her young son but made a comeback at the end of the 'eighties when a re-mixed version of her biggest hit went top ten in France and Germany.

Many of the live shots in this book were taken by local photographer **Frazer Ashford**, who covered rock concerts for the Croydon Advertiser between 1972 -1977. He was a free-lancer at the time, whose monopoly of music photography in the area really began because the Staff photographers working for the Advertiser were refused paid overtime on Sundays. Frazer stepped in, offered to cover the Sunday night rock gigs and the local paper agreed to use them.

Throughout the early '70's, Frazer spent most of his weekends at Croydon concerts, working late into the night processing and printing, often driving up to London in the early hours to sell prints to the national music press. His first rock pics were taken at the Orchid Ballroom in Purley, including the shot of Rufus Thomas on page 75 and he went on to cover gigs at the Star, the Greyhound and the Dog & Bull in Surrey Street. It was here that the rehearsal shots of local favourites Budlippspringer (page 153) were taken.

Through his work at the Fairfield concerts, Frazer was also asked to take publicity pictures for several artists; early New Seekers, Gene Pitney and the Four Tops, amongst others.

Frazer has good cause to remember the Fairfield gig by **Manfred Mann's Earthband**, 12th September 1976. He was working down at the front as usual and had only clicked over half a film, when the manager tapped his shoulder to say that a person was in the foyer insisting they get into the concert to speak to him. Frazer left the concert to investigate and found an anxious mother-in-law with a taxi, waiting to whisk him away to Mayday hospital, where his wife Claire had gone into labour. Frazer arrived just in time to see the birth of daughter Rebecca.

As a further result of his Fairfield work, Frazer moved into the world of theatre and stage photography, covering productions not only at the Ashcroft and the new Warehouse Theatre, but all over the country, holding exhibitions of his work both here and in the USA. Frazer's negative archive now runs to over 36,000 frames! No longer a professional photographer, he has remained working in the entertainment industry, in the fields of T.V., film and video.

The Fairfield Hall concert on September 17th was the opening night of the British tour for Country star **Don Williams**. In attendance were 'fans' Eric Clapton and Patti Harrison; after the show, Eric invited Don and the band back to his house for a jam session that carried on into the early hours of next morning. On the 18th, the tour moved on to the Hammersmith Odeon, where Eric joined Don onstage to play dobro.

Frazer Ashford

Manfred Mann (right) jokes with his lead guitarist during the early part of their set at the Fairfield Hall - 12th September 1976.

Towards the end of 76, the seeds of a new movement were being sown for the next teenage sub-culture that would emerge as PUNK! Out of the unlikely suburbs of Kent came a group of fans who became known as the **Bromley Contingent**, who began by following the Sex Pistols around after seeing them play at Ravensbourne Art College at the beginning of the year.

The 'Contingent' consisted of Steve, Simon, Debbie, Bill and Suzie and from then on they turned up at every gig, including driving over to a Punk festival in France where the five of them slept in a minivan. At the gig in Paris, Suzie was punched in the face after some people objected to her outfit of topless black plastic corset, suspender belt, fishnet tights and swastika armband!

In October, Britain's first Punk rock festival was held at the 100 Club in Oxford Street and a couple of the Bromley Contingent decided to perform. Somewhere down the bill from the Sex Pistols and the Clash, Suzie and Steve Severin put together a scratch band that included Sid Vicious on drums, to perform as **Siouxsie & the Banshees**.

Suzie, sorry - Siouxsie!, grew up in Chislehurst, Kent and attended college in Orpington. But it wasn't only the members of the Bromley Contingent who became famous in the punk movement; Adam Ant (Stuart Goddard) came from Orpington, while Generation X singer Billy Idol came from Bromley, as did the original drummer with the Clash, Topper Headon.

The September gig by **Manfred Mann's Earthband** was part of their 'Roaring Silence' tour and coincided with a hit single - their version of Bruce Springsteen's 'Blinded By The Light'. The set also featured 'Father Of Day, Father of Night', 'Joybringer' and 'Waiter, There's A Yawn In My Ear' from the new album, plus the usual encore of 'Mighty Quinn' from Manfred's earlier days.

I remember the support band as being a bit special - a Welsh group called **Racing Cars**, led by Morty, a barefoot miniature version of Roger Chapman. Unusually for a support act, they also had a single in the charts, 'They Shoot Horses, Don't They', inspired by the film of the same name. As is often the case, the hit was not really representative of the rest of their material - they were very rocky, extremely tight and musically proficient, with a pair of guitarists swapping the lead parts between them.

Forget that extra pint in the bar - never miss the support band, that's my advice.

Croydon Advertiser – 24.12.76

'Black 'n' blues girl'

*SHE USES HER voice like Shirley Bassey uses her body; and if blue jeans, a white shirt and corked feet don't conjure up a picture of sexuality, somehow **Joan Armatrading** at Fairfield on Thursday, overcame the problem. She even managed to make the guitar seem a physical, pulsating part of herself.*

Following the neat, sweet harmonic sounds of a mediocre Prelude, she walked onto a Pinter-esque stage jungled with speakers - plus her four musicians, including ex-Fairporters Jerry Donahue and Dave Mattacks - and sprouting two dozen bulbed beanstalks and a huge goalpost frame of some two dozen lights. There was applause and a sprinkling of cheers: but it seemed that most people had come on the strength of her hit single, "Love and Affection".

She started singing the moment she reached the microphone. Singing rock, ballads and her own particular brand of bruised black'n'blues that ably demonstrated her powerful, volcanic voice. A voice deep, dark and molten like the bowels of the earth, that would suddenly erupt into a lighter, higher purity.

If she started the evening as an unknown quantity, Joan Armatrading ended it - after two strenuously demanded encores - by proving herself to be a lady of considerable quality.

S.K.P.C.

JANUARY

- 1 STRAY **G** (n/a)
- 8 SLAUGHTER & THE DOGS **G** (n/a)
- 20 STRANGLERS **RD** (70p)
- 27 BURLESQUE **RD** (70p)

FEBRUARY

- 3 ALBION DANCE BAND **FH** (£1.25 to £2.50)
- 3 MEAL TICKET **RD** (70p)
- 7 GEORGE MELLY **RD** (70p)
- 10 THE VIBRATORS **RD** (70p)
- 13 RACING CARS **G** (n/a)
- 15 GALLAGHER & LYLE **FH** (£1 to £2.50)
- 21 LITTLE BOB STORY **RD** + MOTORHEAD (70p)
- 24 THE HEARTBREAKERS **RD** + SIOUX & THE BANSHEES (70p)
- 25 KATE & ANNA McGARRIGLE **FH** + FIVE HAND REEL (£1.50 to £2.50)
- 27 PROCOL HARUM **FH** + HERON (£1.25 to £2)
- 27 ALBERTOS Y LOST TRIOS PARANOIAS **G** (n/a)
- 28 ROY ORBISON **FH** (£1.50 to £3.50)

MARCH

- 3 GEORGE HAMILTON IV **FH** + PETE SAYERS + COLT 45 (£1.50 to £3.50)
- 3 THE FLYING ACES **RD** (70p)
- 6 GRAHAM PARKER & THE RUMOUR **FH** + SOUTHSIDE JOHNNY & THE ASBURY JUKES (£1.25 to £2.50)
- 6 CAN **G** (£1.40)
- 10 OSCAR PETERSON **FH** (£1.50 to £2.50)
- 13 CADO BELLE **G** + JENNY DARREN (n/a)
- 17 JACQUES LOUISSIER **FH** (£1.25 to £2.50)
- 17 SAM APPLE PIE **RD** (70p)
- 20 JAN AKKERMAN **FH** (£1.25 to £2.50)
- 24 ULTRAVOX **RD** (70p)
- 27 OSIBISA **FH** (£1.50 to £2.50)

APRIL

- 3 ALBERTOS Y LOST TRIOS PARANOIAS **G** (n/a)
- 7 WAYNE COUNTY **RD** (70p)
- 12 RANDY EDELMAN **FH** (£1.25 to £2.50)
- 14 NASTY POP **RD** (70p)
- 15 TWIGGY **FH** + CHIP HAWKES (£1.50 to £3)
- 17 STYLISTICS **FH** + 5000 VOLTS (£1.25 to £2.50)
- 17 STRAY **G** (n/a)
- 21 DOWNLINERS SECT **RD** (70p)
- 24 JOHN CALE **G** + THE COUNT BISHOPS (n/a)
- 28 BEES MAKE HONEY **RD** (70p)

MAY

- 1 DETROIT SPINNERS **FH** + BRASS CONSTRUCTION (£1.25 to £2.50)
- 1 JUDAS PRIEST **G** (n/a)
- 5 THE VIBRATORS **RD** (70p)
- 8 MR. BIG **G** (n/a)
- 10 JAKE THACKRAY **FH** (£1.25 to £2)
- 12 PETE BROWN's BACK TO THE FRONT **RD** (70p)
- 15 DORY PREVIN **FH** + ILLUSION (£2 to £3)
- 15 FRANKIE MILLER's FULL HOUSE **G** (n/a)
- 22 THE SHADOWS **FH** (£1 to £3)
- 24 CHRIS BARBER **FH** (£1 to £1.50)
- 29 THE RAMONES **G** + TALKING HEADS (n/a)

JUNE

- 2 THE SPINNERS **FH** (£1.25 to £2.50)
- 3 RALPH McTELL **FH** + MAGNA CARTA (£1.50 to £3)
- 5 BURLESQUE **G** (n/a)
- 9 999 **RD** (40p)
- 12 KURSAAL FLYERS **G** (n/a)
- 16 STEPHAN GRAPPELLI **FH** (£1 to £2)
- 16 SKREWDRIVER **RD** (40p)
- 19 THE SAINTS **G** (n/a)
- 23 ALTERNATIVE TV **RD** (40p)
- 26 THE JAM **G** (n/a)
- 30 SQUEEZE **RD** (40p)

Fox Leisure, ever on the lookout to expand their empire, began the year by introducing regular gigs at their new venue, **The Red Deer** on the Brighton Road, South Croydon. Their plan was to 'showcase fringe groups' on a Thursday night, an idea which led to an interesting mix of rock, jazz and punk bands, such as George Melly one week, followed by the Vibrators the next! Kicking off the new regime were **The Stranglers**, and this is what the Advertiser had to say:

Croydon Advertiser – 28.1.77

'Punk Rock was here'

PUNK ROCKERS come to Croydon - thousands hurt, hundreds of innocents shocked!.

No, seriously, it wasn't like that at all. But it is true that this was the first time that the real punks had come to Croydon, and they certainly caused a stir. They came in their tight mock-leather trousers, golden razor-blade earrings and coloured hair. The 'straight' members of the audience thought it was a laugh, but it was sufficiently interesting for French TV to come over and film the event.

So, what about The Stranglers themselves, the ones who actually play the music? Well, in short, not bad.

Oddly enough, they looked fairly normal chaps - shortish hair, jeans and T-shirts. But I had a pretty good idea of the music we were going to have, when the DJ played AC/DC, the Ramones and Eddie & the HotRods in quick succession. I am told by the knowledgeable that The Stranglers are not true punks. "It's called high energy rock, man", explained the razor-blade.

The Stranglers sure do play high energy rock; a sort of combination of early Doors (if you can remember that far back) and Roxy Music. 'Sometimes' was typical of the racy, organ-layered riffs that they shot at you, from behind an undergrowth of bass and drums. 'Hanging Around' took the audience by the proverbial scruff of the neck, dropping them only when the group decided they wanted the bright lights (put up for the TV), turned off.

The polite clapping at the end of the show suggested that the Stranglers had done enough to interest people, but maybe not enough to really captivate them.

Charles Balchin

Although they had played at the 100 Club Punk festival towards the end of '76, the first touring line-up of **Siouxsie & the Banshees** (Siouxsie Sioux, Steve Severin, Peter Fenton and Kenny Morris) made their debut in Croydon on February 24th, as noted by their manager Nils Stevenson: *"As a favour to me, Lee Black Childers and the Heartbreakers let us support them, purely out of the kindness of their hearts, I'm sure! So they did their first gig at the Red Deer, South Croydon. I was just so nervous, so were the band, Sioux's voice was cracking and I just got as pissed as I could. I couldn't cope with listening to it. Oh God! Anyway, everyone came away patting each other on the back saying, 'It was brilliant...' one of those things, first gig! You've got to pretend it was real good. So that was that, first gig over and everyone was relieved."*

From the book 'Siouxsie & the Banshees' by ace photographer Ray Stevenson, older brother of Nils.

Local punks the **Damned** were due to play the Red Deer on 3rd March, but had to be replaced at short notice by **The Flying Aces**, led by ex-Man bassist Martin Ace and described by the Advertiser's Dave Jones as *"an engaging bunch of hippies"*. However, two members of the Damned did turn up at the Greyhound gig by **Alberto Y Lost Trios Paranoias**, as reported by one time-Advertiser journalist Charles Balchin in the short lived music paper 'National Rock Star':

National Rock Star – 5.3.77

THE PROBLEM with the Alberto's is that they're so damn funny. *That may be odd in this day and age when humour is so lacking in music, but it's true. The problem is that you're so busy laughing or looking for the next punchline, that there is never really time to take anything seriously.*

First, let me say that they're very good at what they do - a sort of musical Mike Yarwood and no one escapes their sarcastic scrutiny. There's Ted Nutter prancing around the stage and a 'Bob Marley' who appears in 'The Funky Alberto'; actually it's a woolly hat with about ten black springs draped on it, but from a distance it really does look like dreadlocks. The highlight of the evening is the take-off of punk rock, where the band play a note for note version of the Damned's 'New Rose' - until suddenly Rat Scabies appeared from the sidelines to spit beer into the face of lead guitarist Simon White. Captain Sensible joined in and it became a free for all. The Albertos and the Damned have struck up a friendship in recent weeks and it came to a head when Sensible and Scabies took over on bass and drums - it was a total disaster and the funniest part of the evening.

Frazer Ashford

Kate and Anna McGarrigle relax backstage at the Fairfield Hall, before relaxing a little too much onstage later that evening!

French-Canadian folk rock duo **Kate & Anna McGarrigle** appeared at the Fairfield on Friday 25th February and were their usual contrary selves, judging by the review of Sandy Harrod in the Advertiser. In live performance the McGarrigle sisters can either be breathtakingly brilliant or frustratingly inept; it almost becomes part of their charm but you 'pays your money and takes your choice' when going to see them in concert.

As Sandy put it: *"A pernicious form of creeping paralysis seemed to take over Kate & Anna on Friday night... seemingly free and emancipated, quaint and gauche at first, the duo so completely lacked any taste or talent for showmanship that their music, like their performance, turned to stone... their own compositions are excellent, while they have unusual, interesting voices and both play well enough. But music has to have feeling - it's not enough just to "get it right" as Kate said at one point... if they had purposely tried to sabotage their own act, they could not have done a better job".*

Purley rock band **Maverick** entered the annual Melody Maker folk/rock competition, in search of that elusive recording contract, or at the very least some cash and new equipment. The group, who composed most of their own material, comprised Ian Stuart (guitar), Nigel Horwood (vocals, guitar), Mike Vincent (bass, keyboards) and Tim Clay (drums). Their first step towards fame and fortune came in the area heats held at the University of Surrey, Guildford at the beginning of April. Ian told me - *'We didn't get through the heat, but it was very enjoyable playing on a big stage to such a large and enthusiastic audience'.*

Ian and Nigel, both aged 21, had left Trinity School, Croydon shortly before the contest, to move into further education, but they returned to the school with their group on June 26th to play their biggest ever gig in front of 500 people, supported by Weird Sister.

During the last week in March, two rock bands cancelled out Croydon gigs within the space of a few days. **Motorhead** failed to appear at the Red Deer on Thursday 17th, reason unknown. Prior to that, on Sunday 13th, a capacity 900 crowd had to be turned away from the Greyhound when **AC/DC** quit at the last moment. A spokesperson for the band said that the Foxes management had failed to provide enough stage hands, but Kevin Barry, Foxes promotions manager told the Advertiser - *'I just don't think they wanted to do the show at all'.*

Having left Evil Weasel, Steve Boyce joined forces with Ronnie Sims - guitar, vox, Rick Luck - bass, Jerry Wickins - drums and vocalist Kevin McCrea to form the **Steve Boyce Band**. They became especially popular at the Red Deer, South Croydon, where they played once a month and regularly packed the place out. Two up and coming bands who supported them at the Red Deer were **Iron Maiden** in November '77 and **Samson** towards the end of '78.

The Steve Boyce Band were 'spotted' one evening by Troy Dante (of 'Troy Dante & the Inferno's' fame), who reported back to WEA A&R man Dave Dee, (of 'Dozy, Beaky, Mick & Tich' fame), who subsequently signed them to the label. The group were put into a London studio to record an albums worth of material, but when the people at Warners felt that they couldn't hear a hit single in amongst Steve's songs, they presented the band with a 'surefire' hit written by Keith Chegwin! The song simply didn't suit their style and was recorded but never released. Their career with Warners came to a sudden end when an American Director was installed during a management re-shuffle and proceeded to axe all the recently signed bands.

Their live work continued to pick up a loyal following, playing widely across London and the South East, including gigs at the Rock Garden, The Music Machine and Dingwalls in Camden and the 101 Club, Clapham where the support act was a young Scottish band with a battered van and a sound akin to Genesis - **Marillion**!

Breaking out of the pub rock circuit, **Graham Parker & the Rumour** brought their big, brassy rock'n'soul sound to Croydon on 6th March. The ten-piece line-up included Brinsley Schwarz on guitar and Bob Andrews on piano, both from the late, lamented **Brinsley Schwarz** plus Martin Belmont from pub-rockers Ducks Deluxe. The concert also featured strong support from US band (and friends of Bruce Springsteen), **Southside Johnny & the Asbury Dukes**.

JULY

3 THE VIBRATORS **G** + BERNIE TORME (n/a)
6 MR. ACKER BILK **FH** (£1 to £1.50)
7 BOOMTOWN RATS **RD** (n/a)
14 WIRE **RD** (n/a)

AUGUST

00 JOHNNY MOPED **RD** (n/a)

SEPTEMBER

4 BUZZCOCKS **G** + THE WORST (n/a)
11 LONDON **G** + THE VICTIMS + SWORDS (n/a)
15 GEORGE MELLY **FH** (£1.25 to £2)
18 ELKIE BROOKS **FH** (£1.50 to £3)
18 999 **G** (n/a)
25 HAWKWIND **FH** (£2 to £2.75)
25 STEVE GIBBONS BAND **G** (n/a)
26 WOODY HERMAN **FH** (£1.25 to £2.75)
27 THE DUBLINERS **FH** (£1.25 to £2)

OCTOBER

2 GENERATION X **G** + ART ATTAX (n/a)
8 BARCLAY JAMES HARVEST **FH** (£2 to £2.50)
9 SIOUXSIE & THE BANSHEES **G** + THE SLITS (n/a)
12 BROTHERHOOD OF MAN **FH** (£1.50 to £3)
16 'STIFF'S GREATEST STIFFS' **FH** (£2 to £2.75)
16 THE HEARTBREAKERS **G** + BOYS + SLAUGHTER & THE DOGS (n/a)
23 THE ADVERTS **G** + FRUIT EATING BEARS (n/a)
30 FAIRPORT CONVENTION **FH** (£1.50 to £2.50)
30 BOOMTOWN RATS **G** + BERNIE TORME (n/a)

NOVEMBER

6 THE HEARTBREAKERS **G** + THE MODELS (n/a)
6 JIM CAPALDI & THE CONTENDERS **FH** + MEAL TICKET (£1.50 to £2.50)
8 THE CHIEFTAINS **FH** (£1.50 to £3)
11 SANDY DENNY **FH** + DANNY THOMPSON (£1.50 to £2.50)
13 THE BUZZCOCKS **G** + THE LURKERS (n/a)
13 THE FOUR TOPS **FH** (£1.50 to £3.50)
20 BURLESQUE **G** + BAZOOMIS (n/a)
20 GRAHAM PARKER & THE RUMOUR **FH** + CLOVER (£1.50 to £2.50)
21 BARBARA DICKSON **FH** (£1.50 to £2.50)
24 CLIFF RICHARD **FH** (£1.50 to £3.50)
25 CLIFF RICHARD **FH** (£1.50 to £3.50)
27 TOM ROBINSON **G** + NO DICE (n/a)

DECEMBER

4 IAN DURY BAND **G** + RAT SCABIES' RUNNERS (n/a)
9 JOHN MILES **FH** + TRICKSTER (£1.25 to £2.50)
11 THE JAM **G** + NEW HEARTS (n/a)
18 GENERATION X **G** (n/a)
24 WEIRD SISTER **RD** (n/a)

(n/a) = ticket price not available.

Mid-way through the Queen's Silver Jubilee year and Punk had gripped the live music scene firmly by the lapels and proceeded to give it a damn good shaking. The Greyhound had become 'Surrey's Premier New Wave Venue' according to it's publicity handouts and journalist Charles Balchin was now 'punk correspondent' for the Croydon Advertiser.

In September he went along to see Riff Regan's **London**, but pronounced them to be just 'mediocre'. Balchin's problem with the group and indeed with many of the punk bands, was summed up by their performance of the Easybeat's 'Friday On My Mind'. He wrote: *"On record, it was a mess. On stage, with the electricity buzzing to and from band to audience, it was really quite good. Unless the New Wave can find an answer to this dilemma, I think the whole scene may collapse - because in the end, it is the records which make money".*

My own abiding memory of this mayhem was the **Generation X** gig in October. I had been coaxed into going along by a friend who had just heard the *'Ready, Steady, Go'* single and the pair of us must have stood out in the queue like the proverbial sore thumbs. The rest of the crowd were in full regalia; the black bin liners, the safety pins down the lapels of the ripped jackets, the unbelievable, gravity-defying hairstyles – mind you, I was still at Art college and had been growing mine since 1974 – the punks probably thought the same about Daryl and I !

Despite their aggressive look and occasional anti-social behaviour, they were just another rock crowd out for a good time. When two menacing looking girls approached us we began to wonder what was coming - had they been 'egged-on' by their boyfriends to go and worry the two hippies? In fact they just asked if we would look after their bags while they threw themselves into the mock-fighting! As for the bands, they were loud and energetic but fairly tuneless; the **Art Attax**, led by cartoonist Savage Pencil were dreadful (his artwork for the music paper Sounds was far better) and as for Gen. X's **Billy Idol** - well, who at the time would have believed that he would later become an FM West coast rock star - exactly the same type of music that punk did it's best to destroy.

Elkie Brooks visit on the 18th September was the fourth night of a short eight-date tour and she brought with her a new band that included two musicians from her days in Vinegar Joe; guitarist and at that time, husband, Pete Gage and bassist Steve York. The rest of the band were Trevor Morais - drums, Ken Freeman - synthesisers and Tim Hinkley on keyboards, plus the addition of John Edmed on pedal steel.

The first, and quite possibly the best of the packages put together by the wonderful Stiff Records was the 'Stiff's Greatest Stiff's' tour that hit Croydon on 16th October. A sensational line-up included Nick Lowe, Elvis Costello, Wreckless Eric, Larry Wallis and Ian Dury & the Blockheads. Lowe's group went under the name 'Last Chicken In The Shop' and featured guitarists Dave Edmunds and Billy Bremner. The tour was very democratic; all the bands travelled in the same coach and onstage shared the same P.A. system. Publicity for the tour noted that - "All the acts are playing sets of equal time... but the playing order will change nightly". Somewhere along the way the gigs were recorded and released as the 'Live Stiff's Live' album, most notable for Costello's version of the Bert Bacharach/Hal David classic 'I Just Don't Know What To Do With Myself'.

As a Fairport Convention fan (don't tell me you hadn't noticed), I was privileged to see **Sandy Denny** at the Fairfield in November, on what was tragically to be her last solo tour. The ex-Fairport vocalist turned in a strong performance, despite the inconvenience of a heavy cold and she spent most of the evening seated at the piano, atop which sat various cold cure remedies and some Vicks Synex! Her band contained Pat Donaldson and Trevor Lucas from the short-lived Fotheringay, as well as Fairport drummer Dave Mattacks, but the material was strictly Sandy - any audience requests for old Fairport standards such as 'Matty Groves' or 'Tam Lin', were firmly refused. The support slot was filled by Danny Thompson, no easy task for a man alone with his double bass, but his amiable personality and humourous stories more than made up for the absence of extra musicians.

On 23rd November, punk band the **U.K. Subs** were booked to play at 'Scamps' Nightclub in Crown Hill, Croydon. Due to the licensing laws at the club, the manager was obliged to put on some live music, although his clientele were more used to visiting soul & disco acts. Consequently the U.K. Subs played their 45 minute set *before* the doors of the club were even opened and duly received £35, which was more than their usual fee!

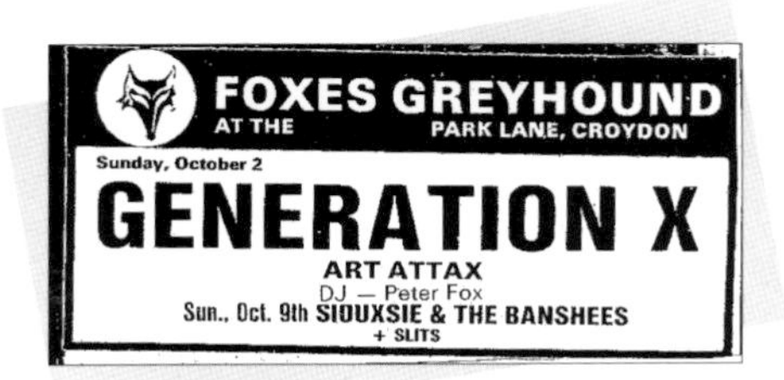

Croydon Advertiser – 16.12.77

'Gay Rule OK'

GAY RULED at the Greyhound on Sunday. I mean, there we all were enjoying the ***Tom Robinson Band****, those self-confessed bastions of Gay Power, when suddenly our Tom pulls out the plugs and says he ain't coming back till everyone stops gobbing.*

I mean you've gotta be confident to pull that kind of stunt. It can easily backfire if people just carry right on spitting. But no, Tom and the boys go off for three minutes and guess what? When they come back on, no spitting.

The Tom Robinson Band sure ain't no punk band, but they've come in on the new wave. Actually they're a good old-fashioned protest band, whether it be against the police, the politicians or the Establishment. Of course, their big thing is gay power, and it came through in quite a few of their songs. But first there was '2468 Motorway' and what a cheer that got.

Then came the band's anthem, 'Glad To Be Gay' and boy, did Tom put some feeling into that. He was damn near choking back the tears. Then it was 'Power In The Darkness' and finally 'We Ain't Going To Take It'. With a title like that, need I say more?

Charles Balchin

Courtesy Steve Boyce

Local guitarist Steve Boyce sweats his way through yet another pub gig.

In amongst all the anarchy and general punk rock mayhem, the Fairfield could still find room for **Cliff Richard** to play his annual brace of Croydon gigs come November. But if a persistent fault in the sound system meant that the show was not quite as perfect as we've come to expect - Cliff of course, was as polished and professional as ever. "Lets do some of the old stuff, yes?" he asked the audience; "I was sure some of the old pensioners would be in tonight... and most of them are on stage!"

Taking a break from The Damned, drummer Rat Scabies formed the short-lived **Rat Scabies' Runners** in November. The band only played two gigs, as Rat told journalist Pete Frame: *"The first, at the Speakeasy, was an absolute disaster. The next night, we supported Ian Dury at the Croydon Greyhound... the audience hated it, the band hated it and I hated it... I suppose in a way it was quite a good gig!"*

The band consisted of Rat on drums, vocalist Kevin Blacklock, Steve Turner on bass and guitarist Denise Mercedes. Denise had flown over from Greenwich Village, New York, having initially met The Damned when they played at CBGB's earlier in the year.

Scabies, Blacklock & Turner carried on together in two further groups, Drunk & Disorderly and the White Cats, before Rat rejoined the Damned in September 1978.

Croydon Advertiser – 16.12.77

'It's hot, like it was in 1965'

THE RAILWAY PUB, 1965, it's hot, unbearably so, kids faint and have to be taken out. Townshend smashes his guitar with cutting chords, violence reigns. The Greyhound pub, 1977, it's hot, unbearably so, kids faint and have to be taken out. Weller smashes his guitar with cutting chords, violence reigns.

Point taken? I mean ***The Jam*** *and The Who are so similar it's just not true. And you've got to say early on that the Jam make no attempt to hide where they get their inspiration from. On the cover of the new album Paul Weller wears a Who badge and looks suitably angry with life. Even the songs are reminiscent - 'Modern World', 'London Traffic', 'In The City' - the titles are grass-roots, the music is grass-roots.*

The Jam are one of the best new wave bands around, with plenty of fire and guts. Weller twirls and splits his body, Bruce Foxton's bass bam-bams through the P.A. and Rick Buckler lays down the beat. Encore time and it was 'All Around The World', great cheers, more heat, more faintings, more violence. Great night, lost three pounds, must go again.

Charles Balchin

JANUARY

1 THE BOYS **G** + THE FORCE (n/a)
8 SLAUGHTER & THE DOGS **G** + MILK (£1)
15 THE DAMNED **G** (n/a)
22 GEORGE MELLY **G** (£1.60)
25 THE DAMNED **G** (n/a)
26 LABI SIFFRE **FH** (£1 to £2)
29 ULTRAVOX **G** + THE DOLL (n/a)
31 MARY O'HARA **FH** (£1 to £3)

FEBRUARY

5 OSIBISA **FH** + SPARTACUS (£1.50 to £2.50)
5 TALKING HEADS **G** + DIRE STRAITS (n/a)
11 WEIRD SISTER **CT** (n/a)
12 SIOUXSIE & THE BANSHEES **G** + THE UNWANTED (n/a)
16 ROY CASTLE **FH** + CLIFF RICHARD + DANA + NEIL REID (£1.50 to £4)
19 WIRE **G** + THE STUKA'S (n/a)
26 THE STRAWBS **FH** + ROY HILL BAND (£1.25 to £2.50)
26 THE ADVERTS **G** + THE NIGHT (n/a)

MARCH

1 GILBERT O'SULLIVAN **FH** + OFANCHI (£1.50 to £3)
5 RICH KIDS **G** + DYAKS (n/a)
12 HOT CHOCOLATE **FH** (£2 to £3.50)
12 MOTORHEAD **G** + PSYCHO'S (n/a)
16 CHRIS DE BURGH **FH** + PHILIP GOODHAND-TAIT (£1.25 to £2.50)
19 GORDON GILTRAP **FH** (£1.50 to £2.50)
19 VIBRATORS **G** + THE YOUNG ONES (n/a)
22 SLADE **T** (£1.50)
26 GENERATION X **G** + THE JOLT (n/a)
27 TANGERINE DREAM **FH** (£1.50 to £3.50)
29 BOOMTOWN RATS **G** (£1.75)
30 JOHNNY NASH **FH** + BLACK GOLD (£1.50 to £3)

APRIL

2 THE BUZZCOCKS **G** + THE SLITS (£1.75)
9 DAVE SWARBRICK & FRIENDS **FH** (£1.50 to £2.50)
9 WRECKLESS ERIC **G** + THE DYAKS (£1.75)
16 RANDY EDELMAN **FH** (£1.50 to £2.50)
16 X-RAY SPEX **G** + SKID MARX (n/a)
20 CHRIS BARBER **FH** (£1.25 to £2.50)
23 MANFRED MANN's EARTHBAND **FH** (£1.50 to £3)
23 SLAUGHTER & THE DOGS **G** + REACTION (n/a)
30 THE NEW SEEKERS **FH** (£1 to £2.50)
30 MAGAZINE **G** + THE MUSE (n/a)

MAY

4 SAD CAFE **FH** (£1.50 to £2.50)
7 SIOUXSIE & THE BANSHEES **G** + THE FALL (n/a)
12 GEORGE MELLY **FH** (£1.25 to £2)
14 LINDISFARNE **FH** + MIKE ELLIOTT (£1.75 to £3)
14 RADIO STARS **G** + THE BOYFRIENDS (£1.90)
21 STEVE HILLAGE **G** + NATIONAL HEALTH (£1.90)
25 BONNIE TYLER **FH** (£1.25 to £2.75)
28 THE MOTORS **G** (£1.90)
31 JOE PASS **FH** (£1.25 to £2.50)

JUNE

1 MADDY PRIOR **FH** + ANDY DESMOND (£1.50 to £2.50)
2 HARRY CHAPIN **FH** (£1.50 to £3.25)
4 GERRY RAFFERTY **FH** (£1.50 to £2.50)
4 FLAMIN' GROOVIES **G** (£1.90)
7 PARAPHERNALIA **CA** - *see text* (£1)
16 GEORGIE FAME & THE BLUE FLAMES **FH** (£1.25 to £2)
22 MR. ACKER BILK **FH** (£1 to £2)
23 RICHARD DIGANCE **FH** (£1.25 to £2)

When the **Adverts** appeared at the Greyhound on 26th February they found that their fans had been banned from doing the 'Pogo' - the punk's own favourite dance! The organisers feared (probably with some justification) that the floor might collapse under the weight of several hundred people leaping up and down; it may have saved the floor, but it ruined the gig for the audience.

The Advertiser saw it this way: *"The concert started well, when the Adverts crashed into 'One Chord Wonders' and the crowd ricocheted into action. Packed in sardine-tight near the front, they had only one way to go and that was up. Then the bouncers waded in to subdue the leaping mob and the atmosphere went dead. The Adverts are definitely a band that sound better when you are being kicked along by the music. Lead singer TV Smith did his 'electrocuted doll' bit, jerking and collapsing, wondering dimly where the other half of the mike stand was, while sultry Gaye Advert stood frozen, staring into space. The hit single 'Gary Gilmore's Eyes' popped up near the end and got the best reception. All good music perhaps, but no real excitement".*

PLEASE NOTE

We are very sorry but

POGO DANCING
OR SIMILAR

IS NOT ALLOWED DUE TO ACCIDENTS & INJURIES DURING RECENT WEEKS

FOX ENTERPRISES

The ban on pogo-ing, however, was the least of the punks problems; the general manager of the Greyhound, Mr Peter Davis, warned that he would stop the Sunday night gigs completely if the wanton damage to the venue did not cease. Fox Enterprises, who organised the gigs, had an agreement with the Greyhound to pay for any damage. Around 500 punks turned out for every Sunday concert and Brian Mason, Fox's managing director said: *"The trouble has been exaggerated - there has been none since 11th December".*

But a maintenance man wrote to the paper to say "...four weeks ago they poured beer over the emergency power system, causing about £5,000 worth of damage..." amongst everything else!

Chris Groom

The original Lindisfarne line-up together again at the Fairfield Hall on May 14th 1978. Shown left to right: Ray Jackson, Rod Clements and Alan Hull, with drummer Ray Laidlaw obscured by his kit.

This year saw the recording debut of **Kirsty MacColl**, singing backing vocals under the pseudonym 'Mandy Doubt' with local group the **Drug Addix** on their EP, 'The Drug Addix Make A Record' - Chiswick SW39. Despite the punk-sounding name, the Addix were actually an R&B band, but as punk was the music of the day, their name helped to get them extra gigs. They were given a recording session by Stiff Records, who were less than enamoured with the results, but when they later found that Kirsty had left the band, she was invited back. Stiff were keen to add another female singer to their rosta and saw her as 'Croydon's answer to Rachel Sweet', a billing that Kirsty hotly disputed.

Kirsty was born on 10th October 1959 and grew up in Croydon, the daughter of Jean Newlove and Ewan MacColl, one of the kingpins of the 'sixties folk revival and a highly respected singer-songwriter. Many of his songs have become contemporary folk standards - 'Shoals of Herring', 'Go, Move, Shift', 'Dirty Old Town' - while Roberta Flack's version of 'The First Time Ever I Saw Your Face' made number 14 in the charts in 1972. However, living solely with her mother, Kirsty's musical influences came more from the radio and her elder brothers record collection than from her fathers folk singing. She attended Croydon Art College and worked as a tele-sales girl for the Exchange & Mart in the Whitgift Centre, before beginning her musical career with the Drug Addix.

By Christmas '78, Kirsty had quit the Addix to begin writing material for her first solo album on Stiff - the early signs showed that she was fast becoming a fine songwriter, with a distinctive style.

Croydon Advertiser – 26.5.78

*IT IS FIVE YEARS since **Lindisfarne**'s last tour - and they got a rapturous welcome back by Croydon fans at the Fairfield on Sunday.*

Their music now sounds less simple - slightly more sophisticated, but it retains the jaunty, traditional flavour of the old days. The band delighted the audience with songs from old albums and introduced them to tracks from their soon-to-be-released LP 'Back and Fourth', which were every bit as good as the oldies.

Their new single sounds destined for chart success; the A-side 'Run For Home' is by guitarist/vocalist Alan Hull and the B-side, an anti-racist song called 'Stick Together', is written in part by the quiet man of the group, guitarist Simon Cowe.

For me, personality man of the group is Ray Jackson, whose harmonica solo made a lovely change from the ubiquitous drum solos.

The concert came to a noisy, happy conclusion with most fans on their feet swaying, clapping, singing and whistling. The show was opened and compered by Newcastle-Brown swilling comedian Mike Elliott.

Diana Eccleston

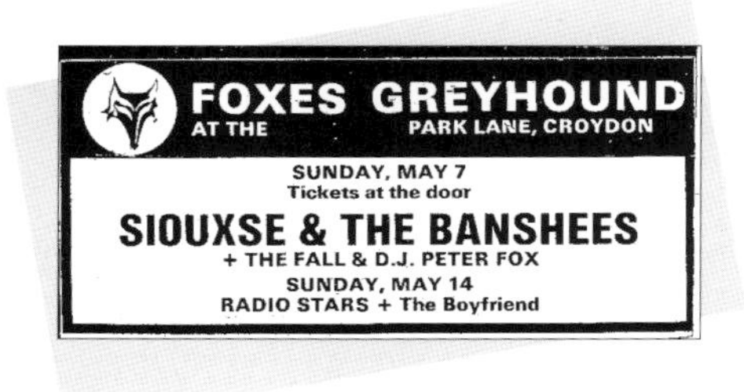

After trouble at the **Siouxsie & the Banshees** gig on May 7th, punks and skinheads were banned from the venue. This resulted in mass fighting taking place outside the Greyhound two weeks later, before and after the **Steve Hillage** concert - bad enough to hit the headlines on the front of the Croydon Advertiser.

Croydon Advertiser – 26.5.78

'Sickening' Attack - 'Pub staff rescue punks' victims'

HORRIFIED STAFF at the Greyhound, Park Lane, Croydon, unlocked a side door to rescue two youths who were attacked by a pack of punks and skinheads.

Barmaids saw the youths, thought to be brothers aged 19 and 20, chased and kicked by a 30-strong mob. One had blood pouring from his face. The other was clutching his ribs and groaning "Help me...".

In another incident a third youth was taken to Mayday hospital with a cut eye. Now punks and skinheads are barred from the Greyhound.

Terror came to St. George's Walk just after 10.30pm pub closing time on Sunday. Upstairs in the Greyhound, guitarist Steve Hillage and the National Health rock band were just ending a concert.

The two victims, described as "quiet boys" had sat in a corner of the downstairs Greyhound bar listening to the jukebox. Outside in the walk the punks and skinheads, including girls, pounced. "One of the boys was kicked to the ground" said one of the staff, "it was sickening. It's lucky it didn't end up as a murder enquiry".

A bar cellarman who witnessed this May madness, unlocked the side door and helped the youths to safety - "What else could I do" asked the Greyhound's good samaritan. Witnesses, who fear reprisals, do not want their names disclosed. One man said "I estimate that at one stage there were 100 punks in St. George's Walk".

Victor Tredger

As part of a local Arts festival, the jazz/rock quartet **Paraphernalia** made a rare appearance in Caterham Valley, playing the Adult Education Centre in Beechwood Road on 7th June. Led by talented saxophonist Barbara Thompson, the group on that evening featured Colin Dudman - keyboards, Roy Babbington - electric bass and Harold Fisher - drums. Barbara and husband Jon Hiseman (who later replaced Fisher on drums) both lived locally at that time, in Sutton. Roy Babbington was previously a member of Soft Machine - his replacement in the 'Softs' was Steve Cooke who had played bass with... Barbara Thompson!

JULY

13 KENNY BALL **FH** (£1 to £2)

AUGUST

19 THE HEROES **RD** (n/a)

SEPTEMBER

3 THE SHADOWS **FH** (£1.25 to £3.50)
4 THE SHADOWS **FH** (£1.25 to £3.50)
8 CHRIS BARBER **FH** + ALVIN ALCORN (£1.50 to £2.50)
10 CAMEL **FH** + MICHAEL CHAPMAN (£1.50 to £3)
10 JIM MULLEN **RD** (£1 to £1.50)
12 STAN TRACEY QUARTET **RD** (£1 to £1.50)
20 HI-TENSION **T** (£2)
24 RENAISSANCE **FH** + THE DODGERS (£1.50 to £3.50)
26 KATHY STOBART QUINTET **RD** (£1 to £1.40)
28 THE DUBLINERS **FH** (£1.25 to £2)
28 OLYMPIC RUNNERS **T** + KANDIDATE (£2)

OCTOBER

5 MIKE HARDING **FH** + HEDGEHOG PIE (£1.50 to £2.50)
7 THE EDGE BAND **RD** (n/a)
8 SMOKIE **FH** (£1.50 to £3)
10 RONNIE SCOTT QUINTET **RD** (£1.50 to £2)
15 HAWKWIND **FH** + PATRICK FITZGERALD (£1.50 to £3)
16 BARBARA DICKSON **FH** + THE BLUE MAX (£1.50 to £3)
21 BUDGIE **G** + STRIFE (£2)
24 BUDDY RICH **FH** (£2 to £3.75)
29 THE FOUR TOPS **FH** + OFANCHI (£2 to £4)
29 THE DAMNED **G** + THE SNIVELLING SHITS (n/a)
31 DON WELLER & TERRY SMITH **RD** (£1 to £1.50)

NOVEMBER

3 OSCAR PETERSON **FH** (£2 to £3.50)
5 GORDON GILTRAP **FH** (£1.50 to £2.50)
5 THE LURKERS **G** + THE NIGHT (n/a)
8 HI-TENSION **T** (£2.50)
9 MILLIE JACKSON **FH** + ROKOTTO (£2 to £4)
11 STEVE BOYCE BAND **RD** + VOYEURS (n/a)
12 THE CHIEFTAINS **FH** (£1.75 to £3.50)
12 SIOUXSIE & THE BANSHEES **G** (n/a)
19 LEO SAYER **FH** (£2 to £4)
26 TAVARES **FH** (£2 to £3.50)
26 GENERATION X **G** + THE CURE (£1.90)
27 TOM ROBINSON **G** (n/a)
29 CLIFF RICHARD **FH** (£1.50 to £3.50)
30 CLIFF RICHARD **FH** (£1.50 to £3.50)

DECEMBER

1 PETERS & LEE **FH** (£1 to £3)
3 THE THREE DEGREES **FH** (£4 to £6)
3 PENETRATION **G** + GANG OF FOUR (n/a)
10 THE REZILLOS **G** (n/a)
11 THE JAM **G** + NEW HEARTS (n/a)
17 FRANKIE MILLER **G** + DARLING (n/a)
18 THE CLASH **T** + THE SLITS + THE INNOCENTS (£2.25 to £2.50)
19 SIOUXSIE & THE BANSHEES **T** + HUMAN LEAGUE + MANICURED NOISE (£1.90)

(n/a) = ticket price not available.

For die-hard fans of Rockabilly and 'fifties Rock'n'Roll, the place to go was the St. Helier Arms in Carshalton. Live music every Wednesday and Saturday night, and bands such as Crazy Cavan, Shazam and the Flying Saucers. Dynamite were booked for Saturday 15th July, followed by Matchbox on Wednesday 19th.

Sixties favourites the **Shadows** played two consecutive nights at the Fairfield Hall towards the beginning of September. Their old lead singer turned up to see them on Monday 4th - Cliff Richard was seen sneaking into his seat after the lights had gone down and slipping out just before the end of the show, with a handkerchief covering his face to try and retain his anonymity. Some hope! Cliff was back at the end of November for his regular brace of concerts - the Shadows were seen, sneaking into their seats...

Wimbledon Stadium was an interesting place to be on 17th September. **Queen** had decided that their next single release should be a double A-side of 'Fat Bottomed Girls'/'Bicycle Race' and their publicity people came up with the idea of getting 65 naked girls to race their bikes round the stadium. The resulting picture and film footage could then be used to promote the single and the band understandably jumped at the idea. The weather turned out to be good, the girls were all hired from model agencies and there was no shortage of photographers and film crew! When the single was released later that October, the cover picture had to be amended by the addition of a pair of black 'undies' *(great British censorship, eh?!)*.

And not only that, but Halfords Cycles, who had generously provided the bicycles, refused to take back all the used saddles and Queen had to pay for the replacements!

Surrey group **The Edge Band** played several gigs at the Red Deer in South Croydon, combining hard driving rock with a macabre, theatrical stage show that owed much of its influence to Alice Cooper (and Screaming Lord Sutch, come to that). Lead singer Gary Challen wore a skull mask and dripped blood from the corners of his mouth, while the band - guitarists Andy Hutt and Colin Huggett, bassist Dixie Wiggins and drummer Rob Adams - kept the musical dynamics at full power.

The group **Cold Comfort** released their new single 'Phone-In' on Jet Records at the beginning of August, featuring local guitarist Nigel Bagge. An ex-pupil of Whitgift School, Nigel spent his early years in Norbury, Sanderstead and South Godstone; after failing to find a job that suited him, he decided to try his hand as a professional musician. In November 1975, he answered an advertisement in the Melody Maker and joined Cold Comfort as lead guitarist, replacing Chris Thompson who had left to become the vocalist with Manfred Mann's Earthband.

Nigel was the only southerner in the group, the other three all coming from Newcastle - their lead vocalist Dave Price being the cousin of Alan Price, one-time organist with The Animals. Cold Comfort toured with the Sutherland Brothers, Medicine Head and Alan Price, with whom they appeared at the Fairfield.

On 27th August I went back to one of my old college haunts, the Lakers Hotel in Redhill, to see local band **The Hotpoints**. They were an unusual mixture of jazz/rock with heavy reggae undertones, led by a huge bearded sax player - the band regularly played there on a Sunday night and had also appeared at a couple of the Art School end-of-term parties. The Hotpoints had released their own 5-track EP on the Crowmium label, recorded in September 1977 at Spaceward Studio in Cambridge with the help of producer Mike Kemp.

I arrived early at the gig to catch the support band; partly out of habit, but also because they too had a record out and there was a bit of a buzz about the group in the music press - the support were a Crawley band called **The Cure**. Previously known as Easy Cure, the group had built up a local following at gigs such as The Rocket and Lakeside in Crawley, plus Felbridge Village Hall and one or two at the Lakers. The Cure were now down to a trio of Robert Smith - guitar and vocals, Michael Dempsey - bass and Laurence 'Lol' Tolhurst on drums and had been signed to Hansa, a German record label, but parted company from them when Hansa refused to release 'Killing An Arab' as a single.

As you entered the ballroom of the Lakers Hotel, the room itself had an L-shaped stagger to it - you turned left and then looked right to see the main stage; but any support group had to play at floor level and were positioned to your right just as you entered the room - so if they were already playing you almost walked into the band as you came through the door!

I remember thinking that the Cure were pretty good, they had an unusual sound for the time and certainly weren't as 'punky' as I had expected. The band played 'Killing An Arab' and '10.15 Saturday Night', the two sides soon to be their first official single. Because unbeknown to me and the other punters at the time, was the fact that Polydor A&R man Chris Parry was there specifically to see the Cure play live. Parry was responsible for signing The Jam and Siouxsie & the Banshees to the label, and found the Cure's demo tape intriguing enough to venture down to Redhill to see them. After the gig, the band took Parry over the road to the Home Cottage - an old Youngs pub that Robert Smith has described as the place *"where everyone used to go after our gigs because it sold such horribly strong bitter"* - and virtually clinched the deal, becoming the first group to sign for Fiction, Polydor's new subsidiary label.

The Cure came back to the Lakers on 19th September and this time Parry brought along journalist Adrian Thrills from the NME, who was not quite so enthusiastic. Robert Smith recalls that the Cure regularly went to see bands either at gigs in Brighton, or at the Greyhound in Croydon rather than travel into London and finally got to play Croydon themselves on 26th November, as support to Generation X.

Jazz trombonist **Chris Barber** seemed to have found the secret of eternal life (on the road) - he stays exactly the same but changes the band around him. The fresh faces this time included 66 year old veteran trumpeter Alvin Alcorn and blues singer Tommy Tucker - of 'High Heel Sneakers' fame, whilst the featured newcomers were Sammy Rimmington (alto clarinet) and John Crocker (reeds). Adding a slight rock edge were Roger Hill on guitar and drummer Pete York.

When progressive English rockers **Camel** sold out the Fairfield on their first major tour three years before, their support act was folk guitarist Michael Chapman. For the gig in September, Chapman was on the bill once again - but the line-up of the main act had changed drastically. Keyboard player and unofficial leader Pete Bardens left the group on the eve of the tour, so Camel drafted in Dave and Richard Sinclair, and Jan Schelhaas all former members of Caravan, plus ex-King Crimson saxophonist Mel Collins. The new group often found themselves deep in jazz rock territory but delighted the Fairfield crowd who stormed the stage at the end of the concert.

Further problems at the Greyhound for **Siouxsie & the Banshees** on November 12th, when their show had to be cancelled on the afternoon of the gig. Bearing in mind some earlier incidents, the stage was declared unfit due to lack of sufficient crash barriers!

Back in September 1977, Punk acts began to appear regularly on the John Peel 'Sessions' - the part of his Radio 1 show that featured a specially recorded 'live' set from an up & coming band of the day. Radio producer John Walters was a regular visitor to the Croydon Greyhound, one of the venues he used for his weekly talent-spotting trips, or "lack-of-talent" spotting, as he put it. Peel himself was too busy and too recognisable to go and see many of the new groups, so Walters did the rounds - the Greyhound on Sunday nights, the Roxy on Mondays and the Vortex were his main haunts.

On 9th October 1977, he attended a double bill of **Siouxsie & the Banshees** and the **Slits**, arriving early to see the Banshees soundcheck. Without the distraction of a baying crowd he was suitably impressed and booked them on the spot. In May 1978 Walters again went to the Greyhound to see Siouxsie, but music journalist Danny Baker had advised him to get there early and watch the support group. As soon as the gig was finished, Walters wrote to the support act to book them for a session - the group were the **Fall**, who went on to be the most recorded group, post-'77, to appear on the Peel sessions and remain John Peel's favourite group to this day.

On 26th November '78, Walters came to Croydon to see Generation X supported by a young trio from Crawley known as the **Cure**. He was 'horrified' to hear that they would only receive five pounds between them (standard Greyhound practice for support bands); not only that, but their manager was actually paying the Generation X sound and lighting engineer a tenner for his services, so the gig was costing *his* band money right from the word go! Needless to say, Walters booked them - and their poverty stricken state didn't last too long.

Chris Taylor, the guru of Caterham-based Goodness Records, helped to set up the Toadstool record label as an outlet for local talent. The first (and as far as I know the only) release was by **Slime** - 'Controversial'/'Looney' TOADSTOOL WOOD1 - which received the thumbs-up from the music paper Sounds, at least:

"Close interest department
Slime is our old chum Slimey Toad (Toadstool records, gettit?), venturing into the harsh world of criticism alone. It needs a few spins to ascertain whether Slimey is a wunderkinder or a prat. I liked it, so it's probably the greatest thing since plastic bananas."

The Caterham branch of Goodness filled their window with the eye-catching sleeve; the word SLIME dripping in fluorescent yellow and green - nice!

JANUARY

7 THE DAMNED **G** + THE COWARDS (n/a)
14 THE DAMNED **G** + THE HEROES (n/a)
28 SHOWADDYWADDY **FH** (£2 to £4)
31 ROY AYER'S UBIQUITY **T** (£2)

FEBRUARY

9 FLYING CLOUD **C** (n/a)
11 OSIBISA **FH** + RAW (£1.75 to £3)
15 THE SPINNERS **FH** (£2 to £4)
16 FLYING CLOUD **C** (n/a)
23 ALAN PRICE **FH** (£2 to £4)
25 CHRIS DE BURGH **FH** + CATHERINE HOWE (£1.50 to £2.50)

MARCH

3 SUMUTA **C** (n/a)
7 SLIM WHITMAN **FH** + CARROLL BAKER + THE HILLSIDERS (£3.50 to £5.50)
11 INNER CIRCLE **G** (n/a)
18 REGGAE REGULARS **G** + TRIMMER & JENKINS (n/a)
24 STAN TRACEY QUARTET **G** (£2.50)
25 THE HOLLIES **FH** (£2 to £4.50)
30 FLYING CLOUD **C** (n/a)

APRIL

1 THE DAMNED **G** + THE COWARDS (n/a)
2 RALPH McTELL **FH** + BOB FOX & STU LUCKLEY (£1.75 to £3.50)
10 STEPHANE GRAPPELLI **FH** + DIZ DIZLEY & JOHN ETHERIDGE (£1.50 to £3)
10 SKYLINE **C** (n/a)
14 DIANE SOLOMON **FH** + BOBBY CRUSH (£1.50 to £3)
20 BURL IVES **FH** (£2 to £4)
22 JOHN MILES **FH** + BANDIT (£1.50 to £3.50)
22 THE DAMNED **G** + THE RUTS (n/a)

MAY

13 RENAISSANCE **FH** + GAY & TERRY WOODS (£2.25 to £3.25)
27 HARRY CHAPIN **FH** + TOM CHAPIN (£2 to £3.50)

JUNE

3 FAIRPORT CONVENTION **FH** + BERT JANSCH's CONUNDRUM (£1.50 to £3)
9 SPECTRUM **C** + THE SHOOTERS (n/a)
7 MR. ACKER BILK **FH** (n/a)
17 MANFRED MANN's EARTHBAND **FH** + DARLING (£2 to £3.50)
27 THIRD WORLD **T** (£2.50)

(n/a) = ticket price not available.

1979

Where else but in Croydon could you find such a ridiculously diverse set of artistes appearing in the same month? Take April, for example, where you could have enjoyed The Damned, Bobby Crush, Stephane Grappelli, Ralph McTell and Burl Ives, all within a hectic twenty day burst.

According to the Advertiser's John McCrone, 'Punk' was all over bar the spitting, after its brief two year reign. **The Damned** returned to the Greyhound twice in April, where *"hordes of 15 year old, second generation punks swamped the stage and hid the Damned from view"*. He continued, *"Playing the Greyhound was a homeground gig for the Damned and they clearly wanted it to be a night for nostalgia. One of the first punk bands, they must have asked themselves who were all these youngsters linked in a sweaty mass standing centre stage?*

Can all the original punks have married, got a mortgage and be spending their Sunday nights washing out nappies?"

At the other extreme, the audience for American folk hero **Burl Ives** was a little more sedate, and probably somewhat older than fifteen. Burl himself was just a couple of months short of his 70th birthday, with such eventful years behind him that even the members of the Damned would envy. He spent three years as a hobo in North America, moving across 46 of the States; at 51 he won an Oscar for best supporting actor in 'The Big Country', although his best known film role is the part of Big Daddy in 'Cat On A Hot Tin Roof'.

He had returned to London to celebrate his wedding anniversary in the city where he was married, only to find that his trip had turned into a nationwide tour. He took the stage alone and captivated the Fairfield audience with charm, a gentle humour and old favourites such as 'The Grey Goose' and 'A Little Bitty Tear' - and with 2,000 'wedding guests' every night, it's a hell of a way to celebrate your anniversary!

Croydon Advertiser – 6.4.79

'Our Gentle Troubadour'

IT WAS an emotional evening at Fairfield on Monday; Croydon's favourite singing son Ralph McTell returned in triumph and collected not only the adulation of his fans, but a plaque to commemorate the sale of more than 100,000 copies of his most famous composition, 'Streets of London'.

There can be no disputing this is a brilliant song, it is sensitive and aware at the same time as being heart-wrenchingly sentimental. But it has tended to overshadow much of Ralph's other work. he is a gifted lyricist, his rhymes are never contrived and his words never wasted.

Ralph's latest compositions are to be found on the album 'Slide Away The Screen', which he showcased at the concert. My favourites from it were the beautifully tender, reassuring love song 'White Dress', which he adapted from a track on a Fairport Convention album by his friend Dave Swarbrick, and the deeply perceptive 'Traces'. This song, about a long-gone relationship painfully remembered, is so simple in lyric and arrangement yet it says so much, conveys a wealth of feeling.

Ralph McTell writes a lot about love but it's far from being the only subject in his repertoire. He composed 'Run Johnny Run' after his brief stint in the army. He used to train on Dartmoor and when he saw the prison he was moved to write about it "as escape was on my mind as well!"

When he was hitch-hiking through Yugoslavia, waiting by the roadside for a lift, he saw a heron sitting in a tree, so he wrote about that too.

And he wrote about his Guyanese friend in 'Harry Don't Go' and about Bob Dylan in 'Zimmerman Blues'. For this latter number Ralph played harmonica - "I believe the Croydon expression for it is gob-iron!" - a la Dylan, "the man who first popularised this particular method of knocking your own teeth out."

The story of how Ralph, who spent his childhood at Howard Primary and John Ruskin Secondary Schools in Croydon, busked his way round Paris is folk legend.

He is now widely appreciated, although not by the less discerning commercial market, as one of the country's finest songwriters. It has lasted until now and will probably last until Croydon's gentle troubadour is old and grey.

Diana Eccleston

Sadly, the days of regular concerts at the Greyhound were drawing to a close, when jazz virtuoso **Stan Tracey** played to little more than fifty people in the St. George's Suite on Saturday 24th March. Hammering out his discordant, strident chords on an old piano that looked as if it had survived years of touring the pubs and clubs of South London, Tracey twice lost a piano key from its slot but carried out the running repair without breaking his stride!

The handbill for the Croydon leg of Chris De Burgh's 'Crusader' tour. The programme for this tour was free - a four page A4 leaflet was put out on every seat before the concert began.

Much as she enjoyed the concert by Ralph McTell, Diana Eccleston was far less impressed with American singer-songwriter **Harry Chapin**. In May, one of his rare UK appearances received an ecstatic reception from the Fairfield crowd, yet Diana *"found his songs for the most part either twee or tedious, as they tend to be lengthy narratives"*. She added, *"Harry is an ebullient chap, full of chat and four-letter words and even more irritatingly fidgety than Michael Parkinson. He and his brother Tom, who accompanied themselves on acoustic guitars, ended the concert by getting everyone to join in 'All My Life's A Circle'. Then they bounded, waving through the audience to make their departure. It was all very cosy and I know their fans enjoyed it; they certainly got value for money as the concert was a long one.*

Too long for me though, and I cannot see Mr. Chapin augmenting his following here when we've got such superior home-grown talent of similar style - Croydon's Ralph McTell for one".

Rock with a heavy classical influence was the order of the day when **Renaissance** returned in May. Set against a background that owed more to Debussy, Rachmaninov and Prokofiev than to Chuck Berry or Muddy Waters, it was vocalist Annie Haslam who drew all the plaudits.

Diana Eccleston described her thus: *"she is one of rock's enigmas, she sings like an angel, her pure voice clear as glass soaring high above the rich tapestry of the music. Annie can hit notes other singers have barely heard of and I would like to bet she could beat Kate Bush hands down in any wailing contest!*

But when she gets down to a bit of cheeky banter with the audience, Annie is a proper 'cor blimey' merchant who frequently subsides into fits of uncontrollable and infectious cackling laughter more befitting one of Macbeth's witches. She also has an ethereal look about her, with her flowing hair, bare feet and long tattered gown she looks a cross between a medieval peasant girl and a wild spirit - an anachronism anyway, when set against the conservative style of dress of the male musicians."

Renaissance were promoting their 'As You Adore' album and a new single 'The Winter Tree', which failed to follow the group's only hit 'Northern Lights' into the charts. The band were joined onstage by eight year old Lee Sullivan, who replaced his dad Terry on drums for the track 'Forever Changing'.

Dazzling lights, explosive fireworks and backdrop projections all combined to overwhelm rather than enhance the music of **Manfred Mann's Earthband**, when they played the Fairfield in June.

They too had a new album to sell, but the tracks from 'Angels At My Gate' proved unimpressive when set against their cover versions of 'Blinded By The Light' and the ever-popular 'Mighty Quinn'. The Advertiser sent along Diana Eccleston, who was far more impressed with the support band, as shown by her cute headline:

Not mad about Mann, but Darling I love you

She continued: *"I'm not usually a New Wave fan but this foursome was a knockout. Their singer is a lady by the name of Alice Spring, her stick thin figure clad in a skintight black outfit and her jagged hair was jet on top, with a vibrant auburn frame around her marvellously expressive face. Darling deserve to go a long way - watch for their new single 'Do You Wanna'."*

JULY

16 THE PRETENDERS **T** + INTERVIEW (£1.50 to £1.75)
20 WOODY HERMAN **FH** (£2 to £3.50)

AUGUST

SEPTEMBER

2 THE SHADOWS **FH** (£1.60 to £4.25)
3 THE SHADOWS **FH** (£1.60 to £4.25)
6 KENNY BALL & HIS JAZZMEN **FH** (£1.60 to £2.65)
11 JOHNNY RAY **FH** (£1.60 to £3.70)
23 THE DARTS **FH** + SCREEN IDOLS (£2.15 to £4.25)
27 THE DUBLINERS **FH** (£1.60 to £2.65) *CANCELLED*
27 MR ACKER BILK & HIS PARAMOUNT JAZZBAND **T** (£3.75)
28 BASIL's BALLS-UP BAND **C** (n/a)
30 LINDISFARNE **FH** + MIKE ELLIOTT (£2.25 to £3.75)

OCTOBER

6 ALLISON BROTHERS **C** (n/a)
11 LOUDON WAINWRIGHT III **FH** (£2.50 to £3.50)
14 DEAN FRIEDMAN **FH** (£2.25 to £3.50)
17 BASIL's BALLS-UP BAND **C** (n/a)
19 SUTHERLAND BROTHERS **FH** + MICHAEL MOORE (£2.25 to £3.75)
21 HOT CHOCOLATE **FH** + NICK VAN EEDE (£2.50 to £5)
22 HOT CHOCOLATE **FH** + NICK VAN EEDE (£2.50 to £5)
23 GERRY MULLIGAN **FH** (£2 to £3.50)
25 TOM PAXTON **FH** (£1.50 to £3)
28 LEO SAYER **FH** + MAINLAND 2 shows (£2 to £3)
29 MARY O'HARA **FH** (£2 to £3.50)

NOVEMBER

5 RICHARD & LINDA THOMPSON **FH** + MICK STEVENS (£1.75 to £2.75)
6 HUMPHREY LYTTLETON **FH** + JOE LEE WILSON (£2 to £2.75)
8 WHITESNAKE **FH** + MARSEILLE (£2.25 to £3.50)
25 GALLAGHER & LYLE **FH** + JUDIE TZUKE (£2.75 to £4.50)
30 BEN E KING **FH** + JIMMY JAMES & THE VAGABONDS (£1.50 to £3)

DECEMBER

12 THE SPINNERS **FH** (£2 to £3.50)
12 DEADRINGER **C** (n/a)
15 QUEEN **T** (n/a)
16 ROCKOLA **C** (n/a)
27 WOOFLER **C** (n/a)
28 DOTTY CROTCHET **C** (n/a)

(n/a) = ticket price not available.

1979

During the second half of '78, I first stumbled across a local band who were to become a firm favourite - the wonderfully named **Basil's Balls-up Band**. For the next two years, Julia and I became regulars at the Cartoon to see this crazy, but musically talented bunch of reprobates; who were led, not as you might think by 'Basil' but by a tall, skinny guy named Randy who performed like an animated cross between Ian Anderson and Frank Zappa. Normally a group whose members have such diverse musical tastes can't hope to survive more than six months, but this lot appeared to thrive on the variety, playing complex pieces such as Zappa's 'Black Prince' and Herbie Hancock's 'Chameolean' one moment and the music hall standard 'No One Loves A Fairy When She's Forty' the next!

I don't think the band ever put down anything on vinyl, which is surprising when you consider that Randy was involved in setting up a local recording studio, but they did sell a live tape at their gigs.

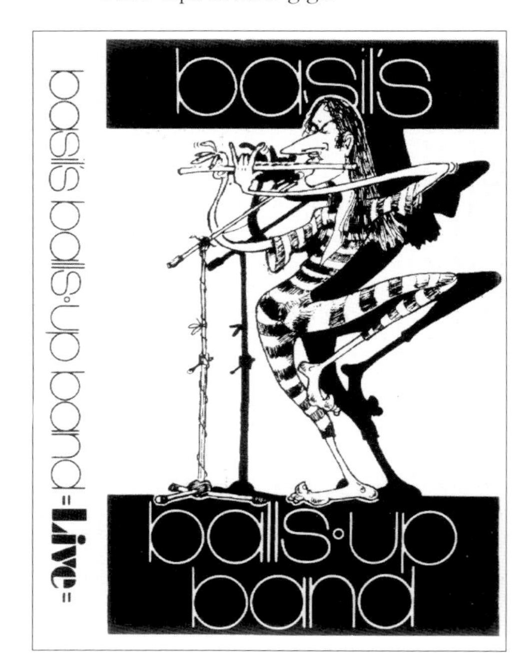

The line-up on this tape was Ranald MacDonald, saxophones, flute and vocals; Steven Donachie, violin and vocals; Steve Watts, bass; Geoffrey Lavender, keyboards; John Morris, guitar and vocals and Dave Bell, drums. Two of the tracks featured a guest appearance by 'Briggsy', their former lead guitarist Dave Briggs. Dave Bell also supplied the cartoon of Randy for the cassette sleeve, shown above.

One set of Cartoon regulars who did record a single were **Flying Cloud**, although just as their record was released the group changed their name, which may or may not have hindered its chances!

Whereas most pub bands tended to play purely cover versions, Flying Cloud had a batch of original songs that were just screaming out to be turned into hit records. So it wasn't too much of a surprise when thumbing through a box of cheap singles in Cloakes record shop, to see the titles of two Flying Cloud songs pressed up on Decca records; 'Get Out, Take Your Mother With You' and 'Gimme A Can Of Spray Paint' - catchy, huh? What I was surprised to see was that the record was released under the name **Airship**, as the band were still called Flying Cloud when we saw them at the Cartoon in the first half of the year. Sad to say, the Airship single didn't take off (pun definitely intended) and I never saw the band again; a real life case of 'whatever happened to...'

In October, Hot Chocolate made yet another visit to the Fairfield, but the gig is memorable for showcasing the talents of a young singer songwriter from East Grinstead - **Nick Van Eede**, who opened the show. In her review for the Advertiser, Diana Eccleston described him as *"an attractive, baby-faced blond with a good voice and engaging personality, Nick already has some interesting material in his repertoire, including a rocker called 'Eye To Eye' and a reggae song that is even better, 'The Whites Of His Eyes'. Nick has already supported major artists such as David Essex, his writing and voice are both versatile, all he needs now is one special single and he could be topping the bill on a show of his own".*

Well spotted Di, for only a few years later, Nick was high in the charts on both sides of the Atlantic with his group 'Cutting Crew' and their single ' I Died In Your Arms Tonight'.

Master songwriter and guitarist **Richard Thompson** returned to the Fairfield with his wife Linda on 5th November to promote their new album 'Sunnyvista'.

The ex-Fairporter and his missus performed songs from the album, including 'Sisters', 'You're Going To Need Somebody', 'Living On Borrowed Time' and 'Civilisation', as well as some unusual cover versions - 'Pipeline', an old surfing instrumental by the Chantays, the Everly Brothers 'Crying In The Rain' and Chuck Berry's 'No Particular Place To Go'. In his band that night were Simon Nicol, rhythm guitar; Pat Donaldson, bass and Michael Spencer on drums.

Croydon Advertiser – 16.11.79

Pale Snake

ROCK & ROLL will never die - but yesterday's heroes get left behind. Few can keep up with the advances in ashion, and ***Whitesnake****, at Fairfield last week, seemed content to rest on their laurels until their pensions come through.*

Whitesnake can boast three members of that truly great band, Deep Purple - singer David Coverdale, drummer Ian Paice and Jon Lord on keyboards. But they cannot claim to have Deep Purple's power and excitement which inspired a host of other bands in the early 'seventies.

They played a fairly competent heavy metal bash - better than most second division bands, but a far cry from their heyday. The two men who could lift Whitesnake into another league were crushed under the white noise crash of guitars. Jon Lord's keyboards - which held Deep Purple's sound together - were almost completely inaudible. And Whitesnake would be light years better if Micky Moody's blues-influenced slide guitar was allowed to dominate the strings section.

Inevitably, the audience treated the ex-Purple members as gods and would have been much happier if Whitesnake had spent the whole night covering old Purple hits. Witness the storm of clapping whenever a Deep Purple riff was touched on during one of the many tediously long solos.

John McCrone

In November, **Queen**, who by this time were more used to playing stadium sized concerts, decided that they wanted to return to some of the smaller venues, to 'get back in touch with their audience'. Having just had a number two hit with 'Crazy Little Thing Called Love', they named the proposed gigs the 'Crazy Tour'; it began on November 24th at a large venue, the NEC Birmingham, and from there on the venues became smaller and smaller. By the time it reached London on December 13th, they were down to the size of the Lyceum, then the Rainbow and then on 15th December, Queen arrived at Tiffanys in Purley, which was at that time more of a night-club and had largely stopped hosting live bands. On the 19th, the band played the Mayfair in Tottenham, which was too small for the bands' lighting rig and they had to make do with the venues' own tiny stage lights.

Croydon Advertiser – November '79

Judie Steals It

BILLED AS 'special guest', one of pop's newest talents, ***Judie Tzuke*** *opened the show for Gallagher & Lyle at Fairfield on Sunday.*

But for my money Miss Tzuke, who is as attractive to look at as she is to listen to, should have topped the bill. She is one of the best things to have happened to popular music this year. Judie has everything going for her; she has an abounding talent for writing original songs (which she does with guitarist Mike Paxman) and a delectable voice.

She is a tantalising child-woman combination with a stunning figure, Bardot pout and a mane of shaggy blonde hair; and an incongruous, but attractive innocence in the way she chats to her audience. Judie's first album "Welcome To The Cruise" was critically acclaimed and her single "Stay With Me Till Dawn" did well in the charts.

Unfortunately, Judie did not have the studio-style balanced instrumental backing she deserved on Sunday. Her over-amplified musicians crowded her and her voice is not the raw and gutsy variety which can compete with an excess of decibels. Sadly, because of this, some of her lyrics were lost, but the band come into it's own for the forceful 'Sportscar', when the sound was more important than the song.

As her encore, Judie sang the beautiful 'For You', unaccompanied except for a tape of her own chanting backing vocals. Even this was played slightly on the loud side, but the total effect of the song and of Judie's vocal abilities was breathtaking.

The same cannot, I'm afraid, be said for Gallagher & Lyle. They were consistently over amplified and as the evening wore on they were increasingly eardrum shattering and head-splitting. Why they need a six piece backing group, I don't know, but the result was that most of their lyrics were inaudible. As many of the numbers were unfamiliar to me and few were introduced, I had no clue as to what they were about. What I did adjust to was unremarkable, although to be fair, the sell-out audience seemed to enjoy themselves.

The duo were at their best on their own and for the old favourites - 'I Want To Stay With You', 'Wear Your Heart On Your Sleeve' and 'When I'm Dead And Gone', which they wrote as members of McGuinness Flint.

If I have been too uncharitable to Gallagher & Lyle, it could be because the second house, due to begin at 7.30, did not in fact do so until 8.10!

Diana Eccleston

JANUARY

5	DANA	**FH**	(£2.50 to £4)
10	GORDON GILTRAP	**FH**	(£2.50 to £3.50)
16	THE COMMISSIONAIRES	**C**	(n/a)
20	THE RAYDERS	**S**	+ KRYSIS (£1)
23	THE DUBLINERS	**FH**	(£2 to £3)
23	BASIL's BALLS-UP BAND	**C**	(n/a)
27	OSIBISA	**FH**	+ HEADLINE (£1.75 to £3)
31	JULIAN BREAM	**FH**	(£2.50 to £4)

FEBRUARY

2	BAD ACTORS	**WT**	(n/a)
3	WISHBONE ASH	**FH**	+ THE DUKES (£2.50 to £3.50)
6	BASIL's BALLS-UP BAND	**C**	(n/a)
8	THE CHIEFTAINS	**FH**	(£2.50 to £4)
11	SPYRO GYRA	**FH**	+ ELECTROTUNES (n/a)
15	THE POINTER SISTERS	**FH**	+ GERARD KENNY (£3 to £5)
18	URIAH HEEP	**FH**	+ GIRLSCHOOL (£2 to £3.50)
24	THE DOOLEYS	**FH**	+ THE HOUGHTON WEAVERS (£2.50 to £3.50)

MARCH

6	CHRIS BARBER	**FH**	+ OTTILIE PATTERSON (£2 to £3.50)
9	YAKETTY YAK	**C**	(n/a)
14	BUDDY RICH	**FH**	(£2.50 to £4)
16	SHOWADDYWADDY	**FH**	+ INVADER (£3 to £4.50)
17	SHOWADDYWADDY	**FH**	+ INVADER (£3 to £4.50)
16	THE MICE	**S**	(n/a)
21	THE SPINNERS	**FH**	(£2 to £3.50)
21	SEVEN YEAR ITCH	**C**	+ ALBERT LEE (n/a)
29	FELIX & THE CATS	**C**	(n/a)
30	SAD CAFE	**FH**	+ THE OUT (£2.50 to £3.50)

APRIL

2	BASIL's BALLS-UP BAND	**C**	(n/a)
4	SPLODGNESSABOUNDS	**S**	+ THE HEROES (£1.25)
4	ANGELWITCH	**G**	+ THE CAROLINE ROADSHOW (£2)
4	SEVEN YEAR ITCH	**C**	(n/a)
6	JOHNNY MOPED	**S**	+ IDIOT DANCERS (£1.50)
21	ROY ORBISON	**FH**	(£3 to £5)
22	RALPH McTELL	**FH**	+ MICHAEL HAUMONT (£2.50 to £3.50)

MAY

5	MIKE OLDFIELD	**FH**	2 shows (£4 to £5)
6	JUDIE TZUKE	**FH**	+ GRADUATE (£2.50 to £3.50)
10	RIO & THE ROBOTS	**C**	(n/a)
11	SUZI QUATRO	**FH**	(£3 to £4)
12	DAVID GATES	**FH**	+ GERARD KENNY (£4 to £5)
14	CITIZENS	**S**	(n/a)
15	SKY	**FH**	(£3.50 to £5.50)
26	ROD McKUEN	**FH**	(£2.50 to £4)

JUNE

7	GARDEN PARTY '80	**CPB**	BOB MARLEY + JOE JACKSON (n/a)
16	DAVID ESSEX	**FH**	(£3 to £5)

(n/a) = ticket price not available.

The new decade began with a name from the past, as the Star Hotel re-opened their music room and exhumed the old Crawdaddy Club title. Local bands the **Rayders** and **Krysis** opened the proceedings and the evening also included a '60's disco'.

Following a couple of years touring with The Damned, bass player Algy Ward formed **Tank** in February, a Motorhead inspired power trio, playing "loud, dirty, mean, fast music". This Croydon based group comprising Ward on bass, Pete Brabbs, guitar and vocals, Mark Brabbs, drums - went on to support Angelwitch, Girlschool and even their own heroes, Motorhead. In fact, they also managed to get original Motorhead guitarist Eddie Clarke to produce an EP and an album for them.

Croydon Advertiser – 22.2.80

Pointer's Way

APPARENTLY the ***Pointer Sisters****' church minister father used to allow them to hear only gospel music and TV soundtracks. But as they proved at Fairfield last week, they have come a long way in their ten years in the music business.*

A large part of their set comprised hard driving rock, with their four-piece band very much to the fore. And there was an interlude when the band had a free rein, with the sisters helping out on tambourines and with the odd forced shriek of delight.

The high spots though, were when they switched to songs with a blues feel, like the moody 'Hypnotised' from their album Energy. It was helped along by the gyrations of Ruth, clad in tight red satin pants. 'Yes You Can Can', their trademark, was a favourite with the audience, as was Bruce Springsteens' 'Fire', their soulful single from last year. And I loved 'Dreaming As One', a slow love song from the new album Priority. It was a shame that they were only beginning to warm up the audience by the end of their performance.

The same can't be said of support act ***Gerard Kenny*** *- he won everybody over at once with his warm, jokey presence. The singer songwriter showed his versatility by ripping through 'Son Of A Song & Dance Man', some rock and roll, the Johnny Mathis recorded ballad 'Love' and the ragtime inspired 'Hollywood Dream'. He finished with his hit single about his native city, 'New York, New York'.*

Sally Bull

Heavy rockers **Uriah Heep** were preaching to the converted on 18th February, when the Fairfield resembled a college concert hall packed to the gunnels by a young, heavy metal-crazed crowd. Still led by guitarist Mick Box and keyboard man Ken Hensley, the band also featured Trevor Bolder (ex-Spiders from Mars) on bass, drummer Chris Slade, fresh from Manfred Mann's Earthband plus a new frontman, 22 year old Welsh singer John Sloman and Heep were supported by all-girl group **Girlschool**, described as "four urchin-like cockneys, who obviously had a large London following."

Under the new management of Roy Burton, Scarlett's Night Club in Purley launched yet another live music night. Jazz was the new theme and in early March he booked the seemingly inspired combination of **Georgie Fame** with local tenor sax man **Don Weller**. Augmented by Harry South on piano, Roy Babbington on bass and drummer Bryan Spring, this fine band struggled to begin with in surroundings perhaps not best suited to a live sound. However, 'You've Changed', 'Good Bait', a slightly uneasy 'Bonnie & Clyde' and a storming 'Yeah, Yeah' eventually brought the club crowd to their feet.

As reviewer Terry Collcutt put it, *"A unique attempt to drag jazz out of the cellar and into the strobe light!"*

Croydon singer/songwriter **Kelvin James** decided to promote his own talent in the best way he knew how - by hiring the Fairfield Hall and putting himself top of the bill! This 'do or die' attempt at self promotion cost Kelvin a few thousand pounds and the problem of selling out an 1,800 seat hall, but the inclusion of his good friend Peter Sarstedt as support, plus a last minute feature on a local television news programme helped to fill the venue.

The association with Peter began in a pub in Putney, where Kelvin was a regular performer - when Peter dropped by one night and found that the gig was cancelled because Kelvin's guitar had been stolen, he immediately 'phoned and offered to lend him his.

The show on 11th April coincided with Kelvin's birthday and followed up the release of his latest single 'Don't Give Your Lies To Me'. The first half featured a selection of his favourite Elvis songs (Kelvin appeared in a Spanish version of 'Elvis - the musical') and for the Croydon show enlisted the help of local producer John Edmed to put together some authentic backing tapes, (see John's interview on pages 60 - 61).

The second half of the concert showcased some of his own rock songs and Kelvin even pre-planned an after-show party to celebrate. As Peter Sarstedt told the Advertiser's Diana Eccleston *"You've got to admire his guts!"*.

Chris Groom

Mike Oldfield pictured onstage at the Fairfield Halls during the first of his two shows on May 5th 1980.

In May, Julia and I attended the first of two shows by **Mike Oldfield** at the Fairfield Hall. Up to that point all I really knew of Oldfields work was the Tubular Bells album (but then who *hasn't* owned a copy of 'the Bells' at some time in their life), plus a few snatches of the follow-up, Hergest Ridge. Expecting to hear a far more 'orchestral' sound, I was surprised and pleased to hear how much of a straight forward rock band they were, with Mike himself proving to be an excellent lead guitarist.

His band included Pierre Moerlen, drummer and percussionist with Gong, Mike Frye also on percussion, Benoit Moerlen on vibes, Peter Lemer and Tim Cross on keyboards, guitarist Nico Ramsden, Hansford Rowe on bass, backing vocalist Wendy Roberts and Pete 'Bimbo' Acock on saxes and woodwind - this was no surprise, as I've lost count of the number of groups I've seen, from the Festival Hall to the Croydon Cartoon, where Bimbo has turned up to play some sort of reed instrument!

Chris Groom

Gordon Giltrap does his best to impersonate Jimmy Page - Fairfield Hall, January 1980.

The following evening, 6th May, we were back at the Fairfield to see **Judie Tzuke**. Having seen Judie steal the show as support to Gallagher & Lyle in November '79 we wanted to see her again, this time headlining her own show. Judie's own support group were a bright, quirky little pop outfit called **Graduate**; dressed in sharp suits, white shirts and black ties, they were riding on the back of the 'mod' revival that had also landed minor hits for the Lambretta's and the Pleasers. Graduate were led by Roland Orzabal and Curt Smith, two names that you don't forget in a hurry. Little surprise when they both surfaced again ten years later as chart topper's Tears for Fears with 'Everybody Wants To Rule The World'. But whatever happened to the other three - Buck, Baker and Marsden?

Monday 12th May saw the return visit of **David Gates**, the mellow voice on, and indeed the songwriter behind such hits as 'Baby I'm A Want You', Everything I Own', 'If', and 'Make It With You' for the American group **Bread**. In fact two of the other members of Bread teamed up with him again for this tour, drummer Mike Botts and keyboard player Larry Knechtel, augmented by Hadley Hockensmith on lead guitar and bass player David Miner, who had previously worked with Leon Russell.

The support was provided another American singer/songwriter, **Gerard Kenny**, a talented pianist who learned his trade in the bars of New York, in a similar style to Barry Manilow, who began his career playing piano for Bette Midler. Croydon fans were becoming used to seeing Mr. Kenny, who had already appeared at the Fairfield in February with the Pointer Sisters and would return again in October with Sheena Easton. 'New York, New York'? Croydon, Croydon more like!

JULY

- 9 BASIL's BALLS-UP BAND **C** (n/a)
- 10 MR. ACKER BILK **FH** (£1.50 to £3)
- 11 SLEDGEHAMMER **G** + THE CAROLINE ROADSHOW (£2.20)
- 16 JO-ANN KELLY's SECOND LINE **C** (n/a)
- 27 TRIMMER & JENKINS **C** (n/a)

AUGUST

- 8 THE BREAKERS **C** (n/a)
- 15 WHITE SPIRIT **G** + THE CAROLINE ROADSHOW (£2.00)
- 22 THE BREAKERS **C** (n/a)
- 26 SOUTHLANDS OUTLAW BAND **C** (n/a)

SEPTEMBER

- 14 THE HOLLIES **FH** (£2 to £3.50)
- 19 THE BREAKERS **G** (£2.20)
- 21 DARYL HALL & JOHN OATES **FH** (£3 to £4.50)
- 24 TRIMMER & JENKINS **C** (n/a)

OCTOBER

- 3 SEVEN YEAR ITCH **C** (n/a)
- 5 THE SHADOWS **FH** (£2 to £5)
- 6 THE SHADOWS **FH** (£2 to £5)
- 7 JUDY COLLINS **FH** (£3.50 to £5)
- 12 SHEENA EASTON **FH** + GERARD KENNY + DENIS WATERMAN (£2.50 to £3.50)
- 15 BILLY CONNOLLY **FH** (£3 to £4.50)
- 15 BASIL's BALLS-UP BAND **C** (n/a)
- 17 HANK WANGFORD BAND **C** (n/a)
- 19 BENEFIT FOR JOANNE STONE **FH** CLIFF RICHARD + CHAS & DAVE + MADELINE BELL + JOE BROWN + PEARLY GATES + TONY BLACKBURN (n/a)
- 26 DARTS **FH** + THE BREAKERS (n/a)

NOVEMBER

- 2 THE FOUR TOPS **FH** + THE MARVELETTES (£3 to £5)
- 4 GORDON GILTRAP **FH** (£2 to £3)
- 5 TRIMMER & JENKINS **C** (n/a)
- 12 BASIL's BALLS-UP BAND **C** (n/a)
- 14 ATOMIC ROOSTER **G** + THE CAROLINE ROADSHOW (£2.20)
- 16 CHRIS DE BURGH **FH** + CHAS & DAVE (£2 to £4)
- 17 BARBARA DICKSON **FH** (£2.50 to £5)
- 21 MUNGO JERRY **C** (n/a)
- 23 SHOWADDYWADDY **FH** + VENUS & MARS (£3 to £4.50)
- 25 EMILE FORD **TR** (n/a)

DECEMBER

- 2 GEORGE MELLY **FH** (£2 to £3)
- 5 VISITOR **C** (n/a)
- 7 OSIBISA **FH** (£2.50 to £4)
- 17 BASIL's BALLS-UP BAND XMAS PARTY **C** (n/a)
- 22 PYEWACKETT **SH** (n/a)

After twelve good years at the Waddon Hotel, Croydon Folksong Club moved into their new home upstairs at The Ship in Croydon High Street. The final 'Worthwhile Wednesday' performance at the Waddon saw a rip-roaring set from Barry Skinner who boasted having 'closed' more folk clubs than any other singer!

Without pausing for breath, the club re-opened at the Ship on Monday 21st July, as Sue Lewis reported for the 'Advertiser: *Any nostalgic sadness about the demise of the Waddon was not to last long. Monday night saw the triumphant opening at the Ship - and things certainly got off to a good start. The Ship's upstairs room was bursting at its oaken seams, with lots of newcomers no doubt attracted by the caperings of the Downs Morris dancers outside on the pavement. Guest stars were* ***Wild Oats*** *- Derek and Viva Smith on guitar and vocals and Ray Tassie on flat-backed mandolin, playing an assorted bag of easy-to-listen-to music.*

So Croydon Folksong Club seem to have found themselves a congenial home in a 'real ale' pub with a landlord who likes folk music. They will meet regularly on Mondays at the Ship. May God bless all who sail in her!

At a time when many publicans were not bothering to renew their music licences, Ian and Creanna Sheppard did the complete opposite and started a country music night every Monday at the Newton Arms in Queens Road, West Croydon. Resident performer was **Dave Wright Gibb** and his first guest was guitarist Mike Lloyd.

Making regular appearances at the Cartoon, Ian Trimmer & Billy Jenkins were former members of Burlesque, a fairly accurate description of the stage act for both band and duo. But don't be fooled - behind the onstage mayhem lay some clever songwriting and fine musicianship.

(n/a) = ticket price not available.

Croydon Advertiser – 25.7.80

Blues on the Line

A LOT OF PEOPLE don't seem to know where the Cartoon public house is. Which is a shame, since it is one of Croydon's few regular outlets for live 'popular' music. Wednesday of last week saw ***Jo-Ann Kelly & the Second Line*** *featuring Geraint Watkins, at the Cartoon in Broad Green for the first time and judging by the reception they received, it will not be their last.*

The band comprising Les Morgan (drums), Pete Emery (guitar), Paul Riley (bass) and Geraint Watkins (keyboards) started with four numbers by themselves and set the tone for the rest of the evening. Best of these was 'Wanna Be Loved' which featured Watkins in form on both keyboards and vocals.

With the appearance of Jo-Ann, the tempo seemed to quicken - she possesses a fine voice which she used effectively on Ry Cooder's 'You're Gonna Mess Up A Good Thing'. To say the band is blues-influenced would be a vast understatement. They rework old blues standards such as 'Let Me Love You Baby' and Bobby Bland's 'Help Me Through The Days', with Jo-Ann exercising her all her vocal dexterity on what I thought was the best song of the evening - very powerful and truly atmospheric.

The band played two Cajun numbers with Watkins on piano-accordion and Riley helping Jo-Ann on vocals. These two numbers, 'Hobo Blues' and 'Take a City Bride' were good fun and the band were obviously enjoying themselves. The choice of material did not allow Jo-Ann to use her voice to the full; I would have liked to have heard her tackling some more modern numbers but both band and audience seemed happy with what they were doing.

The band was somewhat loose at times, a couple of songs fading into obscurity rather than finishing at any recognised point. But they worked hard and finished off with 'Over You', 'Neighbour's Daughter' and 'It's All Over Now', coming back to encore with another old blues classic 'Sweet Home Chicago'.

Simon Sterling

Croydon's Warehouse Theatre announced details of a 'Benefit fortnight' including concerts by various local bands, all of whom offered their services free. The gigs kicked off with Questions and Apocalypse (Dec.2), Maverick and Ash (Dec.3), El Slug and Maineline (Dec.4), Empty Vessels and Fruit Eating Bears (Dec.5), Riders (Dec.9), The Spivs and the Daleks (Dec.10), Childe Rolande and Dr. Cosgill (Dec.11), Anerley Park (Dec.12) and Rhyme & Reason (Dec.13).

In August, a five-piece Croydon band made their debut at the Cartoon and turned in a sizzling set, despite having only played together for five months.

I say 'Croydon band' - they were certainly based locally, but most of the group originally hailed from the North East. **The Breakers** consisted of lead vocalist Maggie Roscoe Norris, Les Dodds - lead guitar, Charlie Foskett - bass, Marty Craggs - saxophone and Ian Hamilton on drums. Under the guidance of manager David Robinson, the Breakers had recently signed a five-year contract with MAM records and released their first single 'Headline News'. Further appearances at the Cartoon were lined up, plus a charity gig at the Greyhound in September and a tour supporting Darts in October.

Bassist Charlie Foskett and Maggie were both in a band called Sandgate, before Maggie left to join Newcastle folk group Hedgehog Pie. Marty Craggs played in Harcourt's Heroes alongside Lindisfarne's Ray Jackson and fellow geordie Charlie Harcourt, while Les Dodds co-wrote a song for Jackson's first solo album 'In The Night'. In 1985, Marty became a full-time member of Lindisfarne and teamed-up once more with Ray Jackson.

On October 3rd I went along to the Cartoon to see **Seven Year Itch**, a solid country/rock outfit who played a mixture of covers including The Band's *Cripple Creek* in amongst some of their own material. While the group were just preparing to go on, a short, curly-haired guy bustled through the crowd, carrying a guitar case - 'that looks like **Albert Lee**' I thought, and when he took his place on stage and began to play, I knew I wasn't mistaken. Earlier in the year, I had seen Albert playing a slightly bigger venue in Hammersmith, as a member of Eric Clapton's band.

The Fairfield Hall turned into the Glasgow Apollo for a week in October, which saw concerts from **Billy Connolly** and **Sheena Easton**. For Sheena it was the opening night of her first major concert tour, although she already had two top ten singles behind her - 'Modern Girl' and '9 to 5'. Her big break came from an appearance on the Esther Rantzen TV show 'The Big Time', but who would have recognised the petite shy Scots lass in the white flying suit from the raunchy 1990's version, hanging out with the likes of Prince.

The concert at the Fairfield Hall on October 19 was a special benefit for the young family of **Joanne Stone**, one half of the hitmaking group R & J Stone, who died of a brain tumour on New Years Eve 1979. Paying tribute were Madeline Bell (Joanne's cousin), Cliff Richard, Chas & Dave, Joe Brown, Pearly Gates and compere Tony Blackburn.

Croydon Advertiser – 28.11.80

Jug with Jerry

MUNGO JERRY were in an ideal location when they played the Cartoon wine bar in Croydon on Friday. The smoky, noisy atmosphere of the bar was well suited to their kind of music.

The band shot to fame in 1970 with their massive hit 'In The Summertime' and they spearheaded a short craze for honky tonk jug-band music. They played a hurried version of the song on Friday but they're not the sort of group who deny the existence of their hits.

Among others aired, all with a great sense of fun, were 'Lady Rose' and 'Long-legged Woman Dressed In Black'. Although the band boasts a superb lead guitarist - Dave Woods - it centres on lead singer Ray Dorset. Dorset wrote 'Summertime' and most of the group's best songs; he has a deep, husky voice and the sort of dark, gypsy looks to get the girls going. The lad makes some strange noises too - lots of growls and shouts of "all right". Unlike many professional musicians he seems cheerful and uncomplicated and was perfectly willing to talk to people in the audience afterwards.

The band set out to make people happy and join in the singing - the only two slow songs they played weren't given much of a welcome by the crowd. Things like 'Margarita' and 'Knocking On Heaven's Door' weren't as well suited to the location and mood of the evening as the old Sonny Boy Williamson song 'Don't Start Me Talking' and an original arrangement of 'See You Later Alligator' which got the audience singing in reply.

Mungo Jerry ended with 'All I Need Is Boogie' and a terrifically fast version of 'Johnny B. Goode'. Although the last two songs included an unnecessary female backing singer, the crowd sent the band off with cries for more.

Alan Hyder

Another local musician, singer/songwriter **David James**, recorded a new single for the Towerbell label. The hugely titled '*The Original Cuckoo Bird Pineapple Truck (Lone Star Boogie Bar Band)*' featured lead guitar from Albert Lee as well as a session band that was pretty well made up from regulars from the Cartoon. Rockola's Dave Christopher played guitar, Bill Aedy played bass, Peter Baron was the drummer and Roger Retig added pedal steel and dobro.

The sleeve featured a somewhat tongue-in-cheek list of credits, with James thanking (amongst others): Eddie Cochran, bacon butties, Scout halls, the Everly Brothers, hangovers, fish'n'chips, Andrews liver salts, B-movies, Del Shannon, A.C. 30's, Saturday nights, and the pie stall at Thornton Heath!

Crystal Palace Bowl - The Garden Parties

Time to take a look at Croydon's celebrated equivalent to Monterey & Woodstock... well, Reading and Bath perhaps; the annual one-day rock festival that took place halfway up Crystal Palace Hill - the **Garden Party.**

The 'Crystal Palace' itself was built for the Great Exhibition of 1851 and the spectacular construction of glass and steel was originally situated in Hyde Park. Once the festivities were over, it was moved from central London to Penge Park and re-opened by Queen Victoria herself on 10th June 1854. This remarkable building burnt to the ground in December 1936, and once the charred metalwork had been cleared away, only a handful of statues, stone arches and the sweeping front steps remained. The largest of the local open air concert venues, Crystal Palace Park contains a natural amphitheatre - a grassy slope contained by trees on three sides, that runs down to a small lake, on the other side of which lies the stage covered by a white semi-circular acoustic canopy. The Garden Parties were extremely popular with rock photographers - the inside of that white canopy is instantly recognisable and can be seen in a huge number of library shots by all the top 'snappers'.

1971 – Pink Floyd / The Faces / Mountain / Quiver

Pink Floyd
The Faces
Mountain
Quiver

The very first event took place on Saturday 16th May, with Pink Floyd top of the bill and tickets at £1.25. An estimated 15,000 turned out (almost every year was reported to be this figure!) and by all accounts, the three supporting groups played in reasonably fine weather - right up until the Floyd took the stage. The Croydon Advertiser's Barry Shinfield reported: *'They were certainly worth waiting for; imaginative, creative musicians, innovators and showmen, the Pink Floyd can rightly lay claim to being one of the leading rock groups of the day. But soon after the Floyd struck up with their opus 'Atom Heart Mother', the skies opened. The audience huddled under miles of polythene, revellers swam in the muddy pond...and the band played on.'* The Floyd provided their usual share of visual tricks - in this case detonating orange smoke bombs, rockets and a giant inflatable octopus afloat in the lake. There was even a special guest appearance by Elvis - or at least an impersonator in a gold lamé suit!

1971 – Elton John / Yes / Rory Gallagher / Fairport Convention / Hookfoot / Tir Na Nog

Elton John
Yes
Rory Gallagher
Fairport Convention
Hookfoot
Tir Na Nog

Saturday 31st July was the date for the second of the Palace Garden Parties. As any festival-goer will testify, the weather is almost as important a factor as who appears on the bill and this time it held out. Barry Shinfield again... *'when the sun shone, it was oven hot and, in these conditions, there was much to be said for settling down on the grass for seven hours relaxation. And so 15,000 others thought, a genial, bra-less, hot panted, hirsute assembly, smoking pot and tossing red coke cans into the still, green, weed-wasted waters of the lake'.*

The compere was DJ Pete Drummond, who took the opportunity to angrily voice his opinion on the verdicts passed on Richard Neville and co. in the infamous OZ trial. **Elton John** was top of the bill, dressed in red jump suit and yellow winged boots he rocked his way through a set that included covers of 'Honky Tonk Women' and 'Whole Lotta Shakin' Going On' as well as his own 'Razor Face' and 'Take Me To The Pilot'. In fact, a bootleg recording of this set is available, the not quite accurately titled 'Live in London'.

Carry-on star Barbara Windsor was one of the assembled throng, personally invited by Elton she relaxed in the crowd and has listed the event as her favourite ever gig. The Melody Maker, ever keen to review the musical content of the day, wrote that Barbara's boobs didn't appear to be as large as they looked on the big screen!

Frazer Ashford

The Crystal Palace crowd catching a few rays during yet another day in the park - anyone recognise themselves in the assembled throng?

1972 – Joe Cocker
Melanie
The Beach Boys
Ritchie Havens
Sha Na Na
David Blue

Saturday 3rd June was a particularly wet afternoon, in true open air festival style. The resilient crowd, around 17,000 of them, huddled under polythene bags and sheets of cardboard while the Beach Boys could only conjure images of sunshine with 'Surfs Up' and 'Good Vibrations'. They were joined onstage by Elton John and Keith Moon - Moon had flown in by helicopter, buzzing the crowd with confetti before rowing across the lake with 'Legs' Larry Smith from the Bonzo's. Sadly, time ran out for David Blue, they just couldn't fit him into the schedule.

1972 – Arlo Guthrie
Stone the Crows
Osibisa
Edgar Winter
Roxy Music
Loggins & Messina

Saturday 23rd July was the date for the years second Palace date, hosted by DJ Pete Drummond. As this ad. from 'Time Out' shows, Pink Floyd loaned out their sound system and the entrance fee was the princely sum of £1.25.

1972 – Yes
Lindisfarne
Capability Brown
Gary Wright
John MacLaughlin's Mahavishnu Orchestra

The third party of the year, Saturday 2nd September claimed a record crowd of 20,000 to see a bill topped by Yes, Lindisfarne and the first UK appearance of the Mahavishnu Orchestra. The Advertiser's Barry Shinfield preferred the lively Geordie's to Yes, whose *'extended and meticulous treatment of their material tends to bore, once you have appreciated their basic skills of playing and harmonising'*. John MacLaughlin's new group contained some excellent musicians in violinist Jerry Goodman and keyboard player Jan Hammer, but was deemed *'too esoteric for rock audiences'*.

The usual high jinks were in evidence - fully clothed revellers in the lake, a male stripper in the crowd - but the free cheese rolls that compere John Peel had promised would be dropped by helicopter, failed to materialise!

1973 – James Taylor
Lou Reed
Beck, Bogart & Appice
Golden Earring
Tony Joe White
Back Door

Saturday 15th September marked the return of this outdoor rock event after missing the annual summer slot. Complaints from locals after three 1972 'Parties' meant that the GLC had to review the application, only granting the promoters a licence at the last minute. *"A licence to print money"* moaned the Advertiser, with over 20,000 punters paying £2.80 on the gate or £2.50 in advance.

The maximum turnout was a result of three things; fine weather on the day, improved publicity, including a rumour leaked to the press that Bowie would appear (he didn't) and the absence of a summer show. Golden Earring, Back Door and Tony Joe White opened the proceedings, but the acts that really got the crowd on their collective feet and into the lake were stunning sets from Beck, Bogert & Appice and Lou Reed. Jeff Beck's new trio played an impromptu encore entitled 'Crystal Palace Boogie'.

The headline act was James Taylor's first British appearance for two years. At the end of the day, as Taylor played 'Fire & Rain', the heavens finally opened to the crash of thunder and lightning.

41 Time Out 21–27 July 1972

MICHAEL ALFANDARY, HARVEY GOLDSMITH and JOHN & TONY SMITH
PRESENT

SPECIAL SUMMER GARDEN PARTY
at the CRYSTAL PALACE BOWL

The first Public Appearance in Great Britain of

★ ARLO GUTHRIE ★

Plus the only British performance this summer of

OSIBISA

with

STONE THE CROWS

and

ROXY MUSIC

Guest starring exclusively from the U.S.A.

EDGAR WINTER

+ LOGGINS & MESSINA

Compere: PETE DRUMMOND

Saturday, July 29th

Tickets only £1.25 Advance. £1.50 Door

SOUND SYSTEM BY PINK FLOYD

DOORS OPEN 11 O'CLOCK

AGENCIES
harlequin
record shops 01-636 1348

CORNHILL 74 CORNHILL
LUTON 12 ARNDALE CENTRE
BOW LANE 4 BOW LANE
CANNON ST. 129 CANNON ST.
LIVERPOOL ST. 41 LIVERPOOL ST.
MOORGATE 121 MOORGATE
CHEAPSIDE 116 CHEAPSIDE
FENCHURCH ST. 150 FENCHURCH ST.
BALHAM 168 HIGH ROAD
OXFORD 12 GEORGE ST.
CAMBRIDGE 4 BRIDGE ST.
BEDFORD 97 HIGH ST.
EPSOM 16 HIGH ST.
CAMBERLEY 14 PRINCESS WAY
FLEET ST. 167 FLEET ST.
50 FENCHURCH ST.
HIGH HOLBORN 36 HIGH HOLBORN
BROMPTON RD. ESCALADE 187
MAIDENHEAD 7 NICHOLSON'S WALK
GUILDFORD 14 TUNSGATE SQUARE
READING 22 UNION ST.
57 THE SOUTH MALL BUTTS CENTRE
WEST END 67 GT. TITCHFIELD ST.
OXFORD ST. 201 OXFORD ST.
MARBLE ARCH 527 OXFORD ST.
NEW BOND ST. 119 NEW BOND ST.
BERWICK ST. 96 BERWICK ST.
HAYMARKET 35½ HAYMARKET
VICTORIA 28 STRUTTON GROUND
CHELSEA DRUG STORE 49 KINGS RD.

One Stop Records
97 Dean St., W1. 734 9096
40 South Molton St., W1.
2 The Square, Richmond.

Mr Fox records
34 Station Rd., West Croydon

Fairfield Hall Croydon
Box Office

TICKETS AVAILABLE BY MAIL.

Send a stamped addressed envelope plus Postal Orders.

Cheques will be cleared and therefore will be subject to about one week's delay; any cheques sent should be made out to "Garden Party".

Please send me . . . . tickets
at £1.25 each, plus S.A.E. to:

Name . . . .

Address . . . .

. . . .

I enclose PO/Cheque for £. . . . .

Frazer Ashford

James Taylor put in his appearance between sets by Beck, Bogart & Appice and Lou Reed.

1974 – Rick Wakeman
Leo Sayer
Procol Harum
Gryphon
Wally

Saturday 27th July. The climax of the concert saw ex-Yes keyboard wizzard Rick Wakeman perform his new epic composition 'Journey To The Centre Of The Earth', based on the novel by Jules Verne. The stage of the Crystal Palace Bowl is by no means big, but Rick managed to cram the New World Symphony Orchestra, the English Chamber Choir and its conductor David Measham, actor and narrator for the day David Hemmings, as well as Rick's own five piece group!

At one point in the performance, a pair of seventeen-foot long, inflatable dinosaurs were launched onto the lake to 'do battle' and barring a few technical hitches, the entire 'rock-symphony' was successfully recreated.

Reporting for the Croydon Advertiser, Alaistair Wright thought Gryphon and Wally to be *'melodic & ingenious'*, but not really rock festival material. Procol Harum, however, *'had the fans on their feet, chanting for more'*.

The gig nearly ended in tragedy for the headline artist. Rick Wakeman had put so much into the rehearsal and organisation of his show that he had barely slept for five days. To add to his problems he had fallen over in his local pub a couple of days beforehand and cracked some bones in his arm. On the day of the concert, Rick was so ill, a doctor gave him three injections of morphine to kill the pain and he remembers little about the day itself. Instead of celebrating afterwards, he was bundled semi-conscious into a car and driven home to Buckinghamshire. Two days later he collapsed with a suspected heart attack and was rushed to hospital.

1975 – Steve Harley & Cockney Rebel
Steeleye Span
Billy Cobham
John Cale
Jack Bruce Band
Back Door

Garden Party 8 was held on Saturday 7th June and guess what?... for once the sun shone. Special guests The Jack Bruce Band included Carla Bley and ex-Stones guitarist Mick Taylor in their line up. Steeleye Span entertained the crowd with a traditional 'Mummers play' and Steve Harley was his usual enigmatic self. Rumour has it that Harley had a wooden platform built just under the surface of the lake in front of the stage, so that he could step off the stage and appear to 'walk on water'!

However it was the crowd, not Steve Harley, who took full advantage of the weather to frolic in the water and judging by Fraser Ashford's pictures, a thoroughly good time was had by all!

1976 – Eric Clapton
Freddie King
The Chieftains
Jess Roden Band
Barbara Dickson
Dick & the Firemen

An estimated 15,000 people turned out on Saturday 31st July for a solid eight hours of music, most of whom came prepared to brave the worst of the weather, although apart from a couple of black clouds and the odd spot of rain, generally the sun shone and the cool beer flowed. Ironically, once it became apparent that it was not going to pour with rain, a large number of the audience left their umbrellas and poly bags and immersed themselves in the lake at the front of the stage! According to Sandy Harrod of the Croydon Advertiser, Clapton was disappointing - *"somehow the euphoria normally attributed to his performance was missing; the music was good, but lacked sparkle..."*

Freddie King was on form, as was Barbara Dickson and it was during Jess Roden's set that the first 'bathers' took to the water. Towards the end of Clapton's set, he was joined onstage by Larry Coryell who jammed on 'Further On Up The Road' while both Freddie King and Ronnie Wood played during the encores. And who were Dick & the Firemen? A scratch band of Steve Marriott and friends, comprising Simon Kirke & Boz Burrell from Bad Company, Zoot Money, Mel Collins, Tim Hinkley, John Halsey, plus Neil Hubbard & Allan Spenner from the Grease Band.

The new Jack Bruce band playing 'the Bowl', June 1975 - featuring Carla Bley and Stone's guitarist Mick Taylor.

Both pics: Frazer Ashford

Eric 'Slowhand' Clapton and backing vocalist Yvonne Elliman - note the characteristic guitar string 'ciggie-holder'.

1977 – Santana
Elvis Costello
Southside Johnny & the Asbury Jukes
Brand X
Crawler

10th September '77 saw Carlos Santana topping the bill of the tenth Garden Party, with the surprising choice of Elvis Costello in second place. In what is now regarded as a rare mistake by manager Jake Riveira, Elvis failed to impress an audience of over 12,000 laid-back Santana fans with his quirky, often aggressive delivery of songs from his first album for Stiff Records, 'My Aim is True'. According to the biography by Mick St. Michael, Costello *'stormed off, leaving a bowl of feedback to express his feelings'.*

Overall, this was certainly one of the more ambitious line-ups - blues/rock from Crawler, jazz-rock from Brand X, brassy US soul from Southside Johnny, 'new wave' angst and anger from Costello and the latin flavoured rock guitar of Carlos Santana, who even named one of their lengthy instrumentals 'Incident at Crystal Palace'.

1980 – Bob Marley & the Wailers
Joe Jackson
Average White Band
Q-Tips

Saturday 7th June and one of the rare appearances in Britain by arguably Jamaica's finest songwriter - Bob Marley. One of the Bowl's largest crowds, nigh on 20,000 people turned out to see the 'High Priest of Reggae', with every possible vantage point taken for a better view of the stage - in trees, up on van roofs, the faithful even climbed on waste bins

Louise Chase was the Advertiser's appointed one and she noted that - *"Marley's coming was greeted with near religious zeal, as people who had sat, lazed and sunbathed their way through a sleepy afternoon's entertainment, rose to their feet craning for a view.... the atmosphere was electric as thousands swayed and danced to insistent reggae rhythms. Even the trees moved in time - something of a puzzle until I realised they were all chock-a-bloc with swinging, clinging fans."*

For his encore, Marley previewed a brand new number - the acoustic 'Redemption Song', which was about to be released on the album 'Uprising' and destined to become a Marley classic.

Earlier in the afternoon sun, the party had been opened by the Q-Tips, an eight piece soul band featuring the vocals of Paul Young and who had only just launched their recording career; whereas the Average White Band had a wealth of experience and hits behind them - material like 'Pick Up The Pieces' and 'When Will You Be Mine' would seem to be ideal for a summer outdoor festival. Following Elvis Costello's striking appearance in '77, this years 'angry young men' were the Joe Jackson Band, and once again the reaction of the crowd was somewhat muted.

But then let's face it, 99% of the crowd had only come to see one man - *the* man - the inimitable Bob Marley.

David Corio / S.I.N.

Bob Marley at the Crystal Palace Bowl - 7th June 1980.

Waddon Makes Wednesdays Worthwhile!

An interview with Peter Twichett, one of the longest serving residents of Croydon Folksong Club and one without whom, it can safely be said, the club would not have survived to the present day.

The Folk Club predates me and my involvement in it, but not by long; I didn't actually know there *was* a folk club in Croydon, but I was living in West Wickham at the time and had been going regularly since about 1966 to one at Catford. I'd been having a whale of a time there, thoroughly enjoyed it and then it was suggested to me that there was a club in Croydon, which was a lot closer than Catford, and might be worth going along to have a look. This I did, but it was a completely different sort of club, not the same atmosphere; the club at Catford was very much one big family, everybody would sing everyone else's songs, to the extent that if a guest singer got up and sang a song that everyone knew, you got the most incredible chorus work. And if it was a very well known song, people would sing not only on the choruses, but add the most wonderful folk harmonies to the verses as well - it was something that when you remember it today it still sends a tingle down the spine - a tremendous atmosphere.

So, the first time I went to Croydon it was completely different, it was very quiet, there were only about ten people there and it didn't make an enormous impression. The club was based even then at the Waddon public house, which is situated at the junction of Stafford Road and Duppas Hill Road, although it ran for a couple of months in another pub in South Norwood which wasn't at all suitable, so to all intents and purposes its home was always the Waddon. It was run at that time by a lovely couple called John and Sue Wallace who were themselves very good musicians and singers and because it was much more local for me, I kept going, got to know a few of the regulars there and they were kind enough to let me sing. Because it was on a different sort of circuit, they hadn't heard many of the songs that I sang, which of course had been done to death at Catford. Eventually, John and Sue moved down to Cornwall and they left the club in the hands of a gentleman called Fred Crook, along with myself and another singer called Tony Powell. We were the resident singers that went along with the club, so Fred did all the booking and that sort of thing, and we supported him and opened both halves of the 'show' by singing on club nights.

Well, that didn't last too long; John and Sue went in the August 196? and during that next year, Tony and I both decided that it wasn't worth staying where we were. To be honest, Fred Crook and I didn't see eye to eye on a number of things and so Tony and I began looking all around the district for a pub back room in which to start our own club. We looked for the best part of three months and the nearest we got was a place up in Crystal Palace but the rent was way too high - it was about eight pounds a week or something! Then one night, Tony 'phoned me up and said 'Hey, they're packing it in, Fred doesn't want to do it anymore and he's left it to me; I can't do it on my own - come down and help me run it'. So this solved our problem, we now had our own club without having to look for premises and we ran it together for about three years until Tony was promoted in his job and moved into Central London.

I ran the club on my own for a while, with various people drifting in and out; that period had its good times and bad times, without putting too fine a point on it, I don't think the club would have got to thirty years old if I hadn't hung in there during those early days. The attendances fluctuated - you see, we had to build up the audience from what it was, which was about twenty people a night and we knew that if it was going to survive then we had to get a much bigger audience than that. We didn't have the funds to go for the big names, so we had to bring people in on reputation and our regulars had to trust our judgement on who we put on. The people got to know that we wouldn't book anybody who was rubbish and I must say that we very rarely 'pulled a boner' - there are only two nights that I can remember wishing I was dead! That trust did build the audiences up and it got to a peak where we were regularly getting sixty people a night. We were also into the business of having a motto, a catchphrase where people could feel that they actually belonged to a stable, well-run club that they could identify with. So because we met on a Wednesday night, the motto became 'Waddon makes Wednesday worthwhile' and this was actually changed into a song about 'walking to the Waddon in your wellies' during the very wet summer of '75 or '76. This was written at the suggestion of the present encumbent Rita Cherriman, who was walking down to us from her house and getting soaked to the skin and when we made some 'sarky' remark she said 'well, at least it deserves a song'. We used the song to open up the club nights in the music hall tradition, you know 'my Lords, Ladies and Gentlemen, pray welcome to the first half...' and we always finished up with the same song as well, to the tune of 'Cwm Rhonda', ending on the words '...please take your glasses to the bar', which was greatly appreciated by the landlady!

We were actually very lucky at the Waddon, because right the way through the clubs time there, from John and Sue opening up, until about 1980, the pub was in the hands of one landlady all that time. She thought the club was wonderful; to the extent that when we were recorded for the BBC programme 'Folkweave', recorded twice, in fact, she was quite happy to give over her lounge and front bedroom to the BBC and all their recording equipment! The presenter of Folkweave was up there doing his stuff and she was quite thrilled by that, and we presented her with a recording of the programme afterwards. It was quite a community pub in those days - sometimes when we had a slack night we would go out into the bar and say 'does anybody want to come in for half price?' and they'd all come in... some would not think much of it, but a lot of the locals regularly came into the club as well. Sometimes they would say 'I see you've got a bit of a crowd in tonight, so we won't come in, but can you leave the door open a bit so we can hear what's going on!'. It was that sort of atmosphere, that friendly spirit, which was so tremendous.

Around 1972/73, there were rumours that another club had opened up in a wine bar in Croydon and we thought we'd better check this one out. So we went down to the Scandis wine bar in South Croydon, and there was a resident

Courtesy Graham Maisey

Croydon Folksong Club in action at the Waddon, circa 1974. Left to right: Sue Rule, Peter Twitchett, Graham Maisey and Grant Rule.

group called **Garden Party** in there, singing away, who were very good. I invited them down to the Waddon and they came, and ended up staying with us for about eight years, as residents! Garden Party were a three piece; Mick Longhurst, Graham Maisey and Dave Greenhough and they really gave the club a second wind when they joined, because they not only bought their audience from the Scandis with them, but they were a complete foil for myself, just as Tony Powell had been. They sang contemporary folk, while I was more traditional and we could put across more of a blend of material. Two of the group eventually moved away, but Graham Maisey stayed on and we ran the club together for what became the longest and possibly the most successful partnership. Once again, we pulled the club through some pretty grim nights, even when, on one occasion it was just Graham, myself and three others, we still did an evening for them, just to keep the club going.

It was during my association with Graham and his involvement with the graphics industry, that we came up with the idea of the 'Penny Dreadful', mainly because we got fed up with the table being covered with piles of other clubs leaflets! Nobody would ever take them and we were left with hundreds of leaflets that we didn't know what to do with; we thought this must be costing somebody a fortune. So instead we produced the Penny Dreadful which acted as a sort of what's on for all the local clubs who wanted to be advertised in it. It started out as A4 and later reduced to A5; it was professionally printed and in it's heyday ran up to about twenty pages. We had a series of people who delivered it to the areas that they wanted it to go to, mainly Surrey and South London and it was good for a lot of the clubs - it made them more organised, and the artists could advertise in it and avoid playing two clubs close to each other in the same week, that sort of thing. It certainly wasn't a money-making enterprise, just an extended club newsletter really.

There were a group of people up in South Norwood who were very interested in folk music, they started out of a Scout group, they belonged to whatever took over from the Scouts in those days, the Rovers or Rangers, and they decided to put on a concert. One of their members was a regular at our club and he asked if some of our residents would add to the list of performers that he was putting together. So we all went along and played and the concert went down very well, but more importantly, three things emerged from it: firstly their folk group became regular performers at Croydon, which boosted our attendances; secondly the concert launched a Morris team which eventually became Northwood Morris and I ended up playing the accordion for them and thirdly, we thought that if we could do a concert like that, we could go out and 'take the folk to the people' much more than we were. This was something we did quite successfully, organising several concerts and ceilidh's outside of the general club nights, including one memorable one during the miners strike and Edward Heath's 'Winter of Discontent'. One of our members worked on the site of the old Croydon Airport, Purley Way, for a firm who exported generators and we had this particular concert booked in the Hall adjoining Croydon Parish Church. It was due to be quite a good night, but of course, when we checked the papers, they announced that there was going to be a strike and consequently a 'blackout' on that night. We all looked at each other and wondered what we could do, and this guy came up and said ' You probably don't know this, but I work for a firm who service and export generators all round the world; we've got one that needs running in and I'll bring it along on the night'! We thought he was stringing us along, but come the night of the concert, he took this generator down to the Parish Hall and we ran the first half hour of the concert on 'real' electricity, then when the lights started to go he switched his machine into the hall circuits and pumped it back up, to a massive round of applause. The generator pumped away all night and of course, no one minded the noise because without it there would have been no concert; afterwards he took it back, let it cool down, crated it up and the next day it was flown out to Nigeria! He also did that for one of our club nights, he sat the generator out in the carpark and ran the leads in through the window.

Some of the guests who passed through are actually now quite famous names, I always like to say that **Jasper Carrott** and **Mike Harding** were regular guests at the club, whenever Jasper comes on the TV I bore the family by saying that he once bought me a pint! And **Barbara Dickson** was playing the folk clubs then and would have appeared but for a 'disagreement' on the telephone! We had **Gordon Giltrap**, who was an absolutely stunning guitarist,

Pete Twitchett (contd.)

Nic Jones, **Stan Arnold**, **Allan Taylor**, **Mike Maran**, **Alaistair Anderson**, **Tony Rose**, **Vin Garbutt** and even **Fiddlers Dram**, pre-Daytrip to Bangor!

Towards the end of the 'seventies, our favourite landlady at the Waddon decided to retire and although she tried to ensure that her replacement would allow the club to continue, it was never quite the same. It was also around that time that the club at the Swan & Sugarloaf, South Croydon 'retired' and we inherited some of their residents as well. So we ended the 'seventies with a good group of resident performers and a strong following, but a new landlord who, although he knew the club was there and was quite happy to take the money for the room, had little interest in the club itself. There was a different set of people coming into the pub, some of the old regulars were drifting away and he started dropping heavy hints that perhaps he could use the room for something else.

So we sent our residents out onto the highways and byways and said 'find us somewhere' and I think it was Chris Roche who found the room over **The Ship**, opposite the south end of Surrey Street. Everybody had reservations about this, because the Ship had a bit of a reputation in those days, but Chris said there is a lovely room upstairs, which is a restaurant during the day, but available in the evenings. We went along to see it and the people were happy to have the club there, so we thought we would give it a go and we moved to The Ship around 1980/81. The club continued there very successfully but it lost 'something' which is very difficult to pinpoint, and I think that it was the feel of the Waddon itself, the actual building, the compactness of the room - which all combined to make the club what it was.

Pressure of work then forced me to take a backseat and the 'benevolent dictatorship' that Graham and I had enjoyed was thrown over to a committee of residents. Other people were coming in and showing more of an interest in the actual running of the club, so eventually I retired gracefully and left the club in the hands of the committee, with Peter Trimming heading the cast and later handing it on to Rita Cherriman, under whom it has thrived ever since. For me the Waddon was the ideal, the Ship was good but lost a little in the move and then possibly a little more when it moved into the Fairfield Halls complex (the club initially took up residency in the Arnhem Gallery and subsequently moved to the Fairfield Bar). I can see the reasons for moving there but personally, it is not a move that I would have made. On occasions, we took the club to the Fairfield Halls to provide entrance and interval music, singing on the stairs when there was a folk act in the main hall, just to show people that there was a local club, which did us a lot of good and helped when we were looking for a new home because the Fairfield said, look, we've got the Arnhem Gallery... but that was after my time, because by the end of 1981 I was gone, I moved up to Suffolk. At the end of the day, it was great fun and given the chance, without question I would do it all again. ”

One of the more elaborate covers of the Penny Dreadful, for December 1974. Illustrated by Lawrence Heath, better known for his contributions to Folk Roots magazine especially the 'Borfolk' cartoon strip.

As advertised in the Penny Dreadful, December 1975, a Croydon Ceilidh with one of the early Albion Band line-ups.

Frazer Ashford

One of the truly great names of British folk music, Ewan MacColl and his partner Peggy Seeger performing in Croydon, circa 1974. Ewan has a long association with the area, living in Croydon and Beckenham and running and supporting folk clubs throughout South East London.

Frazer Ashford

Another stalwart of the folk and blues circuit, Long John Baldry pictured here playing the Star Hotel circa 1969/70. Baldry was a regular visitor to Croydon and during the early 'sixties his drummer was also a Croydon man, Sean O'Malley. While playing for LBJ, Sean first met Jack Bruce and Graham Bond, became a close friend of Ginger Baker and Yardbird Eric Clapton was a visitor to O'Malley's home in St. Peter's Street, South Croydon.

Francis Rossi

Founder member of one of the most popular and enduring of Britain's rock bands - Status Quo. Ask anyone and they will undoubtedly link 'the Quo' to the Croydon area, so I spoke to Mr. Rossi on the telephone to find out exactly what those links were. But first, a bit of background...

Francis was born in Forest Hill, South London on 29th May 1949, his father was part of the 'Rossi Ice cream' family business. The family moved to Park Avenue, Bromley and both Francis, and younger brother Dominic attended Sedgehill Comprehensive in Beckenham, where his teachers noted that *"he lives in a fantasy world, consumed by wild dreams of becoming a pop singer"*. At school, Francis tended to use the name Mike; as he told the Croydon Advertiser, *"I got so fed up with having the mickey taken out of me, I thought I'd change it while I had the chance"*. It was here that he met bass guitarist Alan Lancaster, who *was* born in Peckham and together with guitarist Alan Key they formed their first group, the **Scorpions** in March 1962. After only three months, Key left the band so Mike and Alan changed their name to the **Spectres**, bringing in schoolfriend Jess Jaworski on organ and Barry Smith on percussion. The Spectres continued to play mainly cover version instrumentals - hits by the Shadows, Tornado's and Johnny & the Hurricanes - and would practice next door to the ATC headquarters in Lordship Lane, Dulwich, where they could often hear another group playing. That band turned out to be the Cadets, including Dulwich-born drummer John Coghlan, who had been playing a couple of pub gigs in West Norwood. He had a decent drum kit and seemed to know what he was doing, so Francis asked him to join the Spectres - playing their first proper gig at the Samuel Jones Sports Club, Dulwich in late 1962. As the gigs became more frequent, they began travelling to them in the ice cream van owned by Francis's dad; fairly soon the Spectres got themselves a manager, Pat Barlow, whose main contribution was to get the band a summer residency at Butlins. Around this time the band also played support to the Hollies at Orpington Civic Hall.

By April 1965, the Spectres line-up consisted of Rossi, Lancaster, Coghlan and new organist Roy Lynes from Redhill band the **Side-Kicks**, and the group headed off to play the summer season at Butlins in Minehead. Here they ran into a cabaret trio called the Highlights and Francis befriended their guitarist Rick Harrison, from Woking. The Spectres were offered a recording contract with Pye subsidiary label Picadilly, but none of their three singles made any headway in the charts, including cover versions of 'I, Who Have Nothing' and 'Hurdy Gurdy Man'.

In May 1967 they decided that a change of name might improve their luck, so they became Traffic - only to run straight into legal problems with Steve Winwood and friends. So a quick change again to **Traffic Jam** and a further single 'Almost, But Not Quite There' written by Mike Rossi, that also lived up to it's name - the group made their only money as a touring backing group to people like Tommy Quickly, Madeline Bell and Guy Darrell. Francis had kept in touch with Rick from the Highlights and asked him to join the band - which he did, under the name Rick Parfitt. Manager Pat Barlow came up with another new name for the group and in August 1967 they became **The Status Quo**. The group played all over the country, but tended to shun gigs in central London, as Francis told the Croydon Advertiser - *"In London, everyone seems to think it's their scene, that they're the biggest thing that's ever happened. We want to steer clear of all that and just play good stuff. In the West End they just don't want to give us a chance, so we play anywhere outside of London and we seem to do all right"*.

Still signed to Pye records, their first single as Quo was a Rossi composition called 'Pictures Of Matchstick Men' - it took off immediately and finished up at number 7 in the national charts. The hit was unexpected; in fact, the band were still out on tour as Madeline Bell's backing group when the single entered the charts! A follow up single 'Ice In The Sun' also made the charts, but after that things started to go downhill. Their 'Carnaby Street' image may have looked the part for the psychedelic end of the Sixties, but the group were never really part of the 'underground' scene frequented by Cream, Pink Floyd, Hendrix and the rest. By the end of 1969, Quo were seriously thinking about packing it all in and actually, on a trip to Scotland in 1970 Roy Lynes did just that - he left the train and the band never saw him again.

Time for Francis to take up the story:

"So, live music in Croydon. Does it exist, anymore? It may have done, but I know my sons have trouble getting work anywhere nowadays - there doesn't seem to be any gigs, anywhere for them to play. It baffles me how any young bands get through, and the bands that are coming through, I just don't know who gets to see them and where. And most of the gigs they do get are on a pay to play basis - they get £75 to £100 I suppose and then usually charge them about £50-60 for the use of their P.A. system and then maybe £25 for the guy who is going to mix for them. I've got two sons who are now in the same band; the youngest, Kieran joined earlier this year, the band needed somebody to fill in on bass for a tour - he usually plays guitar - and they're still struggling out there somewhere. Sorry, but you've caught me at a time when that's very much in my mind...

People saw Quo as a local band? well it always felt that way, yeah. I was actually born in Forest Hill and then we went to Balham for a while, my parents brought a business in Balham and from there we moved to Bromley. Then I moved back to Forest Hill when I got married and then here, to Purley. Our manager Colin Johnson lived in Wallington, Alan Lancaster lived around here for a while, in Coulsdon, so all pretty local. Of course a lot of people from the music business lived on the Webb estate for a while; Peter Grant, who managed Zeppelin, the father and son team the Mehams, who managed Black Sabbath and various other bands - all sorts of people at one time. I heard that Brian Ferry may have done at some point and there was also a rumour that David Bowie was going to come and live on the estate - but I've spoken to David a couple of times and he told me he didn't know anything about it. Which is typical.

Our old keyboard player Roy Lynes was a lovely guy, he came from Redhill; our plumber/manager found him or saw him somewhere in about '65 and asked him to join us. He was a nice likable bloke, about four years older than the rest of us, maybe a bit more, which seemed a lot at the time.

There was always a bit of a problem in the band with Alan Lancaster, who could only ever sort things out by 'being aggressive', let's put it that way. I think that got a bit much for Roy, plus we'd all started smoking 'wonga' at the time, pot or hash and he wasn't into that very much, a little bit maybe, nothing special. Roy was really keen on these sports cars, Jaguars and Astons, that sort of thing; anyway he'd brought this car and we were all going somewhere one weekend in two motors, some of us in each. He pulled up to get some petrol, met this girl and that was it, you know, they were off. The following week, we were on our way to Scotland by train and Roy just got off the train at Leeds or somewhere like that and disappeared. We didn't see him again for years, until eventually we heard from him in New Zealand. Last time I saw him though, he was still the same, still Roy, a lovely quiet guy.

Andrew Bown now lives in Barnes, although he used to live in Caterham, but he will now tell you that he lives in the hub of the world! A lot of musicians live around that way - we wind him up by calling them a load of 'schmucks' - schmucks from Barnes. Andrew's been with us for a long time, since about '73-'74 and he's a good man, always very professional in his attitude, we've relied on him for that. He came from the Herd, of course, him and Peter Frampton are both from out Beckenham way.

I've lived in Purley since my early twenties and I really like where I live, I like the whole area. I remember when I was quite young, my mum and dad used to bring us to Croydon to the Caters supermarket in Surrey Street, which may have been the first supermarket in the area. When I was a kid, Caters was donkey's knob, you know?, to go to the supermarket was like, yeah, we were happening! I used to love to go to the supermarket, it's the main thing I remember about Croydon when I was young. I didn't know that this area south of Croydon even existed until I was in my twenties, I really didn't know this part of the world at all. It's a smashing place to be, I love it.

Everyone always figured that Quo came from Peckham, because Alan Lancaster came from there, there was a lot of talk about Peckham, but I mean Rick came from Woking... I wasn't really aware of the other local bands, I'm not the sort of bloke who goes to see other bands. It's very big-headed and probably the wrong way to do things, but once I had decided that I was going to do this for a living I sort of shut everything else out and just focused on what we were doing. Actually one of the disadvantages of being in a band is that, to dance is completely out of the question! I used to be able to dance quite well, but once I started playing in a group...

So I couldn't go out and see another band or any act play live, without spending the whole evening analysing what was going on and how it was being done. I can't just sit there and enjoy a show. And we used to be put off, especially if the band was really good, we'd think 'shit, you've got to be *that* good to get anywhere?' But it was more to do with the focus, you know, 'shut everything else out, this is the way to do it' type of thing.

When we were called the Spectres, we played over in Redhill and at Wallington Public Hall once or twice, which was more the case of our manager putting us in for a local gig. Wallington was a good gig; the place still had half day closing when I first came here - which is what we call Belgium, as it happens - but I quite used to like all that, everywhere would quieten down for the afternoon, it doesn't really happen anymore. We did one at the Bromel Club, which was the old Bromley Court Hotel and played the Castle at Tooting a few times as well; it's weird, I was talking to one of my sons the other day about them trying to get work and I was telling him that I was so lucky because a guy

Fraser Ashford

Rossi in action onstage at the Fairfield Hall - May 1972

came up to me when I was thirteen and said I want to manage you and the band. So I never really had to think about getting gigs, or the ins and outs of the business, all that was taken out of my hands. I wasn't really interested, we had an agent and a manager as soon as we got going. Whereas these guys have got no-one, today.

I said to them, it's amazing - after 'Matchstick Men', after our initial hit, we were going that far downhill that we went back into playing pub gigs and ended up supporting Mott the Hoople. To think of Status Quo and Mott the Hoople playing in the pub round the corner - but it was a good thing, it's like we were saying earlier, all these acts came out of that small gig circuit, built up their own followings - there was something real about it. Maybe it still goes on in parts of the country that we don't hear about, perhaps there is still a club circuit in the North, I don't know.

I also remember us supporting Slade at the Orchid Ballroom in 1971/72; in fact I'm sure we played there as the Spectres too, backing someone or other, but that tour we did with Slade stands out and it was strange to come and play Purley, I'll tell you. I was looking around here for a place to live about that time, but I didn't buy my current place until 1974 and moved in in '75.

There were lots of gigs with Quo at the Greyhound, one supporting T.Rex, and another one with the Groundhogs, I think. Everybody sat on the floor there, and getting them to stand up was something else, it really was some achievement in those days. I haven't been there for some years, but I dare say it's a lot smaller than I remember it. It was a guy

Francis Rossi (contd.)

called Brian Mason who ran it, him and his brother Steve. Brian Mason goes way back, he was around when we were just starting at thirteen or fourteen years old - in fact he probably owes us money from then! Those gigs we did as support at the Greyhound - a fiver, that's what we got - and especially unbelievable after we'd already got to the two or three hundred pounds stage. No band ever got more than four or five hundred quid in those days, that was about as far as you got really.

We did these package tours, everybody did these same package tours from Floyd to the Who, you know, and you'd get Engelbert Humperdink on there, Helen Shapiro, Amen Corner, the Love Affair, a bloke called Don Partridge, us and Gene Pitney! And you'd possibly sell out two houses at the Hammersmith Odeon or Finsbury Park Astoria, that became the Rainbow. It fascinated me that all these acts were usually top ten or at least top twenty in the charts and yet the whole show could just about sell out a place. The idea of playing somewhere like Wembley on your own was out of the question, it was just unbelievable in those days.

" ...those gigs we did as support at the Greyhound - a fiver, that's what we got! "

The packages were split into two distinct halves, we would often be the band to close the first half and down came the fire curtain for the interval. Everyone travelled on the same bus and shared the same gear, there was no P.A. and all that shit. The mike stand came up out of the floor in the middle of the stage and the sound came out somewhere in the middle of the theatre; you just hoped you could get a balance between the stage level and these speakers that were set way up at the back of the hall or in some case up in the roof. I mean, the sound must have been really wacky! Even when we got to playing gigs like the Greyhound, with our six or seven hundred watts of P.A. and people would say 'look at all this gear, how can you bring things this size in here...' but there's nothing in there really, seven hundred watts, it's nothing. You get that going past in a car these days!

The music scene didn't really become a 'business' until the Seventies, it had grown up a bit by then and people were saying 'hang on, there's money here'. You could see it all over Europe too, all the halls suddenly went up in price. It used to be great in Germany, the halls were really cheap and you could make good money and then suddenly it was like everyone fell in, real early Seventies '71 or '72, all the 'straights' as we called them were replaced by a younger hippie set who were suddenly running these gigs and making fortunes. Up went the prices and the whole business got so serious - which was good and bad of course.

We did a tour of Australia which was really fun, with Slade, Lindisfarne and Camel, I think it was; it was a tour where we got ripped off, but it was such fun, dear me. They were all great guys, Slade were all down to earth, reasonable guys, Linda's Tits were a great bunch, there might have been one moody one in there somewhere and I suppose we were a reasonable band to be on the road with - we had a really good time.

Now this year (1996) we've got Steeleye Span on tour with us, I like them. We asked Maddy Prior to sing on a track with us, when we covered 'All Around My Hat' recently and that was great fun. When they had their hit with it in 1976, I sent them a telegram saying 'Congratulations. Love your thing to death. You shitbags'. Or something like that; I always do that, swear at them because I wish I'd done it, you know, it's like the kid stamping his feet. And Maddy later said 'well, we were trying to copy you at the time', which was nice. So we decided it would be good if we could have them on tour and luckily we were able to get them. They could blow us away, no trouble, they're excellent live. That tour's going to be good; especially coming off the back of some European gigs, coming out of two or three big stadiums and then going bang into somewhere like Brighton or Bridlington - WOW! - suddenly there's all these people in your face - WOW! - it's good though because it makes each night different, it makes you react differently and work differently, it's good. 99

The Status Quo on a cold rooftop somewhere in South London, circa 1968. Left to right: John Coghlan, Roy Lynes, Rick Parfitt, Alan Lancaster and Francis Rossi.

Brian Smith

Thornton Heath guitarist who was a guitar tutor at Potter's Music, ran his own successful jazz/ blues group The Wes Minster Five and backed artists of the calibre of John Lee Hooker and Memphis Slim...

I started out by playing my mother's ukelele when I was seventeen - my mother was a pianist, with perfect pitch, although she never did very much with it - and to begin with I wasn't really interested in music, like a lot of kids at that age I preferred football and cycling. Then I discovered skiffle, so I went out and bought a tea chest and made a 'tea chest bass' out of it, which as you probably know is a broom handle, a bit of clothes line and a tea chest. We were doing the Lonnie Donegan thing, touring the streets on the back of a lorry and we thought we were really big time; we went up to the West End playing the same places as Tommy Steele and thought we were even bigger time!

I was watching all these other guys playing guitars, very badly as it turned out although I didn't know that at the time, so I went down to a junk shop in Portland Road, South Norwood and bought an old guitar for twenty five shillings. I tried to teach myself to play and couldn't make head nor tail of it, I couldn't make more than a few chords - there was a little music shop by the clocktower in Norwood, so I went in there and this little old lady said to me "oh, you want a guitar tutor, son". She sold me this book for two and sixpence, which I've still got, it was full of proper music and I thought what's all this about, you know, I thought playing the guitar was copying a diagram, making a shape and strumming a chord. I took this book home and spent the next four weeks learning to play 'I'll Be Loving You Always', as a guitar solo.

In 1955 I joined the RAF, and one of the first things they ask you is does anyone play a musical instrument?, you say 'yes sir' and they send you home on a pass to get it. I rushed home to get my guitar and I joined the station dance band; then they wanted a trumpet player, so I said "well, I'll have a go if you can give me an instrument", which they did, and I began playing in their brass band. All this led to my starting to think of my guitar as a horn, which is what the American players do and the saxophone players in our band said "yeah, you want to listen to Barney Kessel and Django Reinhart, people like that". That got me into this American stuff, playing real modern jazz which became my thing for a while.

When I came out of the RAF in November '57, I looked in the Melody Maker for a band; nobody wanted a guitar player but there was a guy in Sanderstead who was looking for a saxophonist. I 'phoned him up and said "look, I don't play sax but I know how to make my guitar sound like one", so we got together, became great friends and did a lot of work over the years. Working on scores for John Barry, Anthony Newley and Adam Faith, we were working up at Abbey Road studios during the time The Beatles were there and a friend of mine named Andy White, was sitting in on drums for them.

I was the second guitar teacher at Potter's Music shop, the first one lasted about a month; I had only been playing myself for four years when Dave asked me to teach there, I didn't think I knew enough, but he said "well, you know more than our pupils". So I used to cycle down to the shop on a Saturday morning and got three and sixpence an hour for teaching the guitar. My first pupil, Ian Hudson eventually took over from me at Potter's when I decided to start teaching on my own; but I always had a good rapport with Potter's, I knew Ted extremely well and played in his band. Andy White was one of the drum tutors at Potter's, he was a jazz and showband drummer who played Ringo's part on many of the early Beatles records - Ringo used to stand in the corner smoking a joint - he actually admitted that on TV a while back, I couldn't believe my ears!

Around Croydon I started a dance band, the **Brian Collins Quartet** - Jim Collins who provided the other half of the bands name, now runs the Forge at Addington - and he's a very fine keyboard player. I became the guitarist with the Johnny Howard Orchestra, who were the resident band at the Orchid Ballroom in Purley; we worked there four nights a week and to show you how much work there was around, I was part of a fifteen piece band with Johnny Howard, plus there was a quartet who played during the interval, that's nineteen musicians playing four nights a week at the Orchid *and* there were other venues close by that were all doing good business, the Greyhound, the Locarno in Streatham, the Wimbledon Palais, each one had a regular big band. Then I began sitting in with various jazz groups around Croydon, places like The Gun, The Croydon pub in Park Street and the Star at Broad Green, jazz every Tuesday night and some wonderful people played in there who are now international names.

I formed my own group, the **Wes Minster Five** and we cut some records on the Carnival label, which was basically a reggae/blues label run by Radio Caroline. Our singles, 'Shakin' the Blues' and 'Sticks & Stones' are now supposed to be worth about sixteen quid each, although the Record Collector guide spelt the name 'Westminster', which is incorrect. Also, if you listen to some of the West Indian artists who recorded for Carnival, Sugar and Dandy, Louisa, Maynell Wilson, then that's us backing them. We didn't always want our name mentioned, but the Maynell Wilson records are credited as her *with* the Wes Minster Five. At one point we hit a bit of an identity crisis, thinking we had become too much of a jazz band, so we changed our name to **The Beat Roots** in an attempt to appeal more to the pop market! It was a good name really, but it didn't catch on and we soon switched back to Wes.

My first drummer with the Wes Minster Five was Jon Hiseman, around 1963. We also had Dave Greenslade on keyboards, Bobby Brean on vocals, Tony Reeves on bass and also a guy called John Pamenter on bass. I had played with John Pamenter at Ronnie Scott's in 1959, in a band called the Paul Carroll Quintet, which was probably my first jazz experience and when I formed my own group, it seemed the obvious thing to use John when I could. Reeves, Greenslade and Hiseman all came from Eltham. I also did some work with John MacLaughlin, a guitarist who achieved quite a lot of fame, not all of it deserved in my opinion, but we all used to cross over, working with different bands, it was like one big community. I had a Volkswagon van with Wes Minster Five painted down the side and the Who had exactly the same type of van, with their name on the side - we used to pass each other on the road and wave. Eventually I tried to rock the band up a bit, Jon Hiseman and the guys were becoming a bit too 'jazzy'; I got in a very good bass player called Tony Brooks. How the name came about was one time we were in the van and happened to be passing a Westminster Bank, where the 't' had fallen out of the sign. My manager, who knew that one of my jazz heroes was Wes Montgomery, he spotted the sign and said "there you go, Wes Minster, there's your name! Although I was a white guy from Surrey, I had a very black sound and when the American musicians came over I often got the job of backing them - one after the other we backed Sonny Boy Williamson, Rufus Thomas, John Lee Hooker and Memphis Slim. If you see the footage on video of Rufus Thomas doing a couple of numbers on Ready Steady Go! that's us backing him - and on that same show, Paul Raven was the warm-up man!

Mr. Fox

The famous Fox head logo as she appeared from 1972 to 1975.

The Fox 'organisation' played a central part in the musical history of Croydon, particularly the promotion of live music in the area. Its base was at 34 Station Road, West Croydon where **Mr. Fox Records** was the foremost record shop in town, in the days before the multi-media megastores took over. Run by Brian Mason, the shop specialised in imports and also ran a successful mail order business, with a second premises at 44 Station Road used as the office and storage space.

The shop itself was tiny, with some of the floorspace to the right of the door taken up by a descending spiral staircase; originally the basement contained listening booths, essential for all self-respecting 60's record stores, but it later became extra office space, as the Fox 'empire' expanded.

A subsidiary company *Vixen Record Distributors*, was set up to handle the import and sales side of the business; two of the sales executives were Adrian John, later to become a Radio One DJ and Mike Chapman who went on to run Croydons Rock It! record shop. Mike told me that he and Adrian were interviewed on the same day in early '74, when Mike's lack of experience in the music industry was outweighed by his enthusiasm and a sound knowledge of 'the Quo'!.

Fox mainman Brian Mason had been promoting concerts since the early '60's, including one celebrated instance when he booked the Beatles and then received regular 'phone calls from Brian Epstein to inform him of their spiralling fees! Along with Steve Gledhill, Mason also ran the blues nights in the Star Hotel at Broad Green towards the end of the decade, when it was known as the *Zodiac Club*. In the 'blues boom' of the late 'sixties, the club drew the likes of Fleetwood Mac, Savoy Brown, Chicken Shack, Jethro Tull and Ten Years After, but as these groups became more and more popular, the little back room at the Star just wasn't big enough to cope and Brian looked around for a bigger gig. He found his new venue at the other end of the town, over the new Greyhound pub built into the base of St. George's House, the tower block which is now home to Nestlé. Billing the venue as 'Croydon's Blues Club', the first gig was held on 23rd November 1969 and featured Juicy Lucy. Up to that point, the Star had been the main rival to the big Fairfield Hall gigs, but bands were now given an intermediate step in their progression from pub back room to major concert hall. The Greyhound could hold up to 800 people and began booking acts who were either just about to break big or who preferred to play 'stand-up' venues. From blues to 'progressive' rock, the Greyhound became a haven for bands such as Yes, Genesis, King Crimson, Mott the Hoople, Stray, Lindisfarne, Humble Pie, Free - you name them, almost every major British band played there, sometimes three or four times a year!

Mike Chapman remembers that all Mr. Fox staff were issued with a pass card that would admit themselves and one guest to any Fox promoted gig. However, if any concert looked like becoming a sell-out, the staff were expected to turn out as auxiliary 'bouncers'! When Cockney Rebel made their first Greyhound appearance, they played to around 300 people, but on their second visit not long after the release of '*Judy Teen*', the fans began queuing at 5.00pm for an 8.00pm start and the line of people ran halfway around the building. When the band came on, the makeshift bouncers simply retired to the bar as there was no way they could control the enthusiastic but good natured crowd!

As an example of the relaxed atmosphere and the quality of band, former Greyhound regular Arthur Harris wrote in Mojo magazine: *"I remember seeing Love just after I started work in either 1969 or 1970,* (March '70) *at the Greyhound in Croydon (why did they always insist on putting out two rows of chairs?). It cost £1 for an advance ticket, and my friend Tom and I rested our feet on the front of the stage. No heavy handed security in those days. After an excellent 'electric' set, the management clearly thought it was time to call it a night. Not so Love, who were obviously enjoying the evening as much as the audience were and kept on playing until someone had the bright idea to switch off the power to their amps. This hiccup was easily overcome - Arthur Lee and co. switched to acoustics and carried on! The thought still brings a smile to my face".*

Support bands were paid the princely sum of £5 - and remember this included Status Quo, Roxy Music, Thin Lizzy and AC/DC - as to be support act at the Greyhound was considered a prestigious gig for an up and coming group. Most headline bands played the Greyhound for between £300 to £500 although American jazz drummer Billy Cobham commanded £1,000 for his sellout appearance in June 1975.

The importance of the Greyhound as a venue was endorsed by Dave Winslett, an agent working for Terry King Associates, during an interview with journalist Michael Wale; *"There are now a few club circuits doing a similar thing (to the Marquee) in the provinces. People will advertise, the name of the club gets around, even if it is a little dingy pub hall. These places are of great value to an act. The Fox Clubs, in Croydon and around South East London - they are a very good showcase for groups. They have a very good attendance, anything up to 2,000 people* (nearer 1,000 at Croydon) *for a very big act - and obviously if you can put an act that is just starting on that bill - they're good audiences, enthusiastic audiences - then word soon travels, especially amongst student organisations and colleges".*

Fox Entertainments expanded their venues to include (at various times); The Winning Post at Twickenham, the Starlight Club at Crawley, the Toby Jug at Tolworth, the Public Hall at Wallington and the Surrey Rooms at the Oval, Kennington. Consequently they were able to book bands on a monthly rota basis offering them a choice of venues around the South London area. In the late '70's the Greyhound billed itself as 'Surrey's Premier New Wave Venue' (the Fox head logo became 'spikier') and began to cater for the growing punk movement, leading to some strange combinations of bands; 'hippy' guitarist Steve Hillage followed by Siouxie & the Banshees, for example! As Fox Leisure, they also booked bands into the Red Deer in South Croydon between 1976 and 1978, giving early gigs to groups such as Motorhead, Ultravox, Squeeze and local favourites, the Damned.

The Greyhound came within a hairs breadth of staging a gig by the Sex Pistols, shortly after their TV clash with presenter Bill Grundy. The Croydon Advertiser ran a front page piece stating that the band had been pencilled-in to play Croydon on Sunday 12th December 1976, but had cancelled because "the stage was too small." Kevin Barry, described as manager of the Greyhound, said *"we have never had any problems with punk bands. They are the nicest to work with because they have no images to keep up. The more the press say violence goes with punk rock, the more the bands will have to comply to keep in the public eye."* He denied that the cancellation had anything to do with the bad publicity surrounding the Pistols at that time. However, the following week a reply appeared on the letters page from Howard Bossick, the real general manager of the Greyhound, pointing out that Kevin Barry was actually the booking agent for Foxes, and as such his comments were those of the promoters and not the Greyhound itself. He continued, *"In my view, and from telephone calls I have received, the attitude portrayed by Mr Barry is one of condoning the behaviour, attitude and language of the Sex Pistols. I personally do not, nor on behalf of the Greyhound, do I consider they are a suitable band to be booked into these premises, and I would further point out that it was I that cancelled their proposed concert, and not due to the reasons stated, ie that the stage was too small."*!!

By 1980, the regular gigs had all but finished; the Caroline Roadshow had moved in, which basically consisted of a heavy metal disco plus a set from a live band - Atomic Rooster, Angelwitch, Sledgehammer and the like.

Steve Mason, who helped run the Greyhound for the first seven years, moved up to become chairman of Pinnacle Records now based in St. Mary Cray, Orpington. Unfortunately, no-one seems to know the whereabouts of Brian Mason, and at least one report suggested that he would be reluctant to talk about his days as a pop promoter. A pity, because in it's heyday the Greyhound was a healthy rival to the concerts at the Fairfield Hall and some would say that the informal 'stand-up' atmosphere made it by far the more preferable gig.

Glory days! A typical handbill from the Greyhound in 1972. The common problem was the number of gigs that had to be cancelled at the last minute, after the handouts had been printed and the advertisement copy sent in to the Melody Maker. Here, regular devotee Alan Barnes has filled in the new acts as they appeared - but fans of the cancelled groups need not have worried. Genesis returned agin in September and Spirit were back in April 1973.

Frazer Ashford

This shot of the Sutherland Brothers & Quiver gives you a good view of the old Greyhound stage, circa 1973.

Jamie Moses

A guitar-slinger who started his professional career with young glam-rockers Merlin and has barely had time to stop for breath ever since. His CV reads like a 'who's-who' of rock music - Pete Townsend, the Hollies, Denny Laine, Eric Burdon, Paul Rodgers, Chaka Khan, the Pretenders, Paul Young, Brian May - and that's barely scratching the surface. Still living locally, I met up with Jamie to find out how it all started...

Despite the American accent I was actually born in England, in Ipswich; my father was in the US Airforce and was stationed near there. Shortly after I was born we moved to the States, to upstate New York where we lived for a short while before moving to the midwest to Illinois and Washington DC. Because of my dads work I also spent a couple of years in Japan and then we came back to England when I was about seventeen. I did my last six months to a year of school in Shirley, at what was then Shirley Secondary School - which of course I knew nothing about, I mean I was supposed to be studying for my O levels, I had been out of the country, you know, what were O levels? I had learned American geography, American history and even the American way of English language, if you like. Even the methods of simple arithmetic were different in the States, so I really didn't stand a chance with the exams. I got one, I did get English language but all the rest were really a waste of time.

I started playing guitar when I was ten and by the time I was eleven I had a band called the Three J's - which was Jim, Jim and Jeff; we covered songs by the Beatles, Stones, Beach Boys and the Monkees, the Hollies and instrumental stuff by the Ventures. A lot of English bands were big in the States then, but ironically by the time we started playing more American music, I was fourteen and living in Japan. We would play all the clubs on the Airbase, the Officers club, the NCO's club, the Airmen's club and the youth club - and for each place we had to learn a different style of music. The Officers wanted to hear County & Western, the NCO's, who were just a peg down wanted stuff like Creedence Clearwater Revival and a bit of Soul, the Airmen more or less wanted all Soul, Sly & the Family Stone, but we managed to fit a little Hendrix in there somewhere and the Youth club wanted the more 'poppy' end of the scale - 'Venus' by Shocking Blue was big then and stuff by US bands like the Strawberry Alarm Clock. Doing all that was enormously helpful to me as I had to learn just about every style of music going and I liked all those styles too - and that is still the case now. At the moment I'm playing in about eight different bands and I have to drop into a different style at a moments notice.

We lived in Shirley to begin with, Bramley Hill, South Croydon and Brian Avenue, Sanderstead. Eventually the family moved to Coulsdon, where my mother still lives, and I got my first house in Limpsfield, a little two up two down and it was like 'Animal House', it really was - it made Men Behaving Badly look like some sort of convent - and then finally I moved to Caterham.

While I was at school in Shirley I had an appalling band called 'Moses' and another one called 'Everest' - our slogan was 'the heaviest rock around', can you believe that? They were both amateur bands playing anywhere anyone would let us. Then in the early 'seventies I played in a band called Angel, which was Bob Webb on keyboards, George McFarlane on bass and Dave Norman on drums. We moved up a notch to actually playing support to some decent bands - we supported Home at Carshalton Technical college and then the Groundhogs at the Greyhound in Croydon; which was a real buzz because I used to go and *see* bands at the Greyhound all the time - Genesis, Stray, Edgar Broughton, Quo. I remember standing at the bar next to Genesis singer Peter Gabriel, who at the time had that strange haircut where his hair was shaved like a very wide parting right down the middle, he'd calmly walked up and ordered a beer as though he was just another guy in the crowd - I thought they were excellent. I went to see Status Quo one New Years Eve and I swear the floor moved - the place was absolutely heaving and the floor bounced as though it was sprung!

When Angel opened for Home at Carshalton Tech. their guitarist was Laurie Wisefield who as you probably know went on to play with Wishbone Ash. These days I play in a fairly 'fluid' line-up of musicians called the SAS Band, and when I can't make one of the SAS gigs, Laurie stands in for me. Going back to that gig at Carshalton, I remember being impressed by the huge number of WEM amplifiers that Home worked with - and then being horrified that once the gig was over the roadies backed their van up as close to the hall doors as they could and then hurled these valve amps across the ground. I know the cases were on castor's, but they still bumped and crashed across the concrete as they rolled from the door to the van!

There was an open air gig at Beddington Park where we were on the same bill as Stray and a couple of other bands. Before Dave Norman joined, our first drummer was called Jay Scott and we used to rehearse in the garage at his mum's house in Pampisford Road, Purley. I've got some tapes from those sessions and they're pandemonium, we're just playing anything that came into our heads. That's also where I first met Debbie my wife, when Bob brought her along one day to hear us rehearse - Debbie is Bob's sister.

Angel recorded some tracks at a studio up in North London somewhere and I have heard that at least one song was released on a compilation album, but no one has ever contacted me or any other member of the band for approval or royalties for that matter!

My first professional band was called **Madrigal**, which eventually became **Merlin**, but to begin with the band was called Madrigal. We were 'discovered' by CBS and signed up for an album and about five singles and we were sent out as the support act on a nationwide tour with David Essex. Bob Webb also joined Merlin but for some reason he decided to use the name 'Scully Wagon-Lits' - although he is technically my brother-in-law, Bob and I don't really get on and haven't seen each other for about ten years.

Merlin were a very young band - I was seventeen, most were eighteen or nineteen the oldest was twenty four. Paul Taylor was the bass player, Dave the drummer, Bob Webb on keyboards, Alan Love who went on to play in a few stage shows including the lead in Godspell. Although I say we were discovered by CBS, it was actually Roger Greenaway, of the Cook & Greenaway songwriting team. So as you can imagine, they made sure most of the album were their own compositions - they wanted to create a pop band and we were going to be it. We were featured in an article in the Melody Maker, a centre page spread called something like 'Hype in the Pop Market' - comparing us, who were the new band on CBS, to Queen who were EMI's young hopefuls! It's strange because I have since joined Brian May's band - I took the article in to show him and he said "oh, I remember this - so you were in Merlin were you?"

Going back to the album, I managed to get two of my songs on there and Cook and Greenaway only supplied four,

Courtesy CBS Records / Joe Gaffney

The debut album from Merlin. No prizes for guessing the year - it could only be 1974! That's Jamie on the extreme left.

so they were being quite generous. Roger Greenaway - if he ever reads this book you're doing, I'd like to send a message to him, which is to say - "forget about producing rock music because you haven't got a fucking clue". He has no idea whatsoever and he stitched us up something terrible; he is now one of the leading lights in the PRS, or one of those beaurocratic-bullshit music business organisations, but he promised us each a regular wage for the duration of the David Essex tour, twenty pounds a week, which he gave us - and in 1974 that was fine, it wasn't a huge amount by any means, but it was on top of the hotel accommodation which was already paid for. But as soon as we got home, everybody had rents to pay and the deal was that the wage carried on for six months, while we were writing the next album and rehearsing the next tour. The week the tour finished we went along to his office because the cheques hadn't arrived and we said "Rog, what's happening, where's the money, the agreement for twenty quid a week?". And he sat behind his desk and calmly said "Oh yeah, I lied about that" I lied about that, those were his words. We were just completely devastated; because he had made us cancel all of our existing work, between our manager and ourselves we had arranged paying gigs that would have given us a living wage, and we cancelled it all to do the Essex tour and to promote the album. We said well, now that we've cancelled all this what do expect us to do and he said "split up".

I'll never forget another thing he said to me, when we were recording the Merlin album at Air Studios in Oxford Street - I'd done demos before, but this was the first time I'd been in a studio 'mastering' a record. To a young musician it was mind-blowing; Jeff Beck was working in the next studio, George Martin would put his head round the door to check out what we were doing, all that sort of thing. So I was a little bit nervous, but I'm playing the guitar lines they want and at the same time trying to be the band that they saw live, and presumably liked. So I'm bending the odd note or adding a little bit of slide or whatever, because that's the way I play and Greenaway calls through to the studio and says "No style, thank you". You'll play what I told you, you know?

I also played in a band called **Royce**, again with Bob Webb and some other guys from Southend, in fact our lead singer was very good, a guy called Nigel Benjamin. Bill Mitchell was the bass player - all very good players and we ended up playing a residency at the Speakeasy in Margaret Street, up in town - every Friday night for six months. This was the club where all the musicians would hang out after their own gigs, so there was a lot of head-hunting going on and pretty soon it happened to us. One night we saw a couple of guys from Mott the Hoople in the club and after the gig Nigel came up to us and said "sorry guys, but I've been offered the gig in Mott". Ian Hunter and Mick Ronson had gone off on their own and the remaining members of MTH were looking for a new singer and guitarist. They got Nigel from us and a lead guitarist called Ray Majors from Hackensack. We auditioned and auditioned for a new singer but we just couldn't replace Nigel, so that was it - which was a shame because Royce was one of those bands where every one contributed to the songwriting and it seemed to come relatively easily.

After Royce, I put together another band with Bob which was really a very good group, very 'Genesis-like', called **England**. We really thought we could go places; we had these strange plans to conquer the world and it was all a little bizarre, plus we were all very broke - all that is except the drummer, who actually brought us a house! We never asked him where the money came from, there were three Jaguars parked outside this place and every now and then he would turn up with all the shopping, anything we needed - and of course it turned out he was a real crook. He guested at one of Her Majesty's hotels for a while after the band broke up -

but he was a real talented guy, a great drummer. He would say to us "hey guys, we wouldn't do Top Of The Pops if it was offered to us, would we", and we'd look at each other and say "wouldn't we?" - he'd say "no, of course not, that's going the safe route, it would be too easy to do that".

He also came up with an idea called The School's Plan, which was to play at every school in the country - he would set up a deal with the Minister for Education where we would take rock music to all the school's as part of their music lessons and be subsidised by the government. A strange idea, yet it all sounded so credible to us when he explained it and twisted it all round. It meant that we would be constantly working all year round, for very good money *and* we would be selling the album to the school's - in fact he even suggested that it could be shipped around the country by the local councils.

Now it's time for the confessional - at the end of 1975 I joined **Paper Lace**, remember them? I was completely skint and I told the rest of the band (England) "I'm leaving guys, I've had enough, Paper Lace have offered me £100 a week". They really took the piss out of me for joining Paper Lace; Mark Ibbotson said "can't you see further than the end of your nose? It may be a lot of money..." to which I replied "yeah, it's a lot of money. Bye, bye!" I was with Paper Lace for about a year to a year and a half and that gig ended bitterly in a court case. It was basically us, the band, sacking our manager for being useless; and then him counter-suing for wrongful dismissal. Myself and Larry Oliver (Peter Oliver from the New Seekers), who joined with me in Christmas '75, were both on a wage as employees, whereas Phil Wright the drummer and Cliff, who were both great guys, were directors of the company. We won the court case, which took weeks in the High Court but the legal fees and expenses came to about twenty grand; so although it was a moral victory, for the band it was a financial disaster - and people tend to forget that pop groups are run as a business.

The shame of it is that I really had a great time with Paper Lace, they were a very credible band and live it was good, you know, great harmonies. I mean jesus, when we were with them they had the number one selling single worldwide - 'Billy Don't Be A Hero' which went to number one in '74 and 'The Night Chicago Died' made number three, 'Black Eyed Boys' number eleven, you know - they did pretty well.

After that we formed **Up All Night** - which was Larry and his brother Rob, myself and a drummer... actually we got through a succession of drummers but the one who lasted the longest was Graham Walker, who eventually left us to join Gary Moore. Up All Night went on for about seven or eight years, on and off when we weren't away doing other things. We started off playing at a pub called the Midday Sun in Chipstead Valley Road, Coulsdon and that all began because it was my dad's local. Being a six foot six American from Chicago, dad would go in and 'entertain' the locals; one day he said to the landlord "hey, you know my boy plays the guitar, why don't you have him come in and play?". Then dad would come back to me and say "Jamie, I've got you a gig at the Midday Sun". What? I don't have a band. Dad said "do it with Larry, just the two of you". So he fixed the whole thing up; Larry and I played with a couple of acoustic guitars and it went down pretty well - dad covered the bar with bags of popcorn, which is an old American trick to make the punters thirsty, they drink more and the bar sales go up, the landlord re-books the band!

So we said look, would it be possible to get Larry's brother Rob in to play bass, because we can do some good harmony stuff - which we did for the next gig and that went down even better. Finally we told them ok, this is great but it's impossible having a bass player without a drummer, so if you could just pay us a little bit more... Once we got our drummer we had a very good little band and the place just went out of all proportion; we were pulling in 600 punters and the place should have only held about 450, people were standing outside and leaning in through the windows, the pub must have been coining it in. We played there for about a year, this must have been around 1980-81 and from there we went to the Red Barn near Lingfield and then to the Grasshopper just outside of Westerham.

I got the chance to play in **Tommy**, the first incarnation of that show in the West End, in Shaftsbury Avenue, with a cast that included Alan Love from Merlin. This was the first musical I had ever been involved in, and at first I was a bit sceptical, but if you're going to do one then Tommy is the one to play. It's not as if you're in the pit, you're actually on stage with the band and very much part of the show. When that closed I got a call to do the **Elvis** musical and I thought, hmm I don't like the way this is going, but it was good money and a lot of fun, so... in 1980, I played in the house band for the Elvis musical when it went out on tour, this was the one that had Shakin' Stevens as the middle period Elvis, one of the three 'Elvi' that appeared in the show! PJ Proby was in the West End version, but didn't go out on tour and strangely enough Proby has since played with the SAS band, that I'm also involved with.

As for the names on my CV, although I've worked with them all, it was not always as part of a touring band. Freddie Mercury, I did a one off gig with him at the Colosseum in St. Martin's Lane. Kiki Dee and Judie Tzuke both sing from time to time with the SAS band, as does Roger Chapman. Olivia Newton John, I did the video of her album 'Physical' - which was about five tracks, I suppose. Gary Barlow, I did some work on his last album. Swing Out Sister was a Top of the Pops appearance. Bucks Fizz - I toured with them for a while. I was in the Denny Laine band too for a bit...ah, now **Broken English** was my own band, do you know about them? We put out a single called 'Coming On Strong' that was deliberately made to sound like the Stones - and then sent out white label copies to all the DJ's, many of whom assumed that it *was* the new Stones single and consequently played and played it. It eventually went to about number 16 in the charts and the follow-up, even though they knew it was us by then, also made the thirties. Broken English were a three-piece and we got Paul Jones to play some harmonica for us.

I also put together a local band called **Special Offer** that was really a filler when I wasn't away touring with someone else, but I tell you, it stops you going crazy when you've got a couple of months between tours. We would fit in gigs at the Cartoon, places like that.

I played at the old Cartoon many times, in fact we even did it with the **Pacaminos**, the Tex-Mex band that I currently play in that features Paul Young. It is an open secret these days that Paul is the vocalist with us, mainly because I believe there is some contractual obligation with Paul's management that prevents the band trading on his name. But secondly, as Paul says, and he's quite right - as soon as his name goes up we are plagued with people shouting out for 'Wherever I Lay My Hat' and 'Everytime You Go Away', you know? And we don't do any Paul Young stuff, he just wants to be one of the band and have fun, and that's how it is. At one Pacaminos gig, we even had one guy calling out 'Toast', which goes way back into Paul's past with the Streetband and he ended up just turning his back on this guy, you know, who needs it. ”

"...and my only vice is the fantastic prices I charge for being eaten alive*..."

Frazer Ashford

Two views of the wonderful ***Cockney Rebel*** *as seen through the lens of Frazer Ashford. Led by the enigmatic Steve Harley, who cut his teeth as a performer at The Beckenham Arts Lab run by David Bowie, the original line-up produced two classic albums for EMI - 'The Human Menagerie' and 'The Psychomodo'.*

The picture above was taken at the Croydon Greyhound and shows the band early in 1974 - Harley centre stage and Jean-Paul Crocker, right, on violin.

Unfortunately this group split up around the middle of 1974, Harley taking only drummer Stuart Elliott with him into the new band. Whereas the original Rebel had been so quirky and original, the new band released a far more commercial single 'Make Me Smile (Come Up & See Me)' and hit number one almost immediately - February/March 1975.

The second picture shows the new Cockney Rebel playing top of the bill at the Crystal Palace Bowl in June 1975. Either side of Steve are Duncan McKay on keyboards and Jim Cregan on electric guitar.

**Oh yes, the heading is a line from 'My Only Vice'* ©Rak/Trigram Music 1973 *- from the Human Menagerie album.*

Frazer Ashford

Captain Sensible

Croydon's favourite 'punk', railway enthusiast and one of the most popular characters in the music biz. Born Ray Burns in Balham on the 24th April 1954, the Captain was brought up in Croydon and educated at Whitehorse Manor Junior School and Stanley Technical High. Drifted through a variety of jobs including landscape gardening, carpet cutting and working for British Rail, during which time he played in an early incarnation of Johnny Moped...

As far as I remember, it all began in my brothers bedroom in Croydon. We had an upright piano, a Bontempi chord organ from Woolworths, an acoustic guitar and a set of drums. None of us could play that well, but Fred Berk, the piano player was inspired - he never had any tuition, but he was the one who saved the band, he could really improvise. In fact we all thought we could improvise quite well, which is something I've tried to hang on to; we used to improvise whole songs that came out of nothing, right out of thin air. Xerxes and Johnny who were the two singers, would just bounce off each other, one would sing a line... it was like that game where someone writes a line on a piece of paper, folds it over and passes it to the next player to write something, it was exactly like that.

Amazing songs would just fly out of the air - mind you, some pretty bad ones flew out of the air too, from these rehearsals in the bedroom - but we'd tape everything. And Dave Berk has got cupboards full of them, 'the vaults' he calls it, he is the keeper of the vaults! We would play for about three hours at a time, tape everything we did and out of that we'd probably get one blinding piece, that was completely inspired and the rest would be complete crap.

We would listen to the good ones - and only the good ones, mind you - by driving in Dave's Morris Traveller round the back of the gasworks off Beddington Lane. Sometimes we'd sit there all night, drinking brown ale and listening to what we thought were the best of these tapes. After a few beers, listening to these tapes we began to sound really good, we actually thought that everybody else we heard on the radio was garbage compared to us, we said "nobody can do what we do", we thought we were really great. In fact, after giving the band a few names - 'Genetic Breakdown' and 'Johnny Moped's Assault & Buggery' for example, we actually called ourselves 'The Elite' - that's how good we thought we were! I think in all the time we only played about ten gigs, most of the time it was 'rehearsals' either in my brothers bedroom or in Dave's dad's garage in his back garden.

The band were mostly my brothers school chums, my brother is about a year and a half younger than I am, and they all went to Selhurst Grammar School. I was considered too thick to go there, they thought I was much better with my hands and I was packed off to the technical college to study woodwork, metal engineering and cast-iron pattern making, all the things that have served me so well in later life! So yes, Dave, Fred, Xerxes were all Paul's chums; he would bring them home, we were all interested in music and it went on from there. Johnny was one of my biker pals, all the time I was at school I wanted to be a biker. I missed out on the 'sixties by a whisker, I was just too young to really be a part of that generation and I looked on that Mods and Rockers thing as the way to go, I thought that was absolutely wonderful. And a biker was what I wanted to be. I did actually get involved in a brawl at Dreamland in Margate, which was very frightening. I went down with a bunch of bikers, I was the youngest one there and this whole group of mods jumped us by the rollercoaster; there were about seven of us and there seemed to be millions of them. We all took our studded belts off and some mod chucked a chair at us - it was a big stand-off for a while and then thankfully the coppers came along and broke it all up. A few friends of mine from Stanley school also wanted to be bikers, so we got together and formed our own little group - which didn't go down too well with The Nightingales, who were the real local bikers - they would take our jackets from us and rip off our home-made 'colours', and there was another group from Chelsea Bridge, they didn't like us either. So this guy Moped, he wanted to be a biker as well.

In October 1974 Captain was employed as a porter at the Fairfield Halls and by Christmas he had met up with with a fellow employee to form a partnership that would radically change both their lives; this soulmate was Chris Millar - later to become 'Rat Scabies', drummer extrordinaire and a lynch pin in one of the leading groups on the punk scene. Captain worked as a steward at the Sunday rock concerts, getting paid overtime to watch the bands; Mott the Hoople, Alvin Stardust and Marc Bolan. Although part of the job was to watch for the audience rushing the stage, when this eventually happened towards the end of the gig, Captain would be the first down the front! It was these shows that convinced him that it was better to be a pop star than a toilet cleaner.

I went to see Mott the Hoople at the Fairfield and I really wanted Ian Hunter's glasses. I jumped on stage and made a grab for the glasses but I didn't realise that Hunter had them tied on specifically to stop arseholes like me from pulling them off! Trouble was, when I tugged at the glasses I ended up pulling Hunters head forward and banged his face on the microphone. He stopped the song and he was shouting "where is he, where's that bastard..." he would have flattened me that's for sure, but I was back in the crowd by this time and making myself scarce.

I met up with Rat, or Chris as he was then, when we were both working at the Fairfield Halls. He was a floor cleaner and used to walk around the place with a mop and bucket and I had this supermarket trolley with a whole load of toilet cleaners, brushes and bog roll. Most of the time we would sit and talk about music and play each other tapes of our respective bands. I would bring in some of the Moped bedroom tapes and Chris was the drummer in a group called Tor. One day he saw an advert for musicians in the back of a paper and disappeared off up to London; when he came back he had his head shaved and I said "what is this, some sort of skinhead band?" and he said "no, it's a bit weird, I can't really explain it". So I went up to see the same bloke and it was Brian James - by the time he had explained his ideas to me, I could see that he knew what was going on - and I came back to work with a shaven head too! So it was Brian who actually formed the Damned. He had the vision to see what was about to break loose.

By February '75, both had been sacked from the Fairfield, but teamed up again to work for a building company - by this time Captain had left the Mopeds and joined Oasis, a 'cabaret outfit' performing at social clubs for a little extra beer money. Chris Millar meanwhile, had joined a band called London SS, whose members Mick Jones and Tony James later went on to form the Clash and Generation X respectively and also have the dubious honour of naming Chris 'Rat Scabies', allegedly after a rat ran across in front of his drum kit during a rehearsal in a particularly run-down studio. When London SS broke up in January '76, Rat and guitarist Brian James began hanging around the pubs of Portobello Road and Camden High Street, with the people

The Captain looning around under the Croydon flyover - the final version of this publicity shot replaced the destinations on the road sign with 'Chaos' and 'Lunacy' - I wonder which one relates to Purley?

who were to become central to the punk 'movement'. Dave Vanian was auditioned as lead vocalist and Captain was recruited as the obvious choice on bass. By the summer of '76, The Damned was born.

I knew that something was going to change in pop music and I thought the logical progression would be from 'sixties pop to heavy rock to glam rock and the next phase had to be a sort of jazz rock style with lots of improvisation added to some sort of lunacy. That's what the early Moped band were trying to do - to improvise musically and have some sort of visual lunacy going on at the same time. So Johnny Moped would emerge from a dustbin, painted with green food dye - he would sing the first song in a dustbin, stuff like that.

I remember we saw Arthur Brown's Kingdom Come at the Greyhound and sang the first song in a giant syringe, in the middle of the stage this huge syringe and most of the vocals were just feedback, because if you try to use a mic in a confined space like that, it feedbacks like hell. Arthur tried to get out after the first number and he couldn't get out - the roadies were pulling at this thing and it wouldn't come off - it was one of the funniest things I've ever seen. And later on in his set this giant brain came scurrying across the stage, thanks to a roadie at the other side pulling a piece of string, he had traffic lights on stage - total lunacy, it was brilliant.

So I really thought that a bit of improvisation combined with things like that would really be the next big thing, but of course I was wrong. I was right about the lunacy and the visual chaos of punk, though...

The group signed a recording deal with the newly formed Stiff Records, knocking out their first album 'Damned, Damned, Damned' in a total of ten days under the watchful eye of producer Nick Lowe. Their single 'New Rose', is regarded as the first punk single and is arguably one of the best of it's kind. They were signed up to play on the 'Anarchy in the UK' tour, with the Sex Pistols, the Clash and the Heartbreakers, but the whole tour became a farce following the Pistols' swearing match with Bill Grundy on TV. Out of 19 bookings, only a few were allowed to continue by the local authorities. The Damned played one date, at Leeds Poly. and were thrown off the rest of the tour, due to disputes with the other bands.

It really annoys me when I read about Malcolm MacLaren claiming to have invented punk and how he invented The Sex Pistols - "I told them to do this and I told them to do that". Absolute bollocks. They only tolerated him because he gave them a few bob, knew how to hire a rehearsal studio and book the odd gig. We were all rehearsing for the 'Anarchy' tour on the day they did the Grundy interview - MacLaren didn't tell them to say all that stuff, they did it themselves - on the spur of the moment. In fact, after they came off air MacLaren went berserk - he was screaming at them "You bastards, you've ruined everything we've worked for, you'll never work again, it's all over..." And of course it made them. I've heard MacLaren's account and I've since spoken to John Lydon about it - well, let's just say I know who I believe.

I loved going to the old Greyhound, I can't remember who the first band were that I saw there, but it must have been around 1970 - it was probably Blodwyn Pig or Stray or someone like that. But I certainly saw Bowie and Roxy Music, Status Quo several times, Deep Purple which was one of the loudest gigs I've ever heard, absolutely deafening that one was, I saw Keef Hartley, Colosseum, Soft Machine... oh, just loads of people.

Stray were amazing. They used to set off these huge explosions in dustbins along the front of the stage - you knew they were coming but you didn't know exactly when; in fact I don't think *they* knew when they were going to go off, and that was all part of the fun. And Del Bromham was a terrific guitarist, in a sort of Hendrix style - Jimi Hendrix played at the Star, of course, but then I'm sure everyone will have told you that. I didn't see that show, in fact I didn't get to see Hendrix play at all, which is one of the great regrets of my life. God yes, the Star... I was in that pub once when it was raided for drugs, unfortunately it always had that sort of reputation, and I was one of a whole line of people lined up against the wall.

You know, we rarely ever paid to get in to the Greyhound. We had this routine on a Sunday evening which started in the Dog & Bull, which is a Youngs pub in Surrey Street market. A couple of pints there, then stroll up to St. George's Walk where at the far end you could climb on some dustbins to get up onto the covered part of the Walk, which was a pedestrian shopping area. You had to walk carefully across the roof and make your way along to where it met the first floor at the rear of the Greyhound. You climbed along to the windows on the back stairs, and these windows had to be kept open due to the fire regulations; although even if they were closed there was always some helpful hippy halfway through his pint, who would pull back the curtains and see us emploring him to open the window and let us in. Either that, or you could go in through the kitchens, which was the scariest way of bunkin' in for nothing. If you went up through the kitchens you came out by the groups dressing room and there was usually some 'bruiser' hanging about there. We got caught a few times of course, but we didn't have to pay too often.

> *"For two years I couldn't walk down the road in Croydon without getting dragged into a pub and having booze poured down my neck. I'd say to my mum "I'm just off down the shop to get a cauliflower" and come back a couple of days later looking really rough!"*
>
> The Captain talking about the success of 'Happy Talk', from an interview in The Big Issue.

Sitting around the Greyhound bar in those days, a lot of the bands had no problem with hobnobbing with the audience - people like Status Quo and Stray hardly used their dressing rooms, it seemed like they were straight up to the bar, chatting with people both before and after the gig. When the Damned actually got to play at the Croydon Greyhound, which really was a great ambition of ours, obviously because Rat and I lived in Croydon and even Brian came from Crawley originally, so we were definitely a 'south of the river' kind of band, we still went through the old routine. After the soundcheck, we all walked down to the Dog & Bull and sat there almost until showtime - that was certainly a magic moment for me.

By early '77, the Damned had been given a residency at the Roxy in Covent Garden, made their first television appearance on 'Supersonic' and were personally offered the support slot on a tour with T.Rex by Captain's early hero, Marc Bolan. In September, the group went to Europe, but only a couple of gigs into the tour, Rat decided he'd had enough and headed back to Croydon. Johnny Moped drummer, Dave Berk was flown out as a temporary replacement. They managed to finish what was by all accounts a traumatic tour, but the band were just not the same without Rat and by the end of the year Stiff Records ended their contract. In February 1978, the first part of the Damned story was over.

*The Captain returned home to Croydon and formed a new band called **King** comprising Henry Badowski on vocals, Kim Bradshaw, bass and Dave Berk on drums. Captain had returned to playing guitar. Their short-lived career consisted of a five night residency at a club in Paris and a session for John Peel.*

*Over a few beers with Rat back home in Croydon, it was decided that they should revive the Damned. They contacted Vanian, who agreed to come back as vocalist and they pulled in Henry Badowski on bass. However, to avoid any possible problems they toured under the name **The Doomed**!...*

It was funny, because when I started Deltic - which was my own little record label, it ran for about four years at the end of the 'eighties putting out CD's by other bands as well as my old rubbish -me and my colleague went over to Orpington to see Pinnacle Records about a distribution deal and when we met the boss it turned out to be Steve Mason. Steve of course was the guy at the Greyhound who came out and introduced all the bands, together with his brother Brian they ran Fox Enterprises. When I'd had a couple of beers I used to tell Steve that I did an impersonation of him doing one of his introductions - when he came onstage he looked and sounded just like Neil from 'The Young Ones', you know? Dressed in bell bottomed loon pants, long greasy hair and he'd slouch on and say something like "Yeah man, we've gonna have a really great night, we've got Blodwyn Pig... and don't forget next week we've got Uriah Heep, man it'll be really heavy..." and that's what he was like. I didn't realise it, but he ended up being my boss, in a sense, at Pinnacle. Steve never turned into a 'suit' though, he's a music lover first and foremost, he's great.

I remember he said to me "Watch out for Kylie, she's going to be huge" - because Kylie Minogue was part of Pinnacle in those days and pretty much unknown. I got to meet her at a record company do that Steve held down in Brighton and she was such a nice person. She got up and sang a couple of things and she was really very good - I won't hear a bad word said about Kylie!.

When I recorded 'Happy Talk', we went down the Dog & Bull every night; we recorded that at Matthew Fisher's studio just off Croham Road. I love the Dog & Bull because Youngs beers are so brilliant and every time we all went down there, Matthew would start to reminiss and say "Did I ever tell you about the time.." He has got a lot of stories, but his main one is how he came up with the organ part to 'A Whiter Shade of Pale' - the rest of it is all Gary Brooker - but Matthew's bit *is* the song, for Christ's sake, it is *the* famous bit that everyone remembers. And Matthew didn't get any publishing rights.

After a few beers, he will always tell you how he was ripped off and how he didn't get any publishing - and he's right, you know, he should have got something, he's a terrific bloke, Matthew.

There were three of us most nights, Matthew, myself and Tony Mansfield who was producing my stuff at the time. We would get down there about nine, have a few pints and then take a crate back to the studio; we got some really good ideas out of Youngs beers, you know! I got Matthew to play on one of my B-sides once, when I was with A&M, I said "Matt, will you play keyboards on one of my songs?" and he said "of course I will, of course, it's very nice of you to ask". I came down and I had this song that needed a couple of solos at the end of a nice jazz-rocky sort of riff, he said okay I'll just play something on the organ and for some reason I said, "No, you play piano and I'll play the organ solo..." So I fumbled around and just about managed to pick out this organ solo and Matthew could barely keep a straight face; but it was session so what could he do, you know? He said "the thing about organists is that generally, they can't really play the piano too well", most people would think they would be able to, but they are very different instruments, piano is percussive and the organ is all sustain. Anyway, he went in and played this really good piano solo, but he complained all the way through it, it took about two or three takes and he was saying "look Captain, I'm not really a piano player". And this is the bloke who played on 'Whiter Shade of Pale' telling me that! Brilliant.

Courtesy Ray Cork

The Captain revisits one of his old haunts and runs into an old friend.

'Happy Talk' was mixed at Ridge Farm and they actually got the gold disc when it became a hit, which was wrong I think, it should have gone to Matt's place, The Old Barn Studios. Why he called it that I'll never know, 'cause it's a big old Victorian semi in suburbia.

A band called 'New Musik' were playing at the Fairfield Halls, and my German girlfriend at that time was a big fan and wanted to go along; and she said "He is the right man to produce you, come and meet him". I don't think he'd ever produced anybody at the time, but she said you must go and talk to him after the show. I didn't really want to go and see this guy who I'd never met before, but she breezed through the backstage 'jobsworths' and asked this Tony if he would like to produce Captain Sensible. She came out saying he wants to meet you, I went backstage and we agreed it there and then. So he produced four demos with me at a dodgy place in Mitcham called TMC, which we then took to A&M records and got the deal.

Having clinched a record deal, everything else was done at the Old Barn and I chose 'Happy Talk' because A&M told me that I had to have a certain number of songs on each side of the album and I was one short. Most of these songs were all Damned rejects, I had just written a bunch of pop tunes and Tony said go home, go through your record collection and find a song you'd like to cover. I saw 'See Emily Play' and 'Waterloo Sunset', songs that I dearly love - but I put them back because I thought that they were too perfect, you know, you can't better them.

So then I went through my mum and dad's record collection and I found the soundtrack to South Pacific, which I also loved. I took it in to Tony and said I want to do this song here, 'Happy Talk' and he said well, what about 'Some Enchanted Evening' or 'I'm Gonna Wash That Man Right Out of My Hair'? because they were better known songs.

But no, 'Happy Talk' it was and I remember that I was paralytic when I recorded it. Most of the background track is all machines, one of the first of that kind of session I'd done, we had a Roland MC500 playing all the music on it, all of it. In those days it could be a real hit and miss affair, sometimes it worked and quite often it didn't. On the second day of the session, Tony and Matt were trying to get these machines to sync up so that they could spew out the rest of the music onto tape and then I could put the vocal over the top. Tony said, look why dont you nip down the pub and I'll call you there when we're ready. So I went to the Dog at opening time which was five thirty in those days, and at about half ten I 'phoned the studio to see what time they were going to pick me up. Tony came and poured me into the car and it took until about one in the morning before they were finally ready. I ran through it once to get the levels right and I decided to swear my way all through it; and apparently a tape of that really disgusting, abusive version still occasionally does the rounds of the record biz!

But the second take, I sang the whole thing through exactly as it appears on the record, and in places you can really hear how drunk I was, I can spot it everytime I hear it. I'm off key and the vocal wanders all over the place, but I got away with it. The song 'Croydon' came a little later... that's my life story in about two and a half minutes - it did actually sell quite well, but only *in* Croydon!. I've still got a massive soft spot for the place, which is why I'm always tempted to jump off the train at East Croydon whenever I'm travelling up and down from Brighton and pop into the old Dog & Bull for a quick pint. ”

Slimey Toad & Dave Berk

'Berk & Toad' - not the pair of infamous grave-robbers, but the guitar and drums behind Croydon's second favourite punk outfit - Johnny Moped. I caught up with Simon Fitzgerald (Toad) and Dave Bachelor to find out the history of the often elusive Moped's.

Dave: 'The first line-up of **Johnny Moped** was Johnny, Captain Sensible, Phil Burns who was Captains brother, Fred Berk and myself - and we were all at school together except Captain... but Phil, who originally played bass, didn't make the changeover to punk! All good local lads - Johnny was born and bred in New Addington, the Burns came from Croydon; Toad was born in Finchley and I was born in Portsmouth, but we both moved into the Croydon area soon afterwards. Some people thought that Fred and I were brothers, but we just adopted 'Berk' as a stage name. Fred's real name was Colin Mills, and he sat in front of me at Selhurst school, and Phil Burns sat next to me. Johnny Moped started off as just a rehearsal band in a bedroom, before I joined a band called **Tor**, replacing Rat Scabies on drums and Toad was already their guitarist. We tried very hard to play a sort of jazz fusion, at least we tried to...

And then basically, when Captain went off to form the Damned, it was Toad, Fred, Johnny and myself who reformed Johnny Moped.

Simon: Tor were far too serious for their own good. Whatever it was they were trying to do, they were going in no direction and it was all so intense... and if we could make it complicated, believe me we would!

There's an age old story about when I joined the early Moped line-up, because Chrissie Hynde was a sort of part-time guitarist and really, the band never needed two guitarists. At the time it was easy for me to say to the others that the band didn't need two guitars, because somehow I had a funny feeling that I would be the one left in the equation - and that's really the bottom line. Chrissie moved on - to great success with The Pretenders - so really we did her a huge favour! We did actually do one gig at the Roxy with Chrissie playing guitar, just the one gig...

Dave: ...and wasn't Shane McGowan our roadie somewhere along the line? I'm sure he worked with us at some point.

Simon: Shane was just a punk, he was always around at gigs, just a bit of a spare part. Long before he ever joined a band, he got his picture on the front cover of Sounds as a punk, with his spiked blond hair, just part of the scene.

Dave: Chrissie Hynde tried to form a band with Dave Vanien and somebody else, just as the Damned were starting to get together, that's how they knew her. When that fizzled out, Captain gave her a phone number and told her to get in touch with me and Fred Berk, which became a short-lived band called The Unusuals. So it was really the Captain's idea to put that band together - we never did any gigs, but I've still got a few tapes somewhere - and when that finished she played with the early Johnny Moped line-up, until Toad joined.

Simon: She wrote some great songs, but we can't phone her up because she might shout at us, even now after all this time...! Fred adored Chrissie, I'm sure he wanted to keep her in the band.

Dave: Fred planned to record some demos with her and he called me to play drums on them - but I had to turn him down, I told him that I just couldn't work with the woman. They ended up getting the drummer from Steeleye Span, Nigel Pegrum - and he probably made a better job of it than I could have done. Fred came back a nervous wreck from those sessions, but he got paid to do it, so he was happy.

Simon: The name 'Johnny Moped' was all over the walls in Caterham and Croydon. I was living in Addiscombe at the time, so the Caterham graffiti was probably down to my brother and a few of his friends. I must admit to contributing to some of the Croydon slogans; I'd write things like "Slimey Toad is Banal" - so yes, all the graffiti that was self destructive was probably mine.

Dave: Despite all our local connections, we didn't actually play many gigs in Croydon. We supported The Damned at the Greyhound and did one of our own at the Red Deer...

Simon: Things were just taking off for us at the time of that gig at the Red Deer - and Johnny's wife turned up. We were just coming on stage and she decided to pull up a stool and sit right in front of Johnny. The stage was only a couple of feet high, like a little rostrum - as we started to play the crowd went absolutely berserk and all these punks landed on Brenda, who was in her late forties then, and she just got bundled onto the floor. At the end of each number, Johnny would get down off the stage, pick her up, put her back on the stool - and then it would happen all over again! She was there to see Johnny and that's what she did, despite the melee of punks who were all pogoing on top of her.

Dave: Captain disappeared when he got the job playing bass with The Damned, but he still did our first few proper gigs with us. He played on our first ever gig at the Roxy - the band was Johnny, Fred on bass, Captain on guitar and myself - and then he decided he couldn't do both and split for the Damned, and Toad joined.

Simon: We used to drive up the motorway to gigs in Manchester and Liverpool, all over the place - including one in Middlesborough where I almost had a nervous breakdown. I had driven all the way from Cornwall to Leeds for a gig, and then up to Middlesborough, by which time I was exhausted. I was feeling so weird that I tried to bottle out of the gig; I found somewhere in the building, a cupboard or storeroom and just fell asleep until somebody found me. Eventually I came out and played the gig; but I swear that there were these two guys who tried to nick our Neptune SuperFish - we had a plastic model of the Neptune SuperFish from Stingray - I think they nicked it at the gig in Middlesborough and I swear that it was Vic and Bob. Reeves and Mortimer. These guys were pissing me off so much that I thought, let them take the fish and they might just leave us alone. Now about two months later we played a gig in Norwich - and just recently I've seen an article where Vic reckons that our Norwich gig was the best he's ever seen.

Dave: Around 1977 I actually got to play in The Damned for a short time. Probably because I had been sharing a flat with Rat Scabies, because Captain knew I was a drummer and because Rat threw a wobbler and quit the Damned tour with a gig coming up in two days time, I got a phone call at one o'clock - I had to get my birth certificate and passport together - and I had to be on the train at five. I went over to France and did one days rehearsal and then three weeks tour with the Damned. And that's pretty much all I can remember, because the rest is a complete blur. Rat had decided that he was quitting for good, but when we came back after the tour the Damned decided that they didn't want me permanently. I've no idea why, to this day I still don't know the reason and I have asked Captain about it since and he's never told me, but when the band got back to England they advertised for a

Courtesy Chiswick / Ace Records

Hiya, Tomcats! - it's Johnny Moped.

Left to right: Dave Berk, Slimey Toad , Johnny and Fred Berk.

new drummer and Jon Moss got the job, Jon went on to play with Culture Club. The Damned limped on for three or four months, if that, and then completely packed it in.

They made a comeback as The Doomed, having kicked out Brian Jones, they had Henry Badowski on bass, whose charming party trick was to throw up in a beer glass on stage and drink it! It wasn't long before they couldn't stand him anymore, so they kicked him out and got in Algy Ward, another local lad who I believe still lives in Croydon.

Simon: I guess that since Johnny Moped I've tried to retire gracefully... although having said that, the Moped still gets together every now and then, in fact we've probably played more times in Croydon as 'reunion' gigs than we ever did when the band was together the first time round.

We played at the 'Underground', the Star and the Cartoon several times... and Wales, of course! For some unknown reason we drove all the way to Cardiff to play a one-off reunion gig and took a coachload of punters with us. We did a gig at the Marquee as the Johnny Moped Big Band, with Kirsty MacColl as a guest singer. If Chrissie had turned up we would probably have done ourselves in - that or told her the gig was somewhere else!

Dave: Our connection with Kirsty stems mainly from the fact that she's a Croydon girl; but also after the Mopeds, she offered me a job in her band - we made some demos at RMS Studio's - but I was in another band at the time called The Upset and *they* were paying me money...

Simon: She was with a guy called Rick Smith at the time, who was the lead singer with The Drug Addix.

Dave: During the period just after The Damned split up, but before they came back as The Doomed, I played in a very short-lived band called King, which consisted of the Captain, Henry Badowski, a guy on violin and a bass player who went on to play with The Saints. We played about five gigs in Paris, no gigs in England at all, we came back to do one radio session for John Peel and then it sort of petered out, probably because the Damned were about to get back together.

Simon: The only thing I did was to form the Scuba Divers with a guy called Rod Maberley, which was basically a wine bar duo - and we made more money from those gigs than I ever did with Johnny Moped. I was pleased with the Scuba Divers because I got to play songs that were more... let's just say that I got to play four chords instead of three!

We all had an input to the Moped songs, I wrote a few and Fred wrote some cracking songs; it was Fred who wrote 'Darling, Let's Have Another Baby', which as voted Sounds Single of the Week and has since been covered by Kirsty on the B-side of 'Walking Down Madison'. Everyone loved that song, you know, Fred could write quite a good tune; but that was the problem, it was a good tune in a punk world. We should have done more of those really - I wrote a few, but it was all dross.

Dave: Our cover versions of 'Little Queenie' and 'Something Else' were a legacy from the days when we played in the garage in my back garden; they were the first things we could all get the chords to. To try something a bit different we made Johnny sing 'Little Queenie' in a high pitched voice - I've still got the original tape of that - and then it appeared on the Moped Bootleg Tape, which was something we put out before the band really got together. After that caused such a stir with the music press, it kind of stuck in the repertoire, as did 'Something Else' to a lesser degree.

Simon: After that gig at the Roxy, the Chiswick record label immediately picked up on us and said we'd like to record you, it was actually Roger Armstrong who kicked it all off. They wanted to do it, they really did want to be involved

- and a good job too, because I don't remember any other positive vibes coming from the record companies.

Dave: I think we always suffered from a lack of management - in the early days we had no management whatsoever. Tony Robinson tried to do a bit and then we had a couple of guys called Roger and James, but they had no idea, really. Stan Brennan from Chiswick Records did a good job for a while...

Simon: Chiswick were really good for the band. One of our first interviews was with Danny Baker, who was writing for 'Sniffing Glue' one of the early punk fanzines. This was when he still had all his hair and was actually a very amiable chap. We also ran into Tony Parsons and Julie Burchill quite a bit....

Dave: Those two really hated us, Julie Burchill gave us a dreadful time for being mysogynists, we had a reputation for being mysogynists - I can't think why!! 'Incendiary Device' probably didn't help - "Stick it in her lughole, watch it blow her head apart, stick it in her lughole, stick it in her other parts..."

There are plenty of anecdotes about kidnapping Johnny before each gig so that we could actually guarantee that he would turn up. And that goes right back to the early days, even before we were playing proper gigs; we would still have to stand outside his workplace and kidnap him on his way home just to rehearse in the garage! We were all standing around in shades, ready to bundle him into the boot of the car...

Simon: There was a gig in Liverpool and we knew that we would never get him there if we let him go home the night before. So we told him, you're staying in the small room at 29A, and I actually slept under the stairs in the hallway in case he tried to leave in the middle of the night! As a fail-safe in case I fell asleep, we took one of Dave's cymbals and lodged it on top of the doorhandle; of course if he tried to leave the room, this thing would crash to the floor and alert us all.

Dave: We were booked to play another gig at the Roxy and Johnny told us that he was just going out to do his laundry - and that was the last we saw of him on that day. Blew the gig, blew out an agency deal... I've absolutely no idea what the problem was, you'd really have to ask him.

Simon: To be honest, there was always a problem with his missus, to the extent where we even tried to find him a girlfriend, Lisa. We got the pair of them together and found them a flat...

Dave: There's also a story that the members of Johnny Moped used to follow Soft Machine around - and that's certainly true of Fred, Captain and myself. We were real fans; we all went to a Soft's concert on Clapham Common one night and spotted Mike Ratledge leaving the gig. We literally followed him back into town, tailed him - he was doing U-turns in the middle of the road trying to shake us off - and eventually he did manage to give us the slip. He must have thought we were mad... I wonder if he remembers that?

Simon: I was really impressed with guitarist Allan Holdsworth, but mainly from the gigs he did with Tony Williams, which I thought were superb. In fact, believe it or not, Holdsworth played a couple of gigs with Johnny Moped; we met him in a guitar shop up in Charing Cross Road and we collared him. It was the same time that we were voted 'Single of the Week' in Sounds, so at least we had something to shout about... but he was a really amiable guy and I'm sure he would have played with us anyway. It just blew me away... he was brilliant, he really was.

Dave: Not only did he do the gig, but he actually came down to a rehearsal in Croydon, jumped in to the van with us and came down to a rehearsal - and I wanted a tape recording of the gig, which was up at the Music Machine in Camden. So I said to the tour manager, "look, do us a reel to reel and do a cassette as a back-up" - he said "no, we don't need the cassette..." So he didn't do the cassette and of course, the reel to reel was put onto the machine back to front...!

Dave: After playing with The Upset, I went briefly to Jane Aire & the Belvederes around 1981; they're the only band that I've ever been sacked from. I played a few gigs with them, but I had to travel such vast distances just to rehearse with them; we'd just started to get some regular paying gigs together when her brother, who was also a drummer, came over from the States. And that was it, they just sacked me. I also played in a Mod band called The Small Hours, who contributed a couple of tracks to a Mod compilation album - I'll jump on any bandwagon. After the Mod revival came the New Romantics, so I joined a band called The Polo Club - you can't say that I didn't try!

The last band I was in professionally were called **Glory**, whose only real claim to fame was that they had a quarter of a million quid spent on them. Our manager was Billy Gaff, who in his time has been involved with people like The Herd and Rod Stewart. We made a top ten in Q Magazine of bands who have had the most money wasted on them. The accounts for our first year were - expenses: £98,219.00 and total profit - £26.13. You work out the difference - actually I have still got the cheque - I must frame it! ❞

> *"Alright, so Jackson Browne it ain't - but you'll be singing it after the first chorus, easy money."*
>
> Danny Baker, reviewing 'Darling, Let's Have Another Baby' in Sniffing Glue.

After reading this, should you feel the need to rush out and listen to Moped classics such as 'No One', 'Darling, Let's Have Another Baby' and 'Incendiary Device', you can now purchase their complete output on CD - 'Basically: the Best of Johnny Moped' Chiswick CD WIKD 144 - is available from all good record shops or direct from Ace Records.

DID YOU KNOW? So popular were Johnny Moped in the North East, that a Geordie outfit named themselves 'Arthur 2-Stroke', in tribute! Their line-up consisted of Arthur 2-Stroke - vocals, WM 7 on guitar, Ian Thomson - bass and Naughty Norman on drums. Apparently John Peel was a fan of their single 'The Wondersea World of Jacques Cousteau' and played it constantly on his show.

Dee Generate & Eater - get your yo-yo's out!

December 1976 - in the same week that the Sex Pistols made their infamous appearance on Bill Grundy's Thames TV news programme, the Caterham Advertiser realised that they also had a newsworthy punk rocker in town, and published a short piece on Dee Generate, the 14 year-old drummer with **Eater**.

"Punk Rock" has hit Caterham with the news that a fourteen year old de Stafford schoolboy is leading the way in this controversial new trend in rock music" ran the article. Roger Bullen, alias Dee Generate, of Cromwell Road, Caterham and his band Eater played most of their gigs in North London and were still seeking a recording contract when this piece appeared. As one of youngest punk bands on the scene, the music press made a minor fuss of Eater, often picturing the group in outrageous mode, to get the maximum mileage out of their age.

The Advertiser continued - *"Punk rockers, it seems, are out to be as obnoxious as possible. They wear torn and ragged clothes, held together with safety pins, and they enjoy being ill-mannered, foul-mouthed and arrogant. In fact, they want you to hate them".* Well, it was early days for the local press.

Eater were eventually given their recording deal with The Label, distributed by Virgin Records and put out a total of four singles - 'Outside View'/'You', 'Thinkin' of the USA'/'Space Dreamin', 'Lock It Up'/ 'Jeepster' and 'What She Wants, She Needs'/'Reaching For The Sky'. They cut one LP called 'The Album' and released the wonderfully-titled 'Get your Yo-Yo's Out' EP. They also made an appearance on the 'Live at the Roxy' compilation album, performing '15' and 'Don't Need It'.

Mrs Bullen appeared in print on numerous occasions to either plug or defend her young son's punk career, and threw herself wholeheartedly into the new music scene. The music paper *Sounds* printed her reply to a previous week's letter: *"Dear worried punk of Chester, you are not alone. I am 34, have four kids and enjoy punk music and fashions. Maybe it's because my son is Dee Generate of the punk outfit Eater. Hope to see you at one of their gigs. Like me you probably enjoy change and excitement - maybe you're a Gemini too".*

As the initial energy of punk gradually died down (but not completely out), so many of the peripheral bands fell by the wayside and Eater were amongst them. In a recent punk "where are they now" feature, Roger Bullen was reported to be earning his living as a social worker.

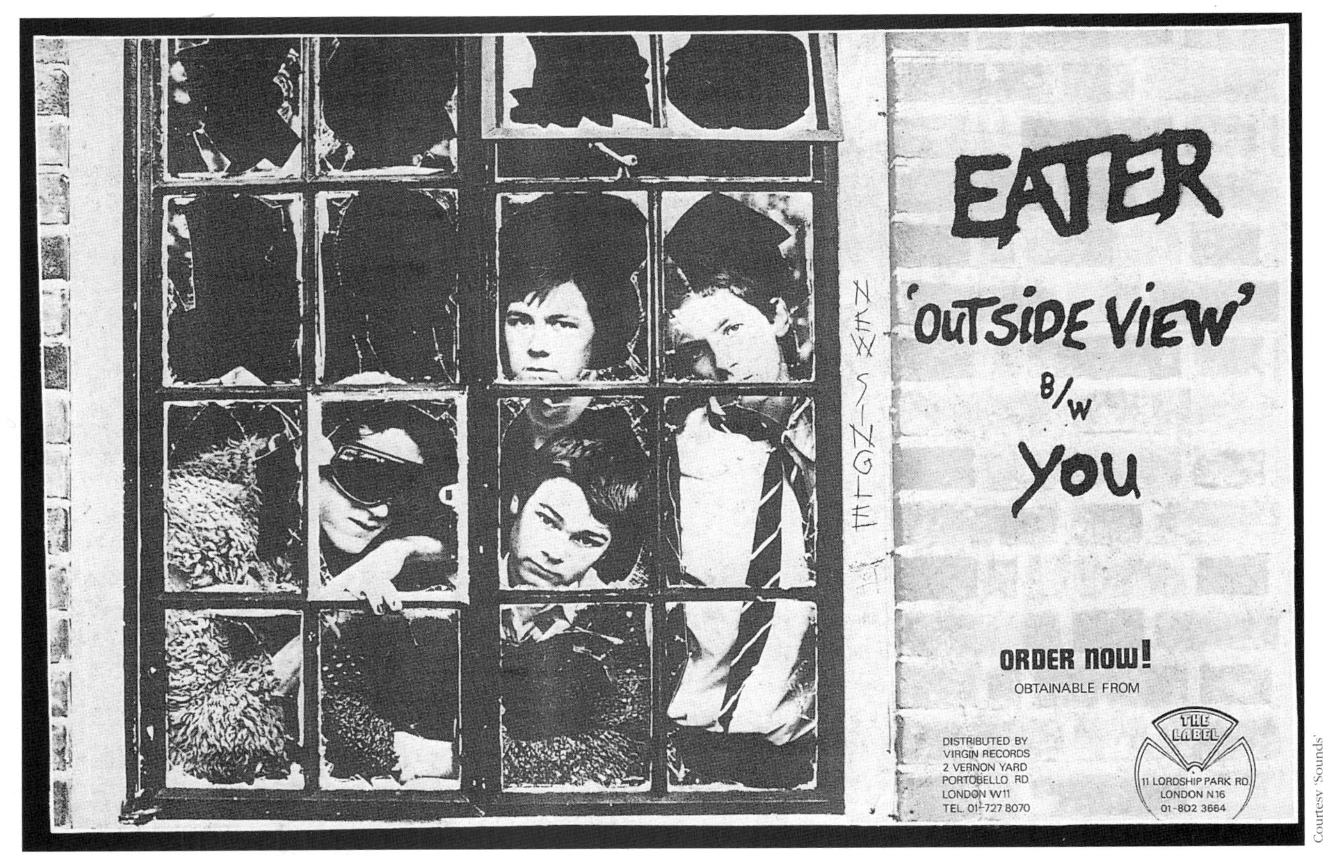

Courtesy 'Sounds'

The press advertisement for their debut single. Dee Generate is framed in the third pane across, third row down.

Dave Holman

The Cartoon at Broad Green became one of Croydon's best known rock and R'n'B venues; as manager during the late seventies, Dave was directly responsible for starting up the 7-nights-a-week live music policy that made the pub so successful.

My family moved into the Croydon area when I was about nine or ten, although I was actually born in Brentwood, Essex, a long, long time ago! So, obviously I went to school locally, Selhurst Grammar in fact and I first started to go and see bands on a regular basis at the Greyhound - early 'seventies onwards. The David Bowie gig stands out, with Roxy Music as support; the Groundhogs who seemed to be everywhere at the time, Edgar Broughton, the Alex Harvey Band, Jon Hiseman's Colosseum and then later on with Tempest, Stackridge, oh, you name them, I went almost every week. Good old Stray, of course, and one of the earliest gigs was Rory Gallagher, the first time I saw him play live he just blew me away.

I went along to see Cockney Rebel, the first time they appeared at the Greyhound; the regular trick was for myself and a couple of friends to hang around the place in the afternoon and help the bands lug their gear upstairs. Usually this meant that we were allowed to stay in there, hide in a corner out of the way and see the show for free. Most bands would let us stay inside for helping them out, but when Steve Harley saw us sitting in the corner, he said 'Who are those guys' - one of the crew told him that we'd helped carry in the gear and Harley said "well I don't want them sitting in here, tell them to piss off!" And they threw us out. I came back and actually paid to get in that night, and I have to say they were really good.

Let's not forget the good old Fairfield Halls, because in those days it could be a real problem deciding which one to go to; you know, do I go and see Deep Purple at the Halls or do I see Stray (again) over at the Greyhound. For a while the choice was unbelievable.

The story of the my involvement with the Cartoon; well, Stewart Wilder used to be the landlord at the Rising Sun at Broad Green, which is just along the road from the Star. He fancied running a place of his own, so he bought a single unit in the new block between the ABC cinema and Cinatra's nightclub and he opened it, as what was really known in those days as a wine bar and probably one of the first of its kind in the area. My wife Shirley had worked with Stewart at the Rising Sun and when he moved, she went with him to the new place, this would have been 1976. It was also among the first places to serve 'real ale', we had barrels of Royal Oak on the bar, that sort of thing and we were in at the start of a trend that you see all around you now, I'm happy to say.

On the live music side, they only 'dabbled' to start with; they tried a sort of folk thing with a girl called Joss, I think her name was, but it only happened at weekends and even then, not regularly at all. This was before I started working there, but I had started drinking there and just into 1977 they put on their first band, which was **Rockola**. They were all very good session musicians, Dave Christopher, Dave Green and various drummers, one of whom was Graham Jarvis, who went out on Cliff Richard's religious tours. Remember, this was still in the single unit, which as you know, was basically taken up by the bar running front to back, with a small free area at the very end, so they were working in very limited space. Dave Christopher, the guitar player, went on the road with Emerson, Lake & Palmer and one of his showpieces at the Cartoon was a guitar version of 'Fanfare for the Common Man'. Before long, that one small unit was overflowing on a Sunday night and you just couldn't move.

By 1978, I had packed in my main job and I asked Stewart if he needed a hand in the bar; he said yes, you can start in the cellar, which I did, throwing barrels around and setting up the pumps. To cut a long story short, the manager left and Stewart asked me to replace him, which I did; with particular emphasis on starting to expand the music side of the business. Stewart knew that I was keen on doing this; I had played in bands myself to a much lesser degree, the Selhurst Grammar School end of term parties, that sort of thing! We called ourselves Ace Thrill & the Stud Stars for those gigs, chains and studs all over our leather jackets, but what a great name!

Anyway, I started to run the bar side of things and then suggested to Stewart that we put on bands on a more regular basis; I decided that if I wasn't good enough to play in bands, at least I could book them and be involved that way. By this time the Cartoon was two units wide; Stewart had bought out the unit next door and knocked through - put in that archway over the staircase, which turned out to be ideal, because you could still see the stage from almost anywhere along the bar - and on a packed night that could be a good thing!

Rockola stayed with the Cartoon throughout; they brought their own crowd with them and were soon selling out the larger place every Sunday night, within a very short space of time. I also managed to leap out from behind the bar and sing with them on a few occasions, which was great fun. Talking of Rockola, around the time I started managing the Cartoon, Jack Good's music show 'O Boy!' was revised on television and they were auditioning for house bands to back the old rockers on TV. We thought that Rockola would be ideal and we all went up for the audition, which was at Cecil Sharp House near Regents Park - the band in their van, Stewart and I in his Jaguar XJS, which at the time was the 'bees knees', car-wise. So we turned up at Cecil Sharp House and as we pulled into the drive, the entire place was crawling with Teddy Boys, which was strange when you think that it is the home of English folk music, the EFDSS! One of them came over and started to say "All right guv? how are you, let me open the door for you..." - they thought we were on the panel of judges! Inside the big hall, they had a band in each corner, just running through some old rock 'n' roll standards; most of them were crap and of course, technically Rockola stood head and shoulders above all of them. And we got the gig! - so we had to go up to Birmingham to record the shows with people like Shakin' Stevens, Fumble, Freddie Fingers Lee and then stay in a hotel overnight before driving back down next day; I remember many nights spent in the hotel bar after the show, standing round a piano singing some good old 'fifties songs.

Stewart could see the benefit of bands like Rockola pulling people into the bar; the amount of beer sold on a good night was phenomenal, and of course once a band built up a reputation, you could also start to charge admission on the door, so I started to bring in other groups. One of the first was **Basils BallsUp Band**, a great band on their day but Stewart really didn't know what to make of Randy, their lead singer and group 'leader' if you like. They just turned up one night and the eccentric guy talked me into letting them play. Word got round the circuit pretty quickly that the Cartoon was beginning to expand as a live music venue and we began to get far more tapes than we could handle, so we started to run audition nights, where we

Julia Revell

The inimitable Basil's Balls-Up Band on a regular night at the Cartoon. Left to right: Steven - violin, Steve - bass and Randy - lead vocals and sax. The bar continued to host a wide variety of 'names' well into the 'eighties - Steve Marriott, Mungo Jerry, Dr. & the Medics, Roachford and rock'n'roll legend Bo Diddley (right) in March 1984.

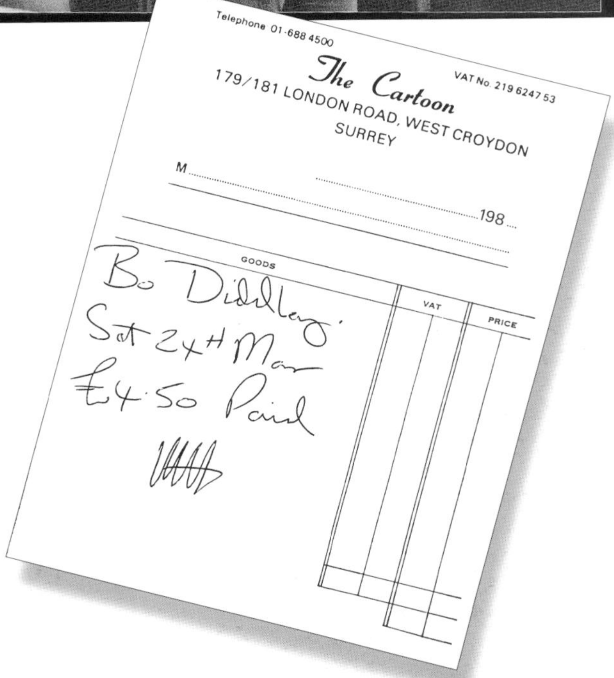

Telephone 01-688 4500
VAT No. 219 6247 53

The Cartoon
179/181 LONDON ROAD, WEST CROYDON
SURREY

M...
....198...

GOODS	VAT	PRICE
Bo Diddley' Sat 24th Mar £4.50 Paid		

would have three or sometimes four new bands playing about half an hour each to try them out. It was good free entertainment for the pub regulars on an 'off-peak' week night and was obviously a better way of seeing how well a band could perform live, but it could be chaotic, with so many bands setting up and breaking down their own gear in quick succession! As we started to get good regular bands on five nights a week, we moved the auditions to a Saturday lunchtime, which was good fun; we once had a one-man band along who insisted his name was Bob Dylan and he was *so* bad, the regular drinkers were lining up at the front of the stage to heckle! In fact some of the real regular drinkers drew up a set of marking cards, you know 0.1, 0.5, etc. specifically for these audition sessions.

The standard of musicianship was pretty high on the circuit at that time, so we turned a few groups away, and one of the bands we did turn down, was **Haircut One Hundred**. Nick Heyward came from over Bromley way and he rang us up for an audition; so they came down one Saturday lunchtime and did their half hour set and I said 'No, no, no, you'd be no good for this pub at all'. The Cartoon was booking rock and blues bands whereas Nick's lot were much too 'poppy' for us, needless to say they were a bit peeved by this and trooped off back to Bromley. However, I'd say that within six months, maximum, they had a number one hit single, and Nick came back to the pub soon afterwards and said "Told you so!"

A band called **Little Sister** came in regularly, made up of very good players who had all been in various bands before; Gary Grainger and the Brewer brothers were members, I think one of the guitar players turned down a job in Rod Stewarts group. **Seven Year Itch** were another excellent band that we booked on a regular basis, a country/rock outfit with Keith Nelson as their main man, a very fine banjo player and I think sometimes BJ Cole would sit in with them on pedal steel; the trouble with session players is that their scene is very incestuous, players would be recommended to several groups and you'd see the same faces sitting in with different bands. Mind you, with such quality musicians that's not such a bad thing. One of the most memorable moments with them, was when Keith asked me if he could bring somebody with him the next time they were down, so I said that I didn't mind and it turned out to be Albert Lee. I was knocked out; I knew Albert's reputation as a brilliant guitarist from way back and here was a guy who had been voted best country/rock guitarist in America, over people like James Burton, and who was now going to play in a tiny pub bar in Croydon. So, two weeks later he turned up and played, superbly, and I was in total awe. He came down two or three times in all and at the time of his last appearance, his 'day-job' if you like, was as part of Eric Clapton's band. I was on the door on this particular night and Albert was late arriving, so I said, 'Hello Albert, you're a bit late tonight, what's the score?' He said 'I've just been doing a session for Eric's new album; I asked him to come down and he was going to, but at the last minute he got a 'phone call from Patti asking him to come home'. Otherwise we would have had Clapton and Albert as guests, now that would have been something! I'm not sure if Seven Year Itch ever recorded anything, all the members were probably too busy doing sessions for other people.

One of the bands we booked who did have a record out were the **45's**, who I believe hold the record for the worst selling Stiff single ever! Personally, I thought they were great, close harmonies, a really good group - and ideal for the Cartoon at the time.

Dave Holman (contd.)

The Fyfe brothers brought a unique electric folk sound to the Cartoon in various line-ups, I think the **Kitchen Band** was the first group of theirs to play for us, in about 1978 or '79. Later on they put together **Eavesdropper** who became regulars at the Cartoon and did pretty well on the festival circuit too, as well as supporting people like Fairport and Paul Brady. I had known Pete and Chris Fyfe since school and being local lads they brought quite a large following with them whenever they played; they certainly kept up the Cartoon's tradition of a high standard of musicianship. Pete also backed **Noel Murphy** whenever he came to the pub.

There was the **Barbara Dickson** incident, of course, which would have been around 1979 (*25th October*) when her backing band decided that they wanted to play a couple of gigs in their own right and booked a night at the Cartoon. The group included Bimbo Acock on sax and Dill Katz on bass, a very proficient band they were. Barbara was there, but she sat quietly near the front with some friends and didn't perform. I went across at the end of the night and offered her a bottle of Champagne if she would get up and sing the last number with them, but she politely declined. Funny thing was, after everyone had gone and the band were packing away their gear, she went round the pub tending to all the flowers, she was a bit of a flower expert and went round saying 'Ooh, you've been neglecting this one' and so on. Which is hardly surprising when the atmosphere was 99% smoke, although there was always plenty of 'moisture' in the Cartoon's famous carpet!

We also had a 'visit' from **Peter Sarstedt**, although this may have been into the early Eighties; what happened was that he played a gig at the Fairfield Halls, which he subsidised himself and a crowd of us went backstage afterwards to meet him. During the chat I mentioned that we ran the Cartoon and he expressed an interest in playing for us and gave me his 'phone number. So I got in touch and he came down one night, just to have a look at the place; but unfortunately we probably offered him one pint too many of Royal Oak and Peter staggered out in the middle of a conversation and I never saw him again!

Let's cover a few others who did play for us on a regular basis; there was the **Dance Band**, which was Lou Stonebridge, Tom McGuiness, Rob Townsend the drummer from Family, they played all the old Soul dance hits, with a big brass section and later merged into the **Blues Band** with Paul Jones and Dave Kelly. And while we're on the subject of Dave Kelly, one of my early bookings was his sister **Jo Anne Kelly**, a lovely lady, sadly no longer with us, she came down and played a lot. Dave and Jo Anne both originated from Streatham and were living in Mitcham, I believe, when they played for us. Dave brought his own band down on a number of occasions, which was basically the Blues Band without Paul Jones, we certainly got our moneys worth out of the Blues Band 'family tree'.

I booked a really fun band called **TattiOllity**, which was formed by two ex-Bonzo Dog members, Sam Spoons and Roger Ruskin-Spear - and Roger still brought with him his 'exploding kinetic wardrobe'. Another couple of nutters were **Trimmer & Jenkins**, a sax and guitar duo from the band Burlesque. One of the highlights of their act was the infamous 'heart attack' competition; at a given point during the song 'I've just had a Heart Attack', members of the audience would be invited to perform their own version of a cardiac arrest, while Ian Trimmer and Billy Jenkins judged the best ones from the stage!

Brett Marvin & the Thunderbolts appeared, still with Jona Lewie in the band and not long before he had his solo hit with 'Stop the Cavalry' and I also managed to get **Chicken Shack** while I was there although I think they have been back to the Cartoon since. Guitarist Stan Webb was superb, he walked across the tables while he was playing, I tell you that surprised a few punters! While we're talking about band members who went walkabout during the set, we had a great band called **Deadringer** whose sax player, a guy called Pete Thomas, used to get up on the bar at the stage end, walk the length of it towards the doors, (scattering a few beers as he went), jump off and run down the stairs and into the gents! When you were in the toilets at the Cartoon you could hear the bands playing above your head and you could always picture these guys in the loo, thinking 'That sax solo sounds a bit loud' and turning 'round to find Pete playing next to them! Deadringer were a bit like Graham Parker & the Rumour, with Pete Thomas and Bimbo Acock again, on saxes and a guy called Steve King on keyboards.

> *" ...you could picture these guys in the loo, thinking "that sax solo sounds a bit loud" and turning 'round to find Pete playing next to them! "*

Rock fans in Croydon will know all about **Dumpy's Rusty Nuts** who were a sort of heavy blues band that played a great many times over the road at the Star - well, before forming the band, we had 'Dumpy' himself at the Cartoon working the P.A. for us. **Nicky Barclay**, who used to be the keyboard player in Fanny, brought her own group down to the Cartoon several times; she had Dave Ball on guitar and Wilgar Campbell on drums - now old Wilgar was at one time Rory Gallagher's drummer and he also went on to play with another local guy, Steve Boyce.

The Cartoon decided to promote two of the regular bands by making a video of their set and hawking it round to all the A&R men. This was still in the early days of video, bands just weren't doing this as a matter of course like they do today and we even had to take a player with us to run it on, as the record companies didn't have their own! So this was a pretty impressive bit of marketing at the time and it worked for one of the bands - we promoted Deadringer and a three-piece 'Police-style' band called **The Drivers**. The main man in the Drivers was singer Nick van Eede from East Grinstead, and the tape caught the eye of Canadian A&R man Terry Brown, who must know a good trio when he sees one because he went on to manage Rush! The Drivers soon changed their name to the **Cutting Crew**; I think they kept Nick and ditched the other two and went on to have a massive hit single with 'I Just Died In Your Arms Tonight' both here and in the States. But Nick didn't forget his roots and he brought the Cutting Crew back to the Cartoon for a couple of really special nights. "

Sadly the Cartoon closed the doors on live music towards the end of 1995 when its music licence ran out and was not renewed. However, the good news is that a new music venue - The Cool Room - has opened on the same site; let's hope it continues a fine tradition.

Shotgun - a shot of South London Rock'n'Roll...

They say that old rockers never die - and thankfully most don't fade away either. Throughout his long career, guitarist Ray Neale has continued to play the music he loves - the style may have changed a few times along the way but the bottom line is - hey, it's all rock'n'roll.

During the late 'sixties and early 'seventies, South London was generally regarded as the birthplace of a British rock and roll revival - the pubs and clubs of the area were packed night after night with rockers and teddy boys - and it was a tremendous melting pot for musicians just itching to get back to basics, back to the wild days of Haley, Vincent, Jerry Lee and Little Richard.

Along with Ray Neale, at the heart of the South London revival were Bob Burgos and Rob Murley, who formed an explosive trio that played for many years on reputation alone, without an official name.

Bob Burgos from South Norwood has a rock'n'roll pedigree that is second to none. He has backed Chuck Berry and been a member of The Savages behind Lord Sutch. He was the drummer with Matchbox during their heyday in the 'seventies and among those who sing his praises are Sonny Burgess, Ray Campi and Dick Richards, the sticksman for Bill Haley's Comets. High praise indeed.

Bass man Rob Murley comes from Wallington. He was also one of the Screamin' Lord's Savages and a member of the highly respected Cruisers, before teaming up with Shotgun. A Fender man through and through, this is how he was described by rock and roll writer Ray Liffen: *"Stand Rob blindfold on a stage anywhere in the world, put a bass in his hands, give him an intro, a note, a beat and he's right there - in the key, in the rhythm and in the music".*

Addington's Ray Neale has already been featured in the earlier chapters, with local 'sixties bands The Kingpins and Those Fadin' Colours. He played guitar with the Mojos and for Aynsley Dunbar, and Ray too was on the payroll of Lord Sutch. He crossed paths with Rob Murley and Bob Burgos throughout the 'seventies, in bands such as C.S.A. with the late Tony Vincent.

In 1978, they finally adopted the name **Shotgun** and among the regular fans who flocked to see them play live was Terry Parker, manager of Billy Goat Records who signed them up to record their first single under their new name in September 1978. Jim Carlise was added as second guitarist for a short time before being replaced by Iain Terry, and the band also brought in piano and saxophone for recording purposes or to add extra depth to their sound on the larger gigs that were consistently coming their way.

The 'legendary' Shotgun line-up. Left to right: Ray Neale, Dave Briggs, Rob Murley and Bob Burgos.

In 1987, the position of second guitarist was ably filled by Dave Briggs from Norwood, who had previously added his rock and blues influences to local favourites Basil's Balls-Up Band amongst others, and who has remained Shotgun's fourth member ever since.

Throughout the 'eighties and 'nineties, Shotgun have recorded several albums, including 'A Shot of Rebel Rockabilly' and 'Red Hot'n'Rockin', in between the constant touring, not only in their own right, but also working with rockabilly stars Mac Curtis, Ray Campi, Johnny Legend, and a host of others.

Having cut their rock and roll teeth in various groups from around the Croydon area, Shotgun remain one of Britain's wildest rockabilly bands.

Thanks to Ray Neale and Ray Liffen for their help and information.

Potter's Music Shop

Situated at 7 South End, right next to the Blacksmiths Arms on Coombe Cross, Potter's was generally regarded as the 'epicentre' of all things musical in Croydon during those ground-breaking days of the early 'sixties. Talk to any local musician from that era, and they can't speak highly enough of its importance to the area and to the development of the local groups.

The history of Potter's Music Shop has its roots in variety and music hall, many years before the advent of rock'n' roll and British Beat.

The shop was very much a family affair, with Mr & Mrs Potter, their son Edward and daughter-in-law Jean all taking turns behind the counter. The Potters had previously run a pub - The Thames Hotel in Hampton Court, but were quick to spot a gap in the instrument market with the advancing interest in popular music, choosing Croydon as the site for their first shop because they considered the town to be a "music-conscious suburb".

Mrs Potter was better known as variety star Gladys Hay, the daughter of comedian Will Hay, famous for his roles in classic comedy films such as 'Oh, Mr Porter' and 'Convict 99'. A one-time resident of Norbury, Will Hay was not only a fine comic actor, but also a keen astronomer who later had an observatory built on top of his Hendon residence.

Customers to the shop were often quite surprised to see Gladys demonstrating the various models of accordian, not realising that she was the proprietor. She had made her name on the radio programme 'Ignorance is Bliss' and even after the Potter's had opened their shop, Gladys continued to make occasional appearances on the stage and on television, including the Ted Ray show during the late fifties.

Not just a place to buy instruments, Potter's Music Shop was ***the*** *place to buy records... and you could listen to them first!*

Her husband Albert Potter was a timpanist in the Royal Philharmonic Orchestra, before forming his own act 'The Six Harmonists' in which Gladys played the piano.

Their son Edward (or Ted as most people knew him), was a top-line modern jazz drummer with the Lenny Best Quartet and by December 1958 was fronting his own band, the Ted Potter AllStars, with a regular gig at Croydon's Park Lane Ballroom. Both he and his musician father gave lessons in the evenings and for any instruments they couldn't cover between them, specialist tutors were brought in; but although the walls of the shop were covered in jazz and rock'n'roll records, the pupils weren't taught any of these styles, at least not to begin with. In an interview with the Croydon Times (February 1957), Gladys Hay told them: *"The queues at the Davis Theatre showed us that Croydon people were interested in music. The musical standards here are very high and an amazing number of youngsters come in who are seriously interested in learning. We teach them to read music and to play their instruments straight - what they do after that is up to them!"*

The family certainly were keen on promoting all forms of music to children, no matter how young. In early 1964, Ted was approached by Ron Earwicker for some advice on local beat groups. Ron was manager of the Classic cinema, just a little further down the Brighton Road from Potter's shop, and he ran a matinee session for kids known as the 'Three C's Club'. Under Ted's guidance, the Classic was the first local cinema to feature live groups playing before and between the films, an idea that proved popular to the beat-crazy youngsters and helped raise Saturday morning attendances.

In the Autumn of 1968, Ted formed the Croydon Drums Club, which at the time was the only organisation in Britain specifically for drummers. *"Drummers should be able to read music"* Ted told the guests at the clubs first annual dinner, including representatives of Premier and Dallas Arbiter, *"we have some fantastic drummers in this country who are just as good as the Americans"*. By April 1969, Ted and Joan had opened another two music shops to add to the South Croydon branch; during the 'seventies a further shop opened in Merstham run by master violin restorer David Newton and this shop is the last remaining branch of Potter's still operating today.

I asked Dave Newton about the early days of Croydon's premier music shop:

"I was twenty one when I joined Potter's, which must have been around 1962 - I'd served an apprenticeship in engineering and hated every minute of it, but I kept up the making and repairing of musical instruments. I sang with various local skiffle groups and eventually I saw a job offered for a musical instrument technician with a company in Jersey. So I packed my bags and went out there and they said "well, how good are you at tuning pianos?" That wrecked my chances of that job, but I didn't have enough money to get back, so I took a building job to earn my fare home. The day I got back I went up to Croydon and got a job with Potter's - and I've been with the company ever since.

The early sixties was an amazing time - it reached a point, at the height of 'Beatlemania' where I would drive up to London and pick up van loads of guitars, making as many trips as possible to build up stock for the weekend. The cellar at Potter's held about 200 guitars and we would reckon to sell most of them during one weekend and then the whole process would start again. In some instances there would be queues of people outside the shop, waiting for the van to return and we'd be selling instruments straight out of the van.

There were a whole load of young musicians who were regular visitors to the shop, that later went on to become famous; **Jeff Beck** was one, he was working as a panel beater just down the road in South Croydon and he would turn up in his overalls during his lunchbreak and sit around playing the guitars. **Manfred Mann** used to come in quite a bit. We also had the little shop over at Kingston, and quite a few bands would come in there - The Nashville Teens and The Kinks were customers, in fact we had a guy called Andy White who used to teach Mick Avory how to play the drums. I believe that Andy White actually played on most of the early Kinks singles, although Mick Avory was a very good drummer.

We had a guitar especially made for **Ronnie Wood**, it was built by a guy named John Bailey who now lives down in Devon. This guitar was a really special thing; it was a black 12 string, a great big beast, with an oval sound hole and a V-shaped head. It was a long way ahead of its time - and when this thing was delivered to the shop it was stolen almost immediately. There was a guy in Croydon at that time called Dave Eggar who was a pretty big bloke, about six foot four and no mean guitarist himself, and I said to him, "Look Dave, this guitar's gone missing..." and he said "Don't worry about it..." and within days it turned up at the shop in a black plastic bag! Ronnie Wood eventually sold it, it moved on and got passed around, but I recently tracked it down and I now know the man who currently owns it, which is quite incredible.

Upstairs at Potter's we also had a little recording studio as well. Martin Nighy who was the singer with Martin Jae & the High Five, got himself a recording deal and needed to put some material down on tape, for a demo I guess and we set up this little studio specifically to do that. Martin also got to sing with **Roy Budd** - and he was another one who was always in our shop. I had known Roy since he was about twelve or thirteen, he was this little hyperactive ginger headed kid, a complete lunatic and he would sometimes come to London with me on those guitar collecting trips. He would sit in the passenger seat drinking coke, trouble was he would always shake the can up first and then fill the van with coke spray when he opened it! But Roy was a brilliant pianist, absolutely brilliant even at that early age. He got himself an audition with one of the big bands and being only about fifteen or sixteen he couldn't afford a suit; so Potter's bought his first suit for him, he got the job and of course he went on from there to become quite famous. He married Katerina Valente. His film score work is hugely popular again now of course. And his brother was a very talented jazz guitarist too. Both of them would come into the shop all the time when they were youngsters and Roy's trick was that he could perfectly mimick any other piano player's style - and this was before he could read music, he had completely natural ability.

The jazz side of the business was very good of course, we were getting a lot of musicians in from the big bands. There's a nice story about the time the Buddy Rich band played at the Fairfield Halls; their lead trumpet player was in the middle of a solo when one of the valve heads snapped off from his trumpet. In the audience was a fellow called Don Wesson, who was the shop manager in Croydon at the time, Don leapt into his car, shot down to the shop, grabbed a trumpet and took it straight back to the Fairfield for this guy to carry on playing!

Soon after the Fairfield first opened, Potter's staged an exhibition that ran for about three days under the banner 'Music Is Fun', which was Potter's trademark in those days. We ferried in thousands of schoolkids from all over the county, we had concerts running all day, with lectures and seminars in between and the exhibits throughout the corridors and in the Sun Lounge, I did some sculpture for the Sun Lounge - it was an amazing thing to do at the time, it cost us the earth. It could have made us bankrupt, but in retrospect it put Potter's on the map as the foremost music shop in the area and I also think it did a hell of a lot of good for music education in Surrey. It made schools aware of how important music was; our idea was to get it added to the National Curriculum, which didn't happen at the time and obviously it would have been very good for business if it had, but it certainly helped move it on a fair way and helped to set in teachers minds where they wanted their school to go musically. Potter's had a separate company within the shop called Educational Instruments which actually funded the exhibition and yes, we did an awful lot of educational business. We do less now, as the funding for music in schools has been cut-back more and more.

Potter's developed and made their own pick-up, the Plato Pick-up, and quite a few were fitted to well known pop guitars - Bill Wyman, the bass player in the Stones certainly had one. Ted also invented an electric metronome, which we called The Electronome and we made hundreds of the things.

Don Wesson ran a 'Glenn Miller' style Big Band, which played regularly at the Dukes Head and was basically a Potter's run band. Ted Potter himself played in quite a few bands, he actually started out as the drummer with the Oscar Rabin Band and the fact that the whole Potter family were involved in the stage world in some form or other, made it a very lively shop. When Ted stopped being a professional musician to run Potter's full time, he injected so much energy and enthusiasm into the shop itself. Of course he still played, one long term gig was with the Lenny Best Quartet, Lenny was a vibrophonist and they would always have regular guest musicians - Ted's musicianship brought in a lot of business to the shop and a lot of interest too. Ted bless him, eventually left the business to start up a jazz pub in Brighton which never really worked out for him. Unfortunately, towards the end of his time at the shop, Ted had developed quite an alcohol problem and a friend of his, Charles Piper who was a member of the Wilkinson Sword family business, was injecting money into the business. But Ted was drinking the money away as fast as Chas was pumping it in and the situation ended up with Chas Piper owning Potter's and having to kick Ted Potter out before the shop went under.

Charles promoted me to managing director and we continued for some time with the same kind of general business; but eventually it was my personal interest in one area which changed the direction of the shop and was one of the reasons we moved out of Croydon, which was something I thought would never happen. I had always been employed by the shop as a repairer and restorer of musical instruments and when the opportunity came to take on more of that type of work, particularly violins, I seized that chance and reduced the other work that the shop was doing. We could see that in all the other areas, the electric guitars, drums, amplification, clarinets, flutes etc, the business was becoming far more competitive and cut-throat. But I knew that the violin world never was and never will be, a cut-throat business.

By this time we had expanded the business to three shopfronts and with the new business rate coming in, the council kept putting the rates up at a colossal pace. So what happened was that I bought the little shop in Merstham and built it up to a position where I could afford to close Croydon down completely and interestingly enough, because of the way we had changed our business, it made no difference to our work whatsoever. I notice that there is now a small music shop in part of our old building in South End. For years I wanted to buy the site in Croydon, but the block was made up of four shops, plus the rooms above - we had three but the council refused to sell unless someone had all four - had we managed to do that, Croydon would have had a music centre without equal and Potter's would probably have still been there today.

In the beat group days, we had an enormous amount of people in the shop who became so famous that they would never think of coming to us again - now of course we get quite a few classical musicians who are very well known in their field, but not known to the general public - there aren't too many people who could name a top violinist outside of Vanessa Mae or Nigel Kennedy! ”

And vinylly... Croydon Record Shops

So you've just got back from the old Greyhound and your head is still spinning after listening to the best band you've heard in absolutely ages... well, at least since last Sunday, and that final number was just so amazing... didn't the singer say it was on their second album?. Yeah, you've simply *got* to get hold of a copy and you know just the place.

Sounds familiar, doesn't it? To cope with such post-gig euphoria, every town has to have it's fair share of record retailers and Croydon is no exception. But todays high street chain stores, the Our Price's and HMV's have taken some of the magic out of record buying. The small, independent record stores are sadly few and far between these days, those pokey little backrooms and basements that no matter how small, always seemed to hold every single or album ever made and where the staff really knew their matrix numbers and could tell a single by it's B-side at fifty paces.

According to Rick and Terry Biddle, one of the best places to buy a record during the late 'fifties was from a stall in Surrey Street market, run by a lady who really knew her rock'n'roll - and oddly enough her stall was situated roughly in front of the shop that was to became Beano's - more about them later. In the late 'fifties and early 'sixties, Kennards arcade offered a fine selection, as did Potter's Music shop and Record Rendezvous in West Croydon - all three supplied sales figures to the pop chart that appeared in the Croydon Times. The Pyramid record store at Broad Green is also well remembered.

Cloakes - at one time home to the greatest 'bargain basement' in the world - erm, probably.

During the 'sixties and early 'seventies, most shops contained soundproofed (or supposedly so) listening booths, where you could ask the proprietor to play Billy Fury's latest single on his turntable, while you disappeared into booth 3 to decide whether or not you wanted to buy it! Cloakes had them, as did Potter's Music on the Coombe Cross junction, before it became solely an instrument shop. At the start of the 'sixties, a 45rpm single would have cost six shillings and three old pence (6s. 3d), an EP cost 10s. 11d and an LP record £1. 14s. 3d (and people wonder why we went decimal!). By the end of the decade the pop single was 8s. 6d, the EP 13s. 3d and the LP cost £1. 17s. 6d.

Cloakes is still flying the flag in opposition to the larger chainstores, but in its heyday, a visit to Cloakes 'Bargain Basement' was a must for every vinyl junkie. A walk down the narrow stairs at the back of the shop took you into another world - every inch of wall was decorated with cuttings from the music press, posters and publicity shots of obscure groups, whose one and only album was in the rack for 99p (and these days is a probably a psychedelic rarity worth eighty quid). Classic albums on the Island, Deram and Charisma labels were yours for £1.99 and french students flocked in to pick up the double album soundtrack to Woodstock for only a pound more.

On your way back to the bus terminus at West Croydon, the headquarters of Mr. Fox Records was to be found. As the gigs at the Greyhound were promoted by the same organisation, there was often a special offer on Sunday-nights-artists-latest LP and you could buy advance tickets for the following week. The shop featured, I remember, an intriguing spiral staircase that tunnelled its way into the floor, but was for 'hey, staff only, man'.

If you were heading back via East Croydon railway station, then Bonapartes was the last port of call on your record buying tour. Later the shop became 101 Records, who stayed in the same building until the redevelopment of the station, when they moved to their current position in Drummond Road. They were always one of the best places to find quality second-hand vinyl and quickly became the local trendsetters in selling second-hand CD's. Around the time of the name change, the old shop front in George Street was dwarfed by an enormous cut-out Elvis Costello, circa 'My Aim is True'!

Almost opposite, on the corner of the cut through to the Croydon College entrance, Virgin opened a store for a short period, but it never really took off. And still in the same road, does anyone remember the record basement underneath the newsagents?. It was run by a jazz buff, but carried a good selection of unusual rock albums and the ever present box of ex-chart singles. Every good record shop had such a box, the point being that in the Seventies every album produced a single, no matter how uncommercial, as a 'taster' for the album. Often only intended for the shop staff or local DJ's, most of the singles in the ex-chart section never even got near the charts and were all the better for it. And all the more interesting to dig out from the bottom of the pile.

There were countless others of course - Rumbelows in St. George's Walk, Gooses in the Whitgift Centre and Broad Green Record Centre, which even published its own magazine - 'Red Hot', for a couple of issues during the mid 'seventies. Goodness Records became a fairly successful local chain started by Chris Taylor from Caterham, from the original shop in Caterham Valley, they opened branches in Tooting, Norbury and Warlingham, before finally closing to concentrate on mail-order and import stock. Goodness also dabbled in making records, their own label Toadstool Records was created to release 'Controversial', the debut single by ex-Johnny Moped guitarist Slimy Toad.

Today, Beano's is probably the best known of Croydon's record shops and proudly boasts the title of Britain's largest 'second-hand recorded music' store - three floors of wall to wall vinyl, CD's and memorabilia, complemented by an unseen back-up of mouth watering stock. Talking of which...

Beanos

The largest second-hand recorded music store in Britain, and probably Europe, if not the Universe!

The Beanos success story can be traced back to 1971, when David Lashmar and his wife Kay opened a boutique at Polperro in Cornwall. In order to liven up the shop, David installed an old jukebox, but when it was delivered it didn't have any records; so he advertised for second hand singles and was inundated with hundreds of them which he snapped up for a bargain price. Later on, while looking around a market in Plymouth, he saw a man selling old records and realised this was how he could sell off any of the jukebox singles that were surplus to requirements.

Starting with just a couple of cardboard boxes on a market stall, David could not have imagined that in 1996 his company would turn over a cool million pounds with profits of £250,000 - and all down to that old jukebox.

Born in Surrey, Lashmar played in a 'sixties rock band but freely admits that he didn't know the first thing about buying and selling records when he started the business. In those days, record collecting certainly wasn't the huge industry that we know today. He began to notice that many of the people sorting through his cardboard boxes only picked out certain records - those on a certain label or ones that were long deleted. Starting with a policy of selling every record for double the price that he paid for it, he soon built up a considerable stock and decided to move back from the West Country to Croydon, opening his first shop in a disused billiard hall off a market street. Bell Hill Cassettes proved to be popular - more so the spare stock of vinyl, consisting of five hundred albums and several hundred singles - plus the new location and the timing proved crucial. In an interview for the Daily Mail's Financial section, David told them: *"There was a big student population who wanted to sell their records for quick cash, and a lot of working kids who had the money to buy them. And later, when those students graduated, many bought their records back!"*

Remember this? - how the empire began, way back in the early 'seventies.

Within ten years of opening his first shop, Beanos had outgrown the premises in Bell Hill and were forced to find somewhere bigger - David didn't have to look far, moving just a few hundred yards across into Surrey Street market itself. This is the shop that really established itself in the hearts of record buyers throughout the country and didn't just capture the imagination of the ordinary punter either; Beanos customers have included Pete Townshend and Diana Ross, both looking to complete their own collections, and the likes of Mark Lamarr, Bob Stanley from Saint Etienne and Tim Burgess of The Charlatans regularly drop in. The rarest and most valuable records have passed through the shop; a South African album released in the 'fifties featuring Elvis Presley on one side and an unknown singer called Janis Martin on the other, was priced at £2,000. After a quick 'phone call, the buyer came in the following day and handed over the full sum - in cash. The 'doo-wop' classic 'Earth Angel' by the Penguins sold for a similar amount, while the hastily deleted A&M single release of 'God Save The Queen' by The Sex Pistols now fetches £2,500. These are records that you only ever *see* once in a lifetime, let alone get the chance to own.

In 1985, the shop launched its own record label to help promote local musical talent; the first two groups to record singles for Beanos Records were Stagefright and Cause & Effect. Stagefright in particular were popular regulars at the Cartoon and David told the Croydon Post - *"We are offering young talent a no-strings opportunity to record their own records and have them issued through our set-up. Beanos have been looking for a new outlet, having successfully built up the store over the past few years."*

David attributes Beanos success to *"loving what we do and being fair with the customer. Every second-hand record is guaranteed; buyers have their money returned if they aren't satisfied - but I rarely buy a scratched disc."* Plus they employ a staff of around twenty enthusiasts, all experts in their own fields, one stalwart has been with the company for 18 years while another started his own record collection buying from Beanos as a fourteen year old. Beanos also offers a valuation service and David has often appeared on radio to answer listeners' questions about rare records - including a regular feature for the Diana Luke show on GLR - and also guested on the Croydon Cable TV channel.

1996 was an eventful year for Beanos; it was their twenty first anniversary and the shop moved to bigger premises yet again, this time to a three-storey, 5,000 square foot Victorian warehouse in Middle Street, still only a 7-inch singles throw from both other shops. Ground floor for albums, first floor for singles, top floor for blues, folk and rock 'n'roll. The shop also sells books and memorabilia - and that crowded top floor also features a coffee bar with authentic '50's soda fountain and mini cinema (a couple of rows of old cinema seats and a TV showing videos!). The shop has hosted occasional live sets from bands such as Rocket From The Crypt and rumour has it that Beanos may open their own local venue.

Beanos are justifiably proud of their success and equally proud of their Croydon heritage; they are always looking at ways of putting something back into the local community - and long may they continue.

Beanos, Middle Street, Croydon, Surrey CR0 1RE

Artists index – *listed here in alphabetical name order & date of appearance. To find particular concert details, turn to the spread for that year.*

THE **CHECKMATES** - 7.12.63,

CHICKEN SHACK - 5.2.68, 1.4.68, 6.5.68, 23.6.69, 19.4.70, 6.12.70, 29.8.71

CHICORY TIP - 23.4.74

THE **CHIEFTAINS** - 15.10.75, 31.7.76, 12.10.76, 8.11.77, 12.11.78, 8.2.80.

CHIFFONS - 25.11.68,

CHILDE ROLANDE - 11.12.80,

CHRISTIE - 30.4.74,

KEITH **CHRISTMAS** - 26.2.71,

CITIZENS - 14.5.80,

THE **CITY WAITES** - 25.4.75, 4.11.75,

THE **CLANCY BROTHERS** - 18.9.64, 5.5.68, 12.1.69, 16.1.70,

ERIC **CLAPTON** - 31.7.76,

ALLAN **CLARKE** - 29.9.74,

THE **CLASH** - 18.12.78,

CLAYSON & THE ARGONAUTS - 19.5.77,

CLIMAX CHICAGO - 5.6.70, 17.6.73,

CLIMAX BLUES BAND - 7.11.76, *(see also Climax Chicago)*

CLIVE'S ORIGINAL BAND *(Clive Palmer's C.O.B.)* - 5.11.72,

CLOVER - 20.11.77,

COAST ROAD DRIVE - 7.4.74, 4.8.74,

BILLY **COBHAM** - 22.6.75,

COCHISE - 22.5.70,

JOE **COCKER** - 16.9.64, 12.2.69, 3.6.72, 4.12.76,

COCKNEY REBEL - 6.1.74, 24.3.74, 7.7.74,

THE **COFFEE SET** - 10.12.66,

FITZROY **COLEMAN** - 5.7.64,

ORNETTE **COLEMAN** - 12.5.66,

JUDY **COLLINS** - 7.10.80,

SHIRLEY **COLLINS** - 5.7.64, 7.2.65, 18.6.68,

COLOSSEUM - 10.5.70, 6.9.70,

COLOSSEUM II - 15.2.76,

THE **COLOURED RAISINS** - 2.9.68, 3.2.69, 9.3.69, 7.4.69, 1.9.69, 22.12.69,

KEN **COLYER** - 19.9.58, 3.6.60, 10.3.61, 27.5.61, 31.3.62, 9.3.63, 20.4.63, 6.7.63, 2.2.68,

THE **COMMANCHES** - 4.4.64, 20.6.64,

THE **COMMISSIONAIRES** - 16.1.80,

ARTHUR **CONLEY** - 24.11.69, 16.2.73,

BILLY **CONNOLLY** - 15.10.80,

CONSORTIUM - 3.12.72,

BERT JANSCH's **CONUNDRUM** - 3.6.79,

MIKE **COOPER** - 10.2.69,

THE **CORRIES** - 13.9.67, 13.9.68, 29.10.71,

ELVIS **COSTELLO** - 10.9.77, 16.10.77,

COTTONWOOD - 29.10.72,

THE **COUNT BISHOPS** - 24.4.77,

WAYNE **COUNTY** - 7.4.77,

THE **COWARDS** - 1.4.79,

MICHAEL **COX** - 3.3.61,

KEVIN **COYNE** - 8.6.75,

CRAZY CAVAN & THE RHYTHM ROCKERS - 13.6.76,

CREAM - 26.9.66, 6.11.67,

THE **CRESTA'S** - 8.1.61,

THE **CRESTERS** - 25.4.62,

THE **CRICKETS** - 2.10.74,

THE **CRUISERS** *(with Dave Berry)* - 23.2.64, 30.4.65,

BOBBY **CRUSH** - 14.4.79,

THE **CRYSTALS** - 17.2.72,

CUPIDS INSPIRATION - 29.7.68, 17.12.74,

THE **CURE** - 26.11.78, 1.6.79,

CURVED AIR - 20.11.70, 10.1.71, 7.3.71, 1.10.72, 30.3.75, 30.11.75, 20.6.76, 10.10.76,

IVOR **CUTLER** - 3.12.72,

THE **DALLAS BOYS** - 4.3.62,

TERRY **DACTYL** & THE DINOSAURS - 27.8.72 *(see also Brett Marvin...)*

DADDYLONGLEGS - 15.3.70,

THE **DALEKS** - 10.12.80,

THE **DAMNED** - 21.11.76, 28.11.76, 15.1.78, 29.10.78, 14.1.79, 22.4.79,

DANA - 16.2.78, 5.1.80,

MIKE **DANIELS** & THE DELTA JAZZMEN - 28.3.58, 27.5.61,

JOHNNY **DANKWORTH** - 21.4.63,

DARLING - 17.12.78,

JENNY **DARREN** - 13.3.77,

DARTS - 23.9.79, 26.10.80.

DAVE DEE, DOZY, BEAKY, MICK & TICH - 27.4.66, 13.11.67,

BOB **DAVENPORT** - 20.8.62, 15.10.65, 6.5.66,

CYRIL **DAVIES** - 23.10.63,

FREDDIE **DAVIS** - 31.3.65,

REV. GARY **DAVIS** - 14.6.65,

D'DANCER - 18.11.75,

DEADRINGER - 12.12.79,

DEAF SCHOOL - 14.11.76,

DEEP PURPLE - 28.12.69, 22.2.70, 14.6.70, 22.11.70, 22.2.72, 12.3.72,

THE **DEFIANT ONES** - 19.2.66,

DESMOND **DEKKER** - 11.12.67, 14.4.69, 15.9.69, 29.12.69, 12.1.70, 10.2.72, 24.10.75,

DELANEY & BONNIE - 7.12.69,

THE **DEL-TONES** - 8.12.62, 8.6.63, 20.6.64,

TERRY **DENE** - 20.10.57, 3.3.61,

THE **DENNISONS** - 17.3.64,

SANDY **DENNY** - 26.3.72, 11.11.77,

KARL **DENVER** - 20.11.62,

THE **DEPUTIES** - 6.4.63, 1.6.63, 8.6.63,

DEREK & THE DOMINOES - 29.9.70,

SUGAR PIE **DESANTO** - 25.10.64,

ANDY **DESMOND** - 23.9.75, 1.6.78,

THE **DESPERADO'S** - 20,6,64,

DESPERADOES - 16.9.81,

THE **DETROIT EMERALDS** - 3.2.72,

THE **DETROIT SPINNERS** - 2.11.73, 13.4.75, 1.5.77,

BARBARA **DICKSON** - 21.11.77, 16.10.78, 6.7.81,

RICHARD **DIGENCE** - 13.3.75, 4.11.75, 23.6.78,

DIRE STRAITS - 5.2.79,

DIZ **DISLEY** - 10.4.79,

THE **DISSATISFIED** - 13.2.65,

WILLIE **DIXON** - 18.10.63, 19.10.64, 25.10.64, 25.11.70,

THE **DOCKS** - 11.3.68,

DOCTORS OF MADNESS - 20.11.76,

THE **DOLL** - 1.1.78, 29.1.78,

LONNIE **DONEGAN** - 5.6.75,

DONOVAN - 15.10.65, 23.6.67, 17.12.73, 22.6.75, 7.10.81,

THE **DOOLEYS** - 24.2.80,

VAL **DOONICAN** - 5.9.81,

DOPPELGANGER - 7.1.78,

LEE **DORSEY** - 6.11.67, 13.10.69

TOMMY **DORSEY** ORCHESTRA - 27.1.64,

DOTTY CROTCHET - 28.12.79,

DOWNES & BEER - 22.11.71,

DOWNLINERS SECT - 19.2.64, 21.4.77,

DR. COSGILL - 11.12.80,

DR. FEELGOOD - 27.3.74, 18.5.75,

DR. HOOK - 6.6.76,

DR. JOHN - 7.5.72,

DR. MARIGOLD'S PRESCRIPTION - 24.11.67,

DR. ROSS - 11.10.65,

DR. STRANGELY STRANGE - 12.3.71,

DRAGON MILK - 30.4.72,

NICK **DRAKE** - 10.10.69,

THE **DRAMATIC DRUIDS** - 20.9.65,

THE **DRANSFIELDS** - 22.11.71,

JUDGE **DREAD** - 8.10.75,

THE **DRIFTERS** - 18.5.66, 30.9.68, 28.4.69, 29.9.69, 9.9.71, 24.2.72, 9.4.74, 6.4.76,

THE **DUBLINERS** - 1.7.67, 26.1.68, 3.11.68, 1.3.70, 4.9.70, 2.5.71, 16.4.72, 1.4.74, 25.9.75, 29.11.76, 27.9.77, 28.9.78, 27.9.79, 23.1.80,

THE **DUKES** - 3.2.80

JOHN **DUMMER** BLUES BAND - 17.11.69,

AYNSLEY **DUNBAR** - 8.4.68, 13.10.69,

AYNSLEY **DUNBAR** RETALIATION - 27.5.68, 13.2.69,

DUNCAN, JOHNNY, & THE BLUE GRASS BOYS - 3.3.61,

CHAMPION JACK **DUPREE** - 13.2.69, 9.11.69, 23.2.70, 25.11.70,

JUDITH **DURHAM** - 23.9.70, 4.3.71,

IAN **DURY** - 16.10.77, 4.12.77,

THE **DYAKS** - 5.3.78, 9.4.78,

VINCE **EAGER** - 16.11.62, 2.7.71,

THE **EAGLES** *(R'n'B)* - 20.8.62, 10.3.64,

EAST OF EDEN - 22.12.69, 16.8.70, 1.11.70, 20.12.70, 4.4.71, 21.5.71, 13.6.71, 21.5.72,

SHEENA **EASTON** - 12.10.80,

THE **EASYBEATS** - 18.3.67, 3.6.68,

EASY STREET - 24.10.76,

THE **ECHOES** - 22.4.63,

ECLECTION - 29.9.68, 24.1.71, 22.9.72, *(See also Doris Henderson)*

EDDIE & THE HOT RODS - 17.10.76, 28.11.76,

DUANE **EDDY** - 21.11.63, 00.5.68,

THE **EDGE BAND** - 7.10.78,

RANDY **EDELMAN** - 12.4.77, 16.4.78,

EGG - 28.7.69, 8.3.70, 17.4.70,

EGGS OVER EASY - 31.7.71, 26.9.71,

EL SLUG - 4.12.80,

THE **ELECTROTUNES** - 11.2.80,

ROY **ELDRIDGE** - 15.4.65,

ELECTRIC LIGHT ORCHESTRA - 16.4.72, 14.5.72, 10.3.74,

THE **ELGINS** - 4.11.71,

DUKE **ELLINGTON** - 25.1.63, 17.2.65,

BERN **ELLIOTT** & THE FENMEN - 7.1.64,

DAVID **ELLIOTT** - 25.4.74,

RAMBLING JACK **ELLIOTT** - 14.6.65,

ALAN **ELSDON** & THE VOODOOS - 18.11.64,

EMERSON, LAKE & PALMER - 25.10.70,

EMILY MUFF - 26.7.70,

EMPTY VESSELS - 5.12.80,

THE **END** - 21.1.67,

ENO - 24.2.74,

THE **EQUALS** - 18.3.68, 26.5.69,

DAVID **ESSEX** - 16.6.80,

THE **ESPRESSO FIVE** - 00.00.62,

SLEEPY JOHN **ESTES** - 25.10.64,

THE **ETHIOPIANS** - 7.7.69,

THE **EVERLY BROTHERS** - 23.10.62, 25.9.72,

EVIL WEASEL - 11.4.76, 23.5.76, 20.6.76, 18.11.76,

EVOLUTION - 17.3.74,

F

F.F.& Z. - 14.5.72,

FABLE - 21.4.74,

FABULOUS POODLES - 31.3.77,

THE **FACES** - 29.11.70, 24.1.71, 30.5.71,

FAIRPORT CONVENTION - 10.10.69, 23.8.70, 15.11.70, 21.2.71, 28.11.71, 23.4.72, 16.12.73, 30.6.74, 8.12.74, 2.11.75, 13.6.76, 7.11.76, 30.10.77, 3.6.79,

ANDY **FAIRWEATHER-LOW** - 22.2.76,

ADAM **FAITH** - 13.4.60, 8.2.61,

THE **FALL** - 7.5.78,

THE **FALLING LEAVES** - 15.6.64,

GEORGIE **FAME** - 24.2.65, 5.5.65, 10.8.66, 27.11.67, 5.2.68, 16.6.69, 4.9.73, 16.6.78,

FAMILY - 16.11.69, 26.7.70, 7.11.71, 4.2.73,

THE **FAMOUS JUG BAND** - 12.11.70,

FANG - 20.5.73,

FANNY - 8.10.72, 27.5.73,

THE **FANTASTICS** - 3.3.69, 2.2.70, 9.3.70,

CHRIS **FARLOWE** - 6.12.65, 3.2.66, 6.7.66,

GARY **FARR** - 31.8.65, 29.1.66, 8.11.66, 17.11.74,

FAT MATTRESS - 8.9.69,

THE **FATBACK BAND** - 25.2.76, 5.9.76,

FELIX & THE CATS - 29.3.80,

JULIE **FELIX** - 14.6.65, 15.10.65, 26.11.65, 23.11.66, 14.6.68, 6.12.68, 5.12.69, 22.7.72, 2.3.76,

THE **FENTONES** - 8.1.65,

ANDY **FERNBACH** - 14.7.69,

GRACIE **FIELDS** - 17.9.64,

THE **FIREBALLS** - 22.10.66, 4.3.67, 12.1.70,

ELLA **FITZGERALD** - 11.5.58, 6.4.64, 15.4.65,

PATRICK **FITZGERALD** - 15.10.78,

FIVE BLIND BOYS OF MISSISSIPPI - 5.2.65,

THE **FIVE DIMENSIONS** - 26.2.64, 29.1.65,

FIVE HAND REEL - 3.9.76, 25.2.77,

THE **FLAMING GROOVIES** - 21.11.76, 4.6.78,

FLEETWOOD MAC - 20.12.70, 22.7.71, 27.5.73,

FLIGHT - 23.7.72,

THE **FLIRTATIONS** - 7.10.68, 9.3.69,

FLOCK - 12.4.70,

THE **FLOWERPOT MEN** - 10.10.67,

EDDIE **FLOYD** - 27.3.67, 24.2.72,

THE **FLYING ACES** - 3.3.77,

FLYING CLOUD - 9.2.79, 16.2.79, 30.3.79,

FOCUS - 12.11.72, 17.5.73,

THE **FOLKVENDORS** - 8.4.63,

WAYNE **FONTANA** - 27.4.64, 24.10.64, 27.5.66, 13.2.67,

FOOSH - 24.2.75,

EMILE **FORD** - 25.11.80,

FOREVERMORE - 14.6.70,

HELEN **FORREST** - 27.1.64,

THE **FORTUNES** - 22.6.66, 17.2.72,

THE **FOUNDATIONS** - 30.10.67, 4.3.68, 30.12.68, 9.3.69,

FOUR TOPS - 24.5.70, 27.9.70, 22.10.72, 2.11.73, 14.11.75, 25.10.76, 13.11.77, 29.10.78, 2.11.80,

FOX & LUCKLEY - 2.4.79,

CHARLIE & INEZ **FOXX** - 9.2.66, 11.11.68, 19.5.69, 17.11.69,

JACKSON C. **FRANK** - 27.1.69,

FREDDIE & THE DREAMERS - 11.10.63, 23.2.64, 27.4.64,

Artists index – *listed here in alphabetical name order & date of appearance. To find particular concert details, turn to the spread for that year.*

BILLY J. **KRAMER** - 25.4.63, 1.6.64, 8.1.65, 9.7.71,
KRYSIS - 20.1.80,
THE **KURSAAL FLYERS** - 31.1.76, 13.6.76, 28.11.76, 12.6.77,

PATTI **LABELLE** - 11.5.66,
LAMPLIGHT - 8.10.76,
RONNIE **LANE** - 25.1.76,
MARIO **LANZA** - 23.3.58,
JULIET **LAWSON** - 5.12.74,
THE **LEAGUE OF GENTLEMEN** - 9.2.66,
MIKE **LEANDER** SHOWBAND - 31.3.65,
ALBERT **LEE** - 21.3.80,
LONESOME JIMMY **LEE** - 11.10.65,
MARK **LEEMAN** FIVE - 5.3.65,
J.B. **LENOIR** - 11.10.65,
KETTY **LESTER** - 23.10.62,
CARTER **LEWIS** &THE SOUTHERNERS - 21.11.63,
DAVID **LEWIS** - 2.11.75,
JERRY LEE **LEWIS** - 9.5.63, 28.5.63,
LINDA **LEWIS** - 18.6.72, 3.9.72, 4.2.73,
RAMSEY **LEWIS** TRIO - 18.9.73,
JOHN **LEYTON** - 6.11.63,
LIFE - 30.10.74,
LIFETIME - 29.11.70,
GORDON **LIGHTFOOT** - 25.2.66,
TERRY **LIGHTFOOT** & HIS JAZZMEN - 9.3.58, 14.3.58,
LIMEY - 22.2.76,
LIMMIE & THE FAMILY COOKIN' - 28.8.74,
PETE **LINCOLN** & THE SUNDOWNERS -
THE **LINCOLNS** - 15.4.67,
LINDISFARNE - 11.4.71, 18.7.71, 28.11.71, 11.6.72, 2.9.72, 15.7.73, 17.2.74, 16.2.75, 14.5.78, 30.9.79,
LITTLE BOB STORY - 21.2.77,
LITTLE TONY - 13.4.60,
LIVERPOOL SCENE - 14.12.69, 1.3.70,
LIZZIE MACK - 7.1.67,
GERRY **LOCKRAN** - 6.4.63, 22.4.65, 2.11.66, 11.11.66,
LOCOMOTIVE - 28.10.68,
NILS **LOFGREN** - 9.11.75,
DAVE **LOGGINS** - 25.9.72,
LOGGINS & MESSINA - 29.7.72,
LONDON - 11.9.77,
LONE STAR - 20.2.77,
JOHN D. **LOUDERMILK** - 25.10.74,
JACQUES **LOUISSIER** - 2.10.67, 10.10.68, 23.10.69, 28.2.71, 18.10.71, 17.3.72, 13.10.72, 30.3.73, 13.3.74, 16.3.75, 17.3.77,
LOVE - 8.3.70, 2.6.74,
THE **LOVE AFFAIR** - 22.1.68, 22.5.68, 4.9.70, 17.12.74
NICK **LOWE** - 16.10.77,
TREVOR **LUCAS** - *(see also Fairport Convention)* 25.2.66,
THE **LURKERS** - 1.1.78, 5.11.78,
TAMI **LYNN** - 1.7.71,
JACKIE **LYNTON** - *(see also Grande)* 12.1.75,
LYSANDER - 18.3.76,
HUMPHREY **LYTTLETON** - 10.10.58, 6.11.79,

M

JIMMIE **MACGREGOR** *with Robin Hall* - 8.10.65,
JOHN **MACLAUGHLIN** - 2.9.72,
MAGAZINE - 30.4.78,
MAGIC CARPET - 23.7.72,
MAGNA CARTA - 26.2.73, 20.9.73, 3.6.77,
TAJ **MAHAL** - 19.4.70,
MAHAVISHNU ORCHESTRA - 2.9.72, 19.1.75, *(see also John Maclaughlin)*
MAINLAND - 28.10.79,
MAINELINE - 4.12.80,
MAJOR SURGERY - *(residency at the Gun, every Sunday throughout 1975 !)*
MIRIAM **MAKEBA** - 15.11.67,
TOMMY **MAKEM** - 12.1.69,
MAKO - 8.10.70,
CURTIS **MALDOON** - 22.7.72,
MAN - 1.7.73, 28.10.73, 23.12.73, 13.10.74, 7.12.75, 5.12.76,
HARVEY **MANDEL** - 31.3.74,
MANFRED MANN - 28.1.64, 25.9.64,
MANFRED MANN CHAPTER III - 8.3.70,
MANFRED MANN's EARTHBAND - 2.12.73, 17.3.74, 16.3.75, 20.7.75, 22.2.76, 12.9.76, 23.4.78, 17.6.79
MIKE **MARAN** - 1.10.72, 6.10.72,
THE **MARK FOUR** - 9.9.65,
THE **MAR-KEYS** - 27.3.67,
MARMALADE - 27.1.69, 12.2.69,
STEVE **MARRIOTT's ALLSTARS** - 8.2.76,
STEVE **MARRIOTT's MOMENTS** - 5.4.64, 24.4.64, 3.8.64, 25.8.64,
MARSEILLE - 28.5.78, 8.11.79,
BOB **MARLEY** - 7.6.80,
JOHN **MARTYN** - 13.1.69, 25.11.71, 25.5.75,
THE **MARVELETTES** - 2.11.80,
BRETT **MARVIN** (& THE THUNDERBOLTS) - 20.9.70, 20.11.70,
MARVIN, WELCH & FARRAR - 29.11.71, 11.5.72,
MASON - 23.12.73,
AL **MATTHEWS** - 23.7.72, 14.11.75,
MATTHEWS SOUTHERN COMFORT - 29.3.70
MAVERICK - 3.12.80,
JOHN **MAYALL** - 17.1.66, 9.5.66, 22.1.69, 31.10.69, 1.5.70, 20.11.70, 26.9.71, 5.10.75,
THE **MAYTALS** - 11.5.70,
TONY **McCATHY** - 15.10.65,
PETER **McCLAINE** & THE CLAN - 7.12.63,
EWAN **McCOLL** & PEGGY SEEGER - 21.9.69, 30.11.69,
MISSISSIPPI FRED **McDOWELL** - 11.10.65,
RORY **McEWEN** - 2.3.63,
KATE & ANNA **McGARRIGLE** - 25.2.77,
BROWNIE **McGEE** - 10.5.64, 25.11.70,
ROD **McKUEN** - 14.5.71, 10.5.72, 27.5.75, 26.5.80,.
DON **McLEAN** - 4.6.72, 12.10.73, 26.5.75,
RALPH **McTELL** - 22.11.71, 21.5.72, 24.11.72, 24.12.72, 8.6.73, 28.2.74, 1.4.75, 17.2.76, 3.6.77, 22.4.80,
MC5 - 13.2.72,
MEAL TICKET - 3.2.77, 6.11.77,
MEDICINE HEAD - 8.8.71, 30.9.71, 3.12.72, 7.2.76,
TONY **MEEHAN** & JET HARRIS - 30.10.63,
MELANIE - 3.6.72,
GEORGE **MELLY** - 5.7.57, 6.5.66, 5.2.74, 27.10.74, 11.5.76, 7.2.77, 15.9.77, 25.1.78, 12.5.78, 2.12.80,
HAROLD **MELVIN** & THE BLUENOTES - 31.3.74,
MEMPHIS SLIM - 18.10.63,
THE **MERSEYBEATS** - 23.2.64, 1.6.64, 16.9.64, 13.11.74,
MICE - 16.3.80,
MIGHTY BABY - 19.9.69, 16.10.70, 6.12.70,
MIGIL 5 - 12.5.64, 20.1.67,
JOHN **MILES** - 9.12.77, 22.4.79,
FRANKIE **MILLER** - 19.9.76, 17.12.78,
GARY **MILLER** - 12.3.58,
MILLIE - 15.6.64,
GARRY **MILLS** - 8.9.61, 1.12.61,
THE **MINDBENDERS** - 27.4.64, 24.10.64, 10.10.67,
GUY **MITCHELL** - 22.2.57,
THE **MODELS** - 6.11.77,
MODERN JAZZ QUARTET - 19.4.64, 21.9.66, 13.3.69,
THE **MOJO'S** - 17.12.74
THEOLONIUS **MONK** - 25.4.66,
MATT **MONRO** - 13.4.63,
MONTAGE - 16.1.72,
CHRIS **MONTEZ** - 21.3.63,
MONTY SUNSHINE - 2.3.58, 3.6.61, 6.4.63, 9.2.68, 5.6.75,
THE **MOODY BLUES** - 29.1.65, 5.3.65,
MOON - 14.9.75, 10.10.76,
MOONDOG - 27.5.73,
MOONRIDER - 5.10.75,
JOHNNY **MOPED** - 15.1.78, 6.4.80,
SONNY **MORRIS** & HIS JAZZMEN - 2.3.58, 23.3.58,
VYVIAN **MORRIS** - 28.10.73,
MICKIE **MOST** - 21.11.63,
MOTHER SUN - 28.4.74,
MOTIVATION - 13.7.65, 20.7.65, 24.8.65, 4.1.66,
MOTORHEAD - *(also billed as Lemmy's Motorhead)* 14.9.75, 21.3.77, 17.3.77, 12.3.78,
THE **MOTORS** - 28.5.78,
MOTT THE HOOPLE - 14.12.69, 18.1.70, 26.4.70, 13.9.70, 18.10.70, 27.12.70, 28.3.71, 18.10.71, 20.2.72, 4.6.72,
THE **MOVE** - 21.10.66, 8.5.67,
MR. BIG - 8.5.77,
MR. MOSES SCHOOLBAND - 30.1.72,
MUD - 25.2.67, 26.5.67, 28.10.67, 24.1.74,
MUFFTY - 2.11.75,
GERRY **MULLIGAN** - 21.4.62, 23.10.79,
MICK **MULLIGAN** - 5.7.57,
MUNGO JERRY - 19.7.70, 21.11.80,
NOEL **MURPHY** - 21.4.68, 2.11.69,
MUSE - 30.4.78,

N

JOHNNY **NASH** - 30.3.78,
THE **NASHVILLE TEENS** - 21.5.64, 4.11.64, 17.12.74,
NASTY POP - 14.4.77,
NASTY TRICKS - 26.12.75,
NATIONAL FLAG - 16.2.75
NATIONAL HEAD BAND - 11.10.70,
NATIONAL HEALTH - 21.5.78,
NATURAL ACOUSTIC BAND - 24.11.72,
THE **NATURALS** - 16.9.64,
NAZARETH - 31.10.71, 28.11.71, 3.6.73,
NEKTAR - 10.2.74, 14.7.74, 24.11.74,
MIKE & TONY **NEVITT** - 22.4.63,
THE **NEW BREED** - 2.4.67,
NEW HEARTS - 16.10.77,
THE **NEW MERSEYS** - 15.4.66,
THE **NEW SEEKERS** - 18.2.70, 7.10.71, 6.5.73, 30.4.78,
THE **NEW VAUDEVILLE BAND** - 7.12.76,
OLIVIA **NEWTON-JOHN** - 29.11.71, 17.11.72,
THE **NICE** - 29.9.68, 22.6.69, 17.10.69, 22.3.70,
NIGHT - 26.2.78, 5.11.78,
THE **NIGHTIMERS** *with Ronnie Jones* - 5.3.65,
NIMBUS - 14.7.69,
NINA & FREDERIK - 27.9.64, 9.4.66, 6.4.69,
HAMMY **NIXON** - 25.10.64,
NO DICE - 27.11.77,
NO SWEAT - 10.9.77,
RAB **NOAKES** - 11.5.75,
PATSY ANN **NOBLE** - 6.3.63,
NOIR - 11.10.70,
THE **NOYSE** - 7.12.65,
NUTZ - 10.3.74,

DES **O'CONNOR** - 12.3.58,
THE **ODDS-ON** - 7.10.66,
OFANCHI - 1.3.78, 29.10.78,
ESTHER & ABI **OFARIM** - 28.3.68, 1.7.68,
OFARIM & WINTER - 6.5.73,
JOHN **OGDON** - 22.3.60, 7.2.61,
THE **OHIO PLAYERS** - 27.6.76,
EARL **OKIN** - 27.11.76,
MIKE **OLDFIELD** - 5.5.80,
OLYMPIC RUNNERS - 28.9.78,
ROY **ORBISON** - 27.4.64, 11.6.72, 19.9.75, 28.2.77, 21.4.80,
THE **ORLONS** - 13.7.66,
MARY **O'HARA** - 31.1.78, 29.10.79,
THE **O'JAYS** - 6.12.73,
GILBERT **O'SULLIVAN** - 14.6.73, 4.3.75, 1.3.78,
OSIBISA - 21.3.71, 12.12.71, 4.3.72, 29.7.72, 2.1.74, 20.1.74, 23.6.74, 17.11.74, 14.9.75, 11.4.76, 27.3.77, 5.2.78, 11.2.79, 27.1.80, 7.12.80,
THE **OTHER TWO** - 21.5.64,
THE **OUT** - 30.3.80,
THE **OUTLAWS** - 9.5.63, 28.5.63,
THE **OVERLANDERS** - 7.12.63, 12.4.64,

P.F.M. - 18.5.74,
PANAMA SCANDAL - 12.11.76,
PAPER LACE - 7.5.74, 14.4.75,
THE **PARAMOUNTS** - *(see also Procol Harum)* 15.9.65,
PARAPHERNALIA *(with Barbara Thompson)* - 26.5.74,
GRAHAM **PARKER** - 6.3.77, 20.11.77,
JOE **PASS** - 31.5.78, 7.11.80,
OTTILIE **PATTERSON** - 2.3.58, 20.4.62, 6.3.80,
BOBBY **PATTINSON** - 30.4.65,
PATTO - 19.2.72, 5.11.72,
TOM **PAXTON** - 14.11.68, 2.10.69, 28.5.70, 11.2.71, 11.11.71, 12.10.72, 30.10.73, 21.11.74, 13.11.75, 26.10.76, 25.10.79,
PEGASUS - 19.10.75,
PENETRATION - 3.12.78,
PENTANGLE - 15.11.68, 25.4.69, 15.2.70, 1.11.70, 12.11.71, 5.11.72,
PERCY - 10.11.74,
CARL **PERKINS** - 21.5.64, 4.11.64,
MARK **PERRY** - 11.11.76,
PETERS & LEE - 1.12.78,
OSCAR **PETERSON** - 6.4.64, 15.4.65, 00.5.65, 7.4.66, 7.10.68, 25.9.69, 10.12.70, 10.3.77, 3.11.78,
PIBLOKTO - 9.10.70,
NICK **PICKETT** - 1.10.72,
THE **PIED PIPERS** - 27.1.64,

Artists index – *listed here in alphabetical name order & date of appearance. To find particular concert details, turn to the spread for that year.*

THE **STATELINE BAND** - 25.5.77,

STATUS QUO - 11.3.68, 2.10.70, 8.11.70, 20.12.70, 14.2.71, 9.5.71, 31.10.71, 26.12.71, 30.4.72, 25.5.72, 6.8.72, 31.12.72, 30.9.73

STEALERS WHEEL - 25.2.73,

STEAMHAMMER - 4.8.69, 12.1.70, 20.9.70, 4.7.71,

TOMMY **STEELE** - 13.5.61,

STEELEYE SPAN - 24.10.71, 9.4.72, 19.10.72, 9.11.73, 18.11.74,

STEPPENWOLF - 24.5.70 *Cancelled*

AL **STEWART** - 11.2.70, 22.2.73, 27.11.73, 18.2.75,

BILLIE **STEWART** - 13.1.69,

ROD **STEWART** - 18.2.64,

BOB **STEVENS** - 20.9.70,

CAT **STEVENS** - 18.12.70,

SHAKIN' STEVENS - 7.6.70, 29.11.81,

STILLIFE - 8.7.73,

R. & J. **STONE** - 5.4.76,

STONE THE CROWS - 6.9.70, 3.1.71, 29.7.72,

THE **STRANGERS** - 00.0.62,

THE **STRANGLERS** - 1.5.76, 20.1.77, 27.3.77,

THE **STRAWBERRY HILL BOYS** - *(see also Strawbs)*, 26.4.64,

THE **STRAWBS** - 31.5.70, 3.6.70, 16.4.71, 30.1.72, 14.2.72, 6.10.74, 26.2.78,

STRAY - 27.10.69, 1.12.69, 8.1.70, 19.1.70, 10.4.70, 8.5.70, 12.6.70, 31.7.70, 24.12.70, 10.1.71, 7.2.71, 14.5.71, 9.1.72, 12.3.72, 14.5.72, 5.11.72, 18.3.73, 16.9.73, 30.12.73, 28.4.74, 30.6.74, 28.7.74, 29.12.74, 27.4.75, 12.10.75, 26.12.75, 8.2.76, 23.5.76, 26.9.76, 2.1.77, 17.4.77,

STRIDER - 11.12.73,

STRIFE - 20.6.76, 15,10.78,

THE **STUKA'S** - 19.2.78,

THE **STYLISTICS** - 28.4.74, 8.4.76, 17.4.77,

SUCKER - 14.1.78, 13.2.78,

SUE & SUNNY - 15.2.66,

HUBERT **SUMLIN** - 25.10.64,

THE **SUNDOWNERS** - 6.11.63,

SUNLINERS *(with Lee Bennett)* - 23.10.64,

SUNNYLAND SLIM - 25.10.64,

SUNRISE - 30.7.72,

SUNSHINE - 18.10.71,

SUPERCHARGE - 31.10.76,

SUPERTRAMP - 2.8.70, 17.9.70, 23.10.70, 16.11.75,

THE **SUPREMES** - 21.11.71, 11.3.73, 7.9.75,

SUTHERLAND BROTHERS & QUIVER - 9.1.72, 18.8.74, 29.6.75, 10.10.76,

THE **SUTHERLAND BROTHERS** - 19.10.79,

DAVE **SWARBRICK** *(see also Fairport Convention)* - 9.4.78,

SWEENEY'S MEN - 21.4.68,

SWEET SENSATION - 26.1.75, 7.9.75,

THE **SWINGING BLUE JEANS** - 9.2.64, 21.5.64, 17.12.74,

SWORDS - 11.9.77,

SYD & EDDIE - 18.11.64,

ROOSEVELT **SYKES** - 11.10.65,

SYMARIP - 12.1.70,

SYNDROME - 31.7.74,

T

TAJ MAHAL - 19.4.70,

TALKING HEADS - 29.5.77, 5.2.79,

THE **TAMS** - 28.10.71,

TANGERINE DREAM - 23.10.75, 14.11.76, 27.3.78,

THE **TANNER SISTERS** - 12.3.58,

TASTE - 15.2.70, 3.5.70, 6.8.70, 6.9.70,

TAVARES - 26.11.78,

ALLAN **TAYLOR** - 15.11.70,

FELICE **TAYLOR** - 21.10.68,

HARRY **TAYLOR** - 00.10.71,

JAMES **TAYLOR** - 16.7.71,

JACK **TEAGARDEN** - 29.9.57,

THE **TEMPERANCE SEVEN** - 30.6.61, 27.2.62,

TEMPEST - 10.6.73, 30.9.73,

TEN YEARS AFTER - 26.2.68, 8.4.73,

CLARK **TERRY** - 30.11.66,

SONNY **TERRY** - 10.5.64, 25.11.70,

JAKE **THACKRAY** - 17.4.70, 22.3.73, 31.1.74, 10.5.77,

SISTER ROSETTA **THARPE** - 25.11.70,

THEM - 2.5.66,

THIN LIZZY - 4.4.71, 8.4.73, 27.10.74, 12.1.75, 1.6.75, 14.12.75, 7.3.76,

THIRD EAR BAND - 20.10.69, 11.2.70,

THIRD WORLD - 27.6.79,

THIRD WORLD WAR - 5.9.71,

BARRY **THOMAS** - 23.3.63,

NICKY **THOMAS** - 2.8.70,

RICHARD & LINDA **THOMPSON** - 29.4.75, 5.11.79,

BIG MOMA **THORNTON** - 11.10.65,

THOR'S ANVIL - 5.7.70,

THE **THREE DEGREES** - 3.12.78,

STEVE **TILSTON** - 29.9.72,

THE **TINKERS** - 27.4.67,

TIR NA NOG - 22.8.71, 4.6.72, 7.4.74,

THE **TODAS** - 31.10.65,

OSCAR **TONEY** JNR - 12.5.69, 23.2.70,

BERNIE **TORMÉ** - 3.7.77,

THE **TORNADO'S** - 23.3.62, 22.4.63, 4.10.63,

STAN **TRACEY** - 24.3.79,

TRADER HORNE - 8.2.70, 16.3.70,

THE **TRAIN** - 14.2.66, 12.12.66,

TRAFFIC - 31.5.70, 6.6.71, 5.5.74,

TRAPEZE - 21.8.70, 30.5.71, 6.2.72,

THE **TRAUMEN** - 19.2.66,

THE **TREBLETONES** - 4.3.62, 6.3.63, 15.11.63,

THE **TREES** (R'n'B) - 5.10.65, 14.12.65, 18.1.66, 25.1.66, 6.12.66,

TREES (FOLK) - 13.11.70,

THE **TREMELOES** *with Brian Poole* - 00.4.65, 10.12.65,

THE **TREMELOES** - 15.7.71, 15.10.74,

THE **TREMORS** - 10.12.65,

TONY **TRIBE** - 22.9.69,

TRICKSTER - 9.12.77,

TRIMMER & JENKINS - 18.3.79, 27.7.80, 24.9.80,

THE **TROGGS** - 3.8.66,

THE **TROJANS** - 6.4.63,

THE **T-BONES** - *(see also Gary Farr)*, 27.6.64, 31.6.64, 27.1.65, 29.1.65, 18.8.65, 25.8.65, 31.8.65, 21.5.66, 22.12.66,

T.REX - 8.11.70, 4.2.71, 23.5.71, 24.10.71,

TOMMY **TUCKER** - 4.11.64,

TWIGGY - 15.4.77,

TWINK - 19.6.70,

TWINKLE - 4.12.64,

BONNIE **TYLER** - 25.5.78,

THE **TYMES** - 10.3.69, 17.3.76,

TYRANNOSAURUS REX - 16.2.69, 27.12.69, 7.6.70,

JUDIE **TZUKE** - 25.11.79, 6.5.80,

U.F.O. - 5.11.72,

UGLY ROOM - 10.6.70,

ULTRAVOX - 24.3.77, 29.1.78,

UNCLE DOG *with Carol Grimes* - 2.1.72,

THE **UNDERTAKERS** - 21.1.64,

UNICORN - 6.6.76,

UNIVERSE - 13.11.70, 15.1.71,

THE **UNWANTED** - 12.2.78,

UPP - 13.10.74,

THE **UPSETTERS** - 8.12.69, 12.1.70,

URIAH HEEP - 28.8.70, 20.6.71, 5.9.71, 21.11.71, 28.5.72, 28.1.73, 18.2.80, 18.12.80,

V

THE **VAGABONDS** - 30.11.79,

RICKY **VALANCE** - 8.1.61,

FRANKIE **VALLI** - 5.4.76,

THE **VAMPIRES** - 18.12.65, 27.9.65, 22.1.66,

VAN DER GRAF GENERATOR - 26.5.70, 11.4.71, 13.7.71,

VANITY FARE - 25.8.69,

SARAH **VAUGHAN** - 18.9.63,

VENUS & MARS - 23.11.80,

THE **VERNON GIRLS** - 23.10.62, 6.3.63,

THE **VIBRATIONS** - 20.4.66, 21.9.66,

THE **VIBRATORS** - 10.2.77, 5.5.77, 3.7.77, 19.3.78,

THE **VICTIMS** - 11.9.77,

GENE **VINCENT** - 3.3.61, 9.5.63, 21.11.63,

VINEGAR JOE - 10.9.72, 26.11.72,

THE **V.I.P.'s** - 16.9.64, 21.10.66,

THE **VISCOUNTS** - 13.5.61,

VISITOR - 5.12.80,

THE **VOYEURS** - 11.11.78,

LOUDON **WAINWRIGHT** III - 5.11.71, 6.5.73, 12.6.75, 11.10.79,

RICK **WAKEMAN** - 27.7.74,

THE **WALKER BROTHERS** - 10.12.65,

JUNIOR **WALKER** & THE ALLSTARS - 20.1.69,

T. BONE **WALKER** - 30.10.68,

BOB **WALLIS** STOREYVILLE JAZZMEN - 23.3.63,

LARRY **WALLIS** - 16.10.77,

HANK **WANGFORD** BAND - 17.10.80,

WARM DUST - 30.10.70,

DIONNE **WARWICK** - 18.11.64,

GENO **WASHINGTON** - 26.4.67, 13.9.67,

DENIS **WATERMAN** - 12.10.80,

MUDDY **WATERS** - 18.10.63, 20.10.63, 10.5.64,

CHRIS **WAYNE** - 3.3.61,

AJ **WEBBER** - 5.5.74,

BERT **WEEDON** - 16.11.62, 15.11.63,

WIERD SISTER - 24.12.77, 11.2.78,

ALEX **WELSH** & THE DIXIELANDERS - 7.3.58, 26.11.58, 3.3.61,

HOWARD **WERTH** & THE MOONBEAMS - 26.10.75,

DODIE **WEST** - 19.3.65,

PAUL **WHEELER** - 13.1.69,

BETTE **WHITE** - 6.10.74,

WHITE LIGHTNING - 3.4.70,

WHITE SPIRIT - 15.8.80,

JOSH **WHITE** - 12.10.67,

TONY JOE **WHITE** - 30.9.71,

WHITESNAKE - 8.11.79,

SLIM **WHITMAN** - 16.2.73, 5.2.76, 13.10.77, 6.2.79, 7.3.79,

THE **WHO** - 8.6.65, 16.7.65, 15.4.66, 24.8.66, 18.1.67, 21.9.69, 8.10.70,

WHY WORRY? - 22.2.76,

WALLY **WHYTON** - 2.11.69,

WICKED NUN - 2.4.72,

THE **WILD ANGELS** - 15.12.69, 9.4.70, 8.7.71, 12.8.72,

WILDMOUTH - 14.7.69,

MARTY **WILDE** - 20.11.62, 4.10.63, 2.7.71, 24.2.74,

BIG JOE **WILLIAMS** - 18.10.63, 20.10.63, 30.10.68,

DON **WILLIAMS** - 17.9.76,

ROBIN **WILLIAMSON** - 23.3.63,

SONNY BOY **WILLIAMSON** - 18.10.63, 20.10.63, 6.12.63, 19.10.64, 25.10.64, 27.1.65,

JOE LEE **WILSON** - 6.11.79,

PETE **WINGFIELD** - 28.9.75 *(cancelled)*

MARTIN **WINSOR** - 20.5.63,

WINSTON G. - 29.1.65,

EDGAR **WINTER** - 19.4.70, 29.7.72,

JOHNNY **WINTER** - 19.4.70,

WIRE - 19.2.78,

WISHBONE ASH - 26.9.71, 6.2.72, 17.12.72, 17.6.73, 13.10.74, 31.10.76, 3.2.80,

JIMMY **WITHERSPOON** - 6.5.66,

WIZZARD - 4.2.73, 11.9.74,

DARYL WAY's **WOLF** - 28.1.73,

HOWLIN' **WOLF** - 19.10.64, 25.10.64,

STEVIE **WONDER** - 9.3.69,

GAY & TERRY **WOODS** - 1.4.75,

WOOFLER - 27.12.79,

THE **WORRYIN' KIND** - 12.4.64, 15.6.64, 20.6.64, 4.12.64,

THE **WORST** - 4.9.77,

WRECKLESS ERIC - 16.10.77, 9.4.78

GARY **WRIGHT** - 2.9.72,

THE **WRITING ON THE WALL** - 9.3.70,

THE **WURZELS** - 7.12.76,

MARK **WYNTER** - 20.11.62,

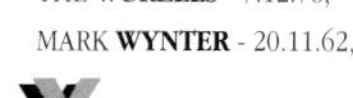

X-RAY SPEX - 16.4.78,

X.T.C. - 22.1.78,

Y

YAKETTY YAK - 9.3.80,

STOMU **YAMASH'TA** - 16.6.74,

THE **YARDBIRDS** - 30.11.63, 4.1.64, 15.2.64, 21.2.64, 16.5.64, 27.5.64, 5.3.65, 3.11.65,

TOM **YATES** - 17.9.72,

THE **YETTIES** - 12.3.76,

YES - 7.12.69, 25.1.70, 2.8.70, 27.9.70, 2.9.72,

THE **YOUNG ONES** - 19.3.78,

THE TERRY **YOUNG** FIVE - 23.10.62,

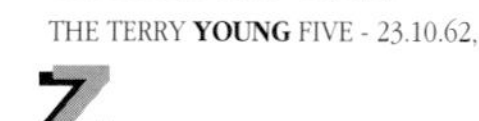

THE **ZEPHYRS** - 30.4.65,

THE **ZOMBIES** - 18.11.64,

ZOOT MONEY'S BIG ROLL BAND - 3.1.66, 7.3.66, 8.6.66, 9.11.66

(OK, I know Zoot should be listed under M, but as Z.Z. Top, Warren Zevon and Frank Zappa never quite made it to Croydon, I needed another Z...!).

AND FINALLY, A FEW NUMBERS...

999 - 9.6.77, 18.9.77,

10 CC - 29.2.76,

30 YEARS WAR - 24.10.76,

1984 - 7.1.67,

5,000 VOLTS - 17.4.77,

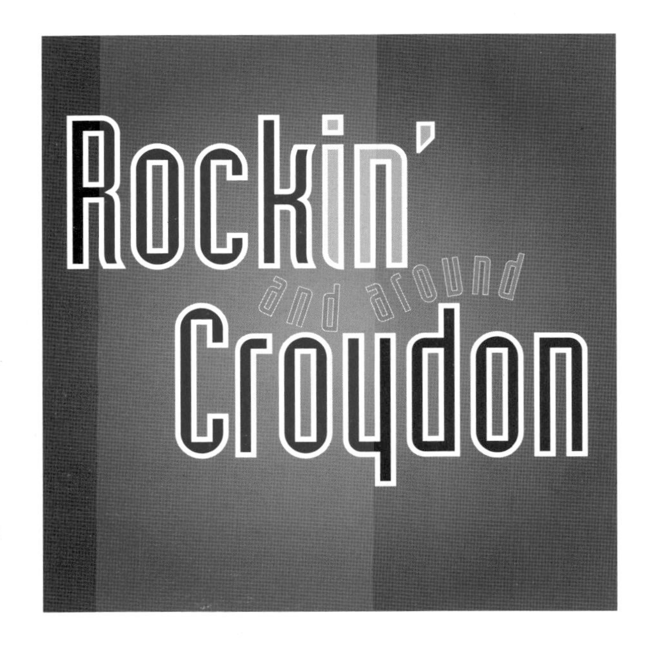

Chris Groom was born at home in Caterham on the Hill, Surrey, in the same month that "Que Sera, Sera" by Doris Day was Number One in the Hit Parade. Grew up to the sound of 'fifties rock'n'roll emanating from his uncle's Dansette record player and to the Beatles and Stones from various transistor radios - decided early on that he preferred the Stones, and that the Fab Four were vastly overrated. Sensibly decided *not* to go into A&R.

Educated at De Stafford Comprehensive School to the sounds of Slade, Alice Cooper and Mott the Hoople; he moved on to Reigate School of Art & Design, where he began listening intensively to Fairport Convention, Frank Zappa and Janis Joplin, thus managing to emerge with his Dip. A.D. (as it was in those days), intact. Also managed to keep his copy of Big Brother & the Holding Company's 'Cheap Thrills' intact, despite constant threats from his mum to smash it to smithereens - thus anticipating 'punk' by a couple of years.

Started work with a Purley design group the very day after he went to his first Dylan concert, much to the bemusement of his boss; yet still works with almost the same bunch of fun people - despite taking away his drawing board and replacing it with an Apple Mac - now based in Orpington.

Wrote his first two album reviews for the late lamented 'Swing 51' (thanks Ken) and then spent five years as a freelance arts reviewer for the Croydon Advertiser, until the tax people finally caught up with him. Has been published by 'Folk Roots' and 'Record Collector' and been turned down by 'Q'. Still never mind; whatever will be, *will* be - isn't that right Doris...?

Bibliography

During the compilation of this book it felt as though I delved into almost every available music publication in the search for Croydon-related information, including ploughing through the back issues of Melody Maker, New Musical Express, Time Out and all the local papers. Great fun, of course! I have taken quotes from some of these and several more are a thoroughly recommended 'read'. Although it would be impossible to list them all, take your pick from:

Stone Alone.
Bill Wyman — Penguin

Mama said there'd be days like this.
Val Wilmer — The Women's Press

Alias David Bowie.
Peter & Leni Gilman — Hodder & Stoughton

The Yardbirds.
John Platt/Chris Dreja/Jim McCarty — Sidgwick & Jackson

VoxPop - profiles of the pop process.
Michael Wale — Harrap

Diary of a Rock & Roll Star.
Ian Hunter — Panther

Beat Merchants.
Alan Clayson — Blandford Press

British Beat.
Chris May & Tim Phillips — Socion

Rock Family Trees - Vol. 1 & 2.
Pete Frame — Quick Fox / Omnibus Press

NME Book of Rock 2.
Nick Logan & Bob Woffinden — Star Books

I Play As I Please.
Humphrey Lyttleton — Pan

The Book of the Damned - the official biography.
Carol Clerk — Omnibus Press

The Electric Light Orchestra Story.
Bev Bevan — Mushroom Books

60 Years of Jazz in Croydon.
Ian King / John Rickard — Kings Jazz Review

The Cinemas of Croydon.
Allen Eyles & Keith Skone — Keytone Publications